EARLY REAGAN

BOOKS BY ANNE EDWARDS

BIOGRAPHY

Sonya: The Life of Countess Tolstoy
Vivien Leigh: A Biography
Judy Garland: A Biography
Road to Tara: The Life of Margaret Mitchell
Matriarch: Queen Mary and the House of Windsor
A Remarkable Woman: A Biography of Katharine Hepburn
Early Reagan

NOVELS

The Survivors
Miklos Alexandrovitch Is Missing
Shadow of a Lion
Haunted Summer
The Hesitant Heart
Child of Night

AUTOBIOGRAPHY

The Inn and Us (with Stephen Citron)

CHILDREN'S BOOKS

P. T. Barnum
The Great Houdini
The Bible for Young Readers

EARLY
REAGAN

ANNE EDWARDS

TAYLOR TRADE PUBLISHING
Lanham • New York • Boulder • Toronto • Plymouth, UK

Published by Taylor Trade Publishing
An imprint of The Rowman & Littlefield Publishing Group, Inc.
4501 Forbes Boulevard, Suite 200, Lanham, Maryland 20706
www.rowman.com

10 Thornbury Road, Plymouth PL6 7PP, United Kingdom

Distributed by National Book Network

British Library Cataloguing in Publication Information Available

The hardcover edition of this book was previously catalogued by the Library of
Congress as follows:

Edwards, Anne, 1927—
Early Reagan.
Bibliography: p.
Includes index.
    1. Reagan, Ronald.   2. Presidents—United States—Biography.
3. Moving-picture actors and actresses—United States—Biography.
I. Title.
E877.2.E39   1987   791.43'028'0924 [B]   87-7728

ISBN 978-1-58979-743-7 (pbk. : alk. paper)
ISBN 978-1-58979-744-4 (electronic)

♾™The paper used in this publication meets the minimum requirements of
American National Standard for Information Sciences—Permanence of Paper for
Printed Library Materials, ANSI/NISO Z39.48-1992.

Printed in the United States of America

IN MEMORY OF
PETER HEGGIE,
WHO DEDICATED HIS LIFE
TO THE CAUSE OF THE AUTHOR
AND THE FREEDOM OF THE WRITTEN WORD.

ACKNOWLEDGMENTS

In the writing of this book, my own past has pointed my hand. Ronald Reagan's Hollywood years often crossed my own. I have known what it is to be under contract to a film studio. We have worked for, and been friends with, some of the same people; we were both survivors of the terrible years of the Hollywood witch hunts; and we had both headed a large guild of artists—Reagan as president of the Screen Actors Guild for six years, and I as president of the Authors Guild for four years. Throughout, I have consciously tried to be as impartial as I could, to make the facts and the people who were close to Reagan reveal the man. Without the constant help of those witnesses and the many hours they gave to answer my questions, this book could never have evolved as it has. Awaking sleeping memories can be a disquieting experience.

Current history has been inclined to regard Ronald Reagan's first fifty years as having only a small bearing on the man who in 1964 gave his famous "A Time for Choosing" speech in support of Barry Goldwater's unsuccessful bid for the presidency. I have tried to provide a reliable chronicle of the events and actions in the first fifty-five years of Ronald Reagan's life that will serve to better understand the very long making of this, the United States's fortieth president.

I owe so many debts of gratitude—to Bill and Jean Thompson and to the people of Dixon—who opened their homes, their hearts and their memories to me; to Dwight A. and Janice M. Wilson and Mr. Reagan's other family members in Illinois who painstakingly helped me trace Mr. Reagan's roots; to the faculty of Eureka College who gave unstintingly of their time; to Ralph McKinzie, Mr. Reagan's football coach, who gave me a day filled with humor and sharp memory that will never be forgotten; to the folks at Radio WHO in Des Moines; and all the marvelous artists and technicians from Warner Brothers who helped me to re-create those years in Ronald Reagan's life.

I must also make special thanks to the executive staff and the board of the Screen Actors Guild, who granted me permission to study the Guild's minutes so that I could reconstruct Mr. Reagan's activities as a labor leader. I understand that I was the first person to have been accorded that privilege, and I am most appreciative of the trust this implied. No words can adequately be found to thank Jack Dales and Chet Migden for their interviews and help, or Mark Locher, National Public Relations Director of the Screen Actors Guild, for his unstinting cooperation and the many weeks he allowed me to sit and work in his offices. Nor would my research at the SAG have been complete without the memory and assistance of Kim Felner.

I have also had the good fortune to work with some of the finest archivists and librarians in the country. I shall never be able to express enough thanks to Anthony Slide and the library staff at the Academy of Motion Picture Arts and Sciences; to Leith Adams and the staff at the University of Southern California Film Archives, who gave me full access to the Warner Brothers Archives; and to Stephen Ourada and the staff at the University of Wisconsin Film Archives.

One of the greatest advantages I had in re-creating Mr. Reagan's life was the use of transcripts of personal interviews made by the Department of Special Collections at the University of California in Los Angeles, and the Regional Oral History Office at the University of California at Berkeley, and by Jean Kinney for her newspaper columns "Around About" in Scottsdale, Arizona. I had the good fortune to be the first author to have the availability of these transcripts. Everyone involved in these programs is truly a dedicated person, working to preserve our history. I cannot say enough about the fine interviewing techniques of Gabrielle Morris, Stephen Stern, Mitch Tuchman and Jean Kinney.

No biographer ever had a better secretary-assistant than I have in Barbara Howland, who has seen me through four complicated books and has become a super sleuth and a grand literary detective. I am also blessed with an editor, Harvey Ginsberg, who never lacks faith in me. With each book, my husband, Stephen Citron's, counsel and astute insight grows as does my dependence upon him. I cannot imagine that I would have had the stamina to complete this challenging book without his love, care and constant help.

Many contributors of known reliability have asked that I not publicly name them. I abide by their wishes, but I do want those confidential informants to receive here my public thanks. And to the many people (they are not names, but people, who have given unselfishly of their time) listed below, please forgive the absence of a larger note of appreciation. All of you have been most generous and I consider myself a very fortunate author to have had your assistance. Here then are my thanks to (in alphabetical order):

Jon Anderson, production manager, WHO-TV, Des Moines, IA; Betty J. Ankle, executive secretary, Monmouth, IL, public schools; Gregory A. Apel, Iowa City, IA; Gregory D. Baker, photographer, Dixon, IL; John M. Bartholomy, president, William Woods College, Fulton, MO; Wayne Bastian, Fulton, IL; Lynn Beer, College Relations, Eureka College, Eureka, IL; John Behrens, CBS Broadcast Group, New York, NY; Lois Bell, Martin Luther King Library, Washington, D.C.; Barry Black, Phoenix, AZ; H. B. Brooks-Baker, Burke's Peerage, London, England; Myrna Brown, Sterling, IL; George T. Bryson, Jr., Richmond, VA; Richard Burdick, Sarasota, FL; Marcelle Cady, Los Angeles, CA; Anne Caiger, UCLA, Los Angeles, CA; John M. Caldwell, archivist, University of Oklahoma, Norman, OK; Gil Cates, Directors Guild, Los Angeles, CA; Edward Chodorov, New York, NY; Debra Cohen, Life Picture Service, New York, NY; Ned Comstock, USC Archives of Performing Arts, Los Angeles, CA; Arlene Dahl, New York, NY; Shirley Davey, BBD&O Advertising Agency, Avalon, CA; Ruth Degenhardt, Berkshire Anthenaeum, Pittsfield, MA; Frank Delaney, London, England; Vernon Denison, Tampico, IL; Alvah Drew, Jr., Dixon, IL; Ralph Eckley, Monmouth, IL; Polly Brown Edwards, Washington, D.C.; Ruth G. Edwards, Reference Dept., Dixon Public Library, Dixon, IL; Nanette Eichell, Danbury Public Library, Danbury, CT; John Elliott, University of Wisconsin; Deloris A. Ferger, Dixon, IL; Joanne Foster, Eureka College, Eureka, IL; Marian Foster, Ronald Reagan Home, Dixon, IL; Jack Gilford, New York, NY; Madelaine Lee Gilford, New York, NY; Alex Gottlieb, Motion Picture Country Home and Hospital, Woodland Hills, CA; Evelyn Greenwald, SCAN, Los Angeles, CA; Stella Grobe, Loveland Community House, Dixon, IL; Benjamin J. Guthrie, clerk, U.S. House of Representatives, Washington, D.C.; James K. Hall, chief, Freedom of Information–Privacy Acts Section, U.S. Department of Justice, Washington, D.C.; Enid Hanks, Galesburg Public Library, Galesburg, IL; Gardner Haskell, librarian, Public Library, San Francisco, CA; Tim Hawkins, Wisconsin Center for Film and Theater Research; George Hearne, president, Eureka College, Eureka, IL; Catharine Heinz, director, Broadcast Pioneers Library, Washington, D.C.; Arthur Hershey, Los Angeles Turf Club, Inc., Arcadia, CA; Dan Heusinkveld, county clerk, Morrison, IL; Richard L. Hill, New York Public Library, New York, NY; Jan-Christopher Horak, George Eastman House,

Rochester, NY; Judy Horgen, Danbury Public Library, Danbury, CT; Janet Horvak, New Milford Public Library, New Milford, CT; John Houseman, New York, NY; Mevelyn Hughes, SAG, Hollywood, CA; R. W. Ibach, Jr., director, Public Relations, Chicago Cubs, Chicago, IL; John Imrie, Scots Ancestry Research Society, Edinburgh, Scotland; Mrs. J. M. Irvin, Monroe, WI; Mrs. Phyllis W. Johnson, Arlington, VA; Nathan Juran, Los Angeles, CA; Melba Lohmann King, Des Moines, IA; Command Sergeant Major Klein, Camp Dodge, Johnston, IA; Robert Knutson, USC Archives of Performing Arts, Los Angeles, CA; Tressie M. Kozelka, Peoria, IL; Pam Kulik, promotion manager, WHO Broadcasting Co., Des Moines, IA; Charles Lamb, University of Notre Dame, Notre Dame, IN; Karen J. Laughlin, Iowa State Historical Dept., Iowa City, IA; Paul Layet; Andrew Lee, Research Dept., Universal Studios, Universal City, CA; Verl L. Lekwa, Columbus Junction, IA; Judy Leonard, Galesburg Board of Education, Galesburg, IL; Paul Lerner, William Morrow, New York, NY; David LeVine, Dramatists Guild, New York, NY; Eleanor M. Lewis, Research Associate, Smith College, Northampton, MA; Fiona Lindsey, London, England; Donald Littlejohn, Eureka College, Eureka, IL; Arthur Lloyd, San Francisco, CA; Reverend Fred Long, Tampico, IL; Pruda L. Lood, Hoover Institution on War, Revolution and Peace, Stanford, CA; Ms. Joan McCollum, Eureka College, Eureka, IL; Mary Ann McFarlane, Latin School of Chicago, Chicago, IL; Mrs. Violet (Winston) McReynolds, Dixon, IL; Wilbert Mahoney, Military Archives, Washington, D.C.; Alice Mappen, Dixon, IL; Melba Matson, Monmouth, IL; Virginia Mayo, Los Angeles, CA; Mark Meader, National Archives and Record Services, Washington, D.C.; Ron Mix, news editor, *Dixon Evening Telegraph,* Dixon, IL; John L. Molyneux, Rockford Public Library, Rockford, IL; Reverend Benjamin A. Moore, Christian Church (Disciples of Christ), Los Angeles, CA; Patricia Moore, Wrigley Museum, Avalon, CA; Winifred B. Moore, Sterling, IL; Emil P. Moschella, chief, Freedom of Information–Privacy Acts Section, Washington, D.C.; Lisa Mosher, Academy of Motion Picture Arts and Sciences, Beverly Hills, CA; Donald Murray, *Fulton Press,* Fulton, IL; Victor Navasky, *The Nation,* New York, NY; Judy Noack, Warner Brothers, Burbank, CA; Gene Nelson, Beverly Hills, CA; Isabelle Newman, Dixon, IL; Paul and Helen Nicely, Tampico, IL; Audrey O'Rourke, Public Library, Rockford, IL; Dixie Painter, genealogist, St. Joseph, MO; Arthur L. Park, Los Angeles, CA;

ACKNOWLEDGMENTS

Bernard F. Pasqualini, The Free Library of Philadelphia, Philadelphia, PA; Anna Pendergast, St. Joseph, MO; Herb Plambeck, Des Moines, IA; Armando Ponce, Universal City Studios, Universal City, CA; James B. Poteat, Television Information Office; Sarah Price, London, England; Roy Prutt; Alejandro Rey, Hollywood, CA; Cheri Ritchhart, *Des Moines Register*, Des Moines, IA; Jill Schary Robinson, London, England; John W. Rogers, Warner Brothers, Burbank, CA; Gertrude Crockett Romine, Monmouth, IL; Mrs. J. Roy, Genealogical Research Specialist, Public Archives, Ottawa, Ontario, Canada; Michael Ruark, Dixon, IL; Rick Ryan, Princeton University, Princeton, NJ; Karen St. Pierre, Museum of Broadcasting, New York, NY; Janet Saunders, Dixon Public Library; Joy Hodges Schiess, Katonah, NY; Tony Schipps, SAG, Hollywood, CA; Chuck Schlesselman, Des Moines, IA; Gloria Scott, Public Library, Corona, CA; James Seale, president, Christ Historical Society, Nashville, TN; Tom Shaw, editor, *Dixon Evening Telegraph*, Dixon, IL; William Shaw, publisher, *Dixon Evening Telegraph*, Dixon, IL; Jack Shelley, Ames, IA; Reverend Tom W. Shepherd, First Christian Church (Disciples of Christ), Dixon, IL; Shirley Shisler, Public Library, Des Moines, IA; Don Siegel; Louis Sindlinger, Dixon, IL; Bette Smith, Bennett, IA; Ann Steinfeldt, University of Wisconsin; Ezra Stone; Dorothy Swerdlove, curator, The Billy Rose Theatre Collection, Lincoln Center, New York, NY; Linda Taetes, Tampico, IL; Frances Tanabe, *The Washington Post*, Washington, D.C.; Raymond Teichman, Franklin D. Roosevelt Library, Hyde Park, NY; Benjamin Thau (now deceased), Motion Picture Country Home and Hospital, Woodland Hills, CA; Ethel Trego, Monmouth, IL; Molly Tuthill, Hoover Institution on War, Revolution and Peace, Stanford, CA; Mr. and Mrs. Richard Ulrich, Grinnell, IA; Diane M. Vicarel, The Public Library of Youngstown and Mahoning County, Youngstown, Ohio; Rudy Villasenor, Los Angeles High School Alumni Association; Mike Walker, Petersburg Public Library, Petersburg, VA; John H. Wetzell, Sterling, IL; Jeremy Williams, Warner Brothers, Burbank, CA; Maggie (Mrs. Lawrence) Williams, Westport, CT; Robert Williams, Verona, NJ; Waverly K. Winfree, librarian, Virginia Historical Society, Richmond, VA; David S. Wolfson, CBS Songs, New York, NY; Roger Worthington, *Chicago Tribune*, Chicago, IL; Jean Wynne, The Authors Guild, New York, NY; Jim Zabel, sports director, WHO, Des Moines, IA; David Zeidberg, University of California, Los Angeles, CA.

CONTENTS

ALMOST THE CONQUERING HERO

SEPTEMBER 14–16, 1941

"See the conquering hero comes!
Sound the trumpet, beat the drums!"
—DR. THOMAS MORELL,
text for Handel's *Joshua*

1

HE STOOD ON THE PLATFORM OF UNION STATION, Los Angeles, narrow as a long knife, an easy smile on his tanned young face, his chestnut hair Brylcreemed to perfect order. Photographers crowded in close. One called out, "Step back, Ronnie . . . you're casting a shadow across Miss Parsons." Ronald Reagan acknowledged the command. The small, dark-haired middle-aged woman beside him held her toothy, smiling pose. Clearly, she knew she was the focal point of the group about to depart. In a few moments, they would board the *City of Los Angeles* for the two-day journey to Dixon, Illinois, and the "Louella Parsons Day" celebration that was being held in her honor. Reagan and Parsons were both former Dixonites, a fact that had given Hollywood's most powerful columnist the necessary angle for the best press coverage of the event.

Reagan was one of Hollywood's most popular young players, on the verge of becoming a major star. The studio felt he needed Parsons and the publicity her name generated to give him a bit of a nudge over the edge. His mother, Nelle, was accompanying her son on what she reckoned was his moment of glory—his return as a celebrity to Dixon. Once considered petite, Nelle now appeared almost frail. But she stood steadfastly behind him like a tin soldier, arms at the side of her white-collared print-silk frock, her proud new hat balanced on her head like the grandest tricorn. She and Parsons were about the same age. Yet Nelle had the aura of an earlier generation.

Fifteen minutes had been allotted to the press. When that time ran out, Virginia Lindsey, one of the publicists accompanying the tour (which would also present the other Hollywood players gathered on the sun-glinted platform), stepped forward. Parsons and her daughter, Harriet, turned and headed for the rear car of the train, where they were helped on board with a mass of hand baggage by several Pullman-car porters. A moment later, Hollywood's first lady of gossip appeared on the rear platform, smiled and lifted her white-gloved hand in a stiff wave—a gesture obviously gleaned from studying royal photographs—and the cue for the rest of her Hollywood celebrity group to follow.

Nelle took her son's arm and skillfully maneuvered her way with him over the microphone wires and through the crowd. Only the white line across the bridge of Reagan's nose gave away his most carefully guarded secret—the thick-lensed, horn-rimmed glasses he wore privately, without which his shortsightedness made the world a blur. Not until the train had pulled out of the station and was well on its way did he replace his glasses. He settled his six-foot frame into the green upholstered seat of his drawing-room compartment across from Nelle, leaving the door open. Ed Oettinger, Parsons's brother, came by to see if they were comfortable. Celebrity-group members George Montgomery and Ann Rutherford peeked in and asked if they would care to join them for a drink. Reagan smilingly refused (Nelle was a teetotaler). Finally, Sam Israel, another publicist, informed Reagan that Parsons wanted to see him. He got up and followed Israel to the rear car, which had been turned into a private lounge, where Parsons, in high spirits, was holding court to the rest of her entourage. Comedians Bob Hope, Jerry Colonna and Joe E. Brown, film stars Bebe Daniels and Ben Lyon, had agreed to join them in Dixon, and there was nothing Parsons enjoyed more than being surrounded by the famous—unless it was to be attended by them.

On this day, September 12, 1941, World War II was two years old, and although America had remained neutral, most of Europe had been overrun by the Nazis and England was suffering an almost nightly blitz from the German air force. Franklin Delano Roosevelt sat in his wheelchair in the Oval Office of the White House preparing for an unprecedented third term, struggling with the burden of operating a vast peaceable democracy in a war-gripped world, trying to hold together his now sagging social-welfare program. But in Hollywood the war in Europe still seemed distant. If not riding high, American films were at least charged with a new vitality. *Gone With the Wind*'s recent grand success had proved that Americans were caught up in their own history. And although movie audiences had responded well to English stars during the previous decade, Hollywood had developed its own stables.

Reagan was at Warner Brothers, where Bette Davis was champion and other players, such as Errol Flynn, Barbara Stanwyck, Joan Crawford, Humphrey Bogart, and James Cagney, jockeyed for top scripts and roles that would bring them into the winners' circle. Below them were the contract players, who were closely watched over by the studio in hopes that one or two might break through and exhibit top-class potential. Reagan had been in this last group for four years and had been given leads only in B films and supporting roles in a few A films. But he had recently made a low-budget picture, *International Squadron* (to be premiered in Dixon on the tour), thought by executives at Warners to have great potential. He had also completed major scenes on an A film—*Kings Row*—and the rushes had looked encouragingly good. For years, Warners had not believed an audience would buy a ticket expressly to see Ronald Reagan in a movie. He had to be, more or less, packaged—either in a supporting role in a feature that starred one of their more popular players, or as a lead in a programmer (a picture that was made as a second feature to accompany the studios' A films—usually those that needed all the help they could get). Louella Parsons's columns were read by millions and her power to thrust a player into the forefront of the movie fans' attention was phenomenal. Therefore, Reagan and the studio readily agreed he should accompany her on this tour to their small hometown, Dixon, Illinois.

Nine years had elapsed since Reagan had lived in Dixon. Despite his celebrity status, returning would not be easy for him, for wherever he turned he would be reminded of some of the more unhappy problems of his youth—the tough times, his father's drinking, the girl he had loved and lost. Yet, this was the town that he felt had formed him. His ties to it were strong. Perhaps some force other than coincidence had guided his return at a critical time of reassessment.

The train was due to arrive in Dixon at ten-thirty A.M. on Sunday, September 14. Reagan spent the last hours of the journey with his eyes steady on the Midwest farmlands that bordered the railroad tracks. As a young boy he had watched the chicken hawks circling over the hen houses of Dixon's outlying farms—the youngest chicks, white feathers coming through the soft yellow, never knew enough to hide, and the hawks would dive and snatch them up in their sharp beaks. The image was disturbing, for in spite of the urge, he was powerless to rescue or warn the chicks. When he grew a bit older and became a lifeguard at Lowell Park, some of this guilt had been assuaged. He had saved seventy-seven lives over the many seasons he worked at the park. People in Dixon respected him for that. Some of the younger kids had even made him a kind of hero. That's what Dutch Reagan (as he was known in Dixon) really wanted. To be a hero. People remembered heroes.

Bill Thompson had been six years younger than Dutch Reagan, but Lowell Park's only lifeguard had not treated the youngster with condescension. Dutch liked kids, and at fifteen he found their admiration for him a boon to his sometimes shaky ego. Thompson was to drive the returning Dutch around Dixon during Louella Parsons's week-long celebration, and he could not wait until his childhood hero arrived. What kept coming to his mind was the great old log that used to sit by the lifeguard station at Lowell Park. It had been large enough for him to teeter on as a kid, his feet not touching the ground, as he watched Dutch take a bead on a bobbing figure struggling to keep afloat and screaming for help. Dutch would throw down his glasses and slash through the rough undertow like "a torpedo in the water" as he struck a straight course toward the distressed swimmer. People on the shore would cheer Dutch on and soon the long, lean teenager would have the drowning person securely in his strong grasp and be heading back to shore. Once there, he would perform artificial resuscitation. Then, when the formerly endangered swimmer had revived satisfactorily, Dutch would replace his glasses and carve a deep notch in the log that young Thompson had been balanced upon.

By the end of seven summers, Dutch Reagan had carved his seventy-seven notches in that log. A few skeptics hinted the young man might have slipped in a few extras, but all agreed that the river—"Dixon's only outdoor swimming facility"—was a treacherous place because of the unexpected undertow. There had been a series of drownings, and the Park Authority had considered closing Lowell Park to swimmers before Dutch undertook the job no one else wanted, an act Dixonites considered of extreme courage.

After Dutch left Dixon, better safety precautions were instituted in the park—buoys were placed to mark off the dangerous areas, signs warned swimmers not to go beyond a certain point, and on days when the current was unduly swift, the river was closed to them. Still, boys played mumblety-peg on the old log with their pocket knives as the older men watching them bragged at seeing Dutch Reagan put in one of the notches. "On hot summer days," one of them recalled, "old men would sit on it [the log], their hats in their hands, fanning themselves while the sun sparked the river and cast shadows on their faces." They exchanged stories about Dutch Reagan too. Different ones. On Saturday nights, they had seen him come to the aid of his father— out cold or barely able to stand on his own after a night of hard drinking. They admired the boy's attitude toward his alcoholic father. Dutch Reagan never publicly displayed anything but respect for Jack Reagan, and when success came to him (and even Hollywood substardom was looked upon as great success in small-town Dixon) he made sure his dad—and his mom too—was right there to enjoy it with him.

One summer, high tides carried the log downstream and it disappeared. But by then the stories of Dutch Reagan's bravery had reached mythic proportions. Dutch had become a well-known actor and Dixonites could say, "I always knew he was going places." Dutch believed this too. However, unlike his fellow hometowners, he already suspected that stardom in films might not be his final destination.

The terrain changed dramatically as the *City of Los Angeles* crossed the Iowa-Illinois border over one of the narrowest spans of the Mississippi and headed toward Dixon. The land loomed straight ahead, flat as the bottom of an old iron. Trees were scarce. During the Depression, Illinois farmers had needed every inch of their land and had planted crops to the edge of the railroad tracks and the highways, cutting down trees that had once given shade to farm laborers and foot travelers and a sense of life and beauty to the land. Too many of the local farms that had fallen under the auctioneers' gavels in the thirties remained unattended in 1941, the paint peeling from their boarded-up buildings, their fields lying fallow. This did not embitter Dutch, for he had confidence that in Roosevelt's third term prosperity would return fully to the land.

Dutch had a great belief in Mr. Roosevelt, who was his own contemporary hero. One of his best party imitations was a loving one of Franklin D. A select group of people in Hollywood realized the depth of his interest in politics—his wife, Jane Wyman, the actress, of course, the crews and actors on his films, and a few close friends. He had been too midwestern, too hick-town unsophisticated, to be accepted by Hollywood's liberal intellectuals, and too prim a Sunday-church–type to travel with the *macho*, womanizing hard drinkers. His best friends were his golf buddies and conservative men like actor Dick Powell and businessman Justin Dart, with whom he enjoyed arguing politics. Lately, he had become more and more involved with unions and the rights of actors, even while he favored cowboy films and read Zane Grey Westerns.

He liked to act, did the best he could, and recognized his own limitations. To his co-workers, he appeared to lack the ambition and dedication needed to be a great actor or even a top star. Those who did not know him judged him by the naïve or brassy characters he generally portrayed onscreen and by his mediocre talent, and pretty much dismissed him. Those who knew him had recognized long before that Ronald Reagan's true passion was politics. He kept at acting because it had not yet come to him what he really wanted to accomplish. At thirty years of age, he considered he still had time. Recently, he had seemed to Jane Wyman, his actress wife, to be devoured by something she could not define, when she heard him pacing the rooms of their apartment at night or discovered he had gone horseback riding alone in the early morning. She noted that he was a good deal more involved when working with the Screen Actors Guild than when shooting a film, and more enthusiastic about discussing world conditions and politics than about his current script.

The train creaked through the dry, hot morning; sun-drenched fields lay scorched between the shabby houses they separated. Thirteen of Dixon's neighboring towns had declared September 14, 1941, "'Louella Parsons Day'—a public holiday to give the folks a chance to attend the festivities." The train crossed over small-town main streets; children waved and gaunt figures came out of luncheonettes or paused at gas pumps (the only businesses left open) to watch the celebrity train pass through.

About ten minutes before they reached Dixon, Sam Israel poked his head around Reagan's door. "Louella wants you—now." Reagan followed him to the last car. Parsons threw her arms around her fellow hometowner as he entered. "They've declared a school holiday just for ME!" she cried in a voice that was part rasp and part coo. "It's a dream come true . . . I am going to break down and cry!"

"What," he laughed as she pulled away. "And spoil that swell makeup?"

Not only was Dixon the town where she had attended school, it was where Parsons had worked at Geisenheimers Department Store as a salesperson in the corset department before being hired at five dollars a week by the *Dixon Evening Telegraph*. Parsons had thought "bitter thoughts many times" during her youth in Dixon, when it seemed to her "that not only my family but all the townspeople were amused and laughing because I wanted to be a writer." Now, Dixon had accepted her generosity in helping raise funds for a Louella Parsons Children's Ward to be built as an addition to Dixon's Katherine Shaw Bethea Hospital. The funds, however, were not to come from her but out of the proceeds from a local banquet and tea to be held in her honor during her visit.

The high school band played a medley of patriotic pieces as the sleek *City of Los Angeles* slithered into Dixon's North Western Station. Crowds waved banners and cheered from behind a rope barricade. Little Louella Oettinger Parsons ("You remember her? She used to *think* she was going to be a writer!") disembarked and led her troop to a specially constructed wood platform. A curious expression flashed across her face. The majority of the banners declared WELCOME HOME DUTCH! As soon as he was visible, the cheer "We love Dutch!" could be heard above all the rest of the cacophony of welcome-home noise. Reagan waved back at his fans. Parsons was presented with a massive bouquet of American beauty roses as she stepped up to the microphone. "Thanks, thanks, thanks—" she began. News photographers and hundreds of candid-camera fans went into action. There was a loud cheer when Bob Hope was recognized as he sprang out of the station house, pushed through the crowd, jumped the barricade and hopped onto the platform, grabbing the microphone from her.

Pointing to a dilapidated hovel on the other side of the tracks, he announced, "Ladies and gentlemen—over there is the birthplace of your townswoman, Louella Parsons. Do you wonder that this glamour girl ablaze with orchids, dressed to the teeth, bedecked and bejeweled, wants to forget it? Do you wonder the little lady is overcome with emotion?" Parsons was not amused—although she forced a laugh. Hope handed her back the microphone. "This is an event, my old friends in Dixon, which I shall never forget," she said. "I will remember this occasion as long as I live, and I know that Ronald will too. . . ." Cries of "We love Dutch" came up again and Parsons turned to Reagan and continued. "Good friends, Dutch Reagan—my boy of whom I am most proud, and who is the same today as he was when he left Dixon."

The huge crowd (an estimated thirty-five thousand people*) shouted "We love Dutch" again as he stepped to the microphone battery. He raised his hand and they grew quiet. Parsons expected him to say a few words and step down. "I do not feel at ease on this platform," he began in an even, melodious, boyishly humble voice, the color rising in his face to an endearing blush. "I would much rather be out at Lowell Park beach calling to the kids to quit rocking the raft and to the smaller ones to stay in the shallow water . . ." The crowd sent up a cheer and Reagan paused, smiling, seeming able to sense the right moment to continue. "When I stepped off the train I was greeted by a Dixon policeman and his star twinkled as he recalled that the last Dixon cop I had an experience with was the means of my paying a fine for shooting firecrackers off the Galena Avenue bridge. . . ." (Laughter and applause.)

"I want all of you to know that I did not sleep last night, thinking of my trip back to Dixon where I could meet my old friends. I counted the seventy-seven persons whom I have been credited with pulling out of Rock River at Lowell Park many times during the night."

Jerry Colonna turned to Louella and quipped, "This fellow must be running for Congress!"

Parsons edged her way back to the microphone and Reagan's side just as he confided to the audience, "It is with sincere regret that I am not able to present my wife, Mrs. Reagan, who in the movie world is known as Jane Wyman, but as you doubtless know, she submitted to an operation a few days ago [a curettage] and while her condition was not serious, the operation was neces-

---

*Dixon's population was approximately eleven thousand in 1941. The crowds came from surrounding towns.

sary. When I left Hollywood she was crying because she could not accompany us on this trip." Parsons leaned into the microphone and Reagan backed away.

"Well—thank you Ronnie and thank YOU—all of YOU—" A few moments later the publicity people hustled the celebrities into open-topped cars to lead the planned parade through town. Reagan insisted his mother ride with him.

"Hi, Dutch." Bill Thompson grinned over his shoulder at his movie-star passenger. "Why, Bill, you old son of a gun." Reagan pressed forward, grasped the man's shoulders and took several minutes inquiring about his family and himself. To Thompson and many others present that day, Dutch Reagan was the real returning celebrity. Jerry Colonna was not too far off target. Reagan could well have run for Congress in this district and won. After all, he had been a local hero, a man of the people, humble with his success, a good son and a true-blue American.

BEGINNINGS

1 9 1 1–2 8

> "Among the three or four million cradles now rocking in the land are some which this nation would preserve for ages as sacred things, if we could know which ones they are."
>
> —SAMUEL CLEMENS
> November 14, 1879

DARK AND MUSCULAR, JOHN EDWARD ("JACK")
Reagan, Ronald's father, was a dashing dresser who possessed a
glib tongue, a great thirst for Irish whiskey and an enormous
pride in his Irish-Catholic ancestry. The Reagans had come from
Ireland to Illinois before the Civil War and had always taken care
of their own members. The men were as well known for their intelligence and charm as for their manly vigor.

Jack's grandfather—the first Reagan to arrive in America—
was Michael Reagan (born O'Regan in 1829), the youngest of
Thomas and Margaret O'Regan's six children. The O'Regans
lived in Doolis, a small impoverished village in the shadow of the
Galtee Mountains in the barony of Iffa and Offa West in County
Tipperary. Doolis was nothing more than a group of crude stone
huts with dirt floors. Thomas O'Regan and his three sons worked
in the fields of a wealthy landowner. William O'Brien, a member
of Parliament from North Cork in 1829, recorded a visit to Doolis,
describing his horror at conditions and at seeing a Widow Conlon
(a neighbor of the O'Regans): "a starved-looking and half-naked

old woman barefooted and shivering with age and pain . . . the unfortunate creature had built [her cabin] herself of sods and bits of timber . . . fastened against the walls here and there to prevent it from falling to pieces. An iron pot was the entire furniture. There were stones for seats, a mound of wild plants for a bedstead. The approaches to the house were swimming in liquid manure and mud."

At night, Doolis peasants kept any livestock they were fortunate enough to own inside their huts to protect them from being stolen, and slept on mud floors on straw or rushes, whole families and livestock often in the same room. They were permitted a small amount of the potatoes they grew, and these were the mainstay of their diet. Even this meager way of life could be threatened by the land baron if he decided to move the family out. The potato blight that began in 1845 and continued for three consecutive years resulted in great famine for the area. Those Doolis peasants who survived and could travel immediately emigrated to England and America. But the O'Regans did not because the women (Michael Reagan's mother and three sisters) were in too weakened a condition to endure such a strenuous journey.

Education was normally out of the question for the potato farmers' children. But Michael was bright and ambitious, and a teacher from nearby Ballyporeen took a fancy to him and surreptitiously taught him to read and write. At twenty-three, Michael ran off to London with a local colleen, Catherine Mulcahy (born 1830), the daughter of Patrick Mulcahy, a laborer.* They were wed on October 30, 1852, at St. George's Roman Catholic Church. The registrar recorded the Irish spelling "Regan," but Michael signed himself "Reagan," taking on the English spelling of his name (the first syllable, however, would still have rhymed with *sea* or *pea* and the name pronounced the same). Catherine could only make a mark and was listed as illiterate. Three children were born to them in London: Thomas, May 15, 1853; John Michael, May 29, 1854 (to become Jack Reagan's father); and Margaret, November 3, 1855 (who was eventually to raise Jack). They all were baptized in the Catholic church.

---

*Patrick Mulcahy's three brothers had all been imprisoned for long periods of their lives. Two had been jailed for manslaughter, which occurred during a drunken brawl in a public house. According to old newspaper accounts, the third brother, James Mulcahy, was sentenced in 1828 for six years after he was found guilty of stealing fifty pounds of wool, committing a further act of "barbarity and atrocity" by ripping the wool off the backs of living sheep, "dragging pieces of skin with it."

Despite the responsibility of three children born in four years, Michael, working as a soapmaker, accrued enough money by 1856 to emigrate with his family and two older brothers, Nicholas and John, to Canada. The family probably left England from Liverpool, the main port for homebound Canadian lumber and cargo ships, their decks packed with immigrants taken on for the extra profits. Because their trip appears to have been well planned, the Reagan family must have saved money from the wages of the three men and their crossing might not have been as horrifying as for most of their fellow passengers, who would have been crowded aboard with little food in confining, filthy, rat-infested conditions. Those with some funds brought food for the voyage with them and often were able to buy slightly better space for their families. Such vessels as the one the Reagans would have had to take to cross the Atlantic were called coffin ships because of the thousands who died en route or shortly after landing.

The Reagans all survived the crossing with enough money left to continue on what must have been a prearranged journey. For they did not remain in Canada more than a few weeks before they boarded a wagon train to Fair Haven Township, Carroll County, Illinois. Once there, they took advantage of the American Homestead Act, which allowed a settler to choose undeveloped acreage without cost and work the land for four years, at which time the land and any dwelling on it became his. In the 1860 census of Fair Haven Township, Michael Reagan (misspelled as "Reigan") was recorded as being a farmer with real estate valued at $1,120 and personal property valued at $150. Four children were recorded, a son, William, having been born in 1859. Michael, with his brothers to help him, had built a small home and cultivated sixteen acres, which were now his.

Michael's elder son, John, who had been born in England, was Jack Reagan's father. As a young man, John Reagan farmed his family's land. He moved into nearby Fulton in 1873 to work on a grain elevator. In 1877 he claimed two sections (21 and 22) near his family's homestead (his Uncle Nicholas had a claim on section 23). He had to clear the scrubby black oak and cultivate his parcel alone, not an easy task. Eventually, he acquired livestock and built a two-room frame house (probably with the help of male members of his family, the custom at that time), seeded corn and planted beans and squash. The black soil was rich, rain was plentiful, but the life was hard and Jenny Cusick, whom he had married in 1878, was frail. Despite this, she had three children:

Catherine (Kate), born in 1879; William in 1881; and John Edward (Jack) in 1883. Jack Reagan's earliest memories were of helping to chase the flocks of blackbirds and crows that came to scratch up the seed of the spring planting. He was still a boy when he went with his father to hunt the raccoons that foraged their fields at night. His happiest times were when his parents called upon their neighboring family—his great-uncle Nicholas and his wife, Maria, and his grandfather's younger brother, Bill, and his troop of kids. Unable to make a go of his farm, John Reagan moved his family back to Fulton, where he again took a job on the grain elevator.

Jack Reagan was a child caught up in fantasy. His mother taught him to read and to memorize the catechism, but his contemporaries frequently referred to him as "a clown of a boy." The Reagans, all practicing Catholics, had a love of music and dance. Family gatherings meant sprightly reels and jigs executed with great enthusiasm. Corn whiskey was consumed in large quantities by the Reagan men, whose thirst was prodigious. To be a hard drinker without becoming drunk was a test of character, a means of demonstrating a man's self-control.

When Jack Reagan was six, his mother and father died within six days of each other, both of tuberculosis. The world he knew came to an abrupt end. His sister, Kate, and his brother, Bill, were taken in by his uncle Bill. If he had been a few years older and able to do more than boy's chores on the farm, he might not have been packed off to the small town of Bennett, Iowa (population three hundred), where his Aunt Margaret and her husband, Orson G. Baldwin, owned a general store. Aunt Margaret had been a spinster until the age of thirty-eight, when she met and married Baldwin, then a bachelor of forty-nine. Neither of Jack's foster parents had had much experience with children. Aunt Margaret was a milliner by trade, an Irish woman with Old World ways, religious and strict in her discipline. Though Baldwin was born in Vermont, his forebears were early Connecticut settlers and his great-grandfather had fought in the Revolutionary War. Uncle Orson was a stolid Yankee, not given much to talk, inclined to keep his business quite to himself. In as small a town as was Bennett, his nephew-in-law's background was never discussed. There were neighbors who did not know that the boy was related.* Nor was Baldwin a public-spirited man. In all the records kept during his residency in Bennett, not one mention is given of

---

* Jack Reagan was listed in the 1900 Bennett census as John Regan, nephew in the household of Orson G. Baldwin.

his involvement in town doings—political, economical or social.

Baldwin's General Store, which Orson owned free and clear, was at the southwest corner of Third and Main streets. The family lived in rooms behind it. An outside iron stairway led to the second floor, which was rented to the Knights of Pythias. The town had been founded only in the fall of 1884, when the railroad decided to place a depot there to augment service between Cedar Rapids and Clinton. One year afterward, Bennett had a two-story railroad station, some stores and a hotel ("conducted by mine host Flater").

Before coming to Bennett, the Baldwins lived in Davenport, Iowa, where Orson had been employed in merchandising. Their new hometown could hardly be called a metropolis, but they had come a long way from the open prairie of the previous year, and the Baldwins were confident enough in Bennett's continuing growth to invest their life's savings in its future. However, since two other general stores, also carrying groceries, hardware and clothes—Templeton's and Buzzard's—opened before him, Baldwin's never was to fulfill its promise.

Margaret disliked the crudeness of Bennett. The predominantly German-Lutheran town not only had mud streets and no sidewalks, but it supported two saloons and a pool hall and did not have enough good Catholics to form a parish.* Baldwin's also sold women's clothes, and Margaret traveled to Chicago several times a year to bring back ladies' hats, dresses and suits. The addition of high-styled city goods did not help too much, and the Baldwins had to continue to struggle to keep themselves and their young charge afloat.

As Jack matured, disciplining him became a problem. Aunt Margaret was not one to dismiss such pranks as placing the post-office sign in front of the lumberyard or upsetting an outhouse. Jack, a poor student, quit school at age twelve after completing the sixth grade. He then helped his uncle and aunt full time in the store, but sports were his real love. Wrestling matches were very popular in Bennett, and he would save his fifteen cents' admission to attend them from the fifty cents a week his uncle paid him. In 1897, Bennett's teenage boys (fifteen or under) organized "a ball nine" (a baseball team) that they called the Junior Tigers, and Jack became an avid member and then manager, "challenging all comers." Once they competed with Dixon (and lost).

---

* *Bennett Buzzings* reported in 1898, "We think [saloons] are coming in a little too thick . . ." The mayor ordered the saloons to remove their blinds "so there won't be any shenanigans going on inside." Tavern brawls were not unusual.

Win or lose, playing baseball on Sundays created a great local controversy. "Why can't these games be arranged for some other day in the week except Sundays?" a reporter on *Bennett Buzzings* inquired. And another reporter suggested, "the ladies of the town should put a stop to our boys playing ball on Sunday," adding a complaint about the players' language. "Baseball is a hoodoo game and some of the expressions that were used on the ground [that past Sunday] were far from what a gentleman would use before ladies."

Finally, by 1899, when Jack was sixteen, he returned to Fulton in Carroll County, Illinois (a distance of thirty-one miles), to live with his elderly grandmother Catherine* and his twenty-year-old sister, Kate, who had secured a job for him at J. W. Broadhead Dry Goods Store, where she was employed in the millinery department. His brother, William, also lived in Fulton, working on the grain elevator as his father once had. For the next two years, Jack visited Bennett often. His relationship with his uncle had greatly deteriorated, and he stayed at the Bennett Hotel (fifty cents a night), registering with exotic addresses such as Dublin, Ireland, and Molasses Junction. Known as a "real joker," he obviously thought this amusing. His last visit to Bennett was Christmas, 1901. The Baldwins had decided to sell their store and premises. They moved to Waterloo, Iowa, in the spring of 1902, and then to Prophetstown, Illinois.

J. W. Broadhead Dry Goods Store was located on Main Street in Fulton. Shoes became Jack Reagan's specialty. He liked children, and particularly admired the graceful turn of a lady's ankle. He talked about some day traveling west to pioneer, as Michael Reagan and his brothers once had. But he remained at Broadhead's for eight years, gaining a reputation as a young man a bit too fond of alcohol, a fact that made the parents of most eligible Fulton women (who were entranced by Reagan's beguiling manner and dark good looks) wary. The West began to beckon seductively, but lost out when small, perky, blue-eyed and auburn-haired Nelle Clyde Wilson, two years his junior and a strong-willed woman, came to work at Broadhead's.

Nelle was the youngest child† of Thomas A. and Mary Anne Elsey Wilson, and she had been born and lived most of her life on a farm in an area known as North Clyde, about eleven miles east

---

*Catherine Reagan died in April 1908 in Fulton.

†Nelle Wilson Reagan's siblings were: Emily T. (1867–1962), John C. (1870–1942), Sarah Jane (Jennie) (1872–1920), Thomas A. (Alex) (1874–1952), George O. (Lug) (1876–1952), Lavina (Mary) (1879–1951).

of Fulton, where her family had moved when she was in her teens. Nelle's grandfather was John Wilson. According to family legend, John's brother, William Ronald Wilson, had married Susan, the daughter of Sir Charles James Napier (1782–1853), a British general who had served with distinction in the Napoleonic wars. The story went that Napier had returned to England to find that the daughter he adored had married—against his will and without his permission—the Scotsman, considered by Napier to be far below her station, and he subsequently disowned her. The Wilson family had either embroidered the truth or been misled. Sir Charles Napier did have two daughters, Susan and Emily, both born illegitimately of his Greek mistress. Napier raised the girls and was, indeed, close to them. But both eventually married soldiers in his command and remained near their father until his death.

Whatever branch of the Napier family William's bride, Susan, descended from, it appears she had been disowned by her parents upon her marriage and the discredited couple went to Wilson's home in Renfrewshire, Scotland. They sailed for Canada in 1853 with William's younger brother, John, arriving in Halifax and then moving on to Ontario, where both men joined the rebels fighting the control of the Church of England in the Patriot War. William was taken prisoner for his activities, but somehow managed to escape.

During the years 1815–32, thousands of immigrants had come to Ontario from Scotland and Ireland. Movements for reform arose when the new settlers found themselves denied political opportunity for religious reasons. The immigrants were either Catholic or Protestant and the powerful group that dominated the government was the Church of England, which was Anglo-Catholic. A journalist and insurgent leader, William Lyon MacKenzie, attempted in 1837 to seize Toronto, but the rebellion was put down. The Wilson brothers were part of MacKenzie's group, but they eluded capture and escaped to the United States.

The two brothers, with other fellow rebels, found their way to Dent's Grove, Clyde Township, Illinois, in September 1839. Soon after, Susan Napier Wilson died. (A handwritten account of the disinherited woman's story and her grief at never having been reconciled with her family was preserved in the Wilson Bible [apparently kept by John] and memorized by Nelle,* who, being the romantic in her family, swore always to forgive and to comfort any "sinner" she knew, and vowed to marry for love.)

---

* Reagan took the presidential oath of office twice on this Bible, opened to Nelle's favorite passage, Chronicles 7:14 ("If my people, which are called by my name, shall humble

John Wilson married Jane Blue on November 28, 1841. Jane was the daughter of another of MacKenzie's Patriots, Donald Blue, from Argyllshire, Scotland, and Catharine McFarlain, also from the Highlands. None of the former rebels was welcomed graciously to North Clyde, where they had staked claims which in turn they had been warned to abandon. They replied to the county committee that they were "in peaceable possession" and would hold their land "at all hazards." They were allowed to remain.

The adventurous brother had been William. The promise of gold in California lured him there in 1852. Donald Blue and John Wilson followed, leaving their families for a period of three years. They returned empty-handed. William remained in California. However, that does not end Nelle's forebears' fascination with gold. A bizarre paper was filed in the Clerk's Office of the U.S. District Court for the Northern District of Illinois; a lengthy narrative written by Daniel Blue, son of Donald Blue, related the details of the horrific deaths of his two brothers, Alexander and Charles, and another man by starvation during an expedition to Pike's Peak "among the Rocky Mountains," where, rumors had it, gold abounded.* The brothers and two others left on their fatal journey on February 22, 1859. Daniel's account claims that within three weeks they were lost, then beset by snowstorms, fierce cold, illness, starvation and finally the death of the others of the party, excepting Daniel. Recounting the events that followed the first death, Daniel wrote:

> We were not strong enough to inter the corpse, neither had we pick or shovel with which to dig a grave . . . The dead body laid there for three days, we lying helpless on the ground near it, our craving for food increasing . . . until driven by desperation; wild with hunger, and feeling . . . that "self preservation is the first law of nature" we took our knives and commenced cutting the flesh from the legs and arms of our dead companion.

But, Daniel continued:

themselves, and pray, and seek my face, and turn from their wicked ways; then will I hear from heaven, and will forgive their sin, and will heal their land"). Written in his hand on the side of this page are the words, "A most wonderful verse for the healing of the nation."

*Alexander, Daniel and Charles Blue would have been Reagan's great-great-uncles on his maternal side.

. . . the corpse began to mortify and to smell and we could eat no more of it.

Days passed into a week. Alexander died:

After he had been dead two days the uncontrollable . . . cravings of hunger impelled Charles and I to devour a part of our own brother's corpse . . .

Daniel recorded that on April 18, 1859 (as nearly as he could figure), Charles died, and several days later he committed his final act of desecration, stumbled on, still lost, and finally collapsed.

An Arapaho Indian found him, nursed him back to life and then got him to the Leavenworth and Pike's Peak Express Company and to a Mr. R. D. Williams who transported him to Denver City. A man named Alexander J. Pullman befriended him at this point, listened to his story and agreed to write to John Wilson (Daniel's brother-in-law) recounting the grisly facts that had been told to him. Daniel Blue's "testimony" reads like a wild tale. But the three brothers did leave for Pike's Peak on the date stated, and only Daniel survived. The bodies of the others were never found. "The History of Clyde County," 1885, records that "Charles and Alexander [Blue] died upon the plains, from starvation during the Pike's Peak gold excitement in '59." Daniel is listed as still being alive as of that date (1885).

Thomas Wilson, Nelle's father, was born to John and Jane Blue Wilson in 1852, the same year John went off to search for gold in California. Being her youngest, Thomas remained closest to his mother's heart. Jane was a woman of staunch faith. The Bible had been her constant companion. Converted when a child of ten years, she became established "in the teachings of the Christ life." The plight of her two brothers who had died on their trek to Pike's Peak, and the three years that she had been forced to manage alone, had made an exceptionally dour woman of her.

A son, Thomas Wilson, married an Englishwoman, Mary Anne Elsey, in 1879. Mary Anne had come to America at age sixteen, after her parents' deaths, as a domestic in the employ of the Frank Cushing family in Coloma Township.* The youngest of seven children, Nelle Clyde Wilson was born July 24, 1883. Seven

---

*Mary Anne Elsey's parents were Robert Elsey (1812–50), a house painter, and Mary Baker Elsey (1819–51). Both were from an area in West Sussex, England.

years later, to the surprise of all, the conservative Thomas took off for Chicago and was not heard from for several years. His brother finally found him and brought him home when his mother was dying. Jane Blue Wilson's obituary relates, "There was one deep-seated yearning in the mother's heart to see once more for the last time the one son Thomas, gone so long, and the son came and mother and son looked into each other's eyes and she was satisfied."

The Wilson family, led by Jane as its matriarch until her death in 1894, found their chief pleasure in their religion. They strictly observed the Sabbath, regularly attended worship and had detailed knowledge of the Bible. Sundays, along with other parishioners, they would listen to a ninety-minute sermon and then reassemble after brief pleasantries for three more hours of sermon, readings, prayers and hymns. Except for medicinal, sacramental or ceremonial occasions, whiskey played no part in their lives.

Mary Anne Elsey Wilson died when Nelle was seventeen. Her father (now returned to the fold) disapproved of Jack Reagan. But that did not deter Nelle. They were married on November 8, 1904, in the parsonage of the Immaculate Conception Church in Fulton (the Catholic church attended somewhat sporadically by Jack). Nelle's brother Alex gave the bride away.

Nelle always forgave Jack his weekend benders, usually shared with his brother, William. An Irishman, she explained to friends, liked to have "a couple of nips." But she never approved of her brother-in-law, who now operated a cigar store and made his own cigars. William, unlike Jack, grew surly when he drank and had served six months in Whiteside County Jail at Morrison for drunk and disorderly conduct and inciting a brawl. Jack, Nelle felt, was reaching for something that he had not been able to find in Fulton or at Broadhead's—a sense of his own worth. The ambition was there, but he lacked direction. He did not think in terms of money, perhaps because he had not known many rich people in his life. To have people look up to him was of greater importance. Nelle persuaded Jack to leave Fulton and William's influence. In February 1906, the *Tampico Tornado* ("so named after several disasters which leveled the town") reported that John Edward Reagan ("Mr. Reagan worked for eight years in Broadhead's big store in Fulton and comes highly recommended") had recently joined the staff at the H. C. Pitney General Store, twenty-six miles away in Tampico.*

---

* Pronounced with the accent on the first syllable and meaning swampy land in the dialect of the Indians who once lived there.

The Reagans moved into a five-room flat over a bakery on Main Street.* There were no toilet facilities. Few homes in Tampico had an indoor toilet, but many did have a bathroom with tub and sink. In the Reagans' Main Street flat, the kitchen was used for this purpose and an outside pump supplied water. A treacherous stairway led from the dining room to the toilet around back. Water was heated on a coal-burning stove that was also a source of heat. The flat had two bedrooms with windows that overlooked the alley behind. Nelle used one as a sewing room, hoping one day to turn it into a nursery. Life was not easy for Nelle in Tampico in the early days, and "hauling coal to the second floor apartment for 3 stoves, carrying water up endless flights of stairs, struggling to keep tidiness without bathroom facilities and indoor toilets took its toll on [her]." Jack was not one to help much with household chores and divided his spare time between the local tavern and his interest in wrestling events.

Tampico (population 1,276 in 1910), about one-third the size of Fulton, was "pretty much all stores then—two drug, two hardware, two lumberyards, two [grain] elevators, two or three meat markets, two or three grocery stores, two barber shops, an opera house . . ." The railway that stopped at Tampico served mainly as a shipping and shopping center for neighboring farmers. No one was rich in Tampico, but no one starved or went without shoes in winter. Social life centered around school or church activities. Patriotic holidays were occasion for picnics and firework displays. The community was fairly cohesive and its residents shared similar educational and economic backgrounds. Very few had gone past grade school. Most had never traveled as far as Chicago and considered nearby Dixon and Fulton—which were an equidistant twenty-six miles—an excursion.

On September 16, 1908, the Reagans' first son, John Neil, was born at home. Father Defore from the Catholic church came to pay the new mother a visit. "'It's time, Nellie, to baptize the baby,'" Neil Reagan reports his mother told him the priest said.

"'I'm still trying to make up my mind, Father,' she replied.

"And Father Defore said, 'You don't have any choice, Nellie, you promised to bring up the children as Catholic when you were married to Jack in Fulton.'

"And she said, 'No, I didn't. Nothing was mentioned about that.'

---

*The structure was then known as the Graham Building.

"And the priest turned to my dad, and said, 'Jack, Nellie says nothing was told to her about bringing the children up Catholic. Why is that?'

"Jack snapped his fingers and said, 'Father, I completely forgot! The priest who married us* told me right after the ceremony that he had forgotten to tell Nellie, and I told him not to worry about it, that I would tell her. I've never thought a thing about it until this very moment!'"

John Neil was baptized, and Nelle and Jack made a pact. Their children would be raised Catholic, but at an age when they could think for themselves they were to have a free choice. The Bible had always been Nelle's companion and she was drawn to the Christian Church,† which derived all its beliefs from the New Testament and was an offshoot of the Presbyterian Church. Their belief was in unity among all Christians and they followed "the primitive and simple gospel."

On Easter, March 27, 1910, Nelle was received into the Christian Church of Tampico, professing her faith in Christ. Not long after, she became pregnant for the second time. "One of the worst blizzards occurred late Sunday [February 5]," the *Tampico Tornado* reported on February 6, 1911. "After the wind and snow had spent its fury, the snow was ten inches to a foot on the level and drifted badly making the highways nearly impassable." Nelle was in hard labor and having a difficult time, and Jack feared for her life. Neil was sent downstairs to stay with the neighbors. Jack managed to make his way to Dr. Terry's house, but the doctor was on another call. Jack then tracked through the snow to the house of Mrs. Roy Rasine, the local midwife, and brought her back to help Nelle deliver. The birth was difficult and long. Finally Dr. Terry arrived and the child's squeals and screams filled the small bedroom. Jack Reagan peered closely at his second son, who the doctor had just informed him would be Nelle's last child.

"For such a little bit of a Dutchman, he makes a hell of a lot of noise, doesn't he?" he commented.

"I think he's perfectly wonderful," Nelle said weakly. "Ronald Wilson Reagan."

---

*The Reagans were married by the Reverend J. L. Moloney.

† Also called Disciples of Christ and Campbellites. In 1906, the Christian Church had separated into two factions because of a dispute over instrumental music being incorporated into the church service. The progressive group, which allowed it, became known as the Disciples of Christ. This was the church into which Nelle Reagan was received. For the purposes of this book, the Christian Church (Disciples of Christ) will be referred to hereafter as simply the Christian Church although the author acknowledges that the latter is not the full and correct title.

The next day the *Tornado* announced, "Jack Reagan has been calling 37 inches a yard and giving 17 ounces for a pound this week at Pitney's store; he has been feeling so jubilant over the arrival of a 10 pound boy Monday."

Jack continued to brag about his "fat little Dutchman" (a term chosen because of the child's robust appearance) and so "Dutch" was what the child was nicknamed and most often called.

(Neil relates that he remained downstairs for several days before he was told, "Now you can go home and see your baby brother . . . for two days after I was home I would not go in the room where my brother and my mother were. I didn't want any part of a brother. I had been promised a sister by my mother and father. That's all I wanted. I guess that shows you early in life I determined not to be queer [laughter]. I was strictly a girl man.")

Three months after Ronald Wilson Reagan's birth, his family moved to a small white-frame structure (known as the Burden House) across from a park that was distinguished by a Civil War cannon and a seventeen-foot memorial column with a statue of a Union soldier atop. Burden House had been built in the 1870s, but the bungalow had an indoor toilet and modern plumbing. The house was also near the railroad tracks. One day when Dutch was about eighteen months old, he toddled after Neil, who had plans to take some ice from a wagon parked on the other side of the tracks. The two crawled beneath a train that was stopped in the station just moments before it lurched into motion. Nelle watched "horrified from the front porch of the house until she saw them emerge [from the other side] safely."

Leaving Fulton had not ended the problems caused by William Reagan's drinking. He became gravely ill in 1912, a result of his alcoholism, and suffered such intense delirium tremens that his mind was affected. Fearing that William might do harm to himself or others, Jack filed a petition in 1914 to have his brother declared insane. The authorities rejected the request. (Neil comments that "[William] really went off the track with his drinking, over a girl . . . he had hoped to marry, but she jilted him. He never recovered.")*

By now, Nelle was active in the Christian Church. More important, the church's doctrine had had a strong effect on her. She

---

*In 1919, after William Reagan seriously injured himself with broken glass from a smashed empty whiskey bottle, Jack Reagan signed a second petition to commit William. This time the court approved. William died in 1925 in the mental institution to which he had been committed.

attended prayer meetings with both children every Wednesday and Sunday nights. Sunday mornings, the boys were taken to Sunday School. ("In between all the churchgoing," Neil said, "I had to run an important errand every Sunday for Dad; it was to fetch a nickel's worth of beer from the local saloon.") Within a short time, Nelle had developed into a visiting disciple, helping anyone she knew who was in distress or moral confusion, praying with or for them, taking more and more time away from her family to help others. She remained close to her sister Jennie, who lived in nearby Coleta. Christmas holidays were spent together with Jennie and her family, traveling by bobsled and teams to Tampico where the children played tag and fox and goose in the snow.

"I can remember," Neil says, "when we were little kids in Tampico, and I can remember very vividly [one Christmas] . . . my mother saying, 'What do you fellas want for Santa Claus to bring you?' I had only one thing: 'I want an electric train.' Now that was the furthest from the family budget, even though they probably didn't cost very much in those days. My mother then started the campaign that maybe Santa Claus didn't have electric trains, you know. Every day, some way or another, she'd get around to the subject, trying to soften the blow when I got up Christmas morning and there was no electric train.

"The night before Christmas, boy, we [Dutch and Neil] heard the *whee*s and laughing and all the noise. We sneaked part way down the stairway and looked across into the parlor (we had a living room, and then we had a parlor) where the Christmas tree was, and here's Jack with the train all set up on the track. It's going around the track—the engine, one car, and this caboose is going around this track, and he's getting a bigger kick out of it than I was getting. We didn't dare let them know we saw it."

Neither parent was ever demonstrative toward their sons. Neil could recall no physical contact except for an occasional spanking. But Jack was a softer touch when it came to giving in to one or the other of the boys' strong wishes, even if it meant no meat on the table for a week or two to pay for it. And to please Nelle, he did join her drama group, which had space above the bank in a building called the Opera House. Jack loved to dance, but acting was another matter. Still, he appeared with Nelle in *The Dust of the Earth*, a play that required a dying child. Nelle carried Neil onstage, his face painted with calcimine to make him look ghostly.

In January 1914, President Woodrow Wilson approved the

landing of U.S. Marines in Veracruz in retaliation for the arrest of U.S. sailors in Tampico, Mexico, during the Mexican Revolution. Nothing as dramatic was taking place in Tampico, Illinois. But the Reagans did begin a series of moves—first to a small cold-water flat on the South Side of Chicago near the Chicago State University campus. Jack was employed as a shoe salesman at the Fair Store on South State Street. Opened in 1897, the monolithic building occupied a square block and was nine stories high and known as the largest department store in the world. The Fair Store was Jack's first experience at punching a time clock and being just one of more than three hundred employees, a difficult situation for him.

Ronald Reagan recalled that one day in Chicago he and Neil had been left alone while Nelle had gone on "one of her periodic goodwill trips. We got scared, with twilight coming on, and went to scour the city for our parents." After carefully blowing out the gas lamp, they wandered about two or three blocks and finally got "engaged in a debate with a friendly drunk who thought we shouldn't be out so late. Nelle [the Reagan sons always called their parents by their first names] arrived just in time to agree with him. Nelle had almost lost her mind, coming home to a gas-filled house with us missing. [For once she lost] her temper and stood as a figure of righteous wrath while Jack clobbered us."

That December, Jack lost his job and they packed up their possessions and took the train to Galesburg, a fairly large man-ufacturing center in Knox County where Jack had relatives who helped him obtain a good job with a prospering shoe store.* The Reagans moved into a rented house on a tree-lined, red-brick street. The house had an attic where the landlord had stored an enormous collection of birds' eggs and butterflies. Dutch would sneak up alone and "sit for hours . . . looking at those glass-encased collections." He was five at the time and the Galesburg school had no kindergarten, but Nelle had taught Dutch to read by sitting with him every evening and having him follow her fin-ger as she read.

"One evening," he recalled, "all the funny black marks on paper clicked into place." He was lying on the floor with the eve-ning paper and his father asked him what he was doing. He re-

---

*Ironically, Loyal Davis, a member of one of the older families in Galesburg, attended Knox College in his hometown before going on to Northwestern Medical School. Dr. Davis was to become Reagan's father-in-law when his adopted stepdaughter, Nancy, took her vows as Reagan's second wife.

plied that he was reading. Jack asked him to read something then, and he did. Nelle proudly invited the neighbors to come in while he recited "such events as the aftermath of a bomb that had exploded in San Francisco during a parade and the exciting details of the two-dead, Black Tom explosion in New Jersey [perpetrated by German saboteurs]."

Europe was at war—Germany and the Kaiser the enemy. After the sinking of the American ship *Sussex* by a German submarine, Wilson issued an ultimatum for Germany to cease such unrestricted attacks. In the November 1916 election, the Democratic campaign slogan "He kept us out of war" helped return Wilson to the presidency, but war was imminent. On February 3, 1917, after the sinking of other U.S. vessels, Wilson broke diplomatic relations with Germany, and on April 6, 1917, America entered World War I. There were rally parades in Galesburg and lines at the Army Recruiting Office. Jack tried to sign up, but to Nelle's relief was not accepted. His younger son recalled, "He always protested his bad timing . . . too young for the Spanish-American—and too old for 'Over There.'"

Dutch had been enrolled in the first grade of Filas Willard School in February 1916. In the middle of his second year (1918), the Reagans were forced to move again (Jack had been fired because of his drinking), this time to a two-story house at 218 Seventh Avenue in Monmouth, Illinois, where Jack was again employed as a shoe clerk in the E. B. Colwell Department Store on South Main Street. Monmouth was remembered most vividly by Dutch for "the parades, the torches, the bands, the shoutings and the drunks and the burning of Kaiser Bill in effigy [in 1918 at the time of the Armistice]." Monmouth was also the birthplace of Wyatt Earp, a fact that gave the small city of about eight thousand a romantic aura.

Entering a new school was never an easy task. Dutch must have found Monmouth tougher than Galesburg. "I remember six or eight of us from old Central School decided he was too new around here," the former Gertrude Crockett said. "We chased him all the way home—up onto his porch. (When he came through here in 1976 campaigning for the nomination [Reagan's first bid for the presidency], he told me it was the only time in his life he'd been truly terrified, scared to death.) I don't know why I did what I did. He lived on Seventh. I lived on Ninth and a huge, big, black gal lived on Eighth. We all walked east from school going home every day. This afternoon, some boys joined us and that's when it happened. His mother was a tough old gal and came out on the porch and gave us a red-hot lecture. . . .*

"Maybe the kids thought he was stuck-up or something. My best girlfriend was Laura Hays . . . she was the smart kid in our class. The day Dutch entered our class for the first time, Laura brought him into the room and I remember that she introduced him to all us staring kids. He was startling to look at (not only good-looking but he had this air about him), and she sensed that he was special and should be introduced. I sensed it too and used to turn around in class just to stare back at him. His jaw was always set—as though somebody was going to take a poke at him and he was ready for the punches . . . I looked at his thrust out chin every day and wondered 'Why?'"

The flu epidemic hit Monmouth when Dutch was in the third grade and "the school closed down and everyone wore masks." Nelle, a victim of the disease, nearly died. "The house grew so quiet," he recalled, "and I sat watching for the guy with the black bag [a Dr. Laurence, who lived around the corner], and when he came down Jack went outside with him and I waited with a lurking terror for him to come back, and he'd say, 'She's going to be all right,' but his face didn't say so, and I went to bed and woke up with a weight dragging at the pit of my stomach till one day Jack said 'she's going to be all right,' and his face looked as if the sun was out . . ."

Nelle had begun to feel she had found her rightful niche in life. The prayers she expended on behalf of Jack's drinking were extended to the husbands and sons of church members. She had a melodious voice, an ability to speak with conviction and she could quote the Bible at length. When words of comfort or hope were needed, she always knew the right and meaningful passage. She became what might be considered a local missionary, dispensing the word of the Good Book. (The promise she had made to Father Defore had long been forgotten. The boys were being raised in the Christian Church.)

The Reagans were unaware of Dutch's poor sight. He managed to do well in school mainly because of his prodigious memory. His third-grade teacher, Miss Luhens, was amazed at the way he could rattle off dates and names and how fast he was at multiplication and division. Monmouth's Central School was a

---

*Gertrude Crockett added, "Maureen Reagan [Reagan's daughter], when she was in Monmouth, told me [Nelle] was a 'tiger.'"

large, foreboding four-story brick building without much land
for a playground and with very few shade trees. Neil adjusted
better and faster than his brother. Gertrude Crockett, however,
points out Dutch's "charisma—everyone was taken with it, Miss
Luhens, Laura Hays—he had a crush on her, although he didn't
think any of us knew . . . I remember thinking—make up your
mind—is your name R*ee*gan or R*ay*gan. He sometimes pronounced it differently. But he had super ability, like Laura, and—
I guess—*class.*"

Winter 1918 was severe, and before it ended Dutch contracted
pneumonia, his first serious illness. After Nelle's siege, the Reagans were on constant vigil. The first day he was up all the neighborhood kids brought their lead soldiers in (apparently a gesture
to make up for their earlier attack). "The sun streamed through
the window and I felt like a king with an army of 500," he recalled. The family's medical difficulties did not end with Dutch's
recovery. A short time after, a truck hit Neil and ran over his leg.
Miraculously, the leg healed without complication.

The country was enjoying a postwar prosperity, but the Reagan family was still suffering hard times. Jack's salary was not
enough to cover inflationary prices, the high medical bills they
had incurred and the alcohol he consumed. Nelle was more than
careful with the dollar, but she never let her kids go without anything she thought important. Life revolved around Nelle in the
home. She read aloud every evening, Jack seated at one end of the
kitchen table with his newspaper, while at the other end the kids
crowded next to Nelle. A huge pan of buttered popcorn stood in
the middle of the table. Apples and salted crackers were other
Reagan staples as Nelle read to the boys about King Arthur and
the Round Table or the Three Musketeers.

During the summer of 1919, Jack's old boss, H. C. Pitney,
blindness encroaching upon him and with no one to help him
manage the store, wrote Jack offering better pay and a chance to
become a partner if he returned to Tampico. The Reagans were
quick to accept. They left Monmouth in August. This time they
moved into a flat above the Pitney Store and across Main Street
from the bakery. Dutch and Neil were delighted with the freedom
the small town gave them to roam the outskirts or play in the
streets. Nelle became involved in the high school theater group;
Jack, however, was restless. After the more cosmopolitan life of
the larger cities they had been living in, Tampico, with two of
everything except a tavern, was claustrophobic. He told Pitney he

did not want to stay. Pitney decided to sell, and evoked a promise from Reagan to remain until a buyer for the business was found.

Summer of 1920 passed and the Reagans were still in Tampico. "Evenings Neil and Dutch sat on their downstairs steps with a bowl of popcorn, giving handfuls to friends passing by," recalls Vernon Denison, a Tampico school chum. "Dutch entered the fifth grade with me in September. School work centered mainly on the 3 R's—reading, 'rithmetic and the Palmer method of 'riting large curves. And there was history," Denison remembers, "American history. We brought our own books and traded or sold them to grades behind us. But in front of the class there also stood a little bookcase from which we could 'check-out' books. Dutch was an 'A' student because he had such a good memory for dates."

Tampico's youth was divided into two factions by Main Street. Dutch led the "West Side Alley Gang," Harold "Monkey" Winchell the "East Side Alley Gang." The Winchells lived almost directly across the street from the Reagans, above their family shoe store. Vernon Denison was a member of Dutch's gang and recalls "racing across the pens of the town stockyards, swinging from pen to pen, jumping from gate to gate, opening and shutting the gates to block Monkey and his gang from catching up with us." If anyone was caught, no violence occurred, but it did mean a loss of face.

The two gangs also engaged in food fights. From the garbage cans of the alley they compiled an arsenal of rotten fruit and tomatoes. "What's the difference?" Denison says. "We didn't shoot people or smoke pot—except a few corn silk cigarettes maybe [six-inch corn silk stogies wrapped in newspaper]."

Most of the time Dutch managed to stay out of trouble, or at least to avoid being caught. Once, Monkey Winchell recalls, "His dad had been on a hunting trip, but he only had a single-shot gun that you had to reload. My dad had a five-shot gun, so we had to go across the street to see it. We stood it up. I don't think we could have gotten shot with it because we weren't higher than a barrel—and we clicked it once. It just clicked.

"We had to pump it and click it again. The next time it [the shot] went through the ceiling." Monkey rolled on the floor, too scared to cry. Bits of mortar and lath showered down onto them.

Reagan later recalled hearing "the thunder of feet on the stairs, the yells of alarm coming rapidly nearer." When Jack and Nelle entered the room, Monkey and Dutch sat huddled together on the couch in a cloud of smoke, "frantically reading our Sunday School quarterly."

Jack administered a licking that his younger son was never to forget, despite Nelle's pleading that the rod be spared in this instance because the good Lord had seen fit to save the boy Himself. "My worst experience as a boy was not the licking I got for that," Reagan insisted later. "My father bought a carload of second-hand potatoes for a personal speculation. My brother and I were ordered to the siding to sort the good potatoes from the bad. . . . [We] sat in a stinking boxcar during hot summer . . . gingerly gripping tubers that dissolve[d] in the fingers with a dripping squish, emitting an odor worse than that of a decaying corpse . . . for days. At last we got so queasy at the very look of spuds that we simply lied about the rest and dumped them all good or bad. My father made a little money on the proposition. We got a near permanent dislike for potatoes in any form."

At Tampico Grade School Dutch fell under the stern but kind direction of Miss Nellie Darby. His best chum was Denison (whom he called Newt), and they attended all the silent Westerns, gaining free admission by carrying coal to the Opera House where they were shown.

"[On Sundays] we wore knee pants and black stockings," Denison confessed, "and when our shoes wore out we put cardboard in the bottoms and when we got holes in our stockings we painted in shoe polish to cover 'em up. We stole a few grapes and some apples. . . . We had this janitor at the school. In the fall we'd all come down and help him rake up all the leaves and we'd stay for a big marshmallow roast. We didn't play ball on Sunday. . . . We had to go to church and then have the family dinner and not much rough play."

Monkey Winchell recalled how they all used to go swimming north of town where the county ditches merged. Dutch was by far the best swimmer and would lead the way barefoot via the railroad cinder path to the deeper, more dangerous Hennepin Canal. "We was poor folks," Winchell admitted, "but [Dutch] and Neil were always dressed clean, not raggedy . . . I was always envious. They had a bicycle [a secondhand model belonging to Neil] and there wasn't too many bicycles in town. When we got a chance to ride it, that was really something." It sat out front near a hitching post when Neil wasn't riding it. At noon, when Jack came home for lunch, Dutch would get up into the seat and Jack would push him around "in the street for a few exhilarating circles."

Next door to Pitney's was Greenman Jewelry Store (Dutch called the Greenmans Aunt Emma and Uncle Jim). They had a special fondness for the youngest Reagan, giving him ten cents a week as an allowance and welcoming him with cookies and chocolate any time he came to visit—which was daily. In his autobiography, Reagan recalled spending many days in an old rocker in the "mystic atmosphere" of the Greenman living room, furnished with "its horsehair-stuffed gargoyles of furniture, its shawls and antimacassars, globes of glass over birds and flowers, books and strange odors." Other times he would remain hidden in a downstairs corner of the jewelry store "with its curious relics, faint lights from gold and silver and bronze, lulled by the erratic ticking of a dozen clocks and the drone [of the voices] of the customers who came in." Greenman's was not quite so exotic as recalled, for it also carried veterinarian supplies and patent medicines.

At Christmastime the Reagans took the train to visit members of the Wilson family who had a farm near Morrison, Illinois. From the station, they rode through the deep winter snow in a sleigh with hot bricks at their feet, buffalo robes as lap blankets and with bells jingling. Dutch loved such adventures. It brought him in touch with ways of life other than his own. He talked about being a cowboy and living out West.

The Reagans did not own a crystal set, but the Wilsons did, and Dutch listened "with breathless attention, a pair of earphones attached tightly to my head, scratching a crystal with a wire. I was listening to raspy recorded music and faint voices saying, 'This is KDKA, Pittsburgh, KDKA, Pittsburgh.'" When the sound faded, he got up in the room of a dozen or so people and imitated the announcer. Everyone laughed and he repeated the performance.

The boy was developing into a dreamer, and he found escape in worlds other than the drab flat on Main Street. Nelle was a good homemaker, but Jack's drinking cut severely into her housekeeping money. The flat came with some simple sturdy furniture and its rent was deductible from Jack's earnings. With all their moving around and having always to make do, Nelle had never been able to own much in the way of her own furnishings and decorations. She dreamed of one day possessing two things—a sewing machine and a kitchen cabinet in which to keep and display the set of dishes she had received as a wedding gift. She did some sales work and alterations at Pitney's and liked the chance to talk to people. Church duties continued to take up a large portion of her time. For relaxation she would go around the countryside giving dramatic readings with "the zest of a frustrated actress." Dutch would sometimes accompany her, watching with fascination as "she recited classic speeches in tragic tones, wept as she flung herself into . . . such melodramas as *East Lynne,* and poured out poetry by the yard."

She shared a closer affinity with her younger son. Jean Kinney, a friend to Neil throughout his life, observed, "Neil seemed always to be defying his mother. I had the feeling he really disliked her and preferred to think he was like his father." A sense of their Irish heritage drew him to Jack, along with shared interests and personalities. Both had a touch of the promoter and a good shake of Irish brash. Jack represented good times and much laughter; Nelle, somber prayer and high standards. And whereas Neil was well built, a good natural athlete, Dutch was "scrawny," a dreamer, somewhat precocious. He had what the family thought was a nervous habit of blinking a bit too much. No one gave much thought to his favorite reading position—flat on his stomach on the floor where his eyes were only inches from a book—or the fact that he insisted on sitting in the front row at the movies. Tom Mix was his favorite movie actor. His private idol was the local taxidermist who had a collection of fierce-looking fish and antlered deer mounted on the walls of his shop. He got along better with women than Neil did because he had a sincere need to please them— Nelle, Aunt Emma, his teacher, the mothers of his friends—and they all adored him. He had an innate politeness—his hat came off as soon as he entered a room, he sat only after the ladies had done so and he was quick to offer his assistance in toting packages. Still, there was not a scrap of sissiness about him.

In fact, skinny as he was, myopic as he would soon be found to be, Dutch Reagan was a leader and a scrappy opponent on any field of sport. The summer of 1920, when he was nine and a half, he played football for the first time. "There was no field, no lines, no goal. Simply grass, the ball, and a mob of excited youngsters," he later recalled. "We chose up sides, backed up to the limits of the field, and one of us kicked off. Then, screaming and waving our arms we descended on the unlucky kid who caught it. Everyone piled on top of him. ["I got a wild exhilaration out of jumping feet first into a pile up," he said another time of this experience.] I worshipped the wild charge down the field and the final melee— but being underneath it all . . . I got frightened to the point of hysteria in the darkness under the mass of writhing, shouting bodies."

Jack's drinking grew in proportion to his dissatisfaction at Pitney's. Somehow, he managed to pull himself together during working hours. Saturday nights were the worst times. Remembering back, Ronald Reagan would recall, "My mother would pray constantly for him. She was on her knees several times a day. And she just refused to give up, no matter how dark things looked." Her lack of success in helping Jack exorcise his drinking demon did not inhibit her from proselytizing to others. The Christian Church was adamantly against alcohol, as they were against the thriving abortion clinics* that operated in major cities like New York and Chicago. Nelle never condemned any woman for illegitimately carrying a child, but she did all in her power to convince such local "misfortunates" to have their babies.

On the night of January 15–16, the eve of Prohibition, the Christian Church held a midnight service. At 12:01 A.M., when the Volstead Act came into effect, bells pealed in the dark, moonless night, proclaiming a great victory. Tampico's one tavern was closed. But Jack's liquor problem was far from settled. One could still obtain a beverage called near beer—a beer that had the alcohol drawn off. However, with a few grains of medicinal alcohol needled into it, its former state was practically restored. The demise of Tampico's saloon hit Jack even harder than the loss of easy access to good whiskey. The tavern had been the only place he could go when he needed the company of other men with whom he could exchange stories and momentarily escape into another world.

Sixteen months after the Reagans had returned to Tampico, Pitney finally sold the store. He gave his former manager a percentage, not of the sale (as Jack had expected and been promised) but of another business he owned, the Fashion Boot Shop, twenty-six miles away in Dixon. The country had great hopes of new prosperity. Warren G. Harding, the Republican presidential candidate, had just won the election over Governor James M. Cox of Ohio, who had thirty-eight-year-old Franklin Delano Roosevelt (not yet crippled from polio) as his running mate. Harding had a special kinship with the press. One cold December night, as he took a walk in the company of some reporters, he confessed, "I

---

*Goeffrey Perrett in *America in the Twenties* wrote: "In the country as a whole it was estimated that up to 1 million women a year [1920] were criminally aborted. There was abortion by knitting needle, coat hanger, and buttonhook. Desperate women swallowed poisonous concoctions in an attempt to induce a miscarriage. Criminal abortion killed as many as 50,000 women a year. Yet it was absolutely against the law to disseminate birth control information and devices under Section 211 of the U.S. Penal code."

can't hope to be the best President this country's ever had, but if I can I'd like to be the best-loved."

On December 6, 1920, the Reagans left Tampico for Dixon. After posing for a neighborhood picture, they crowded into their first car, a secondhand model that had once belonged to Mr. Pitney. Dutch's cat, Guinevere, had had kittens, duly named King Arthur, Sir Galahad and Buster. Jack said they would have to be left behind, but Nelle snuck them into a covered basket and placed it on the floor of the rear seat under the boys' feet. Piled high around them and tied to the roof of the car were most of the Reagans' possessions. Neil and Dutch could hardly contain themselves. Jack had been telling them stories for a week about Dixon ("a big city")—how the circus came there and about the yard they would have at their new house.

3

"DIXON WAS ALWAYS A SMALL TOWN. IT ALWAYS has been and it always will be," Dixon historian George Lamb boasted. With no large nearby metropolitan centers, people were generally born, educated and married there. "Folks had dreams [to move away and become successful] . . . but most never realized them. . . . The real center was downtown; it was a Saturday night town."

Nearly one half of Dixon's population was employed in industry: Brown Shoe Company, the Reynolds Wire Company, Medusa Cement, J. I. Case, which made plows and farm implements, Clipper Lawn Mower Company, and several feed-and-grain companies. The area around Dixon was farm country. The dairy farms supplied the Borden Milk Company, and farmers grew wheat and corn to market. Both the Illinois Central and Northwestern railroads came through, enabling farmers to transport their produce to Chicago, Omaha and the South. Predominantly blue-collar and lower middle class, Dixon prided itself on being "the backbone of the country. Nothing much," Mr. Lamb says, "could shake those foundations."

Dixon first saw life as a way-stop for those seeking their fortune elsewhere. The winding, treacherously swift currents of the
Rock River, which snaked through the area, had to be forded if
the riches of the lead-mining town of Galena were to be reached.
By 1828, a French-Canadian trader named Joseph Ogee had
opened a ferry to transport heavy wagons and draft animals
across the river. He built, and for two years operated, both a ferry
and a tavern, and then sold the enterprise, along with a small
cabin, to pioneer John Dixon, whom the peaceful local Rock River
Indians referred to as "Nada-chu-ra-sak" (white-haired Father)
due to his long, flowing, silver hair. For the same reason, the in-
dustrious settlers who remained in Dixon because of the rich
farmland and the power to be harnessed from the river were to
call him "Father."

Dixon's growth was more steady than spectacular. Once the
riches of Galena had vanished along with its lead mines, the population influx slowed down to a languorous trickle. Nearly 6,000
people poured into Dixon between 1850 and 1860. Fifty years
later, in 1910, Dixon's census recorded a population increase of
only 1,216. Ninety-eight miles west of Chicago by rail and 105
miles by highway, Dixon was too distant to benefit from the
growth of Illinois's major city. By 1920, which saw a boom that
doubled and tripled the size of many Midwest towns as privately
owned companies were taken over by large corporations, the population had reached only 8,191. Despite the advent of the telephone and the telegraph, the radio, the automobile and the train,
Dixon remained a backwater—an isolated and overgrown prairie
village little more than an enlargement of Tampico. Still, a young
boy fed stories by a father with a glib manner and a penchant for
exaggeration might view the town not in "the drab hues of reality" but with a certain enchantment.

Actually, Dixon sat squat in the middle of rich farmland, un-
protected and unprotecting. No great homes were to be found.
People there earned lower wages than the national average. (Reagan was later to state, "We didn't know we were poor because the
people around us were of the same circumstance.") Even the more
successful merchants, small manufacturers, lawyers, doctors and
bankers earned modest incomes and lived in the "gaunt frame
shelters like grocery boxes" that made up the fictional Gopher
Prairie of Sinclair Lewis's *Main Street* and were typical of small
midwestern towns in the earlier part of the century. Front porches
extended in buck-toothed fashion, destroying the natural lines of
the low frame houses. Architectural innovation had never reached

Dixon. Houses built in 1920 looked like spruced-up versions of homes constructed fifty years earlier.

Little choice of merchandise was offered in its Main Street stores. Mail order was used for most household or farm items. Eggs and chickens, bacon slabs and catfish were easy to come by. But fruits and vegetables grown out of the state were as exotic as litchi nuts and escargots. The drugstore had a soda fountain. The hotel was strictly a hotel—no dining room. There were a couple of luncheonettes, but mostly Dixon's workers brown-bagged it or went home at noon. For amusement, there was a movie house (the Dixon Theater), a small playhouse (the Old Family Theater) and Plum Hollows Golf Club. Ladies held meetings at the library or at church. Dances were given in the high school gymnasium. In the summer, Lowell Park offered boating, bathing and fishing; and the Chautauqua, which lasted about two weeks, was located a mile up the highway at the end of the trolley line. The Chautauqua, named for the town in New York where it originated, was a national organization that arranged church seminars and presented visiting lecturers in small towns across the country. People who came from a distance lived in tents during the Chautauqua, and the campsites took on a fairgrounds atmosphere, with concessionaires and picnic areas along the banks of the Rock River.

The river's swift currents bisected Dixon. Catfish from its waters were said to be the best you could catch anywhere. Almost everyone had to cross it at some point on a daily basis. Kids fished on the banks, pants rolled up but never quite high enough to avoid the mud. Heavy rains all too often caused damaging floods, and sighs of "The river's low" indicated droughts. An area on the south bank, Demon Town, contained, until Prohibition, a number of thriving taverns. But in a section farther up the bank, known as Bootleggers' Knob, black-market alcohol could still be purchased.

Instead of driving directly to their new home, Jack took a detour of a few blocks to Galena Street so that they could pass under the recently built wooden Memorial Arch with "D I X O N" emblazoned across it. The arch had replaced a temporary structure that had been raised in honor of "Dixon's Returning Heroes"* after the signing of the Armistice. The *Dixon*

---

*These were H. F. Walder, Walter Smith and Dement Schuller, who repeated the march on July 1, 1979—sixty years later—when a new concrete-and-steel arch (the second of these) had been built to replace the one before.

Evening Telegraph reported that on that occasion, "As the [three Dixon] heroes marched beneath the arch, thousands of flowers were strewn in their path by ladies and to the riot of color was added color-paper streamers thrown from upper floors of the Nachusa Tavern [the hotel]." Painted on the back of the arch were the following words: "A grateful people pause in their welcome to the victorious living to pay silent tribute to the illustrious dead."

The Reagans had rented a boxy two-story white frame dwelling at 816 South Hennepin Avenue, a narrow tree-lined street of similar middle-class houses all set fairly close together and to the street. A front porch extended only across the entryway. The house had been built in the summer of 1891 for William C. Thompson* on a fifteen-hundred-dollar loan from the Dixon Loan and Building Association. The property was now owned by Teresa and John Donovan, who had inherited the deed from Mrs. Donovan's mother. Jack had driven to Dixon on his own a few weeks earlier, signed the lease and paid twenty-three dollars for the first month's rent, high by Dixon's standards.

The house was modest—small rooms and lowish ceilings—but at the top of a narrow staircase were three bedrooms and an indoor toilet. The boys were to share one room, their parents another and the third was to be Nelle's sewing room, where she could keep her new, prized Singer sewing machine. The third bedroom represented a measure of security to Nelle. It meant she could take in a roomer if there should ever be a need. For that reason, the boys were given the smallest room, which held little more than a single bed (to be shared) and a chest of drawers. Downstairs, the front parlor had a tile fireplace.† A back parlor led off this room through an archway. The dining room was actually the alcove between the staircase and the kitchen, but was papered elegantly in a raised rococo design (all the rooms were wallpapered, but not quite so extravagantly). Nelle's first purchase for the house—from a Sears, Roebuck and Company catalog—was a cabinet to hold her china. Out back was an unused and rather ramshackle barn, fourteen feet by twenty-four feet with a loft in it—a perfect clubhouse for Neil and Dutch.

---

*The grandfather of Reagan's future Lowell Park friend Bill Thompson.

†Reagan claims the family kept a penny behind one of the loose tiles of this fireplace so that they might never be "penniless." When they later moved, he took the penny with him and has kept it since as a lucky charm.

The boys were enrolled at South Central Grammar School (a five-minute walk), Dutch in the second half of the fifth grade (he was skipped a half-term, which meant he would now matriculate in the summer) and Neil in the seventh grade. From the time that he moved into Hennepin Avenue until he reached twenty-one, Dixon would be home to Dutch, the first permanent one he would have. "All of us have a place to go back to. Dixon is that place for me," Reagan later wrote. "There was the life that shaped my mind and body for all the years to come after."

Jack Reagan believed that in coming to Dixon as a partner in the Fashion Boot Shop he would soon improve his economic standing. Pitney had put up all the money. But neither the "partnership" nor the profits from it would become effective until some far distant time when Jack had earned his half-interest in the business. This meant that any commissions he could make above his meager salary were to be deducted and applied toward his indebtedness for his share. Not too many weeks had passed before the Reagans realized commerce in Dixon would dictate a much longer period of repayment than Jack had anticipated.* To add to this, the cost of living was considerably higher than in Tampico.

To manage on Jack's small salary, Nelle forfeited such great delicacies as chicken on Sunday. Liver was considered pet food, and the butcher, if requested, would throw a pound or so in with an order. Nelle bought soup bones and asked for liver for the cats. Soup, potatoes and bread were served daily. On Sundays—since the cats ate the mice they caught in the barn anyway—the Reagans ate the cats' liver dressed up with a slab of bacon and some homegrown onions.

Neil made friends and adjusted more quickly to the new environment than his brother. "Everybody thought he [Neil] would go into the movies or go on the stage . . . he was always . . . putting on," Bill Thompson remembers. The kids at South Central nicknamed him "Moon" (from the comic-strip character Moon Mullins) and it stuck. The Reagan boys were now Dutch and Moon. Moon was a good athlete and Dutch tried hard but could not keep up with him. George and Ed O'Malley lived across the street and the four boys played football together—George and Moon squaring off against their younger brothers.

"Dutch was a bit nearsighted," Ed O'Malley says, "but he always wanted to carry the ball." Ed would give it to him and

---

*Reagan wrote: "The Depression made sure that day would never dawn."

Dutch "would go charging ahead." The older boys would let him "just start to get by when they would trip him, sending him flying into the bushes."

Dutch's poor eyesight contributed greatly to his love of football over baseball. He claims it never occurred to him that he was seriously nearsighted. In his mind, "the whole world was made up of colored blobs that became distinct when I got closer—and I was sure it appeared the same way to everyone else." He never cared for baseball because when he stood at the plate, "the ball appeared out of nowhere about two feet in front of me." And he was "the last chosen for a side in any game." This changed when he "discovered football; no little invisible ball—just another guy to grab or knock down, and it didn't matter if his face was blurred." He had trouble reading the blackboard even from a front seat in the schoolroom and bluffed his lessons, receiving good marks despite this.

Not long after his thirteenth birthday, the Reagans went for a Sunday afternoon ride. Neil kept quoting the highway advertising signs as they drove past. The Burma-Shave signs were the best, usually a series of six red panels stuck in the ground along the highway a short distance apart, each carrying a few words of the complete message. Most were amusing bits of doggerel like: DOES YOUR HUSBAND/MISBEHAVE/GRUNT AND GRUMBLE/RANT AND RAVE?/SHOOT THE BRUTE SOME/BURMA-SHAVE! Dutch could not see them and, kidding around, borrowed his mother's glasses. For the first time in his life, he saw "a glorious, sharply outlined world jump into focus . . . houses had a definite texture and hills really made a clear silhouette against the sky." Nelle had him fitted out "with huge black-rimmed spectacles." And though he felt that "the miracle of seeing was beyond believing," he soon began to hate the big glasses.*

Nonetheless, the visual aids made his two favorite pastimes—reading and the movies—much more pleasurable. He remained addicted to Western films, but also liked the new cliff-hangers that starred sports figures like Babe Ruth, Jack Dempsey and Red Grange, "who strutted, grimaced, thrashed the villains, kissed the heroines and, not incidentally, showed off their athletic prowess."

---

*In 1966, in his autobiography, *Where's the Rest of Me?* (written with Robert C. Hubler), Reagan (referring to the glasses) wrote, "I hate them to this day." As early as 1947, he was fitted with contact lenses. During the years that followed, he seldom was seen in public wearing glasses. The horn-rimmed spectacles he had once hated reappeared in 1984 when he began wearing them while giving speeches.

He took out his first library number* when he was ten and checked out an average of two books a week (always on a weekend), leaning toward boys' adventure stories—the Edgar Rice Burroughs Tarzan books and Burt L. Standish's Frank Merriwell series. *Frank Merriwell's Bravery, Frank Merriwell's Foes* and *Frank Merriwell's Sports Afield* ranked as favorites, for they were checked out twice each. The family generally attended the movies together on Friday nights. Whenever he could get Jack to give the extra dime, Dutch would go to the Saturday matinees. ("Think I'm made of money?" Jack would growl. But he usually gave in.) One Saturday *Birth of a Nation* came to town in a revival.

The Ku Klux Klan, whose antiblack activities were featured in the film, were again visible, spreading this time to the Midwest from its beginnings in the South. The Klan's objective of white supremacy had broadened to include opposition to Jews and Catholics. Klansmen violently opposed parochial schools and Catholic candidates for office, flaming crosses were set on the front lawns of Catholic schools and churches, and Jack swore that no son of his "was going to sit through their shenanigans." When he saw that his pleading approach was not working, Dutch introduced what he thought was logic. The Klan in the film, he argued, represented another period of history, not the one Jack loathed.

His father's mouth turned a shade grimmer. "The Klan's the Klan, and a sheet's a sheet, and any man who wears one over his head is a bum. And I want no more words on the subject." Jack's response seemed more logical than his, so Dutch went off to the library.

Of Dixon's twelve black families,† one breadwinner, Tom McReynolds, rode through town with an old horse and wagon collecting junk and carting it away. McReynolds made a respectable living by driving up to Rockford and selling anything good in his wagon to a scrap-metal dealer there. The McReynoldses lived on the south side of Dixon with their two sons, Winston ("Wink") and Elwood. Wink was a pretty good football player, and he and Moon sat next to each other at the back of Molly Duffy's sixth-grade class. The boys became good friends and Wink was often in the Reagan home. Thompson claims, "Nobody in those days

---

*Dixon Library issued numbers instead of cards at that time. Number 3695 was given to Ronald Wilson Reagan on December 20, 1921.

†By the 1940s the black population in Dixon grew to about four hundred.

thought of [Wink's] being black. . . . In Dixon there was no thought of it. There was just Wink . . . and Elwood and Tom, their father."

The individual feelings of certain Dixonites notwithstanding, the town was not free from prejudice. Violet McReynolds (Wink McReynolds's future wife) says there was no equality between blacks and whites. "Dixon was no different than any other city in America at that time. There weren't the same housing and job opportunities." Blacks were not allowed to register at the hotel, a rule that was enforced for many years. Nor could they get their hair done in Dixon's beauty salons or barber shops. They were excluded from membership to the Golf Club, although they did eat at the counters of the luncheonettes, attended the movie houses and never were excluded from any school function. The Reagan household was free of intolerance toward blacks. The Christian Church preached equality of color and had black parishes with black ministers.

Dixonites felt strong ties to their state's favorite son, Abraham Lincoln, who in 1832 had joined a group of Sangamon County men and volunteered for military service against the Blackhawk Indian uprisings in the North. As captain of his company, on Sunday, May 12, 1832, Lincoln led his men into the frontier community of Dixon's Ferry and there saw his only military service, succeeding in helping to drive the Blackhawks farther north. "This was a success," he wrote in 1859, "which gave me more pleasure than any I have had since."

Lincoln returned to Dixon on July 17, 1856, to deliver a two-hour speech from the lawn of the new county courthouse at Second and Ottaway avenues, just a few streets away from the Reagans' future house on Hennepin Avenue. A plaque was placed on the site inscribed with "Lincoln stood here while delivering his Great Speech, July 17, 1856." In it he urged the election of John C. Freemont, then a candidate for president, to help ward off the impending crisis that he foresaw spreading throughout the nation over the slavery issue.

Lincoln was to visit "Governor" Alexander Charters's estate, Hazelwood, several times (actually, Charters was never governor of anything but his own acreage). Hazelwood had been built on a six-hundred-acre tract three miles out of town and could claim to be Dixon's only grand and elegant house. Charters had modeled his mansion after his former home in Ireland. He had come to Dixon's Ferry to parlay his fortune into an even larger one by investing in the lead mines in Galena. When the mines were abandoned, he simply led the life of a landed gentleman, obviously not having lost his entire fortune. After his death in 1878, his son-in-law took over Hazelwood, but shortly after his death the estate became idle. Storms lashed down some of the great trees, and finally, in 1905, Hazelwood burned down. But the townspeople drove the old roads on a Sunday afternoon to see the brooding trees that encircled the charred ground where the mansion had once stood. To them, Hazelwood had been Dixon's Camelot. The only vestige of the grand life that Charters had led in Dixon centered now around the country club. Although it did not have a restaurant and was not the scene of garden parties and social affairs, the low, grass-blanketed slopes represented Dixon's one link with the gentleman's life.

Dixon did have an especially large group of women golfers. The Lincoln Highway and Northern Illinois golf tournaments were often held at the country club. Dutch worked as a caddy there the second and third summers he was in Dixon. He collected bird eggs as a hobby. Jack got him an old display case from the store and they put it up in the hayloft of the barn. Dutch lined the floor of the case with cotton batting. "[He] would punch a hole in both ends and blow the eggs out [from the shell]," Neil recalled. "He was always climbing trees to get them." Moon kept pigeons and rabbits in the barn and developed "a little business. Come Friday night if there were squabs up there, I'd get the squabs and a bucket of boiling water, and I'd snap their heads off and clean them. I'd kill four or five young rabbits, skin them and clean them. Then I'd take a market basket and go out the next day beating on doors, and I never failed to sell all the squabs and rabbits I had in the basket." Dutch could not bring himself to become part of this enterprise.

"The pool hall [in Dixon] was downstairs under a store where your folks couldn't see you if they happened to walk by," Neil remembered. "[Dutch] would never do anything like that. He would rather be up there gazing at his bird eggs."

The brothers never threw punches, but they stuck up for each other when necessary. "When someone started taking picks at me [Moon], he'd [Dutch] stick in, and if somebody started taking picks on him, I'd stick in. But on the other hand, if you were a casual observer, you'd say, 'Well, those two brothers don't have any association at all, do they?' . . . I knew when he had down moments, but I never said anything to him. There was no such thought of, you know, putting my arm around his shoulder and saying, 'Let's talk this over,' or anything like that. . . . I always

operate on the theory that [Dutch] doesn't even know I'm breathing—but that's the way it's always been with my dad, [Dutch]
and myself. Not my mother. She was not that way at all. I guess
all three of us were cut from the same bolt on the male end."

Times were tough for the Reagans. Neil says, "My mother was
a charger. [She] was the one where come rent day and my dad
would say, 'Nellie the rent is due day after tomorrow.' My mother
would just look at him and say, 'Don't worry, the Lord will provide.'" Most times, Nelle gave the Lord a hand and took in a
roomer and sewing to make the money. She had joined the Christian Church of Dixon by letter even before the move from Tampico. By 1921, religion had become a burning issue "in the
cloistered calm of rich seminaries and the dusty streets of poor
mill villages alike." Dixon's working-class population was under
the same strain. To counteract the trend toward doubters and ag-
nosticism, a back-to-basics movement gained tremendous momentum. Called Fundamentalism, this religious revival had as much
an impact on the twenties as Prohibition did. Industrialization
had pushed hundreds of thousands of simple country people into
noisome factories at the same time as it made honest, age-old
craftsmen obsolete. "Damned on Saturday night, they were desperate for Salvation on Sunday." Jack's drinking propelled Nelle
deeper into religion, where she hoped to find answers and prayer
that she could take home to him.

The members of the Christian Church of Dixon saw themselves as liberal Fundamentalists.* The Reverend Harvey Waggoner, a powerful and dogmatic speaker, led the congregation for
the first two years of Nelle's attendance. The church, whose meetings were held in the basement of the YMCA, was vigorously raising funds to obtain a building of its own. Tithing was considered
desirable, although not mandatory, for its members. No matter
how difficult her struggle to keep her family afloat, Nelle insisted
that one tenth of their income (including what the boys earned)
go to the support of the church. Nelle countered Jack's grumbling
complaints with assurances that "the Lord [will] make your
ninety percent twice as big if you [make] sure He [gets] his
tenth."†

---

*The five fundamentals of belief were: "The infallibility of the Bible; the virgin birth of
Christ; the Resurrection; that Christ died to atone for the sins of the world; and the Second
Coming."
†Reagan continued to tithe 10 percent of his earnings directly to the Hollywood-Beverly
Christian Church during his Warner Brothers years. In 1986, the church's pastor, Ben-
jamin H. Moore, stated, "The President still contributes weekly to the church."

Jack's earnings were a disappointment. He took a correspondence course to learn about the bones of the feet, believing that if he knew more he could sell shoes better. In the 1920s salesmanship was considered one of the greatest of the performing arts. Bruce Barton, the son of a poor Tennessee preacher, who had become a supersalesman and a huge success, in 1924 wrote the best seller *The Man Nobody Knows*. In it, Barton compared the art of selling *anything* with the art of selling religion. ("Jesus hated prosy dullness . . . all the greatest things in human life are one-syllable things—love, joy, hope, home, child, wife, trust, faith, God . . .")

"Jesus walked barefoot," Jack was known to say, "but then, he didn't have to deal with our Illinois winters, now did he?" Another favorite was, "I'm glad you chose that pair, they can walk to church and dance a jig on the way home." Even his gift for selling did not help greatly. The money was simply not there to be made at the Fashion Boot Shop. "People in Dixon were careful. Shoes got handed down from one child to another in a family, and folks seldom had more than two pairs—dress and work—and they took both to the shoemaker to repair worn out parts many, many times before they considered buying a new pair." Reagan was to say that he wore his brother's shoes and outgrown clothes until he was in college.

Despite the disappointing performance of his business venture, Jack would have been a better provider for his family if not for his "weakness." Reagan often told stories of his father's drunkenness. "I was eleven years old," he wrote in his autobiography, "the first time I came home to find my father flat on his back on the front porch and no one there to lend a hand but me. He was drunk, dead to the world. I stood over him for a minute or two. I wanted to let myself in the house and go to bed and pretend he wasn't there. Oh, I wasn't ignorant of his weakness. I don't know at what age I knew what the occasional absences or the loud voices in the night meant, but up till now my mother or my brother handled the situation and I was a child in bed with the privilege of pretending sleep. . . . I felt myself fill with grief for my father at the same time as I was feeling sorry for myself. Seeing his arms spread out as if they were crucified—as indeed he was—his hair soaked with melting snow, snoring as he breathed . . . I bent over him, smelling the sharp odor from the speakeasy. I got a fistful of his overcoat. Opening the door, I managed to drag him inside and get him to bed."

Nelle taught the boys tolerance, even of their father's "bouts with the dark demon in the bottle." Alcoholism, she insisted, was a sickness and one should never condemn a man or woman for something beyond his or her control. Jack never understood Nelle's dedication to her church, her obsessive ministering or her interest in theater any more than she could explain his drinking. Jack's cynicism, his frustration, his violent anger at the men behind big business, his growing inclination toward week-long benders, his "lusty, vulgar humor" and his feistiness never seemed to undermine Nelle's optimism. Reagan said, "If [Jack] was occasionally vulgar [Nelle] tried to raise the tone of the family."

Dutch and Moon were the first to be baptized in the new Christian Church at 123 Hennepin (completed only three days earlier) on June 21, 1922. The sacrament of baptism was a personal confession of faith—a symbol of death, burial and resurrection of Christ, and a commitment to the way of Christ. With the immersion the old life is buried, new life is born, and sins are forgiven. The Reverend Waggoner had died only a few days before of a sudden blood disease and it is unclear who officiated at the brothers' baptism (a fire destroyed the church's records in 1928), although it is considered most likely that it would have been Harry H. Peters, state secretary for the Christian Church who functioned as minister until a replacement for the Reverend Waggoner could be found (a matter of only a few weeks). After his immersion before the congregation, as he rose from the waters, Reagan remembered hearing the minister say, "Arise and walk in newness of faith," or, in other words, in a new born-again state.*

So intense was Nelle's faith as opposed to her husband's that Neil claims he did not know until he was eighteen years old that Jack was Catholic. "We [Dutch and Moon] were brought up in the Christian Church, which meant Sunday School Sunday mornings, church Sunday morning, Christian Endeavor Sunday evening, church after Christian Endeavor, and prayer meeting on Wednesdays." But if Moon's compliance in the baptism was meant only to appease or please his mother, Dutch's was a more deliberate act. Both boys had a sense of religion, but Dutch's faith was a more active part of his life. (Reagan told Reverend Adrian Rogers, president of the Southern Baptist Convention in 1980, that he had felt "called" at the time of his baptism, adding, "I had a personal experience when I invited Christ into my life."

---

*The Disciples movement does not believe in infant baptism.

The Reverend Rogers asked him if he knew the Lord Jesus or just knew about him. Reagan replied, "I KNOW him!")

"My Sunday School class is getting paid for janitor work [in a nearby building] and we are using the money to plaster our S[unday] S[chool] classroom," Dutch, at thirteen, wrote a church member who had moved away. Two years later, he taught his own "Sunday School class" for young boys at the church and was a leader of several of the prayer meetings. Class members say he made examples of current sports figures as young men with Christian principle. The congregation was much taken with his voice and delivery, which they believed owed a great deal to the private elocution lessons Nelle gave him. Parishioners of the church like to recount how Dutch could make the Bible seem personal, like a "phrase might just have been written."

"Everybody loved Nelle Reagan and looked up to her as a leader," Mrs. Mildred Neer, the wife of Dutch's Sunday School teacher, said, the expression on her face glowing as she added, "She was always there when anyone needed her. God always heard Nelle Reagan's prayers and answered them." Questioned as to whether she had ever asked [her now deceased husband] what Dutch was like in Sunday School, she replied, "Just a live wire. A real all-American boy."

In discussions about Dutch during the 1920s with Dixonites who shared those years with him, that phrase crops up frequently. *All-American boy. What exactly does that mean?* "Well, a kid who believes in the Lord's word, respects his elders and still has enough spit in him to get into trouble once in a while," confessed one gentleman who knew Dutch. *What kind of trouble?* "Puttin' a buck rabbit into the cage of the female rabbits when we weren't supposed to. Although I think it was Ed O'Malley who done that. Dutch weren't afraid of a rough fight. Never saw him back down. His dad would tan his hide if he didn't win though."

Nelle Reagan's personal ministry grew to extend beyond members of her family and church. "If Nelle had had the education, I think she would have mounted the pulpit," a contemporary commented.* She regularly visited patients at Katherine Shaw Bethea and the state mental hospitals, and scheduled weekly visits to prisoners in the local jail as well. Dixon did not have much of a

*The Christian Church encourages women in the ministry and had two women ministers at the time who were well known for the flamboyance of their millinery choices. At meetings their appearance was referred to as "the war of the hats."

crime problem. Petty theft and drunk-and-disorderly conduct
were the causes of most arrests. Nelle ate a Spartan lunch of soda
crackers on jail-visiting days, but always brought apples or cookies to the inmates along with her Bible. She would read from it
and then give the prisoners the Book to hold in their hands.

"She had a way of givin' out her religion that wasn't offensive.
She was an elocutionist—dramatic readings is what it is called
nowadays," Dixonite Louis Sindlinger explained. "She was very
good at that and she entertained the prisoners with them as well."
Some of them were released in her custody and slept in Nelle's
sewing room until they found another situation.

"She was thin—a real tiny, little thing," Isabelle Newman recalled. "Pleasing voice. She started and headed a True Blue
Class." (This refers to a group of about twenty-five women who
met either at the Christian Church or at Nelle's to read and study
the Bible and exchange stories of how the Book had helped them
through various crises in their lives.) When the class was held at
the Reagan house, Dutch would join in the readings. The Christian Church had a new minister, "an old-time pastor with much
rhetoric, Reverend Ben H. Cleaver. He often stopped by to visit
Nelle at home . . . rather homely, Abe Lincoln type." Cleaver
soon became Dutch's listening ear.

In the summer Nelle dragged Dutch with her to Chautauqua,
to listen to the religious lectures and Bible readings that were in-
termingled with theatrical entertainment. An announcement
dated August 12, 1923, reads:

> Mrs. Catherine Sherer Cronk, in the interest of the Inter-
> Church World Movement, will appear on August 12. Her
> subject will be Lilliputian Heresy.

And one dated August 19, 1923, announces:

> Andreas Bard, the Man with a Message—he hails from Kan-
> sas City, he interests, he captivates, he persuades, he is clear
> in his thinking and he abounds in his humor, his diction is
> graphic, his pictures are real, he is well-known and loved in
> his own city. You must hear him.

And appearing in the *Dixon Evening Telegraph* on the same day
was a photograph of an ample gentleman with a handlebar moustache standing before a machine that looked like a stage prop

from *Dr. Jekyll and Mr. Hyde*. Beneath the photograph was the caption:

> Electrical entertainer, Louis Williams. The demonstration consists of experiments with the latest developments of wireless telegraphy, an experiment with currents and high frequency, in x-ray, luminous wires, lighting vacuum tubes, etc. Many of the demonstrations are really startling in their nature.

Dutch and Nelle (Moon preferred playing football on the school grounds) would take the streetcar out to the picnic area of Chautauqua and lunch on apples and crackers before attending the shows. Mother and son were close, but since Nelle spent so much time in the pursuit of her vocation, she was away from home a lot. Afternoons such as those spent with Nelle at Chautauqua were special occasions for Dutch that gave him a window on an extraordinary life. They had pretty much ended by summer 1925, for Dutch now held full-time summer jobs. His first, when he was fourteen (1925), was with a construction contractor who paid him thirty-five cents an hour for working ten hours a day, six days a week (twenty-one dollars a week, just slightly under the average weekly Dixon paycheck at the time). He was put to work digging the foundation for the future St. Anne's Catholic Church in heavy clay soil. One day Jack came by to pick him up at lunch hour. Dutch had just raised his pick ready to strike a blow when the noon whistle blew. He did not bother to lower it to the ground, but let it drop behind him. The sharp steel implement struck earth inches from the toes of the contractor, who yelled at Jack, "This kid of yours [is so lazy he] can get less dirt on a shovel than any human being that's human!" But he did not fire him, and by the end of the summer Dutch had saved two hundred dollars, which he hoped to put away for college. He still had four years of high school to attend. Many of Dixon's young people quit school at the eighth grade; but Nelle, determined that her boys would have an education, encouraged all of her sons' thoughts of college.

The rent on South Hennepin Avenue became too steep for Jack to pay. By the end of the summer of 1923, he moved his family to a smaller and less expensive house at 338 West Everett on the north side. Dutch and Moon slept on the enclosed porch, which was fine in summer but nippy in winter. Gone were the rabbits, the pigeons, the glass case for the bird eggs and the club house, the small "elegance" and luxury that the house on Hennepin Avenue had represented. Jack considered the move temporary. "No need to put up curtains here," he told Nelle. "We won't be staying that long." ("Jack always wanted to be 'cut-glass Irish'; at best he was 'lace-curtain,' but that never had a way of registering with him," one old friend remarked.)

Dixon had two high schools.* Dutch entered North Dixon High School, while Moon remained at South Dixon where he was starting his junior year. ("I took the long trips across the bridge morning and night," Neil recalls. "Cold, winter weather—oh— the wind [blew] down that river.") Neil claims the south side was rougher than the north side. This might have been because the north side was newer and the families who resided there were more progressive and affluent. With the boys attending schools of different values (sports were stressed at South Dixon, culture at North Dixon), a schism began to bisect the Reagan family as surely as the Rock River divided Dixon. Increasingly, it became Nelle and Dutch, Jack and Moon. The two boys were polarized in their personalities as well. "We [South Dixon] considered them [North Dixon] sissies. . . . I don't think he [Dutch] ever saw the inside of a poolroom!" Neil scoffs, apparently meaning he and his friends from South Dixon ventured into Demon Town to play the evil game.

Moon was an extrovert, a great promoter and salesman for whatever he wanted. The jobs he held in his early youth were more sales pitch than physical. Nelle said Moon possessed brassiness. Dutch was introspective. He read late at night, tried his hand at writing, was earnest about his religion and was more reserved at home than in public. He basked in the acceptance of outsiders and always gave that "extra something"—a special boyish smile, blue-gray eyes "looking straight at you."

"As a kid I lived in a world of pretend," he said later. "But by the time I was [eight or nine] I felt self-conscious about it. People made fun of me . . . 'What are you doing, kid? Talking to yourself?' Enough people make enough cracks like that, and a sensitive boy . . . begins to feel a little silly. . . . So from then on he doesn't pretend openly. . . . That was the way it was with me anyway. I

---

*Dutch started high school at South Dixon but transferred to North Dixon his sophomore year. Sometimes he referred to his activities at South Dixon because the two schools were not actually autonomous; they shared some sports teams, graduation, etc.

had a great imagination . . . and I used to love to make up plays and act in them myself . . . but I soon got self-conscious."

Still scrawny for his age, he remained on the bench during his first two years on the Dixon football team. (Finally in his third year he made the second string.) Wink McReynolds was on the senior varsity team and Dutch greatly respected him.* What free time he had apart from school and church was devoted to memorizing strategy he was not asked to execute on the football field and practicing baton twirling with a broomstick or the top of his and Moon's old brass bedpost. The latter paid off for him when he became drum major of the YMCA band. He tells the story of one St. Patrick's Day parade when he pranced ahead of the band, eyes front, baton twirling, so caught up in his performance that he forgot to turn down the planned route and the band continued without him. When he realized he was all alone, he raced back and overtook them, to much applause and laughter from the crowds on the sidelines.

The great thing about belonging to the YMCA was its supervised swimming program at Lowell Park, a three-hundred-acre naturally forested reserve named after the poet James Russell Lowell, author of "Ode to a Waterfowl" (supposedly written in the area). The Rock River tore through the park with the same vehemence with which it ripped through Dixon. Reagan was to recall, "There was a dam downstream which, when the sluices were opened, gave the ordinarily slow current a quicker tempo and deeper thrust. The bottom sloped swiftly into deep water not too far from the edge. An additional hazard was the other bank, about six hundred feet away; swimming across was a challenge— once started you had to go all the way, or else."

The year Dutch turned fourteen (1925) saw a tremendous change in his appearance. He matured into a tall, muscular young man, and that year he and Moon were roustabouts for the Ringling Brothers Circus when it came to town. It quartered in Demon Town and the boys earned twenty-five cents an hour for dragging the circus wagons into the mud so they couldn't accidentally be sent rolling. (Moon managed to make extra money by scalping the passes they were given as a bonus.) They had to be on the

---

* In 1966, now governor of California, Reagan wrote McReynolds: "My memory [sic] sharp and clear . . . of that young Dixon High School star who had the courage to tell the referee 'yes' he had illegally held on a block. The price was a 15 yard penalty, but the example set was well worth it."

grounds at four o'clock in the morning to feed the elephants before the tents were raised. "In those days it was the elephants who set 'em up by pulling the ropes you know," Bill Thompson explained. "It was a sight."

An only child and a poor swimmer, Thompson had wanted nothing more than to swim as well as Dutch. ("I guess you are notches one, two and three on my log," Reagan wrote him years later.) Because of Dutch's strong crawl stroke and his speed, no one could touch him in a race. But in the spring of 1926, after several tragic drownings, the Park Commission threatened to close Lowell Park that coming summer unless better safety precautions could be assured. Dutch thought what the park needed was a good lifeguard and applied to the concessionaires, Ruth Graybill and her husband, Ed, for the job.

"You're pretty young," Mrs. Graybill scoffed.

"He can do it," Jack Reagan urged. "Give him a chance."

Mrs. Graybill hired him for the summer and Dutch took to the job "like a rodeo rider to a bronc's back." His pay was eighteen dollars a week* and all the nickel root beers and ten-cent hamburgers he could eat. ("Everybody piled all the onion, pickle and relish on so they really got their money's worth." Ruth Graybill grinned.) His schedule called for him to work twelve hours a day, seven days a week (except on heavy rain days when the concession was closed). Extra lifeguards were hired for Memorial Day and the Fourth of July. He began work at ten A.M., when he picked Ruth Graybill up at her home "kitty-corner from South Central School" (then about ten minutes from his house) and helped her pack up the day's food supplies before they drove out to the park (a fifteen-minute drive) in her old Ford truck. On very hot days he remained on duty until ten P.M.

"I kind of had to laugh at myself when I went to work at [Lowell Park] in the summers," he confessed. "You know why I had such fun at it? Because I was the only one up there on the guard stand. It was like a stage. Everyone had to look at me."

"He liked it and we liked him," Mrs. Graybill said. "He was real pleasant to everybody and treated everybody the same. In the morning, if he had time, he would give small children swimming lessons . . . there was never a basket left at closing time. That meant we had a good lifeguard; there was no bodies at the bot-

---

*Reagan wrote in his autobiography that he received fifteen dollars, but Mrs. Ruth Graybill adamantly maintains that it was eighteen dollars.

tom. . . . Oh, when he went after them, he went because they needed help. . . . Some swimmers, well, they would shrug off his help. 'Oh, I could have made it alright,' they'd say. I guess they resented being 'saved' . . . they just felt he was showing off. Maybe. But he was with us six years [seven summers] and we never had a drowning in all that time. . . . He was a wonderful, good-natured young man. I never heard him speak one cross word to the bathers. He was a beautiful diver. He would do the swan dive out on the springboard."

"He was the perfect specimen of an athlete, tall, willowy, muscular, brown, good-looking," Bill Thompson remembered. "Of course, the girls were always flocking around him." Thompson also recalled a white canoe, owned by Honey Glessner, that Dutch would rent out to young lovers for fifty cents an hour and then split the money with Glessner.

He began making notches on an old log (at Jack's suggestion) for those swimmers he had "saved" the very first summer. "How many you got now?" people would ask. "You count 'em," he would reply. But, if pressed, he always knew the current total. Only once did he receive a reward. When he retrieved Gus Whiffleberg's dental plate, which had come loose when Gus hit the water too hard coming down the slide, Whiffleberg gave him ten dollars for his efforts.

One of the "jokes" in a page of the Dixon annual (1928) reads:

DROWNING YOUTH: "Don't rescue me. I want to die."
DUTCH REAGAN: "Well, you'll have to postpone that; I want a medal."

Bee (Elizabeth) Drew* was a year ahead of Dutch in high school, but her best friend ("a sparkling brunette"), Margaret Cleaver, daughter of Reverend Ben Cleaver, who had taken over the Dixon Christian Church in 1922, was in his class. For one entire year, Dutch had not been able to take his eyes off her in church. When he became a lifeguard, she took her first real notice of him.

Bee Drew, her boyfriend, Margaret and Dutch would go out on the river in the white canoe late in the day. Drew recalled that "Dutch had a portable windup Victrola that he used to take in

*Elizabeth Drew was a camera bug and shot pictures whenever she could. Cover photograph of Reagan as a lifeguard was taken by her.

the canoe. There was one record, 'Ramona,' that he played over and over all the time. My boyfriend finally threw it in the river."

In order to get some time to go canoeing with Margaret (his private name for her was "Mugs," although her family called her "Peggy"), he would have to clear the river of swimmers early. To do so, he would skip a pebble into the water and then wait to see the lagging swimmers' startled expressions.

"Oh, that's just an old river rat," he would say drily, thereby emptying the swimming area.

In his graduation annual, he wrote an article entitled "Meditations of a Lifeguard," which gave his view of the day-to-day experience. In it, he was cynical about the swimmers whose lives he came to guard. He refers to a big "hippopotamus," a "frail and forty maiden" and "this motley crew." But then he points out "one ray of hope":

> . . . she's walking onto the dock now. She trips gracefully over to the edge of the crowded pier, and settles like a butterfly. The life guard strolls by, turns and strolls by again. Then he settles in the immediate region of the cause of all this sudden awakening. He assumes a manly worried expression, designed to touch the heart of any blonde, brunette or unclassified female. He has done all that is necessary. She speaks and the sound of her voice is like balm to a wounded soul. . . .

Reagan wrote: "She [Margaret] was (strange as it sounds) grown up enough to know we weren't grown up enough to call this anything but friendship. . . . Me!—I was in love . . ." His classmates insist he never had another high school girlfriend except Margaret Cleaver.

They saw each other on a regular basis. However, the first year they were dating, Margaret was also seeing Dutch's friend Dick McNichol. By the time of the senior banquet, McNichol came to Dutch and said, "I think Margaret has made her choice and you should ask her to the banquet." That ended the triangle and Margaret and Dutch became a couple in the eyes of all who knew them. Members of the church expected that one day they would wed.

Yet, there was something about Dutch that Margaret could not understand, some elusive element in his personality. His charm was overwhelming, his kindness almost extreme. He always left people with a way of saying "God bless you" that made them feel—just maybe—"he had an inside track." Her father hoped the boy might find his way into the ministry and encouraged him along that route.

Dutch had a deep-felt compassion for Jack in spite of his drinking. He admired his father's good instincts, his fury at racial or religious bigotry, his respect for the independence of his sons' thinking, and he loved his father's bawdy stories and locker-room jokes which made father and sons confederates in a manly sect. But Jack was never able to reach out, or to dig in, to understand his sons any more than he could unravel Nelle's mysterious needs and inclinations. Jack took his family on a surface level and showed little interest in their accomplishments. Moon confessed that his father rarely managed to see him play football, at which he was a local star, or Dutch in a school play, in which he also was invariably the star. Whatever his sons achieved did not impress Jack greatly unless the achievements had to do with money earned, and yet he could display a great sensitivity toward his sons.

Moon graduated high school the summer of 1926. "We were poor, and I mean poor—the class decided and voted that for the senior prom and for graduation the fellows would wear tuxes. There was no way. So, the subject came up one evening at home, for dinner, about graduation, and I just remarked at the table, 'I'm not going to graduation,' and my mother said, 'You're not what?' I said, 'I'm not going to graduation.' And she said, 'Well, there's no question about whether or not you graduated, is there?' I said, 'No . . . I passed everything . . . [but] the class decided that the fellas were all going to have tuxes for the senior prom and . . . at the graduation.' And that was the end of the conversation.

"I worked that season part time in the shoe store for my dad. . . . Saturday afternoon [a week before the prom], my dad says, 'Let's take a walk.' Business was not very good, so we [closed the store and] started out walking. All of a sudden, we wheeled into O'Malley's Clothing Store, and no questions asked, Mr. O'Malley says, 'Hi, fellas, how are you?' He turned around and walked away, and went back into one of the cubicles where they had clothes hanging, and pulled something off a hanger. As he turned around before I could even see what he had, he says, 'Take your coat off, Neil.' I took my coat off, you know, and here was a tux coat. He puts it on, and he said, 'Well, we won't have to do anything with the coat. I'll get the trousers. Try them on. We

might have to shorten or lengthen them.' . . . Now this was a sacrifice to my family, don't think it wasn't, even though it didn't
cost probably over twenty-five dollars in those days. But that was
my dad."

Nelle would have much preferred the $25 to go toward Moon's
education, but he did not want to go to college. Instead, he took a
job at the Medusa Portland Cement Company doing cost work for
a salary of $125 a month, which enabled the Reagans to live a
slightly more comfortable life. Moon seemed determined to oppose his mother's wishes. His decision against going to college was
a big disappointment to her; a harder knock was his sudden con-
version to Catholicism. "I was eighteen years old and decided I
was dissatisfied with the church," he explained, "and went out
shopping for a church, and went home and told my mother I was
going to join the Catholic church. She then, with a tear in her eye,
told me [for the first time] I had been baptized Catholic when I
was six weeks old."

For "fatherly advice," Dutch went to either the Reverend
Cleaver or his drama teacher, Mr. B. J. Fraser, or Ed Graybill.
He had a number of surrogate fathers in Dixon throughout his
youth. Jack Reagan and his younger son had little in common. He
was not a mean or brutal drunk. Still, he was an alcoholic, able to
escape from real life, and that generally included the lives and
feelings of his family. Upon occasion he would make a gesture as
with Moon's tux, but Neil attributes such actions to his father's
concern with his own image, his need to appear able to keep up
with the Joneses.

Nelle worried about Dutch's ironclad control, his ability to
block out such things as Jack's binges. But the boys, as the children of an alcoholic, suffered certain humilities and defended
themselves as best they could. Moon threw himself into a frenzy of
physical activity, a host of friendships; he became the life of the
party. Dutch developed two worlds—public and private—and
was acutely alert to the dangers of Jack's benders so that when
they came he could cope with them, a feat that took a tremendous
amount of self-control for a young boy to achieve (which he did,
plus a great deal more). For if Jack's drinking had forced Dutch to
be self-reliant, Nelle's obsessiveness demanded a continuous performance by him in public—being gracious to everyone and accepting social responsibilities, church activities. "Look people
straight in the eye," she counseled him. "Remember people's
names. Let them know you care." Dutch appears never to have

shared the harsh experiences involving his father with anyone, including Margaret, Nelle or Moon. Years later he did discuss these feelings, perversely not with those closest to him but with the press and in his book—for the public.

B. J. Fraser was a young, aggressive English and world history teacher at North Dixon High School. Fraser also was adviser to the Dramatic Club and responsible for school productions. He quickly encouraged Dutch to join, and since Margaret was also a member, it did not take much convincing. Fraser found him "head and shoulders above the rest of them [in the Dramatic Club]. . . . He possessed a sense of presence on the stage, a sense of reality . . . he fit into almost any kind of role you put him into. Wisecracking, hat-over-the-ear, cigarette-in-the-mouth reporter— he could do that as well as any sentimental scenes."

School plays were performed just for the student body until Dutch entered his senior year. He then approached Fraser on a plan to open the productions to the public, and by so doing encourage outside interest. The club elected him president. At the same time he was president of the senior class, vice-president of the Boys' Hi-Y (who had as their aim to promote "Clean Speech, Clean Sports, Clean Living and Clean Scholarship"), on the varsity basketball team and had finally made it as tackle on the varsity football team (over local radio, he also broadcast a game in which he did not play). Another job he undertook was the art editing of the *Dixonian*—the school annual. His line drawings show originality and talent. The *Dixonian* was also filled with several examples of his writing. The following was titled "Gethsemane" (the olive grove east of Jerusalem where Jesus was betrayed):

To every man comes Gethsemane! Some fight the battle surrounded by prison walls, but for all the soul is laid bare. Some fight the battle when old age is creeping on like a silent clinging vine.

This is the story of a boy who fought his Gethsemane on the level sward in the shadow of a deserted grandstand.

An early harvest moon made ghostly figures of the milky mist tendrils, that hung over the deserted gridiron like spirits of long dead heroes, hovering over scenes of ancient triumphs. The level field was silent and lonely to all save the huddled figure who lay stretched out on the close cropped grass. But to this boy the field was crowded with ghosts of former stars.

Great linemen, brilliant backs who had given their all for the highschool were pointing ghostly scornful fingers at him. The quitter cringed before the visions his tortured mind brought up.

The quitter was the greatest half-back the school had ever produced, he was a story-book type, tall, good looking and very popular—or rather he had been popular until the last game the Saturday before. Crippled by ineligibility his team had run into competition harder than was expected. Held scoreless, and held to few gains he had quit—refused to risk his brilliant reputation by being flopped for losses.

His sham injuries were quickly perceived by the coach and team. Now he stood on the field, his mind torn by emotions and desires. His soul was being torn apart and all the petty little egotisms were preying on his mind. He realized his grandstand nature, he saw for the first time how cheap he really was. Great sobs shook him and he writhed before the pitiless conscience that drove him on in his agony of self punishment. Then his sobs ceased and he stood up, his face to the sky, and the ghosts of honored warriors urged him and drew him from the low shadows. A love and loyalty took the place of egotism. His hand strayed to the purple monogram he wore, and as he looked at the curving track, at the level field, he realized that he loved them.

Stubborn pride held him in silence while his team fought a losing battle in the last game of the season, he had been a quitter but now some sense of honor kept him from asking to play. The team filed into the dressing room at the end of the half, beaten and discouraged. The strained silence was broken by a stamping and shouting in the stands above them. Then they cried as the opening lines of the old loyalty song boomed across the field, and as the last notes died away, so died stubborn pride. The quitter rose and spoke. In three minutes the team trotted out to warm up, and eleven boys were wiping tears from their eyes as the quitter took his place by the full-back.

To finish the story right, perhaps they ought to win the game, but this is a story of football, of football when the score stands thirteen to nothing against you.

Time and again the quitter pounded around right end in

a beautiful ground gaining stride that made the coach want to recite poetry, the rhythm was so even. He didn't scurry like so many open field runners; neither did he push and fight his way, but he sailed, and as he side-stepped a man the rhythm remained unbroken, until, as he hit an inevitable tackler his bird-like flight changed to a ripping, tearing smash that gained a last yard every time.

The game ended a tie. The first score was made when he sprinted thirty-seven yards over tackle for a touchdown, after running and smashing his way the length of the field in three short snappy plays. As they carried him off the field he received the perfect tribute; with rooters for both sides standing while the waves of sound broke on the gray cloudy sky, broke and seemed to shriek in the ears of the quitter.

And when a friend asked the coach whether he considered the past season successful or not, he thought of the greatest half-back and murmured to himself, "It matters not that you won or lost, but how you played the game."

R.R. '28

Also included in the annual was his poem called "Life":

I wonder what it's all about, and why
we suffer so, when little things go wrong?
We make our life a struggle,
When life should be a song.

Our troubles break and drench us.
Like spray on the cleaving prow
Of some trim Gloucester schooner,
As it dips in a graceful bow . . .

But why does sorrow drench us
When our fellow passes on?
He's just exchanged life's dreary dirge
For an eternal life of song . . .

Millions have gone before us.
And millions will come behind,
So why do we curse and fight
At a fate both wise and kind?

We hang onto a jaded life
A life full of sorrow and pain.
A life that warps and breaks us,
And we try to run through it again.

Neither work is what others might have expected an all-American type like Dutch Reagan to have penned. In the story "Gethsemane" he revealed a fear of failure, and in the poem "Life" he obviously felt quite comfortable exposing his more emotional side to his peers in Dixon. By now he was a kind of hero (thirty notches had been carved into the log out at Lowell Park), a role model to those younger and less strong than he. From being a skinny, small kid, he had filled out and finally made the varsity football squad. He wore glasses but had won the heart of Dixon's prettiest girl. For him, Dixon had become the embodiment of all he was to hold true and right. Small-town folk stuck together. They were a family, a greater one than your own. You were in the boat rowing together. People were involved with each other's problems, their kids, their kids' futures. Most thought that future meant staying in Dixon, and so everyone was concerned with what was happening to affect their neighbors' lives.

At seventeen, Dutch, like Jack, was a dedicated Democrat, counting the days of the years until he could vote. An anti–third-term resolution had been passed by the Senate in February, making certain Calvin Coolidge would not run again.* When the Republican Convention met in Kansas City early in July, they nominated Herbert Hoover on the first ballot despite strong opposition from the Old Guard, who suspected him of being a Democrat at heart because of his allegiance to Woodrow Wilson during his presidency and his pro-British stands (privately they called him "Sir Herbert"). In his acceptance speech, he vowed (in a midwestern monotone, his head bent as he read the words), "We shall soon with the help of God be in sight of the day when poverty will be banished from the nation."

The Democratic party had virtually fallen apart since Harding's election in 1920. It no longer had either a national headquarters or a publication of its own and was laboring under a huge stack of unpaid bills. Its convention opened in Houston and Franklin Delano Roosevelt delivered the nominating speech, plac-

---

* Later to be excepted when Franklin D. Roosevelt ran for a third term in 1940, and then a fourth term in 1944.

ing the name of the governor of New York, Alfred Emanuel Smith, before the delegates. Smith also won on the first ballot. He had a reputation for decisive action and possessed a winning personality—"congenial, straightforward, unassuming, a wonderful teller of jokes, a man you would enjoy having a drink with." The fact that he had attacked the Volstead Act (antagonizing Prohibitionists nationwide) set well with Jack. More important, Smith was a Catholic, which might have put Jack in his corner but was more damaging to his chances of winning than his stand on Prohibition.

Jack was caught up in the fervor of the 1928 election. The old car sported Al Smith banners. Dutch was putting in too many hours at Lowell Park to help much with the campaigning. But he did demonstrate against outside workers being brought in to labor on the farms or in the local factories by marching with a group over the Galena Street bridge with protest signs. When Reagan was running for governor of California, a *Time* correspondent badgered him into explaining his sudden political emergence. "You have to start with the small-town beginnings," he explained. "You're part of everything that goes on. . . . In a small town you can't stand on the sidelines and let somebody else do what needs doing; you can't coast along on someone else's opinions. That really is how I became an activist. I felt I had to take a stand on all the controversial issues of the day, there was a sense of urgency about getting involved."

The urgency prodding him in the summer of 1928 was the matter of how he would one day make a living. Nelle might privately have wished he would go into the clergy, but she never placed pressure upon him. Moon wasn't setting the world on fire at the Medusa Cement Plant. Jack's business venture had turned into nothing more than a poor-paying job. There never were any commissions to discount for his "share."

In the spring of 1928, Dutch had made some money caddying at the club. After being deserted for so many years, Hazelwood had been sold to Charles Walgreen, a Chicago pharmacist who had parlayed his unique talent as a druggist and entrepreneur into a large national chain of drugstores that gave customers cut-rate prices on drugs and beauty products.* Walgreen was in and out of Dixon often during this time, arranging for the reconstruc-

---

*Walgreen's son-in-law, Justin Dart, claimed his father-in-law "made a million dollars during Prohibition selling prescription drugs with a high alcoholic content."

tion of the one habitable building on the estate, the old log cabin that had once been a gatekeeper's lodge. He came to Dixon to supervise the work, bringing with him friends like Commander Byrd (who had just announced his plan for a flight to the South Pole), who presaged the future glories of Hazelwood. (Mrs. Walgreen recalled how during this time Dutch came to a picnic she and her husband gave for the caddies at the end of the summer, and Reagan added to this memory: "I was stretched out in a hammock and Mrs. Walgreen herself brought me a plate of food. That was my idea of being King.") Between his work at the club and at Lowell Park, Dutch had saved four hundred dollars, which could not have seen him through college even if he had not felt obligated to help out at home.

This was an age of heroes, men like Byrd, Lindbergh and the leading sports figures of the day. Dutch fervently admired a young man, Garland Waggoner, son of the minister whom the Reverend Cleaver had replaced. Six years earlier, Waggoner had been South Dixon High School's star fullback and captain, and then had gone on to Eureka College (a Christian Church school) to become a football star. Dutch thought he would like to go to Eureka (about one hundred miles from Dixon). His dream was to make the football varsity team and to equal Waggoner's success. Fundamentally a theological school, Eureka also offered other degrees. Jack talked to him about the possibility of becoming a salesman—he certainly had the gift of gab it required. But sports interested him the most. He loved football. Sure, he was nearsighted and it was tough to wear glasses on the football field. Yet he had a strong belief in himself, that he could—with God's help—overcome this obstacle.

The Reverend Cleaver had approved Margaret's desire to attend Eureka (her sister Helen was already there and her older sister was a graduate), yet an additional incentive for Dutch, who could not conceive of being parted from her. His one obstacle was money. The tuition was $180 a year, which did not include living expenses. By the end of the summer he had not yet enrolled for lack of funds.

One day he piled into Margaret's coupe with its rumble seat packed with her possessions and drove with her to Eureka where she was registering for classes. Skirts barely touched the kneecaps that summer, but hers fell demurely far below. Margaret possessed a sharp mind and a good sense of humor. Her figure was trim, her dark eyes and hair entrancing. She talked about Eureka as a beginning, not an end. She wanted to see the world—France and the Far East. She had taken a primary course in French and liked to use the little that she knew in conversation. Being the youngest in her family had given her a special security to go with her natural pride, poise and spunkiness. Although Dutch identified with him, the Reverend Cleaver was an awesome parental figure, but Margaret had a way of getting around him.

The road was hot and dusty. It was September and the fields were still high. They passed Chautauqua, where both senior high school classes of Dixon had held their joint graduations. Somehow Dutch knew he would not come back without at least a promise of his dream in hand. He had spoken at graduation (not as valedictorian but as class president), quoting John 10:10: "I have come in order that they have life in all its abundance." He had an appointment with Dean S. G. Harrod when they arrived at Eureka, and arrangements had been made for him to stay the night at the Tau Kappa Epsilon (TEKE) House, one of the fraternities on campus. He would have to talk the Dean into giving him an athletic scholarship and secure work, for he did not intend to take the Greyhound bus back to Dixon in the morning.

MAC'S GOLDEN TORNADOES

"Don't forget who you are and where
you come from, and they can do
nothing to harm you."
—F. Scott Fitzgerald,
"The Diamond As Big As the Ritz"

Eureka. THE VERY SOUND OF THE NAME CONJURES images of Greek gods and glittering gold seen for the first time through the reddened but gleaming eyes of a nearly demented old prospector or the likes of the Blue brothers. The Greek physicist Archimedes, upon his discovery (made while he was taking a bath) that gold, because of its density, displaces less water than an equal weight of silver, streaked naked through the streets shouting, "Eureka! [I have found it!]" The old prospector in Northern California supposedly also exclaimed "Eureka!" as the gold glimmered from the battered bottom of his prospecting pan—and so a town was named. The town of Eureka, Illinois, was, on the other hand, named for the school that was opened there in September 1855, the final dream of two men, Ben Major and Asa Starbuck Fisher. Their discovery was not the usual gold men lusted for, but the golden elixir of education combined with the teaching of the highest spiritual values.

Ben Major was born in Kentucky. A successful farmer and a medical practitioner, he was convinced the system of slavery was

against God's word. In 1830, he determined to liberate the thirty
slaves he had inherited from his father. Realizing they would not
be prepared for such a challenge, he spent late evenings teaching
them to read and write. At first, his lessons were resisted. But
finally, Major's teaching skills succeeded. When he felt his
charges were able to cope with freedom, he left his farm in their
care and, alone on horseback, set out in the fall of 1831 to find a
home in some free state for himself and his immediate family.
After cutting through the forbidding prairie land to the south-
easterly section of Illinois, he reached Walnut Grove, a small settlement on the banks of the clear, rushing waters of Walnut
Creek, founded only six years earlier by a group of about fifty
people from Kentucky, Virginia and Ohio, refugees also from
modes of life based on the ownership and exploitation of slaves.
The majority were followers of Alexander Campbell and Barton
W. Stone, who preached (as did the subsequent Christian
Church) a release from divisive denominational creeds and a
unity of believers in Jesus as Christ. Their theology was ideally
suited to the frontier because it encouraged the spirit of the community.

The Walnut Grove settlers had built log cabins from the
straight-grained wood of the huge walnut trees that dominated
their site. In the center of their settlement an old spring gave
abundant cool water. Strangers passing through were always welcome to refresh themselves and their horses. The community
spirit made a strong impression on Ben Major, and he returned to
Kentucky with a plan that was to take three and a half years—to
send his slaves as free men and women to West Africa, and then
to move his family to the Illinois settlement. This involved trans-
porting the black people to New York and then arranging passage
for them to Liberia, where a man named Jehudi Ashmus and the
American Colonization Society had succeeded in settling nearly
fifteen thousand American freed slaves.* In 1835, Major returned
with his wife and five children to Walnut Grove, where he first
built a two-room log cabin and two years later a fine frame house.
The children were taught at home. In the summer of 1848, Major
wrote his nephew John Lindsay, a student at Bethany College, to
inquire if he knew a fellow student who might consider coming to

---

*The emigration of American freed slaves to Liberia (which means place of freedom) vir-
tually stopped with the advent of the Civil War. Several of Ben Major's former slaves
became government officials in Liberia and later visited Major in Illinois.

teach Walnut Grove's school-age boys and girls (who numbered thirty-seven by then). Classes were to be held in his home until a schoolhouse could be built. The man Lindsay recommended for the post was Asa Starbuck Fisher.

Fisher had been raised on a farm in Dillon Settlement in central Illinois, considered to be the Wild West at that time. He had taken a course of study at Knox Manual Labor Institute in Galesburg, then a small prairie village, and then taught in a small school in Marshall County, Illinois, for two years following his graduation.

The elders of Walnut Grove agreed to pay Fisher three hundred dollars for ten months' work. At the end of the first year, pleased at the caliber of the man they had hired as a teacher, they raised money for a small schoolhouse, which was named Walnut Grove Seminary. An addition was completed in December 1849, when the school was renamed Walnut Grove Academy. The same Christian attitudes and community spirit that had drawn Major to the settlement were the basic tenets of the school. The word spread and Walnut Grove grew.

One day in the spring of 1850, so the story goes, Major and Fisher were walking along the road leading eastward from the school. Major stopped as they neared the edge of the settlement and, turning westwardly, pointed to a slope of land dense with woods. "On that rise," he is claimed to have said, "we [the elders] intend to build a college, and we want you to be President." Fisher did not reply "Eureka!" and race streaking naked through the timberland shrieking the word. Instead, according to the 1894 *History of Eureka College*, he replied in a suitably humble if loquacious Christian manner, "I am not ambitious for such a position, and possibly have not the requisite qualifications, but I am strongly in sympathy with the enterprise, and to the extent of my power will aid the brethren to push forward the noble work they have so generously undertaken."

Three years later Major died. Walnut Grove Academy continued through 1854–55, when on February 6 of that year it was chartered Eureka College.* Fisher was named the school's first president.

Dedicated to helping the economically poor student, the college held tuition prices as low as possible. In 1878, their catalog announced, "We intend to make Eureka College the cheapest

---

* Reagan's birthday, coincidentally, is also February 6, the date of the founding of Eureka.

school in this or any other state." By 1894, the descriptive word had been upgraded to "least expensive." Children of Christian Church ministers (like Margaret Cleaver) received grants, and those studying for the ministry were given education free of tuition. The school maintained ties with the Christian Church. From the beginning of its history, only about 20 percent of the student body was studying for the ministry, but the 1871 catalog stated: "The Bible is a regular textbook, and every student may prepare and recite a lesson in it at least once a week. While everything of a sectarian or denominational tendency is conscientiously excluded, it is designed to enforce the sublime morality of the Divine Volume." Philosophical aims did not alter over the years. Teaching a Christian way of life was, and remained, the main objective. The 1936 catalog stated: "Religious values shall be found in courses of study, in the work plan and in recreational activities. The development of religious attitudes . . . is essential."

Dutch felt perfectly comfortable in a school with strong church ties. However, if he received a scholarship, he planned to work for degrees in social science and economics. Jack's lack of business acumen had alerted Dutch to his own need to succeed on this score. His high school grades had not been spectacular (a low B average). Because he did not plan to go into the ministry or the teaching of religion, his chances of securing financial aid were slim. His only hope was to seek an athletic scholarship.

The walnut trees had all but vanished by 1928, when Dutch and Margaret drove into Eureka. Unlike Dixon, the land rose into soft hills, and verdant pastures marked the spot where they turned off the narrow highway onto the main street. The small town of eighteen hundred people was so integrated into the college that their houses and lawns all seemed an extension of it. There were not enough cars for the establishment of traffic signals. No Bootleggers' Knob either. The school sat on the heavily forested rise exactly where Ben Major had envisioned it would one day be built. Elm trees bordered the wide green lawns of the five redbrick ivy-covered buildings that were arranged in a semicircle (Burgess Hall, Administration Building, the chapel, Pritchard Hall and Vennum Science Hall).

"I fell head over heels in love with Eureka," Reagan later wrote. "It seemed to me then, as I walked up the path, to be another home. I wanted to get into that school so badly that it hurt when I thought about it."

Dean Samuel Harrod was a heavyset, bespectacled man who

looked as though he had outgrown the size of his glasses and of his suit. Dutch knew he would be accepted as a student. All that was required was a high school diploma. The tuition was the problem. At that time, small schools (Eureka had an enrollment of 220 students) competed fiercely for football talent. The last decade had seen college enrollments more than double in most universities, and football had become a favorite college sport as well as a big business. Stadiums of monster size were being constructed—Ohio State had a 64,000-seater, Yale a bowl that held 75,000. Few schools could ignore the revenue football brought to them. A star player and a winning team drew students. Eureka's elders considered football with some disdain. The school's *real* commitment was to teaching a Christian doctrine, not to athletics. But without a competitive football team, a university lost scores of prospective good students—and Christians.

Eureka had been having trouble replacing their last big star, Garland Waggoner. Dutch pointed out that he had played on Dixon's varsity football team his senior year, as had Waggoner, adding a bit more to his accomplishments than they actually were. Harrod sent him to speak to Eureka's coach, Ralph McKinzie. The young man's bravado did not greatly impress him. High school players were given a lot of scrutiny by colleges scouting talent. McKinzie knew Dutch Reagan had not been a star performer. But he did like his enthusiasm and obviously considered his potential good, for he convinced the school board to grant him an athletic scholarship for one half of the $180 tuition. Harrod then secured for him a job washing dishes in the TEKE House for his meals. His room at the fraternity would cost $270 for the freshman year, which he had to pay himself. It did not take a degree in economics to add $270 plus $90 (the other half of his tuition) plus the $5 enrollment fee and see that with only $35 left of the $400 he had saved, he would be broke for most of the year. But he would at least be near Margaret.

His freshman schedule included rhetoric (the study of the effective use of language), French, history, English literature, math, physical education, football and swimming.

The TEKE House, built in the 1870s, was a solid, buff-colored, brick three-story building with a vast front porch. The third floor was a converted attic. Dutch's room was at the top with a dormer window that offered a panoramic view of the campus. (He was to retain this room throughout his college years.) He settled in quickly, adjusting more easily to his new environment than he had ever been able to do before. A good part of this had to do with the segregated nature of the student body, all of whom were of the same faith and similar socio-economic background. American campuses at this time were at the center of a revolt in manners and morals. College students, disdainful of social conventions, were labeled "flaming youth" and were quoted as calling themselves "disenchanted" (a favorite word of the era). This seldom took the form of political or militant action. Students rebelled by exhibiting some eyebrow-raising behavior. They bought contraband alcohol and went on binges. Party crashing was an accepted part of college life, as were petting, raccoon coats and bobbed hair. Compulsory chapel attendance had been abolished in most nonreligious campuses across the nation. At some schools, smoking had been legalized for women, dress codes abandoned, and wild "hooch" parties overlooked by the faculties.

Life at Eureka bore no resemblance to what was happening on other American campuses. Eureka was a small rural college with strict standards of student behavior. The dress code for female students directed that their skirts be of such a length as not to expose the calf of the leg. Slips were to be worn under summerweight dresses and flesh-colored or see-through stockings were not permitted.

Dancing, which was the college rage across the country, was also not allowed. In fact, Eureka's rules about this had grown even more restrictive the previous year. Until then, an annual back-to-school social affair called The Grind had been held, at which an orchestra played as concentric circles of boys and girls moved in opposite directions and the members of the two sexes introduced themselves to one another and shook hands. Then they all sat down and listened to speeches and ate ice cream and cookies. This had now been discontinued. One of the first speeches Dutch heard at Eureka was to be the "annual dancing speech," given by Eureka's puritanical president, Bert Wilson. Wilson was trying to divest the school of its debts by obtaining a church endowment. It did not seem to President Wilson that abandoning "a tradition [no dancing] which was held since the first days of the college could in any way help Eureka win the approval needed for their petition for aid [from the Central Church] when the Disciples of Christ Church does not sanction dancing."

A small rebellion was taking place. Sorority and fraternity parties held off campus were essentially dinners, but after the scheduled programs, students would go off to the garden or some remote room in the house to dance. The town also had a small ballroom called Legion Hall (known as "Damnation Hall" by the elders), and although dancing there was unacceptable behavior, students did so. One night a stool pigeon took down the names of all his classmates who were going into Damnation Hall as he stood hidden behind a bush. He was caught and gleefully tossed into a water tank.

President Wilson responded to the desire of the student body to have a more relaxed code of behavior by tightening restrictions further and recommending discipline (extra work and longer hours) for offenders. The approach was wrong. Rural Illinois, which is where most of Eureka's students were from, was suffering harsh financial problems. Twice in 1928, farm aid had been cut back. High school graduates were finding it difficult to finance their educations. Eureka had suffered a crippling drop of eighty students in one term as young people returned home to help out their parents. Very few of the ones who remained were paying full tuition.

Reagan recalled, "We had a special spirit at Eureka that bound us all together, much as a poverty-stricken family is bound." Eureka's tuition fees were too low to cover the school's operating costs. Even before the Depression, Eureka was "perpetually broke." When times grew bad, professors would go for months without pay and the small-town merchants would grudgingly extend credit "for the necessities of life." The college often had to pay its bills with produce from a farm that was part of the endowment, and which the students helped to run.

Having to do without was no strange philosophy to Dutch, or to most others on the campus. An editorial in the school paper, *The Pegasus* (upon which Dutch immediately became a reporter), on September 24, 1928, addressed new students: "If you notice among your associates a personal interest in another's welfare, if you notice the utter lack of snobbishness on our campus, if you notice an appreciation of any kind of honest endeavor and if you discover a willingness of individuals to sacrifice for the good of the whole, we say you have found our Eureka Spirit."

Eureka was proving to be, in many ways, an extension of Dutch's life at home and in Dixon. Once again he did not feel poor because everyone else was in the same boat. Racial discrimination was virtually unheard of. The Bible was a daily and vital part of his life. He made friends quickly with his peers and the faculty. He had a particular fondness and respect for Henry

("Heinie") Brubaker, the school's engineer and bell ringer (the chapel bell signaled the beginning and end of classes). Heinie could always be counted on to champion the students in any controversy with the faculty. A man with a salty tongue, he was dubbed "Professor of Profane Language" by the student body. Since few of Dutch's classmates were exempt from some form of physical labor to defray their expenses, washing dishes did not have a stigma attached to it. Students ran the laundry, cleaned toilets, shoveled snow and mowed lawns. Pocket money was scarce. A fifteen-cent peach sundae (Dutch's favorite) at the drugstore soda fountain was an extravagance. Eureka had a large music department, and so there was always a recital to attend on weekends, but Dutch was not keen on classical music. Any extra time he managed away from his duties and his studies and Margaret (who was considered his steady girlfriend from the first day at school) was devoted to sports. Compared to life on most American campuses in the twenties, Eureka seems to have been existing in a time warp. Outsiders thought of it as being "old-timey," "out of step," "a Bible school, after all."

Oklahoman Ralph McKinzie had been the athletic director and coach at Eureka College since 1921, which had been his own senior term. During his four years as an undergraduate at Eureka, he had built for himself an athletic record that had placed Eureka's football and basketball teams at their zenith. By graduation, Mac had won the halfback position on the Midwest All-Time Football Team and was a star basketball player on the All-Conference team as well, bringing Eureka glory and himself the esteem of faculty and student body. Mac was young, tough, high-spirited and feisty. His athletic prowess was achieved not only by talent but by tremendous grit and tenacity. Only five feet eight, a trim 145 pounds, he had to hold his own and more on a football field of bruisers; and on a basketball court, where a man several inches taller was considered average height, he was nothing short of phenomenal. In a basketball play-off between Eureka and Bradley College, Mac had scored every one of Eureka's fifty-two points himself, and the Peoria newspaper had proclaimed in a two-inch headline: MCKINZIE BEATS BRADLEY. Mac's teams revered and loved him—if not at first, then by the end of a season.

(At ninety-one years of age [in 1985] and having long ago retired from coaching, Mac remained in Eureka, living alone, still a guiding spirit to the athletes on campus. The toughness of the man was intact and his intense love of sports and the men and women who achieved any small measure of success in the field had not dimmed. With immense effort he pushed himself up from a chair to a standing position, ignoring the canes and walker beside him. "Just because the doctor says I'm disabled doesn't mean I am!" He grinned, blue-gray eyes still flinty. He wanted a scrapbook across the room and insisted on getting it himself. It contained press clippings of Eureka games, photographs of his former team members and of his family, and letters from both, Reagan included.) "Dutch—I put him at end on the fifth string [Eureka actually had four backup strings—nobody who wanted to play football was excluded]. Later he switched to tackle. But the first year I never let him on the field to play a [competitive] game. Guess he hated me for it. But I had a team to consider. He was nearsighted, you know. Couldn't see worth a damn. Ended up at the bottom of the heap every time and missed the play because he couldn't see the man or the ball moving on him. Gotta say he was regular at practice. And took his knocks. When practice was over, I'd say, 'Do the duck waddle.' All the kids hated that. But he'd start across the field almost dragging one knee on the ground. Then when they got to the goal line, I'd say, 'Turn around and go back.' He never quit. Others did. But not Dutch. . . . He was very skinny at the time, and not quite as fast as the other fellows. . . . He was a plugger but Eureka wasn't in a position to gamble because we were not a top team even in the local area. I kept him off the field so that other young men who were a little more aggressive playing football could carry the ball."

"It's tough to go . . . from first string end [at North Dixon High] to the end of the bench before the whistle blows for the first game," Reagan wrote in his autobiography. "I managed to accomplish this all by myself. But in my mind I had help—heaven forbid I should take the blame! I told everyone who would listen that the coach didn't like me. I was the victim of unreasoning prejudice. I needed a damn good kick in the keister, but how can you kick something that's permanently planted on a bench?" He had also assumed he would play basketball at Eureka. "I went to the first practice, looked through the door, adjusted my glasses, looked again, turned and walked away. I saw fellows doing things with a basketball that I just didn't believe."

"Swimming? Well . . ." "Little Mac," as his teams privately called him, remembered, "I don't believe he ever swam in a pool before. Took some time, but when he got the oil off his wings nothing could hold him back. Don't know why he persisted at football. He had this dream I guess of becoming a big football star. He liked being close to the field even when he wasn't playing a game. Used to take an old broom from the locker room and pretend it was a microphone and 'announce' the game play by play afterwards. Never forgot a play either! He understood football—and baseball for that matter, too, better than most of the teams combined. Just couldn't execute what he knew on the playing field. But he never gave up trying."

Both Dutch and Margaret joined the Dramatic Club. ("I always let on that my only interest in the Dramatic Club was that it was such fun going to rehearsals and walking home with the leading lady afterward," he said ten years later. "Secretly I really thought I was communing with the Arts.") As in Dixon, he filled his life with constant school activity. Margaret recalled, "He was an indifferent student." She worried about it, but he always managed to get by. Margaret soared to the top of her class. She was a member of Delta Zeta, as was her sister, Helen. The Reverend and Mrs. Cleaver visited Eureka frequently that autumn. According to the Eureka *Pegasus,* the Cleavers were in town the first and the eighth of October. Margaret went home to Dixon on October 15 and her parents returned to Eureka on the twenty-second; an unusual flurry of back and forth, due perhaps to consultations the Reverend was having with the school concerning the possibility of his taking over the pulpit in the near future.

Ruth and Ed Graybill came to visit Dutch on Thursday, October 27, bringing unsettling news about his family. The Fashion Boot Shop was in a very bad way and Moon had lost his job as a cost accountant and was now working for a substandard wage. The Depression that would not hit the nation for a year had already begun to roll across the corn belt. Herbert Hoover had won the election in a landslide. "A chicken in every pot" had been his campaign slogan. But the farm belt was having problems feeding the chickens.

Things were getting even tighter at Eureka. The school had not received the financial aid it had sought. President Wilson had countered by dropping several courses, including art and home economics, from the curriculum. Students were alerted to the possibility that sports would be next. (Wilson had tried to get the school board to agree to such a plan two years earlier with no success.) The president was of the opinion that football and basketball were demeaning enterprises for a religious school. The students' unrest over the ban of dancing now came to the surface, and these combined issues agitated them and many members of the faculty. At an open meeting in the chapel on Thursday, November 22, Wilson tendered his resignation. At the same time, he went on to make a statement that was a serious tactical error. He spoke in such a disparaging way about the morals of the school and the town (not churchgoing enough for him) that the student body and the townspeople banded together in defense.

"Affiliated churches," he said, "are not supporting Eureka the way they should either with students or money, and these are the reasons: Eureka is too small a town to provide enough jobs for students. There is no daily newspaper to give the school the constant publicity it needs, although," he added sardonically, "the press is doing very well now [referring to nearby Peoria's coverage of this particular meeting]. People are moving away from rural areas like Eureka and into the big cities. Students seem to prefer larger schools. The real question is, Can Eureka College, a small church college in a small town, survive at all in the face of the present trend of education and civilization?"

Directly after this speech, a statement was issued by an Alumni Committee that it would be a forward step if Wilson's resignation was accepted by the trustees. *The Pegasus* printed an editorial saying: "By questioning Eureka's fitness for 'riding the storm,' he has, in the minds of everyone, lost mastery and control of the situation."

The following Tuesday, November 27, the trustees were to meet to consider Wilson's resignation, just before the season's big game against Illinois. All talk on campus centered on who would replace Wilson. The students were due to go home for Thanksgiving break after the game. Dutch was on the bench, "as usual." Reagan recalled that it was one of those "if-anybody-makes-a-mistake-that's-it games. Lump Watts, a [black] classmate of mine . . . who had been all-state full back at Kewanee [Illinois] High— set a conference record by punting one that carried over eighty yards in the air. Late in the fourth quarter he won the game with a drop kick of better than fifty yards. Through some technical error regarding registering the feat, this kick has been kept out of the national records, but he did it for three points.

"In the second half, newsboys hit the stands with extras [the *Peoria Press*] headlining the fact that our petition to the board had been denied [Wilson's resignation had not been accepted]. Looking back from the bench was like looking at a card stunt. Everyone was hidden by a newspaper."

The win over Illinois was diminished by the decision of the board. The students were in a fury. The greatest unrest was among the members of the TEKE House, where the feeling was that the student body had been sold out. Leslie Pierce, the president of the fraternity and a varsity player on Mac's Golden Tornadoes, became the student leader in a move to oust Wilson from the presidency despite the trustees' vote. By evening, very few people on campus had left for their holiday as they had planned. Groups huddled together in fraternities and sororities discussing the crisis. Pierce and some of the other student leaders "flew into action," going from one group to another stirring up their emotions. At 11:45 P.M., feeling the time was right, the leaders banged on the old college bell for fifteen minutes straight. Running through the streets from all directions came students, teachers, townspeople—many still with nightclothes under their overcoats—thinking there must be a fire. Pierce had set up a meeting in the chapel, which filled quickly to capacity. People were standing in the aisles and in the doorways and looking through the windows to see what was going to happen next.

"When the bell rang everyone went to the meeting," another student recalled. "It didn't matter whether you agreed with the movement or not, or whether you even knew what it was all about. Goodness. It was so exciting!"

Pierce and the other leaders had decided that a freshman should put forth the charges against Wilson because that class would have more years at stake. A quick vote in the TEKE House elected Dutch to this task. He was, they all agreed, the best and most enthusiastic speaker they had, and they needed someone whose impassioned words could stir up the student body into demanding Wilson's resignation. The Golden Tornadoes stood guard at the doors of the chapel to counter any possible violence. A professor of music sang spirituals to entertain the crowd while Pierce and his co-leaders were priming Dutch on what he should say. The plan was that he should sell the student body on the idea that they stay away from classes. After their return one week from Thanksgiving break, the strike was to begin, and they hoped it would lead to Wilson's departure.

"I'd been told," Reagan recalled, "that I should sell the idea so there'd be no doubt of the outcome. I reviewed the history of our patient negotiations with due emphasis on the devious manner in which the trustees had sought to take advantage of us. I discovered that night that an audience had a feel to it and in the parlance of the theater, that audience and I were together. When I came to actually presenting the motion there was no need for parliamentary procedure; they came to their feet with a roar—even the faculty members present voted by acclamation. It was heady wine. Hell, with two more lines I could have had them riding through 'every Middlesex village and farm'—without horses yet." When Dutch finished his rousing speech a co-ed fainted in the audience and had to be carried outside to be revived.

The students put forth a written statement adopted unanimously: "We, the students of Eureka College, on the 28th of November [it was now well past midnight], 1928, declare an immediate strike pending the acceptance of President Wilson's resignation by the board of trustees . . ." They stood and sang the alma mater. By two-thirty A.M., the meeting was over and the strike won. Two students, Bruce Musick and Howard Short (president of the student body), took another statement, saying the student body would remain out on strike until Wilson resigned, and placed it under Wilson's door. The Golden Tornadoes, acting as "police escorts," showed all the women to their dormitories and then patroled the campus to make sure there was no disturbance.

Burrus Dickinson (a student and from 1939 to 1954 president of Eureka College) stated, "The agitation was centered in the TEKE House where [Dutch] lived. As far as the students were concerned it was a strike against Wilson's domineering personality and his prohibition against dancing."

Bruce Musick remembered, "The strike climaxed efforts of the majority of the students to bring about a change in what they thought were outmoded rules governing student behavior—rules against dancing and smoking. Wilson and the whole administration were persons steeped in the belief that the then-current wave of liberal thought and action was a sign of moral decadence."

Dutch had finally gotten off the bench, but he had done so in the area of politics, not athletics. He later minimized the importance of this student rebellion. But no matter how inconsequential forcing Wilson's resignation might have seemed to Reagan later, the removal of a man in authority from a job to which he had been elected is an important undertaking, more so when it involves a student rebellion and especially at a time when such things were not occurring on American campuses. The item was news enough to be carried by the United Press and printed in *The New York Times* and the *Chicago Tribune*. Also, from Reagan's own description of his feelings at the time, "Hell, with two more lines I could have had them riding through 'every Middlesex village and farm'—without horses yet," he had experienced a new feeling. He had so connected with an audience that he had been able to sway their emotions into a mass reaction. Nelle's evangelistic talents and Jack's sales techniques had melded together into something new and thrilling for him. It was, indeed, as he had said, "heady wine."

The day before Thanksgiving, the clouds swept down and hung over that part of Illinois between Eureka and Dixon. By night a heavy rain fell that lasted almost without stop for the entire week that followed. The Rock River rose dangerously high. The brown earth turned to black mud. Out of town, haystacks grayed from exposure to the rain and everywhere a penetrating dampness, a smell of mildew and a depressing bleakness persisted.

The situation in the Reagan home was serious. Not only was money short, but Nelle and Jack were having troubles. "We knew she [Nelle] had her problems," Mrs. Mildred Neer recalled, "but we knew God was helping her. She wasn't the kind of person to come and cry on your shoulder and tell you her problems. Neighbors and relatives suggested she get a divorce [because of Jack's drinking] but this was absolutely against her beliefs. Nelle taught very strongly against divorce in her Sunday School class. Once she found out that she had accidentally offended one of the members [of her class] whose parents were divorced and she got down on her knees and asked forgiveness. That was Nelle Reagan."

After the great exhilaration of his part in the school rebellion, the reality Dutch found at home was difficult to face. He talked about returning to Dixon after the term to help out, but Nelle would not hear of it. The Reverend Cleaver invited him on a family outing to Rockford (forty-five miles north) to see "the supposedly original London company play [in] 'Journey's End.'"* The live theater experience, his first with a professional company, coming so fast on the heels of his rousing chapel speech, had a

---

*Since the R. C. Sherriff play opened at the Apollo in London on December 9, 1928, only six months earlier, this would have been impossible. Laurence Olivier, the original Captain Stanhope in the London company, was replaced after a month (because of other contractual arrangements in England), and Colin Clive played the role for a run of eleven months at London's Savoy Theatre. However, *Journey's End* opened successfully at The Henry Miller Theatre in New York on April 22, 1929. American touring companies of the play spread out across the country that summer. Reagan must have seen one of these companies.

mesmerizing effect on him. "For two and a half hours I was . . . on the stage. More than anything in life I wanted to speak his lines [the male lead's]."

Although he had appeared in many dramatic productions and given good amateur performances, Dutch had never been exposed to a play that so absorbed him and a character with whom he could identify. "If I had only realized it," he added, "nature was trying to tell me something—namely that my heart is a ham loaf."

Snow had replaced the rain once Dutch returned to Eureka, and with the snowfall the strike began with impressive strength. Only six students attended classes and among those were President Wilson's two daughters (he had eight, but only two attended Eureka at the time). Regular study hours were set up by the strike committee. The students assigned their own work according to the schedules to be met.

For one week the campus looked like a political convention. Reporters had arrived from all over. A press headquarters and a student public-relations office had been established. *The Pegasus* issued daily bulletins on the progress of the negotiations. Byron Colburn, an alumnus and member of the board, became the acknowledged agent for conciliation. He spent the week talking to the students, faculty, alumni, trustees and President Wilson.

On Thursday, December 6, the United Press reported a rumor that the whole school would be moved to Springfield, arousing the local merchants who feared disaster in such an event. The Alumni Committee issued a statement calling for a "quick end to the turmoil before the college or its reputation is destroyed."

By December 7, the impasse had been resolved. Wilson submitted his second resignation at a closed meeting of the trustees.*

---

*Wilson's resignation speech was as follows: "The situation that has been created makes it impossible for me to continue with any satisfaction to myself or with any possibility of effective results to the College. In leaving my position, I want you also to know that I go bearing no ill will or malice. Other avenues of service are open to me, and a burden will be lifted from my shoulders if tonight I know that I am freed from any further connection with this unfortunate situation.

"As for the students, I have known them all by name, and the towns from which they come. I wish every one of them the best that the future has in store. I am still a firm believer in the idealism and integrity of the present generation of American youth. And for all these here at Eureka, since Christmas time is approaching, I say to them in the language of Little Tim, 'God bless you every one.'"

He added in closing, "It is my desire that this resignation become effective immediately. This is irrevocable. It cannot be reconsidered."

Board chairman Richard Dickinson* was named acting president of the college. By nightfall of that same day, the press decamped. Saturday, regularly scheduled classes met; and by Monday the campus had returned to its usual routines. The students had won. No classes were dropped and dances (one was held to celebrate) became a part of Eureka campus life, but even with the repeal of Prohibition, alcohol was not consumed on campus or at any social affair attached to the school.

Howard Short added, "Bert Wilson was not a good college president . . . [but] he was a great Christian man. He never let this experience affect his relationship to any of us, as far as I could judge.

"Some years later he visited me in Akron, Ohio, as a representative of our pension fund [Christian Church]. This was during the Depression days and nobody had any money. He said, 'Howard, you simply have to belong to the pension fund. You cannot afford to do otherwise. I will take a note for your first three months' payment so that you and your young wife will be protected.'"

"The students were caught up in the changing modes of the times," Bruce Musick remembered. "As I view it there is little or no resemblance between the Eureka affair and the more recent [campus] revolts. . . . We thought we were big shots, important in the eyes of all those who really counted—our friends."

Dutch's good looks and naturalness won him most of the leads (not always the best roles) in the Dramatic Club. No microphones were used in those days and Dutch could always be heard. His college reviews repeat the word "presence." He had a way "of sauntering across the stage" that drew all eyes to him even when he was not speaking. Now he was conscious of his appearance in a way he had never been before. A studied manner can be detected in his appearance in all photographs but those to do with sports. The collar of his jacket is upturned (the only one so worn in group pictures). His hands rest, gunslinger fashion, on the corners of his pants pockets. A lock of hair falls slightly onto his forehead, softening the scholarly look of his horn-rimmed glasses.

"He stuck with the football squad all fall," Short recalled, "although he never even got a first-class jersey. It was difficult not to get one in Eureka! I was the manager of the team that year, and

---

*Dickinson and James M. Allen each served one year as acting president. Clyde Lyon was elected president and served from 1930 to 1936.

so I had a lot of contact with him and respected his nerve and his determination."

What he did not achieve on the football team he made up for in swimming (this never was to satisfy him, however). During the big swimming meet in his freshman year, he won every event (crawl stroke, backstroke, one hundred meter, two hundred meter and relay) except breaststroke. "Everyone admired Dutch, I can't think of anyone who disliked him," classmate Stanfield Major said. He had a personality that was ingratiating. "Other kids on the squad came to me to speak for him," Mac added, "and I knew he didn't put them up to it. He was a leader and used his power well."

All the character traits that he had exhibited in North Dixon High reinforced themselves at Eureka. He never had been or would become a great student. His needs did not lean in that direction. College was a way-stop, a place to refresh oneself for the journey ahead at the same time as one mapped out a route. He managed—*just*—to get passing grades, and Eureka was not a school of extremely high grading. His startling memory and his ear for words got him through English, French and history. But economics was an instinctive science for him. He understood the more complicated theses without a great deal of studying. Had he applied himself just a little more, Margaret Cleaver felt, he could have excelled. But his real interest and constant attention went toward his extracurricular activities, which did not help his grade average—football, swimming, the work on *The Pegasus*, and the Dramatic Club. He said his enthusiasm was in "drama, sports, and politics and not always in that order.

"I was afraid if my grades were good I might end up an athletic teacher at some small school . . . raising other little football heroes," he told an interviewer in 1939. "I was awfully afraid [of] about what was going to happen after college. I wanted more than [Mac] had—not that such a life and such a job is bad; it's wonderful for some people, but I had an idea in the back of my head that I wanted to be an actor. . . . To get a coach's job you naturally had to have a certain scholastic standing, so I was careful not to get it. I even dropped some courses so that I'd be behind in the educational credits. I didn't want to take the chance of weakening when the time came."

Politics had become a form of expression, an art. He felt pride (where Bruce Musick felt shame) in his small involvement in the student rebellion because it had been a "serious, well-planned program, engineered from the ground up by students, but with the full support and approval of almost every professor on campus." He liked order in his world and in his politics.

He saw what was happening around him. Some good friends had been forced to drop out of school. Lump Watts and several others from the football squad had left even before the freshman term ended. By the end of the year, only one black girl of six black students who began the year remained in his class, all victims of family reverses. The auctioneer's gavel had lowered on many farms near Dixon and Eureka. Dutch had not seen the prosperity the rest of America saw in the twenties. His life had been unrelieved pinching and saving, doing without, being grateful for little in the way of luxury. His immediate ambition was not riches, just better conditions—bills paid, money in the bank for an emergency. He feared his own conservative nature would force him to compromise, to abandon a crazy dream of standing alone on a stage as he had at the lifeguard station with everyone looking at him. After all, what kind of sense did such a wild scheme make? He believed in working for the essential needs in life. He did not have the urge to drink, and he did not smoke.

At nineteen the man was fully formed, and that included the charismatic personality that gave him a kind of power over others. He did not use it to any advantage. But after the night of his speech in the chapel, he knew he could do so if he wished.

5

DIXON THOUGHT OF DUTCH AS A YOUNG MAN ON his way up. When he returned for the summer of 1929, he was one of only 8 percent of the Dixon High School graduating class of 1928 who had gone on to college. In his eyes, the year at Eureka had been a failure. Mac's Golden Tornadoes and his basketball team, the Red Devils, were unquestionably the big men on campus, and he had not become one of their elite number. He had grown up in the heroic era of American sports. Football greats like Red Grange and baseball giants like Babe Ruth were more easily recognized by the public than was President Herbert Hoover. They had become legends not only by the yardage they made and the home runs they scored but because the sportswriter had become a major literary figure and the sports announcer a media star.

All-American for three consecutive years, Red Grange, the "Galloping Ghost" of Illinois, was now a professional. "What a football player—this man Red Grange," Damon Runyon rhapsodized. "He is melody and symphony. He is crashing sound. He is brute force." Not to be eclipsed was coach Knute Rockne's stalwart Notre Dame teams, which had won more than one hundred games in a decade and lost only a mere fraction of that number. The year Dutch had entered Dixon High School, Rockne's swift backfield had entered football history with the prose of sportswriters like Grantland Rice: "Outlined against a blue-gray October sky, the Four Horsemen rode again. In dramatic lore they are known as Famine, Pestilence, Destruction and Death. These are only aliases. Their real names are Stuhldreher, Miller, Crowley and Layden."

Dutch wanted so badly to be a football star that his other achievements at Eureka seemed unimportant. But to the folks at home, especially the adoring kids whom he mesmerized at Lowell Park, Dutch Reagan was as big a hero as Red Grange. Or at least he was *their* hero—touchable, near—and knowing him made them feel special. He had a way of remembering a kid. "I couldn't believe it. He was five years older than me and I had five older sisters and brothers at home," Michael Ruark recalled. "They called me 'Peanut.' But Dutch—'Hey, that's a pretty good dive you got there—champ,' he said. 'You sure have made *some* progress since last year.' *Champ.* I felt six feet tall."

When Dutch returned to his job as lifeguard, the notches multiplied and the log soon began to look as if a flock of woodpeckers had chipped away at it. People speculated that Dutch Reagan would end up a famous athlete, a world-class swimmer. Margaret came to the park in pale summer prints, her dark hair waved softly around her young face. They would take out the park rowboat and Dutch would work the oars as she sat facing him, listening to him talk of his dreams in his smooth, confident voice. His hopes to become a professional athlete looked dim. That did not fill Margaret with concern. She valued more serious aspirations. Her warm, safe life had given her a patina of assurance and she was unresponsive to any idea that might disturb the even flow of her emotionally and economically secure youth.

Despite his austere exterior and the basso profundo of his voice, the Reverend Cleaver believed women were born with equal rights and should be given the chance and the responsibility to accomplish more than to waddle in a man's shadow. He had three daughters and no son. Mrs. Cleaver was an extraordinarily intelligent and pleasant woman, active in church affairs and education, and she had inspired her daughters to follow their own independent dreams. Margaret had a fierce urge to travel, to study other cultures, and although the Cleavers were not a family of great, or even moderate, wealth, she had not been discouraged.*

Dutch projected that his summer savings would not be more than two hundred dollars. How was he to return to Eureka with such a meager amount? He talked about finding work in Dixon. Margaret politely hinted that there was more to life than Dixon could offer a young man. Unless it was in sports, Dutch was not convinced that was the case. But her esteem meant a great deal to him. If he could not return to Eureka, then he had to find some alternative, or he feared he might lose Margaret. "He was always a leader," Margaret Cleaver says. "Still I didn't think he'd end up accomplishing anything."

She thought he lacked ambition, a sense of adventure, a cultural curiosity. Yet, while she was in his presence, she found herself inextricably drawn to him. She greatly admired his appearance. His 155 pounds were well distributed on his towering frame and held taut by the enormous amount of swimming that he did. The smooth copper of his summer tan made his blue eyes brighter. The sun had tipped his chestnut hair with glints of red and the light growth of it on his arms and the backs of his hands gave him a real he-man aura. He looked you straight in the eye when he spoke, a flattering attention. A touch of Irish melody edged his voice and his laugh. Yet, a curious self-discipline kept him always in control. He never laughed too hard or gave full vent to his emotions, and these were virtues in Margaret's eyes.

In the last week before the fall term Dutch grew desperate. Lowell Park would close down at that time as well. Then a land surveyor whom he had met at the park offered him a job as rodman, also promising that he would help him get a rowing scholarship with his alma mater, the University of Wisconsin, if Dutch worked for him for a year. Dutch agreed.

Margaret and he had "a last sad date" two nights before her departure for Eureka, with Margaret failing to convince him that he should apply again for a scholarship and see if this time he could get a student loan. The next morning, an unexpected rain engulfed Dixon. There would be no work, for surveyors could not conduct their job in such wet conditions. The rain seemed a sign from a higher hand, and Dutch changed his mind about returning

---

*The Reverend Cleaver earned about thirty-eight hundred dollars in 1929, and considerably less during the Depression.

to school. Nothing could have pleased Nelle more unless it was that Moon was going to Eureka with his brother. Once the idea hit Nelle, she could not let it go. Dutch promised he would speak to McKinzie and the board. But Moon refused to be swayed. The next morning, he left for work before Dutch was up. Dutch and Margaret departed for Eureka a short time later. "God bless little schools," he wrote. "In twenty minutes I was offered a job washing dishes in the girls' dormitory, the college volunteered to defer their half of the tuition until after graduation (my first experience with credit) and I made a call home to tell them I was going to college."

In his opinion, Moon did not seem a candidate for a "mellow, small-town ivy-covered" campus like Eureka. The two brothers had gone separate ways in more than their religion. Moon was a serious drinker, a bit of a ladies' man and fairly careless with money. Dutch was worried about all these undisciplined elements in Moon's personality, but the last bothered him the most because "he'd never paid me back any small loan in his life, and I didn't like to think he might some day treat Eureka the same way." Yet, the very fact that Nelle wanted Moon to have the chance of an education was enough to send Dutch to Ralph McKinzie, seeking help. He claims he "laid it on the line" with McKinzie. Moon had been out of school for three years, but he had been a tough end on his high school's football team and had helped them win the county high school championship; he was an all-around good athlete and he wanted an education badly. McKinzie agreed to Moon being given a partial athletic scholarship, and the board deferred the remainder of his tuition. Next, Dutch talked the school into giving Moon a job "hashing in the kitchen of the girls' dorm." All Moon needed to raise was ten dollars a month for his room at the TEKE House. Moon claims he came home for supper that night and found his brother's trunk set in the middle of the kitchen. "'Nelle, I thought Dutch was going back to school today,' I says [sic], and with a tear in her eye she said, 'He did and you ought to be ashamed of yourself. He left the trunk, thinking you'd change your mind.'

"I went out to work the next morning, and Mr. Kennedy, who was superintendent of the plant and my boss—and before I went into my desk, why I told him this very funny story [that his brother had left his trunk so he could add his clothes to it and join him at school], and I was not aware that he wasn't laughing. About ten o'clock, his secretary came in and said, 'Here's your paycheck, Mr. Reagan.' I looked at the calendar and says, 'Paycheck? It's not payday.' And she said, 'It is for you.' And I said, 'Well, do you mean I'm fired?' And she says, 'Call it what you want to. Mr. Kennedy says if you're not smart enough to take the good thing your brother has fixed up for you, you're not smart enough to work for him.'" Moon was in college by the afternoon of the next day, and with his arrival, life at Eureka changed considerably for Dutch.

The rivalry that existed between Dutch and Moon remained, for the most part, deeply buried, surfacing only when the older brother mocked the youth and inexperience of his younger sibling—on the football field, with women, in hard drinking—and in a brand of locker-room humor. With a cocky smile on his broad Irish face, Moon, in a combination of bully and joker, would rib Dutch. Usually an older brother feels protective toward his younger sibling. But for all his prowess in what he considered manly endeavors, Moon was more immature than Dutch, less settled. He did not involve himself in campus politics or many activities other than those requiring physical aptitude. He managed to find places on the road to Peoria that sold bootleg beer and never seemed to concern himself with finances. He had come to Eureka with some money from his job in Dixon—not a lot, but it never took much for Moon to enjoy himself.

Yet, with all his easy charm, his dark good looks and bruising body, his catwalk strut and his persuasive manner, Moon remained in Dutch's shadow at Eureka. He was referred to most frequently as "Dutch Reagan's brother." Decades later, several of their fellow classmates could not recall a close kinship between Moon and Dutch. "I sort of had the feeling," one said, "that Dutch endured his brother being at the same school with him. Sort of like a penance, you know?" Nonetheless, Moon's proximity brought gratification to Dutch's campus life. By virtue of his one year head start in college, Dutch had become the "older" brother and held rank over Moon, who claimed that as a TEKE pledge, "Anytime I heard the shout 'Assume the position, Reagan' and grabbed my ankles, I knew the whack [from a paddle with one-inch holes all over it to raise blood blisters] I got from him [Dutch] was gonna be worse than the others because he felt he had to, otherwise they'd [the TEKEs] accuse him of showing partisanship." But there were times when Moon induced Dutch into silly, irreverent acts. Dutch went along with some escapades so that he could keep his eye on Moon, but he did manage to loosen up, even to the point of drinking bootleg alcohol "out of a bottle that tasted like gasoline on the fraternity back porch in a parked car."

In his autobiography, Reagan takes great glee in describing a watermelon hunt at the beginning of his sophomore year staged to make some lowly freshmen believe they had been witness to a shooting. "We tiptoed through the [watermelon] patch to build up suspense and at a prearranged location, the place exploded with light. A shotgun blast went off. An upper classman near me collapsed with a scream, gripping his chest, red fluid flowing slowly between his fingers. 'I'm shot,' he screamed, 'My God, I *am* shot!' The freshmen were sent on foot eight miles back to town to fetch a doctor. Of course, the 'injured party' had hot-footed it back to town by the time the doctor arrived at the scene of the 'shooting' with the freshmen as guides." Reagan makes a studied point of explaining that he was just a bystander in this affair. Still, of all the college and fraternity pranks he might have engaged in, he recalls this one with greatest fondness. The fact that each fraternity member paid the doctor ten dollars without protest apparently minimized the immaturity and thoughtlessness of raising an elderly doctor out of bed in the middle of the night to drive eight miles one way and eight miles return for a college prank.

Mac was not unhappy to have Moon on the team, although he left him, along with Dutch, on the second string until the end of the year, despite the grim fact that school dropouts had reduced the Golden Tornadoes to twenty-seven players. Mac did not believe in pushing a player before he was ready. "Moon was a natural player," McKinzie says, "fast, quick-eyed, tough to avoid. I knew he had varsity in him. I held him back so he could season. Dutch did better once Moon was on the team. Seemed he had to prove himself more. I made him guard on second string by the end of second year. But I still didn't think he had it to move up."

The man who helped him finally get off the bench was not Moon or Mac, but another sophomore, Enos ("Bud") Cole. Cole had played his freshman year at Northwestern, then had dropped out to play three years of pro ball. Mac put him in the quarterback position, but when an old knee injury flared up, Mac wisely took him off the field and engaged him to privately coach some of his weaker players.

Reagan recalls of these sessions: "Bud made the decisions and I became a purely physical means to the end he dictated. . . . He would whisper, 'Knife in—they are going the other way.' Doing as he ordered, I was on the ball carrier three plays in a row. 'Now,' he hissed, 'go straight across—they'll try to reverse to suck you in.' Of course he was right . . ."

Most of the action Dutch saw in his sophomore year was in games between the first and second teams. His vision, as he admits, "was limited to one square yard of turf—the one occupied by the right guard on the first team." This was Captain Pebe Leitch, a senior and a fraternity brother. Leitch was definitely the Big Man on Campus, and Dutch held him in great esteem. "I'm a sucker for hero worship to this day [1964]," he admitted, "and teaming with Pebe in mayhem . . . was my dream of Valhalla."

"Eureka opened the season at Wheaton with a drive that netted a 13–7 victory . . . 'Bud' Cole scored in the first quarter after a steady march from midfield . . . 'Bud' turned in some classy running . . . Miller battered the line . . . Leitch played in an aggressive style . . ." Moon leaped right into the front line of the Golden Tornadoes during a singularly tough game at Carthage. In the last two minutes of play with the score 7–0 against them, Moon had "nabbed a twenty yard pass and galloped sixty yards to the goal line. Bud Cole stepped back and booted the ball squarely between the goal posts to make the score board read 7–7." This did not ease the brothers' rivalry. Nor did Dutch turn to Moon as an idol, even though his brother's action was the stuff of which football heroes are made.

He wore his gold and red suit and the enormous E on his sweater with tremendous pride, but Dutch knew he had not made the golden circle of the Tornadoes and it hurt. His interest in theater was just as avid and he and Margaret appeared in many plays performed by Epsilon Sigma, the drama society. Moon had tried out and had been accepted (ten out of thirty-three auditioners were taken).

Dutch and Margaret were still going steady. They had dates in a graveyard nearby (accompanied by other couples), where they could huddle together against an old gravestone. They bought cherry phosphates at the drug counter (only two cents each). They talked a lot about Hoover "and his calm statements on prosperity," and Franklin D. Roosevelt "who was beginning to criticize Hoover from New York [where he had replaced Al Smith as governor]." Margaret was top of her class and honored in the chapel for her grades. She did not share Dutch's interest in politics, but she understood people and their needs. They attended

dances together, including a Halloween party at Camp Lantz on
the Mackinaw River where everyone wore "country fashions—
and square dances were executed with some fancy footwork, a
continuous ghost story was created by the guests and the evening
reached a climax when everyone got a horn or a rattle and proceeded to make some racket." A few weeks later, they attended a
Harvest Moon dance. "Subdued lights and the rosy glow of the
fireplace created an appropriate atmosphere. Each guest as he entered was given a tiny moon containing the name of his partner
for the first dance. During the third dance under the light of the
harvest moon each man discovered his partner for the evening." A
great deal of trading around was done at this time and Margaret
and Dutch managed to end up together. New Year's Eve, Margaret was Dutch's guest at the traditional TEKE New Year's
party and they dined at a candlelit table of four decorated in pink
and green (Pebe Leitch and his girlfriend were the other couple).

For schools like Eureka that existed on the edge of bankruptcy
with a student body whose families had been fighting poverty and
foreclosure for several years, the Crash did not have the element
of surprise that it had for the rest of the country. In his sophomore
year, Dutch kept body and soul together not only by waiting tables but by working with Heinie in the school's steam plant, rak-
ing leaves and thawing out water pipes with a blow torch. He and
Moon did not go home too often for they could afford neither the
fare nor the time away from odd jobs.

In Dixon, Nelle and Jack were feeling the pinch. With both
boys being away at school, no extra income was forthcoming to
supplement Jack's salary (Moon had previously contributed to the
household). Nonetheless, Nelle would not consider her sons quit-
ting college. Moon's decision to attend Eureka had been a great
relief to her. "She always said Dutch would have succeeded if he
had gone to college or not, but Moon was another matter," an old
friend remarked.

By now Nelle enjoyed something of a reputation as a faith
healer. Mrs. Neer recalled, "When our little daughter [Elonwy]
was about four years old, she developed what seemed to be ton-
sillitis. The doctor said it was that and prescribed medicine . . .
we returned to him several times for a couple of weeks, and he
prescribed other medicines, but they did no good. Finally, an abscess developed on her neck, which swelled to twice . . . normal
size. She became so ill she could neither eat nor sleep. . . . On
Sunday morning my husband said to me, 'Why don't you go to

church? It will do you good. . . . [The pastor] spoke on how we as
Christians should accept death. I could hardly take the sermon
because we did not know whether our daughter was going to live.
When the service was dismissed, I couldn't leave my seat. At last,
everybody had left except Mrs. Reagan who was on the platform
gathering up the music that the choir members had left.

"I thought, 'If only I could talk to Mrs. Reagan,' and went up to
her. . . . I told her about our daughter, and she said, 'Let's go into
the back room.' . . . We did. Then Mrs. Reagan said, 'Let's get
down on our knees and pray about it.' She made a wonderful prayer
and when [we stood] I felt the prayer was answered. . . . I went
home. . . . Pretty soon there was a knock on the door. It was Mrs.
Reagan. . . . She spent the whole afternoon [in prayer] with us. . . .
She left about six o'clock. . . . Moments later the abscess burst. . . .
The next morning the doctor said, 'I don't need to lance this.' God
had heard Nelle Reagan's prayer and answered it."

Nelle also gave Bible readings to various groups and was in
great demand. "Many of us believed Nelle Reagan had the gift to
heal," one contemporary admitted. "She never laid on the hands
or anything like that. It was the way she prayed, down on her
knees, eyes raised up and speaking like she knew God personally,
like she had had lots of dealings with him before. If someone had
real troubles or was sick, Nelle would come to their house and
kneel and pray. Maybe she didn't always pray herself a miracle
but folks could bear things a lot better after she left."

Perhaps the one physical attribute Dutch inherited from Nelle
was his voice (he did not resemble either of his parents too closely),
a distinctive, mellow voice, tinged with a hopeful cadence—a voice
that had a timbre to it that impressed people with the honesty of
the words he spoke. Because he believed in himself and his voice so
conveyed this confidence, others picked up on it. Yet, it never
seemed to occur to him that his leadership qualities had anything
to do with natural assurance. Instead, he attributed his popularity
to his minor achievements on the football field and his major ones
as a swimmer. He had a likability, a modesty and a posture that
made him seem at once proud and humble and perfectly matched
his vocal qualities. From Nelle he also learned what to do with his
voice. When trying to be persuasive, he would lower the volume,
speaking "barely above a whisper" to win a confidential intimacy,
and he instinctively knew just the right moments to raise that
volume and lower the pitch for intensity. Unlike the more evangelistic, booming speech of the Reverend Cleaver, which instilled

awe and could both mesmerize and intimidate, Dutch's voice had the humility and passion of a true believer, a manly, ingratiating voice made for promises.

As 1930 ripened into spring, the Depression hit the South and the Midwest hardest. Wheat that had sold in 1929 for $1.35 a bushel now sold for 76 cents. Bread lines had formed in Chicago's windy streets. In Iowa City, where five banks had closed and people had to go to Cedar Rapids to cash a check, eggs were 6 cents a dozen. Factory employment was down 20 percent and payrolls were cut 29 percent, and something like 80 banks a month were closing, most of them the small, family-owned building-and-loan variety that had helped the farmer and the small businessman for decades. People turned to church and religion more and more. A great many weary, bewildered midwesterners tuned in their radios on Sunday afternoons (with no chicken cooking in their pot for dinner) to station WJR, Detroit (a CBS affiliate), to listen to the heartwarming, emotional Irish cadences of Father Charles E. Coughlin. For four years Father Coughlin had broadcast Sunday sermons to children. His simple, clear approach and the richness of his voice appealed to adults to an even greater extent. Coughlin was a Catholic priest from Royal Oak, Michigan, but his paternal quality and the needs of the radio public in 1930 transcended religious and regional boundaries.

During his years on radio, Father Coughlin had so won over his unseen listeners with his ability to bring warmth and a sense of caring and hope into people's homes that his audience had complete faith in the truth of his message. Therefore, when one Sunday afternoon, October 30, 1930, he addressed political issues for the first time, there was a memorable reaction. Thousands upon thousands had been listening when Coughlin complained that "the international bankers have wrecked the country, and the Communists are trying to take it over." His audience let him know they agreed by sending him nearly fifty thousand letters. Coughlin had hit upon the fears of the nation's poor when "he denounced the bankers and the industrialists who had ruled and ruined the country, the greedy politicians and the money changers in the temple."

Coughlin's listeners were able to point a finger. There were men in power to be blamed for their poverty and joblessness. And their fears for the future were not unfounded if the Communists were getting set to take over the country. Within two years, Father Coughlin's audience grew to an estimated thirty to forty-five

million and he became a strong political force. But he had risen
from the Midwest and those states considered his words gospel.
Father Coughlin was no doubt one of the first political voices
Dutch Reagan heard. (Whether or not Reagan was strongly influenced by Father Coughlin, there were striking parallels in their
vocal talent, and later on he shared some of the priest's early, less-
radical political views.) Communicating through the medium of
radio appealed to Dutch, which is why he so enjoyed the act of
pretending to broadcast school games. Wallace Stegner in his brilliant essay "The Radio Priest and His Flock," wrote, "On what
grounds except bigoted grounds could one mistrust a priestly
friend of the poor? What madness would lead anyone to repudiate
so substantial a straw in these drowning times. To many, his
[Coughlin's] was the only voice [in 1930] that spoke the truth."
(Years later, when Reagan went on the road for General Electric,
audiences had the same reaction; how could one mistrust a man
who had appeared onscreen for two decades as American as apple
pie?)

By the end of the thirties, Father Coughlin was to turn into a
hate-monger, a fascist demagogue. Perhaps the priest with the silver tongue was corrupt from the beginning, but in 1930 his future
pro-Nazi theories were a number of years away and the seductive
voice, one of the great speaking voices of the twentieth century,
was a bright-burning candle in dark times, which led the way for
many. A career in radio took on new meaning as a path to fame
and power. Dutch, of course, avidly followed the great radio
sports announcers of the day and confided his dream—that he
might one day join their august body—to Margaret, but she
thought at the time it was only a passing idea. Margaret had been
president of the sophomore class and once again had taken high
scholastic honors while Dutch had just managed to slide through.
Nonetheless, the year was memorable for him. He had won his
varsity letter in swimming. He and Margaret, Homer Jordan and
Enos Cole had appeared in *Aria da Capo* in the national play contest at Northwestern and brought back third place—a tremendous
achievement for such a small school. There had been so many
marvelous evenings shared with Margaret that they had all flowed
into one romantic haze—the spirited Christmas party at Professor
Jones's home and the cold weekend winter nights when they had
trailed into Gish's Emporium to warm up on fifteen-cent bowls of
hot chili.

Both Dutch and Moon returned to Dixon for the summer of

1930. Moon found a construction job and Dutch went back to work at Lowell Park. There was no doubt in either of their minds that they would not abandon college. Dixon offered very little in substantial employment. Boys they had gone to high school with were still jobless two or more years after graduation.

Margaret spent most of the summer in Eureka with her family, but she came up to Dixon several times to visit friends. Never had she looked as beautiful as she did that summer. The round soft-ness of her face and body had slimmed, so that her bone structure could be better seen. Her dark eyes—always lovely—had come alive and flashed with excitement and intelligence. A womanliness had enveloped her. For the first time, Dutch experienced some shyness in her presence. She was a few months younger than he, but suddenly she had taken on an aura of a mature woman. They were still going steady, and people in Dixon remained confident that one day they would wed. Love in Dixon followed a familiar pattern. Boys often married their childhood sweethearts and girls seldom played the field for very long. One could afford to be a coquette at seventeen or eighteen, but a year later such an atti-tude could damage a young woman's reputation.

The summer was a happy one for Dutch despite the signs of the advancing Depression around him—the hard look on Jack's face, the intensity of Nelle's prayers, the shrinking size of Jack's pay envelope, the move to a smaller apartment. Dutch spent every day but Sunday morning at Lowell Park, where the same group of youthful admirers attended him. The notches increased, his local fame spread. Evenings he stopped by Fluff's Confectionery, where his friends gathered for phosphates. When Margaret was in town they had eight-cent ice cream cones at Prince Ice Cream Castle and went roller-skating for fifteen cents at Moose Hill. But mostly he took Margaret to the Dixon Theater (twenty-five cents Mon-days through Thursdays) to listen to the three-keyboard Barton organ and see a double-feature movie, newsreel and cartoon. *Jour-ney's End* had been made into a film (this time he did see Colin Clive, the Stanhope of the London play cast). Fredric March starred in *The Royal Family of Broadway*, Greta Garbo in *Anna Chris-tie*, the Marx Brothers in *Animal Crackers*, Lew Ayres in *All Quiet on the Western Front*, Marlene Dietrich in *The Blue Angel*, Walter Houston as Abraham Lincoln, Richard Barthelmess and Douglas Fairbanks, Jr., in *The Dawn Patrol*, Edward G. Robinson as Little Caesar, the blond bombshell, Jean Harlow, in *Hell's Angels*. But, Johnny Mack Brown as Billy the Kid was his favorite.

At the end of the summer, to Dutch's shock, Margaret told him she planned to spend the next year at the University of Illinois. Her great thirst for knowledge was not being satisfied at Eureka. They would write, she would see him often—after all, the campus at Champaign was even closer to Eureka than Dixon was. Margaret had a strong sense of her own needs. It would have been useless to try to persuade her to change her mind, even if he had thought he had that right.

They said good-bye the first day he returned to school for his junior year. Immediately, he propelled himself even further into the mainstream of college life. He won his second varsity letter in track, and he became the official swimming coach, the cheerleader for the basketball team, president of the Boosters Club, an editor of the yearbook, a member of the student senate, treasurer of the drama fraternity and remained on the football team. He appeared as the lead in four productions, waited on tables and worked for Heinie shoveling snow and helping to stoke the many school furnaces. And his grades improved—although he was not disappointed when he did not win honors.

At the end of the year, he appeared in a school production of a play called *The Brat,* in which he portrayed "the young attractively drunk playboy brother" of a "stuffed shirt." Cast in an Eliza Doolittle–like role of the street urchin he saves from his brother's lust was a shapely senior several years older than her classmates. With Margaret away at Illinois, he contracted a "disease" that he christened "leading-ladyitus," seeing her "in light of the role [she] played." The romance was short-lived, lasting through two weeks of rehearsal and the one performance of the play presented the week before the Christmas holidays, when Margaret, glowing and animated, returned home and promised she would come back to Eureka for her senior year.

Summer 1931 was spent lifeguarding again at Lowell Park (seventy-one notches by the end of summer, eleven that season). The pay had not increased, but he felt lucky that the Graybills had not had to cut his salary. Tough times had hit Dixon with a sharp uppercut to its gritty, outthrust jaw. Newman's Garage had a daily line of weary jobless who queued up for bread and coffee. The factories around Dixon were folding one by one. The foreclosures of local farms had hit an all-time high. The mood in Dixon was somber. As Dutch headed into his senior year, it dawned on him that his degree could well prove useless. Yet, something drove him on. He hoped for a kind of miracle that might make him a football star after all and bring offers from the professional teams. At the end of the summer, the Fashion Boot Shop closed its doors. Jack managed to find a job as a traveling shoe salesman for twenty-two dollars a week including his expenses. Nelle was hired as a sales clerk and seamstress at the Marilyn Shop (women's wear) for fourteen dollars a week. No one worked harder. Her employer, Mrs. J. W. Sipe, recalled, "Sometimes, I would say to her, 'Don't do that. It's too much for you.' She would say, 'I wouldn't ask anybody to do anything I wouldn't do myself.'" Nelle waited on trade, fitted, sewed, pressed, cleaned the premises and often walked a mile or more out of her way home to deliver a package.

In the autumn of 1931, the Reverend Cleaver became the minister of the Christian Church in Eureka and Margaret returned to the college. Shortly after the start of the school term, Dutch was elected senior-class president and Jack lost the job he had on the road. He found another one managing a small store for "a cheap shoe chain outfit" in Springfield, Illinois, two hundred miles north of Dixon with Eureka in between. For three months, he and Nelle were separated, but the boys did manage to visit Jack once when Mac's Golden Tornadoes played a team in Springfield. Seeing Jack as the sole clerk in the squalid "hole-in-the-wall with its garish orange paper ads plastered over windows in front and one cheap bench with iron arm rests to separate the customers (if there was more than one at a time)" was a sobering sight for both Moon and Dutch. The Fashion Boot Shop had been a palace compared to the Springfield store.

The Tornadoes lost to Springfield, but the highlight of the trip for the brothers was bringing Jack back to the college dormitory where they had been put up for the night and having him join the team for dinner. Jack was in rare form. McKinzie recalls how "he started telling stories when they sat down and was still talking when the boys walked him down to the door. He was a gifted storyteller and a pretty rabid Democrat. Talked about how things would change once the Republicans were *shoed* out of office. S-H-O-E he meant, because he said he knew just how to do it. Put the sole of your shoe—well, you know what he meant."

Christmas, 1931, found the Reagans together in Dixon. "Moon and I were headed out on our dates when a special delivery arrived for Jack. I can still see the tiny apartment living room and Jack reading the single blue page the envelope contained. Without raising his head he quietly remarked, 'Well, it's a hell of a Christmas present [being fired].'" After the boys returned to school, Nelle and Jack moved into one room of the apartment on Lincolnway that they had occupied in that year and sublet the remainder. A bedroom hot plate served as their kitchen. Things got so bad that neighbors brought food on trays to keep the Reagans going after the grocer had stopped their credit. Finally (and without Jack's knowledge), Nelle wrote Dutch for help and he sent her fifty dollars and pulled in his belt as far as it could go. Unable to find a job, Jack threw all his energy into volunteer work for the Democrats, convinced that if Hoover could be beaten and the Democrats returned to power, the country would pull out of the Depression.

Eureka's graduating class had dwindled to forty-five as young people dropped out to help at home or simply to keep themselves afloat. The school was in such a bad financial state that publication of the yearbook had to be abandoned. McKinzie fought like a tiger to keep the Golden Tornadoes competing. Trips to games on other campuses became impossible, so he talked and talked until the opposing teams agreed to come to Eureka. In November, Monmouth played at Eureka. Rain had fallen for two days and the team played in a muddy field. During the third quarter, Monmouth's top player, Brownlow Speer, reached for a ball, slid and fell with such force that the leg injury he received required immediate surgery. He was taken to the hospital in Peoria while his team returned home. Dutch showed up about the time that he came out of the anesthesia to assure him his leg would be all right. It struck Speer as odd, because he could not remember Dutch as a child in Monmouth. But there was something in the smiling face of the tall figure who leaned in close to his bed that made him believe Dutch spoke the truth.

Thursday, February 11, 1931, *The Pegasus* ran an editorial, "'Shall We Stay Out of War'—The present agitation for war between the U.S. and Japan should be understood as an opportunity for all college students to show the real value of education. Now of all times is no time to go about talking militaristically. Whether you boys plan to go to war or not, if there is one, it would be much better if you would not discuss your intention with everyone else. Everyone has far more influence on other people's actions than he is likely to think he has. You can't know who you are encouraging to go when you air your opinions." Fears of going out to seek employment where none seemed possible were, however, the real threat to the class of '32.

There were attempts to lighten the gravity of the situation. On April Fools' Day, a cartoon of Dutch in a beanie cap and striped trousers and a little tag that said "Rah for Seniors" was published in *The Pegasus*. A few days later a candid photograph of him taken when he was a freshman also appeared with the caption: "Snap of the late Dutch Reagan taken 4 years ago."

The June afternoon of graduation was clear as crystal. The lawns of the campus had been freshly mowed and a soft breeze carried a heady, grassy scent. Most of the graduating students were broke and in debt (Dutch among them). The day was so perfect that as McKinzie says, "It seemed there was a *right* to hope."

Dutch spoke as president of the class at graduation. Margaret was awarded highest honors for her grades. Clyde Lyon, Eureka's new president, gave a stirring address insisting the graduating class not let the future "bully them into non-achievement." The Reverend Cleaver blessed them and told them to "hold God and God's word in their hearts." All forty-five students stood in a circle holding a rope of woven ivy that had been cut from the brick walls of the school buildings. A tradition that had been going on for more than thirty years then took place. Each student was to break the ivy, signifying his or her breaking with the past and each other and going forward into the future. The exceptions were those students who used the tradition as a way of announcing their intentions toward each other. Couples who wanted to be recognized as such stood side by side and did not break the chain but held fast together. With bright sun overhead in a blue, pacific sky, Margaret and Dutch remained "connected." There were cheers and excitement, then some tears as old friends parted. Dutch Reagan's college years were at an end. Now came the frightening business of having to go out and make a living.

RADIO WHO

"This generation of Americans has a rendezvous with destiny."
—FRANKLIN DELANO ROOSEVELT,
Speech accepting renomination,
June 27, 1936

JACK REAGAN WAS A FERVENT DEMOCRAT IN SOLID Republican country, as were his sons. He did not need Father Coughlin to tell him "Roosevelt or Ruin," he believed this to the core of his conscience. America was caught up in the election and Illinois was especially feverish since the Democratic Convention was to be held in Chicago that July. Jack toiled long and hard in Dixon's small Democratic headquarters. The Reagans were living mostly on Nelle's salary. Jack had applied for any job possible; none was available to a forty-nine-year-old man who had never done physical labor. He managed to hold on to the old Oldsmobile just in case he got a job on the road again, but there was no money for gas and oil. Dutch contributed ten dollars a week to the house from his earnings as a lifeguard. Moon had been rehired at the Medusa Cement Company at a reduced salary. The Reagans were managing to eke by and had even moved into a two-room apartment at 207 North Galena Avenue so that "the boys could have a bedroom to come home to."

Still, the Reagans' adversity could not compare to what was

happening to the local farmers who daily fought foreclosure. No substantial farm aid had been passed when Congress adjourned in July. After much squabbling, the elected body had voted to assist farm families of four with an average relief of fifty cents a day. In Washington that month, President Hoover, fearful that groups such as the angry unemployed veterans who called themselves the Bonus Marchers (twenty thousand strong) might attack the White House, had "the Army [led by General Douglas MacArthur], with fixed bayonets and tear gas," drive the marchers out of Washington and reinforce police patrols surrounding the White House, an act that gave the Democrats great momentum.

Jack had wanted desperately to attend the convention as a delegate and was greatly disappointed when the party rejected his application. This did not diminish his enthusiasm or diligence on behalf of the Democrats or keep Dutch from wearing a "Win with Roosevelt" button on his bathing suit.

In the spring of 1932, Dixon took positive steps "to combat the ravages of unemployment and near starvation that stalked the community." As the number of destitute families escalated, canvassers were hired by the town at one dollar a day to go door-to-door to every house in Dixon urging the residents who could spare any amount of money to spend it locally on improving their homes and businesses or on purchasing items they needed. "These things," the *Dixon Evening Telegraph* reported, "will end idle dollars, fear, perverted thrift and hoarding, and help in a return to prosperity." Individuals pledged to spend $127,579 before June 1. Only a fraction of this was realized, and on July 19 the *Telegraph* stated that the "Paul Rader Pantry of Plenty System has been launched to help feed our own and Chicago's starving thousands." Rader was a Chicago evangelist. The Christian Church and eighteen other Dixon churches backed his plan. Several canning and food experts arrived in town equipped with ten large steam pressure cookers. As a result of their concentrated drive, the churches received donations of fresh fruit and vegetables from small private gardens, and meat and poultry from those who raised their own. These foods were canned over the next eight weeks. When the experts finally departed, they did so leaving town with a total of 5,891 cans to distribute in Chicago, an equal amount remaining behind to feed Dixon's needy.

Since even this was inadequate, the week of August 22 was designated Rooster Week and local farmers were asked to donate old fowls for canning. "The ridding of old roosters from flocks," the *Telegraph* stated, "has long been preached by the University of Illinois College of Agriculture and it is thought that the farmer will thus render himself a service as well as help the poor in this locality." In Dixon, no one looked down on his neighbor's plight; he reached out a helping hand wherever he could. Because pride made Dixon regard Relief with a tinge of disgrace, its citizens rose up, joined hands and worked together to keep their own off the rolls, making its history during the Depression somewhat singular. Distance from a large metropolis and slow growth with few outsiders were partly responsible for this reaction, as was the lower-middle-class economic equality of most of its population.

Dixon's only truly affluent resident, Charles ("Chuck") Walgreen, the cut-rate drug multimillionaire, had a charismatic personality and knew how to use it to his best advantage. Myrtle Walgreen remembered that in the early years of their married life, her husband used to say to her, "Myrtle, when we get $20,000 in the bank we're going to get a place in the country." By 1928 he had accumulated this amount and a great deal more and had bought Hazelwood, which was situated on the Rock River just outside the town of Dixon.

The Walgreens had weekended in the log cabin they had reconstructed for several years before building on a new main house in the spring of 1932. Planned first as "just a long low cottage," it quickly developed into a grand estate complete with "a game room with pool and billiard tables and a wine cellar sunk into the ground . . . a downstairs room—120 feet by 40 feet—with its front wall almost completely made of windows and a stone fireplace scaled to roast a whole ox." Hazelwood also had a swimming pool, stables, and a long underground tunnel that linked "the log cabin [turned into one guest house] and the squash court in the basement of the [reconverted] barn guest house."

To the people in Dixon, Hazelwood was "the castle on the hill." Except for workmen, delivery people and clergymen (Mrs. Walgreen believed in supporting local churches), townsfolk seldom were invited there. No one found it incongruous that a mansion of this order should be constructed in a town that had poor people dividing their own meager rations to share with those less fortunate. Hazelwood gave Dixonites a feeling of importance—a powerful and rich man had chosen their town for his country home. And, they had a grand estate to talk about. More than that, the rebuilding of Hazelwood and the large parties held there brought much needed work and employment to Dixon. It also brought rich and famous people. Millionaire Phillip K. Wrigley arrived with his family and five palomino horses when spending a weekend at Hazelwood. As they passed through town, people on the street stopped to ask if they were a circus.*

The sudden emergence of Hazelwood as a glittering social center was a beacon of hope to Dixon's young men who could not find the most menial jobs. Walgreen had not started from great wealth. His presence bolstered the popular version of the great American dream that, with hard work and proper connections, anything was possible. Dutch shared this philosophy. He later said, "I was trying to reassure myself that I had prospects too." Over the years he had become a fixture among the families who regularly vacationed at Lowell Park. His hope was that through one of the summer people who came from larger cities, he might get an introduction that could lead to a good job. Dutch had taught the two daughters of Sid and Helen Altschuler from Kansas City (Mrs. Altschuler was a Dixon girl) to swim and Sid, a successful businessman, had taken a shine to the young man. One day, as they sat on the bank of Rock River watching the Altschuler girls try out their new expertise, Sid asked him what he thought he wanted to do when the summer was over. "There it was—the question for which I had no answer," he later said. "All I could do was say, 'I don't know.'" Altschuler gave him a few days to think about it, promising to help if he knew anyone in the field he chose.

A few days later, when he met Altschuler again by the river, Dutch announced that what he wanted was a job in radio, broadcasting sports events in Chicago. He claimed he really wanted to tell Altschuler that he wished to be an actor, but "this was a time and place where announcing you wanted to be an actor resulted in a sympathetic committee calling on your parents to suggest a suitable institution." Although Dixon had been hometown to one silent-screen actor, Douglas MacLean, and, of course, Louella Parsons, a career as a performer in either New York or Hollywood seemed too far distant ever to reach, and no other cities could be counted on to pay an actor a salary, or even the promise of one. But Chicago was the Midwest's center of radio.

Altschuler shook his head with great sadness when he made

---

* In 1933, perhaps the worst year of the Depression, Walgreen's advertising budget went over a million dollars and the company was one of the few in America to pay regular dividend payments to stockholders.

this proclamation. "Well, you've picked a line in which I have no connections," he admitted.

Dutch was far from discouraged. The very fact that he had hit upon a career that he knew he would like and be good in bolstered his optimism. For the rest of the summer he would launch into "a rapid-fire routine of 'Here they come out of the huddle up to the line of scrimmage, a hike to the left, the ball is snapped,'" whenever the opportunity arose. He sold ice cream cones for the Graybills when he was not acting as a lifeguard, and this speech was delivered along with every scoop.

On a humid, sweaty night in July, Franklin Delano Roosevelt won the Democratic nomination for president. The next morning, the Democratic nominee, his wife, Eleanor, and two of their sons flew from their home in Hyde Park, New York, to Chicago. To the rousing strains of "Happy Days Are Here Again," the Democrats hailed their new leader. Standing erect with the help of his sons, Roosevelt proclaimed to the delegates who had just nominated him, "A new deal for the American people," a phrase that became immediately popular because it expressed the country's need for "somebody to do something *now*." John Nance Garner was voted vice-presidential candidate. ("The Vice-Presidency," he said in his Texas drawl to Senator Sam Rayburn, "isn't worth a quart of warm piss.")

For the rest of the summer, Jack was caught up in Roosevelt's campaign, the chief topic of conversation at home. This was to be the first presidential election in which either Dutch or Moon was to vote. Dutch cast his ballot for Roosevelt, ". . . because I was a child of the Depression, a Democrat by upbringing and very emotionally involved. Remember his platform? It was all for states' rights, and it also promised to reduce the size of the Federal Government and cut the budget by 25%." (Thirty-five years later, Reagan was to say, "I'm still in favor of that.") But Jack's job, to get out the Democratic vote in Dixon, was not easy. The town feared change would bring upheaval and even worse conditions, and the majority appeared to be solid Hooverites. The *Dixon Evening Telegraph* came out for Hoover. On the same front page was a cartoon drawing of workers carrying their lunch pails home for the last time from the Reynolds Wire Company, which had finally had to shut its doors.

"A job, any job, seemed like the ultimate success," Reagan recalled. As Labor Day approached, Lowell Park prepared to close. Through one of his volunteer workers, Jack learned that there was a job opening in the sporting-goods department of Montgomery Ward that paid $12.50 a week. Dutch rushed down to the chain's small Dixon store for an interview along with several dozen other applicants. The next day, competition had narrowed to one other fellow, George Joyce, and himself. Joyce had played basketball with Dutch at South Dixon High and the two knew each other quite well. By the end of the day the decision was made and Joyce was hired.* The disappointment prompted Dutch to take immediate action.

He would leave with Moon the next morning for Eureka, see Margaret and then hitchhike to Chicago where one of his old TEKE buddies had gone on to study medicine, and with whom he knew he could at least bunk for a night or two. His plan was to get an appointment at NBC and talk them into hiring him as a sportscaster. Margaret was about to start teaching in a small high school near Eureka. Parting was difficult, perhaps more so for Margaret than for Dutch. A realist, Margaret did not have high hopes that Dutch would be successful in his quest. What he sought seemed impossible to her. How could he think he had a chance in a field where he was totally inexperienced and had no connections? And when he failed—then what? Dutch did not have these doubts and at the TEKE House he boasted to old friends, "If I'm not making five thousand a year when I'm five years out of college, I'll consider these four years here wasted." He went off, thumb lifted high and defiantly on the main road to Chicago. Luck was with him. The first ride he got took him all the way.

He had remembered very little about Chicago, which as a small child had seemed to be contained in the few blocks between the Reagan apartment and the Fair Store. The twenties had thrust Chicago forward as "the world's wickedest city" because of its murders and massacres, the police corruption, Black Hand feuds, bootleggers and Al Capone. But by 1932, the city's evil reputation had been overshadowed by the bitter times that were ushered in with the Depression. Gangster blood no longer flowed through its mean, hard streets (or, at least, not quite so often). The Democratic Convention being held there had helped Chicagoans regain a measure of civic pride, increased by the new

---

*When Reagan returned to Dixon in August 1978, Joyce approached him. "You don't remember me, do you?" he asked, referring to their high school basketball team. "Sure I do," Reagan replied. "You're the guy who beat me out of that job at Montgomery Ward."

buildings going up for the Century of Progress Exhibition planned for the following year. The city looked forward to the future with great optimism. Nonetheless, in the elite apartment houses snug to the shores of Lake Michigan, numberless naked windows of empty rooms faced the serene blue waters. Lines leading into soup kitchens were now longer than those to movie theaters offering, for the price of a quarter, four hours of continuous film entertainment and free dishes to lucky ticket-stub holders. Instead of cash, city workers were being given scrip that promised payment at some future date. Few shopkeepers accepted this paper, others turned their backs on old customers. Dutch was not going to find the competition for a job any easier in Chicago than he had in Dixon.

He arrived in the city late on a sweltering Tuesday afternoon in September and went straight to the towering offices of NBC only to be told that the program director interviewed on Thursdays.

Early Wednesday morning, he presented himself at the CBS offices in the Wrigley Building but was unable to get past the receptionist. Out on the street again, he walked from one radio station to another because he was "afraid of the damn buses—as a matter of fact, the city itself scared the bejesus out of me. Everybody seemed to know where they were going and what they were doing and I could get lost just looking for a men's room." By the end of the day he had not obtained even one interview. Thursday morning he returned to NBC. The receptionist informed him that the program director was seeing no one that day. Dutch's disappointment was apparent. The young woman advised him to stay away from the big cities, to try a small town with a small station, that would be more willing to give a newcomer a chance. He thanked her and started back on the hundred-mile journey home.

This time "rides were short with waits between." The heat had broken into a steady warm rain. The last thirty-mile stretch, he caught a ride with "a fellow who told me, somewhat unnecessarily, he'd been trapping skunks."

At home, Jack offered him encouragement and the old Oldsmobile to scout radio stations in sizable surrounding towns. Dutch bought ten gallons of gas and started out early the next Monday morning for a one-day swing, heading first for the farthest point, Davenport, Iowa, which was seventy-five miles west of Dixon. He arrived at radio station WOC, Davenport, "where the West begins, in the state where the tall corn grows," to be told by the station manager and top announcer, Peter MacArthur, that WOC had been advertising for a month for an announcer. Ninety-four applicants had auditioned and a good man had been hired. MacArthur, a vaudeville and music-hall veteran, spoke with a highland burr and walked on two canes, a victim of crippling arthritis. He had come to station WOC by a quirk of fate. The call letters stood for World of Chiropractic and the station occupied space on the top floor of the Palmer School of Chiropractic Medicine, where MacArthur had come in pain and final desperation, orthopedic doctors and prescribed medicine having been unable to relieve him. No surcease from pain was to come from the school either (he still could not use his canes until he was lifted out of a chair first), but he had made his voice the most familiar in Davenport, where he remained to work for the station.

As Dutch turned away, he grumbled, "How does anyone get a chance as a sports announcer if you can't even get a job in a radio station?" MacArthur's interest perked, but Dutch was already on his way down the narrow, dingy corridor to the elevator. About the same time as it arrived, there was a "thumping and cursing in the hallway," and Dutch was sharply rapped on the shin by a cane. "No so fast, ye big bastard," the Scotsman barked, "didn't ye hear me callin' ye?" The door of the elevator opened and closed. "Do ye perhaps know football?"

Dutch told him about his high school and college background, embellishing his accomplishments a little.

"Do ye think ye could tell me about a game and make me see it?"

Dutch quickly said he was sure he could do that. They slowly made their way down another hall and into a studio soundproofed with heavy blue velvet drapes. MacArthur pointed to a red light and told him to start announcing a game into the mike on the table as soon as the red light went on. Then he left. Dutch "was all alone in an acre of blue velvet." The Scotsman had not told him how long he was to talk. He came to a quick decision. The previous autumn, Eureka had played Western State University. At the end of the third quarter Eureka trailed six to nothing.

The red light flicked on. Dutch leaned in close to the microphone. "We are going into the fourth quarter now. A chill wind is blowing in through the end of the stadium," he began, and then re-created the last twenty minutes of play in a voice of growing excitement, much in the way he had "broadcast" games in the locker room or when selling cones at Lowell Park. When he was done, MacArthur threw open the door. "Ye did great, ye big S.O.B.!" Reagan claimed he said.

MacArthur did not offer him a steady job, but instead, "five dollars and bus fare" to broadcast a game from Iowa City a week from that coming Saturday. If he did well with that one, he could announce games on three successive Saturdays. Jack told everyone he could about Dutch's radio debut, and many of the Reagans' friends listened in the day of his first broadcast. The prearranged plan was that Dutch would share the coverage and the between-quarters commentary with another, more experienced, radio man whom he immediately thought of as his competitor. The man was glib, but his knowledge of football was not equal to Dutch's. With bolstered confidence, Dutch let loose all the expertise he could. At the end of the third quarter, MacArthur scrawled a message on yellow paper that was handed to the other man in the booth. "Let the Kid finish the game," it read. After the broadcast, MacArthur told him he was hired at ten dollars a game and bus fare for the next three. It meant traveling back and forth to Iowa City every Saturday and the pay was not exactly a royal sum, but it was employment and Dutch Reagan could now say he was a sportscaster.

Dutch cast his vote for Roosevelt at the polling booth at South Central School, which he had attended as a youngster. The Democratic nominee had spent the autumn campaigning with vigor. "It's a wonder there isn't more resentment, more radicalism in this country, when people are treated like that," Roosevelt had said after the horrifying incidents of veterans being gassed and clubbed during the Bonus Marchers episode in July. On the campaign trail, he promised both public works and a cut in government spending. His inimitable nasal New York voice cut through all classes. What he said made great sense—jobs had to be created. The American farmer, worker and family could not be abandoned. He was a symbol of strength despite (or perhaps because of) his wheelchair. Crowds cheered when he was helped to his feet, as though through his courage they might find their own. America needed a savior. The stage had been set and Roosevelt wheeled onto it a smiling, confident hero, the right man for the time. Money and power had not overcome his need for a wheelchair. But a strong character and a steely sense of survival had enabled him to rise above his own disability. People felt touched by his words. Perhaps there was something evangelistic about his appeal, but if so, the impression was not of his doing.

While Roosevelt put forth plans for government-sponsored aid to American farmers and small businessmen and to the thousands who daily stood for hours in bread lines, Hoover "set his face like flint against the American government's giving one cent to starving Americans." While audiences cheered Roosevelt on his campaign journeys, Hoover was given a reception "that had been afforded no previous American President—not even Lincoln in Richmond in the last days of the Civil War; as the President's train was pulling into Detroit, the men on it heard a hoarse rhythmic chant rising from thousands of throats; for a moment they had hopes of an enthusiastic reception—and then they made out the words of the chant: 'Hang Hoover! Hang Hoover!'" All across the campaign trail grim men and women shouted and shook their fists at his dark shadow concealed behind the glass windows of his limousine. The president's car, along with the Secret Service men guarding their chief, was pelted with eggs and tomatoes.

The country, and the Midwest in particular, was in a state of simmering rebellion that flared up frighteningly during the month preceding the November election. Robert A. Caro reports that "in Iowa, a mob of farmers, flourishing a rope, threatened to hang a lawyer who was about to foreclose on a farm. In Kansas, the body of a lawyer who had just completed foreclosure proceedings was found lying in a field. In Nebraska, the leaders of two hundred thousand debt-ridden farmers announced that if they did not get help from the legislature, they would march on the statehouse and raze it brick by brick. A judge who had signed mortgage foreclosures was dragged from his bench by black-shirted vigilantes, blindfolded, driven to a lonely crossroads, stripped and beaten." The country was in chaos, public authority was being flouted and fear spread dark and murky across the land.

On election night, the results came in with unprecedented speed. By nine P.M., Franklin D. Roosevelt had been elected president, carrying forty-two of the forty-eight states, Illinois included. According to the law at the time, the president-elect would not take the oath of office until March 4, 1932 (four months later). Hoover would preside over a lame-duck government, and no drastic changes could be effected through the long, hard months that faced the nation.

Radio had invaded the lives of millions. Even the poorest could be found huddled around a set in drugstores, club rooms and soup kitchens, listening to the play-by-play descriptions of the World Series games. Those who had radios in their homes listened religiously to *Amos and Andy* weeknights at six P.M. Most programs were reviewed by critics in major cities, and that included sports coverage. In the first football game Dutch broadcast, Iowa lost to Minnesota, 21–6. Radio WOC had relayed the program through NBC affiliate Radio WHO in Des Moines, Iowa, where it was transmitted throughout the Midwest. Heavy rain had fallen on the field that day and the *Chicago Tribune* critic wrote, "[Reagan's] crisp account of the muddy struggle sounded like a carefully written story of the gridiron goings-on and his quick tongue seemed to be as fast as the plays." By the end of the fourth game, Dutch had become a virtuoso in his new field. Yet, as Christmas approached, he did not know how he was going to hang in unless something happened fast. Pete MacArthur called to tell him the station was trying to work things out. For another two rather desperate weeks, Dutch contemplated other, more menial ways of making a living, swinging a pick-ax if necessary. Then MacArthur was back on the telephone to offer him a staff announcer's job to start immediately at one hundred dollars a month—a king's ransom in 1932.

Bridges across the Mississippi connected Davenport (then a city of about seventy thousand) to Rock Island, Moline and East Moline. The four towns were known as the Quad Cities and the combined populations made Davenport, which was the center, a growing and busy metropolitan area. Davenport had started life as a trading post and was the site of a grim battle of the War of 1812 as well as the place where the treaty for the Black Hawk War had been signed. Before the late nineteenth century, the city had possessed a heavy water traffic. Then it became a center for the manufacture of agricultural equipment. With the depressed farm situation, the city had been severely hit and the tone had changed from rushing commerce to desperate times as banks closed, along with factories, and the lines at soup kitchens and unemployment offices grew daily. However, such deprivation fed the box offices of the movies, where people spent the few pennies they had to escape from reality, and ushered in the glory years of radio, which came into people's homes free, providing they were able to afford one in the first place. Time payments became a way of life, with radios and refrigerators as the main items being purchased.

Dutch rented a room for $8 a week, bought a weekly meal ticket at the Palmer Chiropractic School—"three meals a day every day"—for $3.65 and sent Nelle $5 a week. Moon still had to be helped if he was going to continue at Eureka, and so Dutch went to see the pastor at the local Christian Church. "Would the

Lord consider His share as being His, if I gave the 10% to Moon
to help him through school?" The pastor agreed that it would
seem a proper Christian act and so Moon got $2.50 a week and
Dutch kept $5, some of which went to repaying his college loan.
The "king's ransom" had dwindled into "eking by." He had to
live close to the line, but "just to gild the lily" he gave a dime
each morning on his walk to work "to the first fellow who asked
for a cup of coffee," a gesture that did as much to add to his own
sense of well-being as it did to help the recipient of his handout.

His job did not have the glamour or the excitement he had
expected. Locally played football games were few and far between. WOC had him fill in as a disc jockey spinning records for
hours, interspersing the music with the reading of commercials, a
job he did not do too well, being unable, because of his poor eyesight, to read glibly from a script the first time, even with the aid
of his glasses. His co-anchorman at the station was Hugh Hipple,
a Philadelphian with grand hopes of becoming a great actor. Hipple (who later would break into films as Hugh Marlowe) had a
very solemn approach to acting. After three weeks of flipping records and announcing organ music from the Runge Mortuary,
Dutch was told his services would have to be suspended but the
station would call him again to cover sports events. His world had
suddenly collapsed. He turned to Hipple for comfort and encouragement. "I've always believed the kindest thing a man can do in
this business is tell someone when they should get another line of
work," Hipple intoned.

Dutch did not agree. When the station gave him a short re-
prise because his replacement had not worked out, his anger was
diminished and his commercials had a good punch and conversa-
tional pitch. MacArthur asked him to stay on. The relief was
enormous.

On March 2, 1932, Eleanor and Franklin D. Roosevelt and
their son, James, arrived by train in Washington for the inaugura-
tion two days later. They moved into a suite at the Mayflower
Hotel, where they would remain until the transition to the White
House. The following day they were invited to call upon the
Hoovers for tea. Only months before, Hoover had delayed his en-
trance a half hour at a White House governors reception while
Roosevelt stood on the rostrum with James's help, waiting.
Hoover's intent had been to force Roosevelt into exposing his
weakness by asking for a chair. Eleanor had never forgiven him

and she was noticeably cool. "Tea was concluded with minimum conversation." When James went to help his father to rise from a chair and settle into his wheelchair, Roosevelt told Hoover not to wait since the process took some time. Hoover, unsmiling, replied, "Mr. Roosevelt, you will learn that the President of the United States waits for no one," and stalked out.

A cold wind swept Washington on Saturday, March 4, the day of the inauguration. A huge crowd was gathered in the streets surrounding the site of the ceremony. "What are those things that look like cages?" someone in one of the huddled groups asked. "Machine guns," she was told. If the FBI expected trouble, they were wrong. At noon, a bugle blew and Franklin D. Roosevelt, supported by James, walked down a special maroon-carpeted ramp to the platform and took the oath of office on a Dutch Bible that had been in the Roosevelt family for three hundred years. In his resonant, moving voice with the accented Groton *a*, the new president told the nation: "Let me assert my firm belief that the only thing we have to fear is fear itself, nameless, unjustified terror which paralyzes needed efforts to convert retreat into advance." His inaugural speech set forth three main areas where action must be swift—public works for the unemployed, a rise in farm prices and "strict supervision" of the bankers. Action is exactly what the nation wanted, and he gave it to them. By working through the entire first night of his presidency, he was ready the next day, Sunday, to summon a special session of Congress. A bank holiday for the entire country was announced along with a new bank bill. Congress passed this by a voice vote in the House.

On March 12, Roosevelt went on the air with his first fireside chat. "My friends, I want to talk to you for a few minutes . . . about banking," he said in a warm, intimate voice. He then proceeded to assure the nation that it was "safer to keep your money in a reopened bank than under a mattress." The people believed him, and by the end of the next banking day, deposits exceeded withdrawals by a healthy margin. Four days later he sent Congress farm legislation that he hoped would establish and maintain a balance between production and consumption of agricultural commodities. Happy days were not exactly here again, however.

A downward drift in farm prices began toward summer and took a serious dip by autumn. Roosevelt, who had once referred to himself as "the quarterback of the offensive against the Depression," saw the game going against him and tried a forward pass. The government deliberately raised the price of gold, which in turn lowered the dollar in terms of other goods as well. By January 1934 the dollar had been devalued (in terms of gold) to 59.06 cents. But prices had not risen proportionately. Roosevelt's plan was a failure, and as the winter of 1933–34 set in, his New Deal's once-solid support was slipping badly.

In Dixon, Moon's former employer, the Medusa Cement Company, had closed, throwing a thousand more of the city's ten thousand into the lines of the unemployed. Jack was given a job with the Works Progress Administration (WPA) distributing food and paper scrip to Dixon's distressed. The pay would not have kept him off the Relief rolls himself if Nelle had not had her job at the Marilyn Shop. He operated from a desk in the anteoffice of the County Supervisor of the Poor. Daily lines formed at his door. Most of the men and women were people he had known for years. The look of defeat in their eyes was difficult for him to face each day. They did not want handouts, they wanted jobs, and he knew that. Any extra time he had was spent cajoling people with income into making jobs for others. But there were not enough jobs to restore even momentary pride in more than a few. Within a very short time, although almost everyone wanted to work, people had to refuse Jack's offers of a temporary job. By working a few days, they would have their Relief cut off and weeks of no income for their families would pass before they were permitted to go back on the assistance list.

Not until November 26, 1933, with the start of the Civic Works Program, would Dixon begin to find jobs for the unemployed. On that morning, 136 men went to work on several state highway department improvement programs which consisted chiefly "of minor grading projects, removal of brush, trees and stumps." Another 35 men were hired to remove Dixon's old streetcar tracks and an equal number to improve the roads and fences at Lowell Park. The *Telegraph* reported on November 26 that "supplies of shovels, picks and axes, have been practically exhausted and equipment has had to be borrowed to get the work started at once." On the average, men were paid five dollars a day. But two hundred or so jobs did not end Dixon's problems.

Anger and frustration drove Jack on, but they also took their toll on his health. His heart gave him warning signs that he chose to ignore. One good thing had managed to evolve from the pressures of the times. He had curbed his great thirst considerably. The days of Jack's government employment were, perhaps, the finest of his life, more exciting and fulfilling than any previous experience. The desperation and hope had helped him discover a capacity to fight for others as well as himself. The humiliating days of defeat were behind him. Like millions of others of his countrymen, Jack Reagan had caught a glimpse of what he could achieve and what America might become.

7

ON A CRISP, BRIGHT MORNING IN LATE APRIL 1933,
just three months after Dutch had moved to Davenport, Pete
MacArthur sent him to Radio WHO, an NBC affiliate in Des
Moines, to broadcast the Drake Relays, one of the most prestigious amateur track events in the country. Dutch arrived in Des
Moines (home of Drake University, a Christian school associated
with Eureka College) not fully aware of the vast audience for the
track event. The spontaneity involved in live sports coverage
served his talents well. In the forty-eight hours from the time he
knew of his assignment until he was ushered into the broadcast
booth, he had read up on past Drake Relays and memorized biographical material on former champions and current contenders.
His between-race commentaries had the stamp of an expert at the
microphone and his race-by-race coverage contained the surge of
excitement of a knowledgeable, enthusiastic spectator-announcer.

He returned to Davenport after the relay, but within a few
days the owner of WOC and WHO decided to consolidate the
stations. A number of the WOC staff, including Pete MacArthur,

were transferred to Des Moines. Dutch was offered the job of chief sports announcer at double his old salary. A week later, he had packed his one suitcase, left Davenport and moved into a second-floor accommodation in a rooming house owned by a Miss Plummer at 330 Center Street, across from Broadlawns General Hospital and within walking distance of the station. Then he called to tell Nelle and Margaret of his good fortune. Margaret informed him that she was planning to spend a year in France with her sister, Helen, as soon as the school term was over.

"Where does that leave us?" he asked.

"With time to find ourselves," she replied.

Dutch had thought that he *had* found himself and that his rise in income might well support two, but Margaret had made up her mind. She would sail in June. Where exactly *did* this leave Dutch? As one of Des Moines's most eligible bachelors.

Des Moines (population 142,569 in 1932) was the largest metropolitan area in Iowa. It was twice the size of Davenport and, as the capital, boasted a more political atmosphere. Living in a larger city had a great many advantages for a bachelor, the chance to enjoy a fairly private personal life not the least of them. In addition, many well-known celebrities came through on personal-appearance and publicity tours and one of Dutch's new jobs (between sports events) was to interview these people. Within a short time, not only was his voice familiar to most midwestern sports enthusiasts but Dutch Reagan had become a local celebrity and was on a first-name basis with Iowa's top politicos as well as with the stars whom he met in his work. The change in his life had been swift and dramatic. Yet, he took to it easily; in fact, as one associate puns, "as to the *manner* born."

Radio was an "exciting and exuberant" enterprise in the early 1930s. Radio WHO had just become a major station when Dutch joined the staff. They broadcast a good portion of the nation's most popular programs to the Midwest, *Fibber McGee and Molly*, *The Great Gildersleeve* and *Lum and Abner* among them. "WHO had only recently acquired fifty thousand watts of power on a clear channel," the station's farm reporter, Jack Shelley, remembered. "We were serving thousands of people in small towns and on the farms who were ecstatic at what we could give them and who demonstrated a kind of loyalty and appreciation unknown to radio stations today. We [the staff] liked each other and what we were doing; in news, sports, and very shortly, farm service. We were breaking new ground almost every day, thanks to a visionary general manager named J. O. Maland who was one of the great pioneers of broadcast operation.

"[Dutch] was not technically a member of the news staff. Sports was in most respects a separate operation reporting to top management [Maland], just as the news director did. Except for use of such news services as were available (and they were few in the early thirties because the wire services refused to sell to radio), the sports director operated separately and from a separate office."

In addition to being the WHO sportscaster, Dutch was the announcer on the H[arold] R[oyce] Gross newscast sponsored by Kentucky Club, a pipe-tobacco firm, and on occasion substituted for other announcers on noon or evening broadcasts. Because of his tobacco sponsor, he took up smoking a pipe and was seldom photographed in those years without one.

Radio WHO was located in the Stoner Building at 914 Walnut Street in downtown Des Moines. The Stoner Piano Company occupied business and office space on the ground floor, where immense display windows filled with pianos faced the street. Dutch's office was on the opposite side of a long, arcade-lined entrance to the three-story building. At the back of the ground floor were two large broadcast studios separated by the master control room; a much smaller studio ("a cubby hole of a room with a curtain at the door") halfway back was assigned to Dutch to broadcast the sports. The news and program facilities and the administrative offices were on the second floor. Apartments occupied the top floor (there were no elevators). This division of departments meant that Dutch was left on his own a lot. But from the beginning of his employment at Radio WHO he made friends.

Herb Plambeck, who participated in the network's *The National Farm and Home Hour,* recalled that "Dr. B. J. Palmer, head of the Palmer School of Chiropractic, was owner [of stations WOC, Davenport; and WHO, Des Moines]. He was a gruff, somewhat eccentric, likable person, with a world of great personal interest in everything and everybody, and knew most employees on a first-name basis. . . . Dutch Reagan was one of his special favorites. Our 'boss,' Mr. Joseph Maland, a Minnesotan, was one of the sharpest, shrewdest, nicest 'bosses' anyone could ever meet. . . . He had what I would call a compassionate, as well as a business, interest in every one of us [about thirty-five staff members]. He made us feel like one happy family and let us do 'our thing' our way."

Myrtle Williams,* then WHO program director and occasional vocalist and piano accompanist, struck up a close friendship with Dutch, but not without some stress. "It was one of those things," she explained. "He had come in with some of his WOC colleagues and the WHO staff were nervous they might lose their jobs to the newcomers. Dutch didn't seem as aggressive as the others. He understood this was not easy for the rest of us. I could tell he wanted to make friends; he wanted to feel at home with someone." Soon she was won over by him. "He had a presence, a direction. If he wanted to read a certain book you couldn't move him. I admired that."

Myrtle was an attractive, dark-haired woman about two years older than Dutch. She had a good-fellow personality that made her "one of the guys." She, Dutch and news director H. R. Gross (later congressman from the 3rd District of Iowa) often lunched together at a restaurant on the airport road (Fluer Drive) where they had barbecued ribs; they would call this "getting a rib facial" because they got grease from the ribs all over their faces. Herb Plambeck recalled that "Dutch and Mr. Gross used to have great banterings back and forth" (Gross was a Republican and Dutch tried his best—and failed—to sell him the New Deal). His other WHO friends included two announcers, Jack Kerrigan (later program director) and Ernie Saunders. After a late night at the station, the men would stop by Cy's Moonlight Inn for some near beer spiked with alcohol, bought (so Cy Griffiths, the owner, claimed) from government agents (and therefore safe). Cy's was a tradition with the more pleasure-loving of Des Moines's citizens (including some of the coaching staff at Drake University), and even though Dutch did not drink much, he liked the camaraderie of these evenings. He also made good use of the Moonlight's "passion pit," a small dimly lit dance floor where Cy's patrons could dance cheek to cheek to "smooth music" that came from a jukebox—the first and only one in Des Moines at the time. One close friend, Paul McGinn, said that "if everyone else wanted to get tight, Dutch could always drive the car home."

He began dating shortly after his arrival. Though he had not yet accepted the fact that he and Margaret might have broken up for good, he was not sitting home nights waiting for the year of her French adventure to pass. He took out one of the vocalists from the station, but they soon became just buddies. This might

---

*Myrtle Williams was the maiden name of Myrtle Williams Moon.

have occurred because he met a beautiful young woman, Mary Frances,* who was two years younger than he. ("Where are you from?" he asked when they met. "Illinois," she replied. "Where in Illinois?" "Monmouth—you've never heard of it." He said, "No? I once lived there, my dad worked in shoes at Colwell's Department Store." She told him, "My mother was in millinery at Colwell's, how about that!")

Mary Frances was quite the most glamorous-looking girl he had ever known: tall, slim, dark-haired, a sleek catlike quality to her, lithe, graceful, fast-moving, and a superb athlete and horsewoman. She rode in horse shows, taking one blue ribbon after the other. Dutch emceed one of these events, held at the fairgrounds, and was so taken by her that over the loudspeaker he asked her to meet him later, and, indeed, she did. Both were movie fans and they attended all the new films together. Often in the evenings they met at Fort Des Moines Hotel, directly across from the side door of the Stoner Building on Ninth Street ("unquestionably Des Moines's best hostelry and containing the city's finest restaurant," said Jack Shelley) or at the Kirkwood, which had recently opened and was only a few blocks from Reagan's apartment. ("He was a nice man but a terrible dresser," recalled Chuck Schosselman, who became the assistant manager of the Kirkwood. "I'll never forget his tan topcoat that was so long we called him 'Sweet Pea' [from the *Popeye* comic strip]—not to his face, of course, but all regular hotel guests have pet names, and none ever know!")

Mary Frances preferred meeting him away from her home, because when he came to pick her up, "Dutch would clear the dining-room table and with cards and markers re-create the football or baseball game he had just announced that day for her father's benefit and it would be at least an hour before they could depart on their way." A steady relationship soon developed, but Dutch remained noncommittal. Margaret still occupied an important place in his heart. Mary Frances's dedicated Catholicism created a problem for her but not for him. After all, in the Reagan home, Christian Church and Catholic philosophies had co-existed in harmony. But Mary Frances made it clear that when she married, her husband and children would have to share her faith.

One year after Margaret went to France, she wrote Dutch that she had met a young man in the U.S. Consular Service whom she

---

*Mary Frances's surname has been deleted at the request of her family.

planned to marry.* The shock was severe. As if to console himself, he bought his first car, "a smart little two-seater brown Nash convertible" from his savings (the car dealer was his old school friend Enos Cole) and gave every appearance, as he gunned the motor, of being "a dashing young blade around town," with the top down even in inclement weather.

The disappointment in hearing of Margaret's engagement was followed almost immediately by news that Jack had suffered a serious heart attack. After a lengthy convalescence, he was told he could no longer work. Dutch had just been given a raise in salary to seventy-five dollars a week, twenty-five of which now went directly to Nelle. Making money had suddenly become an important consideration. His first year was not entirely clear sledding. Myrtle reports, "Peter [MacArthur] was the one who really brought Dutch along. He'd sit at home and listen to [him on] the radio and I can still hear him bawling Dutch out when he'd mispronounce a word or say something wrong. But Dutch took it."

To augment his income, Dutch took on extra jobs. He was hired for five dollars to narrate a filmed news program (by Burton B. Jerrell, a local man who made short newsreels for release in Iowa theaters). "He was a great announcer with a wonderful voice, but he wouldn't follow the script, so I had to let him go," Jerrell said. He lost another job as interview host on *Parker's Perfect Polish* radio show to Myrtle, when she took over for him one time and the client liked her better.

Despite these small setbacks, within a year of his joining the WHO staff Dutch had become a celebrity throughout the Midwest. Maland took advantage of his ability and his appeal and had him interview numerous visiting greats in the sports fields— Doc Kearns, Ed Strangler Lewis, Max Baer—film stars like Leslie Howard ("I was so stage-struck that I forgot his name as I stepped up to the microphone," Reagan admitted) and James Cagney, as well as controversial personalities such as the famed evangelist Aimee Semple McPherson.

The woman Dutch interviewed was no longer the miracle

---

*Margaret Cleaver was married to James Waddell Gordon, Jr., of Richmond, Virginia, on June 18, 1935, by the Reverend Cleaver in the Christian Church, Eureka. Her sister, Helen (who had accompanied her to France), was her maid of honor. The reception was held at Lidas Wood Hall, Eureka College, where Margaret had once lived and where she and Dutch had spent many romantic evenings dreaming of their futures. On June 22, the Gordons sailed from New York for Glasgow, Scotland, where Gordon was to be an assistant U.S. consul. They later made their home in Richmond.

healer who could draw a crowd of thirty thousand people clamoring for admission, creating pandemonium as the sick and ailing tried to make their way to the platform where she stood. She was at the Fairgrounds in Des Moines on yet another tour that she hoped might turn the clock back for her to better days. Attendance had been disastrously low and she had agreed to be interviewed on radio in order to bolster ticket sales. The famous red hair was now dyed that color, but something of the old "insistent hyperthyroid vitality" (overpowering, to say the least), the high personal magnetism and sexuality remained.

By far, this was to be the most difficult interview Dutch was to conduct. Aimee appeared at noontime wearing a flowing chartreuse ankle-length gown, gardenias at her throat. Dutch had little chance to ask her many questions, for once she began talking she took over the microphone and Dutch was too mesmerized by the potency of her voice to interrupt. ("Her voice . . . was a voice that the ordeal of thousands of sermons, preached on street corners, in outdoor pavilions, in camp meeting tents and in large city auditoriums in the days before microphones, had strained and coarsened. It was the husky vibrant 'contralto of the midway,' a voice of range and power, which she learned to use with rare dramatic skill. Above all," recalled a former neighbor of hers in the thirties, "I remember the deep huskiness of that voice, the occasional throaty richness, the suggestion of stifled laughter.") Dutch wasn't too far into the interview when he realized he had lost control of his own program.

". . . suddenly I heard her say 'good night' to our radio audience," he remembered. "There were four minutes to go by the radio clock. . . . In my most dulcet tones I said, 'Ladies and gentlemen, we conclude this broadcast by the noted evangelist Aimee Semple McPherson, with a brief interlude of transcribed music. [I signaled to] a sleepy engineer [to put on a record]. I expected nothing less than the 'Ave Maria.' The Mills Brothers started singing 'Minnie the Moocher's Wedding Day.'"

The lesson was one he was never to forget. After that time, he did not allow his radio guests to talk at any length and he became adept at forming questions or comments to interject as soon as the other person had made a point, or, for that matter, simply said something pointless.

Baseball was the backbone of WHO's sports department. Shortly after he joined WHO, Reagan was given the job of broadcasting the home games of the Chicago Cubs, remaining in his small studio on the ground floor of the Stoner Building while a telegraph operator in the press box in Chicago tapped out each play. Curly, a young man in an anteroom outside Dutch's studio, received the plays and typed them out in a coded message, which he then slipped through a glass window to Dutch. Without a pause in his reporting, he would translate the cryptic code "S2C" into "It's a called strike breaking over the inside corner making it two strikes on the batter." While he waited for the next message, he would improvise with some fictionalized description. "Hartnett returns the ball to Lon Warneke. Warneke is dusting his hands in the resin, steps up on the mound, is getting the sign again from Hartnett, here's the windup and the pitch." Near at hand was "a turntable with a crowd applause record, the volume of which was manipulated by Dutch with a foot pedal." As he relayed the game, he would dub in stadium sounds to make the broadcast sound more realistic.

Football had always been his game, and as he said, "I knew . . . how it felt to be on the field, and the smell of sweat and the taste of mud and blood . . ." He had never attended a major-league baseball game. Always able to absorb material fast, he managed to sound knowledgeable, but he had to give an impression of being there. Maland remedied that situation by sending him to Chicago (an overnight journey) to talk to Pat Flanagan, a well-known NBC sportscaster and the man who had created the telegraphic-report process. Flanagan gave him an on-the-spot education in the workings of major-league baseball. He advised Dutch to memorize all he saw—the press box, the diamond, the clock, the habits of players, the jargon. By the time Dutch returned to Des Moines, he had an image of Wrigley Field etched clearly in his mind along with a full cast of characters and their idiosyncracies.

Within a matter of a few weeks, he had reason to be grateful for this on-the-spot training. During the ninth inning of a play-by-play broadcast of a game between the Cubs and the St. Louis Cardinals, with a scoreless tie, Dizzy Dean on the mound, Augie Galan at bat, Curly slipped Dutch the news: "The wire has gone dead." For a period of six minutes and forty-five seconds, Dutch improvised, calling numerous foul balls on Galan and describing a "red headed kid who had scrambled and gotten the souvenir ball," along with several other imaginary incidents on the field. This adroit handling of what could have been a disaster for the WHO sports department made Dutch a bit of a hero, a status he unqualifiedly reached a few days later.

Humid weather had prevailed, and on this particular Sunday

evening Dutch had left his windows open as he prepared for bed. About eleven P.M. he heard a scream. Poking his head out he saw a woman (Melba Lohmann) in a white nurse's uniform fighting off a man across the street near the nurses' entrance to the hospital. He grabbed a .45 caliber automatic gun he had just purchased (for target practice) and, aiming it directly at the man, shouted, "Leave her alone or I'll shoot you right between the shoulders!"

The assailant, who turned out to be a mugger, dropped the purse and small suitcase that he had managed to wrest away from Miss Lohmann and ran off. "Are you all right?" Dutch called down.

"I guess so," the young nurse answered.

"Wait there," he shouted. Moments later he was by her side dressed in robe, pajamas and slippers. After ascertaining that she was shaken but not injured, he insisted on seeing her to the hospital entrance. It never occurred to either of them that dressed as they were they made a strange couple. Fifty years later, Dutch was to claim that the gun had not been loaded and that he would have had to throw it at the man to do any damage. Melba Lohmann was taken with the fact that "on a mild, warm night at an hour when people might well be awake, only this young man came forward to help. He was so strong-sounding in his command that the robber believed his gun was loaded—and so did I—and that was the main thing."

Moon graduated from Eureka in June 1933. By late summer he had not been able to find employment. Reagan claimed in his autobiography that at Nelle's instigation, Moon arrived on his doorstep in Des Moines with the hope that there might be work in a larger city. Moon told quite a different story. "Dutch called me and said, 'I just bought a new Nash convertible. Would you drive down and pick it up [in Eureka] and drive it out here? I'll send you some money for a hotel and gasoline.' I said, 'O.K.' Then he says [sic], 'Plan to stay two or three days out here and see the station and meet the guys at the station,' and I said, 'O.K.,' although I had been thinking of going on to law school."

He moved in with Dutch, which was not particularly easy for either of them. The quarters were small and they found they had less to say to each other than ever before. Two or three days extended into three weeks without any job opportunities for Moon. With no pocket money to spend, he hung around Dutch at the station. One Friday night, he sat in the studio as Dutch broadcast a regular spot in his sports commentary—predictions of upcoming league football games. As Dutch spoke glibly, Moon shook his head. Introducing his brother and pushing a live microphone in front of him, Dutch asked why he disagreed. (They had differing political ideologies as well. Moon had rejected Roosevelt and the New Deal six months after the 1932 election and was now a registered Republican, a fact that Jack and Dutch took as a kind of betrayal.) At the close of the program, Dutch promised his audience he would broadcast whether he or Moon had the better percentage the following Friday night.

On the strength of his performance on Dutch's program, Pete MacArthur offered Moon five dollars a week to read the football scoreboard on the Saturday night news broadcast at WOC in Davenport. Moon said he couldn't even starve on that salary. MacArthur expanded this to thirty dollars a week to include Moon's doing a cathartic commercial three times a day, five days a week. Within six months he was made program director at a ten-dollar-a-week increase, a great relief to Dutch, who would no longer have to contribute to his brother's support (which he had been doing for a year and a half).

After Moon left, Dutch moved to a larger apartment at 400 Center Street which he shared with Art Mann, an assistant coach at Drake. His new home was in an old house that had been divided into four apartments, each consisting of "a large living room, a small bedroom and dressing room and a bathroom." The apartment quickly became a busy bachelors' flat. "The house was beautiful," recalled one former friend who added that her most vivid recollection was of the "heavy dark varnished woodwork. Dutch's apartment, on the ground floor, was off the large entrance hallway and had originally been the front and back sitting rooms and butler's pantry."

Art Mann was going steady with Lucille Robinson (a fine athlete who was to win the Woman's State Golf Championship). The three of them became fast friends, and when Lucille and Art married a year later, Dutch was best man. Having a roommate enabled him to afford an apartment better suited to the needs of a successful radio announcer. By the time Art and Lucille had married, he was capable of supporting the apartment on his own. And he had become quite a man about town. Cy's Moonlight Inn remained one of his favorite hangouts, but he had also discovered Club Belvedere, Des Moines's one real night spot. "Club Belvedere was strictly class. It even had a chorus line. Illegal booze, of course, and . . . a casino," explained Des Moines reporter Walter Shotwell. Dutch showed up almost every Saturday night "with many girls." Rich Kennelly, one of Club Belvedere's

owners, remembered that "all [Dutch] ever wanted to talk about
was horses; he knew I kept riding horses."

His relationship with Mary Frances had brought horses into
Dutch's life. He claims that as a youngster he might have "had a
yen to be like Tom Mix." He now dreamed of owning his own
mount, but the prohibitive cost of boarding and grooming a horse
made this impossible. Ernie Saunders suggested that if he signed
up and was accepted as a reserve officer in the 14th Cavalry Regi-
ment stationed at Camp Dodge, not only would he be able to ride
fine cavalry mounts, he would receive invaluable training in
horsemanship.

Lucky for Dutch, an eye examination was not required by the
Reserve Cavalry until the candidate had completed his training.
Dutch reckoned he could prolong that period for a few years. Ultimately, of course, he would reach a place where he would either
have to finish his work and apply for a commission or give up his
privilege of riding cavalry horses. His intentions were not entirely
honorable. He admitted that he had "no particular desire to be an
officer" and that he believed the United States "had already
fought the last war"; but "doing correspondence courses and
going to once-a-week classes wasn't too high a price to pay for
getting astride a horse."

He broke up with Mary Frances not long after he became involved with the Reserve Cavalry. Mary Frances cited their religious differences as the cause. Certainly this had an effect on
their relationship, but Dutch had just discovered his own power
with women. By now he was not only the voice of the Big Ten
football and major-league baseball broadcasts in the Midwest, he
was known to devoted Cubs fans from coast to coast. (No one
would have believed that his "vivid descriptions of crowds and
players, with soaring enthusiasm at the crack of the bat" had been
faked in an Iowa studio.) This had given him a new assurance
that was bolstered even more by Moon's need for his assistance
and his ability to provide it as well as by his sole and continuing
financial aid to his parents. If the attention of attractive women
was not a new experience for him, playing the man about town
was. When an affair broke up, a pattern was to turn to Myrtle for
consolation. Myrtle shared an apartment with her sister, Nell, and
the two women would whip up some scrambled eggs or macaroni
and cheese (his favorite food) for him. Dutch felt drawn to Myrtle,
yet, though on the edge many times, they never entered into a
romantic relationship.

Camp Dodge had been a training camp during World War I and occupied several hundred acres of some of the most beautiful parkland in Iowa. A portion of it had been given over to the city of Des Moines for playgrounds, picnic areas and a "huge pool the size of a football field and end zones." The pool capacity was about three thousand swimmers, who were looked after by seven lifeguards. One of these—Richard Ulrich—struck up a close friendship with Dutch when he began to make a steady habit of swimming there after his riding lessons with the Reserve Cavalry. Photographs of Dutch frequently appeared in the local papers and he was recognized on sight. Ulrich says that "he would wave at the swimmers" as he came to join them much the way "he later waved at crowds of fans and political followers. We first met at a radio broadcast of a game I played with the Des Moines Comets [a professional football team]. He idolized athletes. He was a terrific swimmer, but otherwise only fair. I think he once might have wanted to be a ball player. But now he just wanted to be a 'jock,' one of the boys. He liked to put on riding breeches and ride and make like the cavalry. People liked him right away. He was easy to know, good-looking, an extrovert, and he never made you feel he was better situated than you were. Des Moines was hard hit by the Depression. My lifeguard pay was eighteen dollars a week for six days, and of that six dollars went for food. Many of the people at the pool were on Relief."

Ulrich was married to Lois Hadley, a former model who introduced Dutch to a close friend, Gretchen Schnelle, who was also a model. The two couples would double-date, driving around Des Moines in Ulrich's '29 Ford sedan (larger than Dutch's car) and stopping for near beer at Cy's Moonlight Inn. (Prohibition had ended on December 5, 1933, but the popularity of near beer continued for a time.) Cy now had a large blowup of Dutch seated at a microphone hung on the wall behind the bar. Dutch would notify his friends of just what time he would be at the Moonlight by a verbal code at the end of his broadcast. At the Moonlight, Dutch Reagan reigned supreme. "There was one young man who drove a '33 Ford V-8. He was under twenty-one and Griffiths wouldn't sell him a drink. But Dutch sneaked him a bottle."

He dated the very personable, shapely Miss Schnelle for about a year, although not exclusively, for he had met Jeanne Tesdell, another beauty.* "He [had] bought a Nash convertible . . . new

---

*Jeanne Tesdell Burington.

. . . it was one of the first ever done in metallic brown. He looked very nice in it and he knew it. We went to Club Belvedere just for the floor shows. He didn't drink much and I never saw him gamble. We were seeing quite a bit of each other, but I always had the feeling that I was with him but he wasn't with me. He was always looking over his shoulder, scanning the crowd. I'd say he was a born politician, courting important people, favoring goodwill— wanting it."

"I'd agree with that," Mrs. Ulrich says. "Politics flared so wildly in the early thirties. I remember when Henry Wallace was secretary of agriculture, there had been an overproduction of little pigs that year [1933] in Iowa and he ordered a slaughter of them on a pretty grand scale, reimbursing farmers for their losses. He was an Iowan, a farm man, and Dutch thought he should have known better, that it was wrong to pay farmers to kill pigs. But he defended him in some terrific debates with Voith Pemberthy, a Republican friend of his (our section of Iowa has always been Republican anyway). Voith had a very strong personality. But so did Dutch. He was what we call mind-set. I never will forget how he held his mouth and chin [in these debates]—tight, chin jutting. He wasn't one to back down even if he knew he was wrong."

Jeanne Tesdell recalled that Dutch argued with her father about the same issue (the overproduction of pigs) when he came to pick her up.

Voith Pemberthy and WHO's news director, H. R. Gross, both exerted a great influence on Dutch during his years in Des Moines. Gross, who was known as Hal among the executives at WHO, and as "the fastest tongue in the business," had been born in the small town of Arispe, Iowa, and raised on a 240-acre farm. He attended the University of Missouri School of Journalism and served on the Mexican border in 1916 with the American Expeditionary Forces in France during World War I. Then he had worked as a newspaper reporter and editor, including jobs with the Associated Press and the *Iowa Farmer* (the newspaper of the National Farmers Union), before joining the staff of WHO. Gross was only twelve years older than Dutch, but his experience made him a senior citizen by comparison. Dutch's friendship with him did not take the form of after-hours camaraderie, as it did with other WHO staffers. Except at lunchtime, Hal Gross maintained a distance from all his co-workers. He had an aura of righteousness and a no-nonsense voice that could have made him a fine preacher. Dutch transferred his old awe and respect for the Reverend Cleaver to him. (There had always been an "older" man to whom Dutch turned as a role model—a substitute for Jack whom he loved but did not want to emulate—the Reverend Cleaver, Mr. Fraser [the drama teacher at North Dixon High School], Ralph McKinzie, Pete MacArthur, and Gross. In later years, this list would grow with each new stage in his life.)

"They used to sit over lunch or in the newsroom and harangue each other pro and con about various issues," a former co-worker remembered. "Gross was a Republican but he was involved with labor unions because of his years with the National Farmers Union. He and Dutch would go at each other over FDR's New Deal policies, which Gross strongly opposed. Dutch was always deferential. He sometimes called Gross 'Sir,' and although he could swear just as easy-come as you please, I don't recall his ever using that kind of language in his debates with Gross.

"Somewhere around the last months of Dutch's employment at WHO [1936–37] I recall thinking that maybe Gross was winning Dutch over. He was still a Democrat, or claimed to be, still as enthusiastic about Roosevelt as when I first met him [1933], but he had begun to talk about the [federal] government moving too heavily into people's lives. It struck quite a few of us in Des Moines that Dutch might make a good congressman one day. He was only in his early twenties then. And it seemed like Hal might have seen that, too."

Dutch's life had changed drastically, and his need for acceptance in the new society in which he found himself had altered his attitudes. By 1936, he had given up his fantasies of one day becoming a major sports figure. But he knew now that he possessed a special charm and he had learned how to use it to his best advantage. "He was handsome, charismatic, always joking," Lois Ulrich remembered. "Have you noticed that he seems to have a fetish concerning his left side—his hair parted on the right and combed to the left? He did that back in the thirties. It gave him a 'pouf' on the left side and I asked him once why he combed it that way. He said he thought it gave him a 'rakish' look. He wore hats deliberately tipped to the left for the same reason."

Moon had met Bess Hoffman, a Des Moines girl, a graduate of Drake, and had fallen rapidly in love. In two weeks they decided to get married. Dutch liked Bess, she was cute and slim, a good dresser, a bright young woman, but he tried to convince Moon to wait. "Two weeks—that's way too fast," he told him. "I took Dutch out to the wedding," Bob Dillon, a Des Moines friend of

Moon and Dutch's recalled, "and all the way out he complained bitterly and gave me a very hard time. He said, 'Now here's your very best friend in the world, he's only known this girl for about two weeks, and they're gonna get married, and what kind of a friend are you?' And I kept saying, 'Well, she's a lovely woman, she's a lovely girl.' He says, 'That doesn't make any difference,' and gave me a hard time."

His visits to Dixon were brief but fairly frequent. Even with what he was able to give Nelle, his parents were struggling. His father had aged drastically. The heart attack had affected the nerves in his left arm, weakening it, and his energy level was low. Jack would never be able to work again—and how long could Nelle keep up a ten-hour day, six-day week, on her feet for most of the time? Moon was self-sufficient, but now he had his wife to support. Thoughts of finding a better-paying radio job in New York or Los Angeles entered Dutch's head. He discussed it with close friends. But to leave WHO without the other job secured was simply out of the question.

The values that Nelle and life in Dixon had taught him remained with him. He believed in family, God and country (and perhaps even in that order). He agreed with Jack that Relief was demeaning, abortion a crime, and the big unions controlled by too many thugs. Careful spending was a daily concern. He had a budget and he held fastidiously to it. He shunned credit and bought only what he had saved money to buy. At WHO "Dutch treat" had a special meaning, for he was never known to pick up anyone else's tab and didn't appreciate someone picking up his. But he was the first to offer comfort to anyone in ill health or suffering grief. He had retained his boyish charm, his Irish way with a story and a guilelessness that never ceased to surprise. His smooth-shaven face and his well-tuned physique added to his good looks. Above all, his success had not diminished his extreme modesty, the way he had of holding a slightly receding posture so that people often had to lean toward him to hear what he was saying (a manner that created an almost instant sense of intimacy). And then there was his distinctive voice—hospitable and at the same time persuasive, seductive and without sham. An investigative reporter could search long and hard and not find one man, woman or child who disliked Dutch Reagan in the 1930s. Even Frank Merriwell's creator, Burt Standish, could not have invented a more all-American, likable, true-blue fellow.

It took two and a half years before the army staff at Camp

Dodge insisted he complete his courses (which he did) and submit
to an eye examination (a cavalry officer was required to have good
vision without the aid of glasses). Knowing he would not be able
to see the chart with his naked eye, Dutch employed a bit of strategy. When asked to hold one hand over his good eye, he later
confessed, "I managed to squeeze my fingers down to where I had
the narrowest of slits and [when] I was supposed to be reading
with the uncovered eye, in reality I read with the covered eye,
now corrected by virtue of squinting through this tiny slit between
my fingers [a technique that can greatly aid nearsighted vision]."
Having passed this test, he then had to meet the riding standards
of the Reserve Cavalry.

Astride a large horse which he had never ridden before, in
teeming rain, a mounted officer on each side of him and a platoon
of twenty-seven enlisted men awaiting his commands, Dutch competently executed the maneuvers required to become a cavalry
officer. After more than two hours, with every man "soaked to the
skin," Dutch was given his final test. The company rode behind
him at a gallop over wet, slippery earth. Ahead of him was a high
jump formed by a stack of telephone poles. He claimed that with
twenty-seven mounted men biting at the hooves of his horse, he
had nowhere to go but over the top. "If my horse balked, ran out,
or slipped, there was no way in the world we could escape being
trampled . . . I closed my eyes, grabbed a handful of mane, and
landed on the other side of the jump a second lieutenant."

"Dutch could stretch the truth a bit." Dick Ulrich grinned. He
did, indeed, have a talent for turning any small incident into a
colorful story in the retelling. Jack's influence could be seen at
such times. It seems unlikely that the two cavalry officers putting
him through his paces were not prepared to stop a stampede if he
did not make the jump. Similar tests are given today, with the
company ordered to stay a safe distance behind. But a good part
of Dutch's enthusiasm for most things in his life was his ability to
envelop himself completely in what he was doing. The astounding
realness of his play-by-play broadcasts came out of this skill. No
one could have ever guessed that Dutch Reagan was not in the
press box at the game in Chicago.

His fellow workers were all struck by his lack of arrogance.
Dutch Reagan might "flirt with the truth," but that was because
he didn't take himself too seriously. One WHO staffer commented, "I always thought he was a deeply religious man. Not the
kind who went to church every Sunday. A man with a strong

inner faith. Whatever he accomplished was God's will—God gave it to him and God could take it away."

He put up anyone who came through Des Moines from Dixon. A number of his old friends hadn't found work in over a year and they were forced to move on. Because Des Moines had few jobs to offer, they would come, stay a short time and then leave. The Midwest suffered a double blow when the first of the disastrous dust storms swept across South Dakota on Armistice Day, 1933. "When the wind died and the sun shone forth again," one observer wrote, "it was on a different world. There were no fields, only sand drifting into mounds and eddies that swirled in what was now but an autumn breeze. . . . In the farm yard[s] fences, machinery, and trees were gone, buried. The roofs of sheds stuck out through drifts higher than a man is tall."

During the next two years numberless dust storms of this intensity swept the Great Plains. "Roads and farm buildings and once-green thickets [were now] half buried in sand . . . a farmer, sitting at his window during a dust storm, remarked that he was counting the Kansas farms as they came by."

The refugees "from this new Sahara" fled westward in ancient family jalopies. "They roll westward like a parade," wrote Richard L. Neuberger and Kelley Loe in *Harper's Magazine* in March 1936. "In a single hour from a grassy meadow near an Idaho road I counted 34 automobiles with the license plates of states between Chicago [Illinois] and the mountains."

Some stopped in towns or at farms or government projects along the way to find temporary work. Roosevelt had created many work-relief projects. One, the building of the world's largest earthen dam—two thousand miles up the Missouri River from St. Louis, in northeastern Montana—attracted thousands of migrants who had to pass through Iowa to reach their destinations. Fort Peck City was built to accommodate them when they arrived. Within a year, the place was overcrowded. Six shantytowns sprung up around it—Wheeler, New Deal, Delano Heights, Square Deal, Park Grove and Wilson. There was even a red-light suburb called "Happy Hollow," all "as rickety as git-up-and-git or Hell's Delight." The building of the dam had been intended to aid the grave unemployment problem in Montana. Jobs were available for "as many as 10,000 veterans, parched farmers and plain unemployed parents at a time," but the tremendous influx of out-of-state job-seekers turned "Franklin Roosevelt's Wild West" (as it was called) into a welter of broken-down Fords forced to be used as temporary housing for whole families. Shacks made "of grocers' boxes, tin cans, crazy doors and building paper" were being thrown together, providing little protection from Montana's often subzero winters. Many of these people headed west again and "kept right on rattling toward some other hopeless hope" in "their second-hand cars full of children, chairs, mattresses and tired women."

America seemed a land of displaced people. No longer did this refer to aliens immigrating to the United States. America's own were now on the move. Those who undertook the "Great Trek to the Pacific" were not so much seeking frontier possibilities as some divine haven—sun and sand and sea—fruit to pluck off the trees. Old cars were being pressed to lives far beyond the car manufacturers' expectations. Men and women whose farms had fallen under the hammer rattled homeless through the land, as did their former workers. The days were over when Americans could count on a consistency in their lives. But this fact had not put an end to the American dream, which seemed to have lodged itself in an accelerating wind that blew westward.

Father Coughlin, now rabidly anti-Roosevelt, his Irish voice raised more and more in pro-German propaganda, had lost his network program. The current radio sensation was Major Bowes and his *Original Amateur Hour*. The Depression years had clung too long. Disenchanted audiences no longer wanted sermons of faith or political dogma; they sought entertainment—a glimmer of belief that circumstance could change despair into high hopes. Dance orchestras blared forth the ubiquitous refrain "The Music Goes 'Round and 'Round" while the snappy foxtrot "Blue Skies" spun 'round and 'round phonographs across the country. Astaire and Rogers's nimble feet transported millions of fans into the plush fantasy world of their films, while an eight-year-old Shirley Temple, distilling the innocence of childhood, sang about "The Good Ship Lollipop." More than a million readers buzzed with the question of whether Scarlett got Rhett back in Margaret Mitchell's *Gone With the Wind*. The parlor game of Monopoly, in which players could undertake imaginary feats of financial daring, was all the rage. But no flight of fancy could equal the economic complexity in the government. Federal agencies multiplied with the speed of tadpoles. It took an expert to identify the alphabetical designations—WPA, NRA, RFC, AAA, CCC, SEC, TVA, FAA, HOLC, FCC and NYA.

Roosevelt hit the campaign trail for the 1936 election stressing the continuation of his policies. Eleanor Roosevelt visited Des Moines on June 8, 1936, walking through some of the city's poorest sections, her receding chin set in sadness, a defiant flower on the brim of her hat and a huge corsage (presented to her by J. O. Maland as she greeted Des Moines over the traveling WHO microphone) that pulled down the shoulder of her dress.

Radio played a major role in the 1936 campaign, as it was to do until the advent of television. Roosevelt's fireside chats, which brought him into the kitchens and living rooms of millions of Americans, had made him a close friend. The effect paid off. One workingman said, "Mr. Roosevelt is the only man we ever had in the White House who would understand that my boss is a son-of-a-bitch." The Democratic Convention was held in Philadelphia. "For the first time," Joe Lash wrote, "women were granted parity with the men on the platform committee, a measure of how far they had traveled since 1924 when Eleanor and her feminine colleagues had sat outside the locked doors of the Resolutions Committee." There were 219 women delegates and alternates, as compared to the 60 who had helped to nominate former Kansas Governor Alfred Landon as the Republican candidate. Women made eight of Roosevelt's seconding speeches, their large role at the convention symbolizing the recognition achieved by them in the Roosevelt administration.

The Republican party had not taken into consideration the strength of the women's vote, nor of Roosevelt's tremendous charisma and radio personality—traits not possessed by their candidate. There was optimism in the midst of despair. Yes, hundreds of thousands of young people had given up thoughts of college, farmers had lost their land, millions were unemployed—but the nation was a hundredfold better off than it had been in 1932 when Roosevelt took office. Many millions had also been put back to work, banks were solid, a social security bill giving the elderly a future had been passed, along with other reforms.

"We have conquered fear," a composed, smiling Roosevelt told the hundred thousand people who crowded Franklin Field in Philadelphia and the vaster numbers who listened on the radio as he accepted the Democratic presidential nomination. ("He arrived at the podium on the arm of his son James—after a frightful five minutes when in the crush his steel brace had buckled and out of sight of the crowd he had fallen.") He recalled the problems that beset the nation in 1932 and outlined how his administration had overcome them. He did not shy away from the current problems. But freedom, he declared, was "no half-and-half affair." The language was clear, the tone confident, the style intimate. And as he came to the end of his speech and in a rising cadence announced, "this generation of Americans has a rendezvous with destiny,"* the crowd rose to its feet as one and nearly drowned out his last words with cheers. Harold Ickes, the secretary of the interior, called it "the greatest political speech [he had] ever heard."

Dutch's enthusiasm for the New Deal might have lost some of its fervor (although Jack's had not), but his feelings toward Roosevelt were even more intensified. He put in a radio plug for his candidate whenever the chance presented itself. He also began to perform his first loving imitations of Roosevelt's fireside chats to the amusement of WHO staffers, although not all were in the president's corner. Roosevelt had numerous enemies and detractors. Indignantly the president told his radio audience, "Never before in all our history have these forces been so united against one candidate as they stand today. They are unanimous in their hate for me—and I welcome their hatred." As the election drew closer, the *Chicago Tribune* reminded its readers daily, "Only 5 [4, 3, 2, etc.] days remain to save your country." (The newspaper's switchboard operators were even forced to repeat this message to all callers.) The *Tribune* was also responsible for a vicious story by Donald Day (who later was arrested for broadcasting for the Nazis) that claimed Roosevelt was supported by Moscow. The rival Chicago *Times* proved the story a complete hoax.

Crushes of people cheered Roosevelt's train and motorcade during his campaign journeys. He had the votes of workers he had put back to work and those who believed he would find them employment. He had the votes of farmers who looked forward to his program of rural electrification. He had the votes of northern blacks. The mood of the times is etched in this story of a New Deal official visiting his native Montana and having seen "men I had been to school with—digging ditches and laying sewer pipe. They were wearing their regular business suits because they couldn't afford overalls . . . one man pulled some silver from his pocket and said, 'Frank, this is the first money I've had in my pockets for a year and a half.'" Hoover and the Republicans had cost him everything he had once had. Roosevelt and the Democrats had given him, if not a return to good times, at least money

---

*Reagan used the phrase "a rendezvous with destiny" in his own campaign speeches.

to feed his family. The November election was a landslide for Roosevelt, who carried every state but Maine and Vermont.

The winter of 1936–37 was one of the coldest Iowa had experienced in more than a decade, which could have accounted for Dutch's restlessness as spring approached without any evidence of bringing the smallest signs of fair weather with it. Des Moines had been his home for four years, a residency that had matured and educated him in ways that equal time at Eureka had not. His vision of himself and what he could accomplish had not only changed him, it had drastically altered his perception of the world. He still considered himself a Democrat and a liberal. He blamed Harding, Hoover and the Republicans for the problems the Midwest, and especially his family, had suffered during their administrations. Yet, curiously, despite all the young liberals who had been close to him in Des Moines, the two men who were to remain lifelong good friends and advisers were Hal Gross and Voith Pemberthy, both staunch conservatives and Republicans.

The last two years in Des Moines had sharpened his political knowledge and his desire to learn more. Whenever Pemberthy or Gross made a point, he sought answers from books and articles— cramming up on the information for their next confrontation. He had gone about as far as possible at WHO and he knew it.

Four years earlier he had been embarrassed to tell Sid Altschuler that he wanted to be an actor. But he still thought about the possibility. By now he had learned that power and money went hand in hand. Both appealed to him. Local fame had given him a taste of power. Somewhere up the line he suspected there could be a greater payoff in films than his current seventy-five-dollar weekly salary. At that moment he had no clear idea of how that could be achieved. Then Joy Hodges, a Des Moines girl who had become a successful band singer after years of appearing on Radio WHO (first at age twelve as Eloise Hodges, one half of the Blue Bird Twins, and then as part of the Singing Trio, a teenage group), returned home on a personal-appearance tour. Hodges had appeared in minor roles in several films for RKO, where she was under contract. The Des Moines press promoted her to star status and Dutch was asked to interview her for WHO.

"He sat across the microphone from me in riding breeches, which I found amusing. But he was very good-looking even with his glasses," she said. Slim and willowy with wide-set hazel eyes and bouncy light-brown hair, Hodges was a bundle of energy, as vivacious as she was ambitious. During the interview, she said something to him about his own potential in Hollywood. "After our interview he asked me if I would go riding with him at Fort Des Moines. I said yes even though I knew I had nothing to wear . . . no slacks, jeans, et cetera. . . . When he arrived the next afternoon, I hid in the closet to block out his very determined doorbell-ringing. My folks were out and I just could not face him to tell him I had nothing to wear. He rang and rang, and finally, after about ten minutes, left. I agonized about that broken date . . . some day I think I will confess how vain I was and that I was just another girl who couldn't say no to him and to such a kind invitation [to go horseback riding]."

Being stood up did not seem to perturb him. The interview with Joy had stirred other than romantic emotions. He recalled that she had made a point of telling him that Hollywood was the only place to be if he wanted a film career. Being seen at the right places with the right people was all-important. Her advice rang in his ears for weeks after the interview and was underscored when a musical group called Al Clauser and His Oklahoma Outlaws were guests on WHO's *Barn Dance* program. Also former regulars on WHO, they had just been signed by cowboy star Gene Autry to appear with him in a film (*Rootin', Tootin' Rhythm*), and they dropped a casual "come see us at the studio" when they left.

Des Moines caught Hollywood fever when film promoters came through shooting screen tests for possible future stars. Dutch was approached but did not fall for what he suspected might have been a scam. Nonetheless, he remained optimistic that he could make it in Hollywood as an actor if he could just go out there and see a few "influential people." (His opening remark in the Hodges interview had been, "Well, Miss Hodges, how does it feel to be a movie star?" Prophetically, she replied, "Well, Mr. *Ray*gun, you may know one day.")*

With his conservative nature, he could not consider a trip to California just to bask in the sun on the slight chance that he might be "discovered." Therefore, he came up with a scheme. The Chicago Cubs had their spring-training camp from February 12 to March 15 at Santa Catalina Island, twenty-seven miles southwest of Los Angeles Harbor. He had a month's vacation time coming to him, so he went to see Maland and "talked [him]

---

*Reagan had been sensitive about the mispronunciation of his name and had been correcting his guests before airtime.

into the idea that if they [WHO] put up the money, I would put up the time—and my vacation could be spent accompanying the Chicago Cubs on their training trip to Catalina Island. I made quite a pitch about what this would do for me in filling me with color and atmosphere for the coming baseball season. It worked."

The westward journey that carried him away from his Midwest roots took two nights and a day. Because his departure was in the evening, the most depressed areas between Des Moines and Lincoln, Nebraska, were only a glimmer of lights that came and went as the train chortled through the darkness. By morning it was on its way through the open western plains and the great Rockies. By the second night it was crossing the Colorado plateau and the Mohave Desert. The last sand traces were lost about dawn when—like some biblical miracle—the citrus groves—green and abundant—mile upon mile—appeared, and with them, the shock of fender-to-fender, dented, worn-out, black jalopies—mattresses tied to roofs, gaunt faces staring through windows, figures standing on running boards. Children clambered as close to the tracks as possible, waving on the train's occupants.

Dutch wasted no time when he arrived at Union Station, downtown Los Angeles. By nine A.M. he had checked into the Hollywood Plaza Hotel near the corner of Hollywood Boulevard and Vine Street and hired a taxi to take him to Republic Studios, where the Oklahoma Outlaws were filming with Autry. He had no idea that Republic was such a distance out in the Valley. The cab fare was a lot higher than he had anticipated, as was the thermometer. Los Angeles was experiencing an unusually hot February—with temperatures close to ninety, soaring to over one hundred in the Valley, which was always ten to twenty degrees hotter. The white linen suit Dutch had bought for his California journey was limp by the time he got permission to pass through the gates of Republic Studios. The Oklahoma Outlaws were on location, but he did connect with their representative, who, he later said, "gave sympathetic ear when I voiced my aspirations and introduced me to a casting director who was less than enthusiastic." The man handed him some old scripts to take with him and told him to come back in a week or two and to "pick out a scene that you think fits you, and I'll listen to you read."

As he looked around the Republic lot, which made low-budget quickie programmers—mostly Westerns—an inner instinct warned him that this studio would never offer him the kind of career he hoped for in films. At twenty-six, he was young but not a kid, and he had made a name for himself in radio. The next morning he took the boat from the pier at Wilmington (three dollars round trip) to Avalon, the main center of resort and sports activities on Santa Catalina Island, an hour's boat ride away.

William Wrigley, Jr., the chewing-gum millionaire (who had also built Wrigley Field), had bought the entire island from its previous, unsuccessful promoters in 1919.* Wrigley had the formula and the millions needed to turn the island into a commercial success. The settlement of Avalon, which rested at the mouth of a large canyon along the crescent-shaped shore of the spectacularly beautiful Avalon Bay, was swiftly transformed into a romantic palm-studded haven for tourists, supplying them with a casino, Moorish in design, which had cost two million dollars to build, a boardwalk to equal Atlantic City's, and a vast motion-picture theater occupying the ground floor of the white circular building that housed the casino. Five ramps gave access to the second-story ballroom. A cocktail lounge with a one-hundred-foot-long bar whose walls were covered with fantastic fish murals adjoined it.

Catalina was a year-round resort, but the great crowds came during the summer months. In February, the waters of the many bays and coves were calm and clear, but they were also cold. The tourists of this time of year fished for barracuda, giant tuna and swordfish, and attended the exhibition games of the Wrigley-owned National League Chicago Cubs, held daily at noon at the Catalina Baseball Park at Freemont Street and Avalon Boulevard. This is where Dutch was expected to spend his days. But he did not show up on a regular basis at the practice field. Charlie Grimm, the manager of the Cubs, took him to task for this. "How could I tell him that somewhere within myself was the knowledge I would no longer be a sports announcer?" Reagan said. So sure was he that he'd make it through the golden gates of some major studio that he granted himself a true vacation—horseback riding, boating, "and seeing Catalina scenery."

Catalina indeed possessed some beautiful terrain. The foliage was luxuriant in its numerous valleys, and the rugged higher slopes of its mountains were covered in chaparral. Many film stars (Ronald Colman and Douglas Fairbanks among them) had yachts berthed in the coves and glamorous beach houses on the hillsides, where they entertained lavishly. There were also abandoned movie sets from films that had sought the South Sea island effect,

---

*Wrigley's son was Phillip Wrigley, Charles Walgreen's friend and frequent houseguest.

including both the thatched round house used in the silent picture *Rain* (with Gloria Swanson) and the Continental Hotel set from the sound remake of it (starring Joan Crawford). Dutch was not to meet any film luminaries on Catalina. Evenings he hung around with the ballplayers. Reagan claimed that the sportswriters who were covering the Cubs spring training gave him "some hazing . . . some of it was unkind. . . . Veteran sportswriters are really a breed apart in their ability to coin pungent phrases . . . they were resentful of radio men."

The second week in California he called Joy Hodges, who was singing with the Jimmy Grier Band at the Biltmore Bowl. After the show he sent a note backstage asking her to join him. "I did," she recalled, "and he confessed he wanted to visit a studio. I said that could be arranged. Then he admitted he wanted a movie test. . . . I asked him to stand up and remove his glasses, he did, and it was clear that he was VERY HANDSOME. I told him never to put those glasses on again. The next morning I called my agent [George Ward, of the Meiklejohn Agency] and Dutch went to see him."

In actual fact, "without the glasses I couldn't see him at all!" he quipped. But the major point was that Ward had known instinctively that the young man facing him was a "type" that could easily be sold. He categorized him as "the likeable, clean-cut American," with the kind of sex appeal that emanated from natural charm and a solid maleness. His were the kind of good looks that appealed mostly to young girls and older women. As George Ward sat listening to Dutch exaggerate his acting experience (the Eureka Dramatic Club had suddenly become "The Johnson Professional Players"*) and double the salary Radio WHO was paying him, an idea came to him.

This "big overgrown kid" looked and sounded like another young man, Ross Alexander, whom Warners had been grooming for stardom. Tragically, on January 3, 1937, at age twenty-nine, Alexander had shot himself shortly after finishing *Ready, Willing and Able* for the studio, his suicide paralleling to an amazing degree that of his first wife, Altea, who took her own life a year earlier with the same weapon, a .22 caliber rifle. Warners had covered up the tragedy as best they could. Alexander had recently married actress Anne Nagel† (also under contract to Warner

---

*Reagan used the name of his drama teacher at Eureka, Miss Johnson. This bogus group was to be listed thereafter in his studio biography and reprinted in most publicity releases.

†Also known as Ann Donal, and not to be confused with British actress Anna Nagel.

Brothers), and the two were to leave on a honeymoon the next morning. Echoes of the suicide of Jean Harlow's husband, Paul Bern, allegedly motivated by his impotency, hung over the Alexander tragedy. Replacing him as soon as possible with a similar type would be a smart move for Warners. Ward rang Max Arnow, the studio's casting director, while Dutch was still seated in his office. Arnow agreed to see him that day, and when he had, to shoot a test the following Tuesday (Dutch was scheduled to return to Des Moines by train on Wednesday, March 16). Outside Arnow's bungalow office at Warners, Ward, who now was convinced he had a hot property, said, "Two tests are better than one—let's go to Paramount." Ward's hunch seemed solid when that studio offered Dutch a small spot in a short subject being shot that coming Sunday. (Paramount often cast hopefuls or their contract players in these eight- to ten-minute films that were used as fillers between halves of a double bill. In this way, tests and camera experience for future players were paid for by the exhibitors.)

Early Sunday morning, Dutch appeared at Paramount, submitted to makeup, was given his few lines and then was told to wait. The Cubs were playing an exhibition game at Wrigley Field at noon, which he was to cover. By one o'clock he approached the casting director and asked him when he could be expected to be finished.

"I might not get to you until eleven o'clock tonight," the man replied.

"You mean that you got me here early this morning and you might not use me until tonight?"

"Son, this is Hollywood."

"Well, this is Des Moines," he claimed he said, "and you can shove Hollywood." He left and took a boat to the island. "I could afford to be brave," he admitted. "I had Tuesday coming up, and somehow I hadn't taken this Paramount thing seriously." Sunday evening, Joy Hodges rehearsed with him the scene he was to use as his test. He learned his lines quickly. ("I couldn't believe his ability to read a page and practically recite it back," Joy Hodges said.) He had a good feeling about the test and talked about his return to Hollywood.

His instinct proved reliable. Everything about the test was approached seriously by Warners. His was the only one being shot that morning. Great care was taken in his makeup. June Travis, a promising young starlet, was on hand to do a scene with him from the delightful Philip Barry play *Holiday* (he was playing Johnny Case, the Cary Grant role in the film version made later that year). Both the director (Nick Grinde) and the cameraman (Joseph Patrick MacDonald) were experienced and talented professionals,* and Dutch's choice of *Holiday* to showcase his potential as a youthful, affable and charming leading-man type was a wise one. His performance would not have given Cary Grant any sleepless nights, but Barry's character was interesting and the scene shot for the test, where he explains to his fiancée's sister (eventually played by Katharine Hepburn) his plan to retire young after "making a bundle" (and working again when he gets older), contains some of the playwright's smartest and most literate dialogue. (Coincidentally, Hepburn had won her contract in Hollywood with a scene from the same play.)

This time, he was finished by noon. Ward tried to convince him to remain in California for several days until "Mr. Warner [can] see this film."

"No," he replied adamantly. "I will be on the train tomorrow—me and the Cubs are going home." And home to Des Moines he went, concerned during the entire train journey that he had "blown it" by leaving town. "Actually, I had done, through ignorance, the smartest thing it was possible to do," he said with hindsight. "Hollywood just loves people who don't need Hollywood."

Monday morning, March 22, Dutch returned to work at WHO with stories about his Hollywood screen test, but laughed it off. As he and Myrtle and another member of the staff started out to lunch, a telegram was delivered:

WARNERS OFFER CONTRACT SEVEN YEARS, ONE YEAR'S OPTION, STARTING AT $200 A WEEK. WHAT SHALL I DO? GEORGE WARD MEIKLEJOHN AGENCY.

Dutch wired back:

HAVE JUST DONE A CHILDISH TRICK [leaving Hollywood so soon]. SIGN BEFORE THEY CHANGE THEIR MINDS. DUTCH REAGAN.

He admitted, "Then I yelled."

The same day George Ward called Joy Hodges to tell her of the Warners offer. Hodges swiftly dispatched a telegram to the Des Moines *Register:*

---

*Joseph P. MacDonald (1906–68) became one of Hollywood's top cinematographers. His credits were to include *Pinky* (1949), *Viva Zapata* (1952), *How to Marry a Millionaire* (1953), *The Young Lions* (1958) and *Walk on the Wild Side* (1962).

MAY BE SCOOP. YOU DO HAVE POTENTIAL STAR IN YOUR MIDST. DUTCH REAGAN LOCAL SPORTS ANNOUNCER SIGNED LONG TERM WARNER BROTHERS CONTRACT FRIDAY [March 18]. THEY CONSIDER HIM GREATEST BET SINCE [Robert] TAYLOR WITHOUT GLASSES. JOY HODGES.

"The day Dutch got the telegram advising him he had passed the screen test was a day to remember," Herb Plambeck recalled. "Dutch held court for several hours, sitting on his desk, jubilant, excited, euphoric, accepting everyone's congratulations, mesmerizing all of us with the tales of his Hollywood adventure then, and those yet to be."

That night he called Nelle and Jack, promising that he would send for them to join him in California as soon as he was settled. That was not to be for several months. The Warners contract was to start Tuesday, June 1, and he remained at WHO until Friday, the twenty-first of May. That night the staff gave him a farewell bash at Cy's Moonlight Inn. Early the next morning, his convertible piled high with all his gear, he headed west to a new life.

Dutch Reagan had been left behind in Des Moines. From June 1, 1937, Ronald Reagan would be known by his generally mispronounced proper name.

HOLLYWOOD

"Heart of a continent, the hearts con-
verge on open boulevards where
palms are nursed with flare-pots like
a grove, on villa roads where castles
cultivated like a style breed fabulous
metaphors in foreign stone, and on
enormous movie lots where history
repeats its vivid blunders."
—KARL SHAPIRO, *Hollywood*

Late monday evening, may 31, dutch pulled up to
the front door of the Hollywood Plaza Hotel, the shiny brown
of his convertible obscured by dust and sand. He had driven almost nonstop the last twenty-four hours of the trip, foolishly making the trek across "the burning desert" during the day. Despite
the sunglasses he wore, his eyes were red-rimmed from the glare
of the sun.

Thousands of neon lights up and down Hollywood Boulevard
outlined names and slogans (one read i'd walk a mile for a
camel and showed a cigarette with a red neon tip superimposed
over a camel whose hump appeared to move). Searchlight beams
pierced the sky, but they were too far up the street to ascertain
whether they announced a movie premiere or the opening of a
new hamburger stand. A message waited for him at the desk inside. George Ward would meet him at the hotel at nine a.m. the
next morning and take him out to Warners.

He woke early and walked up and down the Boulevard. Hollywood looked like any other part of its mother city, Los Angeles.

You did not know when you came to it, or when you left it, except for the signs and Hollywood Boulevard, the main street (called in the thirties either the Boulevard or Hollywood Bull), a broad thoroughfare with streetcar tracks up its middle. Both sides of the Boulevard, which runs due east and west, were lined with bizarre, claptrap buildings in pinks, greens and eye-blinding, sunstruck white. White was worn from spring to fall by the suntanned men in polo shirts and sports jackets and by the women in brief informal dresses who, masked by sunglasses, paused at window displays in the colorful storefronts.

South of the Boulevard, ice-cream-colored, one-story stucco bungalows roofed in red tile—thorny branches of scarlet bougainvillaea spreading across the sides of their one-car garages, a single palm growing on the lawn, a pepper tree planted between the sidewalk and curb—lined the side streets that led to Sunset Boulevard and some of the small independent studios. In this area of Hollywood, fake cowboys in chaps and sombreros and extras and featured players in makeup, bright kerchiefs tied around freshly waved hair, dark glasses a must, lunched at corner hot-dog stands and talked shop.

The northern half of Hollywood rose upward from the Boulevard in a network of twisted, sharp roads into the tawny foothills of the Santa Monica Mountains (known as the Hollywood Hills), where larger homes clung tenaciously to the rocky hillsides providing spectacular views for their occupants while daring the fury of the frequent California earthquakes. No greater contrast could exist between the Main Street commonplaceness of Dixon and the midwestern simplicity of Des Moines than the environs of Vine Street and the Boulevard, the location of Reagan's hotel. The unreality of it was awesome. On a warm June day even the air seemed rarefied, as if all of this garish section had been sealed in vaporproof glass.

When George Ward met Reagan, he was struck once more by his clean-cut good looks, his vitality and total naturalness. In the film industry's short career, deception and illusion had developed to extraordinary lengths. For the movies, windows were made of rock candy; stones of tar paper, balsa wood and cork; snow of gypsum and bleached corn flakes; icicles of fiber hair dipped in plaster of Paris. Strawberry gelatin substituted for blood. Warners' prop shop stocked enough artificial apple blossoms for twenty-eight trees and enough fake daisies to cover an acre of field. Studios created new names for players along with totally

fictitious biographies. Image was of optimum importance. Therefore, at Warners, Emmanuel Goldenberg had become Edward G.
[for Goldenberg] Robinson; Ruby Stevens, Barbara Stanwyck;
George Nolan, George Brent; Clara Lou Sheridan, Ann Sheridan;
and Dorothy, Rosemary and Priscilla Mullican—Lola, Rosemary
and Priscilla Lane. The name *Ronald Reagan* had been duly considered by the "front office" and the publicity department, and
since they thought it had a good ring to it as well as marquee
appeal, it had been retained.

Warner Brothers was a family business run by three brothers.
Harry and Albert (Abe) were based in New York, Harry as president of the company and Abe as treasurer. Jack, the only brother
in California, was vice-president in charge of production, ran the
studio and was responsible for all filming. Harry was the pa-
triarch of his family, and his influence on the taste and goals of his
younger brother, Jack, had been enormous. Messianic in his attitudes, Harry believed all films carrying the Warner name should
contain a moral lesson. "The motion picture," he was quoted as
saying, "presents right and wrong as the Bible does. By showing
both right and wrong we teach the right." He possessed "a violent
hatred of all forms of human prejudice" and was obsessively anti-
Nazi. His proselytizing hand could be seen behind all the films his
brother Jack produced.

At Warner Brothers, Jack Warner operated as a "totalitarian
godhead." One observer called him "a bargain-counter dictator."
Even his brightest stars were made to punch a timecard. Warner,
a rabid right-winger, employed a full-time investigator to check on
the patriotism of his employees. No one worked for him without a
private security clearance. The commissaries at most of the other
studios featured three meals a day; Warners served only one. No
socializing on company time was his policy. The studio police at
Warners, headed by F. Blayney Mathews, a former investigator
for the Los Angeles District Attorney's office, was operated along
the lines of the FBI. Warner himself devised a personnel record
which all his employees had to fill out and sign. Questions asked
were about religion, lodge or club affiliation, insurance carried,
assets, debts, and there was one yes or no question: "Are you a
member of any organization, society, group or sect owing allegiance to a foreign government or rule?" Warner was also obsessed with the fear that another studio might get its "spies" on
his sound stages and preempt one of his films. "Clearance" was
not an easy matter, and visitors were few. This gave the Warner

lot an insular quality not found at other studios. But, though he
did not permit much liberty of temperament or freedom of action
among his executives and players, he encouraged liberty of imagination among his producers (often called supervisors) and directors.

Under Jack Warner, the studio had pioneered in sound. Its
current success had been built on its achievement to produce films
that kept abreast with the headlines. It also sought and developed
new stars, directors and production techniques. Jack Warner was
never as involved in the private lives of his employees as was
Louis B. Mayer at Metro-Goldwyn-Mayer, seldom interesting
himself in their affairs, marriages and divorces. At Christmas,
which he and his wife traditionally spent in France, he telegraphed greetings to his closer employees, signing them "Jack and
Ann Warner, Cannes, France," although they were dispatched by
his secretary in Hollywood to save expense. Yet, he did take a
personal interest in Reagan at the beginning of his contract—one,
because he was part of the sports world, which Warner admired;
and two, because he had liked his test and thought him promising. But this was done from the distance of his grand suite on the
lot. Warner and Reagan did not actually meet until many months
after Reagan was hired.

Little that transpired at his studio escaped Jack Warner's attention. Blue memos cascaded from his desk like the waters over
Niagara (all other executives communicated on pink stock). At
the bottom of each sheet of interoffice correspondence was written:
"Verbal messages cause misunderstanding and delays (please put
them in writing)." Since copies of all memos were kept on file,
Warner had a complete written account of studio activities available at all times. Two men, Roy J. Obringer (Warners' general
counsel) and Steve Trilling* (casting director), "equally short [as
Warner], equally stocky, equally bald," functioned as his liaisons,
relaying his edicts, opinions and praise wherever they were to be
directed. When Warner wanted personally to contact one of his
employees (often even when he or she was on the lot), he was
known to do so by telegram, frequently several pages in length.

Reagan started at the studio when Hal Wallis was at the
height of his reign as executive producer (1933–42). Wallis was
largely responsible for Warners' A films, and dealt more on the
day-to-day details of production than did his boss. Bryan Foy was

---

* Later to become his executive assistant.

Wallis's alter ego for Warners' B pictures. Foy's unit produced twenty-six features a year on a five-million-dollar budget, which included his salary and those of his staff. Occasionally, one of Foy's movies received A promotion, but this seldom raised the figure of his budget. B features were the bread and butter of the studio and Foy was well qualified to play Scrooge on their behalf. Raised in vaudeville, he later became "a shoestring independent producer of the most opportunistic stripe." In 1928 he had made the first all-talking feature, *The Lights of New York,* for a total cost of twenty-one thousand dollars. Films like *Sterilization, What Price Innocence* and *Elysia* (filmed in a nudist camp) were made on similar "corner-cutting" budgets and returned their expenses the first week in release. Story costs for his films were virtually nil. He took old Warner scripts and gave them new treatments merely by changing locales or genres (transforming a Western melodrama into a contemporary gangster picture). His films were also strong on the use of inserts such as newspaper clips or newsreel snips (to save the expense of producing the action otherwise required) and close-ups (to minimize the number of actors needed in a scene). Neither Foy nor Wallis permitted their directors to improvise on the script or to make retakes (unless a preview had gone so awry that reshooting was demanded to save the film from being scuttled). Metro-Goldwyn-Mayer worked in reverse. After previews, films were reedited and whole scenes often reshot.

Until Reagan arrived at the studio, he did not know that he had been cast as the lead in *Love Is on the Air,* a programmer to be made by the Foy unit. The feature was scheduled to begin shooting the following Monday morning, June 7, with June Travis, the young woman who had helped him in his screen test, as his leading lady. Only four days remained for the studio to prepare a lead who not only had no camera exposure but no professional acting experience. No matter how low the budget (*Love Is on the Air* was to be made for $119,000), the prudence of such a gamble was questionable. But the decision reflects most pointedly the purpose of the film studios in the thirties: to create their own stable of personalities, hoping that out of every ten contract players one might prove to have star quality.

Warner Brothers had the largest list of stock contract players, of which Reagan was now a member. And, as one observer said, "The studio that had you under contract had to give you consideration, had to try to build you for its own sake. . . . If you didn't make it you were out, and you were a freelance player." Studios also employed freelance performers, of course; Warners hired fewer than others. A freelance player could negotiate each new film, but the competition was fierce and one's livelihood insecure. Nonetheless, many of Warners' contract players griped about the unfairness of the system. "What you, the actor, would have would be a guarantee of six months' [employment], what the producer, of course, would have would be options for seven years . . ." The studio also had the right to place a contract player on suspension if he or she refused a role, the suspended performer receiving no pay for the number of weeks specified by the studio. Like snow days in eastern schools, these suspended periods could then be tacked on to the end of a player's contract. This could mean that the player, now a star, had to make a film on the pay scale of a stock contract player. None of these eventualities troubled Reagan when he started at Warners, nor did the authoritarian attitude that prevailed. Making a movie was the overriding thing. And even there, he gave no thought to its quality or budget.

On April 20, 1937, Reagan had signed a seven-year contract with six-month options to begin June 1, at two hundred dollars a week. This did not mean *consecutive* weeks. Contract players were only guaranteed nineteen weeks' work in twenty-six. In addition, any revenues they made in radio, personal-appearance tours or commercial advertising went directly to the studio. Reagan had only the right to renegotiate his salary after four years (by that time he would be earning six hundred dollars a week), and he could not quit to go elsewhere. Warners could also loan him out to another studio for whatever fee they could get, while continuing to pay him his contracted weekly stipend, a standard arrangement for contract players at that time.* If the performance was well received in his first outing, he would be put in a supporting role in an A film (which usually ran over ninety minutes, whereas a pro-grammer ran approximately sixty minutes) soon afterward. What happened from there depended upon audience reaction. Character actors were not handled in the same way, but Warners had signed Reagan with an eye to grooming him as a leading man.

Almost immediately upon his arrival at the studio, he was taken over by the men and women who created a distinctive look for each player—the makeup artists, hairdressers and wardrobe personnel. The quintessential re-creation of this process occurs in

---

*Warners did not put Reagan on loan until 1941. Whether a request for his services was ever made previously is unknown. However, it seems unlikely that Warners would not have accepted such a proposition if it had been forthcoming.

the Judy Garland–James Mason version of *A Star Is Born,* where Garland's natural beauty is masked by a similar team of experts in an attempt to turn her into a glamour girl. (Reagan was to say, "Apparently I was too big a problem for Perc [Westmore, top Warner makeup artist] to handle at the studio. So he sent me to the House of Westmore [commercial salon for makeup and hair, operated by the six Westmore brothers] on a Saturday for what turned out to be a joint consultation with his brothers. I still remember how they circled around me as if I were a racehorse. They spoke only to each other, not to me. I recall their saying such clinical things as 'What are we going to *do* with him? With his hair parted in the middle like that, he looks like Joe E. Brown with a small mouth!'")

Happily for Reagan, he had been signed for his own best qualities, the boyish charm, the all-American look. The Westmores were most concerned with the deep crevice across the bridge of his nose put there by so many years of wearing heavy glasses. Darker makeup was used on this area, and deeper laugh lines and the intimation of dimples were created to distract the viewer's eye. The pouf he had worn for years was flattened and a suggestion of sideburns penciled in. Without his glasses, one eye had the tendency to turn slightly when tired. Instructions were sent to the camera department that he was not to be photographed fullface in close-up where this would be most evident.

The next day he returned to the studio with two suits from his own wardrobe (which included only one more—the white linen). In all contemporary B films, male contract players were expected to wear their own clothes. The role he was to play, Andy McLeod, did not require much in the way of sartorial attire. His film debut presented him as a crusading small-town radio announcer. The rakish hat brought from Des Moines, the polka-dot ties, the slightly rumpled three-piece suit, even the large Eureka class ring he wore looked so much the part that Nick Grinde, the director, thought they had come from the wardrobe department. Wardrobe also suggested he wear his oversized wristwatch as he had it—the face on the inside near his palm—a habit he had developed at WHO to enable him to glance quickly at the time during a broadcast (this positioning of his wristwatch became a trademark he maintained during his entire film career). He posed for publicity photographs, but was not yet given a script since the writer was still working on it. On the weekend, he moved from the hotel to the Montecito Apartments near the Boulevard with little to recommend his small accommodation except its location. (For many years, Reagan would live in the heart of Hollywood, within sight of those landmarks—the Boulevard, Grauman's Chinese Theatre, Sunset Boulevard, the Garden of Allah and Schwabs Drugstore—which spelled Hollywood to him.) Monday morning he appeared on the set early, ready to shoot his first movie, which—though being made on the Warners lot and distributed by them—was filmed under the aegis of First National, a company they had absorbed in the late twenties and whose banner they now used to protect Warner Brothers's prestige.

Nick Grinde called the cast together, handed out freshly mimeographed scripts and asked for a reading of the scene to be shot. Reagan thought he might be booted out of the studio right then. Reading cold had always been his bête noire. If he had to concentrate on seeing the lines, he could not inject them with any interpretation. The dialogue he spoke for a "fast-talking, high-pitched argument between McLeod and his boss" came out flat, with no personality. Grinde was puzzled. He had shot Reagan's test and had been impressed with his work. But, of course, Reagan had had time to memorize that scene.

Joe Graham, the dialogue director, took Reagan aside. Reagan confessed his inability to read cold and a decision was made to shoot an alternative scene and to postpone Reagan's until the next day. On Tuesday he came in with both his and Robert Barratt's (the actor playing his boss) lines memorized. Everyone relaxed. He conveyed all the personal appeal and enthusiasm that had prompted Warners to offer him a contract. From that day forward, he would never appear on the set without having memorized his lines. Seldom did a scene have to be reshot because of him. Occasionally, he would flub a line, but usually this was caused by a difficulty in coordinating action with dialogue; the sheer concentration of having to react physically to something or someone he could not see pushed the dialogue right out of his mind.

Originally *Love Is on the Air* was conceived as a modest musical. A song had been written for it before Bryan Foy realized the story would not work in that form. So as not to waste the song, Dick Powell sang it in *Varsity Show*, which he was then filming. Powell also made a Decca recording of the song, now titled "Love Is on the Air, *Tonight.*" (Since both Powell's record and movie were released about the same time as Reagan's film, the critics were understandably confused.) The final script of *Love Is on the Air* still retained vestiges of its musical past.

The original story, by Roy Chanslor, had been made only

three years earlier, titled *Hi, Nellie* and starring Paul Muni in one of his few light-comedy appearances. In that version, Andy McLeod had been a newspaper editor demoted by his publisher to lovelorn columnist until he uncovers evidence of a crime syndicate of which the publisher is a part. With the recent success of *Front Page,* Warners thought they might cash in on a trend. When this did not occur, the studio blamed it on its too-close similarity to *Front Page.* The script was then rewritten (by Morton Grant), first as the aforementioned musical, and then in the version Reagan made using the radio networks as a background. McLeod in this rehash is reduced from newscaster to kiddie-show host usurping the job of Jo Hopkins (June Travis), who is resentful for a reel or two before becoming his girlfriend and ally.

The film was shot in three weeks (A films generally had a minimum six-week schedule). The company called him "Ron" or "Ronnie," a new sound to him, but he quickly got used to it. The cinematographer, James Van Trees, proved to be his best teacher, taking him aside to warn him to control his inclination to sway or suddenly lift his chin or cock his head when the camera moved in for a close-up. He also taught him "about chalk marks, those footprints on the floor which marked where you were to come to a halt regardless of how fast you burst into a scene—the problem was you could not look down to find them." (Twenty years later, fellow actors commented that Reagan still could not find the chalk marks easily and would lean forward a bit like Groucho Marx when entering a scene to measure his distance from them.)

The camera did not intimidate him. Once he learned the technique, he was able to play to it in a completely natural way, and the camera responded by transmitting his ease and winning personality onto film. He claims that seeing himself in the rushes at the end of his first day of shooting was a shock to him, for here he was, "plain old everyday [me]—up on the screen. It [was] one hell of a let down." In the beginning, Warners saw him as a beach-boy type. He had a good physique and his first publicity pictures show him bare-chested amid an array of admiring bathing beauties. (Early in the filming of *Love Is on the Air,* the film censor wrote Bryan Foy: "Please be careful that Andy [Reagan] be not unduly exposed in this scene [page twelve of script] where he strips off his pajamas and starts dressing.")*

Once again, Reagan contracted leading ladyitus. He saw Joy

---

* *Love Is on the Air* opened on November 12, 1937, at the Palace Theater, New York, as "decided second fiddle" to *Stage Door* starring Katharine Hepburn.

Hodges, but they would become only good friends ("To my regret," she commented). For the three weeks of filming, he fell quite hopelessly under the spell of the radiant, self-possessed, athletically inclined June Travis, a green-eyed beauty. They had much in common. Her father, Harry Grabiner, was the vice-president of the Chicago White Sox and she had also been raised in the Midwest.* Their weekend dates were spent miles away from the social spin of Hollywood. They went horseback riding in Griffith Park and drove down to Santa Monica Pier at night, where they rode the roller coaster and June "knocked off every clay pigeon in [a shooting gallery] and then rang the bell with that 50 point shot that means sharpshooter. . . . She even managed to beat [him] throwing baseballs at milk bottles." He confessed to being pleased with her show of sports ability that put him to shame. June had grown up in a thoroughly masculine atmosphere and the ballplayers on her father's team had seen to it that she knew how to throw and catch a ball with near-professional precision. Her athletic prowess extended to water sports and hockey. And while attending the University of California (where she was discovered), she had been considered "one of the best feminine hockey players in the country." When production ended on *Love Is on the Air,* so did their romance.

Conservative and as responsible as always, Reagan still sent Nelle and Jack a weekly check and put money aside so that they could soon join him. He found glamour and excitement in his life at the studio—seeing the stars he so admired at lunch in the commissary, or walking in full makeup and costume through the flower-hedged paths between their dressing-room bungalows (he shared a trailer with other members of the cast) and the huge sound stages where the major films were shot. It took a long time for his life to seem real. Nothing in his past had prepared him for his current day-to-day existence. He remained star struck for years. When he was introduced to James Cagney, he was unable to remind him that he had once interviewed him in Des Moines.

Making films is often a boring task. For the actors, it involves hour upon hour of waiting as a setup is being prepared by technicians to shoot three minutes of film. Those three minutes in turn are repeated six, eight, twelve times, as first one actor then an-

---

*June Travis's real name was Dorothea Grabiner. She returned to Chicago in February 1939, did some radio work and married Fred Friedlob, who owned a large mail-order company.

other flubs a line, the lighting goes wrong or a prop is placed on the wrong table. "[Movies are] a specialized sort of business," Larry (Lawrence) Williams, who appeared with Reagan in five films,* commented. "Boredom simply goes with the territory. Movie actors are supposed to be bored, so what the hell, the pay is good.

"Ronnie [however] was never bored. You noticed it at once. There was something about all that idle time on the movie set that seemed to stimulate him in some private way. Far from finding the long dreary hours a drag like the slothful rest of us, Ronnie seemed to embrace them as a happy challenge. To him this time appeared to represent . . . a chance to express his animated views on an infinite variety of subjects to us, his fellow actor-captives on [the] set trapped as we all were for ten hour working days. . . .

"Statistical information of all sorts was a commodity Ronnie always had in extraordinary supplies, carried either in his pockets or in his head. Not only was this information abundant, it was stunning in its catholicity. There seemed to be absolutely no subject, however recondite, without its immediately accessible file. Ron had the dope on just about everything: this quarter's up-or-down figures on GNP growth, V. I. Lenin's grandfather's occupation, all history's baseball pitchers' ERAs, the optimistic outlook for California sugar-beet production in the year 2000, the recent diminution of the rainfall level causing everything to go to hell in summer [in] Kansas and so on. One could not help but be impressed."

As the days progressed, cast and crew also became irritated, and their ability to concentrate flagged. No one quite understood where Reagan came from, how and why he was able to have such an astonishing fund of statistics. Most of his fellow actors were involved with their careers. They read *The Hollywood Reporter, Variety* and Louella Parsons's daily column. A few were deeply concerned with world conditions—the war in Spain, the encroachment of fascism in Europe. Both groups considered him naïve, a memory bank without purpose. One co-worker invited him to a pro-Communist meeting. He refused to attend. Father Coughlin's radio diatribes had not been lost on him. Anything pro-Communist was anti-American where he was concerned.

He missed his Des Moines friends, the camaraderie of Cy's

---

*The five films in which both Reagan and Lawrence Williams appeared were *Girls on Probation, Brother Rat, Going Places, Secret Service of the Air,* and *Brother Rat and a Baby.*

Moonlight Inn, the debates with Hal Gross and Voith Pemberthy, the sense of being number one, as he had been at WHO and in Des Moines. The studio worked on a "cast" system—A casts and B casts (even Hollywood society entertained with A parties and B parties). The commissary had two rooms for lunch, executives and "stars" having a private area, which Reagan did not attend in the beginning. For the first year he was not well known enough to be recognized by studio visitors or by people he came in contact with.

His mind was in ferment, but as was his habit, he kept his confusion to himself. His co-workers and the few outside people he saw (Joy Hodges for one) were exposed to that habitual control on his true emotions that had disturbed Nelle—the easy smile, his rather juvenile sense of humor. On the surface he gave the impression of being shallow. When Bette Davis first met him, she thought he was a "silly boy." No one, therefore, could comprehend how the person they thought he was could have such an incredible store of facts—and a knowledge of complicated subjects. Studio friendships were not at all like those at WHO. They did not carry over after working hours. Left alone for long patches of his private time, he read voraciously.

On the set, according to Larry Williams, "Ronnie might . . . [sit] down next to you peering through his big glasses and suddenly [say] something like, 'Larry, before I run down for you this Far Eastern concept I'm sort of kicking around in my mind, answer me a background question: What would you say is the current population of Formosa?'

" 'Ronnie, I don't know things like that.'

" 'Right. Most Americans don't. No need to apologize.'

" 'I'm glad.'

" 'I've got the figure right here, but before I give it to you maybe I should just jog your memory a bit about Chinese history in the last three thousand years.' . . . [Soon] I began to notice a curious, perhaps unconscious behavior in some of us relating to our lunch hour. When we were released around noontime to walk over to the studio commissary, the thing got to be to see who could come in last—or at any rate behind Ronnie. This way you could figure in advance just where old Ron was going to settle down for lunch before you picked your own table. Once this was established, as if by some mysterious prearrangement . . . our company would then steal off to a corner with our tuna-fish sandwiches and eat them in amiable but total silence. . . ."

During the first few months in Hollywood he saw quite a lot of Joy Hodges. They would go to Dubars, a stable in Hollywood, and ride (Joy turned out to be quite adept once she had the proper clothes). "We discussed politics more than any other subject. I was so fond of him, but he was a passionate Democrat and I a Republican and we used to go round and round about that. . . . He loved anything and everything about Government, History and Politics. So did I and I loved hearing him relate accounts of Indian battles." Hodges had been dropped by RKO without ever having uttered a line of dialogue into the microphone. Reagan now had the opportunity to cheer her up. He did not have to do so for long, as Universal signed her to appear in a leading role in *Merry-Go-Round* (released as *Merry-Go-Round of 1938*). That September she met Moss Hart, who had written a play called *I'd Rather Be Right*. "She's a young Gertrude Lawrence," he told Richard Rodgers and Lorenz Hart, who had written the score. A few days later, she was off to New York to play the lead in the show opposite George M. Cohan.

Reagan's life appears to have been stultifying during his early Warner years. At Radio WHO he had been involved with the news and farm staff. He had met and interviewed people in all walks of life. Once the newness of film acting wore off, he suffered some of the same boredom as his co-workers. The roles he played did not even call for great feats of memory. Six days after he completed *Love Is on the Air,* he began work on *Sergeant Murphy.** Originally developed by Sy Bartlett (who went on to write many major films, including *Twelve O'Clock High*), the script was several cuts above *Love Is on the Air.* Reagan's role was that of a cavalry private, Dennis Murphy, dedicated to his horse (Sergeant Murphy). The horse eventually justifies his master's faith, along with that of Mary Lou Carruthers (Mary Maguire), the colonel's daughter (the colonel was played by Donald Crisp), by winning the Grand National at Aintree after being mustered out of the service and smuggled into England.

Reagan felt comfortable as soon as the company reached the location where the outdoor shooting would take place, Monterey Peninsula, because it was the home of the 11th Cavalry. The scenery was spectacular. The town sat on sloping shores at the southern end of Monterey Bay, protected from high seas and high winds. Settled by Mexico, it still looked as though it belonged

---

*Released out of sequence as his third film.

to that country, with its adobe buildings and red-tiled roofs, white-sand beach and green pines edging a deep-blue bay. On Saturdays, the main street was wide awake. Ford pickup trucks belonging to ranchers and cowboys in blue jeans and high-heeled boots lined up while their occupants shopped for supplies and ended the day in one of the beer halls on the wharf, rubbing shoulders and matching drinks with the fishermen and the cavalrymen from the post. The company stayed at a resort lodge where white tie and evening dress were *de rigueur* in the evening, but for the ten days of location, Reagan preferred to stick with the cavalrymen. (A long-range friendship with Colonel Robert Ferkuson began in Monterey.) After all, he was a second lieutenant in the Reserve.

His director on the film was B. Reeves Eason, who had staged the famous chariot race in *Ben Hur* (1927) and the final masterly charge in *The Charge of the Light Brigade* (1936).* "Breezy," as he was called, had a special talent for directing animals and action. Because of this, the film moved briskly and the race sequences were far above the quality of the rest of the film. He also used Reagan's equestrian skills and his affinity with horses well.†

The leading lady in *Sergeant Murphy*, Mary Maguire, was a winsome eighteen-year-old from Australia. Reagan seemed more in love with his horse than his girl in this movie. Upon the film's release (February 1, 1938), Dorothy Masters, in the *New York Daily News*, wrote, ". . . the most exciting thing about the Brooklyn Paramount show [*Tovarich* with Charles Boyer and Claudette Colbert topped the bill] is that it returned Ronald Reagan to palpitating proximity." Prophetically, she continued, "In the movies only because television isn't yet equipped to do him justice, this erstwhile radio announcer's . . . looks and personality scoop out toeholds for a plot that can barely make the grade. There are the thrills attendant to daring horsemanship, comedy is in abundance, but the scenario . . . has no villain [and therefore no suspense]."

By the time *Sergeant Murphy* was completed, *Love Is on the Air* had been released and Reagan's reception by critics and fans was good but not startling. Warners decided to cast him in small roles in two A films, *Hollywood Hotel* and *Swing Your Lady*. In both his

---

* In 1939, B. Reeves Eason staged, for David O. Selznick, the spectacular burning-of-Atlanta sequence in *Gone With the Wind*.

† Reagan's riding his own horse was okayed by Warner himself, who dispatched a memo to his concerned location man (June 15, 1937): "If any horses are thrown on this I will throw someone myself . . . for $7.50 per day the SPCA will put a man on any picture . . . testifying to the effect that no cruelty to animals was done [in the course of the filming]."

appearance is brief. He comfortably plays an announcer in the first and a sportscaster in the second, wearing his old hat at its set angle. (Reagan said of these early roles, ". . . remember the guy in movies who rushes into the phone booth, pushes his hat to the back of his head while the tails of his trench coat are still flying, drops a nickel in the box, dials a few numbers and then says, 'Gimme the city desk. I've got a story that'll split this town wide open!' That was me.")

Hollywood Hotel starred Dick Powell and introduced Louella Parsons to the screen. Parsons's successful radio program of the same title had been the inspiration for the film story. Although Parsons's few minutes of gossip reporting had been the high point of the program's four-year tenure, each week new players would be introduced. The studios, who saw this as an opportunity to put their contract players before the public, were extremely obliging. Whomever Louella wanted, she generally got.

Hollywood Hotel was a fictionalized account of the weekly broadcast and the young performers who got their breaks on it. Busby Berkeley supplied some lavish musical numbers. Reagan's role was straight and had no connection with the plot.* The most important thing about his appearance in *Hollywood Hotel* was his meeting with Parsons and her discovery that he was also from Dixon. (Frank S. Nugent, of *The New York Times*, commented on Parsons's acting debut: "Miss Parsons plays herself better than anyone else could hope to, or possibly want to.")

His work in *Hollywood Hotel* took only a few days. He then walked into the Humphrey Bogart film *Swing Your Lady*. In the few minutes that he is onscreen in this slapstick comedy, Reagan looks more at home than Bogart, who plays the role of a desperate promoter stuck in a hick town who matches an Amazonian woman (marvelously played by Louise Fazenda) against the professional wrestler (Nat Pendleton) he manages.

After his five-day assignment on *Swing Your Lady*, Warners sent Reagan on one day's notice to Coronado, about a hundred miles south of Los Angeles near San Diego, for the role of a Navy flier in another major film, *Submarine D-1*,† starring Pat O'Brien, George Brent and Wayne Morris. Reagan explained: "Some place in the studio higher echelons it had been decided to provide a surprise

---

* Reagan's name is not always listed in the credits for *Hollywood Hotel* because the role is so small.

† Though films like *Swing Your Lady* and *Submarine D-1* were booked as major films, they actually fell somewhere between A and B and were shown on weekdays. Another, stronger film supplanted them on weekends, when audiences were heaviest.

ending to the picture so that neither [sic] of the three stars would end up with the girl. I would come in as her finacé in the last reel." After a week's shooting, Reagan claimed, the decision was reversed, his footage cut, and "Wayne Morris won the girl [Doris Weston]." However, no one gets the girl in the released film; the men's dedication to the submarine they command wins out.

When he returned to Hollywood from Coronado, the reviews had not yet come in on *Sergeant Murphy*. He feared the worst. To his relief, the studio picked up his option. A six-month stretch lay before him with $250 a week for a guarantee of sixteen weeks' work (standard in Warner Brothers' contracts). The studio could keep him working if they chose, but they could also leave him off salary for as long as ten weeks. He sent Nelle and Jack the railroad fare and rented an apartment for them in the flats of West Hollywood (near Beverly Hills). The location was chosen so that Jack could take a walk, and Nelle, who did not drive a car, could get around on her own. His expenses were going to be hard to meet, but he was determined that he keep his promise to Nelle. He met them at the train and drove them to their new home. Out back was a small yard with rose bushes crowding it and their ground-floor apartment looked out on all kinds of tropical flora. He noted that Jack was more dependent on Nelle than before, that he was often short of breath and that his left hand, the muscles atrophied in it, had a frightening, somewhat clawlike shape. (Jack's unexpected deformity was to have a lasting effect on Reagan, who as the years progressed feared a similar affliction.)

He had learned much in his six months in Hollywood, although not necessarily about acting. Movies were made and players were shuffled around so fast that close friendships had no time to develop. He extended himself in every way possible and was always the first to offer assistance. Aware that his co-workers thought him a bit of an odd fellow, he determined to win them over.

One late afternoon, after a long day at the studio, Larry Williams learned that the work that was to be done on his car had not been finished in time and he was without a ride home. Reagan offered to drive him and the stranded Williams accepted, unaware of the distance between their homes. "I was up at the top of the Mulholland Hills, he was across and somewhere down the other side."* Nor did he learn until he got into Reagan's old car that Reagan had misplaced his glasses.

---

*Reagan was still living at the Montecito Apartments in Hollywood. Mulholland was not only miles out of his way, but involved traveling some precarious roads.

"It was casually taken for granted that Ronnie was blind as a bat without his glasses," Williams said. "He normally wore large, sensible spectacles through which he saw as well as anybody. . . . The drive was a memorable one for several reasons . . . Ronnie was a red-hot Roosevelt Democrat and he took the occasion of our trip home to fill me in on some of the subtler political goals of the New Deal. . . .

"'Now, you take a good man like Harold Ickes,' Ronnie began. 'He's experienced . . .'

"'RON! That big gray truck!'

"'What truck?'

"'The one you just cut in front of when he was making a left turn!'

"'I did?'

"'. . . he's screaming something at you.'

"'Those teamsters! They're tough babies, won't take any pushing around. Building a strong union.'

"We drove on up into the hills.

"'RONNIE!' . . . We were only a couple of inches from the edge of a two-hundred-foot drop on the right side!

"'Your imagination. I stay in the middle of the road. Is that your house? Good. I'll pick you up and take you out to the studio in the morning.'"

Williams declined, but he recalled his co-worker as not being just "fuzzyvisioned" but "eager to be loved."

Right after Nelle and Jack arrived, so did some of his old TEKE fraternity brothers who had followed Dutch west, hoping they too might hit it big in Hollywood in some capacity or other. It did not happen, and since Dutch was the only one employed, he became their sole and uncomplaining support. The next few months were to be the happiest he had experienced since coming to California. With these old friends he could be a "rubber neck" himself. They toured the Beverly Hills homes of movie stars: Charlie Chaplin's at 1085 Summit Drive (and, up the road from it, Fred Astaire's house at 1121 Summit Drive); Harold Lloyd's estate, Green Acres, at 1225 Benedict Canyon ("the second largest [next to Pickfair] in Southern California, includes a 25 room house with 27 telephones, canoe stream and waterfall, private 9-hole golf course, handball court, swimming pool, and a four room playhouse for the Lloyd children. Mr. Lloyd breeds great Danes and St. Bernards"); Ginger Rogers's at 1605 Gilcrest (". . . the highest point in Beverly Hills. There is a shining, well-stocked soda fountain in the house, to fulfill a childhood dream"). He gleaned such other sterling pieces of information (from tour guidebooks sold at stands on Sunset Boulevard) as the fact that Greta Garbo's house had a five-foot wall to ensure her privacy; and that Joan Crawford had a private motion-picture theater.

Such extravagance exceeded any of his wildest dreams for himself. It belonged to the world of millionaires like the Walgreens. He and his Eureka cohorts liked piling into the convertible (you could manage three; the fourth passenger had to sit on the rim and hang on) and driving down to Barney's Beanery on Santa Monica Boulevard (about five minutes from his apartment), where they could argue politics and football. (Two of the gang had been members of Mac's Golden Tornadoes.) Barney's was just a shack with walls precariously angled, a counter, a few tables (none of the legs the same height) and a patio, but for fifteen cents they could buy the best bowl of onion soup in town. Barney (Anthony) also kept a stock of beers in the back that would please any aficionado. Gruff, cynical, "a no-nonsense guy who could see right through you," Barney could "accept your frailties with off-hand tolerance" while defending his own strong prejudice—one only, it seemed—against homosexuals. Behind the bar at Barney's, a large sign was posted that read FAGOTS [sic] STAY OUT. Barney's was a gathering spot for young male actors and its proprietor did not want his clientele "approached."*

Reagan had not become part of Hollywood life and he was not sure he ever would. He confessed to being restless. His friends from college considered him a star. He knew he was not. More than that, he was not sure now that being a star was what he wanted. Less than a year after he arrived in Hollywood, his major concern was how badly actors were treated by studios. He kept talking about the inequities and servitude of a seven-year contract, of the loan out and the lay-off, and the ridiculously low pay of extras. To Bill Meiklejohn's surprise, at the time of his second option he insisted on reexamining every clause in his contract. Meiklejohn told him, in effect, that it was a hopeless exercise.

Reagan grinned less boyishly than usual. "Well, a way has to be figured to turn that around," he replied.

---

* In the early sixties, when the West Hollywood section where Barney's Beanery was located became a center for Gay Rights groups, Barney told *Life* magazine (June 26, 1964), "I don't like 'em. There's no excuse. They'll approach any nice-lookin' guy. Anybody does any recruiting [here] I say shoot him—who cares, anyway?"

9

IN THE TWENTIES, A VETERAN SAN FRANCISCO showman, Sid Grauman, decided that it was "meet and proper" that Hollywood, the film capital of the world, should have "the finest, the most artistic movie theatre in the world." He bought a large piece of property on the Boulevard and built the first "movie cathedral." Bizarre would be a mild word to describe the final result—Grauman's Egyptian Theatre—an architectural crazy house of Chinese, Greek and Egyptian design. The official description of Grauman's (as it came to be called) ran in part: "This temple of art is a replica of a palace of ancient Thebes, profusely embellished with Egyptian hieroglyphics, drawn from the monuments to the Theban kings and presenting the symbolic stories of the gods and goddesses of the Nile. At night it glistens in the aura of brilliant lights. The façade of the theatre presents huge Egyptian columns surmounted by a massive strut of stone. Along the top of the walls all day long silently promenades a Libyan sheik in the garb of the desert. Entering the great foyer, the visitor is greeted by beautiful girls as usherettes, dressed in the manner of handmaidens of Cleopatra. The auditorium is surmounted by a great dome from which hangs an enormous chandelier of Egyptian design, all wrought in colors of gold with golden iridescent rays emanating from an ingenious system of concealed lights, giving the effect of a colossal sunburst."

Realizing that the stars would come to his theater to be seen by their public and that the public would pay huge prices to see the stars in person, Grauman conceived the "premiere," the initial showing of a top super-special film. By three or four o'clock in the afternoon of one of these galas, the huge plaza in the forecourt of Grauman's (a re-creation of a Polynesian village) was jampacked with fans equipped with camp stools and box lunches to help them endure the five-hour wait until "the first royal carriage" arrived. (In the early years, Grauman even had footmen with powdered wigs help the stars out of their limousines, despite the fact that their costumes had no connection with his leitmotiv.)

A premiere at Grauman's offered the greatest publicity a film and its top performers could achieve. The event also gave the studios a chance to parade some of their would-be stars before the public. Warner Brothers's big film in 1938 was *Jezebel,* starring Bette Davis and Henry Fonda. The studio had rushed this pre–Civil War story set in the South into production when they lost out on the bidding for Margaret Mitchell's best seller, *Gone With the Wind.* Reagan was notified he was expected to attend. (He claimed he asked someone, "Do I have to go?" and that person replied, "No, but you'll be around longer if you do.") He was also asked to escort another contract player, Lana Turner, who, though only eighteen at the time, had played small roles in six or seven films, and had been dubbed "the sweater girl" because of her appearance in a clinging knit sweater in *They Won't Forget.*

Turner had been born in Wallace, Idaho, and much of her small-town background clung to her. When she was nine, her father, a mine foreman, had been murdered and she and her mother moved to California where Mrs. Turner hoped to find work as a beauty operator. Lana (then called Julia) had been sixteen when she played a bit part in the Janet Gaynor–Fredric March version of *A Star Is Born.* Young and beautiful, her hair not yet bleached blond, her figure full but a bit pudgy, she was unsure of herself and was as terrified as Reagan was of attending the premiere. In gown and dinner jacket borrowed from the Warners wardrobe department, and having never met before, they headed toward

Grauman's in a taxi because Reagan was too embarrassed to drive up to the theater in his old convertible.*

As their taxi moved slowly up the Boulevard, huge klieg lights scraped the night sky with "monstrous brushes of light." Anne O'Hare McCormick, writing in *The New York Times Magazine*, described the event they attended: "The elite of the movies crossed a high bridge erected across the street in front of the theatre. This 'bridge of the stars' was a temporary gangway ablaze with clusters of huge incandescent flowers and raked by klieg lights like a battery of suns.

"The throng was so dense that the pedestrian could not fight his way within a block of the place. The parade took place under an awning a block long, lighted like an operating table, between solid walls of gaping people. In the theatre the spotlight was thrown upon the audience, always the feature of these entertainments. Here, indeed, were the real figures of the screen in full gala.

"They were a little stiff with awareness of that fact, a little blank with make-up and self conscious."

Not only were Hollywood's stars living in a totally unreal world where obscene displays of wealth were expected, most of the films they played in were equally unreal. The studios hired some of the world's greatest creative and performing artists and then hamstrung them. In July 1938, a distributors' boycott of *Blockade*, Walter Wanger's melodrama of the Spanish Civil War (starring Henry Fonda and Madeleine Carroll), crystallized the artists' discontent. At a meeting of 300 delegates, representing 150,000 members of motion-picture unions, guilds and other organizations, these artists demanded that gag rule be removed from the industry, "so that motion pictures may become as they rightfully should be, a very important part of the democratic structure."

Reagan was not known to discuss the content of films often. He went to the movies to be entertained and his favorites were still those packed with action. If he had a vision of what he wanted to achieve in movies, his image of himself would have been as a John Wayne (who, after all, had gone from football to

---

*Although Reagan has recorded vivid memories of this date, Turner claimed she could not even recall it. Hollywood columns at that time did, however, record that they attended the premiere together, verifying Reagan's statements. The studio thought Reagan and Turner might be a good publicity item and a series of photographs was taken of them together the following week. But they never saw each other socially again (at least not as a dating couple).

cowboy star). But the incident involving *Blockade* had a great impact upon him. He became aware of the potential power of the Screen Actors and the Screen Writers guilds. He had joined the SAG (Screen Actors Guild) when he first came to Hollywood. Now he took a vital interest in it.

Her son's success and her new home had not changed Nelle's habits. Almost immediately upon arriving in California she became an active member of the Hollywood-Beverly Christian Church. "One of the church ladies came to call on me yesterday afternoon to sign me up with the Missionary Group, belonging to this section," she wrote Mrs. Hazel Emmert, back in Dixon, on December 10, 1937. "How I wish you could all see beautiful Hollywood Blvd. with all its wonderful Christmas decoration. Yet it makes my heart ache when I think of all the good that could be done with the thousands of dollars spent on it, which might better be used to alleviate some of the suffering in this old world. Please don't think anything about not receiving a Christmas card from me, for I have decided to just send a greeting to the whole Sunday school and take the money I would have to spend for postage and give it as a gift to your Sunday school instead; but please know that I love you all and am wishing everyone a gloriously Merry Christmas and the happiest New Year you have ever known." Under separate cover she sent a one-dollar contribution to the Sunday School (postage was two cents per Christmas card).

Being exposed to Nelle's "Christian ways" revived many of Reagan's childhood habits. He had not been particularly church-going during his Des Moines years. Now he accompanied Nelle to services on a fairly regular basis. He returned to the custom of giving a percentage of his weekly income to the church, but curiously did not join at this time. The few self-indulgent extravagances he had allowed himself before his parents' arrival were greatly curtailed by the added responsibility of supporting a second household. This could easily have accounted for his spending so much time with old friends who enjoyed simpler, less expensive pleasures than his Hollywood associates (a day at the beach, a beer at Barney's Beanery, a game of bridge at home). Nelle's near presence also might have encouraged his generosity to these old friends, for she held strongly to the idea that one must help one's close associates. His mother's approval was important to him, there was no doubt about that. "Look at your son," he had a habit of saying with a proud smile on his face at a time of accomplishment. "Look at your son—he's making $300 a week now!" he crowed after having his option picked up the second time. "Look at your son—he's starring with Pat O'Brien [in *Cowboy from Brooklyn*]." One of his former TEKE friends who was a houseguest was impressed enough to remember the grown, successful Reagan's courting of his mother's approval. Nelle *was* proud of him, but her values and concerns were not the same as his.

"How is the factory [Reynolds Wire had reopened] running now?" she wrote and asked Mrs. Emmert. "I hope it won't close down through the cold weather, for I think then is the time when more money is needed. One can stand a little discomfort in the summertime so much better." Nelle's heart was always in her missionary work. The second Christmas (1938) she was in California, she wrote that she had just finished wrapping five hundred Christmas gifts "for some needy folks." By now her chief interest was the Olive View Sanitarium for tubercular patients.

Jack was far more impressed with his son's achievements. They were closer during the late thirties than at any other time in their lives. Moon's defection to the Republican party had hurt Jack and he made no secret of it. Jack was completely dry, which might have added to his and Dutch's closeness. But without his old friends, Jack had only Dutch to talk politics with. He listened endlessly to the radio—news and sports. The club chair and ottoman that he lounged on, as well as the radio, were Christmas gifts from Dutch. On Sunday nights, Reagan took his parents to La Rue's (a popular Hollywood restaurant) for spaghetti and meatballs, Jack's favorite. Reagan wrote that every morning Jack took "the slow careful walk the doctor prescribed. . . . He never tired of shaking his head about this new land, insisting that Californians must be the hungriest people in the world. He said, 'There's nothing, by God, but real estate offices and hot-dog stands.'"

Larry Williams remembered Reagan inviting him over to his apartment for a bachelor evening "with some other actors." Two of Reagan's college chums and one Warners contract player were present, and the men played bridge for low stakes and discussed the wisdom of investing in real estate in California.

By the summer of 1938, a year after he had signed with Warners, Reagan's films and the roles he played remained almost instantly forgettable. He projected a likableness even when the part, as in *Accidents Will Happen*, was not totally sympathetic. Warners tried to change his image slightly during 1938 by lightening his hair to auburn for five films. The hoped-for effect was to reinforce his all-American look. (In black-and-white films, darker hair gave a Latin or Mediterranean cast to the player.) Warners picked up his option again in June. Fan mail was coming in; not an overwhelming amount, but enough to reassure the studio that he had potential. His early directors claim that Jack Warner liked and approved his casting because he did his job and never caused any waves. Warners also agreed to put Jack Reagan on the payroll at twenty-five dollars a week to answer the fan letters and requests for photographs that his son brought home.

The noticeable thing about Reagan's first two years in Hollywood is that he was not the same self-assured, cocky fellow he had been in Des Moines. He had lapsed back to his Eureka days (perhaps because of his TEKE friends), with Bryan Foy standing in for Ralph McKinzie. His pattern was to go to the coach to convince him to put him out on the field in action. "I soon learned that I could go in to Byrnie," he confessed, "and tell him I had been laid off [after an assignment was complete],* but couldn't take it at the moment because of all my expenses. He would pick up the phone, call a couple of his henchmen, and actually get a picture going on four or five days' notice—just to put me back on salary." The problem was that Foy, like McKinzie, did not think Reagan belonged on the varsity squad and was perfectly happy to keep him on the second string. Finding competent B leads was not as easy as it might appear. Actors who had been on contract for a long time feared the stigma of B films, and those with obvious star ability jumped from B's to A's and were thus unavailable.

After more than a year under contract, Reagan seemed destined to play B leads and small roles in A films forever, a situation that he encouraged by always pushing Foy to find a film for him. By not being available when a good role came along, he missed out on many opportunities. Wayne Morris and Dennis Morgan (who had also started as a radio announcer) had made the leap after only a few B movies. Morris, in fact, was his strongest competition at the studio, and any role that he played, Reagan could easily have done. Someone should have advised him to fight for better roles, not the reverse. But once Reagan was under contract

---

*Reagan is referring to the period of time between pictures when Warners did not have to pay him his weekly salary.

to Warners, the Meiklejohn Agency did little to help him in this respect.

Unquestionably, his knowledge of the camera improved. His reputation at the studio was as a "dependable guy, never late, hung-over or difficult to work with." Young New York actors like John Garfield were always fighting for the right "techniques." They worried about things like "conflict" in a script, a scene with "enough bottom to it," and they always wanted more time to think about the character's motivation. Reagan did whatever the director or the publicity department asked him to do, never required a stunt man for action scenes, posed tirelessly for publicity photographs and dutifully escorted the starlets chosen by the studio to previews or other public social functions where press photographers would be ready and poised. Privately, he dated Ila Rhodes, a beautiful blond contract player who appeared with him in two films, *Secret Service of the Air* (in a supporting role) and *Hell's Kitchen* (in an uncredited bit).*

"I became the Errol Flynn of the B's," Reagan says. "I was as brave as Errol, but in low-budget pictures. . . . I fought in prisons [*Code of the Secret Service* and *Smashing the Money Ring*] . . . I fought in a dirigible down at sea [*Murder in the Air*] . . . I fought in an airplane which was complete with a trap door that could drop the unwary to an awful death [*Secret Service of the Air*] . . . I swam with . . . bullets, hitting the water six inches from my face [*Murder in the Air*] . . . I even let them shoot a bottle out of my hand with a sling shot [in the same film]."

In all of the above, Reagan is referring to his role as Lieutenant Brass Bancroft of the Secret Service, in a series beamed toward the Saturday afternoon kiddie-show trade and based loosely (to say the least) on the memoirs of William H. Moran, a former chief of the United States Secret Service. *Code of the Secret Service* was so bad that Warners promised Foy they would never release it. They went back on their word, however, and distributed it in small towns where it had no chance to be reviewed.

Reagan made eight films from January 1938 to January 1939, and yet found time in May to return to Des Moines to announce the Drake Relay for Radio WHO after receiving an invitation

---

*In 1980, Ila Rhodes, who was married to a Brazilian industrialist, claimed she had been engaged to Reagan for eight months during 1938–39. Reagan refused to comment. Other close friends of Rhodes at that time say that they knew nothing about an engagement. Friends of Reagan say he dated Rhodes, but not exclusively.

from Pete MacArthur. Myrtle met him at the train. She had recently married. "We realized we had meant more to each other than we had thought," she later admitted. The time had escaped them both. Reagan also found that going back was no longer possible. He visited Cy's Moonlight Inn, the Club Belvedere and saw his old friends. But their worlds had split. He returned to Hollywood accepting that this was now his home.

The studio continued to have him play leads in B films and undistinguished supporting roles in major features. As Lieutenant Brass Bancroft, according to reviewers, he displayed "charm and vitality," "impresses and handles his fists well," "played his role of counter-espionage agent with the customary daring." In *Cowboy from Brooklyn* (starring Dick Powell, Priscilla Lane and Ann Sheridan as well as Pat O'Brien) he had been cast in a role—that of a sharp Brooklyn promoter—in which he had to employ a New Yorkese dialect. "Scene after scene I would discover had been rewritten after one or two of my drawling rehearsals, and the rewrite would wind up with someone else being given most of my lines. I was miserable . . . and beginning to yearn for my good old Secret Service pictures where I was a big wheel." Character actress Elizabeth Risdon and O'Brien helped him to some extent. But in the end his delivery sounded as though he might have been announcing a play-by-play tied game back at WHO, the bases loaded, a second strike called and the teletype machine gone dead.

The Sam and Bella Spewack Broadway hit *Boy Meets Girl* was next. In this one he had a small bit—that of a radio announcer at a major film premiere, which was home ground for him. ("Ronald Reagan, as the radio announcer . . . makes his brief opportunity register," *The New York Times* reviewer wrote.) For Reagan, who called himself at this time "a still worshipping movie fan," the best thing about *Boy Meets Girl* was being in a movie with James Cagney (the other stars were Pat O'Brien, Marie Wilson and Ralph Bellamy). Cagney had just returned to the lot after a court battle with Warners on a breach of his billing clause. (Someone else's name had appeared above his in the credits.) His real aim was to get Warners to limit his films to four a year with a better choice of roles. Cagney was known as the bad boy on the lot at this time. He had grown a moustache in the middle of his last film and he continued to talk to Jack Warner in obscene Yiddish.

Being allowed to join Cagney at a special table in the commissary—"one of the accolades of which I was proudest"—and to sit from time to time with other male stars on the Warner lot—

Bogart, O'Brien and Dennis Morgan—gave Reagan the acceptance he badly wanted. Competency, friendship and admission to the inner circle of those he considered great were the extent of his ambitions. He aspired to be one of *them,* a star, much in the same way as he had once yearned to be a football hero. Unlike many of the contract players on the lot, he did not seek outside drama lessons or work with a little theater group, but doggedly went from one assignment to the other with the same determination with which he had duck-waddled up and down the length of Eureka's football field.

Girls on Probation ("from the Bryan Foy workbench") followed. Reagan co-starred in this second feature with Jane Bryan, whom he greatly admired but who kept him at arm's distance. Also in the cast, in a small role, was Susan Hayward, who was not as aloof. The film was a melodrama with no surprises; the dialogue was embarrassing. *The New York Times* would note: "The cast does not include strong WB marquee talent, but performances by the various members of the company are adequate. Ronald Reagan seems a little lightweight as a d.a. and is perhaps a little too soft for that kind of a job, but otherwise, especially romantically, he serves well."

When Warners cast him as one of a trio of cadets attending Virginia Military Institute in *Brother Rat,* an adaptation of the hit Broadway farce, he had hopes that better times were on the way. *Brother Rat* was the "friendly name cadets had for each other." Reagan, who won his role over Jeffrey Lynn, played Dan Crawford, "who is always going along for the ride." Wayne Morris was Billy Randolph, "who can get into more shakes than you can shake a shako at." Eddie Albert, re-creating the role he had played on Broadway, was Bing Edwards, "who plugs along to accomplish things the hard way." Despite the fact that Albert's role (which had been the starring character on Broadway) had been pared down and the Wayne Morris role built up, Albert still ran away with the film and the reviews. Because Morris's part was bigger and the character more interesting, Reagan—the middleman—was pleasant but otherwise lost in the sandwiching.

The cast of *Brother Rat* also included Priscilla Lane (who had attended school in Des Moines), Jane Bryan, and "pretty, pert" Jane Wyman. Wyman, suing for divorce at the time, was attracted to Reagan, who she thought did his best to ignore her charms. Everything in Reagan's background rejected the idea of responding to another man's wife, no matter how close husband

and spouse were to severing their legal ties. "Ronnie was always going around with his college frat brothers," Wyman later said. "He never seemed to have time for girls. They were all enthused in sports . . . [yet] I was drawn to him at once. . . . He was such a sunny person."

Jane Wyman (her professional name) has always placed an aura of mystery about her birth date in St. Joseph, Missouri. On the surface, it seemed to indicate no more than an actress covering the actual date of her birth to appear younger. Generally, January 4, 1914, was given, but according to a registration blank filled out by her "parent or guardian" and signed by Emma Fulks, she entered grade one of Noyes School in St. Joseph on September 10, 1923, as Sarah Jane Fulks, born on January 28, 1917. Why a young woman should add three years to her age and change her birth date is mystifying but not necessarily of any great importance. In Wyman's case, it has a bearing on the choices she made, the woman she became and the men to whom she was attracted. In 1980, she made a statement that January 5, 1914, was her correct birth date. But it is unlikely that a child would enter the first grade at age nine.

Richard and Emma Fulks, Sarah Jane's parents, were middle-aged. Both had been married before—Richard in 1891 to Nora Christman, who bore him one son (Raymond) before her death in 1894; and Emma (Reiss) to M. F. Weymann, whom she divorced in 1902, the year that she and Richard married. Emma was German by birth and had two children—a daughter, Elsie, and a son, Morie, by Weymann. By 1917, all three of the Fulks children were living away from home. Richard was fifty-two and Emma fifty-one (not a likely age to bear a child). The Fulks' next-door neighbor had two young daughters. "I don't want to get anything wrong," one of them recalled, "but for a time there weren't any children and then there was Sarah Jane. She was about four or five . . . I do know that Fulks was not her real name. Her name was May-field and she was adopted . . . her parents . . . were married and her mother used to come by and visit her some."

A certificate of birth was issued in the state of Missouri to Sarah Jane Mayfield, born January 5, 1917, to Gladys Hope Christian and Manning J. Mayfield (who had been married in Kansas City on May 17, 1916). The Mayfields filed a petition for divorce in October 1921. Gladys Hope had been employed as a stenographer and office assistant for a Dr. Elam, but had been let go. She told the court that she had to move to Cleveland, Ohio, where a job had been promised her so that she could support herself and her child. If the Fulks' neighbor is correct, Gladys Hope Christian Manning left the child, then nearly five, with the Fulks and went off, but reappeared from time to time. (Since Sarah Jane's birth certificate remains under the name of Mayfield and was never changed, one must assume that the child was never adopted by the Fulks and that she simply took their name upon entering school.) Manning Mayfield, Sarah Jane's father, left St. Joseph about the same time and went to San Francisco to take a job as secretary of the Southern Pacific Westbound Conference, a shipping board, and died suddenly a few weeks later (January 21, 1922) of pneumonia at twenty-seven years of age.

It appears to be no coincidence that Mrs. Fulks traveled to California with Sarah Jane in January 1922. Her daughter, Elsie (now Mrs. Wyatt), and her son, Morie (now an eye-and-throat doctor), both lived in Los Angeles. Contrary to what has been written, it is unlikely that Mrs. Fulks took Sarah Jane out to Hollywood to put the child in pictures. Sarah Jane was only five years old and had shown no indication of having undeveloped talent, and Emma had no reason to leave the security of her life with Richard Fulks to become a full-time movie mother. A better explanation is that Mrs. Fulks and Sarah Jane traveled west to see Manning Mayfield before he died to settle the guardianship of Sarah Jane. Mayfield's obituary in the *San Francisco Chronicle* lists him as unmarried (yet, the divorce was not final at the time of his death) and without issue. The *St. Joseph News Press* gives his father, mother and two sisters as Mayfield's only survivors. Since Manning Mayfield's marriage, divorce and legal paternity of Sarah Jane are all documented by the state of Missouri, it appears clear that either he or his family wished not to acknowledge his paternity to little Sarah Jane, perhaps convinced that it would be best for the child if he did not. After two or three months in California, Emma and the little girl returned to St. Joseph.

The Fulks' house was run on Old World discipline and ideals. Emma's heritage (Richard had been American-born) kept her stiff, apart from the child she was now raising. Age had a strong effect on the relationship as well. Emma and Richard were in their late fifties. Richard, a Democrat, was elected county collector in 1916, but served just one term (the only public office he ever held), a great frustration as he had hoped for a political career.* He joined the police force, advancing from patrolman to chief of

---

*Hollywood biographies state he had been mayor of St. Joseph, which is incorrect.

detectives within a few years. He was a strict disciplinarian at home, a remote man, but a good and steady provider.

"I grew up with hurt and bewilderment," Wyman said in an interview in 1943. "A dreadful thing happened to me when I was a child in school. . . . It had to do with a note which was passed to me by another girl at school and which was intercepted by the teacher. The teacher read it and gathered from it that the two of us were planning to run away from home. We were called up to talk to the principal. [Miss Cecil Crawford, the principal, recalled "Sarah Jane's big, brown anxious eyes."] Then our mothers were notified and in due course, we were both suspended from school . . . the other little girl, whom I had considered my best friend . . . put the blame squarely on me. . . . I was bewildered . . . dreadfully frightened, and I felt misunderstood and completely alone.

"Actually, I don't think we had the faintest notion of running away . . . but there was so much confusion and recrimination. . . . I felt I could never trust or confide in anyone again . . . it followed me through my formative years, poisoned my life and my whole outlook until I met Ronnie."

Occasionally on Saturday afternoons, Emma would soften and take Sarah Jane downtown for lunch ("that was exciting in itself, choosing anything you liked from that long, long list of fancy sandwiches—and ice cream . . .") and to the matinee at the Lyceum, St. Joseph's only theater. Sarah Jane, who had dreams of one day being an actress, managed to convince the Fulks to give her dancing lessons at the Prinz School of Dance after a roadshow company musical had played in town.

On March 25, 1928, when Sarah Jane was eleven, Richard Fulks died, leaving sixty-two-year-old Emma in fairly dire straits. She rented their home, packed up Sarah Jane and traveled to Los Angeles where they moved in with Elsie. The Depression years were hard, but Morie helped out as much as he could. By 1932, Sarah Jane had dropped out of high school and taken a job as a waitress at Mannings Coffee Shop to earn enough money for her dance lessons. Somehow, she returned on her own to St. Joseph in the summer of 1933, where she shared a house at 913 North Second Street with Mrs. Gladys H. and Myrtle Johnson. (The similarity of Christian names could mean Gladys H. was Sarah Jane's mother, Gladys Hope.) Another neighbor, Anna Pendergast, claimed Sarah Jane had been married in her teens (never verified), and recalled that she would sit out in the yard "with a pencil and paper in her hand. When I asked her what she was doing she told me writing—that she wanted to write. . . . She was a real sweet person." By 1934, she was back in Hollywood. Leroy Prinz, the son of her old St. Joseph teacher, had become a successful dance director in films and promised her a break as a dancer.

Sarah Jane was not the only teenager trying to crash Hollywood as a chorus girl. Betty Grable was fourteen when she gave her first high kick before a camera. But Sarah Jane's cherubic face and her snub nose made her look even younger (she was claiming to be twenty). Following Grable's lead (who was also coached by Leroy Prinz), she plucked her eyebrows into a pencil-slim arch and bleached her natural brown hair to a Harlowesque platinum. For the next few years she breezed in and out of films—*The Kid from Spain, Elmer the Great, College Rhythm, All the King's Horses, Stolen Harmony* and *Rhumba*—in bits or as a chorus girl. In 1935, she signed with the Small and Landau Agency, who secured her small parts in *King of Burlesque, Anything Goes* (she had a crush on the star, Bing Crosby) and *My Man Godfrey*. The Depression was in full swing and the Fulks-Weymann family barely hung together ("All we had was a roof over our head"). Sarah Jane's meager paychecks were badly needed as Morie's practice dwindled alarmingly.

To her great relief, Warners signed her to a contract on May 6, 1936, at sixty-five dollars a week, after insisting she change her name. Seated in the front office with her agent (William Demarest from Small and Landau, a silent-screen actor who later became well known as a character actor), she had to make a quick decision. Since she had never liked her first name, dropping the Sarah was not difficult. She would call herself Jane—but Jane what? She said "Weymann," it apparently being the first name that came to mind. "Jane Wyman," the studio executive decreed.

For two years Warners cast her in B-picture comedy roles as a brassy, empty-headed blonde. The image was one that carried over into her private life. "She was a fly-away girl, very blonde, liking only the frivolous things," one old friend commented. But another added, "I always thought there was something sad about Janie—like the guy who tries desperately to be the life of the party because he's really insecure. In reality she was never the party girl she appeared. She just wanted to be liked, to be part of the 'in' group." There were many "in" groups in Hollywood—the "kids" (the young potential stars), the big studio "brass," the "head-hunters" (intellectuals), and the "Broadway Joes" (the theater folk who came but protested they would never stay). Jane was terribly ambitious, constantly working to improve her talent. A number of the girls who had danced in films with her were now on their way to stardom—Paulette Goddard, who had become involved with Charlie Chaplin, for one.

Jane's name appeared in movie magazines and gossip columns as having been seen at the Trocadero or the Cocoanut Grove in the company of one or another available man-about-town. Judging by the list of escorts, it seems her inclination was toward older men. In 1936, she met Myron Futterman, thirty-five years old and divorced (newspaper accounts of their courtship erroneously age him considerably). Futterman owned a successful dress company in Los Angeles, although he still maintained ties to his hometown of New Orleans. He had the soft, graceful charm of a Southern gentleman. The father of a teenage girl only six years younger than Jane, he had a paternalistic attitude toward his young girlfriend. They were married in New Orleans on June 29, 1937. Futterman had met her in a period of his life when he was chasing his youth. Once he was married, his needs changed. He expected her to settle down, to do away with her brassy blonde look, to let her career go and become his wife and a hostess to his business associates, whereas she had thought he would help her to succeed. Three months after the wedding, the couple separated.

On November 10, 1938, seventeen months after their marriage, Jane filed suit for divorce on grounds of mental cruelty, claiming Futterman was obsessively jealous, did not want a child (whereas she did), and constantly compared her to his former wife. The divorce was amicable. Futterman gave her a small settlement which included the car he had bought her, the furnishings of their apartment (which she retained), lawyers' fees and a thousand dollars in cash. The final decree came through in December 1938, several months after principal photography had been completed on *Brother Rat*.

To promote the film, Warners did a score of photographic layouts of the cast. Wyman and Reagan were called to the gallery (photography department) to pose together. There had been a mix-up in the appointment, and they had a long wait. "My first impulse, as always, was to resent it," Wyman remembered, "to feel that my rights had been imposed upon, feel that someone was 'pushing us around.'

"'It's just a mistake,' Ronnie soothed. 'It's no one's fault. No one would inconvenience us on purpose. . . .'

"I couldn't help wondering if some of his easy good nature

could be an 'act.' It didn't seem possible that a man could have so even a disposition consistently."

He asked her for a date to the premiere of *Second Fiddle*, a Sonja Henie film. One date led to another until they were seeing each other on a weekly basis. Reagan's attitude to her was protective (he was six years older), and she felt safe with him. Yet, at the same time her self-confidence began to slip. His knowledge overwhelmed her, and his dedication to his mother and his general goodness intimidated her.

"When he took me out to dinner, even at a strange restaurant, we always seemed to receive special consideration and particularly good service. That was because his manner was as kind, as friendly when he spoke to a waiter as it was when he spoke to a friend. The veriest strangers liked him on sight . . . it was no 'act.' It was the real Ronnie. He lived in an apartment not far from his father and mother. When he was between pictures he never let a day pass without dropping in to see them at least for a few minutes. If he was working he called every day from the studio and saw them on the weekend.

"His mother never had rigid rules when he was a boy. He was free to bring anyone he wanted home from school. When I was in [Los Angeles] high school . . . the girls in my group hero-worshipped the boys on the football squad. If one of them spoke to one of us in the corridor it was a thrill. You went to cheer practice and yelled your lungs out, picturing the dramatic spectacle. I was never allowed to see one of the football games . . . I had to be home at a certain hour each day and there were no excuses for not being there. . . . I never had a mother-and-daughter relationship. If I thought about running away from home when I was very young it was because I suffered a sort of claustrophobia—an imprisoned feeling at home [a main reason for her leaving high school to work]. Ronnie had this wonderful relationship with his mother. I sensed it. I wanted to have a part of it.

"I went to work to support myself when I was still in my early teens. I had been punished at home for things I did not understand, things I had thought were the right thing to do. . . . I went around most of the time with a mild form of hate eating into me. After I had the contract at the studio . . . I was constantly on the alert for signs that someone was trying to spoil my job for me. I suspected a hairdresser of trying to ruin my looks for a test . . . a press agent for trying to make me look silly in print. . . . I trusted Ronnie. For the first time in my life I truly trusted someone."

*   *   *

Although *Brother Rat* was the most substantial film he had yet made, his third-place position ("[Eddie] Albert gives a splendid performance . . . Wayne Morris provides a good characterization . . . Ronald Reagan is fine as the third member of the group . . .") did not advance his career. From January to October 1939, he appeared in nine films. *Going Places* (January 9, 1939)* had little to recommend it except a marvelous rendition of the song "Jeepers Creepers" (the name of the horse in this race film) by Louis Armstrong. Once again, Reagan was in a film with Dick Powell. The most that could be said of his role as a member of the wealthy, horsey set was, "Ronald Reagan has a minor assignment that is taken care of satisfactorily." March found him cast as Lieutenant Brass Bancroft in *Secret Service of the Air*† (March 2, 1939). "All we can say," said the *New York Times* reviewer, "is that the Warners have made considerable melodramatic ado about nothing, since the new film is an uninspired reworking of the old story about smuggling aliens across the border."

Despite such reviews, Warners again picked up Reagan's option. Though he was not exactly in the money, his salary allowed him to upgrade his living accommodations. He moved from the Montecito Apartments to 1128 Cory Avenue, a small cottage with a lovely yard on a corner above Sunset Boulevard. Jack and Nelle were only five minutes away, as was Barney's Beanery, but he seldom appeared at the latter anymore. He had not exactly "gone Hollywood," but he had changed his social habits considerably. He dated various young starlets and took them to good restaurants or went dancing (he loved to ballroom dance and was good at it) at places like the Cocoanut Grove.

David Selznick had purchased film rights for the play *Dark Victory* for Merle Oberon and then abandoned the idea of making it. Warners subsequently acquired the property (for twenty-seven thousand dollars) for Kay Francis. Following Cagney's example, Francis, to the studio's surprise, had not accepted the plum role and sued to get out of her contract. Warners cast Bette Davis, who had recently returned to the lot after losing a court case to Jack Warner. Davis had been offered a top role by Alexander Korda and had gone to England—"in the hope of adding a few

---

* Parentheses indicate date of general release.

† One of the most ridiculous bits of film censorship occurred during the filming of *Secret Service of the Air* when Warners was asked (and complied) to cut a scene (page ninety-seven of the script) in which Reagan entered a hallway that contained a door marked REST ROOM.

cubits to her reputation" by appearing in a Korda film—and filed suit there to break her contract. Much chastened and somewhat poorer with her defeat, Davis honored her contract and accepted the secondhand role. But she had not completely swallowed her resentment.

Though the ultimate in soap-opera tearjerkers, the film was Reagan's first journey into the world of the super–upper-crust movie. Davis had recently won the Academy Award for her portrayal as Jezebel and, despite her lawsuit, she remained the studio's top female star. It is always difficult to remember the other performers in a Davis film, and seeing Humphrey Bogart in a supporting role as a horse trainer sexually drawn to Davis's rich society girl comes as a surprise whenever the film is viewed. George Brent as a brain surgeon is the leading man. (The studio had wanted to borrow Spencer Tracy from MGM for this role, but Tracy was unavailable.*) Reagan was given fifth billing as Alex Hamm, a wealthy "frequently inebriated" dilettante hopelessly in love with the giddy socialite (Davis as Judith Traherne) who suffers a fatal brain tumor. *Dark Victory*, with a budget of $517,000, was one of the four truly prestigious films Reagan made during his long Hollywood career,† and he gave a one-dimensional performance. Part of his problem could well have been that while filming *Dark Victory* he had to do retakes for *Secret Service of the Air* (because of censorship cuts), and the transition from Brass Bancroft to Alex Hamm could not have been easy. Still, the character was the kind Lew Ayres (and later Robert Walker and Van Heflin) could have turned into a dazzling cameo even with Davis stealing every scene. Ayres had managed a similar feat the year before as Hepburn's alcoholic brother in *Holiday*.

Reagan claimed his big scene in *Dark Victory* was badly acted because the director, Edmund Goulding, did not give him his head and let him play it as he saw the character. "He was a top director, doing only top pictures [among them *Grand Hotel* and *Love* with Garbo], I was up in that class on a rain check. He didn't get what he wanted, whatever the hell that was, and I

---

* "Tracy was born to play this part," Casey Robinson, the writer of the screenplay, memoed to Hal Wallis on August 9, 1938. "And of course I don't need to tell you what the combination of the names of Bette Davis and Spencer Tracy on the marquee would do to the box office." Basil Rathbone made a test for the role that was so bad, he wrote Warner: "Would you either let me have [the test] or destroy it yourself . . ."
† The others were *Knute Rockne*, *Kings Row* and *The Hasty Heart*, which was his biggest-budget film, $1.25 million, at Warner Brothers.

ended up not delivering the line [s] the way my instinct told me [they] should be delivered." The antagonism with Goulding began early in the production. "I was playing, he told me, the kind of fellow who could sit in the girls' dressing room dishing the dirt while they went on dressing in front of me. I had no trouble seeing him in that role, but for myself I want to think I can stroll through where the girls are short of clothes, and there will be a great scurrying about and taking to cover."

The last statement says quite a lot about Reagan's sense of sexuality, while at the same time it displays a total lack of sensitivity to the actor's craft. He felt that not only was Goulding less than masculine ("He saw my part as a copy of his own earlier life") but also that the director wanted him to play the role with sexual ambivalence. Goulding was right. He understood that Alex Hamm drank because he felt impotent and loved a woman like Judith Traherne because she was unattainable. The character might very well *not* be a practicing homosexual but a man struggling with his sexuality and tragically losing the battle. Reagan could not deal with anything other than black and white. Yet, he was capable of identifying with the roles he played. This was one reason he enjoyed doing the Secret Service films, in which he was the macho superhero.

He had been given a good supporting role in a major film and did not score. His personal dislike of Goulding had been a rare exception to his reputation of always being obliging, pleasant and—better than anything else—noncompetitive. He was shoved into *Naughty But Nice,* another Dick Powell musical potboiler, in which Ann Sheridan (ballyhooed as the "oomph girl") had top billing, and which Bosley Crowther in *The New York Times* would dismiss by writing: "Staffed by a competent cast of pranksters . . . this item might be steady fun if it were anything more than a batch of old gags strung together."

His next two films, *Hell's Kitchen* and *Angels Wash Their Faces,* had him supporting the Dead End Kids. In the first, "Margaret Lindsay and Ronald Reagan are nicely teamed." In the second, "Miss Sheridan is happily married off to the District Attorney's handsome son [Reagan]." Judging by the poor reviews on *Smashing the Money Ring,* his next Lieutenant Brass Bancroft epic (whose title tells it all), one wonders seriously why Reagan's option was picked up again. But he was cast in *Brother Rat and a Baby.*

The entire cast had been reassembled for the sequel to *Brother Rat.* Jane Bryan was now engaged to a man named Justin Dart and planned to marry and leave the screen. Dart, as coincidence would have it, was in the process of divorcing Ruth Walgreen, Charles Walgreen's daughter, although he had maintained his business connections with Walgreen and owned a large piece of the business, given to him during his marriage to Ruth. Dart was a large, gruff man, dogmatic in his opinions. Reagan and Dart hit it off straightaway. They had the Walgreens and Jane Bryan in common. But it was more than that. Justin Dart had a fantastic grasp of economics, and he and Reagan could go around and around debating issues for hours. While Hal Gross had not been able to win many points with Reagan, Dart, also a Republican, did score. During the production of the film, German troops had invaded Poland, bombs fell on Warsaw and Great Britain went to war. Dart was concerned that a war in Europe might provide a pretext for Roosevelt to run for a third term, an idea that had been circulating ever since the 1936 election.* Roosevelt had led the country out of the Depression and the people trusted him. But Dart wanted Reagan to understand that other forces were in-volved—the big-city bosses who were reluctant to lose their power, and the New Deal bureaucrats afraid they might lose their jobs. A lot of Reagan's naïveté was disappearing. Larry Williams noted that for the first time, though still a strong Roosevelt sup-porter, Reagan faulted the Democratic party about high federal payrolls. From this point on, Justin Dart was to have a great in-fluence on Reagan's political views.

Reagan had been dating Wyman on a fairly steady basis dur-ing the making of *Brother Rat and a Baby*.† The cast recognized that Jane was very much in love with Reagan, but he treated her in a casual way, calling her "a good scout," "loads of fun to be with," not exactly the descriptive phrases used by a man in love. At the end of principal photography, Jane suffered a recurrence of an old stomach disorder and was hospitalized. Reagan sent flowers with a card: "Hope you're feeling better, Ronald." When he appeared at the hospital during visiting hours, Elsie Wyatt greeted him in

---

*Reagan was for the idea of a third term for Roosevelt. In October 1986, he publicly endorsed the idea of no limit on presidential terms. "The people should be able to vote for whoever they wish," he said at a Republican fund-raising event.

†The baby in the film was Peter B. Good and the child had a dummy for a stand-in. Elsa Maxwell, famous for her parties given for the Duke and Duchess of Windsor, hosted a publicity party for Warners in honor of Peter B. Good at the Hollywood Roosevelt Hotel preceding the premiere. The invitations noted: "Free parking for tricycles and scooters." Peter B. Good was anything but pleased—he was brought screaming into the room and left, still screaming, fifteen minutes later.

the corridor to tell him that Jane did not want to see him. He returned again the next day. This time he refused to be barred from her room. When he left, they were engaged to be married.

First he told Nelle and Jack and then the studio, who gave Louella Parsons the scoop. Parsons then approached Warners with the idea of sending Reagan and Wyman and other contract players on a tour with her and they agreed. The final group consisted of Parsons, Reagan, Wyman, Susan Hayward, June Preisser, Arlene Whelan* and Joy Hodges, who had returned to Hollywood after her success in the Rodgers and Hart musical and had just had a featured role in Universal's *Little Accident*. "Jane was . . . making jokes constantly, [and was] terribly jealous of Ronald Reagan, with whom she was falling in love," Parsons recalled of the first days of the tour. Susan Hayward's attention to Reagan had distressed his fiancée (who sported a reported fifty-two-caret amethyst engagement ring—which was Reagan's birthstone).

The variety-show format of "Hollywood Stars of 1940 on Parade" met with some indifference when it made its debut at San Francisco's RKO Golden Gate, sharing the bill with Jean Hersholt in a Doctor Christian film. "Hot diggity! Movie stars, movie stars, movie stars!" Paul Spiegle of the *San Francisco Chronicle* sniped. "The Golden Gate is just crawling with them. . . . It's an autograph fiend's dream . . . they [all] pirouetted prettily before their groggy fans, and then Louella Parsons, with 'honey' and 'darling' bubbling from every pore, walked upon the scene." Before this point the audience had had to sit through three other vaudeville acts (Barney Grant, "Hillbilly Humor"; Heller and Ruley, "Songs and Gags"; and the Six Tumbling Jordans) which had seemed endless. Swathed in mink, choked with pearls, Parsons "gurgled in the best high school elocution class manner, 'Hello, am I late?'"

Then out came the Hollywood Stars Chorus, singing "Oh, Louella" to the music of "Oh, Susanna," ending each verse with:

"Oh, Louella, won't you mention me.
For a movie star in Hollywood, that's what I want to be."

This was followed by a screen short ("not short enough," complained *Variety*'s Pat Kelly) of Parsons and the tour group being given a star send-off in Hollywood with the likes of Deanna Dur-

---

*Hayward had recently been featured in *Beau Geste*, Preisser in *Babes in Arms* and Whelan in *Young Mr. Lincoln*.

bin, Errol Flynn, Sonja Henie, Tyrone Power, Eleanor Powell, Fred Astaire, Mickey Rooney and the Lane Sisters all wishing her well. The added "treat" of the show was Parsons dictating and teletyping her daily column. A teletype machine was set up onstage. First Parsons pulled strips of paper from the machine and read off "breathless tidbits, such as William Powell and Ginger Rogers had been seen holding hands . . . and Mickey Rooney's real age [two years older than the studio biography]." Then, from a prop telephone she "talked" to Charlie Chaplin and Claudette Colbert. Finally, she interviewed the members of her group "and told them how she had predicted stardom for each and every one of them, and they all seemed so grateful . . . when the gushing stopped . . . the stars themselves went into their different turns, the show, with a few possible exceptions, got back on its feet and headed in the right direction."

Variety found "Ronald Reagan very personable, deft and obviously at home on a stage. [He] is in and out of the act throughout, talking with Lolly [Parsons], kidding with the girls, and doing brief comedy sketches with Jane Wyman and Susan Hayward."

Wyman, the *San Francisco Chronicle* noted, "looked exceptionally beautiful, got into a silly argument with Ronald Reagan which brought titters from the audience . . . Susan Hayward clowned nicely through a corny murder scene with Reagan." These acts were followed by "Joy Hodges, who ably demonstrates her good voice with a torchy 'Day-in, Day-out' . . . Arleen Whelan . . . who sings, 'South American Way' with mild undulations of her trim torso, and finally, the hit of the show—little June Preisser who has . . . more talent than all the others with her song and dance routine. From the standpoint of audience approval she is the brightest of the stars. The salvo she gets is prolonged, spontaneous and deserved; whereas the applause for some of the others is but the conventional polite acknowledgment tendered all celebs and visiting firemen by generous San Francisco audiences. . . . It [the tour] may go big, but as it looked at its opening stand, it's nothing to stand in line for—and nobody did."

Parsons had chartered a plane to take the group east to their next engagement at the Earle in Philadelphia. They flew all night through a blinding snowstorm and finally were forced down in Chicago, proceeding by train from there. Reagan had never flown before and he vowed he would never do so again.* ("Dutch kept

* For many years after, Reagan suffered a traumatic fear of flying. Only late in his life did he overcome it.

everyone singing until we finally fell asleep. He was a *rock,*" Hodges recalls of the flight.) In Philadelphia the act was tightened, and Parsons traded in her mink for a smart, dark suit. This time they followed five lady jugglers in gold metal cloth with phosphorescent hoops and dumbbells, and two acrobats—an Amazonian woman, six feet six inches, and a male dwarf, three feet eight inches, dressed in identical black velvet ensembles. The group's East Coast reception was more rewarding. They played to full houses and were individually cheered and plagued for autographs. The Earle Theatre was forced to employ extra security personnel to protect the visitors from their "too-enthusiastic admirers."

Except for Reagan, Wyman and Joy Hodges, The Hollywood Stars did not fraternize much offstage. Hodges had been married on September 2 to Gilbert H. Doorly, a newspaper executive on his father's paper, the *Omaha World Herald,* but had returned to Hollywood to finish her Universal contract commitments.* "Dutch was always the 'Father Figure' with the group," she says. "Anything that went wrong we turned to him. He was always patient with everybody. . . . He and Jane were very much in love and she was concerned with the way Susan Hayward beat him up in their little scene on stage. Dutch thought it was funny and the audience loved it. Dutch was our Master of Ceremonies."

On the one free day in Washington, D.C., where they were appearing at the Capitol Theatre, Reagan talked Wyman and Hodges into accompanying him to Mount Vernon, George Washington's home—a long drive for performers who had been doing four shows a day. Hodges recalled how eager Reagan was to go there and how fascinated with everything he was once there— "especially with Washington's personal writing desk." (Wyman later had a replica of it made for Reagan's study.)

The tour ended the second week in January. Wyman and Reagan had set the date, January 26, for their wedding, and Parsons had insisted the reception be at her home. They applied for their license and were married at the Wee Kirk O'Heather Church in Glendale by Reverend C. Kleihauer (a powerful speaker and a nationally recognized church leader), pastor of the Hollywood-Beverly Christian Church.† Of the family, Jack, Nelle, Moon and

---

* Hodges's first marriage was not successful and lasted less than two years. A second marriage to Eugene Scheiss has been a long and happy union.

† The Reagans took formal membership in the Hollywood-Beverly Christian Church on May 12, 1940. The church had a membership of approximately seventeen hundred and was considered to be "a fairly liberal main-line congregation."

Bessie were present, as were Emma Fulks and Elsie Wyatt. Bill
Cook, one of Reagan's TEKE friends, was best man. Mrs. Wayne
Morris and Mrs. Erving (Betty) Kaplan were bridesmaids, and
Elsie was matron of honor. The plans after the wedding were for
the newlyweds to move into Jane's apartment in a terraced building overlooking Sunset Strip only three blocks from Reagan's
bachelor bungalow. Apartment 5, 1326 Londonderry View, had a
sensational view, private entrance, two bedrooms and a maid's
room and bath (which Reagan turned into an office). The wedding photographs made the newlyweds look like paper-doll cut-
outs. Reagan had his hair slicked into place, a white carnation
was poked into the lapel of his dark-blue suit, a white hand-
kerchief folded in overlapping triangles protruded from his breast
pocket. Wyman wore a pale-blue satin princess-style gown, and a
mink hat that perched at a saucy angle with a bridal veil uniquely
reversed into a huge bow at the back of it. A mink muff covered in
orchids completed her wedding ensemble. In the excitement of the
exchange of vows, they forgot the traditional bridal kiss.

They were the last guests to leave their reception and drove off
for their honeymoon in Palm Springs in a new car, Reagan having
given (or sold to) Moon the convertible. Moon had been managing station WOC when he got the idea that what films needed was
a second Reagan, and he and Bessie had taken off for California,
burning all their bridges behind them. An irreversible pattern had
set in between the brothers. Reagan held the dominant position.
But it was not as though Moon walked in his shadow. Reagan
respected Moon's opinion and liked to have him near at hand.

To those fascinated with the lives of film stars, the Wyman-
Reagan marriage was a fairy-tale affair. Reagan had all the attributes of an American hero—a young man with ideals who
treated women (mother, bride and leading ladies) reverently. Wyman was a divorcée, a free-wheeling liberated woman. The public,
Parsons and the general press assumed the "hotcha" blonde had
been redeemed, that what was required for a happy ending, and
perhaps salvation, was a stalwart, old-fashioned American husband.

Rain fell during most of the honeymoon, disrupting the
groom's plans to teach his wife to swim and for them to play golf
(one of Wyman's hobbies). Nonetheless, the future appeared
sunny. Both husband and wife had careers that were going forward. The Depression was over, leaving the country and Americans bound closer than ever. The war in Europe, although
building with a terrible ferocity, still seemed distant. Despite the

rain, the Reagans should have been in a euphoric state. Wyman later claimed that she, at least, was not, having suddenly realized that the man she had just married was obsessed, not by her but by the insidious climate of evil he saw encroaching from two directions—Europe on the one hand, and Communist forces in the United States on the other.

10

BECAUSE HE AND JANE LIKED GOLF, REAGAN AP-
plied for membership (by coincidence at the same time as Jack
Warner) to the Lakeside Country Club, located in North Hollywood a short distance from the studio. The Reagans were accepted; Warner was not. Reagan asked another member how this
could have happened. Lakeside catered to Gentiles, he was told.
"You're anti-Semitic!" Reagan accused. "You're damn right
we're anti-Semitic," was the reply. Reagan resigned. Another
member claims that Lakeside did have some Jewish members and
that Warner was rejected because so many of his employees belonged to Lakeside "and we [didn't] want him looking over our
shoulder and saying the next day, 'Why weren't you at work?'"
Warner was known for his right-wing political views and his tact-
less sense of humor (when introduced to Madame Chiang Kai-
shek, the wife of the Chinese Nationalist leader, he had muttered,
"Too bad I forgot my laundry!") and is reported to have commented on Reagan's defiance of Lakeside's intolerance, "So what?
How soon [would it have been] before they found out his grand-

father was Moishe Rosen, the delicatessen man?" By now, Reagan and Warner had more than a nodding acquaintance. Both Jane and Reagan referred to him as "Boss"; he called them "Ron" and "Janie," or "you kids." But the relationship never left the studio. The Reagans were not part of Ann and Jack Warner's social orbit. Warner, thinking of himself as a kindred spirit to William Randolph Hearst, made an annual trek to Europe with his wife, returning with so many antiques that associates named his Beverly Hills estate "San Simeonette."

Many of Reagan's early notes to Warner reflect a great deference. He admired Boss and tried earnestly to please him, and, indeed, did. Errol Flynn, on the other hand, looked at Warner as a ludicrous man and treated him gruffly. Enmity existed between these two men, but Flynn's popularity kept Warner in line. Although Warner attempted the look of a leading man, his receding hairline, the long white-collared shirts tight around his short, stout neck, the even white-toothed smile that could fade in a flicker, the pin-striped suits gave him a comic look. He also had a sarcastic, juvenile sense of humor. In a restaurant he would often turn to the waiter with an ashtray from the table with the remark, "Here, take this back and have them put some more butter on it." When he saw the French word *poisson* (for fish) on a menu, he would say, "So you serve poison here, eh?" When an interviewer asked, "I understand you're quite a raconteur?" he replied, "That's right, I play a hell of a game of tennis!" Nonetheless, Reagan's stand in Warner's favor and against anti-Semitism earned high marks from Warner, despite his flippant comment.

Ronald Reagan would never have knowingly joined any organization that ostracized a minority. His parents' training was too ingrained. If the person denied membership on grounds of religion or color had been unknown to him, the odds are he would still have resigned. His fellow workers at Warners were as well aware of this as they were of his dedication to Franklin Delano Roosevelt. This facet of his personality and his strong interest in labor convinced the left wing of Hollywood that Reagan was one of them. But there were many issues that the left wing supported and many ideologies with which they sympathized that made it impossible for Reagan ever to join their ranks.

An extraordinary misconception existed for many decades: that a film actor's true self was revealed in the image onscreen, that he or she played the same role in life. A few stars—Garbo, Barrymore, Flynn, Monroe—did attempt to become the creature invented by studio publicists and executives, almost always with tragic results because the private being could never be completely put down. Reagan had more substance than the characters he played, and far from being the scatty blonde she appeared onscreen, Jane Wyman was an intelligent, ambitious woman who had a great need to be loved and perceived as a person of consequence. She *believed* she was an artist, not just a face on the screen. Even early in her career, when she was playing the smallest role, her directors claim she would ask a million questions about the character.

"Janie was always intent on *making it*," one of her longtime friends said. "She never liked the dumb-blonde label. But she played it to the hilt—flashy clothes, heavy makeup at premieres, occasions when she was on display. At home, with friends, she was another person. Whenever there was enough time between films she would let her hair go back to its natural brown. I think she always felt she was playing a part when her hair was blond. . . . Jane was articulate—*very*. She cared about people—*a lot*. I think she saw Reagan as a father figure and she admired his mind. But, in private, she could also be just Sarah Jane with him. She cared about her home, liked to cook, loved animals and was the most loyal friend anyone could have. She had gone to school [in Los Angeles] with Betty Kaplan. Betty was always her best friend. Becoming a film star never changed that."

After his resignation at Lakeside, the Reagans joined the Hillcrest Country Club in Beverly Hills, not far from Twentieth Century-Fox studios. Hillcrest had a large Jewish membership, with many top film names included. At Hillcrest the Reagans became friendly with other golf-loving celebrities—Jack Benny and his wife Mary Livingstone, and George Burns and Gracie Allen among them. Their life as a couple began to take shape. They often drove to Warners together and worked together when the studio cast them in *An Angel from Texas* (based on the George S. Kaufman play *The Butter and Egg Man*). Reagan received fifth billing beneath Eddie Albert, Wayne Morris, Rosemary Lane and Wyman, who played his wife. Somewhat amusing, the film was too lightweight to get much critical attention, and once again Reagan's role as a straight man to Morris did nothing to advance his career.

Wyman had been an active member of the Screen Actors Guild for several years before her marriage to Reagan, helping on committees whenever she could. Her involvement brought Reagan into a closer affiliation with, and interest in, SAG activities. They attended SAG open meetings, played golf at the club on Saturdays, attended church and had the older Reagans for dinner on Sundays. Moon, too, was intent on an acting career. "After the easy way I got in, I had the idea crashing the movies was a cinch," Reagan told a reporter in 1939. "Right away I tried to help a lot of others [his friends from TEKE] do the same thing, and I found I couldn't even get a pass to allow a friend to visit the studio." He did manage to get Moon through the front gate and elicited a promise from Bryan Foy that he would try Moon out in one or two small roles. Moon and Bess had rented an apartment in a bungalow court on Chantilly Drive, four doors south of Beverly Boulevard and Nelle and Jack, now lived nearby at 9031 Phyllis Avenue, in a small but comfortable house with their own backyard and front porch.

Jane had not had as easy an entrée into films as had Reagan, and she believed in making her own breaks, which often meant going after a better role in an active manner. Reagan had an idea that the Notre Dame football star George Gipp, who had died a premature death while at the university, would be a character well suited for the basis of a film and for a role he could play. Wyman encouraged him to act upon it. Reagan did not know how to approach the project—write a treatment, a script, or what. He talked to Foy and several others on the lot, but no one picked up on it. Then, to his amazement, an announcement appeared in *Variety* that Warner Brothers had scheduled *The Life of Knute Rockne*** to star Pat O'Brien† and was looking for an actor to play coach Rockne's most famous player, George Gipp, the great Gipper.

O'Brien claimed Reagan approached him and asked if he would "put in a word" for him with Warner and Wallis. "I've been a great fan of Gipp's throughout his career, and I've read just about everything that's been written on him and Rockne."

"They may want a name actor," O'Brien hedged.

"I can play the part. I won't let you down if I get the assignment."

---

* Later changed to *Knute Rockne—All American.*
† Warners had originally wanted to cast James Cagney as Knute Rockne. His popularity was at a high (number four in the box office for male stars in 1938) while O'Brien had not even surfaced in the top fifty. "It is a simple matter of arithmetic," Robert Buckner, the script writer, wrote Father O'Donnell (business manager of Notre Dame). "Cagney would insure the picture's success. O'Brien would not." Mrs. Rockne, who had final approval of casting, wanted O'Brien, however, and he was cast.

O'Brien spoke to Wallis, who was unimpressed. The role called for a top performer. Reagan was "a hick radio announcer from the Middle West."

"Hal, I've watched this kid around the lot," O'Brien pressed. "He not only resembles Gipp but his knowledge . . . of football should help the picture."

Wallis was still not convinced.

Reagan took his pleas to Foy, who told him to go see Wallis, who was responsible for the production. Wallis told Reagan he could not envision him as a strong football type. "I was still too new in this business and too recent from the sports world to be polite," Reagan admitted. "So I said, 'You are producing the picture and you don't know that Gipp weighed five pounds less than I weigh right now. He walked with a sort of slouch and limp. He looked like a football player only when he was on the field.'" Wallis remained dubious. Reagan left the studio, drove home and returned an hour later with an old photograph of himself as one of Mac's Golden Tornadoes. Wallis, weakening, asked Reagan to test and Reagan agreed.

Graciously, Pat O'Brien did the test with him. (O'Brien had "sweated out a series of tests . . . that were subject to Mrs. Rockne's approval." Still photos had been made of him "in ten different sets of wigs," and he was sensitive to Reagan's uneasiness.) "I really didn't have to learn my lines," Reagan claimed. "I had known Gipp's story for years. My lines were straight from Rock's diary. Our test scene was where Gipp, ordered to carry the ball at that first practice, cocked an eyebrow and asked Rockne, 'How far?'" He got the part, which did not have a lot of footage but was an actor's dream with "a great entrance, an action middle, and a death scene to finish up."

William ("Bill") K. Howard was set to direct. Howard had made a number of successful films in the early thirties, notably the 1932 version of *Sherlock Holmes* starring Clive Brook; in 1933, *The Power and the Glory* (thought by many to have been the prototype for *Citizen Kane*), a story of the rise and fall of a tycoon starring Spencer Tracy; and in 1937, *Fire over England,* made in Great Britain and which produced a memorable portrait of Queen Elizabeth I by Flora Robson and striking portrayals of star-crossed lovers by Laurence Olivier and Vivien Leigh. Howard had remained in England for two years and returned to Hollywood to find studio gates closed to him, partly because of his defection to England and partly because his emotional behavior often made working with him difficult. His temperament would not have mattered had

his more recent films been money-makers, but they had been programmers that had not done well. Hal Wallis hired him recalling
some of the good work he had done for Warners in the past, but
after one week of shooting believed he had made a mistake; Lloyd
Bacon was assigned to the film before Howard had been informed
that he had been fired. Robert Fellows, the associate producer,
was given the job of breaking the news to Howard, and he in turn
appealed to O'Brien (a friend and neighbor of Howard's) to accompany him on this difficult chore.

"We walked over. It was like going to a wake—the 'Dead
March' from the opera 'Saul.' Bill [Howard] greeted us enthusiastically, with the script in front of him. . . . Bob [Fellows] said
softly, 'I don't know how to tell you this, Bill, the easy way.
They're taking you off the picture.'

"Howard walked to the end of the room and beat his fists
together. '. . . this will destroy me,' he cried."*

O'Brien tried unsuccessfully to comfort him and the two men
left. Bacon was on the set early the next morning. "Hell, I'm a
great friend of Howard's," he protested, "and his chair is still
warm." But he plunged into his job with a vengeance.

Nick Lukats, a former all-star halfback and punter at Notre
Dame, and Jim Thorpe (probably the greatest all-around athlete
America had produced—Olympic gold-medal winner for broad
jump, shot put and decathlon and former halfback for Carlisle
Indian School and the Canton Bulldogs) were technical advisers
on the picture, but neither O'Brien nor Reagan used doubles. "I
was forty years old but I blocked and tackled and was on the
receiving end of all the passes in every one of the scrimmage
plays," O'Brien proudly stated. To Wallis's great surprise and
relief, Reagan looked every inch a champion on the field, although
his virtuoso scrimmage scenes were the combined efforts of talented technicians on-camera and in the cutting room. Wallis grew
more enthusiastic about Reagan as the shooting progressed.

Reagan's career looked as though it had taken an upward
swing. He had married a terrific lady whom he loved and who
loved him, his option had been picked up and there were plans to
renegotiate it. Warners had hopes that *Knute Rockne* might make
him a star. A company known as Music Corporation of America

---

*Howard never made a major film again, although he did direct a few low-budget produc-
tions before he was forced into "retiring" in 1946 at the age of forty-seven. He died seven
years later.

(MCA) had bought out the Meiklejohn Agency and Art Parks and Lew Wasserman were now representing Reagan and Wyman. In fact, they represented almost every major star on the Warner Brothers lot.

The MCA/SAG forces that were to bind the restless, disparate parts of Ronald Reagan's personality had clicked into place. The final force, the one that would give him his ultimate direction—his connection with General Electric and big business—would not happen for another decade. Reagan was in Act Two of his career. Hollywood took surprised note. This Reagan guy was not the naïf they thought he was.

A stubby, wispy-voiced, former ophthalmologist named Julius Caesar Stein, but who preferred to be called "Jules," was the man who ran MCA. He had financed his medical studies at the University of Chicago by playing the violin and saxophone in clubs around town, and finally by promoting bands. After two years (1922–24) at Chicago's Cook County Hospital, he realized he could make more money as a booking agent than as an eye doctor. He founded Music Corporation of America with one thousand dollars in 1924. Five years later, he had a 10 percent interest in half of the major bands in the country, booking them into hotels and nightclubs. Radio was the next medium to conquer.

He turned to his boyhood chum, labor boss James Caesar Petrillo, the founder and head of the American Federation of Musicians (AFM). Petrillo was a powerful ally, described in his time as "a small man with a gruff style, [who] speaks salty, ungrammatical English in a grating voice . . . rides around in a bullet proof limousine . . . [and is] a shrewd and treacherous political infighter who rules his union like a dictator." Petrillo exerted his power to block other talent agencies from obtaining licenses to represent band musicians, thereby giving Stein a monopoly over big bands in America. The MCA/AFM alliance smacked of the kind of control practiced by Chicago mobsters. In any dispute between a musician and MCA, Petrillo's union always sided with the agency.*

---

*In 1945, a union official and witness in a Justice Department investigation into the MCA/AFM connection was to claim that there had never been a union member who won a case before the AFM board against MCA. Stein also obtained from Petrillo a "blanket waiver" giving MCA the right to counteract AFM's bylaws and operate "as both agent and production company," a violation of union bylaws he repeated with SAG.

Stein had been dealing with Al Capone and the Chicago mobs since his early agency days, when bootleg whiskey was part of the deal for booking bands. Somewhere along the line, he had arranged a truce with the Chicago Mafia, cutting them in for a healthy percentage of both talent and alcohol. Petrillo's union salary was twenty-six thousand dollars a year at its peak, yet he, along with Stein, was a millionaire by the mid-forties, feeding the fire of accusations that Stein gave cash and other payoffs to Petrillo to build his personal empire.

Mobster tactics were not unknown to Hollywood. Willie Bioff, a minor Capone thug whose Chicago days had included pimping and "shaking down Kosher butchers," had been operating in Hollywood since 1933. Bioff's partner and buddy was George Browne, former head of Chicago's union for stagehands. The two men began their partnership by extorting twenty thousand dollars from Barney Balaban, owner of a midwestern theater chain, under the threat of initiating a projectionists strike. Bioff then took over the International Alliance of Theatrical Stage Employees and Motion Picture Operators (IATSE) and headed for Hollywood. By this time, many craft unions had sprung up in Hollywood and each was struggling for dominance. Bioff's union, although one of the smallest, controlled the projectionists. Bioff's scam (which worked for many years) was to threaten the men who ran the major studios (MGM, Warner Brothers, Twentieth Century-Fox and Paramount) with a projectionists strike. Darkened theaters in the midst of the Depression would have meant economic doom. George Browne became president of the IATSE. Within two years that union went from 168 members to 12,000 of Hollywood's crafts people and technicians, absorbing numerous small unions which had had little clout with the studios. In 1936 Bioff and Browne made a deal with the four major studios for each of them to pay fifty thousand dollars annually (the independents were to pay twenty-five thousand) to "keep labor peace." But IATSE still did not represent all studio workers. SAG was one of the unions that remained independent. Robert Montgomery, SAG president at the time (1938–39),* described his union's situation: "There was an attempt on the part of IATSE to take over the Screen Actors Guild because they felt they would strengthen their organization . . . we were simply between the racketeering union which was attempting to destroy us by force and the attempt on the part

---

*Montgomery served a second term as SAG president in 1946–47.

of the producers to simply demolish the organization through negotiations—we were having a very rough time. . . ."

For the next few years Bioff was at the height of his power and SAG fought grimly to retain its independence. Then Montgomery had a "brainstorm." He appealed to the executive board for $5,000 (guaranteed by him)—no questions asked. They gave the money to him and he hired an ex-FBI man turned private detective to ferret out something in Bioff's past that would incriminate and remove him from Hollywood. Montgomery's daring idea worked; the detective uncovered a 1922 Chicago conviction for pimping that Bioff had "slipped out of serving." SAG urged extradition and California's Governor Olson agreed to sign the order. Bioff might have been able to fight this charge successfully had a $100,000 "loan" to him from movie mogul Joseph Schenk (chairman of the board of Twentieth Century-Fox) not led to the latter's conviction on a charge of income-tax evasion. Schenk plea-bargained to minimize his sentence to one year and told all he knew (which was a lot) about Browne and Bioff's game of extortion. Both were convicted and began twenty-year prison terms in 1941. But in 1940, when Reagan and Wyman attended SAG meetings together, the role these gangsters had played in controlling the Hollywood studios was a major point of discussion. Privately, the meteoric rise and the power of Jules Stein and MCA were hotly debated.

When Stein moved MCA to Hollywood in 1937, he began to represent general talent as well as musicians. His intention was to sign the industry's most famous and established stars. If he could accomplish this, he would have the same strong-arm hold on the major studios that thugs like Bioff had. Without stars, film companies could not make films. By controlling the biggest names, he could get exorbitant deals for lesser players as well. The first star to come through was Bette Davis. It has been said that Stein was so obsessed with landing Davis as a client that he hired her husband Harmon Nelson's best friend, Eddie Linsk (nicknamed "the Killer"), at a high fee to do nothing else but convince her to sign with MCA, a feat that was accomplished in three weeks. Errol Flynn, John Garfield and Barbara Stanwyck soon followed suit. For the next five years, Stein and MCA would purchase a large number of smaller agencies.*

---

* By 1945, they represented an estimated one third of all Hollywood stars and major directors and producers, and earned their nickname—"the Octopus." The expansion did not stop there. MCA "gobbled up" an estimated one half of Hollywood's major talent by 1950.

Power was Stein's objective, anonymity his credo. An air of mystery around MCA was created by design. In the world Stein came from, talk could get a man killed. Publicity was for his clients, not the company. Stein altered the plaid-jacketed, flesh-peddling image of the Hollywood agent. By decree, his management team was ordered to wear only black or dark-gray suits, starched white shirts and conservative narrow ties. Hair was to be trimmed close, nails polished and shoes shined. Competitors soon derisively called MCA's executives "the black-suited Mafia." The dress code for secretaries and receptionists was equally austere.

The offices, housed in a large, rambling, well-manicured complex across the street from the Beverly Hills courthouse, looked as though it could have been an extension of the courthouse itself. Inside, Stein had created the same atmosphere of respectability. All the offices resembled each other and had dark paneled walls and maroon fabrics and carpets. Framed English hunting prints—obviously bought by the gross—decorated the walls. The carpets were so thick that no one could be heard coming or going.

Stein's protégé and MCA's vice-president was Lew Wasserman, a "tall, lanky, soft-spoken" former theater usher from Cleveland, Ohio. At age twenty-two, in 1936, Wasserman had met Stein when he was moonlighting as the publicity director for a local nightclub. Wasserman held only a high school diploma, but he was sharp and Stein immediately recognized his potential. When the Reagans met him in 1940, Wasserman was only twenty-seven, but he was fast becoming both Hollywood's most powerful executive and well on his way to the presidency of MCA. (In 1946, when Wasserman was named president, Stein told a reporter, "Lew was the student who surpassed the teacher. I made him president.") Jack Dales, who was director of SAG, said Wasserman got what he wanted "one way or the other. He had enemies all over town and still does [1981]. But people respect him, because he has power."

Wasserman could have been easily mistaken for a funeral director. Rarely did he smile and he always wore the dark suit–white shirt uniform. A workaholic, he could be found in his office seven days a week, sixteen hours a day. Underlings feared his irascible temper, describing him as a "cold, brusque" man when angry. As a deal-maker, he was a "ruthless, hard-nosed negotiator." Yet, he knew how to be smooth and charming when he needed to win over a client or an adversary. Wasserman had not sought the Reagans as clients. They had come to him as part of the Meiklejohn takeover. But once they were at MCA, Wasserman knew exactly how to use them.

From Reagan's first connection with MCA, he and Wasserman hit it off. Taft Schreiber, a top executive and the man who would later oversee Reagan's personal finances, said that Reagan "accepted MCA's career guidance without a fuss. He only had this one agency. This was it. It wasn't the agent's fault if things didn't go well. Most actors blamed their agents. He understood. He had a very sound grasp of the situation."

The situation was not all that difficult to grasp, especially at the time when the Reagans signed with MCA. Not only was Wyman earning the low Hollywood salary of $500 a week, in the year since her marriage she had played in a succession of forgettable films (*Flight Angels, My Love Came Back, Tugboat Annie Sails Again, Gambling on the High Seas* and *Honeymoon for Three*). Yet, on August 25, 1941, MCA negotiated a three-year contract with Warners for her, starting at $1,500 a week and rising to $2,500 a week. Reagan's contract was renegotiated by Wasserman in November to an increase to $1,628 a week for three years, rising to $2,750 a week in its last year. Wasserman had managed to triple the Reagans' earning capacity. No wonder Reagan was so respectful in doing whatever MCA suggested.

Knute Rockne—All American was ready for release by the first week in September. Reagan called the filming of it "a thrilling experience." (He later said: "I've always suspected that there might have been many actors in Hollywood who could have played the part better, but no one could have wanted to play it more than I did.") Mrs. Rockne was on the set each day as technical adviser. (The writing credits onscreen read: "Original Screenplay by Robert Buckner, based on the private papers of Mrs. Rockne and the reports of Rockne's associates and intimate friends.") Reagan was enraptured as Rockne's widow reminisced about her husband and Notre Dame between takes. And there he was wearing the great Gipper's football number, running eighty yards down a football field with a pigskin clutched tightly in his hand, crowds on the sidelines cheering wildly. His greatest fantasy had been realized.

The story followed the facts of Rockne's life explicitly, beginning with his arrival in the United States from Norway as a boy and continuing through his early struggle for an education, his college football years and, finally, his career as the football coach at Notre Dame. It ended with his own premature death in 1931 in an air crash. But the most moving moments in the film come with Reagan's death scene when he (as George Gipp) whispers to Rockne, "Someday, when the team's up against it, breaks are beating the boys, ask them to go in there with all they've got. Win one for the Gipper." Things got tough and "the boys" did exactly that.*

Reagan was counting on his role in *Knute Rockne—All American* to boost him to real stardom. He had made three films since *Brother Rat and a Baby—An Angel from Texas;* the last of the Brass Bancroft movies, *Murder in the Air;* and *Tugboat Annie Sails Again,* which brought back to the screen the character created by the incomparable Marie Dressler. In the last, Marjorie Rambeau took over as Tugboat Annie. Wyman played a debutante who falls in love with a penurious sailor (Reagan), and Moon Reagan appeared in a small role as one of Reagan's sailor friends (the performance that ended his career). The script demands were few and the humor was of the Billingsgate variety, with Miss Rambeau "lustily tossing harmless oaths and malapropisms." When the executives in Warners' front office saw the first print of *Knute Rockne—All American* in mid-September, they decided to hold back the release of *Tugboat Annie Sails Again,* a decision based on the hope that Reagan's appearance in the former might catapult him into becoming a box-office draw and so carry the latter with it.

Santa Fe Trail, starring Errol Flynn as the Confederate leader Jeb Stuart, was set to start shooting just two days after Warners saw the first print of *Knute Rockne—All American.* Jack Warner had originally sought John Wayne for the role of Custer, planning to make *Santa Fe Trail* a co-starring film. Wayne wired Warner:

I MUST REFUSE THE ROLE OF CUSTER IS NO MORE THAN A
FOIL TO JEB STUART [Flynn's role].

Wayne Morris was cast, but after a few days of shooting he was pulled and Reagan was handed the part. The first day of shooting,

---

*Although Buckner was given sole credit for the script of *Knute Rockne—All American,* the studio had purchased some additional material from a December 1938 *Cavalcade of America* radio script about Rockne. Included in this purchase was the famous "Win one for the Gipper" scene. Upon the 1940 release of the film, the writer of the radio drama threatened to sue. Warners made a settlement granting the studio all film rights but overlooking television provisions. Thus, in 1956, when the film was sold to television, the famous scene had to be deleted.

Reagan recalled being witness "to something I hope I will remember as long as I'm in this business [1964].* On a rack in the fitting room were cavalry uniforms tagged with the name of the actor [Morris] who, until that moment, had been assigned to the part. Into the room rushed a wardrobe man arms filled with uniforms hastily basted together for a first fitting. Without a word, he gathered the completed uniforms in one arm, threw them in a corner and hung the new ones in their place." He had learned how expendable an actor could be in Hollywood, and how cruelly competitive the business was.

Flynn was riding the crest of his popularity after such films as *Adventures of Robin Hood, The Private Lives of Elizabeth and Essex, Virginia City* and *The Sea Hawk.* He became "all the heroes in one magnificent sexy animal package," and offscreen he gained a reputation for his "hedonistic exploits, amorous escapades and barroom brawls" as a rogue and a Casanova. He had recently returned from war-riven Spain, where he had embroiled himself in some heroic (if unnecessary) exploits, and now had a totally confused idea of his own abilities.

Working with the egocentric Flynn forced Reagan to sharpen his talons. One night cast and crew stayed up until three A.M. rehearsing a cavalry campfire scene that had Flynn as a focal point while his men gathered in a semicircle behind him. Suddenly Flynn stopped the action and consulted privately with Michael Curtiz, the director. Curtiz asked Reagan to change his position. He now stood behind a taller man and could not be seen as the camera came in closer to Flynn. "I figured that under the rules of the game I was entitled to protect myself, so as the rehearsal went on I kept quietly scraping a pile of loose dirt together with my feet . . . when the cameras rolled, I quietly stepped up on my newly created gopher mound. When the time came for my one line in the scene it dropped like the gentle rain from heaven on the heads of the men in front."†

Michael Curtiz was a Hungarian whose "inability to observe common English usage in speech was profound." He also had trouble remembering names and sometimes jumbled his casts' real names with those of their characters. The great stage and film actor Raymond Massey, who was playing the abolitionist John

---

* Ironically, Reagan had already made his last film, *The Killers,* at the time of this statement.
† In the final version, Reagan's line was cut.

Brown, became "Joe Brown" (disconcerting to him because of the famous comedian by the same name), Errol Flynn became "Earl Flint" and Reagan became "Ron Custard" (for Custer). Curtiz was renowned also for his brutal treatment of actors.

"He was lining up a shot in the execution sequence," Massey recalled, ". . . John Brown was to be seated on his coffin in the cart with a parson sitting opposite him. . . . Mike, as he used to do, was framing the shot with his hands and stepping backwards to find the camera spot. Behind him was an empty concrete tank used for water shots . . . the parson stood well behind Mike and moved backwards with him. Nobody warned him of the empty tank . . . [suddenly] the little man disappeared into the tank. Before he hit the bottom, Mike muttered, 'Get another parson!' A pile of folded tarpaulins broke the parson's fall and he wasn't badly hurt."*

Robert Buckner's script was a well-told story that somehow managed to blend the pre–Civil War growth of the Atchison, Topeka and Santa Fe railroads with a recounting of the abolitionist crusade of John Brown and the successful campaign to apprehend and execute him. Massey recalled Reagan's enthusiasm for historical accuracy in his portrayal.

In one scene, the squadron leader, Errol Flynn, is informed that John Brown's raiders are nearby and the troops are ordered to take action. "The scene had been rehearsed and the camera was being readied. The action was simply that the three troops mount and move off at the trot. The officers were in the foreground. Ronnie was holding forth about the direction. 'This is a scene of action. We're too apathetic. There should be a feeling of urgency. We wouldn't mount formally by the drill book. I'm going to vault into the saddle and make it look like we're in a hurry.' The other officers, including Flynn, mindful of the potential discomfort of jumping into a saddle that had a pommel, indicated that they would do it as rehearsed.

"The assistant called out, 'All right . . . this is a take . . . AC-TION!' Everybody proceeded to mount 'by the book' except Ronnie who sprang forward with a prodigious leap which carried him with his saber in its sling to an ignominious landing on his behind on the other side of his horse which was being held by an astonished orderly.

"Mike shouted, 'CUT! . . . Acrobat bum!' "

---

*Reagan claimed "he broke a leg."

Later Massey stuck his head in Reagan's dressing room (now a proper trailer of his own) and, quoting *Macbeth* (considered bad luck in the theater), intoned in his resonant, commanding voice: "Vaulting ambition, which o'erleaps itself, and falls on the other." Unfortunately, Massey's classic verse landed pretty much on its backside as well. Shakespeare had not been part of Reagan's curriculum at Eureka.

Life for Jack and Nelle in California provided them with comfort such as they had never known before. Their two-bedroom one-story adobe-colored stucco house in West Hollywood, though modest and working-class by Hollywood standards, was the nicest home they had ever had. The furniture was their own, bought for them as a present by Dutch and Jane. A Spanish-style archway separated the living room from the dining room, which contained a proper suite of furniture and had a large picture window that looked out on a vine-covered patio. The backyard was small but filled with roses and flowering semitropical shrubs. Jack had found he had a talent for gardening and tended the flowers himself.

Although the house was only a few streets south of Sunset Boulevard, they were far removed from the more elite suburbs of Beverly Hills and Bel Air. Each section of Los Angeles had its own shopping district, and theirs was within the boundaries of West Hollywood, with nearby Fairfax Avenue offering its many Kosher markets and Jewish delicatessens. Nelle's day-to-day existence revolved mostly around the church and her missionary activities. In addition to spending many hours with tubercular patients, she had continued her commitment to bring religion and comfort to the men and women in prison.

For the only time in their married life, Jack and Nelle did not have to worry about making ends meet, but they remained careful about their finances. Dutch paid the expenses on the house and gave them a weekly supplement to Jack's salary from Warners. On her part, Nelle could not have wanted more. Yet she could not help but be aware of Jack's growing edginess. He missed his buddies and the fulfillment he had found in his work during the Depression. He had not made the friends she had in California, and was, perhaps, feeling isolated and not quite ready to settle for a slippers and club chair existence.

Upon the completion of *Santa Fe Trail*, the studio notified Reagan that he would be expected to leave in a few days, joined by

Wyman, for South Bend, Indiana, home of Notre Dame University, where Warners had decided to premiere *Knute Rockne—All American.* The minute he mentioned this forthcoming publicity junket (which would include Pat O'Brien, Kate Smith, Anita Louise, Charle. Ruggles, Rudy Vallee, Rosemary Lane, Irene Rich, Ricardo Cortez, Bob Hope, Jerry Colonna and columnist Jimmy Fidler, among others), Jack's interest was aroused. The tour would be climaxed by a College of Pacific–Notre Dame game, and Jack's dream had always been to watch Notre Dame "win one." Nelle took Dutch aside and asked if it was not possible for Jack to go along with him on this trip. They both knew his health had not improved and that time might well be running out. Reagan later said, "Here was an Irishman who had really worshipped from afar; he'd never seen a Notre Dame team play. . . . He thought Pat O'Brien was the greatest man since Al Smith. . . . Still, I felt a chilling fear that made me hesitate. We had all lived too long in fear of the black curse [Jack's drinking problem]."

Nelle's optimism and her pragmatic reasoning finally won out. Jane would be with Jack to cast a protective daughterly eye, and Jack's awe of Pat O'Brien and the monsignor of Notre Dame (in about that order) would hold him in line. Also, they would be in South Bend for only three days (October 3–6). Reagan, though not convinced and more than a little apprehensive and resentful that his big moment might be crossed by a shadow, could not deny Nelle her request. He called the studio and they agreed Jack could go, even offering to pick up his first-class expenses. This was not entirely out of the goodness of their tender hearts. The publicity department had jumped on the news value of Reagan's Irish-Catholic father, which gave them a good tie-in with the trip to Notre Dame.

The city was on the great south bend of the St. Joseph River and shared a physical resemblance to Davenport, Iowa, although larger and more heavily populated. The Warners film party arrived at Union Station, where a special platform had been constructed, on a Thursday afternoon and disembarked from two special cars that had been added to the *Super Chief.* They received a tremendous welcome; nearly a quarter of a million people had poured into South Bend to see in person the men who were bringing Knute Rockne and George Gipp back to life. From that moment, the celebrities were rushed from one appearance to another in dizzying succession. Press interviews had been set up at the Oliver Hotel, where most of the stars (including the Reagans) were staying. From six-thirty to seven P.M., the popular *Vox Pop* radio program, emceed by Parkes Johnson and Wally Butterworth, was broadcast from the lobby of the hotel. Reagan said a few words, but attention was centered on O'Brien, who, in fact, would dominate the press and radio coverage for the entire tour. The role of Knute Rockne was the stuff of which stars are made—and O'Brien's popularity was ensured for a number of years because of it.

A welcoming banquet, held that evening at the university, included a half hour of coast-to-coast coverage by the Mutual network. The graduate manager of athletics at Notre Dame, Arthur Haley (a man in his fifties), was from Dixon and knew Jack. The two men sat together, warmly recalling old times. O'Brien and Bob Hope were in top form, bantering back and forth in good humor. Reagan was expected to say only a few words—O'Brien and aging coach and sports figure Amos Alonzo Stagg were to be the key speakers. But when Reagan stood up, he gave a very well put-together speech in which he talked about his own experiences with Mac at Eureka, his emotion at re-creating those feelings onscreen, and the honor he felt in being chosen to portray George Gipp. He recounted the details of some of the Gipper's greatest games—play-by-play—and ended up by stating: "I hope my performance will win another for the Gipper. I sure wouldn't want to disappoint all those scores of Notre Dame fans."

When the banquet was over, Reagan and Wyman wanted to return to the hotel. Jack chose to remain with Haley and O'Brien. "Don't worry about Jack. I'll see he toes the line," O'Brien insisted. Reagan, on Wyman's urging, left, but not without misgivings since O'Brien was well known in Hollywood for his own bouts with whiskey. About five the next morning, Jack and O'Brien headed unsteadily toward the hotel on foot after a few extended stops at South Bend's local taverns, where, of course, everyone had to buy Pat O'Brien and his fine Irish friend a drink, and where it would have been an insult to refuse.

"It must have been quite a scene," Reagan later wrote. "Jack was sure the empty streets were a trap and that the quarter million fans were lurking in an alley, just waiting to swoop down on Pat for autographs. At each intersection . . . he tiptoed up to the corner and peered cautiously around. Then he would signal Pat to join him and they would scamper across the street to the shelter of buildings."

That day was the "big day," with a luncheon given by Mayor

and Mrs. Jesse I. Pavey at the South Bend Country Club. All four of South Bend's major theaters were screening *Knute Rockne—All American* in its premiere showing that night, and the plan was for the stars of the film who were in South Bend (O'Brien, Reagan, Gale Page, Donald Crisp, Owen Davis, Jr.) to appear onstage at each. The publicity schedule given to the participants states: "You will have to eat dinner on your own from 5:00–6:00 P.M. Car will pick you up at hotel at 6:15 sharp and take you to John Adams High School for the live [7:00–8:00 P.M.] nation-wide, Columbia Network Kate Smith broadcast."

The ebullient and considerable Miss Smith, "America's favorite songstress," shared time on her show with a dramatization of several scenes (including Gipp's last moments) from the film. A caravan of limousines waited outside the school doors to whisk the stars on their round of World-Premiere Showings. Reagan, Wyman and Jack rode in one car. At 8:20, the celebrities marched onto the stage of the Colfax led by Hope, who acted as master of ceremonies. O'Brien said a few words and introduced Mrs. Rockne. Reagan followed (he had been advised that they had only ten minutes and he was to offer no more than his greetings). Then Hope introduced the rest of the notables and, waving, they all departed amid applause as the theater darkened and the projectionist got ready to show the film. This procedure was repeated at the Palace at 9:00 and at the Granada at 9:30. At the fourth theater, the State, they followed the film at 10:15 and there were great cheers. "I guess we really won one for the Gipper," Reagan said during his turn.

A "Grand Ball" at the Palais Royal Hotel climaxed the evening. All the stars were present and introduced by Hope. Roosevelt's son, Franklin junior, had now joined the stellar guests and read "a fine letter from the President." Once again, O'Brien and Jack Reagan disappeared (ostensibly to escort Pat O'Brien's mother back to the hotel), this time about midnight. But neither seemed the worse for it the next morning when they, the Reagans, Gale Page (who played Mrs. Rockne in the film), Donald Crisp and Mrs. Rockne placed a wreath on Rockne's grave in Highland Cemetery. They then attended a luncheon with the female students and faculty of St. Mary's College, the women's school located near Notre Dame. Jack and O'Brien, who were inseparable buddies by now, sat on either side of the Mother Superior. "I picked at my food, conscious that Jack was engaged in a lively non-stop conversation with Mother Superior, not one word of which was audible to me," Reagan said. "On the way out of the dining hall, a beaming Mother Superior informed me my father was the most charming man she had ever met. I won't say I relaxed completely—we were still two thousand miles from home."

The much anticipated College of Pacific–Notre Dame game got under way at Stagg Stadium at two P.M. after the band played an "Ave Maria" as a tribute to Rockne. Jack Reagan was in his glory. ("I think that afternoon was worth dying for," he later told Nelle.) Coach Stagg's College of Pacific team led Notre Dame at half time. Then the visitors were introduced by Hope. "Ten minutes allowed for introduction of celebrities," the publicity schedule informed. "*No speeches please!* Immediately after the above introduction, the celebrities will take their former seats; and the Band will march off the field playing 'The Victory March.' 1 minute allowed. There are only 15 minutes allowed between halves and the above time must be followed closely."

Reagan did not take his seat after the half. He went directly to the press box, where he had been asked by NBC (his old affiliate) to guest-announce a fifteen-minute segment of the last half—a feat he carried off with style and his usual expertise. Notre Dame came from behind to win the game by a touchdown. No better end to the weekend could have been devised. But when the winning play came in the last minutes of the game, the tour party was not around. Stars and press had been commanded to have "baggage packed and in lobby before leaving hotel in the morning for day's activities . . . depart stadium five minutes before end of game (not later than 4:15 P.M.) to waiting buses to take you to station . . . train leaves at 5:00 P.M. sharp . . . Baggage will be transferred from hotel direct to station." By the time the buses reached the station, whiskey flasks were being passed around to celebrate Notre Dame's win (heard over the bus radio) and most of the group (including O'Brien and Jack, but excluding the younger Reagans) continued their alcoholic celebration all the way from South Bend to Chicago, where they had to change trains.

Nelle had miscalculated on two scores: the journey had not drawn father and son closer together as she had hoped, and Jack had fallen off the wagon. Perhaps the idea had been foolhardy, but had she been along and seen her husband's renewed vivacity, the clear happiness of the man, she could not have doubted her instinct of how much the trip would mean to him.

South Bend received *Knute Rockne—All American* a bit more jubilantly than the rest of the country did. But the film unquestionably was the most successful Reagan had yet appeared in. ("Picture is more than a historical document of football during the past three decades—it's an inspirational reminder of what this country stands for . . . Americans will roll up hefty yardage at the theatre box-offices" [*Variety*]. "If some of it is largely sentimental and on the mock-heroic side [i.e., Gipp's death scene]; if some of it is slightly juvenile, that's all part of the sport. And that also makes it one of the best pictures for boys in years" [*The New York Times*].) What puzzled the Front Office was Reagan's lack of good personal reviews. "It's true, I got some unmerited criticism from sportswriters," he said in 1947. "However, this criticism was nicely balanced by some unmerited praise from the same general source. For another sportswriter said I was so accurate in my portrayal of Gipp that I even imitated his slight limp. Actually, I wasn't trying to limp. I just wasn't used to my new football shoes, and my feet hurt."

The tour party returned to California just a few weeks before the presidential elections—one of the most memorable of campaigns. Roosevelt was running for an unprecedented third term. His opponent was Wendell Willkie, a former Democrat from Elwood, Indiana, who had voted for Roosevelt in 1932 and 1936 and then became a leading spokesman of business interests* opposed to the New Deal. Willkie conducted an unforgettable and hard-hitting crusade against Roosevelt's third term. As one reporter wrote four years later when Willkie died: ". . . we will not forget . . . how the country became familiar with his disheveled suits, necktie askew, hair flying in the breeze or falling down over his forehead, his voice getting hoarser and hoarser, as he impatiently used to elide 'Pres-dent-Unide-States.' We will not forget his repeated appeal that 'only the productive can be strong and only the strong can be free.' . . . No American leader saw more clearly than [he] the nature of the Axis threat to the freedom of free men everywhere in the World. The total impact of his leadership was directed toward deflecting that threat, toward defeating that threat, toward forging the Allied coalition which would ultimately win the war into an Allied coalition determined to secure a just and workable peace. During his campaign for the Presidency in 1940, he spurned the most alluring advice on how to win if he would only shut up about the war. He wouldn't."

---

*Willkie had practiced law until 1933, when he became president of the Commonwealth and Southern Corporation, a giant utility holding company.

Willkie's speeches were actually an endorsement of Roosevelt's foreign policy. During the campaign, Willkie's voice gave out and Roosevelt was quoted as saying he hoped the doctors "kept him talking." But he did fight vituperatively against the president's New Deal at home. Roscoe Drummond, then chief of the Washington news bureau for the *Christian Science Monitor,* quoted Willkie as saying to him: "If I could write my own epitaph, and if I had to choose between saying, 'Here lies an unimportant President,' or 'Here lies one who contributed at a moment of great peril to saving freedom,' I would prefer the latter."

At the time, America was experiencing one of its most uncertain, divisive periods. The Nazis were devouring Europe and Roosevelt was doing a juggling act—keeping the Axis as far as possible from the United States while attempting to strengthen the arm of every resisting country. Hollywood became polarized. It had the same proportion of isolationists and of those who felt the United States had to aid Britain as the rest of the country. There were Democrats who believed it dangerous for a president to run for a third term, and Republicans who did not trust a nominee who had so recently switched parties. Seldom had two men of such tremendous charisma and speech-giving talent opposed each other, facts that elicited a higher than usual election fever among the citizens of the film colony. As a result, the town remained politically segregated during the campaign, fearing a confrontation on an issue or candidate with one of the Front Office power men, which could have been a serious misstep. Still, there was a lot of action at Hollywood Democratic Headquarters, and Jack joined Pat O'Brien in doing what he could.

Billboards were pasted across the nation with signs that read *HOLLYWOOD FOR ROOSEVELT*, beneath which were the enlarged personal signatures of Pat O'Brien, Rosalind Russell, Douglas Fairbanks, Jr., Melvyn Douglas, Sylvia Sydney, Alice Faye, James Cagney, Dorothy Lamour, George Raft, Miriam Hopkins, Hugh Herbert, Edward G. Robinson, Andy Devine, Thomas Mitchell, Betty Grable, Henry Fonda, Robert Benchley, Sally Eilers, Humphrey Bogart, Claude Rains, Ritz Brothers, Virginia Bruce, Joan Bennett, James Gleason, Jane Wyman ". . . and hundreds of others." Reagan does not appear to have been active in this campaign, though he was still registered as a Democrat.

Reagan and Wyman spent the evening of Election Day with Nelle and Jack (who paced the floor as he listened to the state-by-state returns on the radio). The election was closer than anyone had predicted, and Willkie was to win more votes than any previous candidate running against an incumbent president. "Jack, please sit down," Nelle kept saying. But Jack was too agitated to do so.

The president, waiting in the dining room of Hyde Park, "news tickers clattering nearby," apparently shared this apprehension. James MacGregor Burns, a member of his staff, recalled of the scene: "The President was calm and business-like. The early returns were mixed. Morgenthau, nervous and fussy, bustled in and out of the room. Suddenly Mike Reilly, the President's bodyguard, noticed that Roosevelt had broken into a heavy sweat. Something in the returns had upset him. It was the first time Reilly had ever seen him lose his nerve.

"'Mike,' Roosevelt said suddenly. 'I don't want to see anybody in here.'

"'Including your family, Mr. President?'

"'I said anybody,' Roosevelt answered in a grim tone."

The room was cleared. Reilly stolidly guarded the closed door as Roosevelt sat alone awaiting the nation's final decision. A short time later the votes began to swing in his direction. He ordered the door open. "Roosevelt was smiling again . . . and in came family and friends . . ."

Roosevelt's reelection was gaily celebrated by Jack Reagan, Pat O'Brien and the workers at the Hollywood Democratic Headquarters. Early in the morning on May 18, 1941, one month after Roosevelt was sworn in for his third term, Jack Reagan died. Reagan wrote: "I'm sure he knows that Pat and his new friends were there in the little church off Sunset Boulevard to say goodbye."

The monkey on Reagan's back—the fear that his father would be overtaken by the "black curse" to his and his family's humiliation—was now also dead.

11

BEHIND JANE WYMAN'S EASYGOING, WISECRACKING exterior lurked little Sarah Jane Fulks, always seeking approval and love. Her insecurity drove her to set near-impossible goals for herself, which kept her on edge but also propelled her forward. Reagan's self-assurance gave him an authority and implacability that were difficult for a less secure person to oppose. In the Reagan-Wyman household, his word was pretty much law regarding what he considered the more masculine considerations: family economics and planning for the future. He left household matters to Jane—not costs, just the "feminine-frivolous"—decoration, entertainment, and orders to the maid who came in five days a week.

Firmly convinced that to want was to have before this marriage, Wyman had lived up to every penny of her modest salary and more. "I don't know how I ever did it, but I was up to my neck in debt," Wyman once admitted of this period. "I knew the way Ronnie [felt] about debts, and decided the best thing to do was to pay every last living bill before the big event. After it was all over, I had $500 to my name. 'That's swell,' Ronnie assured me. 'That's the beginning of our savings account.'"

While still on their honeymoon, Reagan sat her down and worked out what he called "a viable budget. This meant that we saved half of everything we made. That first month was tough sledding. We literally didn't spend a dime. Every one of our checks was banked away, half in a savings account and half in a checking account . . . charge accounts took care of our living expenses—food, gas, oil, dining out—so we had no bills to pay until the first of the following month. . . . Ronnie has a phobia about bills. If a bill is ten days old, he starts having a fit. As a result every bill is paid and out of the way by the 10th of every month . . . and he made sure we never charged more than what we had set aside for living expenses."

Even with their combined incomes, they lived modestly for Hollywood, where spending habits are often a gauge to success. Because Wyman wanted a baby and a house, the percentage of their earnings going toward savings increased. (Wyman refers in one early article to the day when she would have their "savings account baby.") Outsiders found them curiously mismatched. "Janie always seemed about ten years younger," one friend says. "She could be the life of the party. . . . [Ronnie] was a good storyteller, but he often used Jane as the butt of his story—you know, how she had been duped, or a silly thing she had done. She'd get flustered but she never said anything. I had the feeling that they weren't really communicating. In 1940 and 1941 all he talked about was world conditions. He was very serious—even during football season. Only it was the game that he was serious about then."

Another friend adds: "I'd say Janie was a lot quicker than Ron. She had a sort of streetwise intelligence. She did everything fast, made up her mind on the spot. Ron always thought things out. I think she admired him greatly and considered him a hell of a lot smarter than she was. Their friends were more the Old Guard in Hollywood, not their contemporaries or the in-groups and swingers."

(Wyman said of the first few months of their marriage, "Neither Ronnie nor I were stars, we were both featured players making $500 a week. I wasn't a glamour girl and he wasn't a matinee idol. We were just two kids trying to get the breaks in pictures.")

Reagan took a scholarly interest in wine and liked to play host at small dinner parties. They bought two Scotties (the same breed of dog as Roosevelt's beloved Fala), and named one Scotch and the other Soda. Wyman claimed Soda took after Reagan and Scotch after her. "One day Scotch got mad and started snapping at Soda," she told an interviewer. "For a moment, Soda watched him tolerantly—'Pipe down, brother, pipe down.' When that didn't work, he lifted his paw and laid it quietly on his brother's nose. It worked like a charm. Scotch subsided. Soda removed the paw and they trotted off together in brotherly love. And if those aren't my husband's tactics, I'll eat my hat."

"There was a snobbism in Hollywood," Joan Fontaine recalled, "the second leads didn't get invited." The snub did not affect the Reagans much. Late nights were out completely when they were filming, and they worked steadily throughout 1940–41. "When employed there are the long hours of activity, which meet personality needs," Hortense Powdermaker explained in her anthropological study, *Hollywood, the Dream Factory*, written in the 1940s. "Then the picture is finished and a period of inactivity follows. Even if the actor is under contract and there is no financial worry, the situation is not an easy one. There is the well-known lost feeling when not acting." This was true of Wyman, who tried to cram her free time with other activities. Compulsive by nature, she polished silver and brass and constantly rearranged furniture. She went house hunting and priced antiques for the home they could not quite yet afford. She played golf and kept up with current novels, hoping always to find in one a meaty role that she could convince the studio was right for her. Her ambition had grown, her dedication to acting, her sense that she could make it big. Her interest in SAG activities continued. She could always be depended on to pinch-hit on a committee when needed.

Reagan has been quoted as saying, "I think Jane started talking about a baby the day after we were married. I wanted one too, but I used all my male logic to persuade her that every young couple ought to wait a year. She agreed I was right as usual and she was wrong. So we had a baby." The portrait painted of the Reagans in the hundreds of magazine articles published during their marriage point up Reagan's practical nature and Wyman's emotional sensitivity, her need for self-expression and for roots.

Just five months after they married—in June 1940—Wyman became pregnant, and the impending event threw her into more intense activity. She differed from stars of the past who feared children might reduce their popularity. To the contrary, in her case it could reverse her screen image, add maturity and depth of

character. She did not, however, tell the studio about her condition until after the tour to South Bend in early October, when she
was already four months' pregnant.

Reagan, at thirty, was to become a father, but his concerns
were more political than personal. Anticipating the approach of
war, he argued at social gatherings or on the set for American
involvement, solid in his belief that only with our help could the
Axis be defeated. Holland had fallen, France was on her knees.
Only Britain stood strong, but how long could it hold out?

Roosevelt was alert to the danger signs. "Each night as he
relaxed over his stamp collection, the President would confide to
his personal physician, Admiral Ross T. McIntire, 'England *has* to
be saved . . .'" The problem remained that if Germany should
triumph over Britain, how could the United States face the resul-
tant threat to its safety? Roosevelt successfully demanded from the
Senate that the country aim for a production of fifty thousand
planes within the year, and requested a budget increase of $500
million plus an additional $70,000 per plane for annual mainte-
nance. "Even the Republicans," noted Secretary of the Interior
Harold Ickes, "will have to go along with this program because
the country is for it and they dare not do otherwise."

Reagan's co-workers found him more talkative than ever. Defense figures were rattled off at a dizzying pace. "No one was
quite sure he was accurate, but he sure as hell sounded accurate,"
one former colleague commented. As Republicans pushed for the
same goals as the administration—a solid American defense—
war clouds drifted close. (The *New York Herald Tribune* bluntly suggested, "The least costly solution in both life and welfare would
be to declare war on Germany itself.") The passion and fears of
the time found listeners and new friends for Reagan. No longer a
"repository of fact," he was an articulate man with political
knowledge that was of pertinent interest. His friendship with Justin Dart grew. Dart was becoming one of the top fund-raisers in
the Republican party and through him Reagan was meeting many
influential men, among them Goodwin Knight (future Republican
governor of California) and banker Charles Cook. He socialized
often with actors George Murphy and Dick Powell, both Republicans. The war in Europe brought his thinking closer to the Republican view, although he remained a loyal Roosevelt admirer.
He did not think his opinion on joining the fight against Germany
was hawkish. Rather, he spoke of American involvement as a
pledge to help the underdog and defend the weak. But he re-

mained adamant in his belief that Roosevelt would not enter a war until America was ready. What Reagan and his friends debated was the manner in which that readiness was—and was not—being achieved.

"They had made many films together, but arguing politics drew them together," explained Powell's widow, actress June Allyson. "It was a riot to listen to Ronnie, a staunch Democrat, trying to convert Richard [Powell] while Richard argued just as hard to turn Ronnie Republican. I figured the only way to get into this conversation was to pop some basic questions at Ronnie.

"He answered me carefully, methodically. When Ronnie got through explaining something to me, Jane Wyman leaned over and said, 'Don't ask Ronnie what time it is because he will tell you how a watch is made.'"

Wyman had been in *Gold Diggers of 1937* and *The Singing Marine* with Powell when he was a musical-comedy leading man. In the early forties, about the time he met and married Allyson, Powell made a sudden transition to straight dramatic roles. This change coincided with an increasingly serious interest in business and politics and brought him into an active alliance with the Republican party. As early as 1941, he saw Reagan's potential as a political figure. His opinion of him as an actor was less favorable. He not only tried to convert Reagan to Republicanism, he kept insisting that if Reagan became a Republican he might have a future somewhere other than films. Allyson and Wyman, on the other hand, shared a distaste for politics. "He'll outgrow it [Reagan's obsession with politics]," Allyson told Wyman. "To [Jane] it wasn't funny," she later commented. "But even more annoying to her was the fact that it took Ronnie so long to make up his mind about anything she asked him. . . . I thought it was wonderful that Ronnie was so vitally interested in everything and was always studying a new subject . . . he showed the same thoroughness in matters other than politics and he was . . . always studying. He was a wine connoisseur and once after I asked some questions about wines, he sent me a book on the subject." Allyson recalled that during their meetings, "a certain sad sweetness radiated from [Wyman's] large soulful eyes."

Whenever Reagan got together with his men friends, the talk would shift to politics. Wyman's aversion to such evenings was not so much that the subject was boring but that a social occasion would either turn argumentative or place Reagan on a soap box. She was not as apolitical as her distress might indicate. She stood up to be counted whenever an issue seemed important to her, and she had exceptionally sound reasoning ability—which was why SAG called upon her services so often. But Reagan's living-room polemics had more to do with an attempt to convert than to reason. And they echoed something unsettling in Wyman's past.

Many parallels existed between Wyman's father, Richard Fulks, and Reagan. Both were Democrats with strong, conservative attitudes (seemingly a contradiction); both were men who believed in the work ethic, in law and order, in America and American ideals; and both were obsessed with politics and power. Fulks never became a successful politician, not from his lack of trying but because of his austere personality and his mediocre ability. Wyman's reaction to those qualities Reagan shared with her father was to withdraw, to become even more of a private person than ever. Reagan's attention was so diverted by his involvements that he could not recognize the danger this could pose to their marriage. He called her "button nose" and every year sent red and white roses for Valentine's Day. To the world they lived in, he projected a grand-fellow, good-husband image.

"He had a wonderful store of marvelous and funny stories and had that great gift of being *so* articulate," Jane Bryan Dart remembered. "[He] followed the political news as enthusiastically as he followed events in the motion-picture industry." Where he had once monopolized gatherings with his play-by-play descriptions of sports events, he now dominated any group with a replay of speeches given in Congress. This involved a prodigious amount of time spent reading a large number of newspapers: *The Wall Street Journal, Washington Post, Christian Science Monitor* and even printouts, obtained through friends, of the daily *Congressional Record.*

Maureen Reagan was born on January 4, 1941. The Reagans were referred to as the perfect family by the press. (A few months later, Jane told the *Dixon Evening Telegraph* in a telephone interview: "I wanted a boy . . . and was terribly disappointed for a few moments. I can't for the life of me understand why . . .") The Londonderry View apartment soon proved to be too small. On Maureen's arrival, the couple had taken over an adjoining bachelor apartment and made it a nursery and bought new furniture for Reagan's small office (including a copy of the George Washington desk) and the living room. At best, Jane found their housing situation inadequate and finally convinced Reagan that they had to move. The savings-account baby was followed soon by a savings-account house. The Reagans attended a showing of a Rosalind Russell film, *This Thing Called Love*. The house in it appealed to them and Wyman asked the film's designer to let her copy the plans. He agreed. They then bought a lot with a spectacular view on a twisting, steep hill above Sunset Boulevard, less than five minutes from their apartment, and began construction on an eight-room house, which Wyman supervised. Her life during this period was taken up with domestic matters, Maureen, the building of the house and its decoration and furnishing, which was to be in a style that both called "comfortable Reagan" ("We don't want to go out on a limb," Reagan kept reminding her), and her career. She made four films in 1941, none of them substantial.

John ("Jack") Dales, executive secretary of SAG, called Wyman in early July and asked her if she would consider being an alternate on the board for Heather Angel while she was on location. Wyman said she would think about it and let him know later that afternoon. To Dales's surprise, she turned up at the SAG offices with Reagan. "Jack," she said, "I don't think you've actually met my husband, Ronald Reagan, but I think he'll make a better alternate than me." Dales claimed "a bright look came in her eyes" and she added, "He might even become president of SAG one day—or maybe America."

Dales had no objection to Reagan's taking a seat on the board as an alternate, but he had to put the matter before the other members, some of whom knew Reagan from Warners (Powell and Cagney were both on at that time) and "spoke up" for him. But Dales added, "It was primarily Jane Wyman's boost for him" that convinced the board to accept him. "He certainly made himself felt . . . not immediately but in the weeks and months that followed. He was articulate. He spoke with reason, not with experience. Yes, he made an impression." What was more pertinent was the impression the SAG made on Ronald Reagan. His interest deepened with each board meeting. He could see how important good negotiation and political action were to getting actors the most favorable terms for employment. Friends noted a change in him from the time he went on the board of the SAG. He took each issue that came before the board with great seriousness. Studio and union problems began to share equal time with world conditions in his heated discussions.

"Reagan was an unbelievably strong Roosevelt supporter," Jack Dales says. "He idolized him as some people would idolize a film star—he thought he was almost a godlike man. . . . He felt very much that he could work with the Guild in the same way that Roosevelt worked with the country." Dales was a mild man with a pedantic manner and a slow smile. He lived perhaps a little too vicariously in his work and never seemed to lose his admiration for actors or his great pleasure in being able to associate with so many famous members of that profession. He got on especially well with Reagan.

Reagan felt proud of being a movie actor, a career he had coveted since childhood. But what had been the strong attraction—money, fame, adulation? Certainly it had not been a dedication to the art of acting. Except for his years at school, he had never pursued any form of dramatic training. Viewing the films he made in his first five years in Hollywood (and there were thirty of them), one can see little growth in the depth of understanding of a character or in mastering the craft of acting. He appears almost consistently "boyish of face and gleaming of tooth," as a *Time* correspondent described him. His best early performances were given in the films in which he played a brash radio announcer and in the Brass Bancroft Secret Service serial, where he engaged in comic-strip heroics. Warners might have developed the qualities he exhibited in these films and found him able to fulfill top-star potential. But, he lacked friction, passion, the kind of presence that rivets an audience. His likability, his voice, his ease before the camera got him through. None of his performances was wooden, but he often appeared shallow. Even his portrayal of George Gipp did not stir the emotions until Knute Rockne evoked his dead spirit to rouse a losing Notre Dame football team to victory.

His idols and role models were the actors who played heroes on the screen. Such had always been the case. Since childhood, he often fantasized about ridding the West of the bad men, rescuing those unable to save themselves, dying for honor, for love, for country. The intensity that should have been channeled into his craft was spent in his passion for economics, politics and now union tactics. Except for his one desire to play the Gipper, he had not displayed any initiative in seeking a good role, nor had he ever refused an obviously inferior part.

Warners had loaned him to Metro-Goldwyn-Mayer in January 1941 for the juvenile lead in *The Bad Man*, a Wallace Beery–Lionel Barrymore film. (Metro paid Warners two thousand dollars a week for Reagan, who under his old contract received five hundred dollars per week from Warners.) Metro had not sought out his services. Instead, he had been part of a trade that involved other contract players. Metro had many actors on salary who could have put some sparkle into the lackluster role of Gil Jones—Van Johnson, James Craig, Richard Carlson, Lew Ayres and Robert Walker to name a few. But the part was not one that could have displayed any one of these actors to good advantage. Also, stealing a scene from two such veterans as Beery and Barrymore would have been an impossible feat for even the best of players. Certainly, Jack Warner could not have thought the loanout would improve Reagan's status, for he was to receive fourth billing after Beery, Barrymore and Laraine Day.

Porter Emerson Browne's *The Bad Man* had been filmed twice before, and although one version had starred Walter Huston, both had been dismal failures. One wonders what else other than Beery's marquee appeal could have decided Metro to try again. But by now Beery's screen personality had become a cliché. Whatever good footage is contained in *The Bad Man* Barrymore commands. Beery portrays a Mexican bandit (shades of his famous *Viva Villa!*) who shows up at Barrymore's hacienda to rescue it from foreclosure because Barrymore's nephew (Reagan) had once inadvertently saved his life. Laraine Day was cast as Reagan's childhood sweetheart, married unhappily but returning to Reagan's side at his time of need.

"I had been warned about Beery," Reagan recalled, "but no one said anything about Barrymore. . . . Lionel was, of course, theatre through and through, and you were made better by his great ability—provided you kept from being run over. He was confined to his wheelchair at the time and he could whip that contrivance around on a dime. It's hard to smile in a scene when your foot has been run over and your shin is bleeding from a hubcap blow."

"Ronald Reagan makes an ineffectual hero," wrote the reviewer on *The New York Times,* words that could not have raised Reagan's stock when he returned—as he put it—"to the meat and potatoes atmosphere" of Warners (Reagan had referred to MGM as "sort of the Tiffany of Hollywood"), where he continued to make "some shaky A pictures with now and then a lesser role in the class product."

The contents of Reagan's films could not have been farther from the realities of the times. As German armies closed in on Paris, a grave Roosevelt had gone before a hurriedly convened joint session of Congress to reassure a deeply frightened country and call it to arms. Despite Roosevelt's support of a Selective Service Act and the overwhelming public approval for America's preparedness, Congress was extremely reluctant to enact a peacetime draft (for the first time in American history). Angry congressional debates followed. Many members of Congress did not want to be burdened with the responsibility of having voted for peacetime conscription if the necessity of America having to defend itself in a war somehow disappeared. Despite much opposition, Congress passed the act in August 1940, and the country went to work to build and supply planes, ships and ammunition to the new recruits. Everywhere there were flags as Americans shook the mothballs off their patriotism. All the musical shows on Broadway featured the national anthem as a curtain raiser or finale. Hollywood was dragging its tail. Chaplin poked fun at Hitler and Mussolini in *The Great Dictator,* but most major filmmakers seemed not to hear the trumpets of approaching war.

As an officer in the reserves, Reagan received his first induction notice on February 9, 1941. Jack Warner personally wrote the army on behalf of Reagan and his company asking for, and receiving, a deferment in view of the films Reagan was then signed to do. Reagan had dependents and would have never passed an eye test, so Warner felt certain that he could be kept out of the service as long as the country remained at peace.

The studio next cast him as Peter Rowan in a ridiculous film called *Million Dollar Baby,* which also starred Priscilla Lane, Jeffrey Lynn and May Robson. His co-workers noted that he was unsettled by his deferment, displaying guilt. The inconsequential screenplay could not have helped assuage his unrest. The original story by Leonard Spigelgass, titled *Miss Wheelwright Discovers America,* had been considered a hot property when Warners bought it, and they proceeded to give it a production and running time (102 minutes) commensurate with its advance publicity. Unfortunately, "[The screenplay] seems to be put together like a prefabricated house, strictly according to blueprint, with each piece turned out of a mold," wrote Bosley Crowther. "It is one of the most formula-made pictures ever to come along and smells of antiseptic." The formula chosen was simply boy-meets-girl in reverse. An old grumpy lady (Robson) gives a young girl (Lane) a million dollars. Her boyfriend (Reagan) is a struggling concert pianist who breaks off their engagement because she is now too rich for him and she gives away the money to win him back. Spigelgass's original script had been larded with sharp wisecracks.

The adapters replaced these with "a string of old gags that a third-rate m.c. at a fourth rate bistro would have ducked."*

Reagan's most vivid recollection of *Million Dollar Baby* was of the two weeks preproduction, during which he spent considerable time every day at a dummy piano following "the hand movements of a pianist at a real piano playing Chopin and all the music the picture called for." A memo from the film's director, Curtis Bernhardt, to Jack Warner gives an even clearer vision of Reagan's fortnight of piano practicing. "Max Rabinovitz of the music department saw me yesterday after having worked with Ronald Reagan for his piano playing and said that the man is without any musical feeling and sense, and that it would be impossible to ever show his hands while playing the piano." In the end, Reagan was seen seated at the piano, hands *poised*, and then cuts were made to a professional pianist playing.

Curtis Bernhardt had been known in Germany as Kurt Bernhardt, but he was renamed by Warners in 1940 when he escaped the Nazis and came to America. The name change reflected Hollywood's acute awareness of the anti-German sentiments sweeping the country at the time. Warners also displayed a total lack of judgment in assigning a director with a heavy European hand who had not yet mastered English to a project that relied on the subtleties and innuendo of language.

Reagan next did *Nine Lives Are Not Enough*, a "classy little B film" directed by a former protégé of Charles Chaplin, Edward Sutherland, who had contributed a lot to the early musical film. The pace of the movie was above par. Sutherland saw the quality in Reagan that gave him some extra dimension onscreen—that flip brashness. Reagan's character was "a frantic newspaper reporter who's always getting in a jam, but invariably seems to land on his feet," *Variety* commented. "Ronald Reagan is not only a brash reporter to end all screen reporters; he's also hilariously scatterbrained and devilishly resourceful. . . . Reagan gives a superbly helter-skelter performance." The script was "a blazing whodunit, with suspense piled up and action so fast that the average spectator won't have time for the moment of calm thought needed [to discover the villain]."

On seeing the rough cut of the film, Jack Warner had written Foy:

---

*The screenplay of *Million Dollar Baby* was by Casey Robinson, Richard Macaulay and Jerry Wald.

Dear Byrnie,

I saw Nine Lives Are Not Enough and it is a peachy picture. . . . I have about a half dozen more revamping shots,
inserts, and effects to put in, and I cannot understand why
they were not done in the first place, especially in the off-
scene fight where [Reagan] slugs the newspaper reporter and
throws him off-scene. Undoubtedly they had mufflers on
their black jacks.

Warner wanted to retitle the film (made in twenty-one days),
but this was never done.

Nine Lives Are Not Enough, with its cumbersome title, low budget, short running time (sixty-one minutes) and weak marquee
value (Reagan was the major name in the movie), had too many
strikes against it to make the grade as a sleeper. Reagan's performance did set the front office to reevaluating his career, and they
cast him in the starring role of *International Squadron,* an up-classed
B script with plenty of action. Previously filmed as *Ceiling Zero*
with James Cagney (in the Reagan role) and Pat O'Brien only
five years earlier, the story had been reset from World War I to
the Battle of Britain. Reagan played a cocky American who joins
the RAF, creates havoc among his buddies' fiancées and grows up
after his breaches of discipline have cost the lives of two of his
companions.

All the care usually given an A film was lavished on *International Squadron,* except that the cast and the director were not from
the more select company of players, which kept the budget low.
Warner had originally wanted the old *Ceiling Zero* script refur-
bished for Errol Flynn and John Wayne (he seemed determined to
team these two, but was never to succeed). When this did not
develop, Warner turned to Hal Wallis for suggestions for substituting a less stellar cast. Wallis sent back a list of contract players he thought adequate, Reagan among them. His performances
as the Gipper and in the action film *Nine Lives Are Not Enough* won
him the Flynn castoff. Lothar Mendes, a German-born director,
was assigned the film. Mendes worked well with Reagan, appre-
ciating his professionalism. He was not, however, able to draw
from him the sexuality that Flynn might have given the daredevil
role. Nonetheless, the brash Jimmy Grant in *International Squadron*
is one of Reagan's better roles. (Mendes was also a taskmaster.
One scene called for Reagan as an RAF pilot to take a mop,

which was saturated in oil, light it inside the cockpit, pull back the hood and hook it outside the plane as a decoy for the Germans. The hood jammed before he could release the mop and Reagan was overcome by smoke and oil fumes during the minutes it took to pry open the hood. Mendes refused to bring in a double, and the next morning Reagan repeated the scene—this time without incident.)

Warner and Wallis sensed a new and more enthusiastic audience reaction for Reagan when they saw the rough cut of the film—at least three full months before its release. Both agreed that the "hick midwest sportscaster" might have star potential; and by casting him in their biggest budget film yet that year, *Kings Row,* in the co-starring role of Drake McHugh, they exercised their confidence.

In June 1940, Warner had paid thirty-five thousand dollars for the Henry Bellamann best seller (he had offered only five thousand dollars more five years earlier for *Gone With the Wind*). Wallis was ecstatic about the purchase since he considered the project one of social importance, but his task in assembling staff and cast would not be easy. Within a week of the *Kings Row* acquisition, Wolfgang Reinhardt, who had been assigned as associate producer, wrote Wallis:

Dear Hal,

It is only with reluctance that I bring myself to report unfavorably on a prospective assignment as important as *Kings Row*. Yet I prefer not to kid myself or you regarding the enormous difficulties that a screening of this best seller will undoubtedly offer. As far as plot is concerned, the material in *Kings Row* is for the most part either censurable or too gruesome and depressing to be used. The hero finding out that his girl has been carrying on incestuous relations with her father, a sadistic doctor who amputates legs and disfigures people willfully, a host of moronic or otherwise mentally diseased characters, the background of a lunatic asylum, people dying from cancer, suicides—these are the principal elements of the story. The balance of the plot-elements, the ones that are not objectionable, unfortunately are very much on the hackneyed side: A banker who steals trust funds, real estate speculations and some other typical occurrences of a small town. In my opinion the making of a screenplay would amount to starting from scratch, practically writing an original story about the life of a small town, using the same characters but inventing more or less new circumstances for the action. . . .

The quintessence of the author's [Henry Bellamann] ideas is an accusation against the hypocrisy, the narrow-mindedness and the cruelty of the typical midwestern rural town or if you will, of American society as a whole. In the novel this is done in a rather mellow way, without too much bitterness, in the style of a philosopher who knows too much about the evilness of men to get too excited about it.

In the picture we would have to hit much harder, we must let facts speak for themselves, we cannot rely on a Greek chorus to explain the meanings of the plot. We would have to build up dramatically the contrasts that are rather mildly touched upon in the novel. . . .

Casey Robinson, who had successfully scripted *Dark Victory, The Old Maid* and *All This and Heaven Too* (all Bette Davis films), was assigned to write the screenplay.* Before he had a chance to begin, Joe Breen, of the Production Code Administration, which censured all American films, sent Wallis notification that the film script should not be attempted and the project should be abandoned because his administration would unequivocally ban the film:

> . . . Before this picture can be approved under the provision of the Production Code, *all the illicit sex will have to be entirely removed;* the *characterization of Cassandra* will have to be *definitely changed;* the mercy *killing* will have to be *deleted;* and the several suggestions of loose sex, chiefly in the attitude of Drake with reference to the Ross girls, will have to be *entirely eliminated.* In addition, the suggestion that Dr. Gordon's nefarious practices are prompted by a kind of sadism will have to be *completely removed from the story.*
>
> You will have in mind, also, I am sure, that a picture of this kind could not be released in Britain, where *any* suggestion of insanity is always *entirely eliminated* from films. . . .
>
> To attempt to translate such a story to the screen, *even though it be re-written to conform to the provisions of the Production*

---

*Robinson, as noted, had also worked on the script of *Million Dollar Baby.*

Code is, in our judgment, a very questionable undertaking [and] . . .

. . . even though your present script is re-written to bring it within the provisions of the Production Code, it will still be necessary, before approval can be given to the script, that a decision as to its acceptability, *from the standpoint of industry policy*, be rendered by the Board of Directors of this Association in New York.

I am sending a copy of this letter to Mr. [Will H.] Hays [President of the Motion Picture Producers and Distributors Association of America and author of its strict Production Code] for such comment, or observation, as he may care to make in the circumstances.*

Despite the fact that Breen and Hays had the power to stop production of the film or at least to forbid its distribution, Robinson plowed into work on the script† and, on February 4, Steve Trilling, Warners' casting director, sent his first memos to Wallis and Warner on casting. As was the custom, all possibilities were included. Every player on contract who was approximately the right age for a role was listed, no matter how bizarre the choice would have been, along with players from other studios who were considered "right." The lists looked like score sheets for a tournament. Trilling placed his top choices at the head of each column under the characters' names (added to those below were lists for six other characters):

Parris	*Drake*	*Cassandra*
Ty Power	Dennis Morgan	Ginger Rogers
Henry Fonda	[Warners]	Ida Lupino
Laurence Olivier	Franchot Tone	[Warners]
Cary Grant	Fred MacMurry	Olivia de Havilland
Robert Taylor	Ray Milland	[Warners]

---

* Italicized words are underscored in original letter.

† Wallis, Warner and Robinson went personally to see Breen to argue the case. Finally, Breen agreed to reconsider if the script had no reference to incest or nymphomania (dementia praecox was to be used instead). The characters were not to go to bed together. The mercy killing was to be removed, as was a nostalgic scene of young kids skinny-dipping. Robinson had no idea how all this could be taken away and the story still be valid—but he agreed to try.

Douglas Fairbanks	Lew Ayres	Vivien Leigh
Glenn Ford	Robert Cummings	Joan Fontaine
Alexander Knox	Robert Preston	Linda Darnell
[none of the above	Eddie Albert	Adele Longmire
was under contract	[Warners]	[Warners]
to Warners]	Ronald Reagan	Anita Louise
Michael Ames	[Warners]	[Warners]
Arthur Kennedy	John Garfield	Bette Davis
John Garfield	[Warners]	[Warners]
Errol Flynn	Arthur Kennedy	
Ronald Reagan	[Warners]	
[all Warners]	Michael Ames	
	[Warners]	

The list was soon narrowed down. Tyrone Power and Henry Fonda were Wallis's first and second choices for the idealistic Parris Mitchell, but both were under contract to Darryl Zanuck, who would not release either of them. Olivier had abruptly returned to his war-plagued England (with Vivien Leigh). Wallis next turned to Michael Ames, a "young, handsome actor . . . he had a fresh quality that made up for the fact that he had no name." Ames had played one of the juvenile leads in the Broadway production of *My Sister Eileen* before being signed by Warners, where he was given minor roles in *Now Voyager* and *Dive Bomber* and appeared as the Frenchman in *International Squadron* with Reagan, his few moments onscreen registering well. Wallis tested him three times as Parris and finally agreed to his having the role, at which point Ames was drafted into the army. Warner could possibly have tried for a deferment, but war clouds were hovering and Ames, although married, had no children. What good would it have been to star him in a film and then lose him to the army anyway? Therefore, Ames went off to boot camp and Trilling sent a new casting memo, which now placed Robert Cummings's name in the top position for the role of Parris since John Garfield and Errol Flynn were thought by Wallis to be too sexy. Cummings had been Wallis's choice for Drake McHugh. With the switch, he turned to a revised list:

Drake McHugh

Eddie Albert
Ronald Reagan
Arthur Kennedy

In April, the Breen office rejected Robinson's screenplay as still unsuitable. The veteran writer went back to work again. Final casting had not been made. Reagan did not know that he was being seriously considered for the film. While he had a direct line to Bryan Foy's group, he was not close to anyone in the Wallis camp. *International Squadron* was filmed in May and June. After Wallis viewed the rushes, he decided Reagan would play Drake McHugh. When notified, Reagan had not yet read the script and had no knowledge of the complexity of the role.

Second, third and fourth drafts of the screenplay had been submitted to Breen and rejected. Start of production was postponed a month. Cummings now had to fulfill a commitment to Universal—*It Started with Eve*, a Deanna Durbin picture. Production on *Kings Row* finally began the second week in August. Cummings was a much-harried star making both films simultaneously, one a musical and the other heavy drama, shuttling back and forth between Warners and Universal and "changing costumes and characterizations en route." The delay in production had also forced the distinguished English actress Judith Anderson, another performer in the film, to make two films at the same time, but at least she was on the Warner lot for both.* The movie still had no Cassandra and all scenes involving that character were scheduled for the end of shooting. However, Drake McHugh's girlfriend, Randy, was being played by Reagan's former co-star, Ann Sheridan.

While the battling over the casting of Cassandra raged,† and Cummings and Anderson sweated out the pressures of two coinciding schedules, director Sam Wood juggled Reagan's scenes to fill in. As usual, Reagan was extremely cooperative, a fact well appreciated by Wood, who reciprocated by giving Reagan a large slice of his directorial attention. (Reagan would later say: "I owe

---

*Anderson was simultaneously filming a Warner spy thriller, *All Through the Night*. In 1960 she was named Dame Commander of the British Empire. Dame Judith had been one of the leading performers of the English stage. Her most memorable film role had been that of the housekeeper, Mrs. Danvers, in *Rebecca* (1940).

†Warner had fought long and hard to cast the untried studio player Adele Longmire as Cassandra. As late as September 13, 1941, he wrote Wallis: "The woman is a *great actress*." Wallis, the only man with the power to veto final casting, disagreed. "Warner made some [other] ridiculous suggestions," Wallis recalled, "among them Joan Leslie, Susan Peters, and that buxom example of normal, middle-class, healthy womanhood, Priscilla Lane. In mid-August [with production in progress], I was still trying to get Gene Tierney, whose unusual face and temperament made her ideal casting, but Darryl Zanuck got her first [for *Tobacco Road*] . . . Marlene Dietrich's publicist announced that she had won the role, which gave us all a much-needed laugh."

Sam Wood a great debt. If he were alive today [Wood died in 1949], he could tell me on the phone he had a part for me and I'd say yes without waiting to hear the title of the script let alone read it. It was a long, hard schedule and my first experience, I suppose, with an acting chore that got down inside and kind of wrung me out.") Wood and Reagan shared an enthusiasm for politics which carried over on the set. The often underrated Wood, once Cecil B. DeMille's assistant, had made some diverse and entertaining films, ranging from the Marx Brothers' comedies *A Night at the Opera* and *A Day at the Races* to the sentimental *Our Town, Kitty Foyle* and *Madam X* to the adventurous *Rangers of Fortune* (he had also directed several uncredited scenes of *Gone With the Wind*). About one thing he was unequivocal: Sam Wood was dedicated to conservative-hawkish politics and was president of the Motion Picture Alliance for the Preservation of American Ideals.

(One day after Wood and Reagan had been expounding politics between takes, Bob Cummings asked him, "Ronnie, have you ever considered becoming President some day?"

"President of what?" he asked.

"I told him President of the United States."

"What's the matter, Bob," he replied, "don't you like my acting either?"

Because of Wood's conception of the role of Parris Mitchell, Cummings wore heavy makeup. A critic later wrote: "Bob Cummings plays Parris Mitchell like the third girl on the line.")

Reagan wore contact lenses for the first time during the making of *Kings Row,* but although he tried to convert the nearsighted Nancy Coleman (cast as the girl whose doctor-father amputates the legs of her boyfriend, Reagan) to their use, he never was able to rely on them for any length of time.

Actress Marguerite Chapman remembered that one day during the shooting of *Kings Row* she sat across from Reagan in the commissary and called to a friend at the table behind them to join her at mass on Sunday.

"'Are you a Catholic?'" Reagan asked.

"I said, 'Yes.'

"He said, 'Why?'

"I said, 'I was *born* one.'

"He went on, 'That doesn't mean you have to stay one. . . .' He continued to put me on about it and embarrassed me in front of everyone . . . I never liked him since then."

Joseph Breen had provisionally approved the shooting script, which had been laundered about as Oxydol clean as possible, but he still had objections to a scene in which Drake (Reagan) said to his friend Parris (Cummings), "You have to bunk with me. I hope you don't mind the change." Wallis protested vainly that the men and the actors who played them "were entirely masculine and the line contained no suggestion of homosexuality." Breen was adamant and Reagan's line was changed to, "You have to bunk with me. I hope you don't mind, Mr. Mitchell!"

But of greater consequence to Reagan's role was the famous amputation scene, which gave him his finest moment onscreen and his most famous film quote: "Where's the rest of me?"

This time Sam Wood created the problem. He did not want Drake McHugh's legs amputated after a freight-car accident "because he was afraid the audience would assume castration and regard Drake as a freak." Wallis pointed out that legs were "normally . . . amputated just above the knee. Drake might be affected psychologically, but not sexually. Wood refused to accept this. He insisted that the surgeon who hated Drake would have wanted to take his manhood." But by the time the scene was to be shot on September 7, Wood had had a complete turnaround in thinking. On September 4, David Lewis, the associate producer, memoed to Wallis: "On the matter of shooting the lines to cover the possibility of only taking off one of Drake's legs . . . I think you should discuss this with Sam Wood. He [now] feels it means a total rewrite of the end of the picture . . . and feels very strongly about it [retaining the original]."

Reagan claimed that the night before the scene was to be shot, he was so terrified of what it would demand of him that he could not sleep. Drake McHugh was to recover consciousness in an upstairs bedroom after the amputation, and had to come "from unconsciousness to full realization of what had happened in a few seconds . . . worst of all, I had to give my reaction in a line of no more than five words ["Where's the rest of me?"]."

They shot the scene without a rehearsal on Reagan's request. There were cries of "'Lights!' . . . I heard Sam's low voice call, 'Action!' There was the sharp *clack* which signaled the beginning of the scene. I opened my eyes dazedly, looked around, slowly let my gaze travel downward. . . . I can't describe even now [1964] my feeling as I tried to reach for where my legs should be. 'Randy!' I screamed. Ann Sheridan (bless her), playing Randy, burst through the door. She wasn't in the shot, and normally wouldn't have been on hand until we turned the camera around to get her entrance. . . . I asked the question—the words that had been haunting me for so many weeks—'Where's the rest of me?' There was no retake . . . and it came out that way in the picture. . . ."*

Reagan's major scenes were complete the same day that Wallis finally signed Betty Field (who had tested earlier and was borrowed from Paramount) for the role of Cassandra. On August 29, Reagan received another letter from the army calling him to active duty, and obtained a second deferment based on the studio's claim that he was set to go from *Kings Row* to *Juke Girl* and could not be replaced without great hardship to the company. He received a deferment to October 10, 1941.

Jane Wyman, pressured by the building of the new house, the baby and her heavy working schedule, had not been well and Reagan went almost directly from the shooting of his "Where's the rest of me?" scene to the hospital where she had undergone minor surgery (a curettage). Although she was doing well, they decided she would remain at home while he joined Louella Parsons on another tour—this time to Dixon, a personal appearance that had been planned and scheduled before the delays in the filming of *Kings Row*, and during which *International Squadron* would hold its "world premiere."

He would be returning to Dixon for the first time as a movie star, having just played his best role and at a time when another picture touted as very good and in which he was the major star was to open, and Nelle was going to accompany him. Life had given him more than he had even dreamed of possessing when he had left Dixon for Davenport back in 1932.

---

*When the first print of the film was shown to Sam Wood on October 20, 1941, he had reservations about this scene. Paul Nathan, Wallis's assistant, memoed to Wallis the next morning: "Wood was greatly disturbed . . . by your cutting Dr. Gordon's line, 'Amputation—both legs' (scene 159). He felt that this would take away from the rest of Drake's scenes and the audience wouldn't feel sorry enough for him. For Wood insists that many people will think it might have been a toe, or perhaps just one leg—and wonder why the hell this guy feels so sorry for himself.

"Last night I agreed with Wood. However, I have thought about it since then and now think it is wrong. For the scene is certainly gruesome enough and horrible enough no matter what Gordon cut off, later when Drake calls to Randy and screams, 'Randy, where's the rest of me?' you surely know that *both* legs have been cut off." Dr. Gordon's line, "Amputation—both legs," remained in the final cut so that there would be no doubt that Drake had lost both extremities.

12

Reagan and nelle—with pullman-car bedrooms adjoining—remained much to themselves during the two-day train ride
from Los Angeles to Dixon. Louella Parsons occupied a private car
with her daughter Harriet, her publicists, Sam Israel and Virginia
Lindsey, and several of the other members of the tour (which included Ann Rutherford, George Montgomery and Parsons's
brother, Ed Oettinger). Joe E. Brown, Bob Hope, his radio sidekick, Jerry Colonna, and Bebe Daniels and Ben Lyon were to meet
the group at their final destination.

Mother and son were not antisocial. They met with the others
for all meals except breakfast (the Reagans rose at dawn), and sat
around after dinner in Parsons's car, laughing at the ebullient
Oettinger's comments and jokes. Parsons made note that Reagan
was a "far more serious fellow" than the young man who had
accompanied her on the 1939 tour less than two years before. She
attributed it to his concern for Jane and his loneliness without her.
Perhaps, but except for the fact that they earned their living in the
same profession, Reagan had little in common with his fellow pas-

sengers. He also had a great deal on his mind. Returning to Dixon was only a part of it.

That week, Dick Powell had indicated to him that if he joined the Republican party, friends of his would finance a campaign to help elect him to Congress. Reagan had laughed it off with a quasi-joke about the "Democratic Reagans." Powell had countered with his usual arguments—Roosevelt was *not* the Democratic party; the president's liberal left-wing friends *were,* and the liberal Left was being infiltrated with Communists and fellow travelers. Reagan was naïve if he thought the Democrats were the party of the people. He was being duped, deceived. The Republicans were the true people's party because they had become the keepers of "the American Way of Life."

"Why me?" Reagan might well have asked. The answer was simple. Reagan was a celebrity, articulate, a passionate speaker, had an impeccable past and was as American as hot dogs at a baseball game. He had said no, but the discussion had planted a seed in a newly plowed garden of ambition.*

Sitting across from Nelle during the long train ride was a constant reminder of Jack and his dedication to—and his mother's belief in—the Democratic party. Moon's defection to the Republican party in 1932 had hit Jack hard. Reagan feared his own might well disturb Nelle, who was unmovable in her faith that Mr. Roosevelt and the Democrats would see the country safely through its current crisis.

The 1941 climate in America was tense. As apprehension of entering the war grew, waves of hysteria began to roll over the land. Private citizens were all too ready to campaign against the swift undertow of espionage, sabotage and subversion. It seemed everyone was suspect—"aliens, ethnic and religious minorities, labor unions, Communists, non-Communist radicals and the simply idiosyncratic." As early as the summer of 1940, George Britt's *The Fifth Column Is Here,* which claimed there were more than a million subversives in the United States, was a best seller. A congressional bill required that defense workers sign a loyalty pledge, and that the two million WPA workers swear an oath that they were

---

*During the several hundred interviews conducted for the purpose of this book, a pattern began to form. As Reagan's political influence began to grow, his personal detractors multiplied significantly. After 1941, private opinion became jarring in its diversity. Some coworkers still found him "a wonderful guy" and "thoroughly likeable," but a considerable segment referred to him as "power hungry" and "dangerous," or as "boring," with "no depth," "a cardboard figure."

not members of the Nazi or Communist parties. June 1940 found the Justice Department receiving tips on spies and subversives from ordinary citizens at the rate of three thousand a day. The government agency that most exacerbated the escalating hysteria was the House Select Committee on Un-American Activities, generally known in the late thirties as the Dies Committee, after Congressman Martin Dies of Texas, its chairman, and thereafter as HUAC (House Un-American Activities Committee).

HUAC owed its existence to Samuel Dickstein, a Jewish representative from Manhattan's East Side who wanted "a congressional investigating committee to expose the activities of native Fascists [Nazis]." Dies recognized the power the chairman of such a committee would wield and joined forces with Dickstein. Together, "out of real events, imaginary fears and personal ambitions," they created a mostly fictitious enemy-within of half a million Nazis, and, in 1938, one very real House investigating committee. Dickstein was then maneuvered out of power by Dies, who became HUAC's chairman.

Riding with the swift winds of war hysteria, the Dies Committee published the names of 563 government employees as Communists or Communist sympathizers, claiming they had belonged to a Communist front, the League for Peace and Democracy. (Dickstein's original purpose, to alert the nation to an internal Nazi threat, had been lost with his departure.) From the point that Dies took over HUAC, the committee seemed unconcerned about Nazis and concentrated on the danger of the Communists, who were, ironically, to become the allies of the United States. The only evidence HUAC had against the 563 was the inclusion of their names (in many cases unbeknownst to the person) on the league's mailing list. On December 6, 1939, the *New Republic* had stated that the United States was "on the edge of a Red Hunt." By September 1941, when the *City of Los Angeles* snaked through much of the heartland of America, objectivity had all but vanished. Well-known liberals such as Walter Lippmann had given the Dies Committee their blessings. They agreed "its methods . . . were disgusting but un-American, unjust methods were necessary because the Committee was dealing with un-American, unjust activities—'it takes a crook to catch a crook.'"

Sheer mindless violence pervaded the land with not only aliens and Communists at its mercy but the small sect of Jehovah's Witnesses. During 1940, they had suffered more than fifty attacks that resulted in injuries and death to more than 500 people, many of

them women and children, because their religion explicitly forbade them to salute the flag.* The religion was considered to be a
hotbed for conscientious objectors, by groups who fed upon unsubstantiated rumors. The Ku Klux Klan doubled its membership to 300,000 in the single year of 1940, and killings and
floggings by the white-sheeters whom Jack Reagan had so de-
spised rose proportionately. Fear had overridden all common
sense and destroyed intelligent restraint, fear that European refugees could be Nazi spies and that America could fall under Communist influence. Germany's attack on the Soviet Union on June
22, 1941, had almost no effect. Liberal journals such as *The Nation,
New Republic* and *Saturday Review* became "more and more worried
about democracy and more and more militant on its behalf." Reagan's philosophies had also moved in that direction.

As they neared Dixon, Nelle and Reagan read the Bible together. He retained the same ardent belief in the Book. He had
also been restudying the Constitution, which he described to
someone as "the Bible of democracy." The train journey was the
first time in many years that he had spent such an uninterrupted
span of time in Nelle's company, bringing back memories of those
hot, humid summer afternoons of the Chautauquas. Nelle still remained the most remarkable woman he knew. Since Jack's death,
she had become even more obsessed with what she called "her
Christian duty." She had decided to join him on this trip only
after she realized she could share her new experiences with her old
friends in Dixon, with whom she had never stopped corresponding
and to whom she remained bound.

Reagan claimed "he never felt that far from the Rock River."
He had not forgotten the old friends. He remembered names,
could attach them to their proper faces. Providing Dixon had not
been leveled by some catastrophic stroke of nature, he could have
found his way to any town landmark, street or former friend's
front door. Dixon was imprinted on his mind as indelibly as if a
cartographer had inked it there.†

As the *City of Los Angeles* drew haltingly into Dixon's North
Western Station, Reagan stood in the doorway of his Pullman car

---

*Jehovah's Witnesses believe the Second Commandment made the saluting of the flag a
crime against the Lord ("You shall not make for yourself a graven image or any likeness of
anything that is in heaven above or that is in the earth beneath or that is in the water
under the earth. You shall not bow down to them or serve them.")

†Upon meeting old Dixon acquaintances in 1980, he had been able to pinpoint the exact
locations of homes they had occupied fifty-five years earlier.

spotlighted by the glare of the midday sun. The thousands of hometowners and neighboring residents who had waited patiently for the celebrity train began to shout and wave their WELCOME HOME, DUTCH! banners before Parsons had made her appearance. He returned the waves, helped Nelle down onto the platform and then called out, "It's good to be here!" If he was aware that Parsons was not exactly overjoyed at the homage being paid him, he did not show it by pulling back, nor did he limit his words when she handed the microphone to him, expecting him to say a gracious sentence or two and then return it to her. Nor did the spectators want him to cut short his speech. Louella Parsons might well have lived in Dixon, but Dutch Reagan had been a part of their lives.

The Reagans, mother and son, along with the other thirty members of Parsons's group, were to stay at Hazelwood, the guests of Myrtle Walgreen. According to his own admission, nothing that had previously happened to him in his life had made Reagan feel such a grand success. Charles Walgreen had died in December 1939. Life went on as usual at Hazelwood, which meant that a great many celebrity guests came and went. But Mrs. Walgreen was to remember Louella Parsons Day as "one of the gayest events in Hazelwood's history."

The celebrities were put up in the main house, the others in the guest "cottage" (which had nineteen bedrooms). "The fall weather was so fine that we could eat most of our meals out-of-doors under the trees," Mrs. Walgreen recalled. "We had a hilarious time . . . every time our old-fashioned country telephone rang its five rings on a party line [Bob Hope] would grab the receiver to answer, 'Walgreen's Sanitarium for Tired Movie Actors.'" Her prized memento was a photograph of Joe E. Brown seated alone at a very long table covered by a checkered tablecloth with more than a score of places set. At the bottom, the comedian had written, "'Joe E. Brown and His Friends.' Someone had snapped it when he sat down before the big bell rang."

Ruth Walgreen Dart was also at Hazelwood that week, but her relations with her ex-husband had remained fairly amicable and Reagan's friendship with Dart did not create any difficulties.* Reagan was in such high spirits, it is doubtful that anything could

---

* Ruth Walgreen Dart went on to become a writer and poet (*The Flight, My Crown, My Love* and *Prelude to Poetry*) and publisher (*The Tiger's Eye*, a literary magazine).

have dampened them. Mrs. Walgreen claimed that his "forthright candor won everyone. We became real friends." He told stories of his caddying days at the club, his adventures as a lifeguard at Lowell Park, and his awe at being a guest at Hazelwood, "the castle on the hill." Nelle rode with him in the opening parade, waving to the crowds in an uncharacteristically royal attitude while a movie camera on top of a truck revolved constantly, filming the procession.

On Monday night, after two days of accelerating activities, *International Squadron* was shown for a benefit world-premiere performance (for the Dixon Hospital), with tickets at the high price of five dollars at the Dixon Theater. This had not been Dixon's or the theater's first experience with a world premiere. On January 25, 1924, "movie-goers of this locality witnessed the first showing of Wesley Barry's film, 'George Washington, Jr.' . . . The popular young star . . . appeared in person at the showing . . . and awarded prizes of pencils to winners of a contest." Contemporaries of Reagan's claim he attended this gala premiere, but did not, unfortunately, win a pencil.

Nelle strode up the red carpet on the arm of her son as blazing searchlights crisscrossed the skies in Hollywood-premiere fashion. She faced the battery of flashbulbs, cameras and cheering crowds with surprising calm. The premiere was the exciting climax to the trip to Dixon, and she had been the guest of honor with her son in a series of local festivities. Attending the premiere as Nelle and Reagan's guests were all the members of Nelle's former True Blue Bible class. Nelle "acknowledged the plaudits of the crowd and a huge ovation greeted her son. . . . Dutch described his feelings as 'the thrill of thrills' to return to the motion picture theatre where once he, too, had been merely a member of the audience." "Only once before," he said, "have I appeared on this stage. That was back in the days when we had a Y.M.C.A. and I was the lower-end man of a pyramid during a gymnastic demonstration which collapsed just before the curtain was drawn.

"Folks have reminded me since I have been here," he added, "that I was born in Tampico, but until the time I stepped off that train yesterday morning I hadn't started to live. Dixon is my birthplace from now on.

"Some day," he concluded, "I'm coming back to Dixon with my wife and I want to sit down and talk to all the 10,000 people here."

The crowd went wild. Finally, the lights in the theater

dimmed, then went out. In the same theater where he had seen so many movies and formed so many dreams, Dutch Reagan watched himself on the screen.

The next day, the *Dixon Evening Telegraph* reviewer wrote, "While 'International Squadron' will not go down in film history along with 'Birth of a Nation' and 'The Covered Wagon,' it is a technically accurate record of the defense work being done in the skies over Britain.

"Its climaxes, although not new in theme and plot, nevertheless are supported by good dialogue and offer Ronald Reagan a part which displayed his capabilities as an actor. The 'Jimmy Grant,' smart, wise-cracking American pilot, who demanded that life serve him on his own terms—often at the cost of tragedy to others—is not the 'Dutch Reagan' which Dixon knows best." (When the film was finally shown in New York on November 13, 1941, *The New York Times* would comment: "Ronald Reagan is excellent as the slap-happy hell-diver who finally pays for his moral failures with his own death in combat." And the *New York Post* confirmed: "Reagan's performance is tops in breezy, even style . . . he carries the starring burden and proves he can shoulder it." Even *Variety* would state that he was "excellently spotted as the expert flyer"—and promised that the picture would "elevate his audience standing.")

The audience at the Dixon Theater that night found the film "pulse quickening entertainment," and applauded a good three minutes after "The End" glided across the screen, bringing Reagan to his feet and onto the stage where he gave a second speech, this time a thank you that might have been a bit more appropriate to an Oscar recipient. The audience then remained seated for the presentation, live, of Louella Parsons's network-radio program *Hollywood Premiere*, with short appearances by all the stars on the tour. To great enthusiasm, Reagan then repeated his musical debut in the film and sang two choruses (noticeably off-key) of "The Man on the Flying Trapeze."

The tour prepared to leave the afternoon of the next day. Reagan announced to a reporter that he was working on "an original story": "I Knew Them Better in Five Minutes Than Their Mothers Did in a Lifetime," purportedly dealing with his experiences as a lifeguard at Dixon's Lowell Park. "Each person reacted differently," he told the *Dixon Evening Telegraph* reporter. "Only one or two ever thanked me [for saving their lives]. . . . It's hard to understand. You'd think nothing would make a person more grateful. But I believe it's a combination of embarrassment and pride. Almost invariably they either argued they weren't in any trouble or were so mad at themselves they wouldn't admit someone else had succeeded where they had failed." He then smiled knowingly. "One of the first things a life-saver learns, is that the person who can shout for help isn't in serious trouble. It's when their lungs are so full of water they can't sound off with more than a gurgle that they need attention." Confidingly he added, "I remember one time when Dixon's most popular girl waved to me. At least I thought she was waving. My chest puffed out a little and I waved back. Then I turned away for a moment. When I looked again, she was going down. She had tried to signal for help.

"The one time I was really scared was about a blind man. He started for a float guided by a friend's calls. But the river current pulled him away. He was a big fellow—outweighed me by 60 pounds or so—and he was thrashing badly. It looked like a tough time. But amazingly the moment I touched him, he relaxed completely. Just to know that someone was near was enough. He's the one who thanked me."

Bill Thompson drove Reagan and Nelle to the station for the group's departure in the same open-topped car in which they had ridden in the Celebrity Parade. By now Nelle had become quite adept at white-gloved, measured waves. In what proved a tactical miscalculation, Parsons boarded the train first—the Reagans last. The hometown boy who made good in Hollywood despite his humble origins stood in the Pullman-car doorway as the diesel train slowly drew out of the station. Therefore, the last glimpse the crowds caught of Louella's entourage was of a smiling, waving, youthful Ronald Reagan.

Interviews, a trial to many of his fellow performers, held no terrors for Reagan. He granted them readily, talked entertainingly and answered even the most hackneyed questions as though they were fresh and original. His radio experience in Des Moines had honed his talent for public conversation. But that was not entirely responsible for his ease. Reagan liked being a public figure and had always enjoyed being in the limelight. First there had been his days as a lifeguard at Lowell Park, then the "heady wine" when he presented the motion to strike at Eureka. His memories of Des Moines centered on the star interviews he conducted and the events he emceed, a curious fact in view of his main position as sportscaster and his intense love of sports.

Movies had fed him his earliest fantasies. He had always been able to see himself as the hero of these celluloid dramas. His desire to be an actor was propelled by his strong drive to be recognized—preferably as the stuff of the heroes. He remained an avid moviegoer. The new house was to have a screen and projection machine. His idols were Spencer Tracy, James Stewart and Gary Cooper. He had seen Cooper in *Mr. Deeds Goes to Town* and *Meet John Doe* several times each, as well as Tracy in *Boys Town, Stanley and Livingstone* and *Edison, the Man,* and Stewart in *Mr. Smith Goes to Washington* and *Destry Rides Again.** The main characters in these films represented his idealized version of a real man and a real American—humble but strong, dedicated but vulnerable, impervious to corruption; men who took the fate of others in their hands with the faith and knowledge that this was right because their principles were solidly American. It seemed never to occur to him that only in films could things be so black and white, that the real world was made up of a spectrum of grays, often muddied.

His triumphant Dixon trip had buoyed his spirits and given him a new and stronger sense of self-confidence. "He came back [from Dixon] looking like the last reel in a Gary Cooper movie," one old friend commented. He went straight to work, first on short retakes for *Kings Row,* and then, with only a weekend off, opposite Ann Sheridan in *Juke Girl.*† Sheridan was a good friend of Wyman's, the kind of woman able to be best friends with both sexes. A tall, well-built, red-haired Texas beauty, Annie (as her friends still called her) had given her first truly dramatic performance in *Kings Row.* She was also madly in love with George Brent (whom she married a few months later). *Juke Girl* had actually been developed for English actress Ida Lupino (who liked to refer to herself as "the poor man's Bette Davis"). Lupino had scored strongly in three successive films—*The Light That Failed, They Drive by Night* and *High Sierra*—and her loan-out fee had soared to seventy-five thousand dollars per film, while Warners still paid her fifteen thousand. The good economics of this could not be overlooked by the studio. Lupino was loaned out to Twentieth Century-Fox for two films‡ and Sheridan inherited the castoff *Juke Girl,* which had a strong resemblance to *They Drive by Night.* Jack Warner wanted Adele Longmire for this role too, but once again could not convince Wallis that she could carry the part.

---

* In later years, Reagan used lines from these films in many of his political speeches to underscore or make a point, treating the film line or situation as reality.
† Originally titled *Jook Girl.*
‡ *Life Begins at Eight-Thirty (The Light of Heart* in Great Britain) and *Moontide.*

Juke Girl dealt with fruit workers in Florida who become enmeshed in a murder. The film was overly melodramatic and filled with some outright, overboard hokum. Yet it did distinguish itself from other films of the same genre by its enlightened view of the agricultural scene. It did not match the realism of *The Grapes of Wrath,* but in its own jazzy vein it was a movie story with a sense of social responsibility, unlike most of Reagan's other films from this period. Reagan and Sheridan turned in extremely good performances (one of his best in this author's opinion). A chemistry that never existed in any of Reagan's other films flowed between the two. (Alex Evelove, Warners' publicity director, to Ken Whitmore: "Ann Sheridan and Ronald Reagan had a hot love scene that took them all through Wednesday to Friday. The next Monday they did the spot in the story where as strangers they meet for the first time and have a falling out.") Curtis Bernhardt once again directed Reagan. Most of the film was shot on location at Burbank and the Calabasas ranch and involved much night work. One night the temperature dropped to 27 degrees and ice formed on the tops of cars and trucks; breaths of players became so visible that filming had to stop.

The Reagans' home life was chaotic during the fall of 1941. Both husband and wife were under a great deal of work pressure. In addition to the five films she made in 1941, Wyman had to engineer the moving of the household to their new home in September, when Reagan was filming *Juke Girl* and putting in extremely long hours. On October 10, he received another army deferment, this time until January 1, 1942. He had a respite in November and he and Jane began to settle in and enjoy their new affluent life-style.

"On Sunday afternoons up at his house above Sunset Boulevard," Moon recalls, "you could look down on Doheny Drive, the corner of Doheny and Sunset . . . there used to be a big gathering of the [Jack] Bennys and the George Burnses . . . ten or twelve people—then we'd all go out to dinner someplace on Sunday evening. If they were all out around the pool, in about thirty minutes, the Reagan brothers would have driven everybody into the house with our battles on politics. His statement to me always was: 'That's the trouble with you guys. Anybody who voted for Roosevelt is a Communist,' and I used to agree with him heartily, at which point he'd get the screaming meemies."

Wyman was not finding life with Reagan easy. As he became more and more political and an increasingly forthright speaker, and as he began to enjoy whatever moments he had in the public eye, she became more withdrawn and involved in Maureen and her career, which had not been at all satisfying to her. They seemed to have little to talk about and she was the passive half, the listener. At premieres, Moon noticed that when people gathered around them as they entered, reaching out, grabbing for them, wanting to talk with them, she would take her husband by the hand and he would reluctantly follow her away from the crowd. Moon added, "He's really not a demonstrative guy . . . he was a great swimmer but I taught Maureen to swim before she could walk. . . . He didn't bother with her. . . . I was always a pigeon for children* but Dutch thought children should be on their own. . . ."

On November 18 Reagan signed a new contract with Warners. This was not the "million dollar contract" he wrote about in his autobiography. That came in 1944 and he is mistaken in placing it three years earlier.† Nonetheless, the terms were favorable. [Reagan writes: "Lew Wasserman of MCA reminded me of a war that was going on, of Hollywood stars like Jimmy Stewart who had already been drafted, and of my own reserve officer status. He said, 'We don't know how much time you have—let's get what we can while we can. . . .'"] On August 19, Jane's salary had also been renegotiated upward ($1,450 a week for the same time periods as those in Reagan's contract).

Reagan's world looked bright and secure. Europe was still ravaged by war, but most Americans felt certain their country would not be physically involved. He claimed he was sleeping on Sunday, December 7, when the flash came over the radio, midday, that at dawn the Japanese had attacked Pearl Harbor.

It had been 1:50 P.M. EST when E. E. Harris, Radioman First Class USN, received an alert to stand by at Radio Washington, the navy's largest communication station, for an urgent message by the Honolulu operator. Moments later, he transcribed the following message:

NPM 516
Z0F2 1830 0F$_3$ 0F$_4$ 0$_2$ F0 0

---

*Neil and Bess Reagan are childless.

†The 1944 contract negotiated by Lew Wasserman designated that one million dollars be paid to Reagan over seven years at the rate of thirty-five hundred dollars per week for forty-three weeks in each of those years. It also stipulated that his option could be dropped at any option period if he refused to appear in films that were assigned to him.

FROM: CINCPAC

ACTION: CINCLANT CINCAF OPNAV

AIR RAID ON PEARL HARBOR THIS IS

NOT A DRILL.

The brass hands of the ship's clock on Roosevelt's desk—where he sat eating lunch from a tray—stood at 1:57 when the news came over the wireless. At 2:30 EST (three hours earlier in California), the bulletin was flashed to the country via national radio. Even in California, the morning was gone. By the end of the day, fifteen hundred Hawaiians were dead, fifteen hundred others seriously wounded, and an American battleship and a destroyer had been sunk. *Time* reported, "At noon next day . . . the President moved slowly into the House of Representatives. In the packed still chamber stood the men and women of the House, the Senate, the Supreme Court. The heavy applause lingered, gradually began to break into cheers and rebel yells.

"Mr. Roosevelt gripped the reading clerk's stand, flipped open his black, loose-leaf schoolboy's notebook. He took a long, steady look at the Congress and the battery of floodlights, and began to read:

"'Yesterday, December 7, 1941—a date which will live in infamy—the United States of America was suddenly and deliberately attacked by naval and air forces of the Empire of Japan . . .'"

By 4:10 P.M., December 8, the House and the Senate had voted almost unanimously for a declaration of war.* Reagan was stunned along with the rest of the Western world, and his service status had suddenly changed. A few months earlier, he had taken a physical at March Field and because of his poor eyesight was assigned to "limited service—eligible for Corps area service command, or War Department overhead only." It seemed unlikely this conclusion would be reversed. He had little chance of being sent to the front. But before December 7, Warners had banked on the premise that he could win a permanent deferment.

The studio was going through its own problems with the government. Isolationist factions in Washington were investigating Hollywood's so-called "war mongering." On September 25, 1941,

---

*The vote in the Senate was 82–0; in the House, 388–1. The lone dissenter was Jeannette Ranking, a Republican from Montana "who sat with a bewildered smile, muttering over and over that this might be a Roosevelt trick."

Harry Warner had read a prepared statement before the Subcommittee of the Committee on Interstate Commerce, United States Senate, Regarding Moving Picture Propaganda answering charges that Warner Brothers was producing films "relating to world affairs and national defense for the purpose allegedly of inciting [the United States] to war," and that these films "twisted" facts dealing with world affairs and national defense for ulterior motives. Reagan's recent *International Squadron* was one of four of Warners' films cited by this committee.*

Pleading eloquently, Harry Warner made the case that "if Warner Brothers had produced no pictures concerning the Nazi movement, our public would have had good reason to criticize. We would have been living in a dream-world. Today 70% of the non-fiction books published deal with the Nazi menace. Today 10% of the fiction novels are anti-Nazi in theme. Today 10% of all material submitted to us for consideration is anti-Nazi in character. Today the newspapers and radio devote a good portion of their facilities to describing Naziism. Today there is a war involving all hemispheres except our own and touching the lives of all of us. . . ."

He went on to counter a second charge by the committee that Warner Brothers supported Britain and opposed Naziism because the studio had a financial stake in Britain.

"Warner Brothers receives a net revenue of approximately $5,000,000 a year from Britain," he admitted. "If we were to stop receiving this revenue, we would continue to operate. . . . In truth this charge challenges our business judgment and our patriotism.

"No one with any business judgment could possibly have acted on the assumption that the policy of this country towards England would be influenced by the relatively small investment of our industries in England. . . .

"When we saw Hitler emerge in Germany, we did not try nor did we ask our government to appease him. We voluntarily liquidated our business in Germany. . . . If, God forbid, a similar situation should arise in Britain, we would follow the same course as we did in Germany.

". . . I will not censor the dramatization of the works of reputable and well informed writers to conceal from the American peo-

---

* The four films were: *Confessions of a Nazi Spy, Sergeant York, Underground* and *International Squadron*.

ple what is happening in the world.* Freedom of speech, freedom
of religion and freedom of enterprise cannot be bought at the price
of other people's rights. I believe the American people have a
right to know the truth. You may correctly charge me with being
anti-Nazi. But no one can charge me with being anti-American. . . ."

The hearings collapsed shortly before the attack on Pearl Harbor. Warner Brothers had always been known for their action pictures, just as Metro specialized in musicals. And as that studio
seasoned their product with generous measurements of idealistic
portraits of American life and momism, Warners heaped on the
ingredients of antitotalitarianism and the right of violence against
it to reap the best profits in the marketplace. Box-office receipts
proved that Americans bought the theory of "justifiable" violence.
With America at war, Warners now had a no-holds-barred situation and, under the banner of patriotic fervor, swung into production with a platoon of war films, whereas the other major film
companies moved toward escapist entertainment.

On January 1, 1942, Reagan received another deferment, requested by Jack Warner on behalf of the studio, this time until
April 9, 1942. He was cast with second billing to Errol Flynn in
an original Arthur Horman screenplay (then titled *Forced Landing*,
later renamed *Desperate Journey*) about a British bomber on a mission over Nazi Germany. Once again, Raymond Massey joined
them. Raoul Walsh was to direct, perhaps the most prestigious
director Reagan had yet worked with. Walsh's films were well
known for a great sense of adventure matched by pathos and vul-
nerability, and he was considered by many critics "as one of the
great primitive artists of the screen."

The film went into production at the end of January. Arthur
Horman's original screenplay remained the basis for the film, but
in usual Hollywood fashion, other writers, though uncredited—
Vincent Sherman and Julius and Philip Epstein in this case—had
a hand in improving the weak story line.† The film was actually a
series of chases sparked by some bright dialogue by the Epstein
brothers. What story there was dealt with the five survivors of the

---

*Warner Brothers' position and the testimony of Jack Warner during the proceedings of
HUAC less than a decade later contradict this statement. A blacklist existed at Warners
throughout the fifties and most of the sixties and scripts were closely vetted for any pro-
Communist philosophy, which was cut without the screenwriters' approval even if the
excision was a truthful statement in terms of world conditions.

†Raoul Walsh to Hal Wallis, February 13, 1942: "The Epstein boys have added a little zip
to the script, why not let them continue with it and keep ahead of me?" (They did.)

crash of a British bomber in Germany. The five begin an arduous trek on foot back to England, encountering and eradicating Nazis by the bunch on their way. Two meet glorious but violent deaths early on, leaving three—Flynn, Reagan and the robust Alan Hale—to reach Holland, seize a British plane from the Nazis and fly back to England with military information acquired.* (One reviewer called the film "Three Musketeers 1942.")

Reagan felt his "high spot in the picture was a solo effort in which I knocked an arrogant Gestapo officer kicking, and calmly helped myself to his breakfast."

"There is quite a bit of joking in the script now," Walsh wrote Wallis two weeks after the start of principal photography. "I like it, I think it might be a good twist to have a sort of a 'Musketeers' feeling of great comradeship between our men. Frankly, they don't think they have a Chinaman's chance of ever escaping, so they are going to have a 'Roman' holiday, and do all the damage they can, blow up all the military equipment they can lay their hands on . . ." Flynn, however, was not too pleased at the fast snappy lines handed to Reagan by the Epsteins, and on four different occasions stalked off the set claiming to be ill. Walsh refused to be cowed by his star and retaliated by giving Reagan some additional bits of humorous dialogue.

Flynn's interest in the scripts he performed, an interest Reagan seldom shared, prompted him to make his opinion known. He wrote Hal Wallis on February 23:

> Since we had not come to it as yet, I haven't mentioned to you the very bad feeling I get from having [Arthur] Kennedy dead in the bomber while I talk cheerfully to Reagan and jokingly to the CO in England over the short wave. It is, to say the least, callous and I don't think the audience will forget for one moment the corpse flying with us in the back seat while we ignore him. Can he be wounded, or killed outside the plane?†
>
> Please let me know.
>
> Regards,
> Errol

---

*A British film, *The Invaders*, starring Raymond Massey (who appeared as the German colonel in *Desperate Journey*) had almost the identical story line in reverse. A Nazi landing party is stranded when its submarine is sunk in Hudson Bay—and the six Nazi survivors trek across Canada, being murdered one by one.

† In the final cut, Kennedy was wounded, not dead, during the interchange, and *then* died.

A week after filming began on *Desperate Journey, Kings Row* was released, and never were reviews so at odds. The *New Yorker* decreed: "'Kings Row' will give you that rare glow which comes from seeing a job well done crisply, competently, and with confidence. It has such distinction that it is plainly too good for the shoddy fellowship of the 'ten best pictures of the year.' Let us simply record that in February, 1941, Warner Brothers produced a good movie. . . . I wish I could understand the mechanics of the picture—how they combined dialogue, costuming, and set design to convey the variety of the social structure in an American town of the nineteen-hundreds. Anyway they did . . . Ronald Reagan capably breezes through the part of the town sport who becomes a victim of Dr. Gordon [Charles Coburn]. . . . Reagan has never appeared to such excellent advantage."

Taking a different view, *The New York Times* reviewer felt, "Warner Brothers bit off a great deal more than they could chew when they tried to make a cogent motion picture out of Henry Bellamann's gloomy and ponderous novel, 'Kings Row.' . . . Just why Warners attempted a picture of this sort in these times, and just why the corps of high-priced artists which they employed for it did such a bungling job, are questions which they are probably mulling more anxiously than anyone else. For the disappointing fact is that 'Kings Row' . . . is one of the bulkiest blunders to come out of Hollywood in some time . . . and Ronald Reagan and Ann Sheridan make only casual acquaintance with the characters [they play] . . ." If Reagan believed the film would make him a major star overnight, he had miscalculated. Nonetheless, it did extremely well at the box office, perhaps because the turgid soap-opera quality of the film afforded a kind of masochistic relief from the torrent of horrific war stories both real and on film.

For a brief few days in March, Warners considered Reagan for an upcoming film, *Casablanca*. Publicity releases stated he would star opposite Ann Sheridan (the Ingrid Bergman role). Exactly which male role he was to play was never specified. In the original concept, the idealistic Laszlow (played by Paul Henreid) and Rick (Bogart) had equal billing as co-stars. Howard Koch, who shared screenplay credit on the film, claimed the role for which Reagan was considered was Laszlow (the casting list in Warners' file substantiates this). Reagan never knew which part he might have had or why he lost it. At the time, it did not seem important in view of his army status.

On March 30, 1942, Jack Warner had written the U.S. Army

asking for an extended deferment for thirty days (from the pregranted April date already set) on the basis that Reagan had not completed the "patriotic" film *Desperate Journey*. On April 2, Warner received this telegram:

REGRET TO INFORM YOU THAT ANOTHER DEFERMENT CANNOT BE GRANTED 2ND LT. RONALD WILSON REAGAN CAVALRY STOP SHORTAGE OF AVAILABLE OFFICERS PREVENTS FAVORABLE CONSIDERATION—HORACE SYKES, COLONEL AGD, ADJ. GENERAL, FT. DOUGLAS, UTAH.

Reagan's remaining scenes were given top priority for completion before his departure.* His major concern was money. In spite of Jack Warner's patriotic bravado, players' salaries were suspended the same day they went off to war.

With all the expenses of the new house, Jane was not going to have an easy time budgeting, despite her increased salary. Then there was Nelle, whom Reagan had been supporting. He wrote Steve Trilling (now Jack Warner's assistant) asking if his mother could be paid $75 a week by the studio to answer his fan mail. Trilling sent a memo to Warner, who refused the request with: "We can't start a precedent." Reagan then approached Warner for a loan of the $75 a week to be paid directly to Nelle while he was in active service. Warner rejected this idea as well, but finally Reagan signed a note for $3,900; Nelle was to be sent $75 a week for one year. And Reagan, upon his return from his war service, was to repay the loan, interest free, to the studio at the rate of $200 a week for eighteen weeks and $300 on the nineteenth week.

He entrained for Fort Mason, California, near San Francisco, as 2nd Lieutenant Cavalry Reserve U.S. Army on April 19, 1942. He had learned beforehand that he would be on the staff there as a liaison officer loading convoys, so the physical he had on his first day of military service was redundant. But he claimed that after the eye examination one of the two doctors said, "If we sent you overseas, you'd shoot a general." And the other doctor countered, "Yes, and you'd miss him."

---

* Reagan turned in a creditable performance in *Desperate Journey* despite a fairly mixed bag of reviews. ("Reagan scores solidly," *Hollywood Reporter;* "Folks who will sacrifice reason for fast action and the joy of seeing 'Nazis' foiled should find it entirely gratifying. Terry and the Pirates will do as well for the rest of us," Bosley Crowther, *The New York Times.* Charles Einfeld, director of Warners' publicity department, wrote Warner, "The critics take the picture for a ride, kidding it as though it was a Horatio Alger yarn. I'm not at all concerned, because the business is terrific and the audience loves it.")

REAR
GUNNER

"Yes, and the Rear Gunner—the little fella in the flying fish bowl—the
hawk-eyed shooting man who clears
the sky in the rear so that his plane
can fly forward . . ."
—*Rear Gunner*, a Warner Brothers
short subject made with the cooperation of the Army Air Force, with
Ronald Reagan as narrator

13

TEN DAYS BEFORE REAGAN ARRIVED AT FORT MASON, Bataan had surrendered to the Japanese, and General George Marshall and Harry Hopkins were in London discussing aid for Russia by launching a second front. A few weeks later, Corregidor fell, the Japanese had taken Mandalay, forcing the British to withdraw along Chindwin Valley to India, the Germans launched the V-2 rocket and Vyacheslav Mikhailovich Molotov, representing the USSR, signed, in London, the Anglo-Soviet twenty-year alliance. The world was at war and America and her allies were suffering the worst blows.

Reagan was Fort Mason's only movie star. His commanding officer, Colonel Phillip Booker of the regular army field artillery, was a short, trim Southerner "with the wiry physique of a horseman." An intraservice rivalry existed between the cavalry and the artillery. "Never knew a cavalryman who knew a damned thing," Booker would grumble. A sharp, no-nonsense man, he was not much impressed with Reagan's background.

"Colonel Booker, you and I have something in common,"

Reagan remarked over dinner on his first evening at the fort.

"How's that, Reagan?"

"Well, I understand that you are a graduate of Virginia Military Institute, and I once played in a picture about VMI called *Brother Rat*."

With a cold stare, the colonel replied, "Yes, Reagan, I saw that picture—nothing ever made me so damned mad in my life."

In many ways, Reagan found army life satisfying. He much enjoyed the company of men, the chance to ride daily (Fort Mason was primarily a cavalry post) and to dress in cavalry uniform, which included riding breeches, boots and spurs. His one complaint was the fact that he could not put his spurred boots on the glass top of his desk, and he tells the story of another lieutenant who took off his spurs and slipped them into a drawer so that he could swing his feet to his desk top without fear of breaking the glass. At that moment, "Colonel Booker came swinging through" the office the lieutenant shared with Reagan. "The Colonel didn't pause in his stride," Reagan recalls, "and it didn't seem that he looked down as he passed the spurless younger officer. 'Aren't you afraid you'll catch cold, son?'" he commented and was out the door before an answer could be given.

Despite the cool attitude of the colonel, Reagan was a celebrity at Fort Mason; and although he did not receive special treatment, the men on the base were impressed. Reagan was bombarded with requests for information, introductions and statistics about many of the more glamorous women stars, which he good-naturedly answered when he could. At the end of two months, most of his fellow officers were transferred to other bases preparatory to being sent overseas. Clearly, the army was going to have to find a domestic post for Reagan, and he was more than apprehensive as to what that might be, realizing he would have to sit out the war there. Luckily, he was granted a weekend leave to be present "at a giant rally of picture people [in Hollywood] for the purpose of launching the newly created USO program."

Jane appeared with him. She seemed to be managing well in his absence. Nelle was taken care of, and on August 14, 1942, Jack Warner sent Reagan a "bonus check" of six hundred dollars. (On July 29, 1941, Warner had also sent a like amount as a gift, "to buy something for your home . . .") Warner was now a Lieutenant Colonel, Public Relations Division, Army Air Force, with offices at 4000 West Olive Street, Burbank, which in fact was the studio.

A short time after Reagan returned to Fort Mason from his Hollywood weekend, he was ordered to prepare a program at the base to celebrate "I Am an American Day."* Colonel Booker helped him work out the details of the military part (parade, etc.), but he introduced the idea of obtaining a celebrity to sing the national anthem. *Who?* the general wanted to know. "My newly acquired instinct led me to hesitate and avoid a direct answer long enough for the General [("Hap") Arnold, commanding officer of the entire base] to express his own preference." General Arnold turned out to be a Jeanette MacDonald fan. One hour later, Reagan had managed to contact the gorgeous forty-year-old soprano and get her to agree to appear, not as difficult an assignment as one might imagine, for Metro, where she had reigned for nine years as the prima donna of film operetta, had just terminated her contract and she was happy to be given something to shore up her shaken ego. The ceremony was held at a nearby dog track. Standing on an improvised stage made in the box seats, the glorious Jeanette, still in fine voice, sang the national anthem as well as her most famous film songs. The audience of seventeen thousand soldiers loved her, and she had them standing, singing along with her, when she closed with "The Battle Hymn of the Republic." Reagan's instinct had proven hugely sound.

The air force remained part of the army until the end of the war, and so it was not as curious as it might sound today that Reagan, an army cavalry officer, was soon transferred to the air force, which had begun a First Motion Picture Unit at the old Hal Roach Studios in Culver City, newly dubbed "Fort Roach." Although he would be billeted during most of the week at Fort Roach, he would be able to see Jane and Maureen frequently. "I would regret one price I had to pay for this assignment: no more boots and breeches . . ."

Fort Roach (also sometimes called "Fort Wacky") was a strange mixture of the real and the surreal. Thirteen hundred enlisted men and officers—most without previous military training—were stationed there. Air force regulations stipulated that only flying officers could command a post. Paul Mantz, a film stunt pilot, was the only flying officer at the fort who qualified and

---

*Newly designated by Franklin D. Roosevelt and the 76th Congress to be observed on the third Sunday of May, annually. The 82nd Congress, by Joint Resolution, February 29, 1952, designated September 17 of each year "Citizenship Day" and repealed the resolution authorizing "I Am an American Day."

so he was made post commander. Very few of his men had ever been up in a plane. They had been writers, actors, directors, cameramen, cutters, sound men, wardrobe men, prop men, makeup artists, special-effects men—many of them the best Hollywood had ever hired. Their assignment at Fort Roach was to make training and documentary films and to prepare aerial photographers for combat camera crews.

Reagan began his new job as a personnel officer (Assistant AAF Public Relations), "interviewing and processing applicants for commissions. . . . For the most part," Reagan recalled, "our volunteers were ineligible for regular military duty and simply and sincerely wanted to serve. . . . A great many people . . . harbor a feeling that the personnel of the motion picture unit were somehow draft dodgers avoiding danger. The Army doesn't play that way. There was a special job the Army wanted done and it was after men who could do the job. The overwhelming majority of men and officers serving at our post were limited service like myself." (At one time or another during the war, Arthur Kennedy, Burgess Meredith [there with Reagan], Clark Gable, Alan Ladd, Van Johnson and George Montgomery, among other film performers, were also stationed at Fort Roach.)

Within a matter of weeks, Reagan's job shifted to his prewar expertise—acting before the cameras. On August 5, 1942, a request was made by Colonel Jack Warner, through the Burbank public-relations office, on behalf of 2nd Lieutenant Ronald Reagan for a promotion to 1st Lieutenant. This was denied by the War Department by command of Lieutenant General Arnold and signed by Clifford P. Bradley, Colonel A.C. Chief, Military Personnel Division, Washington, August 25, 1942.

Reagan's first army film was *Rear Gunner,* in which he was the narrator. The film (script by Edwin Gilbert) dealt with the poignant story of one Pee Wee Williams, a young gunner in the Army Air Force, his education and his brave action under fire. Warner Brothers "produced and paid for the film," which meant the army supplied personnel and technicians while the studio paid for processing and prints. The original interpretation of the deal was that Warners would receive credit and therefore goodwill by contributing to the war effort. That was not how Jack Warner saw it, however. His plan was to release the short commercially, which caused a furor in Washington. (Coincidentally, on August 14, the day principal photography was completed, Warners issued that second six-hundred-dollar check to Reagan without any explanation of it on the payroll stub in the Warner file. In theory, no serviceman was permitted to accept pay from civilian companies for work also paid for by the army.)

July 14, 1942

MEMORANDUM TO: Col. Minton Kay
AAF Photo Division
Maritime Building
18th & H. Streets, N.W.
Washington, D.C.

The War Department Bureau of Public Relations imposes no objection to the production of the script "Rear Gunner" for release to military personnel exclusively. However, the release of these pictures through commercial houses for paid admissions, exploiting picture personalities [in this case, Reagan] involves policies which the Bureau of Public Relations is not prepared to announce at this time, hence such approval on this script is withheld.

FOR THE DIRECTOR, BUREAU OF PUBLIC RELATIONS
V.F. Shaw
Administrative Executive
Bureau of Public Relations

October 2, 1942

MEMORANDUM: Chief, Pictorial Service
Army Air Forces
Maritime Building
18th & H. Streets, N.W.
(Attn: Major Keighley)

Subject: "Rear Gunner"

1. This office has screened the picture and disapproved any consideration of commercial release because the production violates standing War Department policy in that professional actors who have been commissioned in the Army play leading roles [Reagan and Burgess Meredith]. Under the present decision screen actors now in the Army will not be loaned out to studios for the purpose of producing commercial pictures.
2. Should you decide to purchase this picture from Warner

and pay print costs, this office will be glad to reconsider release as an Air Force project through the War Activities
Committee.*

> FOR THE DIRECTOR:
> W.M. Wright, Jr.
> Colonel, G.S.C.
> Chief, Pictorial Branch

On January 28, 1943, a War Department memorandum
signed by Curtis Mitchell, Lt. Col., G.S.C. Acting Chief, Pictorial
Branch stated:

Release of the film [*Rear Gunner*] fills what appears to be a
morale need, [but it also] allows Warners to exploit or to
profit from a picture which by a combination of circumstances remains their own property and permits them the use
of an officer who was formerly their own star [Reagan] and a
free lance star [Meredith].

In the end, Warners was given commercial rights and *Rear
Gunner* was released as a short to accompany other Warner films.
As propaganda it was acceptable and might well have improved
the image of the rear gunner. It also was good public relations for
Warners and, at the same time, kept one of their players on the
screen so that he would not be forgotten. The army must have
been pleased with Reagan's work, for on October 1, 1942, the
request for a promotion was resubmitted and subsequently approved. Reagan was now a first lieutenant.

Reagan claims that those men who did not experience combat
had "an almost reverent feeling for the men who did face the enemy." At Fort Roach this feeling was heightened by the constant
viewing of millions of feet of combat film that was processed there,
bits and pieces to be used whenever a real effect was needed—air
crashes, men enveloped in flames, strafings—all the horrors of
war. Reagan might be said to have been sitting out the war on the
bench, as he had done the football seasons at Eureka, viewing on
a daily basis the players who were in the action. He was not the
only one, of course, and he had legitimate reasons for being there.

---

*Why, in that case, the army accepted financing of the short by Warner Brothers, agreeing
to "loan out" Reagan's services and allowing the film to be shot on army ground with
other army personnel, is not explained.

But heroes did not sit on the bench while other men carried the ball. And that thought must have rankled.

The biggest Broadway hit of 1942 was Irving Berlin's *This Is the Army*—dubbed "TITA" by the cast (book, music and lyrics by "Sergeant Irving Berlin," production assembled and staged by Ezra Stone—performed by men in the service [female roles as well], with all proceeds after costs going to Army Emergency Relief). Berlin, the erstwhile sergeant from World War I, was also in the cast and sang "Oh, How I Hate to Get Up in the Morning." The song was originally sung by him in a play titled *Yip Yip Yaphank* (1918), and he nightly stopped the show with his appearance. One other song, "Mandy," also came from that show. Otherwise, the score was new and mostly crowd stirrers ("This Is the Army, Mr. Jones," "I Left My Heart at the Stage Door Canteen" and "American Eagles").

Jack Warner wasted no time in pursuing it. (Warner appeared to be in the enviable position of holding the rank of colonel while remaining in Hollywood actively engaged in running his studio. All through the war years studio memos flowed from "Colonel Jack L. Warner.") "I was in California and immediately contacted . . . Irving Berlin," he explained to the *New York Post*. "On the next day, July 4, 1942 [the day of the Broadway premiere], there were fourteen calls between Berlin and me. 'Put your bid in,' Berlin said. I said, 'We'll advance you $250,000 for Army Emergency Relief and in addition will give you 50% of the profits.' I immediately called my brother [Abe in New York] and said, 'Go right over to Berlin and close the deal.' He appeared and gave Berlin the 250,000 bucks and closed it. Then I called my other brother Harry, and said, 'I've been thinking we should give the Army Emergency Relief the complete profits.'" Harry reclaimed the contract, tore it up and wrote a new one.

George Murphy (a navy seaman in 1917 but not a serviceman during World War II) was cast in the role of a former musical-comedy star who turns impresario for the war effort. Reagan portrayed his army private son, Johnny Jones, and carried the romantic lead opposite Joan Leslie (as Eileen Dibble, daughter of a former vaudevillian, played by Charles Butterworth). Other players, including such stellar and disparate names as Kate Smith and Sergeant Joe Louis, had smaller, often walk-on appearances. The service cast received no other remuneration than their usual monthly pay, but the civilian performers were on salary. George

Murphy was paid $28,333.33 for his role, for which the studio had originally wanted Pat O'Brien (shooting schedules had conflicted. O'Brien was making *Bombardier*).

Berlin literally moved into the studio during the making of the film. He appeared only in the "Oh, How I Hate to Get Up in the Morning" number, wrote one new song ("What Does He Look Like") and was not responsible for direction (Michael Curtiz), screenplay (Casey Robinson and Captain Claude Binyon) or production (Jack Warner and Hal Wallis). Yet, as Warner wrote his brother Harry, Berlin was "100 men in one" and functioned on all these levels.

"We [the company of about two hundred men] were welcomed to the film capital like conquering heroes." Ezra Stone recalled. "We got off the train six or seven times (so it would seem like six or seven times as many of us in the picture) and marched the several miles to the studio as the [battery of publicity] cameras continued to grind. The entire studio personnel had lined the street to cheer us wildly . . . as we passed through the gates.

"After the Major [Ambraz] had approved a vacant field adjacent to Warners' back lot as the site for our camp . . . overnight there sprang up thirteen wooden-floored, steam-heated, electric-lighted, furnished tents [outfitted by the studio prop department] in a neat double row . . . a shower house, administration and dispensary room, three latrines, a PX . . . and a flagpole court landscaped with trees and shrubbery still bearing nursery tags. We christened it 'Camp TITA.'

"The nineteen tents at the camp could not hold the 310 man unit. It barely held the night shift of our most unmilitary guard duty unit. So we all stayed in a great variety of personally secured lodgings from flophouses on Main Street to Cole Porter's Bel Air mansion," Stone added.

Reagan was back on the old lot and, permitted to go home at night. He has said he was introduced to Berlin five times during the first week of shooting ("Each time he was glad to see me."). After viewing the early rushes, Berlin approached him. "Young fellow, I just saw some of your work. You've got a few things to correct—for example, a huskiness of the voice—but you really should give this business some serious consideration when the war is over."

To augment the cast, Warners hired extras and dressed them in uniform. Confusion reigned throughout the first weeks of filming, for it was impossible to recognize the real officers from the fakes and a lot of frenzied saluting was wasted. Finally, the studio

ABOVE *Jane Blue Wilson and John Wilson, Reagan's maternal great-grandparents, circa 1860. (COURTESY THE WILSON FAMILY)* BELOW *Dutch Reagan, age two, driving his go-cart with its American flag waving in the backyard of his Tampico, Illinois, home. (DIXON EVENING TELEGRAPH)*

ABOVE *Ronald "Dutch" Reagan (third from left) with parents, Jack and Nelle, and brother, Neil, 1913, Tampico, Illinois. (DIXON EVENING TELE-GRAPH)* BELOW *With baton, far left, front row, in Dixon, Illinois, 1920. Shortly after this was taken, Dutch marched up the wrong street ahead of the band and had to run back to catch up with it. (DIXON EVENING TELEGRAPH)*

The brothers caddied summers at the country club in Dixon. Pictured here after the Women's Golf Tournament, Dutch (far left, front row) and Neil (far left, second row), circa 1922. (*DIXON EVENING TELEGRAPH*)

ABOVE *In front of the Reagan home on South Hennepin Avenue, about the time he had to carry his drunken father up the steps of the porch and into the house. (BILL THOMPSON)* RIGHT *Ralph McKinzie, Dutch Reagan's football coach at Eureka, still active in 1985. (EUREKA COLLEGE ARCHIVES)*

ABOVE *As one of Mac's Golden Tornadoes,*
Eureka, 1929. (EUREKA COLLEGE ARCHIVES)
BELOW *He never became a great football player*
at Eureka, but he was the star of the swimming
team. (EUREKA COLLEGE ARCHIVES)

ABOVE *The Dramatic Fraternity at Eureka. Dutch is wearing glasses, third from left, rear row; sweetheart Margaret Cleaver is far left, front row; and Neil Reagan is second from right, rear row (1930). (EUREKA COLLEGE ARCHIVES)* BELOW *Radio WHO, Des Moines, Iowa, 1934. His sports program's sponsor was a tobacco company. The Irish setter at his feet was named Peggy, after lost love Margaret Cleaver. (BILL THOMPSON)*

He signed with Warner Brothers in 1937, and became "the Errol Flynn of the B's . . . as brave as Errol, but in a low-budget fashion." He did most of his own stunts, above as Brass Bancroft, Secret Service hero in Code of the Secret Service *(1939). (WARNER BROTHERS ARCHIVES, UNIVERSITY OF SOUTHERN CALIFORNIA)*

ABOVE *He began dating Jane Wyman in 1938 when they both appeared in* Brother Rat. *Here they take in the sun at Santa Monica Beach. The man in white is Bill Cook, a friend from Reagan's college days (1938). (BILL THOMPSON)* RIGHT *Time-out with boxing coach Mush Callahan, preparing for Warner Brothers' 1939 film* Queer Money, *released as* Smashing the Money Ring. *The film was so bad, Reagan pleaded with Jack Warner not to release it. (WARNER BROTHERS ARCHIVES, UNIVERSITY OF SOUTHERN CALIFORNIA)*

ABOVE   *Onstage in San Francisco with the Louella Parsons vaudeville tour, January 1940. (From left to right) Announcer, Susan Hayward, Jane Wyman, June Preisser, Parsons, Joy Hodges, Reagan, and Arlene Whelan. (JOY HODGES SCHIESS)*   BELOW *The newlyweds, Ronnie and Jane, with Nelle and Jack Reagan in January 1940. Fellow Dixonian Louella Parsons held the wedding reception at her home in Beverly Hills. (WARNER BROTHERS AR-CHIVES, UNIVERSITY OF SOUTHERN CALIFORNIA)*

ABOVE   *The world premiere of* Knute Rockne—All American *in South Bend, Indiana, home of Notre Dame University in October 1940. (Second row, third from left) Peggy Diggens, Jimmy Fiddler, Irene Rich, Gail Patrick, Anita Louise, James Roosevelt, Bonnie Rockne (Knute Rockne's widow) and Gail Page (who played Mrs. Rockne in the film). (Front row, from left) Charlie Ruggles, William Marshall, Bob Hope, Kane Richmond, Donald Crisp, Pat O'Brien, and Reagan. Jane and Jack Reagan also were present at the festivities. Reagan's dad and fellow Irishman O'Brien managed to close most of the bars in town.* (WARNER BROTHERS ARCHIVES, UNIVERSITY OF SOUTHERN CALIFORNIA)
BELOW   *The conquering hero returned to Dixon with Parsons in September 1941 for a gala homecoming, and was a guest at Dixon's one grand mansion, the Walgreen estate. Here, Mrs. Walgreen takes a ride with him through her property.* (DIXON EVENING TELEGRAPH)

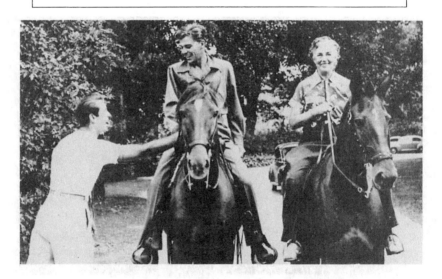

LEFT *Dutch Reagan (movie star) and friend Bill Thompson during the homecoming event.* (*BILL THOMPSON*) BELOW *Dutch and Neil having lunch at the Brown Derby Restaurant in Hollywood during one of Reagan's weekend passes from nearby Fort Roach where he was stationed during the war (1943).* (*ACADEMY OF MOTION PICTURE ARTS AND SCIENCES*)

Reagan made Stallion Road *upon his return to civilian life. He fell in love with the black thoroughbred mare, Tar Baby, that he rode in the film and bought her from the trainer in two installments. This scene was shot five times before Tar Baby cleared the jump, but Reagan refused to let someone else take it for him.* (*WARNER BROTHERS ARCHIVES, UNIVERSITY OF SOUTHERN CALIFORNIA*)

ABOVE *Happy days. Reagan, his wife, Jane Wyman, and children, Maureen (five and a half) and Michael (one), by the pool of the dream house they built overlooking Sunset Boulevard (1946).* (COURTESY OF THE WISCONSIN CENTER FOR FILM AND THEATRE RESEARCH) BELOW *On the board of the Screen Actors Guild in 1946 when Robert Montgomery was president. (From left to right) Edward Arnold, Walter Pidgeon, Jane Wyman, Dick Powell, Montgomery, George Murphy, Reagan, Alexis Smith, Robert Taylor, and Gene Kelly.* (SAG ARCHIVES)

Reagan was elected president of the Screen Actors Guild (1947). He began his first term of five during the chaotic time of an industry strike and was immediately recognized as a rousing speaker. (SAG ARCHIVES)

Once again saving someone from drowning. This time Shirley Temple in the ill-fated That Hagen Girl *(1947). (WARNER BROTHERS ARCHIVES, UNIVERSITY OF SOUTHERN CALIFORNIA)*

ABOVE *Recuperating from a broken leg at the time of his divorce from Jane Wyman. Note the watch worn face on the inside (a style he always adopted) and the large Eureka school ring which finally was removed after he met Nancy. (GEORGE EASTMAN HOUSE, ROCHESTER, N.Y.)* BELOW *In 1948 Jane Wyman won both the Academy Award and the Golden Globe for Best Actress for her performance as the deaf mute in* Johnny Belinda. *Boss Jack Warner was also presented a Golden Globe (Foreign Correspondents Award), as executive producer of the film, which he had never wanted his studio to make. (WARNER BROTHERS ARCHIVES, UNIVERSITY OF SOUTHERN CALIFORNIA)*

ABOVE   *Eight years later, Nancy Davis was act-*
ing in films and had fallen in love with Ronald
Reagan. They were married only a few weeks after
this photograph was taken. (GEORGE EASTMAN
HOUSE, ROCHESTER, N.Y.) BELOW   *With co-*
star Doris Day in The Winning Team, *the last*
film he was to make at Warners (1952). He and Day
had once dated. (WARNER BROTHERS ARCHIVES,
UNIVERSITY OF SOUTHERN CALIFORNIA)

ABOVE *At the nadir of his career—appearing with the Continentals in Las Vegas. (GEORGE EASTMAN HOUSE, ROCHESTER, N.Y.)* BELOW *Dr. Loyal Davis (Nancy Reagan's father), Nancy, Edith (her mother), Nelle (Ronald Reagan's mother), and Reagan at the christening of Patricia (1954). (LIFE PICTURE SERVICE)*

ABOVE *Ronald Reagan and family. Movie actor and aspirant for the GOP nomination in California's gubernatorial election at home in Pacific Palisades with son Ronald and daughter Patricia.* (LIFE PICTURE SERVICE) BELOW *Home to Dixon. The Reagan brothers show Nancy the bedroom they shared at South Hennepin Avenue when they were young boys (1982).* (BILL THOMPSON)

issued arm bands with a "WB" shield, which all the civilian actors dressed as military officers or enlisted men were required to wear off-camera. "What kind of insignia is that," one outside observer asked Richard Burdick (one of TITA's three original dialogue writers brought to the Coast with the film).* "War Bureau," Burdick replied. "Special agents sent from Washington to report any laxity in duty." He later added, "Everything was four times larger than the stage show, of course . . . sets, cast, band . . . really quite overwhelming."

Stone also remembered that as far as Hollywood was concerned, "we rated as stars only in the service flag. We weren't allowed to eat in the same room with the studio's featured players, or talk to stars or the director [Reagan generally ate with co-star Murphy and director Curtiz]. We had no dressing rooms and had to check on and off the sound stage when we went to the latrine."

George Murphy made much of the fact that he was (like George M. Cohan) a true Yankee Doodle boy born on the Fourth of July. Only nine years older than Reagan, he had to wear heavy makeup to appear paternal. The two men played well together. Reagan had a great deal of respect for Murphy and they shared many interests. (They also had numerous strong differences of opinion.) Murphy's father had been a dedicated Democrat and a noted track coach who had prepared the U.S. team for the 1912 Olympics. From youth, Murphy's interest in politics had been as strong as his involvement in theater and films. A Democrat like his father, he arrived in Hollywood in 1934 after a successful career on Broadway as a duo dance act with his wife, Julie Johnson. For eight years he tap-danced through a series of musicals, and in 1939 switched allegiance to the Republican party, becoming active in politics and in the Screen Actors Guild, where, in 1943, during the filming of *This Is the Army*, he was vice-president.

Unquestionably, Reagan's army years imbued him with an even deeper sense of patriotism and shifted him to a somewhat more conservative viewpoint. Murphy's influence during the making of *This Is the Army* cannot be discounted. Throughout the film they were constantly seen by others in "animated debate." And Reagan's already keen interest in the Screen Actors Guild intensified during this time.

Breen's censorship office presented the one major hurdle in Warners' way in the making of *This Is the Army*. Breen at first

---

* Burdick, with Horace Sutton, while stationed at Fort Slocum in New York, had written the book, music and lyrics for the first World War II full-length soldier show, *Spring Fever*.

flatly refused to allow the soldiers to masquerade as women performers in the show within a show. These female impersonations had provided some of the best scenes in the stage version. After an exhaustive exchange of letters in which the approval of the U.S. Army was noted, the studio was allowed to include the footage. The film was rushed through postproduction with the hope that the premiere could be held on July 4, but Warners' technical departments simply could not meet the deadline.*

On July 17, a day decreed "This Is the Army Day" by Mayor Fletcher Bowron of Los Angeles (the entire week was dubbed "This Is the Army Week" by California's Governor Earl Warren), "a powerful display of military equipment, a glittering assembly of motion picture stars and society leaders . . . marked the [Los Angeles and Hollywood] premiere of Irving Berlin's 'This Is the Army' . . ." The film opened in five local theaters simultaneously, each with bands blasting, army exhibits and movie stars. Included in the outdoor displays were four-thousand-pound "Block Busters" (bombs), General Sherman tanks, howitzers, machine guns, half-tracks, jeeps and antiaircraft guns never before on exhibit. (The Block Busters were identical to those that had been used just that week in destroying Hamburg, Berlin and Rome.)

At the Hollywood Theater, the crack drill cadre of forty men from Santa Anita (by December 1942, Santa Anita Park had been converted for use as an army ordnance training center under the command of Brigadier General B. W. Simpson) performed spectacular maneuvers with the accompaniment of the Santa Anita Band led by Sergeant Skinny Ennis. Hundreds of other soldiers from Camp MacArthur massed in drill formation. Just about everyone who was anyone in Hollywood was there, and just about all the women, in a touch suggested by the premiere committee, wore black or white gowns. Jane, escorted by Lieutenant Reagan in dress uniform, proved the exception and attended in a short dinner dress of shocking cyclamen with a wide gold kid yoke at the neck, a silver fox cape over her shoulders (the temperature was 82 degrees that day) and massive amethyst jewelry.

"It's socko entertainment . . . dynamite. . . . It's democracy in action to the hilt. It's showmanship and patriotism combined to a super-duper Yankee Doodle degree," the Hollywood trade papers

---

* Jack Warner offered President Roosevelt a print to be shown at the White House before the premiere. On July 9, 1943, Edwin M. Watson, major general secretary to the president, replied: "Quite frankly, the demands of his [the president's] time during these critical days seem to grow heavier as the War progresses and he has practically no time in which to see movies."

pronounced. And eleven days later, on July 28, Broadway welcomed both productions—the street display and the film. "Broadway strollers flocked into the area [from Fifty-first to Fifty-second Street] as though drawn by a giant magnet. They stood in silent wonderment as the battle-clad gun crews pointed long muzzled 44mm AA and five 50-caliber AA machine guns into the night sky, maneuvering them as though enemy planes were streaking down in attack. . . . Military airs and [musical] numbers from the movie filled the air from 8 to 9 P.M. when a bugler sounded assembly inside the theater and the show . . . got under way."*

New York was as enthusiastic as Hollywood. *This Is the Army,* the critics agreed, had "the unslackening tempo and the high-hearted spirit of a country that can keep its songs and its humor even in a war. . . . It is from beginning to end, a great show." Reagan was not singled out for any praise. In fact, the *Times* reviewer did not even mention his name. Still, he did acquit himself well as Jerry Jones—the butt of the song "This Is the Army, Mr. Jones," and was believable throughout. The film made more than ten million dollars, a sizable gross in 1943, and Warner Brothers did turn over all the profits to AER. That is not to say the studio came away empty-handed. Part of the acceptable expenses was the rental of their sound stages and equipment. The salaries of their nonmilitary contract players—George Murphy, Joan Leslie, George Tobias, Alan Hale, Una Merkel and Rosemary De-Camp—were deducted, as were the pay of the director and all technical staff (which meant the studio did not have to pay these salaries as per their employees' contracts). In essence, the film cost Warner Brothers nothing—and received for them the exhibition fee when shown in their theaters in addition to overwhelming publicity and goodwill. Additionally, like *Rear Gunner,* it kept Reagan before the public without any investment on the studio's part.

Jack Warner considered *This Is the Army* one of the best films ever made for the studio, and his part in it of prime importance. This fact was, however, to cause an irreconcilable rift between him and Hal Wallis.† On November 23, Wallis gave the *Los An-*

---

*Tickets in Hollywood were scaled from $75 to $2.20 (earning for Army Emergency Relief $62,500) and from $55 to $2.20 in New York (earning an additional $28,340 for AER).
†Hal Wallis claimed he had first seen the show in a pre–New York engagement. He then wired Jack Warner and together they decided to film it. He later said, "Irving came West for preliminary work with Casey [Robinson], Mike Curtiz . . . and me, and then we accompanied him back to New York by train [the *Silver Chief.* Berlin returned to Hollywood for the filming]. We worked on the script from the time we left Union Station. Somewhere in the Middle West, we got stuck in a snowdrift overnight, and had to be dug out with snowplows. We were hardly aware of it. As the snow piled up around the train, we outlined

geles Times an interview about his responsibility for *This Is the Army* and other Warner films. Warner telegraphed him a few days later:

> I RESENT AND WON'T STAND FOR YOUR CONTINUING TO
> TAKE ALL CREDIT FOR . . . *THIS IS THE ARMY, GOD IS MY*
> *COPILOT, PRINCESS O'ROURKE* . . . I HAPPENED TO BE ONE
> WHO SAW THESE STORIES, READ PLAYS, BOUGHT AND
> TURNED THEM OVER TO YOU. YOU COULD AT LEAST SAY
> SO, AND I WANT TO BE ACCREDITED ACCORDINGLY. YOU
> CERTAINLY HAVE CHANGED . . .

Wallis wired back:

> . . . ARTICLES APPEARED WITHOUT YOUR PROPER CREDIT
> DUE UNFORTUNATELY TO OMISSION BY INTERVIEWERS.
> SORRY YOU FEEL I HAVE CHANGED. I HAVE NOT CHANGED
> AND DON'T WANT TO IN MY REGARD FOR YOU. HAL.

Warner, refusing to accept this explanation, telegraphed Charles Einfeld (Warners' director of publicity):

> MEAN WHAT I SAID MY WIRE [TO WALLIS] AND WILL DEFI-
> NITELY TAKE LEGAL ACTION IF THIS ISN'T STOPPED . . .
> SICK, TIRED EVERYONE TAKING ALL CREDIT AND I BECOME
> SMALL BOY AND DOING MOST OF WORK . . .

The same day [November 30] he dispatched the following to Wallis:

> STOP GIVING ME DOUBLE TALK ON YOUR PUBLICITY. THIS
> WIRE WILL SERVE NOTICE ON YOU THAT I WILL TAKE
> LEGAL ACTION IF MY NAME HAS BEEN ELIMINATED FROM
> ANY STORY IN ANY FORM, SHAPE OR MANNER AS BEING IN
> CHARGE OF PRODUCTION WHILE YOU WERE EXECUTIVE
> PRODUCER . . .*

---

the whole production. Irving disappeared from time to time into the adjoining bedroom to compose new songs. . . . He sang lustily as he worked, quite oblivious to the fact that we were snowbound.

   "We continued working in my suite at the Waldorf Towers in New York and at [his] house on Seventh Street in Greenwich Village. . . . He was never satisfied, and Casey . . . was miserable. Finally, Irving took over entirely, and Casey went on to another project."

*Wallis's and Warner's animosity flared again at the Academy Awards in March 1944. *Casablanca* was named Best Picture of the Year. Wallis stood up, intending to go to the

Reagan returned to his desk at Fort Roach, where he was "swept up" in what he refers to as "another frantic bit of picture-making." Hap Arnold (a good friend of Jack Warner's) thought it might be amusing to present to his fellow officers a film compiled of humorous outtakes of documentaries and training pictures made on the post that year. Jack Warner had pulled the same gag on various occasions for his own staff with his own films. Outtakes were pieces of film where performers blew or forgot their lines—using profanity or some outrageously amusing reaction, or where the camera or sound crews miscalculated. However, at Fort Roach, outtakes were not saved. Reagan, rather than disappointing the general or gaining his wrath, set about to fake it.

Colonel Owen Crump, who had been a producer at Warners, "called an emergency meeting and gave the unit's top writers, including Norman Krasna, forty-eight hours to come up with a script. A week later General Arnold's guests [all top-ranking officers] are sitting back at the Pentagon party. Lights dim. The film rolls. Reagan, chewing on a cigar and stabbing his pointer at a wall map, briefing a squadron of bomber pilots on a vital mission [stands there].

"'This is our target for tonight,' he declared. The wall map rolls up like a runaway window blind, and there stands a naked girl."

Don Dwiggins remembered another incident when a Fort Roach commando, Sergeant Charles Tanne, an actor and a clever impersonator who "one night when Reagan had the duty [telephoned from another office]:

"'Uh, Lieutenant,' he said in a Southern accent, 'we all jus' arrived at Union Station from Ft. Leavenworth. I've got me 500 cavalry troops here with their horses. Would you kindly tell me the best route to Fort Roach? And has the hay arrived yet?'"

For about "a minute and a half" Reagan bought the gag.

Night-duty officer could be a boring assignment, and Reagan lightened it by writing some arresting entries in the log. One such entry read: "3 a.m.—Post attacked by three regiments of Japanese infantry. Led Cavalry charge and repulsed enemy. Quiet

---

stage to receive the Oscar, but Warner leaped to his feet and rushed to the stage, beating Wallis there. With "a flashing smile and a look of great self-satisfaction" he accepted the award. "I tried to get out of the row of seats and into the aisle but the Warner family sat blocking me," Wallis claimed. "I had no alternative but to sit down again, humiliated and furious." The Academy apologetically sent Wallis another Oscar, but Warner did not apologize.

resumed." Another time, he noted: "Special instructions passed on to New Officer of the Day. New Officer indeed! Did they see me in those West Point pictures?"

The first Allied air raid on Rome took place on July 19. By the twenty-third of that month, Palermo was occupied; and on the twenty-sixth, Benito Mussolini fell from power and a new government was formed. Within three months, the Allies had invaded Italy, the Fifth Army occupied Naples, and on October 13, Italy declared war on their former ally, Germany. But the war was far from over, and indeed, some of the most bitter campaigns, both in Europe and in the South Pacific, remained to be fought.*

Reagan was stationed at Fort Roach throughout the war and helped in the making of several good training films. He also retained an ongoing working relationship with Warner Brothers. On March 18, 1943, Warner had telegraphed:

DIRECTOR, WAR DEPARTMENT BUREAU OF PUBLIC RELATIONS, WASHINGTON: WARNERS REQUESTS PERMISSION FOR LT. RONALD REAGAN TO APPEAR 15 MINUTE PROGRAM BLUE NETWORK [NBC] NIGHT 3-27-43 STOP THIS IS VETERAN OF FOREIGN WARS ANNUAL PROGRAM STOP REAGAN WILL ACT AS NARRATOR OF PROGRAM TAKEN FROM AIR FORCE WARNER PICTURE.†

The War Department granted Lieutenant Reagan permission. Reagan was not personally involved in this request or its granting, but by his appearance on the show the War Department was technically approving the film. Patriotic though it was (it focused on a bombing crew over the South Pacific), *Air Force* was still a commercial venture. ("Fried Jap going down," a bombardier sneers after scoring a hit.) Warner Brothers seems to have had a relationship with the War Department not accorded the other major studios.

The war created a bonanza for Hollywood. Within a year of Pearl Harbor, movie attendance went up 50 percent as each week eighty million customers bought tickets. Across the country,

---

*In early 1943, Reagan bet Captain Edwin Gilbert (the writer of *Rear Gunner*) that "the war would be over by Labor Day. When it didn't end, Reagan paid off the bet—twenty-five dollars."

†Short sections of the sound track of *Air Force,* which starred John Garfield, Gig Young and Arthur Kennedy, were used in this NBC radio show. Reagan held the excerpts together with a running narration.

boomtown movie theaters remained open around the clock to accommodate swing and graveyard shifts. The studios increased production to fill the growing demand. To keep the films rolling, they turned to whatever resources they had at hand. In most cases, they relied on stars who were too old or who had other reasons for being unable to serve. (At Warners, Errol Flynn, for instance, had once had tuberculosis and suffered a weakened lung; Bogart, forty-three at the beginning of the war, had been injured as a seaman during World War I; James Cagney and Paul Lukas were even older; Paul Henreid [born in Trieste] became an American citizen in 1940, but his birthplace made him exempt from service). Warners, which had a great many women under contract, made a large number of films calling for more mature or older men and melodramas that featured women. Former casting director Steve Trilling had now become Jack Warner's production chief, but with his background he had a practiced eye for star-making roles. Bette Davis, Barbara Stanwyck and Joan Crawford had to battle for the best roles as Trilling worked to create a wartime roster of new stars from among those under contract—Lauren Bacall, Olivia de Havilland, Ida Lupino, Joan Leslie, Susan Hayward, Ann Blyth, Brenda Marshall, Julie Bishop, Ann Sheridan, Priscilla Lane, Alexis Smith and Jane Wyman, to mention a few.

Wyman was cast in one inane comedy after the other. A Warners film always had a special stamp that identified it—well described in one film history as: "Murky and somber, with every cocktail bar seemingly full of cigarette smoke, streets and piers gleaming with rain, and heroines mink-clad and ready with convenient pistols to be produced at moments of stress to the strains of rich scores by [Max] Steiner, [Franz] Waxman, or [Erich Wolfgang] Korngold." But the wartime public desired lighter films, and comedies did well at the box office. Warners, however, had under contract only a few writers and directors who were adept at comedy and no star performers (with the exception of Eve Arden) who were known in this medium. Wyman's pert looks, bantering past roles and likability made her a natural candidate.

What Trilling and Wallis did not see, for the simple lack of looking, were Wyman's large sad eyes—those brown wells of emotion that everyone else, from her first-grade teacher to June Allyson, had observed. Wyman had a depth of character that scratched its way through the sleek veneer of such roles and made her dialogue seem more inane than it was. Finally she decided to do something about it. She spoke to Trilling. She wanted a chance to try a straight dramatic role. She was told that the studio had enough dramatic stars. How about a loan-out then? she asked. Warners was amenable.

Current on *The New York Times* best-seller list was *The Lost Weekend,* Charles Jackson's stark, unrelenting novel of a man's descent into the hell of alcoholism. The book contained one woman's role of depth, although quite small.* Paramount had bought the rights and Billy Wilder was to direct. With the advent of war, the problem- and social-conscious films of the Depression and post-Depression were almost obliterated by topical or escapist material. But Wilder was riding high. His *Double Indemnity,* an "archetypical *film noire,*" brilliantly made and incisively written (by Wilder), had just won him an Academy nomination for best picture, script, performance by a female star (Barbara Stanwyck, also borrowed from Warner Brothers for this film), cinematography (John Seitz) and music (Miklos Rozsak). Technically a suspense/crime melodrama, *Double Indemnity* dealt with the themes of greed and middle-class tragedy. The war had turned Wilder, a German Jew whose family had either died or were still incarcerated in concentration camps (all to perish), away from his early Lubitsch-like comedies (*Ninotchka, The Major and the Minor*). A Billy Wilder film had stature and would be seriously considered at award time. No matter how small the woman's role, appearing in such a film could only help a career. Wyman wanted such a chance desperately, and once she had convinced Lew Wasserman, he fought hard to sell Wilder on the idea that "pert" Wyman could pack a wallop if given the opportunity.

By this time, Wilder and his collaborator, Charles Brackett, had adapted the book *The Lost Weekend,* and to give it a slightly more upbeat quality, they had created a new character, Helen St. James, a woman in love with the alcoholic. To pass censorship demands they had also substituted writer's block for the character's latent homosexuality. Wilder (director and co-producer and co-writer) tested Wyman for this role—a sympathetic, winning young woman who could, when called upon, be tough—and she was signed to co-star with Ray Milland. The role was subordinate to Milland's, but it was solid. She began shooting on October 1, 1944 (all New York location scenes had been filmed without her). Principal photography was completed ten weeks later. She ex-

---

*A barfly played by Doris Dowling in the film.

pected the film to turn her career immediately around. But the liquor industry lobbied against its release, exerting strong pressure on Paramount.

The Reagan marriage was in a holding pattern. Wyman was frustrated and depressed with her situation at Warners, where she felt she was not getting the proper attention. The war bore on longer than American optimism had thought probable. Even so, the Reagans were one of the luckier couples. Reagan stood no chance of being sent overseas and he got home frequently. But their lives were pulling apart. He lived totally in a man's world, removed from the everyday concerns of being dependent on the film industry. She suffered some of the isolation she had felt when he was surrounded by his old TEKE buddies or debating with his political friends. The day-to-day care of Maureen was her responsibility, as was supporting the household and Nelle, Warner's loan payments having stopped in April 1943. The couple's time together, though frequent, was brief and seemed inappropriate for a discussion of small concerns and anxieties.

Early in 1944, Wyman went on a grueling twelve-week personal-appearance tour for the studio. The tour (which promoted U.S. bonds and Wyman's last Warner film, *The Dough Girls,* a wartime comedy that also starred Alexis Smith, Jack Carson and Ann Sheridan) took her home to St. Joseph for the first time in sixteen years. Few people she had known were still there, but she went back to the school she had once attended, visited the classrooms and had dinner with the Rudy Hofheimers, former classmates of hers. When she arrived back in California, she was exhausted and had only a week to prepare for a supporting role (Alexis Smith was assigned the female lead) in Warners' musical biography of Cole Porter (played with a poker face by the usually smoothly charming Cary Grant). The studio next cast her in a watered remake of *The Animal Kingdom,* fifth billing with Ann Sheridan and Alexis Smith again, in a role that was a throwback to her old hotcha-blonde days.

Wyman had always wanted another child. Maureen claims that as a youngster she "wanted two things in this world—a baby brother and a red scooter. And they [her parents] kept telling me that if I wanted a baby brother, I would have to save up. And one day they said I was going to get what I wanted that night [March 18, 1945]. I was sort of looking for a red scooter. But sure enough, it was a four-day-old baby brother. And my father [who was still in uniform and recently promoted to captain] said, 'Where is it?'

And I went up the stairs. I had ninety-seven cents. So I gave the lady from the adoption agency my piggy bank."

Three days earlier, the Reagans had disappeared for the day. Wyman says, "Michael [the baby] was only twelve hours old when Ronnie and I got him. . . . As far as we're concerned, we're blood. What else can I say? He's my baby boy." They sent out the following announcement:

Heavenly H.Q.
Special Order #2

Par. 2. Michael Edward Reagan is relieved from assignment and duty with present station and is assigned to the Reagan Base Unit, 9137 Cordell Drive, Hollywood, California. Duty assignment, "Son and Brother." Rations and quarters will be provided. Travel by stork authorized. Effective date of change on the Morning Report, 18 March, 1945.

The Reagans issued a statement that they had "decided to adopt because so many children in the world are in need of care and love, and a real home life. Therefore, we felt it was important for people who want more children and can provide for them to add from the outside to their family as we have. . . ." Certainly, Michael's adoption must have been the result of a combination of motives rather than of a single social issue. Wyman might well have felt she could not take time from her career to carry a child. And both could well have believed that an infant would help draw them closer as a family.

While Wyman was still working on *Night and Day*, *Lost Weekend* (having won its battle over the liquor lobby) was released. Hollywood took a second look at her. Wilder had photographed her with her natural, darker brown hair. Makeup had been minimal, playing up to the depth and size of her eyes, and her wardrobe had been attractive but simple and in good taste. True, her role was small, but when she was onscreen her performance was telling, and Wilder kept coming in for close-ups on the emotion held in her eyes. The delay in the film's release, although a disappointment to Wyman initially, now worked in her favor.

The Yearling, Marjorie Kinnan Rawlings's moving story of a young boy's attachment to a fawn, had been a best-selling book in 1940–41. Metro had bought the rights, and in the summer of 1941 production had begun in Florida with Spencer Tracy as the boy's father. Within a week, filming had been suspended because of the miscasting of the youth and the project was temporarily shelved. But in the past year Metro had seen the phenomenal rise of one of their new young players, Gregory Peck (barred from military service because of a serious back injury incurred in his youth). In the space of that year Peck had starred in *Keys of the Kingdom* (receiving an Academy nomination for his work), *The Valley of Decision* and *Spellbound*. Peck had many of Tracy's qualities—the projection of moral and physical strength, intelligence, sincerity. Metro had also recently signed eleven-year-old Claude Jarman, Jr., who was perfect for the role of Jody Baxter. The project was taken down off the shelf. Playwright Paul Osborne rewrote the screenplay, tailoring the man's role more to Peck's style than to Tracy's, and a search was begun for an actress to play the difficult part of Ma Baxter, the young, backward, inarticulate mother. Clarence Brown, the director, needed an actress who could eloquently express her emotions with her eyes. One look at the close-ups in *The Lost Weekend* and he felt certain he had found his Ma Baxter. Warners agreed to loan her out if her test with Peck proved successful. It did, and Wyman's improbable dream of being accepted as a serious actress became reality.

Brown's reputation had been built on his talent in bringing a stirring beauty to his leading ladies—Greta Garbo (*Flesh and the Devil, A Woman of Affairs, Anna Christie, Romance, Inspiration, Anna Karenina*), Norma Shearer (*A Free Soul, Idiot's Delight*), Joan Crawford (*Possessed, Chained, The Gorgeous Hussy*), Irene Dunne (*The White Cliffs of Dover*) and young Elizabeth Taylor (*National Velvet*). Wyman began the film in the heat of mid-July, thrilled to be working with such a prodigious director. As shooting of *The Yearling* progressed and she saw the early rushes, her hopes rose even higher. Because she had so little written dialogue, her eyes (almost in silent-screen fashion) caught all the poignant longing and caring of Ma Baxter's character. Jane Wyman was on her way to becoming a major star.

Roosevelt had run for a fourth term in the fall of 1944 against Thomas Dewey. The great pressures of the war had taken their toll on him. He was withdrawn and indifferent to the prodding of his party that he must campaign. Even Eleanor felt he was remiss in this, for "only through the actual sight and feel of the crowds [does] the man in public life really get to know what the people who back him believe in," she wrote him. But Roosevelt refused to get "into . . . the dusty political arena." "I don't think Pa [Roosevelt] would really mind defeat," Eleanor wrote her son James. "If elected he'll do his job well. I feel sure and I think he can be kept well to do it but he does get tired so I think if defeated he'll be content. . . . I am only concerned because Dewey seems to me more and more to show no understanding of the job at home or abroad."

Eleanor's proddings were finally effective, and on September 23, Roosevelt surprised the press by making a political speech to the Teamsters Union. The speech became a classic:

"These Republican leaders have not been content with attacks on me, on my wife, or my sons. No, not content with that. They now include my little dog, Fala. Well, of course, I don't resent attacks, and my family doesn't resent attacks, but Fala *does* resent them. . . . He has not been the same dog since."

All of Roosevelt's four sons were overseas the night of the election, but Eleanor and their daughter Anna and her son Johnny were with him at Hyde Park when "at 9 p.m. the dining room table was cleared and the real business," as Eleanor put it, of tabulating the votes began. At 11:40 the traditional torchlight parade from the village arrived, and this time Roosevelt permitted himself to be wheeled out to address them from a wheelchair, instead of putting on his heavy braces and standing up. At 3:15 in the morning, Dewey conceded.

The Yalta Conference took place just two days after the inauguration; his daughter, Anna, accompanied him. The results of the conference were announced on February 11, 1945, in a joint statement by Roosevelt, Churchill and Stalin. The Allies were planning Germany's unconditional surrender. Germany's defeat was near at hand.

Roosevelt returned from Yalta a weary traveler. He addressed Congress to tell them of the conference sitting down "because of the weight of his steel braces." Eleanor was alarmed, fearful he was accepting "a certain degree of invalidism." She convinced him he should rest for a few weeks at Warm Springs, where he often went for the waters. He departed without her. She was to join him on April 12 but was delayed. Late that afternoon, Franklin D. Roosevelt died. When Eleanor was told, her first words were, "I am more sorry for the people of this country and of the world than I am for ourselves [the family]." Harry Truman, vice-president, was immediately summoned to the White House and ushered into Eleanor's sitting room. The widow stepped forward and placed her arm gently on his shoulder. "Harry," she said quietly, "the President is dead."

Roosevelt's death hit Reagan hard. The president had been a fixture and a hero in his life—as he had for most Americans—for thirteen years. What did he know about Harry Truman? What did anyone really know about the feisty little haberdasher from Independence, Missouri? If Roosevelt had survived eighteen days longer, he would have learned that Adolf Hitler had died; eight days after that (May 8, "V.E. Day"), Germany surrendered. One political commentator wrote that "Hitler's fate—or the world's— was that he met Roosevelt, who understood better than Hitler did the calculated risks which must be taken in the politics of the world." On August 6, the United States dropped the atomic bomb on Hiroshima, and on August 9, on Nagasaki. On August 14, Japan surrendered, ending World War II. Reagan had been discharged a month earlier on July 11, 1945. "All I wanted," he wrote, "was to rest up a while, make love to my wife, and come up refreshed to a better job in an ideal world. (As it came out, I was disappointed in all these post war ambitions.)"

Jane was hard at work on *The Yearling*. She rose at five A.M. to be on location at six, and she came home at night tired and totally absorbed in her scenes for the next day. Reagan rented a cabin at Lake Arrowhead, about two hours from Hollywood, and drove there alone. Then he rented a speedboat for twenty-four hours each day. He claimed the boat owner thought he was crazy. "'It's all right,' I assured him, 'I just want to know that the boat is there at the dock any time I want to take a drive on the water. I can't walk on it anymore.'"

THE SAG YEARS

"Let me say here that I believe in the SAG with all my heart. It is a damned noble organization . . ."
—RONALD REAGAN in
Where's the Rest of Me?

14

THEIR CAREERS WERE GOING IN DIFFERENT DIREC-
tions—"hers up, his down," June Allyson says, adding that it
caused a serious problem in the Reagan marriage. But that is far
too simplistic an appraisal. Wyman's career was ascending, and
would continue to do so with breathtaking swiftness. Reagan,
however, had already begun to place his increasing interest in politics above his own film career. Had Wyman encouraged him at
this point, he might have overcome his growing dilemma over
party affiliation (increased since Roosevelt's death) and Nelle's
reaction to a switch and moved earlier into the political arena.

For six years, while other Warner actresses—Bette Davis,
Olivia de Havilland, Lauren Bacall—were being suspended for
refusing roles, Wyman remained docile. Even when Warners began their wartime buildup of female players, she accepted fifth
billing and superficial parts in support of less-experienced performers. Had she not gone to Paramount to make *The Lost Weekend*
and then to Metro for *The Yearling*, the kind of incendiary fame she
had in 1945–47 might never have been lighted.

"We speak of her as 'Wyman' because she is now important," commented one columnist during that time. "You don't refer to Oscar P. Socrates and John N. Cicero, do you?" In the same vein that the press used only the last (or first) names for certain stars—Dietrich, Garbo, Bacall, Cagney, Davis, Olivier—Jane now frequently became "Wyman" in print, while Reagan was written about as "Ronald Reagan"—as though the inclusion of the first name was to avoid confusion with another *Reagan*.

The Lost Weekend, as grim as any war film could have been, won the Academy Award for Best Picture of 1945. Ray Milland's stunning performance as the drink-driven protagonist brought him his first Oscar.* Until the making of this film, Milland had been thought of as a romantic comedian, just as Wyman was associated with the kind of roles she had played. Hollywood did not suspect that either could ever rise to dramatic heights and power. In *The Lost Weekend*, Wyman gave a solid performance but left the histrionics to Milland. Then came *The Yearling*, and all through 1946, while Reagan was either at leisure or working with inferior material in second-rate films, Hollywood talked about the possibility of Wyman winning the Academy Award for her performance as Ma Baxter.

When Reagan returned from Arrowhead, Wasserman was in final negotiation for Reagan's famous million-dollar contract. During a two-week break in the shooting of *The Yearling*, he and Wyman went to New York for a vacation, and while there, at the Waldorf-Astoria Towers, he signed (on August 21) the contract that would pay him thirty-five hundred dollars a week for seven years, with only nine weeks' layoff each year.† That same day, he wired Warner:

DEAR JACK VERY HAPPY MYSELF. NOTHING WRONG AN ARMISTICE WON'T CURE. LOVE TO YOU AND ANN [Mrs. Warner]. JANE AND RONNIE.

He appears to be referring to the peace armistice which came a short time later, but the telegram could well have had a double meaning.

Warners obviously believed in his ability to regain the momen-

---

* *The Lost Weekend* also received the award for Best Direction, Billy Wilder; and Best Written Screenplay, Charles Brackett and Billy Wilder.

† Reagan was to earn a minimum of $150,500 a year. His 1946 tax return shows he earned $169,750 (Bogart earned $432,000, Bette Davis $328,000, and Errol Flynn $199,999).

tum that had built up with *Kings Row* and *Desperate Journey* just before his induction into the service, or they would not have agreed to Wasserman's high terms. Yet several months passed with Reagan drawing a check but with no film in the offing. During the war a number of new male stars had burst forth: Van Johnson, Peter Lawford, Robert Walker, Tom Drake, Cornel Wilde, Gregory Peck and many more. All-time favorites like Jimmy Stewart, Tyrone Power, Robert Montgomery, Henry Fonda, Clark Gable, Gene Kelly and numerous others had been released from service at the same time as Reagan. And Old Guard stars such as Bogart and Cagney had become further entrenched. Most stars had contracted to return to their studios after their wartime service, and film vehicles had to be found for all of them.

About this time, Warners bought Stephen Longstreet's best seller *Stallion Road* for Errol Flynn, but Flynn's popularity was on the wane and his drinking problem had become so acute that often shooting was held up on his films.* A decision was made to star Bogart and Bacall. (Reagan later said, "I felt a great tragedy surrounded [Flynn]. Physically he was a magnificent piece of machinery. He could have been a fantastic athlete in any sport.") William Faulkner, who had been under contract to Warners for three years, was assigned to write the screenplay.†

---

*Undated memo circa 1946–47 from Jack Warner: "Notes for talk with Wasserman regarding Errol Flynn [an MCA client]. . . . If Flynn is late, if liquor is being used so that from the middle of the afternoon on it is impossible for the director to make any more scenes with Flynn, if liquor is brought on the set or into the studio—we must hold Flynn legally and financially responsible. . . . We may go so far as to abrogate the entire contract and sue him for damages. Flynn . . . [has become] incoherent . . . repeatedly during the last pictures we have made in which Flynn has appeared and we cannot permit it any longer." Warner was referring to *Cry Wolf, Escape Me Never* and *Silver River*. All three had far exceeded their budgets because of Flynn's inability to perform, causing shooting to halt.

†Faulkner's screenplay for *Stallion Road* is in the Warner Brothers archives at the University of Southern California.

In 1945, Faulkner had already written *The Sound and the Fury* (1929), *As I Lay Dying* (1930), *Sanctuary* (1931), *Light in August* (1932), *Absalom, Absalom!* (1936), *The Unvanquished* (1938) and *The Hamlet* (1940). On October 15, 1945, after Warners rejected his screenplay of *Stallion Road*, he went home to Oxford, Mississippi, and wrote Jack Warner asking to be released from his studio contract:

"I feel that I have made a bust at moving picture writing and therefore have misspent and will continue to misspend time which at my age [forty-seven] I cannot afford. During my three years (including leave-suspension) at Warners, I did the best work I knew how on 5 or 6 scripts. Only two were made and I feel that I received credit on them [*To Have and Have Not* and *The Big Sleep*] not on the value of the work I did, but partly through the friendship of Director Howard Hawks . . ."

Faulkner shared credit with Leigh Brackett and Jules Furthman on *The Big Sleep*. Furthman receives a co-credit with Faulkner on *To Have and Have Not*. However, very little of Faulkner's draft appears in either film. He had also written unfilmed screenplays: *Air Force, Background to Danger, Northern Pursuit, Mildred Pierce* and *Stallion Road*. Jack Warner denied his request and he attempted a dozen more unfilmed scripts in the four years remaining on his contract. In 1949 he won the Nobel Prize for Literature.

In Hollywood because he was in dire need of money, Faulkner, like his literary colleague F. Scott Fitzgerald before him, felt deeply compromised by his association with films. *Stallion Road*, a melodrama that verged on soap opera, was about a dedicated veterinarian who fights an outbreak of anthrax on his breeding farm and wins the love of a young attractive neighbor from a rather jaded writer. Faulkner obviously took the position that the only way to write such a pedestrian story was to pretend someone else had the assignment. When producer Alex Gottlieb finally got the script, he knew Bogart and Bacall would never agree to appear in it.

"Faulkner, as you probably know, was a drunk," Gottlieb confided. "All the time he'd sit on the couch in his office with a pipe in his mouth. People would pass by and say, 'Now there's a writer who's really thinking.' He had a bottle of liquor by his side and he was dead drunk. If you went over and touched him, he'd fall down. I waited for ten days—didn't hear a word from him. Called his secretary and asked how he was doing. She said, 'Fine. We'll have pages for you any day now.' Three weeks go by. Finally, she called and said, 'Mr. Faulkner is sending over ten pages.' I get the ten pages and I read them. I call up and said, 'Bill, have you got a few minutes to stop by my office?' He came in, sees what's on the desk and asks if I had read the ten pages. I said, 'I certainly have. They don't have anything to do with the novel. Different characters. Different background.' He said, 'I know, but aren't they great!' "

Faulkner went back to work and finally completed a draft. Reading Faulkner's screenplay for *Stallion Road*, one would have no indication that he had written any part of it. The characters have no insight or depth, the story lumbers along and the dialogue is stiff.

Stephen Longstreet was called in to adapt his book and the Faulkner script was tossed on the scrap heap. Bogart and Bacall were now involved in *The Big Sleep* and would not be available. Reagan was cast in the role of Larry Hanrahan, the veterinarian, but shooting would not begin until late spring, 1946.

Hollywood was taken aback by Reagan, the World War II veteran. "During the War Ronald changed considerably. Or at least so it seemed to me," W. H. Mooring, who had served with Reagan at Fort Roach, recalled in 1947. "He would attend some of the press showings of United States Army Air Force propaganda films. Wearing heavy, horn-rimmed glasses and with a wider chin than I had ever seen him wear before, he would get up before the film started and deliver some kind of official talk to the Press.

"He did so well I began to see him in the role of politician. He put on weight, his shoulders broadened out and the boyish air gave way to a stronger, more manly presence.

"By this time he was Captain Ronald Reagan. Quite clearly his command of the situation as a sort of Press relations man was bringing back to him the public slant he had on life before he ever became an actor at all [a reference to his WHO days] . . .

"Get the subject [acting] around to him and he'll shuffle in embarrassment. . . . It may be due to the fact that in his heart he has never really felt like an actor at all. His real interest might be in public service. Maybe politics."

On December 12, 1945, Reagan took his first step into politics when he gave a speech at a mass meeting at Hollywood Legion Stadium, sponsored by the Hollywood Independent Citizens Committee of Arts, Sciences and Professions (HICCASP).* The committee had originally been formed by a large segment of the film community who admired Franklin Delano Roosevelt and his New Deal policies and saw the organization as an instrument to further their support of the Roosevelt program. Norman Corwin's controversial radio play *Set Your Clock at 9-235,* which dealt with the dangers of world extinction by the atomic bomb, was read.

Reagan referred to himself as a "hemophiliac liberal" in the early forties. But by the end of World War II, "wartime contacts with self-serving Government bureaucrats" had led him to agree with Hal Gross about waste and greed in federal spending. Since these wartime contacts were at Fort Roach, the government bureaucrats he refers to would necessarily have had to be connected with the War Department public-relations division. Even so, he still considered himself a liberal (and would for several more years) because of his early education and his interpretation of the word. He believed deeply and sincerely in equality of race, religion and sex. His Jeffersonian view of the Constitution was accomplished by a faith in his country's rightness. And he felt that fortunate men must contribute to the care and support of the more unfortunate. It obviously never occurred to him in the for-

---

*Also on the program, called "Atomic Power and Foreign Policy," was Dr. Harlow Shapley (U.S. delegate to World Cultural Conference, London) and Colonel Evans F. Carlson, USMC.

ties that a conservative Republican might share his convictions.

"They wanted him to run for Congress," Jane Wyman told the *Los Angeles Daily News* on June 18, 1946. "He's very politically minded. I'm not." A few days later, Reagan was quoted as saying, "Politicians have asked me to run for Congress. Heck, I couldn't do that. If I did, I'd be the subject of criticism as a politician. I couldn't go around making speeches without feeling I was doing it for self-glorification. No, I don't want to have any ax to grind." Neither of them state *who* had asked Reagan to run for Congress or on what ticket. Five years earlier, Dick Powell and Justin Dart had suggested he should consider a congressional race—as a Republican. But Jack Dales states that Reagan told him that he had now been approached by the Democrats. His continuing friendship with George Murphy, president of the SAG, had greatly influenced his thinking; the Democrats were good children being tempted and seduced by evil powers, while the Republicans, although too authoritative, had the moral strength to overcome the intruders. Apparently the power brokers of the California Republican party had come to believe they needed a film personality to win the Republican vote in the southern half of the state, which had always been polarized by San Francisco in the north and Los Angeles in the south.*

Despite the "Heck," the humble pie and the Jimmy Stewart shuffle, Reagan was beginning to feel the excitement of near power. The young man who dreamed of being a hero and became a lifeguard began to evolve into the man who believed he had the ability to save his country from sliding on a treacherous downward path. First, though, he had to make those notches in a new log.

As a Broadway star in the twenties and early thirties, Helen Gahagan Douglas had been considered one of the world's most beautiful women. She had married actor Melvyn Douglas in 1931. Drawn to social work and politics, she had organized relief campaigns for migrant workers during the Depression, and then, in 1939, presented seminars throughout California to alert women in the Democratic party to the Nazi threat. ("If Hitler couldn't be stopped in Europe, it wasn't likely that America would escape attack . . .") Within a few years she had become a strong voice

---

*George Murphy served as chairman of the Republican National Committee from 1953 to 1954 and was elected U.S. senator from California, defeating Democratic candidate Pierre Salinger in 1964.

and state vice-chairman in the California Democratic party, and in 1944 she ran a successful campaign for the Fourteenth Congressional District. When the war ended, the country was bombarded with nightmarish photographs of the devastating deaths and horrifying injuries caused by the atom bombs dropped on Hiroshima and Nagasaki. Americans suffered guilt and fear. Gahagan addressed Congress in October 1945, touching on her concern and stressing: "The first order of business of this Congress and the people of the world is the question of the survival of mankind."

The HICCASP meeting on atomic power was already set when Congress broke for Christmas and Gahagan returned home to California. For the first time, Reagan was heard speaking publicly on a serious issue. Gahagan had not been too enthusiastic about his inclusion on the program, but had been swayed by the organizers. She was impressed and surprised by his eloquence and charismatic presence and Hollywood took note with her.

One of Reagan's first acts after being discharged from the army was to narrate a film for the American Veterans Committee on providing housing for the returning servicemen. Then he was voted back on the board at the SAG while an industry-wide strike catapulted him into the eye of the storm.

The Screen Actors Guild's official birthday is June 30, 1933, the date of the organization's incorporation.* Actually, it came into being in March of that year, when the industry's producers decided to beat the Depression by halving the salaries of all actors under contract. Because the actors had nowhere to turn, they took the cut, but six of them—Ralph Morgan, Grant Mitchell, Berton Churchill, Charles Miller, Kenneth Thomson and Alden Gay Thomson (Kenneth's wife)—met in the Thomson home to discuss forming a self-governing union of film actors. By the end of the evening, the Screen Actors Guild was conceived and the six set

---

*The first recorded minutes of the SAG, dated July 12, 1933 (Ralph Morgan elected president), lists these members: Alan Mowbray, Morgan Wallace, Leon Ames, Bradley Page, Richard Tucker, Reginald Mason, Tyler Brooke, Kenneth Thomson, Alden Gay Thomson, James Gleason, Ralph Morgan, Lucille Gleason, Ivan Simpson, Claude King and Boris Karloff. Within a few months, Charles Starrett, C. Aubrey Smith, Groucho Marx, James Cagney, Ralph Bellamy, George Raft, Eddie Cantor, Chester Morris, Robert Montgomery, Fredric March, Adolphe Menjou, Edward Arnold, Lyle Talbot, Gary Cooper, Spencer Tracy, Miriam Hopkins, Otto Kruger and Paul Muni, among others, had joined. The SAG now had collective power. Eddie Cantor replaced Ralph Morgan as president in October 1933. Kenneth Thomson became a member of the paid staff of the SAG, and was Jack Dales's assistant during Reagan's years on the SAG board and as an officer.

out to sell it to their co-actors. For the next few weeks, huddled whispering groups formed on studio sets and clandestine meetings were held in actors' homes. A few years earlier, the theater union, Actors Equity Association, had unsuccessfully attempted to organize Hollywood, resulting in the motion-picture blacklisting of those involved. This time the actors succeeded, but they had a four-year struggle ahead until they had a contract with the producers, and it had taken a threat of a strike by actors to achieve it.

Several thousand motion-picture actors had filled Hollywood Legion Stadium on the hot, sticky Sunday evening of May 9, 1937—"all of them ready to strike for recognition of their union," a member of the SAG staff recalled. "For weeks small, private meetings had been held in the homes of various stars, for the stars added immeasurably to the economic bargaining power of the Guild. Every star had been asked: 'Will you support a strike by the Screen Actors Guild if it is necessary to win a contract with the motion picture producers?' More than 98 percent had answered 'Yes!' . . . Heated meetings of the SAG president, Robert Montgomery, a negotiating committee and the producers, led by studio heads, had continued up to the last few hours before the mass membership meeting.* Everyone in the stadium nervously waited to hear if there would be a strike as Montgomery waved a paper in his hand and then read the contents:

"'We wish to express ourselves as being in favor of the Guild [union] shop. . . . We expect to have contracts drawn between the Screen Actors Guild and the studios before expiration of this week. [Signed] Louis B. Mayer and Joseph M. Schenck.'"

The actors went wild. An hour later, newsboys stood on the busiest Hollywood intersections shouting the page-one headline: ACTORS WIN! AFL GUILD WINS. The SAG had affiliated with the American Federation of Labor in 1935, which had a membership by 1937 of well over four million. The AFL was conservative, apolitical (cautiously so), avoided all affiliations with extremists or left-wing groups, and found it a point of pride that in the 1932 election they had refused to support either socialist or communist candidates. The original board and officers of the SAG were to a great extent conservative Republicans and would remain so for

---

* Rumors later circulated that Ken Thomson had passed money to labor leaders Bioff and Browne in a "little black pay-off bag." Reagan claimed that Thomson told him the black bag held a typewriter "to take down an account of the meeting in which he told those characters—on behalf of the Guild—to go to hell." Bioff, Thomson said, held a Colt .45 on him during the entire meeting.

several decades, whereas the Screen Writers Guild had a more balanced board.

Until 1937, there was little left-wing activity in Hollywood. The political climate in Hollywood began to change during the Spanish Civil War. Nancy Lynn Schwartz, author of *The Hollywood Screen Writers Wars*, wrote, ". . . the Thirties was the era when Hollywood, especially Warner Bros., was turning out a batch of 'socially conscious' pictures that dealt with issues like crime and unemployment. However . . . the movie companies would have willingly followed Stalin in those days had that made for commercially successful entertainment." Screenwriter Paul Jarrico added, "Warner Brothers had made a reputation as good, patriotic Americans, and they made some of the best anti-Nazi films and more political films than were made anyplace else. But they also, when they decided to be anti-Communist (1945 on), were more anti-Communist than anybody else and made more anti-Communist films. . . . The Warner brothers and L. B. Mayer thought politically. They had political motivations, intent and drive. They cared. Harry Cohn at Columbia and Darryl Zanuck at Fox were more open to progressive content if it could be sold to them in terms of its commercial attractiveness. They didn't care what the picture said. They just wanted to know whether it would make money."

The presence of "Communists" or "fellow travelers" in the membership of the film unions became a weapon in the hands of the union leaders. Nothing had to be proved to place the accused under suspicion. Theoretically, a union's fight for better wages or working conditions for their members should have nothing at all to do with the politics of those members, any more than with their race or religion. But by threatening a studio with disclosure (names of "Communists" or "fellow travelers" revealed to them through "private, secret" sources), a union could endanger a box-office star. It took no time at all before the studios began developing their own weapon—they would expose the "Reds" or "pinkos" themselves. The coalition between Right and Left in Hollywood bound together because of the war began to unravel in 1944 with the formation of the Motion Picture Alliance for the Preservation of American Ideals, which announced in a full-page two-color ad in *The Hollywood Reporter,* "we find ourselves in sharp revolt against a rising tide of Communism, Fascism, and kindred beliefs. . . . We resent the growing impression that this industry is made up of, and dominated by, Communists, Radicals, and

crackpots. . . . We want only to defend against its enemies that
which is our priceless heritage. . . ." The ad was signed by its
president, Sam Wood (Reagan's champion in *Kings Row*), Walt
Disney (who in 1941 had successfully squashed a strike by his
underpaid cartoonists, claiming that he would "close down the
studio and sell toys" rather than meet the cartoonists' union's demands), James Kevin McGuinness, Rupert Hughes and Howard
Emmett Rogers. (The last three with Disney had been known as
"the Four Horsemen" when they attempted in 1936 to break up
the formation of the Screen Writers Guild. In a hearing before the
National Labor Relations Board, Rogers was asked, "Ever hear of
Benedict Arnold? You know what they call him, don't you?"
Rogers replied, "I think they called him a traitor . . . I might add
that he was also a very good soldier.")

"The Alliance's strength was concentrated mainly at MGM,"
Nancy Lynn Schwartz said. "The most celebrated film star
among the group's supporters was Gary Cooper, who was known
as being one of the most politically naïve reactionaries in Hollywood. During the late Thirties, he had gotten caught up with
Arthur Guy Empey's Hollywood Hussars, a reactionary vigilante
army that was preparing, with the help of gun-toters like
McGuinness, Victor McLaglen, and Ward Bond, to do a little
housecleaning in their community—their targets, preferably, anyone slightly pink."

As a graphic illustration of the political polarization of Hollywood at this time, screenwriter William Ludwig remembered:
"One really startling day which began when two writers—and I
will not mention their names—came into my office. As they came
in, one of them locked the door, and I asked them what it was
about. They said that they had been observing me and watching
me carefully and they felt I was very good material, and they gave
me an invitation to join the Communist Party. I said that I didn't
think it was for me, I wasn't the kind of fellow who liked to be told
what to think before I had a chance to figure out what I wanted to
think. And then I went to lunch.

"After lunch, King Vidor [the director], for whom I'd written
An American Romance, came in, and he wanted to talk to me, and he
wanted me to join the American [*sic*] Alliance for the Preservation
of American Ideals. I said, 'What are they *for*, King?' And he
said, 'We're against this and against this, and against this, and
especially against the Communists.' I said, 'I know what the Alliance is against, but what are they *for*?' And he said, 'What do

you mean?' I said, 'King, I have made up my mind that I'm not going to join things just because they are against something. I want to find, if there is such a thing, something that's *for* what I'm for. What is your organization *for*, King?' There was a long pause, and King said, 'I'll have to talk to Sam Wood about that,' and he got up and left the office."

In response to the Alliance's cries to rout from the motion-picture industry the "totalitarian-minded groups" working in the industry for "the dissemination of un-American ideas and beliefs," Martin Dies and his committee of "sleuths" arrived in Hollywood on April 21, 1944. The industry began to take militant sides. Sidney Buchman, a top producer-writer at Columbia, issued the statement that "The Alliance's unsupported charges of 'subversive activities' in films are a threat to Hollywood management and labor alike." Screen Writers Guild president Mary McCall, Jr., accused the Alliance of union-busting intentions. "We don't believe union busting is an American ideal."

Dies was not the only "right-wing, publicity-seeking Communist-hounder" who saw the Red menace as the answer to his own need for power. California State Senator John ("Jack") Tenney had also grabbed hold of the Red bait to catch himself a power fish. In the autumn of 1944, he set up the Tenney Committee and began his own hearings into the color of Hollywood's politics. "Years later," recalled Pauline Lauber Finn, "after having testified before Tenney, I watched McCarthy, and it was incredible— the same verbiage, attacks, chanting. They were cut from the same mold. Tenney was physically similar to McCarthy too— beefy without being fat."

The SAG kept an extremely low profile during this period. Nonetheless, celebrity actors' names were being used in support and in defiance of the Alliance and of Tenney's committee. With more naïveté than seems possible, the American motion-picture industry, containing the most international celebrities in the world, had allowed itself to be conned into a publicity tool for Leftist and reactionary demagogues.

Reagan states, "Like most of the soldiers who came back, I expected a world suddenly reformed. I hoped and believed that the blood and death and confusion of World War II would result in a regeneration of mankind. . . . If men could cooperate in war, how much better they could work together in peace.

"I was wrong. I learned that a thousand bucks under the table was the formula for buying a new car. I learned that the real-estate squeeze was on for the serviceman. I discovered that the rich had got just a little richer and a lot of the poor had done a pretty good job of grabbing a quick buck. I discovered the world was almost the same and perhaps a little worse."

He also discovered that his wife had gone on merrily with her career while his had been put in cold storage, that Jack Warner was in no hurry to see to it that this particular returning serviceman be given his place in the sun. With nothing to do and his wife hard at work, he filled his days with constructing two model boats, each about two feet long—the *USS America* and a freighter. If he had any concerns that the industry was being pulled apart by a strike and by polarizing political ideologies, he managed to scuttle them temporarily.

By Christmas, 1945, he got bored with his models, encased them in glass and "blindly" and "busily" joined "every organization I could find that would guarantee to save the world." He adds that he was "hell-bent on saving the world from Neo-Fascism," and claims he was not "sharp about Communism" and "by reason of deception" considered the American Communists in Hollywood liberals like himself. He became a member of the American Veterans Committee after he "observed that more than forty [other] veterans' organizations . . . seemed to be highly intolerant of color, creed and common sense." According to him, he "became a large wheel" in AVC.* He did, indeed, take up the battle of the studio employees who were returning veterans, and the SAG was a natural place for him to seek action. The SAG president, George Murphy, suggested the board ask him to return as a permanent member, and it was agreed.

"When I walked into the board room . . . I saw it crammed with the famous men of the business. . . . I knew that I was beginning to find the rest of me," he once wrote. He overlooked the women on the board—his wife, Jane Wyman, Anne Revere, Louise Beavers and Agnes Moorehead. The famous men gathered around the huge director's table included Murphy, Robert Montgomery, Franchot Tone, Dick Powell, Leon Ames, James Cagney, Henry Fonda, John Garfield, Boris Karloff, Pat O'Brien, Edward Arnold, Walter Pidgeon, Gene Kelly and Robert Taylor. Shortly after this meeting, Murphy stepped down and Robert

---

* Reagan quit AVC one year later, when rumors circulated that it had been "infiltrated with Communists."

Montgomery once again took over the reins of the SAG as president. Montgomery was a political activist with a conservative viewpoint, as were Murphy, Powell, Arnold and Taylor.

With Truman in the White House, Reagan's former presidential fervor was dissipated. Truman was "as inspiring as mud. To listen to a Truman radio address was an experience devoutly to be missed." Reagan would perhaps have liked Truman better had he known him personally. For in private, his manner was lively and his speech direct. Occupying the White House had not changed his proclivities toward playing poker, drinking whiskey and talking politics. He was impulsive, plain-spoken and possessed a crass streak in his nature, but was openly deferential to his wife and daughter. He dressed absurdly in shirts too small for him and wore two-toned shoes. He loved the ceremonial and redesigned the presidential seal and the presidential flag. But behind this public image was a man possessing a great sensitivity to the human condition. Viewed as a failure until nearly fifty, he had fought adversity with great nobility and had deep concern for struggling farmers, the small businessman, the old, the poor and minority groups. Bold ideas did not intimidate him. Truman's complex personality baffled the country the first year he was in office. With the war's end, he was being blamed "for every shortage, all the inflation, intractable foreign problems, and the mediocrity of the people around him."

Communism was one of the principal issues of the 1946 congressional elections. In California, Richard M. Nixon, formerly a lawyer but at the time a lieutenant commander in the navy due for release, was approached by the Republican Committee of 100 and asked to run, all campaign costs paid, against Jerry Voorhis, a Democratic incumbent who had been an effective member of Congress for a number of years and who had just sponsored the National School Lunch Act. Nixon quickly accepted the offer and cast himself as "the Fighting Quaker" and engaged in a "scurrilous smear campaign" to label Voorhis as "the candidate of the Kremlin." He attempted, unsuccessfully, to link Voorhis to two "communist-dominated" organizations and to prove that Voorhis followed the Communist party line in his voting record. By this kind of innuendo and unsubstantiated attack, Nixon won the election.

In the wake of the Nixon-Voorhis campaign, with communism becoming a central issue, Reagan—waiting for Warners to put him to work—dedicated his time to giving speeches denouncing fascism for the various organizations to which he belonged, always to thunderous applause. Then, on one occasion, he ended his speech by denouncing communism and calling it fascism as well. Silence greeted his words. He claims this had a strong effect on him, propelling him to do some heavy homework, which in turn alerted him to the danger of communism and the presence of Communists in Hollywood. This hardly seems to present the full facts.

The meeting Reagan refers to, under the auspices of HIC-CASP, was on July 11, 1946, and several others spoke first. Reagan said he felt "honored" when he was notified (June 1946) that he had been named to its board of directors. The July 11 meeting was his first board meeting. Jimmy Roosevelt (whom Reagan was thrilled to meet) made a speech asking the board to adopt a resolution against communism.

"Jimmy Roosevelt was an employee of HICCASP in New York," Elenore Bogigian recalled, as was Harold Ickes (secretary of the interior). "And then he came out to California, where he was the executive director of HICCASP, and I was legislative director. He had the office right next to mine, which he moved into with his complete staff. The Democratic primaries were approaching, and . . . there ensued a fight between Ellis Patterson and Will Rogers, Jr., who both wanted the office [of senator from California]. . . . HICCASP was split over whom to endorse . . . Patterson or Rogers."

"Everybody who was anybody was active in HICCASP," recalls Joan LaCoeur, the organization's recording secretary. "There was this upbeat feeling of power in the support of both the artistic and scientific and the professional communities. Everyone assumed Jimmy Roosevelt would one day be president [of the United States]—there was still this awe of him, based on his father. . . . The Red-baiting [had] reached such a pitch that people began to quietly withdraw [from HICCASP]. There was a board meeting and some of the right-wing members wanted to make an anti-Communist statement to clear HICCASP. People like Johnny Green and Olivia de Havilland—not strong people, middle-of-the-roaders—began to panic early in the fight. It was decided that if a statement could be arrived at that all could subscribe to, people would stand fast. . . . A six man committee was appointed representing left and right. . . . The committee met for three days and three nights. [John Howard] Lawson and [Dalton] Trumbo represented the Left; Reagan and [Don] Hartman represented the

Right; Linus Pauling and Jimmy Roosevelt represented the middle; and writer True Boardman was Chairman."

"Reagan took a leaf from the supposed Communist book and organized a faction," Elenore Bogigian continued. "The Left and Right were, at this point, at each others' throats. . . . I remember gruesome meetings."

At the end of three days, the tripartite committee arrived at a statement that declared the HICCASP was a totally independent organization without ties to any one group. "It was . . . ridiculous," Bogigian recalled. "Everybody jumped overboard . . . the board resigned . . . the middle weakened . . . the Right resigned. This was how the 'Communists' supposedly took over. It was the beginning of the end of the organization. . . ."

LeCoeur's and Bogigian's recollections of Reagan's association with HICCASP are very much at odds with his, for he disclaims any intensive involvement and has never mentioned his work on the statement committee.

Moon Reagan remembered "when he was in [this] organization. . . I used to beat him over the head, 'Get out of that thing. There are people in there who can cause you real trouble. They're more than suspect on the part of the government, as to their connections that are not exactly American, and one thing and another.' Now, in those days, I was doing little things for the FBI. You know, 'Neil, we'd like to have you go out and lay in the bushes and take down the car numbers off of the cars that are going to be at this little meeting in Bel-Air. Put it in a brown envelope, no return address. And always remember, if you get caught in the bushes, you can just forget about saying, well, you're doing this for the FBI, because we'll just look him right in the eye and say, "We never saw the guy in our lives." Forget it. . . .'

"I talked to him and talked to him about this organization. One evening he calls me—evening, hell, it was about midnight— he had stopped up at the Nutburger stand (there was a Nutburger stand at the corner of Sunset and Doheny at the time, across the street from the drugstore). He says, 'I'm having a cup of coffee, come on up.' I said, 'Do you know what time it is?' 'Yeah.' 'Well, I've been in bed for three hours. Have your coffee and go on home and go to bed.' 'No, I want you to come up.' And I said all right; so I put a pair of trousers on and a shirt and drove up the hill. Here he is—parked. I got in, and—he's a member of the board [HICCASP]—he says, 'You wouldn't believe it. It just came to me tonight. We have a rule that if a board member misses two meetings without being excused, you're automatically off the board. There's a gal out at the such and such studio,' and he says, 'I've been a little suspicious of her. All of a sudden, we had one of these cases come up tonight, that so-and-so had missed two board meetings, and so they were off, and now we've got to find somebody else. It suddenly dawned on me that over the last several months, every time one of these cases came up, she had just the individual that would be excellent as a replacement. I managed to filch the minute books before I left. I can show you the page where her board members became a majority of the board, with her replacements.'*

"I just looked at him and said, 'Junior, what do you suppose I've been talking about all these weeks and weeks and weeks?' He looks me right in the eye and says, 'Why, you never mentioned a word about anything like that. . . .'"

Jimmy Roosevelt has said that "part of my work for the Committee [HICCASP] included making speeches in other cities. They wanted me to submit my speeches to them in advance and I noticed they always removed any critical references to Russia and Communism. Of course, I always put them back in." Roosevelt left the organization several months after the July 11 meeting, although later he put the meeting as the date he severed his ties.†

The HICCASP was under surveillance by the FBI—a fact that Reagan knew. Reagan had, in fact, been in contact with the FBI since September 17, 1941, when an FBI agent in Washington (whose name was later inked out of the papers the author obtained through the Freedom of Information Act) sent a memo to Hugh Clegg, assistant special agent in charge of the Los Angeles division.

> As a result of my previous position as [obliterated], I became intimately acquainted with the following persons who might be of some assistance to the Bureau. [I will be] glad to contact them and give them the name of the special [Hollywood] agent involved.

---

*No explanation was given as to why Reagan took HICCASP's minute books or what became of them.

† By autumn of 1947, HICCASP was concentrating its efforts on the cause of the Hollywood Nineteen, and later the cause of the Hollywood Ten.

A list of eleven names followed, but all are heavily crossed out except for one: RONALD REAGAN, WARNER BROTHERS STUDIO, HOLLYWOOD. Whoever the agent was, he would have had to meet Reagan (as an employee of a company or organization both belonged to) often to become an intimate. The possibilities include someone at the studio, the SAG, Nino Pepitone's ranch in Burbank,* or the Hillcrest Country Club. Further FBI memos indicate Reagan must have agreed to supply the FBI with any anti-American or pro-German information that came his way (considering the war, not an unreasonable acquiescence). On November 18, 1943, Reagan (at Camp Roach) met with an agent and in the interview told of "nearly coming to blows with a German sympathizer at a cocktail party [this could have been during the production of *This Is the Army*] because [name obliterated] made several anti-Semitic remarks.

"Due to the nature of the remarks made by the subject, Reagan became highly incensed and withdrew from the conversation . . . although he emphasized that considerable drinking had been done by all persons involved."

Records obtained through the Freedom of Information Act also make clear that Reagan and Wyman met with FBI agents on April 10, 1947. Reagan claimed three men appeared unannounced at his home one evening and identified themselves as FBI agents. One asked, "We thought someone the Communists hated as much as they hate you might be willing to help us?" He protested that he did not want to "go in for Red-baiting." They then rattled off a list of names, dates, places and conversations that he had been privy to and others that, as he said, "opened my eyes to a good many things." One quote given by the FBI agent, claimed to have been said by an actor Reagan trusted, was: "What are we going to do about that sonofabitching bastard Reagan?"

According to the Freedom of Information Act records, Reagan, after being assured that HICCASP was a Communist front group, "stated that he was present [at the July 11, 1946, meeting] and that this meeting was precipitated by the fact he and nine other members of HICCASP had attempted to create the issue to justify their resignation. . . . Reagan's group advocated a resolution condemning Communism as well as Fascism, a proposal that [he claimed] faced a heavy opposition.

* Where Reagan boarded his horse, Baby, and where Pepitone trained horses and riders for films.

"Reagan advised considerable discussion pro and con ensued and finally [name obliterated] took the floor and stated . . . , 'Regardless of how much discussion occurs here, I can tell you this much for certain: HICCASP will never pass any resolution condemning Communism or condoning capitalism.' . . . The resolution was voted down by 60 to 10 at an ensuing meeting and Reagan submitted his resignation by telegram the next night."

Besides Reagan's membership in the allegedly Communist front HICCASP, there were his activities on behalf of the equally suspect American Veterans' Committee. The previous August, in an Open Forum letter in *The Hollywood Reporter* in answer to an accusation by Billy Wilkerson, the *Reporter*'s publisher, Reagan had written: ". . . you referred to our outfit (A.V.C.) as 'fronters' . . . that seems a little strange when a few months ago the members of any veterans group were 'heroes' who were defending their country. . . . I would like to call to your attention the fact that at a recent A.V.C. National Convention in Des Moines, Iowa, a tentative pink infiltration was met and dealt with in true democratic fashion, with the result that everyone was convinced that the vast majority of A.V.C. members were interested only in perpetuating our forms of democracy. Of course, to deny that there are some 'Commies' aboard would be ridiculous as those guys inkle in just about everywhere." Obviously, the FBI visitors convinced him Wilkerson was right because he quit the AVC shortly after he met with them.

However, the April 10, 1947, FBI meeting was geared not to warn him of Communist front organizations but to enlist both Wyman and Reagan as informants on the activities of the SAG. Of the two, Reagan appears to have taken the lead and told the FBI agents that he was aware of "two cliques within the Guild that on all questions of policy follow the Communist Party line." These two cliques were not "particularly close," Reagan said, "but they [unite] on electing individuals to office." There follows a long list of inked-out names provided, according to the agent, by Reagan and Wyman, although only Reagan is quoted in the report. A request was made by the agent to check the names to determine which were known Communist party members.

Reagan (not Wyman) was given a number—"T-10"—as a confidential informant. His job was to report the names of any SAG members whom he suspected of contributing to the "Communist Infiltration of the Motion Picture Industry" (a lengthy Bureau report on December 19, 1947, carries that title and discusses Reagan's cooperation in giving names to the FBI).*

Reagan's lifelong hatred of Communists came to the fore at this time. The Nazis licked, he feared a second bully was expanding its power—this time right on U.S. soil. He neglected to recall that Hitler's power grew as the German people turned informer against friend, neighbor and one's own family. One of the most unaccountable actions in all of Reagan's life was that he not only continued his SAG activities, agreeing to be an FBI informant, but did so at a period when he had just been elected to the presidency to succeed Montgomery. As president, he would have access to privileged information and gain firsthand observations earned through more intimate relationships. With this step, he was to lose his wife and the home and family he considered dear. But he never understood why.

When they had returned from New York in August 1945, the Reagans were reconciled and apparently happy and Reagan had just signed his one-million-dollar contract. Then, while he worked on his ship models waiting for Warners to put him in front of the cameras, Wyman fought through several long months of steamy Florida-location hardships as she filmed *The Yearling*. In late March 1946, Reagan finally returned to work on *Stallion Road*, and Wyman, without any time off, began shooting *Cheyenne*, a rugged Western, opposite Dennis Morgan. Although *Cheyenne* was an A feature, Wyman knew that the role she played and the movie itself were a major comedown after her last two films, and she had unsuccessfully tried to convince Jack Warner not to cast her in it.

Reagan had been able to use his own horse—Baby (considered stubborn by his co-players)—in *Stallion Road*, and to cast his friend Nino Pepitone in a small role (also to help with the horse). The film was shot on location in Hidden Valley, forty miles from the studio. But he did not mind the distance, the work or the heat. He loved riding and the fact that (except for one scene) he was able to go through the film tieless. He took all jumps and did all his own stunts. One day, he made seven jumps on Tar Baby (the horse's name in the film) in the hot sun and tipped the bar each time. The director, James V. Kern (a former

---

*Reagan was one of at least eighteen informants used by the FBI to gauge Communist infiltration in the film industry. The reports on Reagan's activities for the FBI obtained through the Freedom of Information Act reveal numerous missing pages and contain several dozen blackened paragraphs.

lawyer who had also directed Wyman in *The Dough Girls*), wanted to have a stuntman double. Reagan refused and on the eighth try made it. At one point in the picture, a horse (not Baby) was being filmed crossing a water hole when it slipped and panicked. Reagan dived in, fully dressed, and led the animal to shore (to a chorus of enthusiastic applause). The genre of horse story pleased him. He wanted to do a Western and spoke to Warner about it, but could not engender any enthusiasm.*

As one reviewer said, "In 'Stallion Road,' the human beings don't come off as well as the horses." Reagan did not have to wait to see the final cut to know this. While he enjoyed being literally back in the saddle again, he had no false illusions about the film.

During the early shooting of *Stallion Road*, a labor union strike threatened to shut down the entire film industry. The SAG board (and membership) was overwhelmingly in favor of a no-strike policy.†

In 1945, Herbert Sorrell, a former boxer who had become a business agent of the Motion Picture Painters Local 644, had drawn together nine unions including the Screen Cartoonists, Office Employees, Film Technicians, Machinists and the powerful Carpenters Local, an amalgamation of ten thousand workers. They called themselves the Conference of Studio Unions (CSU) and were looked upon as a democratic and honest alternative to the other, more massive IATSE, the union that had been run by Willie Bioff and George Browne before they were sent to jail. Sensing the CSU as a major threat, the IATSE strengthened its executive forces and sent Roy Brewer (an officer in the Alliance for the Preservation of American Ideals) and IATSE president Richard Walsh into action.‡

On March 12, 1945, the CSU Local 1421 struck on behalf of the set decorators (350 jobs), for whom they claimed exclusive bargaining rights. The IATSE contested this, declaring that the

---

*Baby made enough money with his appearance in *Stallion Road* to "take care of his own feed for seven months," a proud Reagan declared. After the filming was completed, he entered the horse in the Northridge Horse Show. When the horse refused to take a hurdle, Reagan flew over his head, to the horror of the audience (who all rose to their feet). Stunned, Reagan got up in a matter of minutes and rode the horse back to the stable.

†On September 27, 1946, a strike ballot was sent to the SAG membership. Out of 8,740 ballots, approximately 40 percent, or 3,257 ballots, were returned. A breakdown revealed that 2,748 voted no, 502 voted yes, and 7 ballots were unmarked. At this time, Montgomery was still president and Reagan third vice-president.

‡Roy Martin Brewer rose from obscurity to national prominence during his eight years as leader of Hollywood craft labor. On September 13, 1953, he resigned after having led the fight to rid the union of "Communist elements."

CSU contract with Local 1421 had lapsed in January and not been renegotiated. The IATSE union, Local 44, insisted they had jurisdiction over the set decorators and proclaimed their adherence to labor's "no-strike" wartime pledge. At the same time, IATSE president Walsh issued an ultimatum to the studios that if they settled with the CSU, "every movie projectionist in every theater in the United States would take a walk." The strike continued, the studios refusing to be strong-armed by threats and yet not willing to give in to the demands of the CSU. An impasse had been reached and there was "escalating violence and bitterness on the picket lines."

In December, the IATSE and the CSU agreed to abide by the decision of three arbitrators appointed by the American Federation of Labor (AFL) Executive Council to settle their dispute, which involved the contested 350 jobs.* The AFL arbitrators decided in favor of IATSE (which meant they now controlled the Carpenters Union). But the decorators (carpenters), represented by their president, William Hutcheson, refused to accept this decision. The unions were at loggerheads again and the question of those 350 jobs could—if an all-industry strike was called—have thrown 30,000 people out of work.

Accusations spread by the IATSE began to fly that the CSU was infiltrated with Communists. The labor dispute now took on the particularly ugly hue of Red-baiting (CSU president Herbert K. Sorrell was accused of being a Communist by IATSE, an unsubstantiated accusation). From this point on, the labor dispute would be inseparable from the exploitation of, and investigation into, a Communist party takeover of Hollywood. Actor Sterling Hayden (who joined the party in 1946) later claimed he was part of a nucleus group within the SAG who worked to solicit support from his fellow actors for the strike. "The inner nucleus finally simmered down to about 10. They would hold special meetings to devise methods of procedure in advance of SAG meetings," he said.

Reagan, then (summer 1946) still a member of HICCASP and also a confidential informant for the FBI, raised his profile at the SAG by speaking out more at board and special meetings in opposition to the nucleus group's tactics.

"There was an agenda drawn up, which was to be followed if

---

* The three arbitrators (known as the "Three Wise Men") were William C. Doherty, president of the International Postmen's Union; Felix H. Knight, president of the Trainmen's Union; and William C. Birthright, president of the Barbers Union.

any member of the group was able to get the floor and speak [a filibuster in favor of the CSU]," Hayden later testified.

Reagan was appointed by the board to the (Strike) Emergency Committee.* He later stated that while he was shooting the last scenes of *Stallion Road* out at Hidden Valley, he "was called to the telephone at an oil station. . . . I was told that if I made a report to the Screen Actors Guild that the strike was jurisdictional, rather than over wages and hours, a squad was ready to take care of me and fix my face so that I'd never be in pictures again." The threat was real enough to Reagan, who for several months thereafter carried a gun in a shoulder holster.†

As the summer progressed, the strike threat increased. Meetings of the Emergency Committee and dissenting (strike-oriented) SAG members were held at various private homes. Hayden recalled one meeting at Ida Lupino's when Howard da Silva "roughly pulled" John Garfield from the house when Garfield sought a "hearing" for Reagan. "Da Silva clutched Garfield by the lapels, shook his fists in Garfield's face and waved a finger at him violently," Reagan added to Hayden's statement.

The IATSE, according to Roy Brewer, was in direct danger "of being raided" by the CSU, for if the IATSE surrendered the 350 decorators, other small unions under their aegis would be forced out of IATSE and into the CSU. "I thought he was an alarmist," Reagan said. "I thought he was just being uncooperative. Later a representative of the CSU [he did not state who] said that was exactly the case—they were making further raids on the jurisdiction of IATSE."

Max Silver, a former CSU member, testified in 1954 that "the [Communist] Party was very much interested in the success of the CSU. Its interest lay in the main to establish what we called a progressive center in Hollywood instead of the IATSE, the unions who are affiliated with the IATSE, which was at that time the center of influence, and you might as well say control of the work of the trade unions in Hollywood. The Party was interested in

---

*The Emergency Committee consisted of SAG officers and board members Reagan, Robert Montgomery, George Murphy, Jane Wyman, Alexis Smith, June Allyson, Dick Powell, Walter Pidgeon, Robert Taylor, Edward Arnold and Gene Kelly. Within the group there was really only one strong liberal voice—that of Kelly—and no one who might have been part of the "inner nucleus."

† Reagan claimed that the police insisted he be "fitted with a shoulder holster and a loaded .32 Smith and Wesson," which he "mounted . . . religiously every morning and took off the last thing at night."

establishing a nerve center that would be to some extent influenced by Party policy and Party people."

"It was pretty well established," Reagan later said, "that the objective of the strike was to force the studios to accept an industry-wide union [CSU] by Harry Bridges."*

Reagan was attempting to juggle three balls at one time—the SAG, his marriage and his career. The only one he seemed to have a firm grip on was the Guild. As a member of the Emergency Committee, he met with local representatives of the IATSE, the carpenters, and the producers in an effort to find some means of avoiding the threatened work stoppage.† "If IATSE puts replacements for carpenters in the studios in order to keep them in operation," Jack Dales explained to the board in its September 17, 1946, meeting, "picket lines will immediately be established by the carpenters. If the producers decide to close the studios entirely, the IATSE has indicated that it will take some other kind of action against them, which means the closing of theaters throughout the country."

In the event of a strike that would close the studios for many months, actors would have been one of the groups hardest hit. Members of most of the craft unions could obtain work outside the industry, but that was not true of actors. A motion was made and passed by the board (Anne Revere and Boris Karloff being the only dissenting members) that "members of the Guild be instructed to go through picket lines and live up to their contracts . . . and that the Guild make every effort to see that the studios provide adequate physical protection for its members when crossing picket lines."

A letter with this information was sent out to SAG members on September 19, creating tremendous controversy among them. A mass membership meeting was called by the Emergency Committee for October 1. Montgomery was to chair it, but he was unable to attend. The committee voted Reagan to take his place.

---

*Harry Bridges, director of the Congress of Industrial Organization (CIO), was accused of Communist affiliation in 1939 but officially absolved the next year. In 1948, he was ousted as head of the CIO because of his support of Henry A. Wallace for president. For many years a conspiracy to deport Bridges to his native Australia on grounds that he was a Communist was fought through the courts. Finally, in 1955, a federal district judge ruled that there was absolutely no proof of this accusation. But Bridges's power in Hollywood had been obliterated.

† The SAG minutes of September 17, 1946, state: "The Guild is not interested in the merits of the case, but feels that all possible steps should be taken to prevent a strike."

"Reagan had always struck me as being quiet, unassuming, and not the two-fisted fighter we [SAG] needed for the position," actress-columnist Hedda Hopper opined in the *Chicago Tribune*. "I was never more wrong." The meeting was fraught with anger from both sides. "Reagan was a one-man battalion," Sterling Hayden recalled. His refusal to allow "the Red nucleus" to gain the floor alerted Hollywood to a new political presence in their community. Only the naïve could have been unaware of Reagan's emerging power, and only those who wore mental blindfolds could have remained under the impression that he was still the young and ideological bleeding-heart liberal.

Robert Montgomery, following a new trend in Hollywood, had begun to produce his own films, placing him in the three-headed category of actor-producer-director—a growing concern in the Guild, which felt this could lead to a conflict in interests.* His new pressures also called for greater demands on his time, and Reagan began to step in for him.

A convention of the entire AFL had been scheduled to take place in Chicago on October 7. Montgomery had planned to attend with a member of the SAG staff, "blond, affable, Englishman" Pat Somerset, who was in charge of SAG labor relations. In a private meeting, the Emergency Committee, led by Reagan, had decided "that consideration should be given to sending a much larger delegation to Chicago in order that sufficient importance may be given to the issue" (to make every effort to force acceptance of the theory of arbitration of jurisdictional disputes). The board agreed and so the committee flew from Los Angeles on October 6 on a flight "which involved recalcitrant landing gears and conked-out motors." Reagan arrived in a nervous state from the trip (he still had a tremendous fear of flying), but seemed to have regained his full energies by the next day. (Montgomery was to stay in Chicago only a day—he had a theater commitment in New York.)

The SAG minutes from October 21, 1946 (when the Emergency Committee made its report to the board), reveal that in Chicago the group met with William Green, George Meany, Herbert Sorrell, Matthew Woll, Richard Walsh, William Hutcheson

---

*Montgomery accelerated his political activities at this time. He headed (1947) the Hollywood Republican Committee to elect Thomas E. Dewey as president. That same year, he testified as a "friendly witness" for HUAC. In 1951, he worked for Dwight Eisenhower's election and was "Special Consultant" to the president on TV and in public communications during his term of office.

and the three members of the AFL Executive Council who wrote the jurisdictional arbitration award of December 26, 1945, and later issued the clarification of August 16, 1946. Edward Arnold was the major spokesman for the SAG group, Reagan its organizer. Arnold spoke for the Guild before the convention "in the strongest wording," urging the passage "for the establishment of permanent arbitration machinery."

Reagan and the rest of his committee met first with William Green, president of the AFL, and told him they were prepared "to fly stars to every key city in the United States to make personal appearances and show films of the violence outside the studio gates, and to tell the people that one man—the first vice-president of the AFL, Bill Hutcheson, was responsible." This was a heretofore unprecedented extension of the use of executive power—and was without Guild sanctions. (Green supposedly "burst into tears," a bizarre image for a strong labor leader.)

The committee next went to see Hutcheson, "a jolly, Santa Claus of a man who became far less jolly as the discussion went on, well past midnight. Hutcheson was not willing to give an inch. Finally the group rose to leave. 'Tell Walsh [IATSE president] that if he'll give in . . . I'll run Sorrell out of Hollywood and break up the CSU in five minutes. I'll do the same to the Commies.'"

Sorrell was present at the next morning's confrontation. "It doesn't matter a damn what Hutcheson says," he told them. "This thing is going on, no matter what he does! When it ends up there'll be only one man running labor in Hollywood and that man will be me!"

"One of us (old liberal me) was so wide-eyed by this time it seemed my eyes could never close again," Reagan commented about this meeting.

On the last day of his stay, Somerset (remaining one extra day) was told by Walsh "that jurisdiction over set erection [the set decorators] should definitely belong to IATSE, and that if the award were repudiated, it was IATSE's further intention to resign from the AFL Executive Council." The situation was still at an impasse.

While in Chicago, Kelly, Pidgeon and Smith had also discussed with IATSE official Matthew Woll his attack on various motion-picture players as being Communists and informed him of his error. "It is hoped," the minutes of October 21, 1946, state, "that some retraction will be forthcoming."

Reagan had been asked to speak at a meeting of film technicians (IATSE Local 683) that had voted to observe the CSU picket lines. "The invitation was not received until late in the afternoon on Friday [October 18], and as the meeting was to be held that night it was possible to get in touch with only part of the Executive Committee. However, inasmuch as there was no secret about what went on in Chicago, it was felt that it would be proper for Mr. Reagan to give a factual report to the technicians meeting in spite of the fact that such a report had not yet been made to the Guild Board of Directors." The contents of his speech convinced the film technicians to reverse their decision.

Reagan and the Guild received letters of protest from the CSU immediately afterward. In the SAG board meeting held Monday, October 21, Reagan moved that all AFL studio unions be invited by the Emergency Committee to attend a "round-table discussion [at the SAG] to find some means of settling the current motion picture strike"—a motion that was unanimously carried.

Reagan was stepping into the center of the arena.

Father George H. Dunne, a young rebel Jesuit priest who taught at Loyola University in Los Angeles, was committed to Christian Advocacy and very much involved in labor strife in Hollywood. What Dunne believed was what the most progressive edge of the Democratic party—men like Hubert Humphrey—supported. A man with a colorful, if disjointed, way of describing happenings, he emerged publicly in 1946 and immediately became popular with the press—who were always looking for a good story.

"[I can tell you just how] the gangsters took over the IATSE. Willie Bioff, the former pimp from Chicago, had come out with two gunmen, and Willie Bioff dropped off in Phoenix, the two gunmen came on to Hollywood . . . each one with a violin case under his arm," Father Dunne told an interviewer in 1981. "They just walked into a union meeting one night [this would have been 1933] in Union Hall (which then was on Santa Monica Boulevard near Western, as I recall), just walked into the union, and announced that they were taking over. They telephoned Bioff in Phoenix and said, 'We've taken over the union,' and Bioff came over the next day. . . . [In 1946] I went to see Roy Brewer who had succeeded Willie Bioff [actually there had been a four-year interval]. . . . He said to me, among other things, he was rather bitter and angry at his own IATSE workers. He spoke about them the way you might expect to hear a management man talk about a unionist. He complained bitterly about, you know, 'They always want more money, more money, more money.' And he said to me, 'There's not room in Hollywood for the IATSE and the CSU.' (That's Herb Sorrell's group.) It's a war to the finish."

Father Dunne's opinion was that the "whole strike had been manipulated in a conspiracy between the major producers and Roy Brewer and the IATSE union . . . to precipitate a situation in which the CSU would have no choice but to strike, then, once they were out of the studio, freeze them out until time, attrition, and everything else simply destroyed them." The week before the Chicago convention of the AFL, "there was a series of hush-hush, very top secret meetings in Hollywood between the major producers . . . and the IATSE union. Brewer, himself, attended some of the meetings [and guaranteed] the [producers] that if they forced the CSU people out on the streets, he could supply IATSE people if they refused to take their jobs, to work on what they called 'hot sets,' he himself would force them to do so."*

Herbert Sorrell had called the set decorators (Carpenters Union) out on strike on September 24, 1946, just two weeks before the Chicago convention. Three days later, he said he had been kidnapped at gunpoint by hired gunmen of the Chicago syndicate, driven up into the foothills (in Los Angeles), beaten badly, pistol-whipped and left for dead. The next day he was found and hospitalized, and released on the following Sunday with head bandages, both eyes badly blackened and bruises on his face. There were rumors that the beating was "a put-up job." "I don't think even Herb, who had all kinds of courage [he had been a boxer] would submit to getting badly beaten up," Father Dunne insisted. "The doctors in the hospital certainly examined him. They never gave any support to this theory."

Father Dunne was now revved for action—violence, which he strongly opposed, had been used. Believing that the key to ending the strike was held by the SAG, he went on the air (KXLA, February 5, 1947) and declared that if the members of the SAG "would simply refuse to cross the picket line" the strike would be "settled in twenty-four hours." Explaining this at a later time he said, "The producers, as long as they could continue to make pictures, would be making money. But the moment the actors and

---

*Minutes for these "hush-hush" meetings between Brewer and several producers' representatives were produced by Congressman Carroll Kearns years later in a congressional investigation into labor. How Kearns came to have these minutes was never revealed, but they do validate Father Dunne's allegations.

actresses stopped coming into the studios to make pictures for
them, they'd have to shut down, you see. That's the end of their
flow of income, cash. . . . This brought an immediate reaction
from Ronald Reagan. . . . [Late] the very next night he came
down here to Loyola . . . and into [the] parlor . . . downstairs. . . . He was accompanied by Jane Wyman, and by George
Murphy [Jack Dales was also present]. . . . Jane Wyman contributed nothing to the discussion except her charming looks, you
know. . . . [Murphy had] an arrow-collar kind of good looks. . . .
He contributed very little except an embarrassed smile from time
to time . . . the leader, the articulate spokesman for the three, was
Ronald Reagan . . . we were together for about three hours' discussion . . . until two o'clock in the morning, as I remember. The
whole thrust of his discourse was to persuade me that Herb Sorrell and the CSU and all these people were Communists, and this
was a Communist-led and inspired strike, and that I was simply
being a dupe for the Communists.

"He said, and I don't question that it was true, that he and
Murphy, the two of them, had made a trip back to [Chicago]
where they had discussions with . . . Doherty, Knight, and Birthright [the three men on the AFL arbitration committee] . . . and
the committee men told them that it was definitely their intention
that this work [the set decorators] should go to the IATSE union.
[This statement was later contradicted by "the Three Wise
Men"—as they were called—during a congressional hearing into
labor activities.]

". . . [The meeting between Father Dunne and the SAG
group] was calm and collected. . . . Reagan . . . was very aggressive of course. . . . I had the very definite impression, this is a
dangerous man. I remember saying this to myself. Murphy was
totally harmless. . . . But Reagan, I had a definite view, this is a
dangerous man, because he is so articulate, and because he's
sharp. But he can also be very ignorant, as he clearly was, in my
judgment, interpreting everything in terms of the Communist
threat, you see, Communist danger." Father Dunne then adds,
"He had his facts wrong both to the alleged Communism of Herb
Sorrell and the CSU union and as to the rectitude of the jurisdictional issue. He was all wrong . . . then [he ran around] trying to
solve it . . . being a Rover Boy."

Dunne did not believe that Reagan had been a "mouth piece"
for Brewer, but he did feel certain that "he was doing a job for the
producers. . . . I have never had much use for [Reagan] ever since

my dealings with him in the Hollywood strike, because he played a key role in cooperation with . . . the thoroughly immoral Chicago gangster outfit [IATSE] to destroy what was the only honest and democratic trade-union movement in Hollywood [the CSU]. They [IATSE and the producers] did this to them, and Reagan played a key role in that destruction."

Reagan gave a different version of his meeting with Father Dunne. "[He] took to the air waves and blasted the SAG and opponents of the CSU eloquently and with vigor. . . . George Murphy and I decided he must be a victim of a snow job. We knew he had never been exposed to the Guild side of the controversy, and he was saying some pretty harsh things about us. We called and asked if we could see him, and then went down to the university one evening, armed with our records. We were a little taken aback when he introduced us to his lawyer, and coldly informed us he had asked the lawyer to sit in on our meeting. It was a short meeting. The next night he was back on radio kicking our brains out. But not for long; someone else began to teach political science [at Loyola] and he was on the other side of the country."

Father Dunne was transferred to Phoenix for a time, but did eventually return to Loyola. He has insisted the meeting with Reagan, Murphy, Dales and Wyman (who was not mentioned in Reagan's version) lasted hours and that the only other person present in the early stages of the meeting was the university public-relations officer, who departed very soon after the SAG delegation arrived.

15

DURING THE TIME OF REAGAN'S STRIKE ACTIVITIES,
he had been filming *Night Unto Night,* a dramatization of a Philip
Wylie book, playing opposite Viveca Lindfors, who had begun a
prestigious stage career in her native land (Sweden) before signing a
Warner Brothers contract earlier in the year. After many months
had gone by with her only appearance in front of a camera having
occurred in the studio's still photography gallery ("Wet your lips,
Viveca. Look this way or that way, up or down, over your shoulder.
Look sexy"), Lindfors threatened to leave America and go home to
her two small children and her husband. "Warners have a picture
for you," her agent called to say. "Beginning September 15th [1946].
'Night Unto Night' starring Ronald Reagan."*

"Who?"

"Never mind. A young star under contract."

Lindfors says, "The formula was to match a new foreign girl

---

*The title is derived from Psalm 19: "The heavens declare the Glory of God . . . Day unto
day uttereth speech, and night unto night showeth knowledge."

with a big American star. Ronald Reagan was not that. The director was fairly unknown, too [Don Siegel]. He had made only one film so far [*The Verdict*]." Why Warners ever made *Night Unto Night* is puzzling. They had bought the book at a time when they were making emotional dramas, gray in tone, social in content. (Audiences now wanted to be entertained.) The story dealt with a widow (Lindfors) who believes her dead husband is communicating with her; Reagan played a scientist, a hopeless epileptic, who cures her delusion as they fall in love. Then she saves him from attempting suicide. Even Laurence Olivier could not have given credibility to the solemn pretentiousness of this story, which was filmed in a gloomy beach house [also used for *Mildred Pierce*] on inclement days to give the picture an even more somber atmosphere.

When the company was not on location, more drama occurred at the studio gates than on the set. Filming on *Night Unto Night* began on September 20. All the actors and the crew had to pass through an extremely hostile picket line to make their way into the studio. Jack Warner had obtained big buses driven by members of the Teamsters Union, whose rank and file had voted unanimously not to cross the picket lines.* Four days into the production, violence erupted, cars were overturned and set on fire, people were screaming, many were injured. "I heard one studio patrolman tell another, 'Take Reagan home and stay on patrol all night,'" Lindfors recalls. "'He is established in the picture now and we don't want to take any chances.'" Two weeks later, he flew to Chicago for the convention, a three-day trip.

Lindfors recalls him as being "bland and smooth and seemingly pleasant. . . . I don't remember a single conversation of any substance. I do remember some chit chat about sex, which was up my alley, since I was in love with Don [Siegel, the director; they married subsequently]. . . . 'It's best in the afternoon after coming out of a shower,' he said, and then he laughed [an] embarrassed laugh. . . ."

The film ran over schedule because of the strike interference and the difficulty of obtaining the proper light on the beach loca-

*During an investigation into labor by Congress (1953), Joe Tuohy, business agent for the Teamsters, admitted that he had ordered his men to cross the picket lines and had threatened that if they didn't do so, he would bring in drivers from outside to take their jobs. A few months later, Warners offered him a job for $500 a week (he was making $175 with the Teamsters). Coincidentally, the Teamsters was the only trade union that endorsed Ronald Reagan's campaign for the presidency.

tion. Thanksgiving passed and Christmas approached. The cast worked the morning of Christmas Eve, "grey, heavy, humid. . . . Eggnog was served all over the place. . . . By two o'clock in the afternoon, everybody was drunk . . . except for me [Lindfors]." Reagan had left early to go to the SAG offices. The film was finished on December 29. In February, Jack Warner saw the first print of *Night Unto Night* and decided to shelve it. While Reagan waited to begin his next film, an adaptation of John Van Druten's successful play *The Voice of the Turtle,* he immersed himself in the SAG, which was attempting to renegotiate its contract with the producers during the adverse conditions caused by the strike. This contract, upon which Reagan, Murphy and Arnold did most of the negotiating, was viewed by many of the membership as a sellout. Rumors persisted that the three men—all of whom had gone to Chicago—had agreed in secret meetings for SAG to cross the picket lines so that production would not be held up on any films. In return, the producers had acceded to certain favorable points in the new contract.

Rains came to California in biblical force in January 1947. Above the Reagan house on Cordell Drive, the mud was sliding, carrying trees and brush with it, undermining the less substantial homes. Despite the violence of the weather and the violence inside the industry, Jane Wyman was in high spirits. She had been nominated for Best Actress of 1946 for her performance in *The Yearling* and she was pregnant.

The Reagans' marriage had been suffering difficulties since his return from the service. She earnestly tried in 1946 and part of 1947 to share his new involvement in the SAG with him. Some of his viewpoints she agreed with, but not all, and none could she approach with his intensity of purpose.

The SAG had become an obsession with Reagan. He spoke of almost nothing else. Wyman found it difficult to discuss with him her own concerns, which seemed lightweight against such heavy issues as the strike, violence at the studios, gangsterism in the unions, talk of Communist infiltration in the industry, or the negotiations on the producers' contract. At home, he was either on the telephone in conference calls, working with various members of the Emergency Committee or writing speeches. He had very little time for the children, but Wyman hoped that once the strike was settled things would go back to some sort of early, dimly remembered normalcy. She hated guns, and he now had a collection mounted on the walls of the den and wore a loaded one, holstered to his shoulder, during his waking hours. At night, it rested on the bedside table; she told one close friend there had been more than one night that she had awakened to see him holding the gun, sitting up in bed, having thought he had heard noises in the house.

On March 14, Reagan escorted an apprehensive Wyman and Mary Livingstone (whose husband, Jack Benny, was master of ceremonies) to the Academy Awards, being held for the first time at the massive Shrine Auditorium. Wyman smiled bravely when Olivia de Havilland's name was called for her performance in *To Each His Own*.* Her disappointment could not be helped, although she much admired De Havilland. Proving to Hollywood that her two roles (*The Lost Weekend* and *The Yearling*) were not "dramatic freaks"—that she was of Academy Award caliber—became all-important to her.

"Maybe we'll call him [the baby due in September] Oscar," Reagan kidded to the press. "Jane deserves one around the house."

Monday night, March 10, the Reagans attended the regular meeting of the board of directors of the SAG. Seven members submitted their resignations that evening: Robert Montgomery, president; Franchot Tone, first vice-president; Dick Powell, second vice-president; and John Garfield, Harpo Marx, Dennis O'Keefe and James Cagney, all of whom now had a financial interest in the production of pictures in which they appeared.† Upon a motion made by Gene Kelly, seconded by George Chandler and unanimously carried, Reagan was nominated for the presidency. Nominations for Gene Kelly and George Murphy for the same office followed. The election by the board members was held right then by secret ballot, a majority vote required for election. Paper slips were passed out and tabulated by Jack Dales's secretary, Midge Farrell.‡ A nervous silence followed. Then Jack Dales read the results.

---

*Other nominees in the same category were Jennifer Jones (*Duel in the Sun*), Rosalind Russell (*Sister Kenny*) and Celia Johnson (*Brief Encounter*). *Best Years of Our Lives* won the award for Best Picture, Best Actor (Fredric March) and Best Director (William Wyler). *The Yearling* took the Cinematography and Interior Decoration awards, and Claude Jarman, Jr., was voted the outstanding child star of the year and given a miniature Oscar.

† Cagney had recently left Warners to produce, with his brother, William Cagney, his own films. Two years earlier Warner had called him into his office. "'You've got two more years on your contract. Want to make another contract?'" Warner asked. "I said no," Cagney recalled. "He said, 'Why not?' And he had a whole line of those pills on his desk. I said, 'There's your reason.' He said, 'What?' I said, 'You're taking pills for your stomach, aren't you?' He said, 'Yes.' I said, 'That's the reason. I don't want to.' Head man of the studio, and every time he felt bad, he took another pill."

‡ The majority of artists' unions, then and now, require a ballot be circulated to the membership. The SAG today requires election of their officers by the membership.

Ronald Reagan was the newly elected president of the Screen Actors Guild.* Exactly one month later, Reagan had his meeting with the FBI and agreed to be an informant by reporting names of any members of the SAG who he thought had Communist associations. Wyman, a close friend asserts, was in an emotional state, torn, not knowing what to do but not agreeing with his decision.

Reagan had begun filming Van Druten's stage hit *The Voice of the Turtle* (for which Warners had paid the playwright $500,000 plus 15 percent of the total gross receipts) in February. Although this would be a starring role and the film was one of the studio's top productions for that year, he had not been anyone's first choice. Warner had tried for Cary Grant, Hal Wallis for Tyrone Power. Both actors had been unavailable for loan-outs from their home studios. Steve Trilling finally suggested Reagan, and all three men agreed. The film was to be promoted on its reputation as "the greatest stage hit in many years and the most appealing love story of the decade." For the first time, Reagan was being given a romantic lead in a major A picture. The hope was that he might display the sexual appeal of a James Stewart or a Henry Fonda. Eleanor Parker, a Warner contract actress, was getting her big break in this film, which co-starred Wayne Morris and Eve Arden. Reagan had finally overtaken Morris in the jockeying of players' credits. However, Jack Warner was banking on Van Druten's name and the popularity of the stage play to help sell the film.

The Voice of the Turtle was nothing more than boy (Sergeant Bill Page, a charming back-home type in New York on a weekend pass) meets girl (Sally Middleton—young, beautiful, disappointed in love—whose apartment he is forced, through a set of circumstances, to share). John Van Druten's bright, slick, double-entendre dialogue and amusing situations gave it a fresh luster. Jack Warner had a screenwriter (Charles Hoffman) add some dialogue to Van Druten's adaptation. The playwright, in a pique, promptly wired him to remove his own name from the credits. Warner wired back:

RAN PICTURE LAST NIGHT BEFORE TURNING IT OVER FOR
SCORING. AND WANT YOU TO KNOW WE FOLLOWED YOUR

---

*Gene Kelly was elected first vice-president; William Holden, second vice-president; George Murphy, third vice-president; Anne Revere, treasurer. Present and voting at this meeting were Paul Harvey, Anne Revere, Leon Ames, Robert Armstrong, Edward Arnold, George Chandler, Ben Corbett, Rose Hobart, William Holden, Marjorie ("Babe") Kane, Warner Anderson, Boris Karloff, Gene Kelly, Cliff Lyons, Kermit Maynard, J. Carroll Nash, Jeffrey Sayre, Larry Steers, Tudor Williams and Jane Wyman.

SCRIPT VERBATIM. THERE ISN'T OVER ½ PAGE OF
CHANGES. IN VIEW OF EVERYTHING THAT'S HAPPENED IN
THE PRODUCING OF THIS PICTURE [conflict between Van
Druten and Warner over the casting] IF YOU HAVE ANY
IDEA OF REMOVING YOUR NAME FROM SCREEN I FEEL YOU
WILL BE DOING IMMEASURABLE HARM TO THE DISTRIBU-
TION AND SELLING OF THE PICTURE. AM DEEPLY SORRY
FOR EVERYTHING THAT OCCURRED OVER WHICH YOU AND
DE LIAGRE AND I HAD NO CONTROL. BUT WANT TO ASSURE
YOU AGAIN WE HAVE PHOTOGRAPHED THE SCRIPT YOU
WROTE . . .

That same day, Warner also wired his New York office:

KEEP AFTER DE LIAGRE AND VAN DRUTEN . . . CAMPAIGN
ON RONALD REAGAN WILL EMPHASIZE HIS QUICK RETURN
TO FAME SINCE HIS RETURN FROM THE ARMY AND HIS
QUALITY OF EVOKING WARM RESPONSE FROM ALL TYPES
AND AGES OF MOVIE FANS AND WITH HIS PART AS BILL
PAGE HE GAINS NEW STATURE . . .

Irving Rapper had directed a number of successful dramas for
Warners. *The Voice of the Turtle* was his first comedy. "John Van
Druten . . . was to have made his debut directing the film version
[of his play]. But he despaired when he realized the studio preferred to cast its own actors under contract. He therefore quit and
asked Warners to let me direct it. . . . I reluctantly accepted
Ronald Reagan, whom no one took too seriously [as an ac-
tor] . . ." Rapper recalled.

By the first week in May, filming was completed and Reagan
was able to devote almost full time (for a month) to the SAG. He
took over an office in their building on Sunset Boulevard. Despite
Jack Warner's plans to give him a new image as a romantic comedian of Cary Grant's stature, interviews and articles began appearing in which he was referred to as a "stout citizen
representative of the Hollywood folk who think and vote and are
the back bone of America." Accompanying photographs of him
wearing his glasses and speaking from a podium bore such cap-
tions as "Ronald Reagan refuses to be a glamour boy."

A lengthy interview titled "Mr. Reagan Airs His Views" appeared in the *Chicago Tribune* and was syndicated to numerous
other newspapers. (The *Mr. Reagan* was a new form of public address, one seldom applied in print to other actors.) "Our

[America's] highest aim should be the cultivation of freedom of the individual for therein lies the highest dignity of man. Tyranny is tyranny, and whether it comes from right, left, or center, it's evil.

"I believe the only logical way to save our country from all extremists is to remove conditions that supply fuel for the totalitarian fire. I'm not, however, in favor of outlawing any political party. [The Communist party was legal in the United States and on the presidential ballot.] If we ban the Communists from the polls we set a precedent. Tomorrow it may be the Democratic or the Republican Party that gets the ax. . . . The Reds know that if we can make America a decent living place for all our people, their cause is lost here. So they seek to infiltrate liberal organizations just to smear and discredit them. If you don't believe this, name me one conservative organization that is Communist-infiltrated. I've already pulled out of one organization that I joined in good faith. One day I woke up, looked about, and found it was Commie-dominated [HICCASP] and did I pull out of it—but quick!

"You can't blame a man for aligning himself with an institution he thinks is humanitarian; but you can blame him if he deliberately remains with it after he knows it's fallen into the hands of the Reds." To the accusations that he "had sold out to the producers," he replied that he was "not particularly disturbed" because he was "passionately interested in the working man" and recognized faults in labor as well as management. His answer to the slowdown in production posed by the strike was, "The film industry is suffering from prosperity as far as the actor is concerned. . . . Usually if a man sees customers lined up in front of a store, his impulse is to build another store in the neighborhood to take care of the surplus." The studios were not keeping up with the demand, he said [ignoring the strike issue]. His answer: "Build more theaters and make more pictures. In a period of prosperity [postwar] people are ready to spend money at the box office."

Jack Warner asked him to do *That Hagen Girl* opposite Shirley Temple. The script raised the same question of poor judgment as had *Night Unto Night*. Charles Hoffman—the writer who had contributed the "additional dialogue" on *The Voice of the Turtle*—adapted Edith Roberts's turgid story of an adopted illegitimate child (Temple) taunted all her life (she is now seventeen) by the residents of the small town in which she lives. She ends up in the somewhat surprised arms of a man (Reagan) old enough to be her father—and, indeed, long suspected as such. To Reagan's everlasting credit, he did try to get out of doing this film. But Warner insisted, and with a baby due in four months, Reagan chose not to go out on suspension. Production was started on June 4 with a seven-week shooting schedule.

Temple (actually nineteen at the time) had recently married actor John Agar and wanted an opportunity to play a mature role. *That Hagen Girl* probably destroyed any chance she might have had to move from child to adult performer. To add to the awfulness of the film, Reagan and Temple had no chemistry together and ended up looking ridiculous. (Reagan tells the story of an incident at the sneak preview. At the point in the film when he denies to Mary Hagen that he is her father, "There was a loud chorus from the audience [when he ends the scene with "I love you"], 'Oh, No!' I shrank down in my seat and wouldn't leave until the audience had filed out." The scene was cut.) About a week into the production, Reagan and Temple had to shoot the sequence where she jumps into a lake to drown herself and he dives in to save her. To add to the bleakness, Peter Godfrey, the director, ordered rain. Reagan refused a double, and the scene of him jumping off the pier into the cold water of the river location had to be reshot a number of times. The following day, June 19, he awoke with a fever. Wyman called in to tell the studio they would have to shoot around him. Five days later (June 24), his condition grew worse and he was taken to the hospital with pneumonia.

Wyman went into labor and was also rushed to the hospital (Queen of Angels; Reagan was at Cedars of Lebanon). A premature girl (six months) was born, survived in an incubator for twenty-four hours and then died. Wyman had to go through the ordeal alone and return to the house alone, while Reagan remained hospitalized. He resumed work on the set of *That Hagen Girl* on July 14. At home, his wife was withdrawn, relations were strained. At the studio, he was making a bad film that he knew was no good and that had fallen behind schedule. The Guild afforded him his best escape, although he did spend time at Nino Pepitone's (where he now boarded three horses). He spoke to Nelle almost every day and on Sunday the family gathered at his place. But Jane kept more and more to herself. Everyone attributed it to postpartum depression.

*   *   *

Jane Wyman had seen *Johnny Belinda* on Broadway in January 1940, when she and Reagan had been on the Louella Parsons tour.* From that moment, she later confessed to a reporter, she had wanted to play the part of the deaf mute, Belinda, onscreen. At the time, because of the subject matter, no studio had bid for the rights despite the play's great critical and commercial success. Not until June 1946 did a film company express interest. The fact that the studio was Warners was a stroke of tremendous luck for Wyman. Still, selling the idea of making *Johnny Belinda* to Steve Trilling and Jack Warner had not been an easy task for producer Jerry Wald, even though he was thought of as the "bright-eyed genius" on the lot. On June 15, 1946, Wald wrote Trilling:

> I can't stress to you enough the great box-office picture there is in this material . . . the basic story of "Johnny Belinda" is a thousand times more commercial than "To Each His Own." Why nobody has purchased this property before is somewhat beyond my comprehension. In a very slick fashion you are dealing with the most primitive emotional subject in the world—an unwed mother who is having her child taken away. The mother, in order to defend the child, kills the man who is attempting to do this. . . .
>
> Don't you think it's high time that you guys [Trilling and Warner] acknowledged that I do have a good mind for stories? . . . Consistently, Steve, I've had to sell you and Warner on properties [that have become big grossers like *Mildred Pierce*]. . . . When are you going to get wise to the fact that you can tell a corny story with basic human values, in a very slick, dressed-up fashion? . . . Okay, Doctor—I'll go quietly.

Wald finally got the go-ahead from Warner, who had originally memoed him: "Who the hell wants to see a movie where the leading lady doesn't say a word?" By summer 1947, Wald had an acceptable screenplay and was looking for a director. He turned to Jean Negulesco, who had done a good job for him on the Joan Crawford film *Humoresque*. Negulesco wrote Steve Trilling on July 2, 1947: "Jerry Wald gave me a copy of 'Johnny Belinda' to read this morning. . . . I must say it's one of the most exciting, human and colorful scripts I have read in a long time. I am terribly en-

---

* *Johnny Belinda,* by Elmer Harris, opened at the Belasco Theatre on September 10, 1940, for 321 performances. Helen Claire originated the role of Belinda.

thusiastic about the possibility of doing it, because I know I could make a good job of it. . . ."

When Wyman heard that the studio had purchased the play, she went to Wald (a personal friend) and asked to be considered. Having just seen Wyman in *The Yearling* (also an unglamorous role), he had no difficulty in visualizing her as the drab, tortured Belinda. The casting sheets begun in July show he had not considered anyone else for the role, although Trilling had suggested Teresa Wright. Almost immediately after the death of her baby, Wyman began preproduction work on *Johnny Belinda*. She had to master sign language and lipreading by the time the film was to go before the cameras in September. She worked with Elizabeth Gessner, a woman who taught both and then befriended a teenage Mexican girl who had been born unhearing. The young woman and Wyman spent several days a week together at the Reagan house communicating in sign language. Evenings, Wyman ran the sixteen-and thirty-five-millimeter films that the studio had made of the girl so that she could study her eyes, trying to capture "a certain quality," an "anticipation light," the look of one who wants "to eagerly share in things." Something kept eluding her. And then she realized it was that she could hear. She spoke to Wald and Negulesco and they agreed that she might do better if she blocked out sound by putting wax in her ears, both for rehearsals and for the film.

Johnny Belinda was now as great an obsession with Wyman as the Guild was with Reagan. Both had withdrawn into their own worlds.

The role of the doctor who befriends Belinda was to be played by Lew Ayres, but the two were not to meet until they had arrived at Mendocino, California, two hundred miles north of San Francisco, where the location shots would be filmed. Reagan drove up with Wyman and remained for a day before returning to Los Angeles. A jumble of weathered, gabled wooden buildings fronting dirt streets, edged by the ominous pine woods of encircling hills and perched on the northern shore of a half-moon–shaped bay at the mouth of the Big River, Mendocino—with a population under one thousand, almost all greatly dependent on intermittent lumbering—could easily have been Belinda's real village. Seldom had a film company seemed more at odds with its location and a town's inhabitants, most of whose ancestors had traveled in covered wagons across the country from New England. People in Mendocino had retained their forefathers' reserve. They left the

movie folk pretty much alone and expected the same in return.
For this reason, the cast and crew became a tightly knit, insular
group. They moved to the site of a former logging camp. Housing
was fairly primitive. Evenings they sang around an open campfire.
"We felt so isolated, yet oddly at peace," Wyman recalled, "that
no one wanted to play cards or dance. It was as though the spirit
of the simple people of Belinda's remote world hung over and
around us."

Negulesco was a fine painter and, under his tutelage, Wyman
found she had some artistic talent. During her free time in the first
six weeks in Mendocino, canvas and paints under her arm, she
would get into the company pickup truck and drive to Russian
Gulch, where the fern-banked canyon cut deep among the red-
woods; or to the wild, rocky coastline of Fort Bragg; or to Noyo by
the winding Noyo River, crowded with small fishing craft tied up
alongside tumble-down warehouses. Sometimes Agnes Moorehead
(who was also in the cast) joined her, sometimes Negulesco. More
often, it was Lew Ayres. "Just sitting there painting away
with . . . Lew gave me a warm feeling," she later said.

In March 1942, less than four months after Pearl Harbor and
with America seething with war preparations, Lew Ayres had announced to the world that he would not bear arms.

"Now let us consider war," he had said in a prepared statement which he read to reporters. "It is not strange that no one
really wants war, yet few think that life can be successfully or even
respectfully lived without it. We all shake our heads sadly over
our predicament and then wait for the other fellow to stop it first,
each side perhaps eager to be the benevolent victor.

"In confusion we stumble blindly along with prayers for peace
on our lips and bloodstains on our hands, afraid to go forward,
afraid to stop, and troubled by strangely perplexed hearts,
wherein savagery and virtue reside intertwined.

"So in my opinion we will never stop wars until we individually cease fighting them and that's what I propose to do. I propose we proclaim a moratorium on all presumed debts of evil
done us, to start afresh by wiping the slate clean and continuing
to wipe it clean . . . my views have been on file [with the army]
for over a year . . . and have long been taken for granted by my
personal friends.

"Furthermore I am, and have been, fully aware of the possible
consequences arising from such an action as mine in these emo-

tional times, but against all eventualities I am fortified with an inner conviction that seems to increase proportionately with every obstacle I face . . . this decision is . . . the mature result of hours, days, and years of research and reflection."

Ayres was sent to a conscientious objectors' camp at Cascade Locks, Oregon. The story pushed the war news off the front pages of newspapers across the nation and created an incredible furor in Hollywood. Theaters banned his pictures. A front-page editorial in *The Hollywood Reporter* asked the public not to blame the motion-picture industry for Ayres's stand. Whole pages of advertisements were taken in newspapers from Los Angeles to St. Louis vilifying him for his action—and Ayres had been a particularly loved performer, especially since his recent Dr. Kildare films. At twenty, he had burst into stardom in *All Quiet on the Western Front* with his never-to-be-forgotten portrayal of the young German soldier who is unable to kill the enemy but gets killed himself finally by a sniper on the edge of a World War I shell hole as he reaches out to hold a butterfly in his hand. Ayres had been married twice—to actresses Lola Lane and Ginger Rogers—but he had always been a bit of a recluse, an intellectual given to independent ideas. He had a quiet, almost diffident manner, a warm natural voice, all-American good looks and eyes that contained a surprising element of sadness. For many years he had been a vegetarian espousing the creed of passive resistance to evil. Nonetheless, what was a socially acceptable philosophy before Pearl Harbor branded him a coward after America entered the war.

He had been born in Minneapolis, Minnesota, where his father played the cello with the Minneapolis Symphony Orchestra. His paternal grandmother had been a well-trained pianist and teacher. He took up the jazz banjo and at nineteen landed a berth with Hank Halstead's Orchestra and made some of the first Vitaphone jazz recordings. An agent in Hollywood saw him and got him a film contract with Metro. A year later, he was cast as the bewildered soldier in *All Quiet on the Western Front*.

"I have a very simple philosophy," he told one reporter. "I believe that each man is born with certain limitations and capacities. And it's up to him to find them. A tree bears in its seed the possibility of growing to a maximum height, of spreading to a maximum width, of putting forth a maximum number of leaves. Now, if that tree grows as high, spreads as far and produces as many leaves as it is capable of, it has performed its function as fittingly as it can in the eternal scheme of things. We call that tree beautiful. Then, why not the same thing for the lives of men?"

Not long after Ayres had arrived at the "conshi camp," as detractors called it, he asked to be put in the Army Medical Corps and sent to the front lines. After a short training period, he was shipped to the South Pacific as a medical corpsman. Six months before the war's end, he was made a chaplain's assistant and promoted to sergeant. The men who served with him found him brave beyond the normal interpretation of the word. He displayed no personal fear as unarmed and under fire he administered medical assistance and prayers to men injured and dying on battlefields. He also turned over his entire army pay to the Red Cross.

"War was more horrible than I had ever imagined it," he said later. "Maybe you don't know what a bombed city looks like; or what it feels like to hold a child in your arms while it bleeds to death, or to stand by while kids watch their parents being dumped into mass graves. It got me, and for the first time in my life I understood the callousness of medics around suffering people. They have to be that way. When I felt myself cracking I went aside and had a talk with myself. I knew if I didn't get hold of my nerves and emotions I would be no good to anyone. So I did."

After the storm created by his declaring himself a conscientious objector had passed, some of the most conservative industry figures came to his defense. The violently right-wing Hedda Hopper took space to say: "Lew Ayres [is a] man who had the courage to stand up for his convictions in the face of public criticism and at the sacrifice of his career. That's all that a man's God asks of him. It took courage—far greater courage—to do what he did than to wheedle and pull strings to get an officer's uniform, as many, without the courage and ability to measure up to it, have done. Lew could have landed a cushy job. It's unfortunate that he had to go against the prevailing sentiments, but to crucify a man for standing up to his own convictions, even if it meant national ridicule and professional suicide, is un-Christian and un-American."

He had come out of the service several months after the war's end, having been transferred from battlefield to hospital work. He had first considered becoming a minister and then decided he might do more good if he could make films that had "some kind of universal message of faith and understanding." He expected Hollywood to bar its doors to him. But people had come to respect his strength of character. Louella was one of the first to interview him upon his return. "He's one of the finest characters in Hollywood," she concluded. He made one film, *The Dark Mirror* (playing a psychologist), opposite Olivia de Havilland for Universal. It did well. Now Warners had cast him as the doctor who saves Belinda and her child and stands up against a bigoted, self-righteous town. He was thirty-eight, only two years older than Reagan, but his exposure to the horrors of war had aged his appearance. The youthful good looks had given way to "a spiritually remote look in the eyes . . . greying hair . . . and an older, surer, more solid appearance."

Wyman's time in Mendocino was unique for her, because of the isolation of the town and because of the long periods of living in silence when she wore the wax in her ears. During those hours of filming, she became an unhearing person. She claimed she and Ayres did not have an affair while they were making *Johnny Belinda*, that they engaged in talk, not sex, in the time they spent together off the set. Quite probably, this was the truth. Wyman was a woman with a strong sense of loyalty. She had been through, and was still being subjected to, great emotional pressures—the loss of the baby, the strain in her marriage, the intensity of her preparation for Belinda and the knowledge that Reagan had become an informant for the FBI (as she also had for a time) and was carrying a gun, working with union leaders and being courted by rich businessmen such as car dealer Holmes P. Tuttle, who had begun to win him over to the idea that he had a place in politics if he chose the Republican side of the ticket. Being a politician's wife was not what she had envisioned for her future when they had married.

Wyman held some conservative views herself and was as patriotic as anyone else about subversion, spies and foreign takeovers of American industry. But she had genuine trouble in accepting the simplistic doctrine that to oppose a strongly conservative viewpoint, to not be irrevocably anti-Communist, meant a person was therefore a Communist. She was having considerable trouble in getting Reagan to listen to her ideas. He seemed to want her to fall into the role of "the little woman." She had difficulty with that, and she could not have had a greater contrast between two men than the pragmatic Reagan and the idealistic Ayres.

Ayres had been listening to the confused beliefs of men at war, counseling them. He was easy to talk to, comforting, strong. A close relationship evolved. This in itself must have caused Wyman to reevaluate her marriage. In addition, Wyman and Ayres were survivors together in what looked at the moment to be a sinking ship. "They're up there shooting fog and a bunch of damned seagulls! . . ." Jack Warner was purported to exclaim after viewing some of the footage. Warner now felt he had made a mistake in giving Wald the green light on this film and none of his memos was even the least bit encouraging.

Ten days before the end of the location shooting, Reagan went to Mendocino to spend time there with Wyman before driving her home. The cast and crew said that "he haunted the set." On October 17 the company returned to Los Angeles to film the remaining interior scenes. The schedule called for two and a half more weeks before the cameras, but the film fell behind and soon was ten days late.

Reagan has said, "The Communist plan for Hollywood was remarkably simple. It was merely to take over the motion picture business. Not only for its profit, as the hoodlums had tried—but also for a grand world-wide propaganda base. In those days before television and massive foreign film production, American films dominated 95 percent of the world's movie screens. We had an audience of about 500,000,000 souls. Takeover of this enormous plant and its gradual transformation into a Communist gristmill was a grandiose idea. It would have been a magnificent coup for our enemies."

Inside the Screen Actors Guild, fevers raged and anxiety prevailed. Fear of personal jeopardy caused acts that destroyed careers and lives, using the very tactics of the philosophy that the accused were said to follow. No doubt there were Communists in the Screen Actors Guild. No doubt there were some who were duped and fell into line behind the Communist leadership. There was, however, a much larger group that did not belong in either of these categories: those people with strong liberal beliefs who viewed Red-baiting in America with the same cold terror as they might have regarded Jew-baiting in Nazi Germany. Suddenly, artists were being fired and blacklisted, not on the basis of irrefutable evidence but by innuendo and association. In well-known restaurants, industry figures would turn away from old friends, co-workers and even family members who had any taint at all. Fascists and demagogues feasted gluttonously on such fears.

One such man was Myron C. Fagan, the author of numerous inconsequential and badly written plays. On Christmas, 1947, he had produced one of his plays (*Thieves' Paradise*) with a rabid anti-Communist theme at the Las Palmas Theatre in Hollywood. One critic wrote, "Thieves' Paradise will win the mythical title of 'worst play of the year.' Even the commercial variety of little theatres would be hard put to assemble a production that could invest so much bad taste in so much comic-book nonsense. . . . [It is] an incredibly bad play." *Thieves' Paradise* closed three days after it opened. Fagan claimed that Communist forces rallied against him, forcing the closure, and that the unfairness of it "burst into the front pages all over America." In fact, the play received only two Los Angeles reviews and the indexes in the five major American papers made no mention of it. Nonetheless, Fagan's bitterness began fifteen years of the most vicious, irresponsible Red-baiting in Hollywood. He formed a publishing company called Cinema Educational Guild, Inc., which put out (for two dollars) a pamphlet updated every few months that listed "some 300 top RED STARS and FELLOW TRAVELLERS in Hollywood." In Fagan's first indefensible hate pamphlets, Reagan's name was among the RED STARS on the basis that "the Screen Actors Guild . . . was CONTROLLED by its Red and Fellow-Traveller members [and] they elected . . . Reagan to the Presidency of their Guild. Can anybody be so utterly naïve as to believe that they would tolerate an enemy of the Conspiracy in that office?" Fagan regularly sent his list to the HUAC and they accepted and investigated those he charged with being Communists. "There are a number of items [from the pamphlet] I expect to call to the Committee's attention," Frank S. Tavenner, Jr., counsel to the HUAC, wrote Fagan. "I want to take my hat off to you and the rest who have stood in vanguard of the fight against Communism in Hollywood."

At the September 12, 1947, Monday night board meeting of the SAG, a proposal had been put forth that Guild members be required to sign a loyalty oath. Reagan reported that "a sub-Committee of the Motion Picture Industry Council had studied the problem, with particular emphasis on defense of the innocent, not only of those wrongfully accused of being Communists or having Communist tendencies, but also of other members of the industry who may be in or connected with pictures starring persons so accused against whom boycotts have been instigated by the public. The committee felt that a compulsory loyalty oath would not solve the problem inasmuch as there would be no reason why Communists would not sign it since it would give them a screen against any persons who failed to sign such an oath." Reagan, therefore, recommended a "voluntary statement of affirmation be prepared which could be signed by any persons in the Guild who wished to do so."

The statement suggested by the MPIC read as follows:

> In support of our soldiers as they take their oath upon induction, I affirm that I will bear true faith and allegiance to the United States of America and that I will serve the United States honestly and faithfully against all its enemies.
>
> I hold Stalin and the Soviet Union responsible for the war in Korea. I support the resistance of the United States and the United Nations against this act of imperialist aggression.
>
> History having proved that Stalinism is totalitarianism, I repudiate its teachings and program, as I do those of every other form of dictatorship.

Reagan then recommended that the loyalty oath be amplified to include a section in which the signer would volunteer to take an active part in Americanism programs, such as the Crusade for Freedom, and to make appearances for the anti-Communist Hollywood Coordinating Committee.

What this meant, of course, was that those who refused to sign such an oath on any grounds would immediately be placed under suspicion as being a Communist or a Communist sympathizer. The board was in a turmoil about the matter. Discussion became fairly heated, pro and con. (As Reagan had pointed out, the "guilty" could also sign it as a cover-up.) In the end, the majority voted that the proposed statement of affirmation be adopted as a policy.*

At the same meeting, each officer was asked to sign an affidavit stating that he or she was not a member of the Communist party. This was now a requirement for labor-union officers because of the recent passage (over President Truman's veto) of the Taft-Hartley Act,† which also established federal control of labor disputes and empowered the government to obtain an eighty-day

---

*This is not to be confused with the Loyalty Oath voted for in 1953 by 96 percent of Guild members, which was required for membership until 1974. "I am not now and will not become a member of the Communist Party nor of any other organization that seeks to overthrow the government of the United States by force or violence." Reagan was on the board but not president when the SAG approved this oath, which was removed when members of the rock group Grateful Dead and others refused to sign.

†Sponsored by Senator Robert A. Taft and Representative Fred Allen Hartley.

injunction against any strike that it deemed a peril to national health and safety. In addition, the act forbade unions to contribute to political campaigns.

The Screen Actors Guild had seven officers: Reagan, Gene Kelly, William Holden, George Murphy, Paul Harvey, Anne Revere and Murray Kinnell.* Anne Revere was treasurer and had been a diligent worker for the Guild since her arrival in Hollywood from the New York theater in 1940, a member of the board since 1944. One of the industry's finest character actresses, she had won the Academy Award (for Best Supporting Actress) in 1945 as Elizabeth Taylor's stoic yet soft-hearted mother in *National Velvet*. And she had just given a startling performance in *Gentleman's Agreement*, for which she would be nominated again.† She was at the peak of her career. Her gaunt, patrician face, the large, dark, expressive eyes, the well-modulated articulate voice made her an unforgettable film personality. Offscreen, unlike many of her co-actors, she had as strong an impact.

Revere had always contributed intelligent debate to the board meetings. "The thing that I found was most extraordinary when I came on the Board," she recalled, "was there was a minimal concern with the membership. I remember my first session with the Board. . . . When I started to speak [on behalf of the membership] it was as though a cataclysm hit. All eyes were on me. There were some clear problems . . . no one [the membership] ever came to [mass] meetings and they couldn't understand why.

"I said, 'Well, I think there's a good reason. . . . You have it once a year on Sunday night and you read a financial report and shortly thereafter they can read that in the [trade] magazines. So why should they come?'" Revere then recommended they hold four meetings a year and give the membership "some definite participation in the evening. The board agreed. Meetings began to be well attended. Then, in the second year (1945), the board took exception to a great many of the resolutions [being made by members] . . . and the four meetings were cancelled and no more resolutions."

Although Revere did indeed take the part of the membership in most meetings, she had never been known to be disruptive (in fact, no one on the board had been linked with the "disruptives").

---

*The thirty-one directors of the SAG were not affected by this law.
† Revere had also been nominated for her supporting role in *The Song of Bernadette* (1943).

The majority held her in high esteem and personally liked and respected her. On September 25, she wrote the members of the Screen Actors Guild board:

139 So. Camden Drive
Beverly Hills, Calif.
Sept. 15, 1947

Members of the Screen Actors Guild Board
7046 Hollywood Blvd.,
Hollywood, Calif.

Dear Fellow Board Member:

It is with extreme regret that I tender to you my resignation as Treasurer of the Guild. After prolonged consideration, however, I cannot bring myself to sign the affidavit prescribed by the Taft-Hartley law. I hold membership in a number of organizations. None of these in my opinion seeks to overthrow the government by force or by illegal or unconstitutional methods. My opinion, however, is not shared by certain gentlemen who, today, hold rather strategic positions: Mr. Rankin, Mr. Thomas, Mr. Wood, Mr. Tenney, to name but a few. Membership in an organization which seeks to dislodge these gentlemen from public office in the customary democratic American tradition, constitutes subversive activity in their opinion.

Furthermore, if charges were brought against me by these self-appointed judges and I were found *not* guilty, one would likely find the acquittal buried among the obituaries. My name would never be cleared even tho my innocence were established.

I stand ready to go to jail for the Guild whenever her welfare so requires, but then let it be for principle, not for perjury. I also stand ready to serve the Guild in less spectacular fashion if it should be so ordered. If not, my thanks to you all for hearing me out.

Sincerely yours,

[signed] Anne Revere

Revere was asked to resign as treasurer and was eventually replaced by Olivia de Havilland. However, for the time, she remained on the board. A new atmosphere hung heavily over the Monday night meetings. The officers and board were predominantly conservative, or right wing. And no one was quite sure where Reagan stood. They had no idea that he was cooperating with the FBI. They knew he had quit HICCASP and was anti-Communist. But, on the other hand, he still seemed to be a Democrat and had backed Helen Gahagan Douglas.

"We all thought he was 'walking the line,'" the late Dorothy Tree Uris, who served on the SAG board from 1937 to 1946, said. "Meaning he was playing both sides. We [the left wing] weren't sure we could trust him, so we kept pretty much out of his way."

Reagan had received a pink subpoena dated September 25, demanding he appear before the Un-American Activities Committee of the House of Representatives, of which "the Hon. J. Parnell Thomas of New Jersey is Chairman." He left the day he and Wyman returned home from Mendocino, along with Adolphe Menjou, Gary Cooper, Robert Taylor, George Murphy, Walt Disney, Robert Montgomery, Rupert Hughes, and Ginger Rogers's mother, Lela—all to be "friendly witnesses." Most of this group would name men and women they had worked with as Communists infiltrating Hollywood. The purge was on. So far mainly writers and a few directors had been named. Now, members of the SAG who veered Left held their breath, expecting the worst.

16

THE MEN WHO LED THE ANTI-COMMUNIST PURGE
were often out to settle old scores. Others saw the House Un-
American Activities Committee as a means to notoriety and
power. Some honestly believed that the Communists were undermining the country. Public support of HUAC mushroomed in
1946 and 1947. A costly war had been fought. The pain was still
fresh, emotions high-keyed. HUAC appropriation requests were
granted and Congress left the committee to its own devices. A new
chief investigator, Robert E. Stripling, and a new chairman, J.
Parnell Thomas, were installed in the fall of 1946. Shortly after,
HUAC was granted the power to subpoena witnesses. The committee's chief objective was to declare the Communist party—
which they viewed as a criminal conspiracy—illegal. But the
hearings into Communist activities in Hollywood often became
exercises in harassment and were to leave behind them broken
families, shattered careers and suicides—as well as compromised,
victimized and disillusioned men and women, some never again
able to function properly in society.

The first investigations in Hollywood had had more to do with the number of Jews in the industry than it did with Communists. John Rankin, Thomas's predecessor, had claimed that "Communists [Jews] crucified Christ then gambled for his garments at the foot of the Cross."

J. Parnell Thomas, born John Philip Feeney, had been a Democrat for twenty years before he became the Republican representative from New Jersey and HUAC's chairman. Raised a Catholic, he became an Episcopalian. Flabby and pasty-faced, he was also short and squat, so that when seated he slipped a District of Columbia telephone directory topped by a red-silk pillow beneath his generous buttocks, thereby adding several inches to his presumed height. The hearings were begun on October 20, 1947, a Monday, in the Caucus Room on the second floor of the Old House Office Building in Washington, D.C. The room was large, but still overcrowded. A battery of nine newsreel cameras was lined up on one side of the room. Opposite them were rows of broadcasting equipment, manned by several dozen radio technicians and announcers. Press tables accommodated ninety-four newspaper men and women. An overflow of spectators stood at the back of the room leg to leg with newspaper photographers. Bulbs of high intensity blazed in the massive crystal chandelier and powerful photographic lights had been set up. The illumination was so bright that the room looked like an operating theater. Loudspeakers amplified every sound. Thomas sat in a chair behind the rostrum, his bald pate glistening in the hot glare of the klieg lights. Below him sat the members of his committee, which included John McDowell of Pennsylvania, Richard B. Vail of Illinois and Richard M. Nixon of California.* Robert E. Stripling, tall, lean, gaunt—a Southerner and former FBI man and clerk of the Dies Committee, sat at the end of the committee row, ready to jump to his feet and come around front to point an accusing finger. Nineteen men† in the motion-picture industry had been publicly accused of being agents of un-American propaganda. The

---

*The HUAC committee for the 1947 hearings consisted of Thomas, Stripling, Vail, Nixon, McDowell, Karl E. Mundt (South Dakota), John S. Woods (Georgia), John E. Rankin (Mississippi) and J. Harden Peterson (Florida).

†The nineteen men were Alvah Bessie, Herbert Bibberman, Lester Cole, Edward Dmytryk, Ring Lardner, Jr., John Howard Lawson, Albert Maltz, Samuel Ornitz, Adrian Scott, Dalton Trumbo, Robert Rossen, Bertolt Brecht, Larry Parks, Lewis Milestone, Irving Pichel, Gordon Kahn, Richard Collins, Howard Koch and Waldo Salt. One thing all of these men had in common was that none of them had served in the army, having been too old, not a citizen, or deferred for health reasons. For that common reason, no veterans' committee would stir up problems.

investigation would last ten days and was a mockery of American justice. Perhaps that is why the American flag was nowhere to be seen throughout.

The friendly witnesses, Reagan among them, were to come first. Then the nineteen would be asked to answer these charges and were expected to name more names to prove their American allegiance.

Jack Warner had secretly testified before the committee on May 15, 1947, as a friendly witness, supplying them with most of the names of the nineteen now cited. Dapper as always, his hair combed sideways to cover his increasing baldness, his moustache trimmed perfectly, he wore a pin-striped suit and black patent shoes on his small, narrow feet, and looked a bit like a song-and-dance man in an English revue. Everyone in the industry knew Warner enjoyed public speaking. He once spoke uninterruptedly for three hours and twenty minutes, after work, to his own employees. In May he had been "a windy and cheerful witness. . . . In all, he fattened up the record by approximately 57,000 words." Warner stressed his belief that screenwriters were "injecting Communist stuff" [into scripts] and then added: "Anyone I thought was a Communist or read in the papers that he was, I dismissed at the expiration of his contract." Stripling asked him how many employees this had involved. He replied six, but named sixteen.*

"Ideological termites have burrowed into many American industries," he read from an opening statement at his second HUAC hearing on October 20. "Wherever they may be, I say let us dig them out and get rid of them. My brothers and I will be happy to subscribe generously to a pest-removal fund. We are willing to establish such a fund to ship to Russia the people who don't like our American system of government and prefer the Communistic system to ours. . . ."

Although he personally still retained the title of colonel (used on memos to and from his staff) he was addressed as *Mr.* Warner throughout his long morning session (he did not step down until noon).

MR. STRIPLING: Doesn't it kind of provoke you to pay them [the writers he had named] $1,000 or $2,000 a week and see them on the picket lines and joining all of these organi-

---

*Guy Endor, Howard Koch, Ring Lardner, Jr., Emmet Lavery, Alvah Bessie, Gordon Kahn, John Howard Lawson, Albert Maltz, Robert Rossen, Irwin Shaw, Dalton Trumbo, John Wexley, Julius and Philip Epstein, Sheridan Gibney and Clifford Odets.

zations and taking your money and trying to tear down a system that provides the money?

MR. WARNER: That is absolutely correct.

Warner was followed at the witness table by Louis B. Mayer and then by Walt Disney.* On Tuesday, Adolphe Menjou appeared right on cue. Nattily attired and wearing a pair of heavy horn-rimmed glasses, he "sauntered jauntily up to the witness stand. As the applause quickened, he turned, bowing and smiling to his expectant audience, maneuvering his profile skillfully in the fuselage of exploding flashbulbs. With forefinger dramatically outstretched, he raised his hand for the oath. To the first identifying question he replied: 'Motion picture actor, I hope.'" He then proceeded to call off several names, though he could not guarantee to the committee that they actually carried party cards. Twirling his moustache, mugging for the cameramen, he replied to Stripling's question of how he spotted "Reds": "Anyone attending any meeting at which Paul Robeson appears and applauds, can be considered a Communist."

The next day, Wednesday, the crowds increased and formed even earlier because of the scheduled—and leaked—appearance of the sleekly coiffed, dark-haired, Romanesque-profiled film star Robert Taylor. (The dates and times of appearances of witnesses had been deemed classified information.) He offered much the same cure-all as Warner—"send them back to Russia or some other unpleasant place." When he had been dismissed and headed for the door, spectators clustered around him, begging for autographs while following him out of the building and to his car.

Not nearly the same clamor met Murphy, Montgomery and Reagan when they arrived at the Old House Office Building on October 25. Reagan, wearing his glasses and a beige gabardine suit that was somewhat large for him, sat earnestly listening to Montgomery and then Murphy. Murphy was asked, "To what extent has Communism infiltrated into the Screen Actors Guild?"

MR. MURPHY: Well, in my opinion there has been a constant irritation from a very small group. The group is constantly

---

*Of the three, Mayer was the least "friendly," but still gave the names of Edward Dmytryk and Adrian Scott. Scott's first wife, Joan LaCoeur, stated that "Adrian was a vague left-winger. He and Eddie Dmytryk were subpoenaed not because they were . . . in the Party or because they were big names, but because of 'Crossfire' [a picture that dealt with anti-Semitism among soldiers]. Two or three weeks before the subpoenas came out, federal agents came to the studio and demanded to see 'Crossfire.' It was totally because of the content that they were subpoenaed."

changing. . . . I don't think they amount to 1 percent of the Guild membership.*

He was then asked: "Do you feel there is any Communism in the motion picture industry?"

> MR. MURPHY: Yes . . . I think that the screen has been very successful in keeping any attempts to propagandize off the screen. . . . I am an actor. I am not as conversant as some others who have testified. . . . Once in a while I try to change a line or two or a word or two and maybe add a dance step, but that is about the extent of my business. However, I think there has been definite evidence that there are Communists at work in the picture industry.

Murphy was not called upon to give names and proffered none on his own. Asked whether he had ever been "smeared" by the Communists in Hollywood, he replied:

> MR. MURPHY: Well, during the strike there was a routine of handing out throw-aways around the studios and around town every day and they made up three characters that were known as Ronnie, Eddie, and George—Ronald Reagan, Eddie Arnold, and George Murphy. . . . We were called "producers' men" . . . stooges . . . and I think the proof of whether we are stooges or not is evidenced by the contract that the Screen Actors Guild concluded . . . with the producers, and I think one of the best labor contracts ever written.

The outside light had dissolved into metal gray, indicating rain, when Reagan moved into the witness chair at 11:10 A.M. The microphone let off a high whistling sound when he replied "I do" to the oath, and he knowledgeably adjusted it before answering the next question.

(Testimony of Ronald Reagan before the House Un-American Activities Committee, October 25, 1947, follows.)

> MR. STRIPLING: Mr. Reagan, will you please state your full name and present address? [Stripling pronounced the name "Ree-gun."]

---

*SAG membership in 1947 was about seven thousand five hundred.

MR. REAGAN: [Correcting] Ronald Raygun, 9137 Cordell Drive, Los Angeles, 46, California. [He did not include his middle name, Wilson.]

MR. STRIPLING: When and where were you born, Mr. Raygun?

MR. REAGAN: Tampico, Ill., February 6, 1911.

MR. STRIPLING: What is your present occupation?

MR. REAGAN: Motion-picture actor.

MR. STRIPLING: How long have you been engaged in that profession?

MR. REAGAN: Since June, 1937, with a brief interlude of 3½ years—that at the time didn't seem very brief.

MR. STRIPLING: What period was that?

MR. REAGAN: That was during the late war.

MR. STRIPLING: What branch of the service were you in?

MR. REAGAN: Well, sir, I had been for several years in the Reserve as an officer in the United States Cavalry, but I was assigned to the Air Corps.

MR. STRIPLING: That is kind of typical of the Army, isn't it?

MR. REAGAN: Yes, sir. The first thing the Air Corps did was loan me to the Signal Corps.

MR. MCDOWELL: You didn't wear spurs? [Laughter]

MR. REAGAN: I did for a short while.

THE CHAIRMAN: I think this has little to do with the facts we are seeking. Proceed.

MR. STRIPLING: Mr. Reagan, are you a member of any guild?

MR. REAGAN: Yes, sir; the Screen Actors Guild.

MR. STRIPLING: Are you the president of the guild at the present time?

MR. REAGAN: Yes sir.

MR. STRIPLING: When were you elected?

MR. REAGAN: That was several months ago. I was elected to replace Mr. Montgomery when he resigned.

MR. STRIPLING: When does your term expire?

MR. REAGAN: The elections come up next month.

MR. STRIPLING: Have you ever held any other position in the Screen Actors Guild?

MR. REAGAN: Yes sir. Just prior to the war I was a member of the board of directors.

MR. STRIPLING: As a member of the board of directors, as president of the Screen Actors Guild, and as an active member, have you at any time observed or noted within the organization a clique of either Communists or Fascists who were attempting to exert influence or pressure on the guild?

MR. REAGAN: Well, sir, my testimony must be very similar to that of Mr. Murphy and Mr. Montgomery. There has been a small group within the Screen Actors Guild which has consistently opposed the policy of the guild board and officers of the guild, as evidenced by the vote on various issues. That small clique referred to has been suspected of more or less following the tactics that we associate with the Communist Party.

MR. STRIPLING: Would you refer to them as a disruptive influence within the guild?

MR. REAGAN: I would say that at times they have attempted to be a disruptive influence.

MR. STRIPLING: You have no knowledge yourself as to whether or not any of them are members of the Communist Party?

MR. REAGAN: No, sir; I have no investigative force, or anything, and I do not know.

MR. STRIPLING: Has it ever been reported to you that certain members of the guild were Communists?

MR. REAGAN: Yes, sir; I have heard different discussions and some of them tagged as Communists.

MR. STRIPLING: Have you ever heard that from any reliable source?

MR. REAGAN: Well, I considered the source as reliable at the time.

MR. STRIPLING: Would you say that this clique has attempted to dominate the guild?

MR. REAGAN: Well, sir, by attempting to put over their own particular views on various issues, I guess in regard to that you would have to say that our side was attempting to dominate, too, because we were fighting just as hard to put over our views, in which we sincerely believed, and I think we were proven correct by the figures—Mr. Murphy gave the figures—and those figures were always approximately the same, an average of 90 percent or better of the Screen Actors Guild voted in favor of those matters now guild policy.*

---

*This figure is not truly representative, as 90 percent of the Guild membership did not vote in the elections. In fact, only 50 to 55 percent of the membership voted. The 90 percent figure, therefore, could represent as little as 45 percent of the membership.

MR. STRIPLING: Mr. Reagan, there has been testimony to the effect here that numerous Communist-front organizations have been set up in Hollywood. Have you ever been solicited to join any of those organizations or any organization which you considered to be a Communist-front organization?

MR. REAGAN: Well, sir, I have received literature from an organization called the Committee for a Far-Eastern Democratic Policy. I don't know whether it is Communist or not. I only know that I didn't like their views and as a result I didn't want to have anything to do with them.

MR. STRIPLING: Were you ever solicited to sponsor the Joint Anti-Fascist Refugee Committee?

MR. REAGAN: No, sir; I was never solicited to do that, but I found myself misled into being a sponsor on another occasion for a function that was held under the auspices of the Joint Anti-Fascist Refugee Committee.

MR. STRIPLING: Did you knowingly give your name as a sponsor?

MR. REAGAN: Not knowingly. Could I explain what that occasion was?

MR. STRIPLING: Yes, sir.

MR. REAGAN: I was called several weeks ago. There happened at the time in Hollywood to be a financial drive on to raise money to build a badly needed hospital in a certain section of town, called the All Nations Hospital. I think the purpose of the building is so obvious by the title that it has the support of most of the people of Hollywood—or, of Los Angeles, I should say. Certainly of most of the doctors, because it is very badly needed.

Some time ago I was called to the telephone. A woman introduced herself by name. Knowing that I didn't know her I didn't make any particular note of her name and I couldn't give it now. She told me that there would be a recital held at which Paul Robeson would sing and she said that all the money for the tickets would go to the hospital and asked if she could use my name as one of the sponsors. I hesitated for a moment because I don't think that Mr. Robeson's and my political views coincide at all and then I thought I was being a little stupid because, I thought, here is an occasion where Mr. Robeson is perhaps appearing as an artist and certainly the object, raising money, is above any political consideration, it is a hospital supported by everyone. I have contributed money myself. So I felt a little bit as if I had been stuffy for a minute and I said, certainly, you can use my name.

I left town for a couple of weeks and when I returned I was handed a newspaper story that said that this recital was held at the Shrine Auditorium in Los Angeles under the auspices of the Joint Anti-Fascist Refugee Committee. The principal speaker was Emil Lustig, Robert Burman took up a collection, and remnants of the Abraham Lincoln Brigade were paraded to the platform. I did not in the newspaper story see one word about the hospital. I called the newspaper and said I am not accustomed to writing to editors, but would like to explain my position, and he laughed and said, "You needn't bother, you are about the fiftieth person that has called with the same idea, including most of the legitimate doctors who had also been listed as sponsors of that affair."

MR. STRIPLING: Would you say from your observation that that is typical of the tactics or strategy of the Communists, to solicit and use the names of prominent people to either raise money or gain support?

MR. REAGAN: I think it is in keeping with their tactics; yes, sir.

MR. STRIPLING: Do you think there is anything democratic about those tactics?

MR. REAGAN: I do not, sir.

MR. STRIPLING: As president of the Screen Actors Guild you are familiar with the jurisdictional strike which has been going on in Hollywood for some time?

MR. REAGAN: Yes, sir.

MR. STRIPLING: Have you ever had any conferences with any of the labor officials regarding this strike?

MR. REAGAN: Yes, sir. In fact, some 14 days or so before the strike actually took place our guild, feeling that we were representing our actors to the best of our ability, and this being a situation in which the studios might be closed, we met with the producers, met with both factions in the jurisdictional dispute in an attempt to settle that strike. We continued meeting with them separately and together. I believe the Screen Actors Guild committee which put these people in one room and tried to settle the strike perhaps is better informed on the situation and on the jurisdictional strike than any other group in the motion-picture industry.

We met repeatedly and we met continuously for 7 months and then intermittently from that 7 months' period on. The strike is still continuing.

MR. STRIPLING: Do you know whether the Communists have participated in any way in this strike?

MR. REAGAN: Sir, the first time that this word "Communist" was ever injected into any of the meetings concerning the strike was at a meeting in Chicago with Mr. William Hutch[e]son, president of the carpenters union, who were on strike at the time. He asked the Screen Actors Guild to submit terms to Mr. [Richard] Walsh, for Walsh to give in the settling of this strike, and he told us to tell Mr. Walsh that if he would give in on these terms he in turn "would run this Sorrell and the other Commies out"—I am quoting him—and break it up. I might add that Mr. Walsh and Mr. Sorrell were running the strike for Mr. Hutch[e]son in Hollywood.

MR. STRIPLING: Mr. Reagan, what is your feeling about what steps should be taken to rid the motion-picture industry of any Communist influences, if they are there?

MR. REAGAN: Well, sir, I would like to say, as Mr. Montgomery and Mr. Murphy have indicated, they have done it very well. I have been alarmed by the misapprehension, the feeling around, that it was a minority fighting against a majority on this issue in our business, and I would like in answering that question to reiterate what those gentlemen have said, that rather 99 percent of us are pretty well aware of what is going on, and I think within the bounds of our democratic rights, and never once stepping over the rights given us by democracy, we have done a pretty good job in our business of keeping those people's activities curtailed. After all, we must recognize them at present as a political party. On that basis we have exposed their lies when we came across them, we have opposed their propaganda, and I can certainly testify that in the case of the Screen Actors Guild we have been eminently successful in preventing them from, with their usual tactics, trying to run a majority of an organization with a well organized minority.

So that fundamentally I would say in opposing those

people that the best thing to do is to make democracy work. In the Screen Actors Guild we make it work by insuring everyone a vote and by keeping everyone informed. I believe that, as Thomas Jefferson put it, if all the American people know all of the facts they will never make a mistake.

Whether the party should be outlawed, I agree with the gentlemen that preceded me that that is a matter for the Government to decide. As a citizen I would hesitate, or not like, to see any political party outlawed on the basis of its political ideology. We have spent 170 years in this country on the basis that democracy is strong enough to stand up and fight against the inroads of any ideology. However if it is proven that an organization is an agent of a power, a foreign power, or in any way not a legitimate political party, and I think the Government is capable of proving that, if the proof is there, then that is another matter.

I do not know whether I have answered your question or not. I, like Mr. Montgomery, would like at this moment to say I happen to be very proud of the industry in which I work; I happen to be very proud of the way in which we conducted the fight. I do not believe the Communists have ever at any time been able to use the motion-picture screen as a sounding board for their philosophy or ideology. I think that will continue as long as the people in Hollywood continue as they are, which is alert, conscious of it, and fighting. I would also like to say that I think we can match the record of our industry in the contribution to the social welfare against that of any industry in the United States.

MR. STRIPLING: Mr. Reagan, you have testified here concerning the Screen Actors Guild and the record that you people have made within that guild. You are not aware, however, of the efforts which the Communists have made within the Screen Writers Guild, are you?

MR. REAGAN: Sir, like the other gentlemen, I must say that that is hearsay. I have heard discussions concerning it.

THE CHAIRMAN: I think we have had testimony with regard to the Screen Writers Guild. These people are more fully acquainted with the Screen Actors Guild.

MR. STRIPLING: Mr. Chairman, these three witnesses were brought here simply to testify, as president and past presi-

dents of the Screen Actors Guild, as to the possible infiltration within that organization. As you are aware we have
heard numerous witnesses on the Screen Writers Guild.
Those are all the questions I have at this time.

THE CHAIRMAN: Mr. Woods?

MR. WOODS: No questions.

THE CHAIRMAN: Mr. Nixon?

MR. NIXON: No questions.

THE CHAIRMAN: Mr. McDowell?

MR. MCDOWELL: No questions.

THE CHAIRMAN: Mr. Vail?

MR. VAIL: No questions.

THE CHAIRMAN: There is one thing that you said that interested me very much. That was the quotation from Jefferson. That is just why this committee was created by the
House of Representatives, to acquaint the American people with the facts. Once the American people are acquainted with the facts there is no question but what the
American people will do a job, the kind of a job that they
want done; that is, to make America just as pure as we can
possibly make it.*

We want to thank you very much for coming here today.

MR. REAGAN: Sir, if I might, in regard to that, say that what
I was trying to express, and didn't do very well, was also
this other fear. I detest, I abhor their philosophy [the
Communists], but I detest more than that their tactics,
which are those of the fifth column, and are dishonest, but
at the same time I never as a citizen want to see our country become urged, by either fear or resentment of this
group, that we ever compromise with any of our democratic principles through that fear or resentment. I still
think that democracy can do it.

THE CHAIRMAN: We agree with that. Thank you very much.

Unlike the other friendly witnesses, the three SAG representatives had not been asked to name people they suspected of being

---

*The chairman, J. Parnell Thomas, was found guilty of embezzling government funds one
year later and was sentenced to three years at the Danbury, Connecticut, Federal Correc-
tional Institution. Two of the Hollywood Ten (Lester Cole and Ring Lardner, Jr.) were
fellow inmates in 1950 when they were sentenced to one year for contempt of court.
Thomas stood on his constitutional rights and pleaded nolo contendere to avoid taking the
witness stand in his trial.

Communists. However, Reagan through his FBI contact, already could have done so.

Reagan was in good spirits when he left Washington, D.C., by train to return to Hollywood. After his departure, ten of the nineteen men who had been subpoenaed as unfriendly witnesses defied the committee. Articulate men of words, they reduced Thomas to "impotent gaveling," but they refused to give names. With sixty-eight witnesses (friendly and unfriendly) to be called, Thomas dismissed the hearings because he and the committee were taking a beating in the press. But the investigation and the persecution that followed were far from over.

In Reagan's opinion, he and the two former presidents of the SAG had acquitted themselves well at the HUAC hearings. They had said that there was a small Communist faction within the Guild, but publicly had not pointed a finger at any one individual.

On November 10, two weeks after Reagan had returned from the HUAC hearings, the Guild board voted that no officer or board member could serve without signing an affidavit "that he is not a member of the Communist Party nor affiliated with such a party." Guild board meetings during this time revolved around little more than discussions on the problems and dangers of communism and what the Guild's position should be in the matter. During the November meeting, Marsha Hunt read a letter which she asked the Guild to send to President Truman, calling upon him to tell the American people "whether or not the Communist Party is a subversive organization" and appealing to him for help and advice (the letter was not sent). "The last Guild meeting that I went to," Anne Revere remembered, "I was no longer treasurer. I had been called to [appear before] the Committee [HUAC]. I was sitting there, and Ronnie was in the chair, and he said, 'You know anybody that's got a problem? All they have to do is come and talk to us.' There was silence after that and I said, 'I have a problem, what's your suggestion?'

"'It's so simple. All you've got to do is just name a couple of names that have already been named.' I said, 'That's it. I can't climb up on somebody's neck,' so that's the way it ended. As I went out, one of the boys said, 'Don't go away mad.'"*

"Anne Revere was such a good actress, and she was such a strong, firm union member," Dorothy Tree Uris later said. "What

* Anne Revere went before the HUAC, took the Fifth Amendment, refusing to name any names, and was blacklisted in Hollywood for eighteen years. She eventually returned to Broadway and co-starred in *Toys in the Attic* to extraordinary critical acclaim.

happened to her was outrageous. . . . I think a good deal of what happened in Hollywood—meaning the way the people turned to politics and to left politics and Marxism . . . was because of the very nature of Hollywood itself. There was nothing to do . . . you either went out to dinner at one another's homes or you just stayed home . . . it was such an arid country . . . we naturally turned to politics and groups of discussion. . . . We studied the great writers. We also read right through Marx, Engels and Lenin. . . . We became interested in local politics in a sort of liberal fringe of the Democratic party. California was quite left. And it was kind of fun. . . . I kind of wonder if we had all been in New York at that time and had all the stimulation of the city and all been exposed to each other, I doubt if we would ever have been so left. . . . I remember when Japan invaded China, we formed the League of Women Shoppers. . . . We only bought things made in the United States. We boycotted Japanese silk stockings and wore cotton lisle instead. You saw them all over [the cotton lisle stockings].

"Some [of us] were more to the left than others, but there was very little difference between left and liberal [until 1946]. It was great. I suppose it might be called the United Front in Hollywood and we got along awfully well. It was remarkable to me that so many people held firm and refused to name names and to cheapen their lives . . . even though they [were blacklisted] . . . and no longer participated either in politics or in affairs of the Screen Actors Guild. Still they never became informers."

The Screen Actors Guild had since its inception been split by two groups—one that believed the union existed "to improve the wages and working conditions of actors. Period . . . [and] the reformers, who believed . . . that unions are supposed to bring about progressive change, not only in the union but in the greater society beyond," Kim Felner, former public-relations officer of the SAG, recalled. "They supported farm-workers striking in Salinas, the Republicans in the Spanish Civil War and the Hollywood Anti-Fascist League . . . and urged involvement onto their fellow union members."

"I am sure that many of the actors and actresses of that particular time had strong political feelings one way or another [Left or Right]," the late Robert Montgomery said in 1979. "And that they wanted to inject those political feelings into the organization." Politics was a very big chunk of the SAG activities during Reagan's tenure as president. "The Guild's position in the case of pursuing 'Communists' and cooperating with the blacklist did not even pretend at neutrality," Fellner has stated.

Eventually, a motion that every member of the SAG sign a loyalty oath, was passed. Reagan was presiding over a hotbed of political activism coming from both Left and Right.

17

ONE NIGHT IN LATE NOVEMBER, AFTER THE LAST take of *Johnny Belinda* had been filmed, the Reagans were overheard exchanging angry words as they left the Beverly Club, a restaurant in Beverly Hills. That afternoon at the cast-and-crew party, Wyman had announced that she was taking a rest. Somebody asked, "With Ronnie and the kids?"

"No," she had angrily replied. "Just me."

As the parking attendant drove their car up to the curb in front of the restaurant, Wyman said in a loud voice, "I got along without you before and I certainly can get along without you now!" She slid in behind the wheel and drove off alone. Reagan went back inside and left later in a taxicab. The next day, Wyman flew to New York to visit friends. After a week she called from New York to tell Reagan she was thinking of leaving him.

"If this comes to a divorce," Reagan told Hedda Hopper, "I think I'll name *Johnny Belinda* corespondent."

While Wyman was away, Reagan returned to Eureka to attend the fifth-annual pumpkin festival. During his two-day trip (he stayed at the TEKE House), he visited Mac, saw the Golden Tornadoes win a game, rode in a parade, placed the crown on the head of the Pumpkin Queen, Joan Snyder, and danced with her at the coronation ball. According to the local newspaper accounts, Mr. and Mrs. Ronald Reagan had given seventy-five thousand dollars to Eureka's building fund toward the construction of a new speech-and-drama building. The amount sounds astronomical considering his income that year (which had been a little more than double that before taxes) and given his standard of living. Wyman had made about eighty-five thousand dollars before taxes, but it seems unlikely she would have donated such a large sum to Eureka College.

She returned home before Christmas, and there was talk of a reconciliation, but a few weeks later they separated again and Reagan moved into the Garden of Allah, an apartment hotel on Sunset Boulevard that had a legendary history. The apartments weren't luxurious. In fact, they were old fashioned and somewhat baroque. Most of them encircled the pool and were so close together that privacy was impossible. Evenings the occupants gathered at the bar and exchanged industry stories. The Garden's best days had been the thirties, when Robert Benchley and Scott Fitzgerald had lived there. Reagan moved in and out of the Garden twice as he and Wyman reconciled and then broke up again. Finally, in the summer of 1948, he managed to rerent his old apartment on Londonderry View. Wyman began to be seen publicly with Ayres and filed suit for divorce. Reagan told the press, "It's a very strange girl I'm married to, but I love her. . . . I know we will end our lives together."

Warners was finally planning to release *Johnny Belinda* with what they called in Hollywood a proper launch—major advertising, publicity and a glittering premiere. Wyman had a new chic to her appearance, a sleek, short bob, her clothes expensive and understated. She looked poised and happy. She and Ayres were constant companions, seen holding hands "unostentatiously but firmly." At one Hollywood party to honor Danny Kaye, she had blurted out, "Lew is the love of my life." Ayres said nothing, but he smiled warmly at her between puffs on his pipe. When *Johnny Belinda* opened on October 13, it was obvious that Wyman had fulfilled her ambition. Reviewers found her performance "surpassingly beautiful." The town was talking about the Academy Award, and Jack Warner now claimed credit for producing such a fine film.

*   *   *

They dined together on January 26, 1948, their eighth anniversary. The press was filled with rumors of a reconciliation. Two weeks later, Wyman's attorney, Loyd Wright, announced that a divorce was imminent and a financial settlement had already been reached.* On June 29, Wyman filed suit and was granted a divorce on grounds of mental cruelty. "In recent months," she told Superior Judge Thurmond Clarke, "my husband and I engaged in continual arguments on his political views . . . finally, there was nothing in common between us . . . nothing to sustain our marriage. . . . Despite my lack of interest in his political activities, he insisted I attend meetings with him and be present during discussions among our friends. But my own ideas were never considered important."

Reagan did not contest the divorce. Nonetheless, he seemed unable to accept the finality of the decree. On the surface Wyman and Reagan were amicable. The house on Cordell was sold. Wyman found a house in Malibu for herself and the children. Their father was free to visit them whenever he wished, and in the early months he did so frequently. "I suppose there had been warning signs," Reagan said later. "If only I hadn't been so busy, but small-town boys grow up thinking only other people get divorced. The plain truth was that such a thing was so far from even being imagined by me that I had no resources to call upon."

He returned to the bachelor life he had led in Des Moines. Reasonably young and his fame established, he had a comfortable income, a Cadillac convertible, three horses, an apartment with a fabulous view and he knew some of the most beautiful women in the world. However, he was not inclined toward the glare of the nightclub circuit. He dated a few attractive ladies, but he spent most of his time at the Guild (where he had been reelected president), keeping his film commitments and seeing his children and Nelle.

Warners had cast him in February in the film adaptation of Norman Krasna's successful Broadway play *John Loves Mary*, a "bit of fluff" about a soldier (Reagan) who as a favor weds his

---

*Reagan had agreed to contribute $500 a month toward the support of the children. Wyman was to receive alimony of $500 a month only if illness or injury prevented her from work. Otherwise, the pact provided for virtually equal division of some $75,000 of community property (the equity in the house). Reagan was to pay half of the upkeep and taxes on the house until it was sold and maintain $25,000 insurance policies on his life in each child's name. Each also retained their own personal possessions (cars, etc.), Wyman the furniture, Reagan his horses.

married buddy's British girlfriend (Patricia Neal) so that she can come to the United States. Mary does not know her boyfriend has a wife and John has been sworn not to reveal the fact. The two fall in love. This all occurs in the first fifteen minutes of the screenplay. The remaining ninety minutes are devoted to the couple's attempt to deny their love to themselves and each other, and to be loyal to John's pal. In the end, Mary discovers she has been deceived by a married man and so she and John are free to wed.

John Loves Mary had the aura of a present-day television situation comedy. It made 105 minutes move comparatively without pain and it introduced the talented and intelligent Patricia Neal to the screen. (She had made her stage debut in 1946 when she replaced Margaret Sullavan in *The Voice of the Turtle* on Broadway.) Neal and Reagan dated, but he was still in the process of attempting a reconciliation with Wyman (who had originally been cast to star opposite him in the film). "My first meeting with him took place at a New Year's Eve party in Los Angeles," Neal recalled. "His wife, Jane Wyman, had just announced their separation, and it was sad because he did not want a divorce. I remember he went outside. An older woman went with him. He cried . . ."

Jerry Wald, the executive producer on *John Loves Mary*, memoed Reagan on January 19, 1948: "Dear Ronnie: Just saw Saturday night rushes of 'John Loves Mary' and you can send your laundry out. The stuff looked wonderful. However, the idea that you get paid for all those kissing scenes with Pat Neal is beyond my comprehension. In the new contract between the producers and actors, I'm planning to have a clause inserted regarding kissing scenes, that a refund be made by the actors to the studio . . . you're certainly putting everything into your work."

Reagan went from the Krasna comedy into *The Girl from Jones Beach,* a breezy film about an illustrator who sets out to find a perfectly proportioned female as a model (this was in the heyday of girlie illustrators Petty and Varga). Lauren Bacall took a suspension rather than play the female lead. This time it was to be Virginia Mayo who would debut in a Reagan film. "The day I walked out of my dressing room," Mayo says, "wearing [for the first time] one of the daring white swimsuits required for the part, I expected my knees to bang together and my teeth to click. Then . . . Ronnie, who has the manner of a grand duke under ordinary circumstances, whistled at me. That wolf call did more for my ego and my self-confidence than a hundred words could have done. . . . He [also] put me wise to a good many things. Whenever any one of the dozens of department heads or studio officials came on the set, he managed to be near me and to point out important people, giving me the correct names and titles, before I was officially introduced."

Actress Arlene Dahl also recalled a "paternal" kindness at this period of Reagan's life. "Gary Cooper had the same quality." Dahl had just been signed by Warners and cast in a small role in *Life with Father*. The first day she came into the commissary, Reagan got up and went over to her table. "'I understand we're both from the same part of the country [Dahl's home was Minneapolis],' he said, 'so I thought I should be the one to welcome you to the lot.'"

He was not romantically involved with either of these beautiful women. "We did very little offscreen conversing," Virginia Mayo confessed of her work with Reagan on *The Girl from Jones Beach*. "I was shy, I guess, and I was newly married [to actor Michael O'Shea]. He did have, occasionally, young ladies on the set. . . . His charm was overwhelming and I think that was the basis of his career as an actor." A sense of fun pervaded the set. "Eddie Bracken was always playing magic tricks—like making your watch disappear. And Dona Drake kept me laughing all the time," she reminisced. "We went to the beach to film and play leapfrog. I jumped over Ronnie's back."

Bracken recalled an incident that turned out to be amusing. "Reagan was supposed to be running away from, or after Virginia Mayo . . . and I was in hot pursuit of Dona Drake. I came up with the idea for a comedy bit where we'd get confused and chase the wrong girl for a minute or two, then turn around and bump into each other. That's when Ronnie broke some vertebrae." Reagan's version of the incident: "Eddie got so goggle-eyed he stepped on my heels, tripped me and cracked my coccyx."

"Reagan was a lonely guy [during the making of *The Girl from Jones Beach*] because of his divorce, but a very level-headed guy," Bracken later said. "He was never for the sexpots. He was never a guy looking for the bed. He was a guy looking for companionship more than anything else."

The director, Peter Godfrey, who had previously worked with Reagan on *That Hagen Girl*, shot around him for three weeks while he was hospitalized for his back injury and then recuperated at Wyman's Malibu home while she was vacationing in Hawaii. His ties to Wyman remained strong and would for another year. When *The Girl from Jones Beach* was finished, both Reagan and

Wyman had cameo bits (but not together) in *It's a Great Feeling,* a spoof on Hollywood studios. During the time had been making lighthearted comedies, which were destined to do more for his female co-stars than for himself, Wyman was fast becoming a critically acclaimed box-office star.*

"Supplies of headache powder are running low and there's moaning and groaning in the 'land of make believe'—for Hollywood and the entire amusement industry are caught in the throes of revolution," Reagan wrote in July 1948 as guest writer for labor columnist Victor Riesel's syndicated column. The revolution Reagan referred to was the fast ascent and availability of television, which had brought the Screen Actors Guild smack-dab into a dispute with the motion-picture producers that once again threatened to shut down the Hollywood studios. Reagan went on to explain the dispute:

"All actors, whether in low or high salary brackets, take the position that when they sell their services for films intended for exhibition in theatres, such films should not be used in another medium, i.e., television, without additional payment to the actors. Obviously, the producer of the film is not going to give it to television free of charge.

"The actors feel they should get a reasonable portion of the additional revenue from theatre films when used in television . . . all we are asking is that when theatre films are televised—and hundreds of old ones are being sold or leased for television right now—the actors should get a reasonable percentage of the additional revenue.

"The producers' position is that once a picture has been made, they have the right to use that film for any purpose they desire. They claim they made a mistake in granting to the musicians the very principle the Screen Actors Guild is asking for actors."†

The dispute over the new producers' contract with the controversial television clause momentarily pushed aside the issue of Communist infiltration in Hollywood. Reagan's life in the summer

---

* In January 1949, Wyman and Gregory Peck were named the world's most popular film actors, according to moviegoers and the Foreign Press Association. Wyman's closest competitor was Ingrid Bergman.

† The musicians had won the copyright to their filmed music. No filmed music made to the date of their contract with the producers could be televised without negotiation of a separate contract. The Writers Guild was fighting for the same stipulation. Reagan added in the Riesel column: "A playwright who sells a play for the legitimate stage collects additional money if the play is made into a movie. And in television itself even prize fighters whose bouts are televised get a portion of the money paid by television stations to the fight promoters."

of 1948 revolved around the negotiations for the SAG with the producers. He was the sole actor in the three-man team that included Jack Dales and the Guild's counsel Laurence W. Beilenson. The big issue in the new proposed producers' contract was the television residual clause, but the actors were also fighting for compensation for overtime hours put in and for close-ups shot after the film's completion (a general practice at the time). The producers wanted to pay the actors by the hour for these services. Reagan wanted a minimum weekly wage to be applied. Finally, the producers gave in on this but were immovable on the point of the residuals from television.

"The conference with the producers," Jack Dales recalled, "went on so long that finally we decided to break for fifteen minutes to go to the toilet or whatever. There had been a very big bowl of M&M's [candies] in the middle of the table as Ron always liked to eat something sweet as he was talking and it was M&M's then. As he got up he angrily pushed the bowl over to the producers' side of the table. 'Eat these and I hope they're poison,' he said and walked out of the room." Once they were outside, he turned to Dales. "'You know, I don't think it's good that they're going to have to pay minimum if an actor has to have a close-up. It's not good for the actor. That may decide to tell the producer not to do the close-up and it's very important for an actor to have those extra close-ups.' So he did the unprecedented thing. . . . He went back into the producers . . . and he said, 'I'll give you one for you. . . . I don't think we'll take the deal on the close-ups.'"

Dales also remembered another tough negotiation. "The producers were just not giving in at all and he kept pushing and pushing and pushing and pushing, and finally he said to them, 'I'll tell you'—cause everything he'd suggest they said no—'How about a piece of green cheese?' Everyone laughed. It was kind of a corny moment [but] it broke the tension and they were able to come back at that point and renegotiate what they were doing. He always said that he believed, because of Roosevelt, in the impossible dream—he absolutely believed in the impossible dream—and he believed he could get for an actor or anyone that he fought for—the impossible dream and make it possible."

The negotiations with the producers broke down on June 1 and Reagan presented the SAG board with three choices:

1. To request a renewal or extension of the present actors-producers' contract for one year.

2. To strike.

3. Not to renew the contract and not to strike.

The producers, he told them, were convinced that the time was ripe for a showdown, not merely with the SAG but with all labor. And they had no "firm conception" of what the impact of television was going to mean to them. They would undoubtedly stand firm.

A strategy committee was formed, headed by Reagan. Three weeks of frantic meetings in board members' homes followed. Then negotiations were opened again with the producers. "Ronnie acted like a professional [negotiator]," Dales said. "We were balancing so many balls in the air all at the same time. We'd meet with the Hal Roach group on a Monday, and then on a Wednesday we'd meet with the majors on the same issues. We intended to break the majors down by making a deal with the Roach group. All of them were adamant that there was no such thing in their world as ever paying for reuse of a film . . . both sets of producers were absolutely adamant that this was utterly . . . well practically un-American. 'How dare you? You buy something. You pay for it. We pay you adequately. We pay you people munificently. Now you tell us we can't use the stuff? It's ours!' And we said . . . 'You're talking economics of the 1900s. . . . It's a whole new ball game.'

"I can remember sitting around with the independent group, big Hal Roach with that big chin and his pipe in his mouth and furious, red, and Ronnie saying, 'Now Hal, this is not an offer, but let me ask you: You wouldn't give an actor a thousand dollars for a repeat. You wouldn't give him a hundred. Would you give him that pipe you're smoking? Would you give him a pencil? Would you concede the principle at all?'

" 'Absolutely not.'

"So it looked to us like we were going to have two strikes going against both sets of producers. Ronnie was, I think, marvelous. What happened was the major producers, the people we were trying to break by using the independents, actually gave in first. I think the thing that convinced them, if there was one final thing, was . . . their fear that if we got reruns for television, somehow we would ask for the same thing for . . . reissuing of films, and Ronnie was fairly honest about that. He told them, 'That's a dream. Actors can have it. They can dream. But not in our time.' And they had to believe him . . . and they gave in, and that broke the other producers then. We got our first contracts. But it was endless days of bouncing between groups of producers."

The negotiations came to a "successful conclusion" on July 7. The producers had agreed to certain new work compensations coming out of the advent of television. But the new contract was more or less a truce that gave both sides until the following March to reach an agreement on points yet to be negotiated.*

One of the industry problems hotly discussed at this time was the problem of "runaway" films. In England, American films could be exhibited, but the profits had to remain in that country. The only answer appeared to be to make pictures in Europe with the frozen dollars. The SAG was fighting against this practice, as were most of the other trade unions, for obvious reasons.

His image had changed considerably. Before he became president of the Screen Actors Guild, he had dressed informally, showing a preference for sports coats, slacks and sweaters. He now wore suits, neckties and, in the evenings, formal clothes more often. He still read every book he believed important as well as most of the political columns. He wore contact lenses in front of the camera, but his glasses at other times. He took the women he dated out to dinner, quite often to Chasen's, and talked away most of the evening. The charm was retained, but the boyishness and the down-home quality were fast disappearing. What remained merged with the political side of his nature, the easy smile, the solid handshake, the eye-to-eye contact on meeting, the ability to remember everyone's names (co-workers, Guild members, negotiating teams) and some small personal facts—like a husband or wife's first name, a recent illness, birth, wedding, award. On the lot, he always waved at the people on the tour bus. ("They came to see Hollywood stars. I think the least I can do is to send them back home saying one waved at him," Reagan told movie columnist Sidney Skolsky.) He good-naturedly signed autographs, even when it was an intrusion on his privacy (at a restaurant or in a theater).

Bob Cummings remembered that about this time he kiddingly said to Reagan, "One day you should run for president—his answer was, 'Yes.'" His political interest had always been (and remained) national, not regional. He concentrated part of his attention on Hollywood and the industry and the rest on Washington and the world. However, if he had intentions of moving into the national political arena, he still gave no real evidence of

---

*The labor dispute ended, but had not been settled, in the first week of November 1947.

it. The problems and politics of California were not in his area of expertise. (Close associates concur that until the mid-sixties he was never as well-informed about the political climate of California as he was about that of Washington, D.C.) What he appeared to want now was a chance at better film roles. Throughout 1948 and 1949 he wrote Jack Warner, suggesting roles he thought better suited for him than the ones the studio gave him to play. His choice would have been to look tall in the saddle like John Wayne or Gary Cooper, or to have an opportunity to portray a Jimmy Stewart *Mr. Smith Goes to Washington* kind of character.

In January 1945, the John Patrick play *The Hasty Heart* had opened on Broadway. Jack Warner had not been overly enthusiastic about the film potential of a story whose locale was a hospital in Burma just after the war where five convalescent soldiers of assorted nationalities are being tended by a wise but soft-hearted nurse. The play had one outstanding character, a Scotsman with quick changes of mood who was alternately heel and hero. Jerry Wald had seen the play when it opened and had asked Warner to purchase it. Unable to rouse Warner's interest, he wrote him on February 20, 1945:

Dear Jack,

On Sunday you wanted to know why I thought I should produce "The Hasty Heart." In the last election [1944] they had a very good slogan called "Look at the Record."

During the past year you have purchased quite a flock of important properties . . . of all the juicy assignments I didn't receive a single one, nor was I considered for any of them. Don't you think in the name of fair play there should be some compensation made to me in the way of a good assignment in the light of all the originals I have turned in and old novels I have dug up [therefore lowering the story cost]?

Certainly I like whipping up original stories, but I do feel once in a while—*just once*—I should be shown some consideration. . . .

Wald, who was part-model for Budd Schulberg's *What Makes Sammy Run?* had been doing a lot of action films for Warner. A dynamic, indefatigable worker, he also could be counted upon to doctor any script in trouble. Warner did not want to lose him and he bought the property, which Ranald MacDougall adapted.

Warner was not much more enthusiastic when he read the screen-play. It took Wald two years to finally get the go-ahead, but the budget he was given was too low for the quality of film he wanted to make. Finally, to circumvent this problem, Wald and Warner agreed *The Hasty Heart* should be made in England with the studio's frozen revenues, and where salaries for cast and technicians were considerably lower than in Hollywood. The studio wanted only two American performers in the cast—also to keep expenses down.

When Reagan was given the script in September 1948 and asked to star in *The Hasty Heart,* he assumed that Wald was offering him the role of Lachie, the Scotsman, and was not aware that the film was to be shot abroad. He had just been renominated to a second term at the SAG and was working on the strategy for a second series of meetings with the producers in the next sixty to ninety days. After he signed to do the film, he discovered two things: he was cast as Yank, the secondary role (although guaranteed top billing); and he would sail on the *Britannica* with his co-star Patricia Neal and the director Vincent Sherman on November 2 for England. Lew Wasserman convinced him that he should not take a suspension, and that, because of the favor he was doing for Warner, when he returned from abroad the two would be in a strong position to renegotiate Reagan's contract so that he would have more freedom in the choice of his material and be able to accept outside films. The talk within the Guild was that Reagan was being shipped overseas by Jack Warner so that the producers would have the upper hand at the negotiations (in which first and second vice-presidents William Holden and Paul Harvey would now represent the SAG).

This was to be Reagan's first trip abroad and he should have been at least slightly enthusiastic about the chance to see another part of the world. Such was not the case. The crossing was wet and windy. He received the news en route that Truman had won the election against Thomas Dewey. "A single handed fight against the sneers of his enemies and the lack-lustre resignation of his friends," Sir Harold Nicolson, English historian and diplomat, observed, ". . . a bitter blow for Dewey . . . and Dr. Gallup and all those Republicans who were counting on jobs. There is a nasty streak in human nature which gives one a mean sense of *Schadenfreude* [pleasure at other people's discomfort] when such confidence, such actual hubris is punished by the Gods." Dr. Gallop had forecast a Dewey victory, and one newspaper had even prematurely headlined DEWEY WINS. Reagan had found himself in a quandary in this election, publicly stating his dislike of both candidates. (He claimed he voted for Truman in the end.)

The *Britannica* docked at Southampton on a terribly cold day with a real northeaster howling at her decks. A limousine met the *Hasty Heart* contingent and drove them to London. The day was gray; and much of England was still suffering from the after-effects of the war. For a man who was seldom out of sunny California, the drabness must have been overwhelming. Along with Vincent Sherman, the director, Reagan and Neal stayed at the Savoy Hotel, in adjoining suites. ("Although I was a young, pretty girl, he never made a pass at me," Neal declared. ". . . There were splendid reasons. I was wildly in love with Gary Cooper [with whom she had just played in *The Fountainhead*] and he was still in love with Jane Wyman.") While Sherman was setting up the production, Reagan and Neal made some appearances for the benefit of actors in Cardiff, Wales and Dublin. Virginia Mayo and her husband, Michael O'Shea, were in England, also at the Savoy, and had been scheduled to make the tour. "Because Mike was divorced he was told he couldn't go," Mayo says. "Well, they sent Reagan who also had been divorced!" However, Reagan's passport still listed him as married since his divorce was not yet final.

From the beginning of his first meetings with the staff at Elstree Studios, where *The Hasty Heart* was to be filmed, Vincent Sherman realized the budget he had was unrealistic. Technicians and cast were paid about one half of what Americans would have received. But the English worked at a much slower pace, and fewer hours (despite the fact that the British film industry was suffering a serious recession and many employees were out of work). Sherman wrote Steve Trilling, who replied that he must pare down to the very lowest budget he could and cut any extra expense, because: "You probably will read soon about our 'slow down' at the studio here. . . . We want to carefully analyze and estimate the values of our future properties before going into production, so that we are able to meet present world picture conditions . . . we will not start a picture until the script, cast and *price* are right. If we feel a picture will cost too much or present difficulties, we will fold it rather than hazard any extreme gamble. . . ."

Sherman struggled to reduce costs, and finally on December 10 was able to telegraph Warner (who was in the hospital recuperating from a gallbladder operation):

ENGLISH SCHEDULE SET FOR NINE WEEKS OR 45 DAYS OF
SHOOTING. REAGAN AND NEAL HAVE RETURNED FROM
A PUBLICITY STINT AT CARDIFF AND DUBLIN AND WE
ARE DOING MAKE UP TESTS AND WARDROBE OF BOTH TO-
MORROW.

Reagan and Sherman had both started at Warners in 1937,
when Sherman was a writer on B films. Their paths had crossed
at least twice. He had directed a scene of Reagan doing a radio
broadcast for *Hollywood Hotel,* and had stepped in to do some retakes for Curtis Bernhardt on *Juke Girl.* "He [Reagan] had really
hoped to play the dramatic part of the Scot, 'Lachie,' [in *The
Hasty Heart*]," Sherman confirmed. But a young Englishman,
Richard Todd, was cast in the role. Although Todd had only
made one other film, he had worked in repertory for a number of
years and was a fine and sensitive actor.

While Reagan waited for the filming to start, he interested
himself in British politics and spent a large chunk of his time
reading what he could to get a better understanding of them.
These months he had in Great Britain, unhappy as he was at the
time, did have a strong influence on him. He began to see the
world beyond the boundaries of the United States. On November
29, Bertrand Russell had created quite a furor by stating in *The
Times* that the West should make war on Russia "while we have
the atomic bomb and they have not." Harold Nicolson commented, "I think it is probably true that Russia is preparing for
the final battle for world mastery and that once she has enough
bombs she will destroy Western Europe, occupy Asia and have a
final death struggle with the Americas. If that happens and we are
wiped out over here, the survivors in New Zealand may say that
we were mad not to have prevented this while there was still
time. . . . It may be true that we shall be wiped out, and that we
could prevent this by provoking a war with Russia at this stage. It
may be true that such a war would be successful and that we
should then establish some centuries of Pax Americana. . . . But
there is a chance that the danger may pass and peace can be
secured by peace. I admit it is a frail chance—not one in ninety.
To make war in defiance of that one chance is to commit a
crime."

Reagan liked to go down to the bar in the Savoy and expound
on such weighty topics. But he also would hire a car and driver
and go sightseeing in the English countryside. He was not generally known in England—his films had not had much international

appeal—and he was seldom recognized. "Toward the end of one such day [a ride in the countryside]," he later recalled, "we stopped at a pub and it was getting twilight. The driver apologized because this one was only 400 years old. He called it one of the younger ones." England's history did, indeed, fascinate him and he was quick to tell everyone that his ancestors came from Ireland and from Surrey. He also told a few people that he was related to General Napier ("looking proudly out from his pedestal in Trafalgar Square").

On November 1, he had been included in the list of notables invited to the Royal Command Film Performance of the film *Scott of the Antarctic* starring John Mills. "It was a thrilling evening," Virginia Mayo recalled. "The Queen [the present Queen Mother] was so charming and beautiful. Princess Elizabeth was pregnant so she didn't attend, but Prince Philip and Princess Margaret were on the reception line and we all bowed and did the appropriate things. While watching the movie, Mike and I were in the same row with Ronnie, Pat, Alan and Sue Ladd and Vivien and Larry Olivier. Vivien fell asleep (the film was terribly dull and this was her one night off from playing the demanding part of Antigone in her husband's production), and her breast popped out. Sue and Alan were next to us. Alan said to Mike, 'Tell her.' Mike said, 'You tell her.' No one did."

The fog was so thick some nights in November and December that it rolled in through the doors and windows of the hotel and filled the lobby and corridors. Food rationing was still in effect, and central heat nonexistent. Reagan sent Warner an envelope addressed: "To the finder: Please see this letter reaches J. L. Warner, Warner Bros. Studio, Burbank, Cal." The contents read:

Dear J. L.

I am putting this letter in a bottle and throwing it on the tide with the hope that somehow it may reach you. Perhaps my report of life here in this dismal wilderness will be of help to future expeditions.

You will recall with what light hearts we set out such a long time ago—optimistic about an ability to find and thaw the "frozen dollar." If we could have known then what lay ("lay"—there's a word I no longer experience or understand) before us how different would have been our mood.

Our first glimpse of this forbidding land was almost as

frightening as a look at "The Horn Blows at Midnight."*
There seemed to be a heavy fog but it had the odor of cow
dung and coal soot—fearing an explosion of this gaseous
stuff, I ordered "no smoking." Better I should have ordered
"no breathing."

The natives were friendly in a sort of "below freezing"
way but were won over by gifts—mostly cash. We were quite
generous in this inasmuch as it was YOUR cash. They speak
a strange jargon similar in many ways to our language but
different enough to cause confusion. For example—to be
"knocked up" here refers in no way to those delights for
which "Leader swam the Hillespond." It merely means to be
awakened from a sound sleep by a native device somewhat
like our telephone. Another instance of this language difference is the word "bloody." You could see a native cut
stern to stern but to describe the spectacle as "bloody" would
get you thrown out of a saloon in London. Mentioning a pain
in my "fanny" (which is easy to get here) I was distressed to
learn that even this standard American term has an opposite
meaning. If I had what they call "a fanny" I could be Queen
of England!

Another misleading term has caused me some distress.
There is a cleared space near the center of the native capital
called Piccadilly Circus. I have gone there many times and
have yet to see an elephant or an acrobat. In fairness I must
admit how even there are some characters (mostly female)
who seem to be selling tickets to something. They keep pulling my sleeve and saying "two bob, Governor."

One of the most interesting customs of the higher class
natives is something of a sport. They all wear red coats to
chase some dogs which in turn are chasing a fox. I should
add the natives are mounted on horses. This affair is mistakenly called "a fox hunt." I say mistakenly because the red
object has nothing to do with the fox, they actually are doing
this to muscle up the horses which are then served for dinner.
I have been very lucky so far in that I have been able to
avoid the horse and eat only the saddle and harness.

In connection with this let me write a word about English
cooking. What they do to food we did to the American Indian. The average meal should go from "kitchen to can" thus
avoiding the use of the middlemen.

*The title of a Jack Benny film that had received bad reviews.

My strength is failing now, so I'll hasten to put this in the bottle before I'm tempted to eat the cork. We think of you as we sit around the campfire and what we think could curl your hair and make H.M.'s horses seem backward. Come to think of it that might be an improvement.

Cheerio! (that is the native word for goodby. It is spoken without moving the upper lip while looking down the nose).

Ronnie

P.S. Due to the fuel shortage we are keeping the fire alive with "frozen dollars"—(yours).

Dollars were not the only thing frozen in England that winter. The weather was bitter cold, one of the worst the country had experienced in three decades. Since the film was set in a hospital ward (supposedly in Burma in the blazing heat of summer), the wardrobe for the actors portraying patients consisted of pajamas and shorts and nearly all the cast came down with bad colds at one time or another. Pat Neal was under tremendous pressure, in love "wildly," as she told Vincent Sherman, with Cooper, who was married and in the States.

Vincent Sherman wrote Warner on December 23, the first day of shooting:

> . . . practically everything happened to drive a director crazy . . . about 10:30 we were lining up and rehearsing for the first sequence and suddenly we had trouble with the arcs [lights]. Then as we were ready to shoot—came a tea break. This meant that everybody from way up high on down—had to stop to get tea!! From the time that the tea break was called until the men got back, a half-hour was consumed. Then the actors had to be warmed up again, and we finally got our first shot around 11 o'clock. In the afternoon the machine which produces fog broke down (we should have moved outside). We finally got it fixed and when we started to roll along in the afternoon, the sound broke down for almost an hour. Then when the sound was fixed and we were ready to start again, came another tea break.

Sherman feared from the start that the film would never be done on schedule and it is obvious he was preparing Warner for the worst. To Steve Trilling, he confessed on January 3, 1949:

Working Pat Neal hard. Wanted to keep her crisp which is an English quality, perhaps, and to take away the Southern drawl [Neal was from North Carolina] and I believe that what is coming through is good even though it's hard to get. . . . On Friday [she] began to cry in the middle of the day because she could not get one of the scenes right, and I spent a little while comforting her, trying to assure her that she was doing very well. I think she is a very fine actress . . . she has problems at home [Cooper] and is quite nervous and really only 22 years old. She said she felt she was not right for the part, perhaps, that it needed a British girl. Anyway . . . she cried a lot of things out of her system and last night we all had dinner together [Reagan, Todd, Sherman, Neal] so I feel there will be nothing but sweetness and light generating from her henceforth. The scene where Ron has to recite Bible names—there were nine takes . . . because in seven, the arcs were flickering or the bamboo [set decoration] was popping.

The first rushes were flown out to Warner ten days after the start of production and he immediately wired back:

GET PROTECTION SHOTS OF ALL CHARACTERS YAWNING IN OPENING [shots] YOU PUT AUDIENCE TO SLEEP BEFORE PIC-TURE STARTS CONVEY TO NEAL REAGAN REST [of] CAST THEY [are] DOING EXCELLENT JOB.

The last frame of the film was miraculously finished on March 31, just five days over schedule. Eight days remained before Reagan, Neal and Sherman were to sail on the *Queen Mary*. Reagan decided to drive from England across to France with a Warner executive (living in England), and then on to the Riviera for some "sunshine and warmth." Reagan, who had had two years of high school French, was the only one who spoke even a smattering of the language. He counted the journey "a huge success" and won sixty-five dollars in Monte Carlo. The trip contained sad moments too, for "On the ride south our heads were on swivels, turning from burned-out tanks that still could be seen in peaceful grain fields, to temporary graves along the road. Clusters of white crosses, each hung with a helmet." The drive to Monte Carlo was two days each way, which left the two men only a few days on the Riviera.

With all his complaining and sarcasm about the foibles of the

British, Reagan did feel close to the English people and sad about leaving them. "I wished that my own country could slow down just a little to have time for such graciousness," he wrote later. "There were friendships made and cherished to this day [1964] with these wonderfully cheerful, warmly humorous people. . . ."

The day he docked in New York, *Variety* carried a story that Errol Flynn had been slated by Warners to star in *Ghost Mountain*, a film Reagan had wanted to do and had spoken to Warner about before leaving for England.* One can visualize Reagan's self-image by the choice of the role he became incensed at having lost—that of a courageous Yankee army officer who joins forces with his Rebel equivalent to fight off an Indian attack during the Civil War. The script was lumbering, dull, and the Yankee officer was a John Wayne clone.

Without consulting Lew Wasserman, he wired Jack Warner that he simply could not believe the studio had given the role to Flynn.

WHEN I'VE ALWAYS BEEN GOOD AND DONE EVERYTHING YOU'VE ASKED—EVEN "THAT HAGEN GIRL."

But while Reagan had been in England, *Night Unto Night* had been released to devastating reviews, *John Loves Mary* had already been a disappointment to the box office and *That Hagen Girl* was a disaster.

He arrived back in Hollywood ready to do battle with Warner ("pull all the tricks that had ever been invented in past studio feuds to induce ulcers at the executive level . . .") and to attend the Academy Awards. Wyman was up for best actress for *Johnny Belinda* against such formidable performances as Ingrid Bergman as Joan of Arc, Olivia de Havilland in *The Snake Pit*, Irene Dunne in *I Remember Mama* and Barbara Stanwyck in *Sorry, Wrong Number*. Wyman came with director Clarence Brown and his wife, but left with Lew Ayres. Dark-haired, wearing a high-necked, long-sleeved classic gown with two strands of pearls and no other jewelry, Wyman, in one of the shortest acceptance speeches on record, took the Oscar and said, "I accept this very gratefully for keeping my mouth shut. I think I'll do it again," and elegantly

---

* *Ghost Mountain* (1950) was filmed as *Rocky Mountain* and starred Flynn and his wife, Patrice Wymore.

walked offstage to thunderous applause.* Jerry Wald was the winner of the Irving Thalberg Award for "most consistent high quality of pictures," an honor given Hal Wallis twice and which Warner, to his great disappointment and long-lasting bitterness, was never to receive.

Wyman, "escorted by her beau," Lew Ayres, attended Jack Warner's celebration party for her at the Mocambo, at the time one of Hollywood's most popular and exotic nightclubs. Reagan was not present, but at a second celebration the next evening at the Cocoanut Grove, Wyman and Reagan both appeared. They each came and went alone and spoke for only a few minutes during the evening. The inevitable item appeared in the Hollywood gossip columns, hinting at a possible reconciliation, especially when shortly after the Academy Awards Wyman and Ayres were no longer seen together. But on July 16, with one final stroke of a judicial pen, Superior Court Judge Joseph B. Maltby severed the marital ties between Reagan and Wyman. Ironically, Reagan, recuperating from yet another accident inadvertently caused by Eddie Bracken, in which he had broken a leg while both were playing in a charity baseball game, was staying at Wyman's beach house with his children, whose mother had gone to England to co-star with Marlene Dietrich in the Hitchcock thriller *Stage Fright*.

Reagan's bachelorhood was now official.

---

*The 1948 Oscar for Best Picture went to *Hamlet;* Best Actor, Laurence Olivier (*Hamlet*); Best Director, John Huston (*Treasure of Sierra Madre*); Best Supporting Actor, Walter Huston (*Treasure of Sierra Madre*); Best Supporting Actress, Claire Trevor (*Key Largo*).

ENTER
NANCY

"Love is lovelier the second time around,

Just as wonderful with both feet

on the ground . . ."

—"The Second Time Around,"

by Sammy Cahn and

James van Heusen

Copyright © 1960 Twentieth Century

Music Corporation

18

NANCY DAVIS WAS BROUGHT TO HOLLYWOOD IN March 1949 to make a screen test. She possessed neither spectacular talent nor great beauty. She had appeared in small, forgettable roles in summer stock and a few Broadway shows and had been seen briefly in two documentary pictures for RKO Pathe, New York—one for the National Foundation for Infantile Paralysis and the other a propaganda film titled *This Is America*. Despite the apparent lack of razzle-dazzle in her background, the great George Cukor directed her test and Metro star Howard Keel played a scene with her from *East Side, West Side*, an adaptation of a Marcia Davenport novel that the studio planned shortly to film. "I don't know what I would have done without them [Cukor and Keel]," she wrote ten days later in her first studio biography. "I had always thought reading for a play was difficult—but I didn't know about screen tests! Most terrifying experience I've ever had—not only making it—but then having to *see* it!"

What she saw was a somewhat antiseptic-looking twenty-eight-year-old, stilted in speech but with an ability to pose gracefully and attentively while listening to someone else. George Folsey, a master at photographing women at their flattering best (Harlow, Hepburn, Crawford, Lamarr), moved in close to her dark-brown eyes and backlit her brunette hair to soften her look and bring up some highlights. Cukor coached her painstakingly in her lines, allowing her to react more than to act. Keel did his best to put her at ease. (Asked on her Metro biographical questionnaire what she would do if out of pictures, Davis typed in, "Lord knows!" To the question "What is your greatest ambition?" she replied, "Sure to have successful marriage." She confessed that she followed the rule "Do unto others as you would have them do unto you—I believe strongly in the law of retribution—you get back what you give." And she added, "My most treasured possessions are two baby pictures of my mother and father*—never am without them, and a locket of my great grandmother's with a baby picture of my mother inside. Why? Because I'm a sentimentalist, I guess.")

The test was not as bad as Cukor expected it to be (he had been extremely negative about her potential). When Dore Schary, head of production at the studio, viewed it, he thought Davis showed enough ability to sign her to a term contract. Louis B. Mayer did not agree, but he had given his new "fair-haired boy" a free hand and did not veto the decision. Outside circumstances were involved. Davis had been brought to the attention of Schary and the studio by two top box-office stars—Spencer Tracy and Clark Gable—who had met and dated her in New York. And both Cukor and Schary were Tracy's good pals.† Additionally, Schary thought Davis had a bright look, a quality that could be put to good use in the more intellectual films he hoped to make for the studio.

Metro-Goldwyn-Mayer had not made a successful transition from wartime entertainment films. Audiences now wanted more substantial stories with strong themes. At a time when Metro's stock was at its lowest ebb, Mayer's yearly salary was the highest paid an individual in the United States ($1,250,000).‡ The studio's board of directors was chomping at his heels. He had hired

---

*Davis most probably is referring to Dr. Loyal Davis, her adoptive father.

†Dore Schary had begun his career as an actor, had made his Broadway debut in support of Spencer Tracy in *The Last Mile,* and had gone on to co-author the story and screenplay of one of Tracy's most successful films, *Boys Town.*

‡Mayer was dethroned as studio head less than two years later (1951), and was engaged for the next six years (until his death) in a bitter and futile attempt to regain his position.

Schary in 1948 in the desperate hope that the younger man could bring to Metro the same flash of brilliance he had shown as head of production at RKO. Almost immediately, a clash of personalities developed. Mayer was a staunch conservative, active in politics, and had been the California state chairman for the Republican party. Schary was a liberal who actively supported numerous civil-liberty causes. Most of the stories he chose inevitably became message pictures conveying a liberal philosophy Mayer did not support.

Schary cast Davis first in a minor part in the film she had originally tested for, *East Side, West Side,* which had Barbara Stanwyck, Ava Gardner and James Mason in the starring roles. Davis had tested for the Gardner role, that of the other woman in businessman Mason's life, but ended as the obsequious secretary who guards his privacy.* Schary decided she handled herself well but needed experience, and gave her a larger supporting role in another film, *The Doctor and the Girl,* which starred Glenn Ford as a young doctor who renounces an attractive offer for a private practice to help the poor. The girl in the title was Janet Leigh. Gloria DeHaven appeared as Ford's emotionally unbalanced sister, Davis as "the less rebellious sister." One critic commented, "Nancy Davis is to be favorably noted."

Schary now had sufficient footage to judge her potential. Despite the talent of the Metro technical staff—makeup, lighting and camera—onscreen, Davis projected what Spencer Tracy called "all the passion of a Good Humor ice cream—frozen, on a stick, and all vanilla." Offscreen she was "a straightforward, honest young woman with a fine sense of humor whom almost every man including most writers, attached and unattached [at Metro], were fond of and tried to date," former MGM writer Edward Chodorov remarked. Nonetheless, Schary saw a future for her in portraying sincere, unglamorized types—the faithful wife, the dedicated nurse, sister, daughter. As luck had it, he was working on a screenplay that contained exactly this kind of character.

Shadow on the Wall had no particular message, but it was a slick psychological murder story, albeit a poor spin-off of the far superior Hitchcock film *Spellbound.* Davis supported Zachary Scott, Ann Sothern and child actress Gigi Perreau. "Nancy Davis is convincing as the psychiatrist," *Variety* noted.

---

* *East Side, West Side* was released after Davis's second film, although made first. She received no mention in the major reviews of the film.

With writer Charles Schnee, Schary had developed a kind of modern morality play into an unusual film script titled *The Next Voice You Hear*. The original story was by George Sumner Albee, who claimed the idea had come to him while lunching with a friend in New York and discussing world affairs. The topic so distressed him that he exclaimed, "Only a second coming of Christ can save the world now." His companion commented that the idea would make a good basis for a story and Albee acted immediately upon this suggestion.

Published first in the *Saturday Evening Post, The Next Voice You Hear* dealt with the voice of God coming over the radios of the world and proving itself divine by a series of miracles such as sinking the Australian continent under water for some minutes, making the Russian war machinery disappear and transforming parading atheists into winged angels. Schary thought a dramatic yet deeply spiritual picture would appeal to the mood of a cold war generation, but he could not go along with the interplanetary atmosphere in Albee's original story. The adaptation dealt with an average American family, Mr. and Mrs. Joe Smith, their son, an aunt, Joe's boss in a factory and some of his fellow workers. God's voice was not heard but referred to as having been heard, and there were no spectacular miracles, just everyday miracles "which are climaxed by the greatest miracle of all," life itself in the birth of Mrs. Smith's child.

The Next Voice You Hear was the archetype of the message films Schary made in this period of his career. He handled the story with deadly reverence and was so sincere in his belief that he had a great spiritual movie in the script that he became obsessively protective about it. He cast Davis and another newcomer, craggy-faced James Whitmore, as Mr. and Mrs. Smith because he wanted unfamiliar faces so that the characters would seem more real. William Wellman was the director.

Wellman (whom actor James Mason once called "a tough little bastard") rehearsed his cast for four days and then shot the film in eighteen, as much in sequence as possible—at Metro a miracle worthy of the picture's theme. Davis, as the very pregnant Mrs. Smith, was made up with pounds of cotton and gauze placed in the proper position. So realistic was her costuming that the cast and crew treated her with a certain deference. Wellman ordered austere makeup, no rouge or lipstick, hair neat but unglamorously coiffed. She had one big scene where she becomes hysterical, and it may be her best moment on-camera.

Wellman's touch was delicate, always in good taste, and the film has a benign charm. The reviews were raves. "A once in a lifetime film fare that seems destined to raise hosannas wherever shown," wrote *Variety*. "A star maker for James Whitmore, Nancy Davis and Gary Gray."* Another reviewer wrote, " 'The Next Voice You Hear' seems to me one of the finest motion pictures of the year—and it is quite possible that it will turn out to be one of the most popular." He was wrong. The film was a dismal failure at the box office, perhaps because audiences felt uncomfortable with the premise. The role that had been publicized as Nancy Davis's ticket to stardom was to place cement blocks on her film career. Her performance was adequate and handled with a great deal of dignity, but there was never any genuine chemistry between her and the camera.

Looking back about fifteen years later, she was to admit publicly, "I never was really a career girl. I just didn't want to be a post-deb in Chicago." This was not entirely the truth, because there had been a time when being a post-deb in Chicago would not have been the least distasteful to her if she had been confronted with the prospect of marriage to a man who could give her the name and status that Loyal Davis had bestowed on her mother, the actress Edith Luckett.

Edith Luckett was born in Petersburg, Virginia, in 1889, the youngest child of Charles Edward and Sarah Frances Whitlock Luckett, but she grew up in Washington, D.C. The Lucketts and the Whitlocks were old Virginia families and the South and being Virginians meant a great deal to them. To their distress, Charles was transferred from the Adams Express Railway office in Richmond to the company's D.C. offices in 1872 before his first child, Thomas, was born. ("I'm Southern and that's the cute thing about it," Edith confided at the age of ninety-three. "My father and mother had to move up to [Washington, D.C.] but my mother went back to Petersburg to have all [five] of her children born so they wouldn't be born damn Yankees! Don't you love that?")†

---

*Gary Gray was a child actor at Metro. His career went down, not up, after *The Next Voice You Hear*.

†Petersburg and Richmond, Virginia, are neighboring cities. Edith Luckett Davis has claimed 1896 as her birth year. However, Washington, D.C., census records for 1890 list her birth as the previous year. Succeeding records disclose five Luckett children born to Sarah and Charles Luckett: Joseph, 1871; Charles W., 1874 (died 1884); Raleigh, 1880; Virginia, 1882, and Edith, 1889.

Sarah Luckett would never make peace with the life she was forced to live. The wounds from the Civil War were not healed and her soft-voweled speech immediately identified her Confederate background. She missed her family and mourned the lost beauty of her youth. The Whitlocks had once owned vast land and a house that was the equal of any other comfortable plantation in the county. But on Charles's modest salary, the Lucketts could not afford to live in the fashionable section of D.C. and had to settle for one closer to the railroad yards. The neighborhood, with its similar houses all in a row, was depressing. The Lucketts' house had a small yard and a vegetable garden, hardly compensation for the warmth of Petersburg, the gentleness of speech and manner. And in Virginia, no matter how small her husband's weekly wages, Sarah would have been able to hire a black servant to do her menial work.

As it was, she saved furniture advertisements and planned rooms for the house they would have one day when they moved back to Petersburg. Often she would share with Edith her dream of bright warm rooms, of broad steps and white columns beside a gracious door. She was closer to Edith than to her other daughter, Virginia, perhaps because Edith was the baby, or because she reminded her more of herself. Edith was pretty and feminine with blue eyes as dense as a Petersburg summer sky and a flawless rose-pink complexion. She had the sound of sweet wisteria in her voice and a generous passion in her feelings. From the time her daughter began to mature, Sarah was certain Edith would one day marry some particularly important Southern gentleman. Edith had other ideas. She wanted to be an actress.

Edith's oldest brother, Joseph Luckett, was a co-owner of the Columbia Stock Company in Washington, D.C. Once, when Edith was about six, the child performer in a play took ill. The part required the young actress to remain in bed languishing, and finally to die at the curtain. Edith substituted in the role. "I had no lines to say. I just laid there in the bed looking sad. When the curtain went down I was supposed to die. I could hear people in the audience crying. I hopped out of bed and I said, 'Don't cry, I'm alive!' I talked to the audience!"

In 1904, at age fifteen, she joined her brother's stock company where she played everything from little girls to ingenue leads. A year later she had the opportunity to audition for the Irish tenor Chauncey Olcott—then at the height of his fame. "He asked me if I could play the piano and I said I could, but I couldn't do a damn thing. So I went out and hired a piano and put it in my hotel room and all that night I picked out a tune from a piece of music—'My Wild Irish Rose'—and the next day I played it and of course Chauncey thought that was wonderful . . . and he said, 'I'll hire you.'

"I was fond of Chauncey Olcott and his wife. People said to me, 'Don't go with Olcott, his wife is a bitch.' She wasn't at all. She was a darling and she was very sweet to me and anywhere they went they used to take me with them. [Not long after I joined his company,] Mrs. Olcott and Mr. Olcott came to my mother and father and wanted to adopt me [she was sixteen] because they didn't have any children. My mother said, 'Oh no! I don't mind her working with you, I think that's fine,' because they were good Christian people. They were Catholics. I wasn't a Catholic. I was Presbyterian, but who cares."

Olcott then went off the road to appear in a Broadway show, and for a number of years Edith worked with various touring companies. In 1910, she came to the attention of George M. Cohan, who, besides writing and composing several Broadway shows a year, kept up his trouping. The four Cohans were now three—Cohan and his parents, Jerry J. and Helen F., his sister Josephine having gone out on her own. The Cohans would tour the principal cities from New York to Chicago with about sixty others in the ensemble. When Cohan left to return to Broadway, his father would headline the tour. Edith was considered a supporting player and had more or less replaced Josephine.

"You do the damnedest things when you don't know what you're doing, don't you?" she laughingly reminisced. "I used to work with George all the time—duets, just the two of us—song and dance. His father had a little lisp kinda—and couldn't hear very good either. I would wait right directly off stage for him to give me the cue to come on with George—who was always bouncing around [backstage] attending to something until the very moment of our entrance.

"I remember we were in Cleveland and I was leaning forward so I could hear old Mr. Cohan's cue to come on with George. I was listening very carefully—and George and the manager passed in back of me and the manager goosed me. I didn't know what the hell a goose meant. I had no idea. And I went right flat on the stage—right on my fanny—took the scenery with me.

"George called for the curtain and he said, 'Luckett, what the hell's the matter with you, can't you stand on your feet?' I said,

'Mr. Cohan, I apologize to you. I slipped and fell and I'm sorry and I apologize,' and I walked away from him, and I went into his mother, and I said, 'Aunt Nellie, I don't have to take this crap. I'm going to New York.'

"My brother's daughter was Nellie Cohan's dresser. And she roomed with me because it was cheaper for us. We always had our dinner together at night. We'd have a chicken sandwich and if it was hot weather we had a chocolate milk shake. If it was cold weather we had a hot chocolate. Well, that night we went to a nearby restaurant to eat and George passed the table with the manager and he said, 'Luckett, will you girls have dinner with me?' (My niece was only a year or two younger than me.) And I said, 'No, thank you.' And with that I turned my back on him. My niece then leaned in close and whispered, 'Don't talk like that to him. He's the money in the family.' And then she spoke up and said, 'Yes, we'd be very glad to have dinner with you tonight.' And then she said to me, 'Be nice to him, do you hear me?' and I said, 'Yes, dear, I will.' So we went over [to his table]. In the meantime the manager had told him how he had goosed me and that was why I had fallen flat on my fanny. George was furious with him and made him apologize. He was very nice to me—very nice—he used to do nice little things for me, and so did the whole family. I loved them."

In the time that Edith Luckett toured with George M. Cohan, she had developed into a competent, reliable trouper. But Cohan did not have enough faith in her to cast her in one of his New York shows. Edith had a pleasant voice, a pretty face and a well-turned ankle. Cohan's act required little more of her. She spoke the straight lines that set up his gags, and stepped back as his dance partner when he executed his nimble solos. Her work with the Cohans ended on January 31, 1914, Jerry J. Cohan's sixty-fifth birthday, when George M.'s parents retired from the stage. For the next three summers she worked with a stock company in Pittsfield, Massachusetts, and it was here that she met Kenneth Seymour Robbins, a young man five years her junior, slim, natty and having a way with words. Ken was the son of Anna A. and John M. Robbins, a conservative New England family who did not think a traveling actress a proper person for their son to be seeing. Despite the touch of old Virginia that clung to her speech, Edith had a gritty way of phrasing things that the New England Robbinses found common. And there was the question of what a young unmarried woman was doing living away from home.

John Robbins's family had been well respected for years. Robbins was the vice-president of a prosperous local mill and he had plans that his son would go into real estate and banking. Ken had other ideas. He and Edith married in July 1916, and when her summer-stock season ended, they went to New York, where Edith had the promise of a small role in a play starring Alla Nazimova. Ken tried his hand as a booking agent, but a few months later America entered World War I and he enlisted in the army, leaving Edith alone for the duration. Edith managed quite well, and when he returned in January 1919, the two set up housekeeping in New York City once again.

Ken Robbins could not thrive in a metropolis, nor was the theater of particular interest to him. He found it difficult to make a living as a booking agent. What he liked to do was tinker with cars. In 1917 his father had died and left him a small inheritance. His mother was alone and she had been willed the greater share. Robbins wanted to return to Pittsfield, and when Edith refused to go, he left without her. She was several months pregnant.

On July 6, 1921, Anne Frances Robbins was born, but Edith called her daughter Nancy, almost from the beginning. Ken laid down an ultimatum: Either she and the child join him in Pittsfield or the marriage was over. Edith took a job with a touring company.

She moved from one stock company to another. As each season ended, she would return to New York, make the rounds of theater managements, and then, having landed a spot in a company, go back out on the road again. Within two years she had performed in forty-two plays (everything from Dearest in *Little Lord Fauntleroy* to Raina in *Arms and the Man*), shuttling back and forth from St. Paul to Washington, D.C., to Chicago. With Nancy out of the cradle, her care became more difficult. Edith decided to leave the child with her sister and brother-in-law, Virginia and Audley Galbraith, who lived in Bethesda, Maryland. The Galbraiths had a daughter named Charlotte who was two and a half years older than Nancy, promising good companionship for both girls.

Edith went back on the road. As Pat O'Brien once recalled, "In those days actors playing in stock companies were doing four things simultaneously. They were *playing* the play, *forgetting* a play, *studying* a play, and *rehearsing* a play. All because each week we did a different production, and in many of the companies around the nation, they did two plays a week. It was hard, brain-tormenting, bone-breaking work, but gratifying." For Luckett, the best part of this treadmill was meeting other young actors and actresses, most of whom approached their work with an enthusiasm and dedication that, except for Cohan, she had not previously known. She appeared with Alla Nazimova, Zasu Pitts, Spring Byington, Pat O'Brien, and Louise and Spencer Tracy.

"Spencer was darling—he was just a darling," she recalled. "And I liked his wife [Louise]. We played anywhere that anyone wanted anything [Winnipeg, Canada; Pittsburgh, Pennsylvania; and Grand Rapids, Michigan]. Spencer and I would always be there. We'd always play because we both got paid for it you see. So we didn't care where we went. I had Nancy to take care of and he had Louise and then their son, John."

While Edith was on the road, Nancy lived comfortably. The Galbraiths were people of steady but modest income and lived up to every dollar they had. Their house was in a nice middle-class neighborhood. The girls shared a room and together attended Sidwell Friends School on Wisconsin Avenue in Washington, D.C., a private school. Nancy began prekindergarten classes there in September 1925. In the summers, Edith would take her on the road with her or to New York. "Nancy was good, she was so good, so well-behaved," Edith boasted. The child would sit patiently through long performances of plays she could not possibly understand. But she did enjoy the excitement of being backstage and of being with her mother and her mother's friends.

Ken Robbins had little interest in his daughter. He had not made much of a success of his return to Pittsfield, and in 1922 he moved with his mother to Glen Ridge, New Jersey, and went into the real-estate business.

Anna bought a many-bedroomed old house (that had once seen grander days) on Fairview Avenue in nearby Verona. Ken then rented this to a Mrs. Mae Palmer for use as a sanitarium. The Robbins family did not take a great interest in Nancy and the child saw her father and grandmother infrequently. (On one trip that Nancy did recall, her father locked her in the bathroom for speaking up when words were said against her mother. She also recalled that her stepmother finally opened the door. Since Ken Robbins did not remarry until 1935, Nancy must have been fourteen at the time.)*

---

*One book states that Nancy visited Anna Robbins at "the family estate in Verona, New Jersey . . . in the evenings they sat on the porch of the big old house, or walked around the tennis courts." Though Anna Robbins had purchased the house in 1928, she and her son

In the summer of 1927, Edith was asked to join a company of players in England. She sailed on the *S.S. New York*. On the voyage over, she met a Chicago neurosurgeon, Dr. Loyal Davis. He was seven years younger than she, unhappily married and the father of a two-year-old son, Richard; the two fell in love.* Davis was on his way to England for a medical conference. The two saw each other again in London. That fall Edith came to Chicago with a touring company of George M. Cohan's *The Baby Cyclone*. The shipboard romance was rekindled. Loyal Davis later said that his wife "made the decision to take Richard and visit friends in Los Angeles. It was but a week or so later that she informed me that she was going to Reno, Nevada, to seek a divorce." Edith returned to Chicago the next season with Walter Huston in *Elmer the Great*. On May 21, 1929, after both their divorces became final, Edith and Loyal Davis were wed, with Nancy as her mother's bridesmaid. Soon after, Nancy left the Galbraiths and joined her mother and Dr. Davis.†

"She came to live with me in Chicago and I loved it," Edith recalled. "Her life changed then. She was very beautiful—but she was a lady, you see. Nancy was a lady, always—always. . . . Everyone wanted to meet her . . . all the people I worked with . . . George M., Olcott, [John Philip] Sousa . . . I kept up all my friends in the theater. . . . Loyal was very fond of theater people. . . . Walter Huston used to spend summers with us up in the mountains [at the Huston home in San Bernardino, California] and they were—oh, I'll tell you, Walter and Ann [Mrs. Huston] were lovely. We were crazy about them. [In Chicago] I could go out and come home and find Walter in bed—in one of [our] beds."

"I remember one time," Dr. Davis added, "we were at their home up in the mountains. I had seen Walter in *Dodsworth* many times. 'Let's do something from *Dodsworth*,' he said. 'You pick the scene.' So I chose the one where he and Mrs. Dodsworth have an

---

Kenneth (and his new wife, Patricia) did not move into the large house until 1935. It had never been a family estate, and there were no tennis courts. Between 1928 and 1935, the Robbins family lived in a modest house at 93 Baldwin Avenue in Glen Ridge, New Jersey.

*Nancy wrote that "[Edith] came to Bethesda to tell me that she'd met this wonderful man and she wanted to marry him, but she wouldn't marry him unless it was all right with me. And I often think, what in the world would have happened if I had said no? I think she would have gotten around it somehow, but I said yes, of course . . ."

† In his autobiography, *A Surgeon's Odyssey*, Dr. Davis writes of his first marriage to Pearl McElroy: ". . . my driving urge to be successful as a doctor . . . was too much for my immaturity to combine successfully with our marriage."

altercation in the hotel. He had the script there. Nancy was Mrs. Dodsworth [she was fifteen or sixteen at the time] and I was Dodsworth. He just sat back and Nancy and I did this—and of course, I killed her. I was very intent about this. [Walter said,] 'You're marvelous, very good. Now, let's do something else.'

"By this time I was an actor, ready to go onstage to make my living, forget about surgery and everything else, and so he said, 'Let's do a scene from Othello. . . . Nancy did Desdemona, I did Iago and he did Othello . . . and when he spoke—he was Othello—this was Othello sitting there, you see, without a script, without anything. . . . The next day we were all by the pool, looking at the mountains. He put his hand on my knee and said, 'Kid'—he always called me *kid*—'Kid, the first time I saw you operate I thought I could do it too.'"*

And Davis added, "Edith . . . taught me to change my asocial tendencies and habits, to develop a sense of humor, to retain my desire and energy to succeed but to relax and enjoy the association of friends." Nancy had come to regard Loyal Davis as her father. From the beginning she had needed to win his love. There had been all those years without a father, never quite feeling a "daughter" to her Uncle Audley, although she lived in his home. Robbins had certainly been no father to her. A close bond developed between Davis and her. He could be stern, a "rock-hard disciplinarian," but Nancy clung to him and guilelessly charmed him in the way of little girls. And she became as important in his life as he was in hers. Richard lived with his mother in Beverly Hills, and the distance made his visits infrequent. But even when Richard did join his father, Davis found it difficult to display overt affection for a son. A daughter was a different matter. Some portion of the restraint he had placed on his own natural emotions to become the "brilliant" Dr. Davis, the respected scientist and authoritarian teacher, could be eased in his relationship with Nancy. Richard Davis has said, "Dad never raised his voice with Nancy. He did with me occasionally."

She loved Edith, who brought a lightheartedness into their small family, but Loyal Davis was the center of Nancy's life. He wrote her small poems and slipped them under her bedroom door. He discussed his deepest feelings with her, and answered all the

---

*Dr. Davis was an attending surgeon at Chicago's Passavant Memorial Hospital from 1929 to 1963. He was also associate professor of surgery (1923), progressing to chairman of the department of surgery at the Northwestern University Medical School in Evanston, Illinois, until his retirement in 1963.

questions she posed, no matter how mature or complex they might be. She called him "Dad" and, though she knew Kenneth Robbins was her father and she had seen him from time to time, she refused to face the fact that Davis was not her true, her only, father.

She believed everything that Davis believed—from the pursuit of excellence to the doctrine that men were to be the leaders and women to follow. Davis loved Edith with an equal devotion, but with greater public reserve. His life had been pedagogic before he had met Edith, and despite her help and his claims, he had not learned how to relax completely. He had to resort to the slips of paper under Nancy's door, and hiding behind an implacable smile when Edith in her own childlike way would suddenly get up and do a little soft-shoe dance to some old-time music on the radio.

Nancy had been enrolled in 1925 in Girls Latin School, originally under the name of Anne Frances Robbins, a source of embarrassment and confusion to her. She endured her unhappiness over this for a number of years, but wanted desperately to be Nancy *Davis*. Even the *Anne Frances* belonged to ancestors of Kenneth Robbins. But not until 1935, when she was fourteen, would she have the courage to speak to Davis about it. Davis said he could want nothing more than to adopt her legally, but without her real father's legal permission this could not be achieved. And so Nancy took the train to Verona, where he was now living, to talk to him herself. She seemed to have no problem in securing Robbins's signature on the proper document (this could well have been the occasion when Robbins locked her in the bathroom). Edith claimed, "Nancy always handled things very mature. . . . It makes her so damn mad when people call Loyal her adopted [*sic*] father. Oh, God, he hates that too! He's always been a father to her and he doesn't like anybody to say he's her adopted [*sic*] father. Burns the tail feathers off him he gets so mad.

"We both liked Nancy to have her friends come to the house . . . and I'd always invite them to dinner or lunch or *what have you*, you know? Our house always had exciting people walking around in it . . . Jimmy Cagney was always there. . . . I was very fond of Jimmy and I liked him because he was going down the road one day and [someone in] a car in front of him threw a dog out and he said, 'Stop this car—let's go back.' And he was so damn mad, picked up the thing, and brought it to our house (he was on his way there at the time)—and he said, 'Do you mind if I have this dog here—or I'll go to the hotel?' 'No,' we said, 'we'd love it.'

And he had that dog for ten or twelve years. He's a wonderful man, that Cagney."

Home for the family of Dr. Davis during most of Nancy's life in Chicago was an expansive apartment with a magnificent view at 199 East Lake Shore Drive. Dr. Davis was an honored and influential man of medicine and a heavy contributor to the Republican party. Although the Davises were invited to almost all society fund-raising events, they were not included in the inner circle of Chicago's social register. Their close friends came mainly from the theater, the world of medicine and the Republican party.

As a father, Loyal Davis expected a great deal from his children. Edith's favorite maxim was "pretty is as pretty does—that's what my mother taught me and that's what I taught Nancy." Dr. Davis was in complete accord. He also insisted his children understand that they had been privileged and that this imposed certain responsibilities toward anyone less fortunate.

"I can remember when Nancy was in school [Girls Latin School]," Edith said. "We had a lady that came and did our laundry and she [Nellie] was upstairs. And Nellie said, 'Mrs. Davis, I can't do the laundry today, I'm so sick. Do you mind if I take a street car and go home? I'll come tomorrow.' And in the midst of this, Nancy came in from school and she says, 'What's the matter?' And [I told her]. Nancy went upstairs, took her piggy bank, cracked it open, took all the money out of it . . . and gave it to the girl. And she said, 'Now I want you to take a cab and go home. I don't want you on a street car 'cause you're not well enough. So you take this money and you go home and if you're all right tomorrow, that's fine. And if you're not, my mother and I will do the laundry.' Well, I'll tell you! Loyal thought that was pretty terrific!"

A classmate of Nancy's at Girls Latin School confided, "Nancy was never comfortable with the girls. She always seemed older than she was. I was at her house several times. I never met Dr. Davis, but Mrs. Davis was a good sport. Very earthy. I remember Nancy reprimanding her for using a word like darn or damn—I can't remember exactly what it was. She was very warm too [Mrs. Davis]. She called people 'honey' and 'dear' a lot and you felt she really meant it. . . . I always felt Nancy took us [the girls] home, not because she wanted us there so much as she needed to show us how fine her home was. At the time I thought she was a show-off. Later, I suspected she was insecure."

During the early years of her second marriage, Edith had continued her career locally, "Whenever I was asked."

"Always wanted to be an actress," Nancy declared on her studio biography. "Used to watch my mother and stay backstage as much as I could."

Nancy's growing-up years were spent in Chicago except for a short sojourn when, in 1934, Dr. Davis took his family to Europe for a holiday. She became the president of the dramatic club at Girls Latin School, and had the lead in several plays. She was resolute in her drive to become an actress. Nonetheless, Dr. Davis insisted she have a coming-out party and join the 1939 list of debutantes, and that she attend college for a prescribed time before setting out for a life in the theater. She promised only that she would attend a year at college. Her society debut at the Casino Club in Chicago was a great disappointment and not well attended. Nancy has commented that the entire Princeton Triangle Club finally showed up to save the day.

One member of the Princeton Triangle Club, Frank Orville Birney, Jr., certainly was present, and it is entirely possible that he brought other members with him. Birney's father was a Chicago banker and a friend of Loyal Davis, and Frank and Nancy had been close friends since childhood.

In the summer of 1939, Richard's mother died and he came to live full-time with his father and Edith. Nancy left for Smith College at Northampton, Massachusetts, that September, a drama and English major. Her grades were not good, but she managed to pass. Life on campus appealed to her more than she had anticipated. For one thing, she met an Amherst man whom she soon dated on a steady basis. For another, she enjoyed the extracurricular activities that a college had to offer—the football games and parties. She had developed into an attractive young woman—not beautiful, but possessing a good figure and an innate sense of style. She knew how to dress to her advantage and how to accentuate her best features. At the end of the academic year, she went home, did some amateur stock and returned to Smith for the next term, a pattern that was to be sustained over the next few years.*

Her years at Smith were blighted by two things—the advent of war, and the shocking sudden death of Frank Birney. On December 7, 1941, America entered World War II. The nation's young men were understandably in emotional chaos during the dramatic week that followed. The schools were getting set for their

---

*In the summer of 1941, Davis joined the regular company of the Bass Rocks Theatre, Gloucester, Massachusetts. She was a member of the Coach House Players at Oconomowoc, Wisconsin, the summer of 1942.

Christmas holidays, but Birney, who was studying geology, had received a bad report and was told he had to remain at Princeton through a portion of the break to make up his grades. He had fallen into a deep depression, and a call to his brother and sister-in-law in New York City had so alarmed them that they telegraphed him to come to New York for a night so they could talk. The young man agreed to take the evening train into the city. His sister-in-law also contacted Nancy at Smith, and she offered to come down to see if she couldn't help to cheer up the despondent Birney.

At six P.M., Birney left the room he shared with R. E. Pate and walked to the station to catch the local that would in turn take him to the Junction where he would change for the New York train. Fog caused the walk to take longer than he had anticipated. Dean Christian Gauss of Princeton reported that "the train pulled out while he was rushing across the platform. A taxi man drove him to the Junction but too late for the connection. [Birney] gave him a dollar. He was seen pacing the platform for twenty minutes or so. Then, he walked down the tracks one third of a mile toward Philadelphia." No one knew the details from there. But a train was coming from the opposite direction—traveling at seventy miles an hour. When the engineer "saw the victim leap from behind the pole to the track, McGoldrick [the engineer] said he gave a long blast of his whistle and applied his brake but was unable to bring the train to a stop before it struck the man." Dean Gauss wrote, "It is odd that his ring was missing and there was nothing, not even a penny, in his pocket when he had at the outset clearly intended to go to New York."

Nancy was at Birney's brother's home when the call came through that he was dead. Whether he was a suicide or the victim of robbery and murder, his death marked the first time that real tragedy had entered her life. Birney has been described as her fiancé, but if this was the case, no announcement had been made. Even so, Frank Birney was an old and valued friend and his violent death must have been a great shock to her.

After this terrible incident, she involved herself almost exclusively in acting. In the spring of 1942, Smith had, for the first time, included a musical comedy in its drama projects. That next spring she was cast in a thirty-minute production entitled *Make with the Maximum*, composed, written, assembled and produced by students and staff of the Smith College Department of Theater. It was advertised as "a Factory Follies—the first musical show ever staged by college girls to entertain war workers," and for several months during this last term of Nancy's college years, the thirty-three members of the cast toured thirteen war plants in the Connecticut Valley. Visiting such arsenals as the government's Springfield Armory and Westinghouse Electric Company as well as the U.S. Rubber Company plant in Chicopee, Massachusetts, they performed before more than five thousand workers at their lunchtime breaks. Nancy loved it. Her role was that of "the Glamor Gal—a Sophisticated Singer." Wearing a slinky black lace dress, gloves over her elbows, she sang in a recitative voice:

Cocktails at five and
Dinner at the Stork,
Long drives in the country
To get away from New York.

She returned home after graduation to be with Edith while Dr. Davis was overseas with a medical unit. He returned in the summer of 1944 and Nancy took a job in summer stock in the New England area. By the end of the season, Edith realized her daughter was serious about wanting to go on the stage and contacted her old friend Zasu Pitts, who hired her to play the minor role of Alice in the touring company of *Ramshackle Inn,* in which Pitts had appeared earlier that season in New York. Pitts took Davis under her wing in more ways than one. A reactionary and ardent Red-baiter, Pitts lectured Davis on the dangers of Communist infiltration in theater and films. Her words did not fall on uninitiated ears. Dr. Davis was also a strong reactionary, and had pointed out to Nancy some of the same threats to the medical profession. Nancy and Pitts hit it off well.* At the end of the out-of-town tour of *Ramshackle Inn* ("a dreary piece of hocus-pocus with a soporific first act and a helter skelter second and third"), Nancy moved into a small but comfortable New York East Side apartment subsidized by her parents. She posed for a Colgate advertisement and took a few smaller modeling jobs. Finally, just before Christmas, 1945, she was cast as Si-Tchun, a lady-in-waiting in *Lute Song,* a musical which starred Yul Brynner and Mary Martin.

---

*Three of the four plays in which Davis appeared during the six years between her graduation from Smith and her contract with Metro-Goldwyn-Mayer starred Zasu Pitts. Pitts had built up a large audience who enjoyed her many humorous, addled-lady performances in films during the 1930s, and her plays did well out of New York on the basis of her screen successes.

"She had been hired before I arrived as director," John Houseman recalled, "at the suggestion of Mary Martin. During the second or third week of rehearsal I suggested to the producer that she was not physically convincing as a small Chinese hand-maiden. He said, 'Talk to Mary [Martin],' and I did. Mary said, 'John, I have a very bad back and Nancy's father Loyal Davis is the greatest [neurosurgeon] in the U.S.A. *We are not letting Nancy go!*' And that was that."

When *Lute Song* closed five months after it had opened, Zasu Pitts once more came to the rescue. Nancy was cast in the minor role of Millicent in *Cordelia,* which was to star Miss Pitts. George Batson, the playwright (also the author of *Ramshackle Inn*), had tailored the comedy to the star's talents. The show opened in New Haven on August 23, 1946 ("a road jaunt might survive on [the] strength of the Pitts name, but as a Broadway enterprise the venture looks as futile as some of [Zasu Pitts's] well-known limp-wristed gestures"). Nancy toured with the show for its short exis-tence and then returned to New York.

In October 1947, a revival of *The Late Christopher Bean,* again starring Zasu Pitts and film's lovable comedian Guy Kibbee, opened out of town with Nancy playing Kibbee's younger daugh-ter ("nicely sweetened without saccharin"). But the material was hopelessly outdated and characters that had once been good, ser-viceable stock dummies had become "blighting bores." *Ramshackle Inn* was being adapted for television and Zasu Pitts once again asked Nancy to play Alice. The camera did not flatter her, but she enjoyed the experience.

By early fall 1948, Nancy was unemployed, twenty-seven, and with no steady beau. Edith made one more call—this time to Spencer Tracy in Hollywood, and he seemed genuinely glad to hear from her. They had kept in touch through the years. Re-cently, when he had been in a place near Chicago resting after one of his severe bouts with alcoholism, Edith had been gracious to both him and Katharine Hepburn, though he knew she preferred his wife, Louise, to Hepburn. "Sure, I'll see what I can do for Nancy," he agreed. A few days later, he was on his way to En-gland to film *Edward, My Son* (Hepburn was to join him a week later), and he had a stopover in New York. He called Nancy and met her for dinner.

Nancy was fascinated by film stars and films. Tracy promised he would see what he could do to get her a screen test. Although this was a difficult time in Tracy's life, he did, before his departure for London, call his old buddy Clark Gable, then a bachelor, and give him Nancy Davis's telephone number. Gable was in worse shape than Tracy. Since Carole Lombard's tragic death in 1942, he had gone into a steady decline. By 1948, he had gained considerable weight, made several successive money-losing films,* and was dropping in popularity. Alcohol had become a serious problem. His nerves were so shattered that he frequently was unable to face the cameras. More than happy to meet a young woman unconnected to his world and with Tracy's word that she was attractive, he telephoned Nancy on a trip to New York. They had several dates, but shortly thereafter he met Lady Sylvia Ashley, whom he married in 1949.

Nothing had changed in Nancy Davis's life. Although she had met and dated two of Hollywood's greatest stars, she remained unemployed. Then Benjamin Thau, vice-president of Loews (Metro-Goldwyn-Mayer),† called her to have dinner and see a show with him. Gable had passed on her telephone number. Thau might have lacked Tracy's and Gable's glamour, but in 1948 and 1949 he wielded a great deal more power at Metro than either of them. At fifty-one he appeared to be Hollywood's most confirmed bachelor, but his casting-couch exploits were legendary. At the end of the evening, he suggested the possibility of a screen test. Nancy picked up on this idea. Skeptical that Thau would carry through his promise, she called Edith, who in turn reached Tracy, just returned from England. Tracy agreed to speak to Thau. The test was set in motion when Tracy told Dore Schary that New York actress Nancy Davis might be a good bet for one of his upcoming intellectual films. "The girl knows how to look like she's really thinking when she's onstage," Tracy told Schary (although when Tracy saw Davis onstage is in question). With Schary's interest piqued, a test was arranged and Tracy asked George Cukor, his and Hepburn's good friend as well as his landlord (the actor lived in the guest house on Cukor's estate), to direct the test. All lights were *go* for Nancy. She was going to have to deal with Benny Thau, who might feel she owed him something in return, but as Edith Davis has insisted, "Nancy was a lady—always— always . . . people thanked me for my daughter's dignity onstage . . . never once did Nancy ever cross her legs or do anything . . . she was a lady. . . ."

---

* *Any Number Can Play, To Please a Lady* and *Key to the City.*

† Thau was administrative head of Metro-Goldwyn-Mayer for a relatively short span in 1956. He married St. Louis socialite Elizabeth Jane White in 1955.

Rumors about her association with Benny Thau shadowed Nancy's happiness during her first months at the studio. She was unmarried and living alone, and Hollywood assumed no woman in their business under those circumstances had not "been around." Marriage was the answer. Most of her life it had been her one true ambition anyway. She had seen how marriage to Loyal Davis had transformed her mother's life, and she wanted a man with the potential stature of her father, a man who might need a dedicated wife as much as she needed a successful and respected husband. She knew she would gladly give up her career for such a partnership.

According to a co-worker at Metro, one day Nancy jokingly displayed a list of names that she had compiled of Hollywood's most eligible bachelors. The list contained directors, producers, agents and lawyers as well as actors. Ronald Reagan's name occupied the top spot.

Dore Schary's wife, Miriam, was not one of Hollywood's most social wives. Several factors entered into this. Miriam exhibited the usual snobbism of the New York intellectual forced to live in vulgar Hollywood. She pursued her own interests—art, her family, her home. A facial disfigurement, caused by some paralyzed nerves, discomfited certain people. Therefore, she had to feel right with a person before she extended herself. Nancy Davis had been sincere and straightforward with her from the first time they had met. And so, when Nancy mentioned to Dore that she would like to meet Ronald Reagan, Miriam arranged a small dinner party to which they both were invited. As with most dinners at the Scharys', the children were present, and their daughter, author Jill Robinson, recalled the evening clearly. "There was a lot of political talk and some arguments. Reagan made his [anti-Communist] views very clear. He was terribly articulate. Nancy listened to him attentively. She was sitting opposite him at the dinner table and she kept smiling at him in agreement." Schary considered Red-baiting a serious danger and the evening had an edge to it.

Miriam had planned for Reagan to drive Nancy home. But since he was scheduled to leave for New York early the next morning, he was the first to leave. For the hostess to suggest that Nancy depart with Reagan and he escort her home would have been a breach of etiquette, so she said nothing and he left unaccompanied.

19

REAGAN HAD COME TO THE SCHARYS' DINNER PARTY the night he met Nancy leaning on a cane. An accident at the charity baseball game—caused when his nemesis Eddie Bracken tripped him as he was sliding into first base—had resulted in a triple fracture of the leg and was to cause him pain and to need medical attention for many years. He was more concerned about the loss in revenues it had caused ($150,000 he claimed—the salary for two films he had not been able to make) and the time it had taken away from his SAG activities.

The SAG had hit serious stumbling blocks in its negotiations with other artists' guilds and unions for the organization and administration of filmed television under a joint-venture agreement.* There were many complicated issues involved. The main split was

---

*The unions worked under a parent organization, the Associated Actors and Artists of America, which was generally referred to as the Four A's. These unions included the SAG and SEG (Screen Extras Guild) on the West Coast, and AGVA (Associated Guild of Variety Artists), Actors Equity and AFRA (American Federation of Radio Artists) on the East Coast.

caused by regional divisions. The eastern unions wanted a merger
with the SAG. This meant that all television matters dealing with
SAG members would be governed by the East by paid executives,
not by working actors. Reagan, Dana Andrews, Lee Bowman and
Richard Carlson, representing the SAG along with Jack Dales and
Buck Harris, arrived in New York for the meeting on October 4,
1949, hoping they could evolve some sort of partnership in the
solution of the giant bugaboo called television.

Reagan led the SAG team. "He was an aggressive man," Jack
Dales observed. "Depending upon the situation he was two men
. . . aggressive fighter across the table, then in conference among
ourselves in our caucuses . . . most realistic—'Look, what are we
going to get, what do we need? If we can go this far with A maybe
we can go that far and then we can get a hunk of B'—most reasonable, realistic in conference, but aggressive to the point of temper in negotiations, of losing his temper."

The SAG team ended up believing that the other unions were
intent on blocking any solution to the problem. "It was like trying
to sit down and in theory create a U.S. Steel industry without first
building even one blast furnace," Lee Bowman commented. The
New York unions were fighting to keep control in their hands.
"You don't seem to understand," one of the East Coast union
leaders told Bowman. "When we call a strike we've got to be able
to pull you guys out with us—and if we haven't control how do
we know you'll go out when we say?"

Reagan returned to Los Angeles and to another kind of controversy. He did not feel Warner Brothers was doing right by him.
He remained particularly unhappy about his role in *The Hasty
Heart,* which he considered had been subordinate to Richard
Todd's. His contract had three years to go, but Lew Wasserman
went in and renegotiated it so that Reagan could do outside pictures. In exchange, Warners was to reduce Reagan's salary to half
his yearly income, although he now had to make only one film a
year at the studio. Wasserman then went to Universal and made a
five-year deal for him for seventy-five thousand dollars a film.
Reagan "felt rich" and had visions of two or three films a year at
that figure added to his yearly Warners stipend. However, it was
now October and he had not been before the cameras since
March (*The Hasty Heart*) because of his injury, forcing Reagan, in
order to meet his family commitments, to take a personal advance
on his 1950 earnings from Jack Warner. Immediately thereafter
he was cast in a film that Jerry Wald had been developing (even-

tually titled *Storm Warning*) about mob violence and the Ku Klux Klan in a small town.

Another controversy arose when Wald could not get an actress to play opposite Reagan. Lauren Bacall had risked suspension rather than take a role "for which I consider myself unsuited."* Ginger Rogers felt otherwise and was signed. Actually, Wald had written Warner four months earlier: "Rogers . . . will be happy to do 'Storm Center' [the working title] if you want her." Rogers had read Richard Brooks's script and liked it, but Steve Trilling wasn't too keen on her.

Reagan's leg presented a problem until Wald decided to give the character a limp. But it looked as though the injury might have time to heal with all the delays that were placed in Wald's way. A director was not easy to find, nor was the required small-town location.

To prepare Reagan for the realistic role he was to play, Wald inundated him with background material (dozens of articles and books). A note was attached to one titled *Blue Ridge Country Story:* "This is the kind of background [Rainey, the character Reagan would play] should come from." A picture of Marlon Brando in the stage version of *Streetcar Named Desire* was accompanied by the suggestion, "Note outfit Brando wears for this role."†

On November 3, with Reagan and Rogers poised to go, Wald was working on a second draft of the script with Daniel Fuchs, to whom he wrote: "We have seen the Rainey character act the way he does in so many pictures whether it be played by Dana Andrews or John Wayne or Ronald Reagan. But why shouldn't this D.A. have problems too? Wouldn't it be more interesting if he were a man who after years of trying to get the Klan is discouraged, also wants to rush things through, knowing it is hopeless. I would like to see him much less firm, heroic & fearless. Then we would see how really powerful the Klan is, and get away from the pattern of the new sheriff cleaned up the town . . . at times the script strikes me as being a trifle B-picture-ish."

Whatever its final alphabetical rating—A or B—in *Storm*

---

* Bacall stated: "I told [Warner] he had a fine picture but that the part wasn't for me. I've asked him for my release many times, thinking I would be doing him a favor. I'm tired of being suspended." This was Bacall's sixth suspension in a year. For refusing one script she had been laid off for twenty-two weeks.

† Wald to Charlie Mack (wardrobe) on November 10, 1949: "Ronald Reagan's clothes too formal. Must loosen them up. Shirt and tie need small town look . . . if his clothes don't fit so well, it might do a lot to help his character. We should try testing him with a hat—flannel shirt—small knotted tie—off-the-rack clothes."

Warning, Reagan was going to "lick the KKK. . . . I'm braver than Errol Flynn or Vic Mature," he wrote a friend back in Dixon. "Wouldn't Jack have been pleased!" ("They're all bums [the KKK]," Jack Reagan had once told him.)

The articles kept coming from Wald—"South Chicago, Memorial Day Riot," "Scottsboro Boys," "The Crooked Cross," "Prelude to American Fascism," "Who Killed Huey Long?" The list was impressive. Serious stuff. Doris Day was signed for the second female lead, the role of Ginger Rogers's sister, and Reagan, who had met her previously, dated her.

"There were two things about Ronnie that impressed me," Day said later, "how much he liked to dance and how much he liked to talk. . . . There was a little place on La Cienega that had a small dance floor where he often took me. . . . When he wasn't dancing, he was talking. It really wasn't conversation, it was rather talking *at* you, sort of long discourses on subjects that interested him. I remember telling him that he should be touring the country making speeches. He was very good at it. He *believed,* or at least he made you think he believed.

"One night we went up to his apartment [Londonderry View], and it was the first time I had seen the view from high up there in the Hollywood hills, with the lights of the city spread out below . . . high above the city lights with that celestial view. . . ."*

Day had recently completed a supporting role in another Wald production, *Young Man with a Horn.*† Brought to Hollywood as a singer, Day had scored in this film both musically and dramatically. But, given the totally nonmusical content of *Storm Warning,* she had been skeptical about playing in it. She went to see Jack Warner. "[It was] the only time I can remember being in his cavernous, rococo office. . . . 'So you're a big star already,' he shouted in that gruff voice of his. 'She's made a coupla pictures

---

*At this time, Reagan was also dating Patricia Neal (who was still in love with Gary Cooper). On December 14, 1949, they attended the premiere of *The Hasty Heart* at Warners' Hollywood Theatre along with "the entire consular corps in Los Angeles, in formal attire and wearing the decorations of their respective nations." Jack Warner was so elated about the film's prospects that he went back to his office after the premiere and wrote a memo to one of his staff: "2800 people at our premiere tonight had many tears and much more laughter than I have heard in any picture. We have been trying frantically to write or buy a great comedy about the war. One with some heart, pathos and much laughter. Tonight I rediscovered this is the very picture we have in 'The Hasty Heart.' . . . Maybe we should go after a big campaign to sell this picture giving it importance which we have time to do before its [general] release."

† *Young Man with a Horn,* a film biography of the great trumpet player Bix Beiderbecke, also starred Kirk Douglas, Lauren Bacall and Hoagy Carmichael.

and already she's telling the front office how to run the studio. . . . I've got people here I pay five times what you're getting and they've okayed this script and you're coming in here and telling me how to run my business. . . . You just do what you're told to do and let those who know the movie business take care of things, you understand?'"

Storm Warning went into production in the town of Corona, California (population approximately ten thousand), on November 15, 1949, the date pushed up to accommodate Ginger Rogers, who had had another commitment. The screenplay was still in the process of being rewritten when the company arrived. Immediately this community of rich citrus ranches thirteen miles from the larger city of Riverside and once called South Riverside was transformed into a red-necked small Southern town. Leo Kuter, the film's art director, claimed they had chosen Corona because on the four corners of its main street were the courthouse, the library, a combined church and undertaking parlor and a service station. "That's what turned the trick for Corona," Kuter said. Stuart Heisler, who had finally been assigned director, explained their "idealistic" choice. "There before you—law and order, education, religion, death, and gas and oil." He did not mention their impatience to start the cameras rolling, which precluded a longer location search, or the fact that Corona was conveniently less than a two-hour drive from the studio.*

The town took to the invasion of a film company with good humor. Fans fought for autographs and handshakes. The local newspapers ran daily accounts of the stars and the film's progress. The police force went on twenty-four-hour duty as Coronians learned to live by night, for most of the shooting took place on city streets after sundown, lasting until the early-morning hours.

Reagan donned his makeup in the stock room of a ladies ready-to-wear shop across the street from the courthouse, but he used an unoccupied jail cell to rest between takes.

Although Jerry Wald had visions of this film becoming another *Crossfire*,† his early fear that the script had a B-picture-ish quality to it was well founded. The story of a crusading county

---

*Publicists and Reagan himself claimed Corona was a hotbed of the Klan. It seems unlikely the studio would have taken such a chance and there is no substantive proof to back up this claim.

† *Crossfire* was a critically acclaimed film (1947) that dealt with mob violence and anti-Semitism with taste and intelligence. It was directed by Edward Dmytryk, who was included in the Hollywood Ten persecution.

prosecutor (Reagan) out to rid his small town of the Klan by making the townspeople recognize their own responsibility did bear similarity to *Crossfire* and to the future *High Noon* as well.* The failure of *Storm Warning* to become a memorable film rests with the director Stuart Heisler's concentration on grisly and repellant violence (people are flogged and pistol-whipped, a pregnant woman is brutalized and killed) and his inattention to the dialogue, which ought to have been less ideologically preachy and more telling in confrontational scenes.

Reagan gave a fevered performance. All the literature Wald had swamped him with had been carefully ingested. The character of Rainey has a true sense of the reformer and Reagan delivered what was needed in the Klan scenes. But the private man never did come through. Ginger Rogers seemed less comfortable in her role as a New York fashion model who, while visiting her newly married and pregnant sister (Doris Day), witnesses a murder by hooded Klan members, one of whom turns out to be her sister's husband (Steve Cochran). Reagan learns of Rogers being a witness to murder and subpoenas her to appear in court. As she packs to leave to avoid having to do so, her brother-in-law makes an overt and humiliating pass at her. The sister intercedes, and both women are brutally beaten by Cochran. Reagan then persuades Rogers not to leave town. Cochran forces her to a Klan meeting where she is saved from a flogging by Reagan, the sister and the police. In the melee that follows, the sister is gunned down accidentally by the police, Cochran is arrested, the Klansmen told to leave town, and Reagan wins Rogers's love. How a New York fashion model would come to live happily ever after in such a town is never settled. Nor could anyone believe that the Klansmen—all local businessmen—would accept Reagan's edict that they be good boys and ride off into the sunset.*

Time and again, Nancy Davis told how she met Reagan. In her version, the dinner at the Scharys' was forgotten. Nancy claimed that another actress named Nancy Davis had been known to have Communist connections and was the victim of a blacklist, which in turn—because of the confusion in names—created cast-

---

* *High Noon* (1952), produced by Stanley Kramer and directed by Fred Zinnemann. Jerry Wald's first choice for director on *Storm Warning* had been Zinnemann, but he had been unavailable. *High Noon* was about a sheriff (Gary Cooper) who tries unsuccessfully to get his town to rid itself of a band of desperadoes. With the support of his new wife (Grace Kelly) he accomplishes the task.

† The denouement of the *High Noon* screenplay (story by John W. Cunningham, adaptation by Carl Foreman) has the newly married sheriff and his wife leaving the town he has saved, in disgust.

ing problems for her. She said she called Reagan at the SAG some time during September 1949 and asked for his help and if they could discuss the situation. He invited her to have dinner at LaRues (not far from the Guild offices) if she would agree to a fast meal; he had another appointment later. They met and the chemistry was so immediate that he forgot his former engagement and they talked until two or three A.M. The facts contradict this account of their meeting (even if this tête-à-tête is interpreted as being a second meeting).

Reagan wrote in his autobiography that Mervyn LeRoy, while directing *East Side, West Side* (which means July–September 1949), called him at the Guild on behalf of Davis who "was very much distressed because her name kept showing up on rosters of Communist front organizations, affixed to petitions of the same coloration, and her mail frequently included notices of meetings she had no desire to attend, and accounts of those meetings as covered by the *Daily Worker.*" Correspondence and SAG records show this (or at least the basis for this claim) actually occurred in January 1953—three years later. Also, in 1949, Davis was under contract to MGM. It is unclear why she or LeRoy would not have gone directly to the studio for help and clearance since it was generally known that studios at that time had agencies on retainers who checked for anything of a subversive nature in the backgrounds of their employees.

A notation in the SAG minutes reveals that in October 1949 (shortly after the dinner at the Scharys'), Nancy Davis contacted Reagan at the Guild offices and "indicated her willingness and desire to run for the Board [the following month in the annual November elections]." The next year, on July 24, 1950, "Lee Bowman urged that Nancy Davis be considered . . . to replace Ray Collins until the [next] election [November 1950] . . . due to some confusion in membership (two Nancy Davises) her name was not included on the last ballot."

The other Nancy Davis was also a member of the SAG. Her real name was Nancy Coffman, but when she came to Hollywood in 1942, after five years as a member of the Ice Vanities, she took the name Nancy Lee and signed with Twentieth Century-Fox, where she appeared as a skater in several of the Sonja Henie pictures. The studio changed her name to Nancy Davis. She left Hollywood for New York in 1945, when her husband became terminally ill. In "confusion and distress" she had forgotten to take the permissible leave of absence from the SAG, which would have eliminated the expense (and debt) of yearly dues. She did not return to Los Angeles (with two small children to support) until 1952. But her name had been on the SAG membership list during all the years she had been out of the industry (and her yearly-dues debt mounting).

A SAG law prohibits duplication of actors' names. Normally, when Nancy signed with Metro in 1949 she would have been forced by SAG rules to alter her name to avoid any confusion with Nancy (Lee) Davis. But because Nancy (Lee) Davis was on the inactive list, her name had been overlooked. When Nancy chose to run for the board, someone made a more thorough check. Nancy Davis was thought to be Nancy (Lee) Davis and her name removed from the ballot (because of the outstanding dues debt). It makes considerable sense that she would enlist Reagan's help in clearing this matter up—after all, he was the president of SAG. But since Nancy (Lee) Davis did not work in the industry between 1945 and 1952, she could not have been on any studio blacklist. Nor does it seem likely a producer casting a film would have confused the two women. Nancy (Lee) Davis was listed in the casting directory as an athlete—horsewoman, aquatics and ice skating—and had never played a speaking role of any size. Her parent guild was not the SAG but the Screen Extras Guild (SEG). And the two women had never had the same agent.

When Nancy (Lee) Davis returned to California in 1952 and asked to be reinstated as an active member of the SAG, the Guild demanded she alter her name since another member, who had been active and in good standing, claimed it. Nancy (Lee) Davis thereafter became Nancy Lee Davis.

What seems clear is that after meeting Reagan at the Scharys' in September 1949, Nancy was determined not to let it go at that and a mutual interest in the SAG certainly would help. That following November she contacted him at SAG and they met for dinner. In 1950, during the time she was a replacement, she and Reagan saw each other every Monday night, having dinner together either before or after the board meetings. Reagan also took her to meet Nelle, Neil and Bess. Neil observed to a friend, "It looks as if this one has her hooks in him." In November 1950 (she had now been dating Reagan for a year), her name was placed on the ballot. There were fourteen nominations and ten were to be elected. Nancy lost.*

---

*In 1951, she was nominated again. This time she was elected and served on the board with Reagan until she and Ronald Reagan resigned their positions on July 9, 1960.

Nancy Lee Davis was to reappear in Nancy's life in 1953 (by this time she was married to Reagan and no longer under contract to Metro) when she was being considered for a role in a Columbia Pictures film. The investigative firm that checked such things for the studio reported that a Nancy Davis had signed the Amicus Curiae brief for the convicted Hollywood Ten. A letter was dispatched to Nancy Reagan asking for an explanation. Nancy revved into action. Both Jack Dales and Reagan contacted Columbia vice-president B. B. Kahane with much indignation and explained that there was *another* Nancy Davis who must be the subject of the investigative organization's "slovenly and inaccurate report." Nancy then wrote a scathing letter to Columbia casting director Victor Sutker, which he passed on to Kahane, who replied with a lengthy letter of apology.*

One of the highest moments of Reagan's life occurred on February 6, 1950 (his birthday), when six hundred Friars (representing the film's most glittering members) honored him at a banquet held at the Beverly Hills Hotel. Speeches were given in tribute to his work for the industry by Harry Cohn, George Burns, Pat O'Brien and Cecil B. DeMille, among others. The evening was far more serious than most Friars' affairs. There was no roast. "Hollywood and the industry love him," George Jessel said. Reagan attended with a beaming Nancy.

By the spring of 1950 he was seeing Nancy often but remained uncommitted. A series of women had passed through his bedroom. ("One morning I awoke and couldn't remember the name of the lady sharing my bed. That was it.") Wyman had built a life of her own and he found the thirty-mile distance to Malibu from West Hollywood somehow too far to see the children as often as he formerly had. Although he still called Nelle every day, his visits were not as frequent. The machinations of union clashes, of pro- and anti-Communists, of the major film agencies and the studios whirled around him. He was deeply involved in all these issues,

---

*Kahane to Nancy Davis Reagan (January 7, 1953): ". . . of course, we could have taken it for granted that the wife of Ronald Reagan could not possibly be of questionable loyalty and could have disregarded that report. But as the citation was merely the signing of the Amicus Curiae brief and many persons signed this brief who we have been convinced are not now and never were Communists or sympathizers, we informed you of the citation, believing that a satisfactory explanation would be forthcoming . . ." Despite this explanation and apology from Columbia with its clear message that a signatory to such a brief was not necessarily a Communist sympathizer, Mrs. Reagan repeatedly referred to the other Nancy Davis as such, although no proof that this is the case exists.

giving speeches, writing articles,* presiding over meetings and hotly conspiring in small conclaves to win a point or two for the SAG (or at least for his position on various controversies raging at the SAG).

His partnership with Nino Pepitone in the Northridge Horse Farm took time as well, and he still had a career to pursue, one which was not moving in a direction that suited him. The very fact that Warners planned to hold up the release on *Storm Warning* revealed their disappointment with the film.

He became insistent that in the one picture he owed Warners for 1950 he be cast in a Western or a war film that had a role with the macho quality John Wayne was then portraying (*She Wore a Yellow Ribbon, Sands of Iwo Jima* and *Rio Grande*). Wayne remained a role model. Reagan admired his outdoorsmanship and shared his political philosophy. On May 15, 1950, just two days before Reagan delivered one of his own diatribes against communism, Wayne, as president of the Red-baiting Motion Picture Alliance for the Preservation of Ideals, had stated: "America is insisting on a delousing [of Communists and Communist sympathizers]," and urged "all organizations within the film industry and all civic or-

---

*Typical of Reagan's speeches and articles in 1950 were his guest columns for Victor Riesel, the labor columnist:

"... Day after day in this year's hearings by the House Committee on Un-American Activities, the same story has been unfolded—a story of Communist frustration and failure in the party's bold plot to seize control of the talent guilds and craft unions, through which the subversive brethren hoped eventually to control content of films and thus influence the minds of 80,000,000 movie goers ... the Red propagandists and conspirators in this country ... were trying to carry out orders from Joseph Stalin, who had said: 'The cinema is not only a vital agitprop (active propaganda) device for the education and political indoctrination of the workers, but is also a fluent channel through which to reach the minds and shape the desires of people everywhere. The Kinofikatsiya (turning propaganda into films) is inevitable. The task is to take this affair into your hands, and vigorously execute it in every field.'

"So the Red enemies of our country concentrated their big guns on Hollywood. And they failed completely. But not before they had succeeded in bringing about two years of disastrous strikes and bloody fighting in which American workmen battled other American workmen at the studio gates. And, unfortunately, not before the Communists had fooled some otherwise loyal Americans into believing that the Communist party sought to make a better world. Those dupes know today that the real aim of the Communist party is to try to prepare the way for Russian conquest of the world. . . ."

He ended the article with this personal statement:

"'. . . I believe that all participants in the international Communist conspiracy against our nation should be exposed for what they are—enemies of our country and of our form of government.' And any American who has been a member of the Communist party at any time but who has now changed his mind and is loyal to our country should be willing to stand up and be counted, admit 'I was wrong' and give all the information he has to the government agencies who are combatting the Red plotters. We've gotten rid of the Communist conspirators in Hollywood. Let's do it now in other industries."

The column was also the basis of a speech he gave at a convention for LAMBDA fraternity members.

ganizations in the community to press for a resolution to require
registration of all Communists."

But Jack Warner did not believe Reagan had the chemistry to
become a star of John Wayne's magnitude. The rumor that Errol
Flynn would play the lead in *Ghost Mountain,* the script Reagan
had once helped develop, deepened his growing bitterness toward
his employer, and the stake was driven in deeper by exploding
problems among MCA, Reagan's agents and Jack Warner (a situation that would soon erupt into a full-scale government investigation of MCA's monopolistic methods, which would considerably
change agency-studio relations).*

An interview published in the *Los Angeles Mirror* on January 6
set off further sparks between Reagan and his boss. Reagan had
told the Associated Press reporter Bob Thomas that the parts the
studio gave him were so bad that "[he] could telephone [his] lines
in and it wouldn't make any difference." (After reflecting on this
statement, he shrugged, "Well, I can always go back to being a
sports announcer.") Warner was incensed and that day wrote
Reagan a letter.

> Dear Ronnie,
>
> Now that "Storm Warning" is over and you are working at
> Universal, I am wondering if you did or did not give the
> enclosed interview to Bob Thomas, the A[ssociated] P[ress]
> correspondent. If in fact you did this interview I think it was
> very unfortunate of you to do so. . . . If you are not satisfied
> with the roles you have portrayed in the past, undoubtedly
> you will have the same attitude, with respect to future roles.
>
> I would greatly appreciate your sending me a letter can-
> celling our mutual contract obligations with respect to the
> two remaining pictures you are to do with this company.
>
> I have always considered you as a very good friend and I
> would rather have you remain as such than to have business
> matters interfere with such friendship. Recently your agent
> asked me to advance you certain monies on your contract. I
> was happy to do so. However, I do not feel that I personally,
> nor our company, nor the pictures in which you have
> appeared for us, deserve the uncomplimentary and erroneous
> rap that is reflected in the interview.

---

*Warner claimed he was being forced to hire additional and undesired MCA talent in
order to secure a desired client.

Instead of sending this letter, Warner filed it and had Ray Orbinger speak to Reagan. The memo from Ray Orbinger to Warner, dated February 17, 1950, reads:

Reagan felt he had a "beef" playing 2nd lead to Todd in "The Hasty Heart"—that he was blamed for the poor showing of "That Hagen Girl." After he got the steam off I told him that the implications from the interview were very damaging to his pictures, [since] practically all of which were produced here, and that it reflected his attitude towards future pictures—and that while you considered him a very good personal friend you felt it would be best from a business stand point to call off the contract deal amicably.

Reagan went into some more alleged abuses and particularly the fact that he lay in the hospital for six weeks with a broken leg without anybody from the studio contacting him . . . also he said that when he returned from England he talked to Steve Trilling and that Steve told him he was not clicking at the box office and the company was a little cold on him, but this was all due to the fact that he had been a good enough sport to do "That Hagen Girl" which he knew from the beginning would not go over. . . . He also said he thought he was being double-crossed in not getting "Ghost Mountain." He stated that he had a contract for two more pictures and expected to perform under it. He also stated that if he ever has the occasion to see you personally that he proposes to tell you his personal feelings with respect to his not getting "Ghost Mountain."

On May 3, Reagan, feeling more conciliatory, wrote Warner in longhand:

I don't know anything about your difficulty with MCA nor do I care to know. Naturally, it is none of my business. They have just notified me of my right to utilize the Wm. Morris office [in order to deal more amicably with Warner]—a right which I waived. Having been with MCA almost as many years as you and I have been together, I don't feel that strangers can suddenly take over and represent my best interest.

I hope that where our relationship is concerned you will allow Arthur Parks to negotiate in my behalf. Actually he is personally involved in the particular item of business I wish to discuss.

I know that you will recall our discussion some time ago in regard to "That Hagen Girl." You agreed the script and role were very weak, but asked me to do the picture as a personal favor, which I gladly did. At that time you encouraged me to bring in a suitable outdoor script which you agreed to buy as a starring vehicle for me. I found such a property in "Ghost Mountain" and the studio purchased it with me, through MCA, acting as go-between to close the deal with the author.

Of late there have been "gossip items" indicating you plan to star someone else in the story. Naturally, I put no stock in these rumors—I know you too well to ever think you'd break your word.

However, I am anxious to know something of production plans—starting dates—etc. in order to better schedule my own plans. Frankly, I hope it is soon as I have every confidence in the story.

Sincerely,
Ronnie Reagan

Ray Orbinger reported to Warner on May 26:

I talked to Reagan regarding his May 3rd letter. Advised him that the "Ghost Mountain" situation developed when he [first] refused "That Hagen Girl," which, of course, he did not have the right to do, and that there were no promises made by you or Trilling that if he brought in an outdoor picture or suggested properties—they would be his. Other artists bring in stories—many of which are bought, some of them are—and that the ones that are bought are not necessarily produced with the artists being assigned for many reasons.

I also told him that with respect to "Ghost Mountain" that the company's attitude had changed considerably since his article about phoning in his lines to the studio and did not want to risk assigning him to a picture of heavy costs when he had such an attitude and frame of mind about his work. I then stated that in view of his apparent unhappiness, etc.— that maybe, it would be a good idea to effect a mutual cancellation of his contract.

(Reagan obviously did not agree to this for he was eventually to film the two pictures left on his Warner Brothers three-picture deal.)*

When Reagan signed with Universal, it had recently merged with International Films and its former B-picture product was gradually abandoned as major stars and technicians were signed to its banner. The fact that most of the new blood at the studio were MCA clients was more than a coincidence. Within twelve years (1962), it would become a subsidiary of MCA. By 1950, the "Star-Spangled Octopus," as MCA was dubbed, represented the services of nearly 60 percent of the industry's talent. ("I've never seen anything like it in my life," a deputy district attorney would one day exclaim. "You can't even go to the bathroom in Hollywood without asking MCA's permission.") Under Wasserman, MCA also moved aggressively into television production.

No wonder men like Jack Warner bristled at the mention of Wasserman's name. The major studios had been made hostage to his demands for his clients. The "package deal" had been an MCA invention, begun by founder Jules Stein. Wasserman refined it to an art. If a studio desperately wanted a particular star for a film, they often had to take co-stars or a director or writer also represented by MCA in the same package.

No one knew the true extent of MCA's hold on Hollywood, nor its yearly gross income. The company kept its business—in the tradition of Jules Stein's early Capone connections—a closely guarded secret; so close that Dun & Bradstreet had not been able to compile a credit rating on it. Guesses ran from forty to one hundred million dollars. Since MCA did not allow anyone to see a full list of its clients, there was no way to narrow the gap. None of the accepted business reference books (*Moody's, Poor's* or *Standard Statistics* in 1950) published any information on MCA or its many interlocking corporations. Only Stein, his right hand, Wasserman, their auditor and their income-tax collector knew. Incredibly, both Stein and Wasserman avoided being listed in the 1950 *Who's Who in the Motion Picture Industry,* "a staggering compilation of practically everyone in Hollywood above the status of stagehand."

Stein was already the second biggest stockholder in Paramount Studios and now he was going to take over Universal. MCA had moved away from its roots in the overworked band,

---

*The two films were *She's Working Her Way Through College* (1952) and *The Winning Team* (1952).

radio and nightclub fields (although it never gave up its toehold) and into film and television production—the *really* big money.

Reagan later said the Universal film comedy *Louisa* was "a good and healthy plus to any list of screen credits." The film was pleasant and did have a grand cast of sturdy, disarming character performers—Charles Coburn, Edmund Gwenn and Spring Byington. But it was not in the same league with *The Hasty Heart,* or even some of the Warners comedies—*The Voice of the Turtle, John Loves Mary*—that he complained bitterly to Jack Warner had not done him justice. Certainly, the role of Hal Norton, a good-natured, middle-class, middle-aged architect who has to deal with the arrival in his home of a dotty mother-in-law, Louisa (Spring Byington), was not going to bring him head to head with Duke Wayne. He appears to have needed money and his fee for the film was substantial (the agreed seventy-five thousand dollars). However, film veteran Coburn, also represented by MCA, received equal money and co-star billing. As Louisa's imperious suitor and Reagan's boss, he also got the best lines in the script. The truth was a dozen other actors could have played Reagan's role; but for the success of the film, Coburn was essential.

Louisa was shot in thirty-five days at a cost of $792,954, a good portion of the budget going to the artists and crew brought in by Wasserman. On March 7 (a week before completion), Stage 18 of the studio was turned into a ballroom for a huge party to mark Coburn's sixtieth anniversary in show business. Many stars who had worked with or knew Coburn during his long career showed up (including Jane Wyman), and newspapers and magazines were flooded with photographs of the publicity-inspired event.

Ironically, Reagan, while making his most forgettable films, was earning more than he ever had, while sliding dramatically downward in his box-office appeal. He claims the caliber of the roles he was offered by producers was colored by his hard-hitting position as SAG president and negotiator, which implies the studios were taking their revenge on him for fighting for the rights of the SAG membership. But had Reagan felt strongly enough about his roles, he could have taken a suspension (as had Cagney, Davis, Bogart and Bacall, to name a few) rather than accept them.

Nor does his cry hold true that the studios typecast him. From 1950 to 1954, he chose many of the scripts in which he played. The parts were varied enough and included everything from a worried father (*Louisa*) to a Confederate cavalry officer (*The Last Outpost*) to a western marshal (*Law and Order*). Reagan had simply reached middle age, a state that ends more Hollywood careers than bad films do. The youthful glow had begun to leave his body. Lines were beginning to mark his face. If he had been a romantic figure like Cary Grant, or had the star appeal and acting ability of a James Stewart, Henry Fonda or Paul Newman (who at the same age was to make *Butch Cassidy and the Sundance Kid*), the freedom to have a say in the roles he played could have taken him from weakness to strength. He is right in placing the blame on his SAG activities, but not for the reasons he claimed.

When it came to choosing where his great passion rested, as an actor or as a negotiator-politician, there was no contest. If Reagan had done little to improve either his performances or the quality of his scripts before his association with the SAG, he did almost nothing in this area afterward. He needed money to maintain his life-style. Films offered him this and with MCA's clout he knew his chances for making large sums were good.

His old friend Sam Israel (Parsons's former publicity man) was working for Universal and was assigned as a press agent for *Louisa* (the Coburn shindig had been his idea). On March 8, 1950, he memoed the head of publicity, Al Horwits:

> A good idea would be to send Reagan on a tour to Dixon, Illinois and hold one of the premieres [of *Louisa*] there. Reagan once saved 76 [*sic*] natives from drowning and is the town's outstanding hero, also I was on an earlier tour there [with him] and know the coverage we will get. All of which is by way of suggesting that we might plan to hold at least a regional premiere in Dixon in conjunction with a local festival there in August [a three-day Indian Summer Fest]. Ronald is going there anyway,* and he tells me that Warners is trying to swing him behind one of their pictures. But he is at *outs* with Warners and would much prefer to do business with us.

This plan was set into motion in June. "[*Louisa*] must be sold by word of mouth and I propose that we engage in an extensive job of 'giving away samples' [personal appearances of stars at pre-

---

*Reagan had received an invitation to this festival the previous November when he was filming *Storm Warning*. No mention of sending Reagan to Dixon to promote a film (presumably *Storm Warning*) appears in the Warner Brothers publicity files.

mieres] throughout prime cities in the same manner in which other industries successfully use samplings to get favorable comment."

Reagan was therefore sent out on a public-appearance tour in August.* Al Horwits accompanied him on the train journey that took him from Los Angeles to Des Moines on August 14, then on to Clinton, Iowa; Omaha, Nebraska; and then down to Dixon (August 20–23), Denver and San Francisco; and back in time to appear with the film at the Los Angeles Orpheum on September 7. In each city he spoke to the press and said a few words from the stage of the theater in which *Louisa* was playing.

The trip home to Dixon was to be the high spot and he was looking forward to it. Because he was corresponding with Bill Thompson and knew the town had big plans, he arranged for Nelle to join him in Omaha, Nebraska. Reagan stood on the platform waiting for her. She looked tired, somehow smaller, as she greeted him. Al Horwits noted, "He grabbed her up and took her in his arms," then they boarded the train and mother and son continued on together to Dixon.

---

* *Louisa*, though made after it, was released before *Storm Warning*.

20

THE TOUR HAD TAKEN HIM BACK TO DES MOINES, where he was scheduled to crown an Iowa beauty "Miss Jaycee of 1950" at the Paramount Theatre after a "preview showing of 'Louisa.'" He arrived "all done up in cocoa brown suit and tie—which matched his complexion." He introduced red-haired Piper Laurie (who made her debut in the film as Reagan's daughter) with the remark, "They didn't tell me the girls were dressing." Laurie wore an emerald-green strapless gown, rhinestones massed and glittering at her neck and on her ears, and a silver-blue dyed-muskrat coat (the prize for the beauty-contest winner) flung *femme fatale*-style over one shoulder. Outside, the thermometer soared to 89 degrees, while the Paramount, filled to its two-thousand-seat capacity, had no air conditioning.

At the mike, Reagan spoke of the days when he broadcast daily from Radio WHO and of his prediction that Max Baer would defeat Joe Louis in a heavyweight boxing match. "So many memories pop up and have since I arrived that I have to watch out I don't just go on." Of course, he did and the audience appeared to love it.

"I have another home town," he admitted in closing. "Hollywood. I didn't take to it easy. But I have learned that show people make up a fair cross section of American life. I know that if you could get acquainted with Hollywood, you would find the people very fine and wonderful. They are not like the stories that get out."

When eighteen-year-old, blue-eyed, five-foot-two-inch Jackie Jay was declared Miss Jaycee, she hopped up on her toes and planted a kiss on his cheek. "Now that was what I was planning to do to you," he said with a wide grin.

He saw Myrtle Williams and whatever old friends remained at the radio station. The years had changed Des Moines. Wartime prosperity had pushed the city up and out and brought an influx of out-of-town workers. He had changed as well. In the 1930s, Des Moines had seemed sophisticated to him. It was in Des Moines that his dreams had been honed and he had tasted his first heady cocktail of fame and riches. Thomas Wolfe perhaps was right— one can't go home again. But the journey homeward did not end in Des Moines.

"There was quite a crowd at the station [Sunday morning, August 20]—the whole town had turned out to welcome Dutch and Nelle [home to Dixon]," Zelda Multz, the international president of the Ronald Reagan fan club, recalled. "Finally someone noticed the signals of an incoming train. The band played 'California Here I Come' and into sight came the streamliner *City of Los Angeles,* which made a special stop in Dixon to allow Ron and Nelle to detrain. Passengers aboard the train were quite amazed at the procedure. . . . Ron had a big grin on his face and was so excited, and . . . he sure was tan!"

A few moments later, the train had moved on and Reagan was given the key to the city by Dixon's Mayor Fred Hoffmann and Nelle was presented with a massive bouquet of flowers that she had difficulty in managing to hold without obscuring her vision.

Miss Multz remembered shaking hands with Reagan ("a firm grip!") and his "sort of cocking his head to the side, and saying in a very deep voice, 'Well, hello.'"

Bill Thompson drove Reagan and Nelle out to Hazelwood where they, the publicity staff and Miss Multz were to stay. Just about every store in town had Reagan's picture in the window. Banners were strung across the streets exclaiming WELCOME HOME DUTCH. This time there was no one with whom to share the glory. He was taken by the drugstore where he had once bought ice cream sundaes for Margaret Cleaver, past the house on

Hennepin Avenue (now in considerable disrepair) and the statue of Lincoln as a young soldier.

A harsh midday August sun bore down on the town as the first event of the day, the Horse Parade, got under way. Reagan, astride a handsome palomino, led the parade through town. He wore sunglasses, a yellow turtleneck sweater (the sleeves rolled up high to display his muscular biceps), tan breeches and well-worn knee-high boots and was the only hatless figure in the parade. At trail's end, Reagan's old friends from his Rock River lifeguard days had organized a barbecue buffet. A special table had been set up for him and Nelle, but he moved around the gathering, "playing the audience," as one observer noted.

The film was "premiered" yet again at three-thirty that afternoon. Reagan had not been scheduled to speak until after the showing, but the applause was so thundering after he was seen getting into his seat that he mounted the stage. "Such an experience for anyone," he exclaimed, "could only happen in America."

"A banquet was scheduled for Monday evening at the Masonic temple," Multz recalled. "In the large dining hall were eight or nine tables set up to seat about four hundred people. The pianist and vocalist hired for the occasion serenaded us with old-time songs, and suddenly, Nelle took the mike and joined them singing 'In the Good Old Summertime.' . . ." Multz was overwhelmed at the chance to be so near her idol. "Ron liked his food. . . . He takes a little cream in his coffee and half a teaspoonful of sugar—then just a little more. 'That's the story of my life,' he grinned. He laughed when he told a joke—and remembered so many of his friends, and when meeting their children would say, 'I used to throw your father across the river.'"

Reagan next attended the dedication of Dixon's first public swimming pool. "You must be a bunch of sissies," he exclaimed good-naturedly. "The river was good enough for the rest of us." He then surprised everyone by stripping to a pair of bright-red bathing trunks, handing his glasses to Nelle and swimming several laps.

Nelle was honored with a dinner at The First Christian Church (also attended by Reagan). She renewed her friendships, and even found time to give a Bible class. When they departed early Wednesday morning, she cried. Reagan, still grinning, held her close to him with one arm as they walked toward their train. With the other, he waved enthusiastically to the gathered crowd. With Nelle safely ensconced in her compartment by Al Horwits,

Reagan stood in the doorway of his car and continued waving until Dixon's North Western Station was lost from view.

Film people were tougher than they looked. They had survived innumerable scandals, the evolution of sound, the advent of radio, the Depression and a war. Pioneering greats like Warner and Mayer didn't scare easily. But in 1950, Americans owned more than five million television sets. Neighborhood theaters had closed by the hundreds with former box-office stars unable to draw audiences. Harry Cohn at Columbia said, "There's nothing wrong that good pictures and showmanship cannot cure." Jack Warner and Louis B. Mayer never admitted harboring fear, but both studios had cut back considerably in production.

"It is not the golden time [1950]," Bob Thomas observed. "The boom is long past. It is not the world that Hollywood would have chosen for itself. But the essential thing is survival, and it appears contrary to all consensuses, that Hollywood will survive."

George Cukor added wisely, "The secret of survival is not to panic and not to wilt . . . and not to ape the times when you feel you're not part of them. Just try and understand them and continue on your own feet . . . [in Hollywood] you need a great deal of character to withstand the way you're treated sometimes. With a successful picture you're good news. When you're not, people become rather offhand and casual."

Reagan did not fall into either category—success or failure. He was somewhere in the lower end of the great yawning inbetween. Despite Miss Multz's enthusiasm, he was not what the studios referred to as a hot property—a phrase which in 1950 would have applied to Marlon Brando (*The Men*) and Marilyn Monroe (*The Asphalt Jungle, All About Eve*). Television was squeezing out the second feature. Method theater had ushered in a new kind of film hero. Hollywood did not know what to do with the ones they had. Jerry Wald realized, sensibly, that Reagan's clean-cut appeal was too ingrained to change. Hollywood was in considerable confusion, and Reagan, as usual, had a few things to say about the current condition.

"Did you know there are 65,000,000 people who *don't* go to the movies with any degree of regularity?" he asked an interviewer for the *Chicago Tribune*. "Most of them are over 30 years of age. That's the group we need to bring back into theatres. We've been using the selling psychology of the carnival midway, whose sole object is to shill people into the shows and get their quarters. . . . Exhibitors could do a little experimenting. . . . Let them try shifting their showtime, for instance. The average American probably would like to go to theatres at 8:15 in the evening. But if he does, under the present system, he arrives right in the middle of a picture."

Reagan eventually got around to his own films. "I think we've got a good, solid picture in 'Louisa.' . . . I have 'Storm Warning' coming out at Warners. That's about the Ku Klux Klan. I'm doing 'Bedtime for Bonzo' in which 'I'll try to steal scenes from a chimpanzee. Then, after all these years, I finally snagged a western with Pine and Thomas. It's called 'The Last Outpost.' My screen career is in good shape." He did not feel that confident when he saw the first ad copy for *Storm Warning*. Ginger Rogers had received top billing.

As always, none of the films that he had on his agenda touched upon any issue that occupied any part of his life. Truman was halfway through his second term. The shadow of the Bomb hung over him and the Democrats. Postwar prosperity had peaked and deflated, and people blamed the Democrats for that as well. No Democrat running for office in 1950 had been a shoo-in. Senate races across the nation were particularly nasty. Smear campaigns were common, as television was used for the first time to sell or abuse a candidate. Red-baiting became a political sport, and Reagan's old friend Helen Gahagan Douglas kept getting caught on her opponent Richard Nixon's hook.

Nixon called the liberal Democrat "decidedly pink," then "pink shading into deep red." He toured the state with Pat Nixon in a station wagon equipped with a record player and a loudspeaker. He hoped that by having Douglas tagged a Communist (which she was not) he could win both the Democratic and the Republican primaries. "If he could win both," Douglas wrote in her autobiography, "he would be spared the need for an election. Murray Chotiner, his campaign manager who was introducing a personality-based, media-blitz campaign . . . sent out one piece of literature which was titled 'As One Democrat to Another.'"

Douglas's political career had continued to prosper since the HICCASP meeting five years earlier. "[Helen] had been dedicated heart and soul to the development of the Central Valley of California," Leo Goodman, who had worked for her in this campaign, said. "That was part of a campaign which actually started back with Abraham Lincoln to establish 'family farms' (small— under 240 acres as a rule) in this country. She and Sheridan Downey [who backed Douglas's opponent] clashed head on whether or not one supported the family farm as against the great big agricultural interests owning tens of thousands of acres."

No one knew much about Richard Nixon in 1950. He had been on the HUAC and in the House of Representatives (1946–50) and had been instrumental in bringing Alger Hiss to trial to be sentenced for perjury. But there was no real indication of the kind of campaign he would run. Goodman claimed Nixon had bales of hay thrown at Douglas when she spoke and that Murray Chotiner was the author of many similar humiliating tricks.

"It took the Watergate investigation to really go into it in depth [Nixon's alleged dirty tricks] and show how despicable it really was," Goodman explained. "Back then when you alleged these things, people would look at you. And, of course, there was the obfuscation there—The Pink Sheet [a list of Douglas's activities published on pink stock] . . . was, of course, the symbol, and how could you attack a Pink Sheet? She had a great attribute of picking a social issue and carrying it to the public, to the Congress, so that it would have a chance for consideration. As a matter of fact, when she lost in Congress, they didn't have too many like her."

Douglas's advisers felt what her campaign needed now were supporters who could command media attention and knew how to use the camera to their advantage. Reagan was asked for his support late in April, and he pledged it. He would later state that his switch to the Republican party did not come about until 1962, but in fact it took place during the Douglas-Nixon campaign. He might well have been registered as a Democrat, but his position was aligned with the Republican ticket.

Reagan was dating Nancy during the campaign. One night she took him with her to listen to a "particularly vicious" speech given by Zasu Pitts (campaigning for Nixon) on the subject of communism and Helen Gahagan Douglas. "The Pink Lady who would allow the Communists to take over our land and our homes as well."

Robert Cummings recalled that shortly after this date, "A telephone rang in the middle of the night. I was sound asleep. I had to film in the morning. Groggily, I picked up the receiver and someone said, 'It's Ronnie.'

"'Ronnie who?'

"'Ronnie *Reagan*. I'm trying to help a senator [Nixon] get elected and we're giving a party for *him* tomorrow night. Can you come?'

"I said, 'You know I'm not political, Ronnie.' And he answered, 'Couldn't you just come and be there anyway?'"

Neither Douglas nor her staff was ever aware that Reagan had quit in his support of her in favor of Nixon. The campaign had moved into its last and most vitriolic stages after he had gone on the road to promote *Louisa*. Douglas subsequently lost the election, but many Democrats working for her still assumed Reagan was with them. Reagan, in talking about his switch in parties, would refer to a time when he suddenly realized that most of the people he admired were Republicans. In fact, his closest friends had always been Republicans. With his father's and FDR's deaths, his own connections to the Democratic party had become increasingly tenuous. Since taking office as president of the Guild, he had moved closer and closer to the Republican philosophies. This is not to say that the SAG's battles, principles or decisions were motivated by the executive board's allegiance to any one party. On major issues, the membership had a vote and could and did overthrow propositions of their board. But during the Reagan years (1947–60), the board was overwhelmingly conservative. Reagan was a union leader, but this did not translate into meaning he was also a liberal. His stand on HUAC, on blacklisting, on the taking of a loyalty oath, and his constant preaching that the liberals were being duped by the Communists indicate his beliefs.

Between 1947 and 1960, of the more than two thousand men and women who were black- or graylisted, less than one hundred were ever proven to have any Communist connections.* A great many did contribute to charities and causes that also had Communist members. However, to sign the Amicus Curiae for the Hollywood Ten was to register a voice in a battle to sustain the Constitution, the First and Fifth Amendments having been grievously abused in their trials.

The dark cloud of McCarthyism did not appear until 1950. In the late forties, Joseph Raymond McCarthy was a new senator from Wisconsin. He studied engineering, nearly flunked his first-year courses and switched over to law, where he received the lowest grade in a course called Legal Ethics. Nonetheless, in 1940, at the age of thirty-two, he became a circuit judge. He fought with

---

*These figures are compiled by going through the many lists of supposed "travelers" or "fellow travelers" submitted by investigative agencies to the major studios. Those on the blacklist were denied work. Those on the graylist (meaning they had associations with those on the blacklist that made them suspect) were to a great extent denied work also. If those on the graylist were important to the economy of a studio, they stood a better chance of retaining their jobs than those who were not.

the marines during the war, rising to the rank of captain, and was elected to the Senate on the wave of returning servicemen who ran successful campaigns in 1946. For two years he remained resentfully obscure. Then, in 1948, he saw a way of making both money and a name for himself.

Aligning himself with Lustron, one of the giant manufacturers of prefabricated housing (McCarthy received ten thousand dollars cash, a twenty-thousand-dollar unsecured loan and payment of his steep gambling debts by lobbyists during this time), McCarthy went on the road to decry the false promises of public housing; his solution was veterans' loans to finance private prefabricated houses (sold by Lustron). He left no brick unturned to defame every public housing development he visited. After a trip to the 1,424-unit Rego Park Veterans' Housing Project in New York City [in early 1949], he pronounced the place "a breeding ground for Communism," and for the first time received national press coverage. Throughout the rest of the year McCarthy's name frequently appeared in the national press, almost always with a similar accusation.

One witness to McCarthy's rise wrote: "He was the master of the scabrous and the scatological. He understood the perverse appeal of the bum, the mucker, the dead-end kid, the James Jones–Nelson Algren hero to a nation . . . in which everyone was sliding, from one direction to another, into middle-class respectability. . . . He was a fighter who used his thumb, his teeth, and his knee. . . . Hitler discovered the uses of the Big Lie—the falsehood so large and round that reason, which deals in particulars, was almost powerless to combat it. McCarthy invented the Multiple Lie—the lie with so many particulars . . . that reason exhausted itself in the effort to combat it. He said so many different things about so many different people . . . that no one could keep it all in focus. . . . He brought to perfection a kind of shell game to be played with facts, or what George Orwell called 'unfacts' . . . and he knew how to get into the news even on those rare occasions when invention failed him and he had no unfacts to give out."

Another contemporary historian reported: "One night in January 1950, [McCarthy] dined with several acquaintances, including the dean of Georgetown University's foreign-service school, Father Edmund Walsh. McCarthy confessed to him that he needed an issue on which to base his reelection campaign, and Father Walsh suggested, 'How about Communism?'"

McCarthy was scheduled to give a speech over the Lincoln birthday weekend to three hundred members of a women's Republican club. As he stood staring out at the group assembled in the Colonnade Room at the McClure Hotel in Wheeling, West Virginia, "he suddenly brandished a sheet of paper which he contended bore the names of 205 known Communists working in the State Department. . . . Shortly after the Wheeling speech the cartoonist Herblock coined the term 'McCarthyism'—he wrote it in crude letters on a drawing of a bucket of mud. . . . The newspaper columnist Max Lerner took up the new coinage and spread it further." Clearly a term of opprobrium, McCarthy delighted nonetheless in the notoriety it brought him and would crow, "McCarthyism is Americanism with its sleeves rolled up."

Nancy Davis was a lively, attractive and intelligent companion. Unlike Jane Wyman, she was vitally interested in politics and listened with glazed, admiring eyes to Reagan's retelling of his day-to-day conflicts at the SAG. He has claimed he "did everything wrong, dating her off and on, continuing to volunteer for every Guild trip to New York—in short, doing everything which could have lost her. . . ." Nancy had no intention of being lost. The pride in her glance when they were together was not just a feminine wile. Nancy Davis was wholeheartedly in love. All the statements she had made and written about wanting a marriage above a career, of knowing when the important man came into her life, were now valid.

She did not complain when he chose Guild business over a date. She played no games, made no attempt to make him jealous or to pressure him into a proposal. *The Next Voice You Hear* had not made her a star. She was cast in *Night Into Morning,* a well-meaning but maudlin melodrama about a college professor (Ray Milland) who loses his wife and child in a fire and falls prey to alcoholism and attempted suicide. The film did not do well. Davis had then been given a cameo with Fredric March in *It's a Big Country,* an episodic film with guest appearances by many Metro stars. On September 7, 1951, she was told the last option on her three-year contract would not be picked up.

She and Reagan no longer frequented the nightclub circuit where he had originally taken her dancing. Most of their dates were spent at his apartment or at the homes of their mutual good friends, such as Bill and Ardis Holden. Ardis had been known on the screen as Brenda Marshall. A ravishing brunette with marvelously exotic eyes, she had walked away from a successful career as a leading lady in Warner A films to marry Holden.* She returned to make two more films, but in 1950 quit for good to devote herself to her family. William Holden was one of the friends Reagan has claimed to have much admired. The two men could not have come from more different backgrounds. Holden (real name William Franklin Beedle, Jr.) was the son of a wealthy family in the chemical business. He had lived a privileged life, traveled abroad with his family and attended Pasadena Junior College, where a Paramount talent scout spotted him in a school production and signed him to a film contract. At age twenty, with his first real screen role,† he became a star as the boxer-violinist hero in the film version of Clifford Odets's *Golden Boy*. In the years of his close Hollywood friendship with Reagan (1949–53), Holden had moved into the golden circle of film immortals with *Sunset Boulevard, Born Yesterday* and *Stalag 17* (for which he won the 1953 Best Actor Academy Award), and was well on his way to becoming a multimillionaire. Despite the differences in their backgrounds, Holden and Reagan had much in common personally—they liked horses and were wine connoisseurs. Holden was first vice-president of the SAG and they shared the same political philosophies. For that matter, Holden was born in O'Fallon, Illinois, and his parents were personal friends of the Walgreens.

Reagan had brought Holden into the "inner workings" of the SAG and, according to Jack Dales, had "made him an interested, active participant." But Holden's influence was greater on Reagan than the other way around. In his next few films, Reagan can be seen modeling his performances on those of Holden. He copied a trick Holden had of lighting a cigarette. He wore clothes that had a decided Holden look to them. He even aped Holden's raised-eyebrow cynical expression.

When *Louisa* was finally sent out into general release (October 24, 1950), the reviewers found it a "jovial little picture about a gloriously giddy romance between a pleasantly plump grandmother [Spring Byington] and a beamingly sixtyish swain [Charles Coburn]." Both *The New York Times* and the *New York Post* devoted almost two columns to the delights of the geriatrics in this film (which also featured Edmund Gwynn). Somewhere

---

*Brenda Marshall was perhaps best known for *Espionage Agent* (opposite Joel McCrea), *The Sea Hawk* (Errol Flynn) and *Whispering Smith* (Alan Ladd). She and Holden divorced in 1970.

†Holden had made two brief previous appearances as an extra.

around ten lines from the end of the reviews, Reagan is mentioned.*

Late in 1950, Reagan went into the Universal production of *Bedtime for Bonzo.*† Playing stooge to a chimpanzee was a losing battle. The film was referred to as "an animal starrer," and indeed, Bonzo held the camera for most of the action, either mugging away or getting psychology professor Reagan and his housekeeper, Diana Lynne, into complicated and humorous situations. ("They haven't a chance," wrote Abe Weiler in *The New York Times*, "Bonzo makes monkeys of them.") He had fared far worse under his Universal contract than at Warners, where reviewers might have ignored his performance in *The Hasty Heart* but the film at least had stature.‡ And when *Storm Warning* was finally released, his personal reviews had been good ("Reagan gives a splendid performance"), however mixed the critics felt about the melodramatic nature of the film.

He took out the disappointment he felt over the properties given to him by Universal on Warners. Warners had chosen a musical, *She's Working Her Way Through College,* as the second of Reagan's three-picture commitment. The Warners musical was an adaptation of *The Male Animal,* but the central role of the professor (played by Henry Fonda in the nonmusical film version) had been diminished to showcase Virginia Mayo as the burlesque star who decides to continue her education. Gene Nelson co-starred, and his spectacular acrobatic dancing and Mayo's bumps and grinds were almost stiffer competition than a ga-ga chimp.

"We had a rather feisty little director named Bruce Humberstone," Nelson recalled. "He liked to have his scapegoat on the set whom he would tease and make the brunt of his lame jokes. . . . I had to nail him one day because he was making some unnecessary remark . . . [another time] I'm bringing Virginia Mayo home [in a scene] and I'm kissing her good-night and then, suddenly the hall lights go on and there's Ron, the professor . . . now when Virginia Mayo came in they had lit for dark for a silhouette effect, and Bruce kept saying, 'Cut, let's do it again.' He'd never tell me why he wanted to do it again. Then he came over to

---

* "Ronald Reagan is amusingly befuddled as the lady's (Louisa's) anxious son-in-law." (*New York Times*, October 25, 1950.) "Ronald Reagan and Ruth Hussey have little to do except exclaim about the way Grandma is carrying on." (*New York Post*, October 25, 1950.)
† Reagan also made his television-acting debut in 1950 in an episode of CBS's *Airflyte Theater.*
‡ Richard Todd was nominated for the Best Actor Academy Award for his performance in *The Hasty Heart.*

me and he says, 'I can keep on retaking this as much as you want
if you give me a case of champagne.' That was not only juvenile it
was damned insulting to Virginia, and I got very angry. 'You
know, you're a pretty smart guy. You oughta be a director!' I
said. He was a real pain in the ass. . . ." Reagan had his problems
with Humberstone, which prompted Jack Warner to send him one
of his habitual telegrams:

IT IS OUR UNDERSTANDING THAT YOU HAVE STATED TO
THE DIRECTOR [H. Bruce Humberstone] OF THE MOTION
PICTURE—QUOTE—SHE'S WORKING HER WAY THROUGH
COLLEGE—UNQUOTE—THAT YOU WILL NOT WEAR THE
TYPE OF WARDROBE DEEMED NECESSARY TO PROPERLY
CHARACTERIZE THE ROLE YOU ARE PORTRAYING . . . NOR
WILL YOU COMPLY WITH SAID DIRECTOR'S REQUEST THAT
YOU WEAR . . . GLASSES TO CHARACTERIZE YOUR SAID
ROLE STOP WE DESIRE TO CALL YOUR ATTENTION TO THE
FACT THAT YOUR CONTRACT WITH US PROVIDES AMONG
OTHER THINGS THAT YOU WILL ACT, POSE, SPEAK OR OTH-
ERWISE APPEAR AND PERFORM AS REQUESTED BY US AND
YOUR FAILURE TO COMPLY WITH THE REQUESTS AND DI-
RECTIONS OF THE DIRECTOR IS NOT IN COMPLIANCE WITH
YOUR OBLIGATION TO US . . . YOUR FAILURE [to comply]
SHALL NECESSITATE THE SUBSTITUTION OF ANOTHER ART-
IST TO PORTRAY THE ROLE YOU ARE NOW PORTRAYING
. . . AND WE SHALL HOLD YOU ACCOUNTABLE FOR ALL
DAMAGES, COSTS AND EXPENSES SUFFERED BY US IN CON-
NECTION WITH THE ENTIRE PRODUCTION OF "SHE'S
WORKING HER WAY THROUGH COLLEGE."

Reagan wired back:

YOUR TELEGRAM PURPORTING TO RECOUNT MY ACTIONS
TOWARDS THE DIRECTOR OF YOUR PHOTOPLAY "SHE'S
WORKING HER WAY THROUGH COLLEGE" IS A MISSTATE-
MENT OF THE FACTS STOP ALTHOUGH I DID ENGAGE IN
CONVERSATION WITH THE DIRECTOR REFERABLE TO AT-
TIRE TO BE WORN BY ME SUCH WAS A MERE FERVENT AP-
PEAL OCCASIONED BY MY ENTHUSIASM FOR A REALISTIC
INTERPRETATION OF MY ROLE AND WAS NOT NOR WAS IT
INTENDED TO BE A REFUSAL TO COMPLY WITH ANY REA-
SONABLE REQUIREMENT MADE BY YOU OR YOUR DIREC-

TOR. I HAVE COMPLIED WITH ALL MY OBLIGATIONS UN-
DER MY CONTRACT AND SHALL CONTINUE TO DO SO.
RONALD REAGAN.

Reagan wrote in his autobiography that he decided not to send
his reply, and that he called Warner the next day and said, "Jack,
when I got your wire last night I felt pretty foolish. We've been
together thirteen years and something is awfully wrong if we start
sending telegrams to each other. I've done a lot of things for
which I'm sorry and I want you to know there won't be any
more." However, the above original telegram is in the legal files of
the Warner Brothers archives, so Reagan must have sent it.

Reagan's private life appeared to be doing better than his reel
life. In March 1951, he dissolved the Northridge Horse Farm and
bought 290 acres in Malibu Canyon to use as a horse breeding farm
which he named "Yearling Row Ranch" (a name that would appear, curiously enough, to combine Jane Wyman's film *The Yearling*
with his own *Kings Row*). A portion of the eighty-five-thousand-
dollar initial cost of acquiring the property had come from the sale of
the old farm and several horses.* He kept Baby, whom he was now
breeding. Reagan named the first foal born at Yearling Row Ranch
"Nancy D."

His relationship with Nancy had shifted into a more serious
commitment. Despite the problems and disappointments she was
experiencing in her own career, Nancy was always cheerful, always supportive of Reagan and always more concerned about his
trials than her own. People like the Holdens and the Scharys felt
she considered his career of greater importance than her own. She
commented that the studios were purposefully placing him in demeaning situations and that "Marlon Brando got all the good
scripts." She was equally sympathetic over his problems at the
SAG. Jack Dales recalled that she was "quiet, very quiet" at the
meetings. The minutes have almost no mention of her name, except in acknowledging her attendance or when she seconded a
resolution Reagan had instigated. Another SAG staff member
said, "I don't know how she got reelected. I suspect the board did
it as a favor to Reagan. People *REALLY* hated her, thought she
was nasty. I literally never heard anyone say anything nice about
her. But also I have never heard anyone say anything substantive
about her. She came across like a nasty ditz. . . . I never saw her

*See page 440 for the financial questions raised by this purchase.

do anything at the Guild other than sit at meetings and ogle Reagan. She would just—sit." Other board members recalled her "rapt attention" when Reagan spoke. Reagan was speaking out and writing articles at a prolific rate, all of an anti-Communist nature. Since he was the SAG president, these public statements appeared to be Guild policy as well.*

One of the gravest issues the Guild had to deal with was the blacklist. Gale Sondergaard, one of the great character actresses in films, known for the mysterious and evil women she portrayed (*The Letter, Spider Woman*), was subpoenaed to appear before HUAC on March 21, 1951, following her husband director-writer Herbert Biberman's conviction as one of the Hollywood Ten. Sondergaard had always been active in the SAG, and on March 13 she wrote Reagan and the board members:

> I am addressing you . . . not only as the directors of our union, but also as fellow actors. I am addressing you because I have been subpoenaed, together with other members of our union, before the Un-American Activities Committee. I will appear next Wednesday.
>
> I would be naïve if I did not recognize that there is a danger that by the following day I may have arrived at the end of my career as a motion picture actress. . . .

---

*On January 22, 1951, Reagan published a two-thousand-word article in the magazine *Fortnight* titled "How Do You Fight Communism?" In it he stated: ". . . we know how the Communists have sought to infiltrate and control certain key industries. We know they operate with a 1% minority but depend on organization. At meetings they 'come early and stay late' and they get confused 'liberals' to front for them at all times. . . .

"The real fight with this new totalitarianism belongs properly to the forces of liberal democracy, just as did the battle with Hitler's totalitarianism. There really is no difference except in the cast of characters. On one hand is our belief that the people can and will decide what is best for themselves, and on the other (Communist, Nazi or Fascist) side is the belief that a 'few' can best decide what is good for all the rest. . . .

"The Congressional Committee accuses the industry of employing Communists—but several elected members of Congress are known Communists and the law says no employer can even question an employe [*sic*] as to his political beliefs. The Taft-Hartley law says every union official must sign a 'non-Communist' oath, but the same law says 'no union can expel a member and keep him from working as long as he pays his dues.' . . .

"A small group (about ten) of us in an independent political organization here in Hollywood a few years ago proposed an anti-Communist statement of policy. We did it to (as we naively put it) smoke out some suspected board members. . . .

". . . suppose we quit using the words Communist and Communism? They are a hoax perpetrated by the Russian Government to aid in securing fifth columnists in other countries and to mask Russian aggression aimed at world conquest. Every time we make the issue one of Communism as a political philosophy we help in this hoax. Substitute 'Pro-Russian' for the word Communist and watch the confusion disappear. Then you can say to any American . . . the so-called 'Communist party' is nothing more or less than a 'Russian-American Bund' owing allegiance to Russia and supporting Russia in its plan to conquer the world."

Surely it is not necessary for me to say to this Board that I love my profession and that I have tried to bring to it honesty of feeling, clarity of thought and a real devotion. Surely it is also unnecessary for me to state that I consider myself a deeply loyal American with genuine concern for the welfare and peace of my own countrymen and all humanity. . . .

I believe in freedom of speech and religion and association as described in our First Amendment. Unfortunately, our present Supreme Court has not seen fit to spell out its legal availability to us in our own days. But it has done so in respect to the oldest right of the individual in recorded history—the right of silence—the right under the Fifth Amendment.

I intend to avail myself of this right before the committee.

Many Guild members called before the Committee will not agree with my choice. They will take other roads looking to their protection from the attacks, insinuations, and sneers of the Committee. But surely no one will believe that the economic well being of our members or the security of our union or the welfare of the industry is being served by the Committee.

I must earnestly and fraternally ask the Board to consider the implications of the forthcoming hearing. A blacklist already exists. It may now be widened. It may ultimately be extended to include any freedom-loving non-conformist or any member of a particular race or any member of a union— or anyone. . . .

For my own security—for the security of all our members, I ask our Board to weigh this hearing carefully—to determine whether it can afford to witness its approach with passivity.

. . . I most especially appeal to the Board, to my fellow actors, to consider whether it will not be proper and necessary for it to make a public declaration that it will not tolerate any industry blacklist. . . . I can find no reason in my conduct as an actress or union member why I should have to contemplate a severing of the main artery of my life—my career as a performer—because I hold to views for which during the last war I was an esteemed member of the Victory Committee and the recipient of the thanks of my government, industry and union. . . .

In an unprecedented action, Sondergaard published this letter as a paid advertisement in *Variety*. The SAG was forced to reply publicly. A special meeting was called, although only a small number of board members attended, presumably because of the short notice given (a matter of a day). The Guild's position was discussed, a course agreed. Jack Dales drafted a letter based on the board's decision. Reagan and Holden approved, and the letter addressed to Gale Sondergaard was published in *The Hollywood Reporter* on March 20.

> The Board of Directors of the Screen Actors Guild has received and carefully considered your letter of March 13th which you saw fit also to publish in the press. The Guild's answer should be equally available to the public and will be published.
>
> Your letter (1) attacks as an inquisition the pending hearings by the House Committee on Un-American Activities into alleged Communist Party activities by a few individuals and (2) asks that the Guild protect you against any consequences of your own personal decisions and actions.
>
> The Communist Party press also has attacked the hearings as a "warmongering, labor and freedom-busting . . . witch-hunt . . . by Congressional inquisitors." The Guild Board totally rejects this quoted typical Communist Party line. We recognize its obvious purposes of attempting to smear the hearings in advance and to create disrespect for the American form of government.
>
> The deadly seriousness of the international situation dictates the tone of our reply. This is not the time for dialectic fencing. Like the overwhelming majority of the American people, we believe that a "clear and present danger" to our nation exists. The Guild Board believes that all participants in the international Communist Party conspiracy against our nation should be exposed for what they are—enemies of our country and of our form of government.
>
> It is not the province of the Guild Board to decide what is the best method of carrying out this aim. It is our hope that the current House Committee hearings will help to do so, in an objective and intelligent manner. We are informed that the Committee will guard against smearing of any innocent individuals. We will watch with extreme interest the way in which the hearings are conducted and any and all developments stemming therefrom.
>
> The Guild as a labor union will fight against any secret blacklist created by any group of employers. On the other

hand, if any actor by his own actions outside of union activities has so offended American public opinion that he has
made himself unsaleable [*sic*] at the box office, the Guild cannot and would not want to force any employer to hire him.
That is the individual actor's personal responsibility and it
cannot be shifted to this union.

(Signed) BOARD OF DIRECTORS
SCREEN ACTORS GUILD

Gale Sondergaard took the Fifth Amendment when she appeared before the committee. Her husband had been sentenced to
six months in jail for his silence. Sondergaard had all her existing
contracts canceled and was denied work for more than fifteen
years.

"I think . . . it will do no good to search for villains or heroes
or saints or devils," wrote another member of the Hollywood Ten,
Dalton Trumbo. ". . . There were none; there were only victims.
Some suffered less than others, some grew and some diminished,
but in the final tally we were *all* victims because almost without
exception each of us felt compelled to say things he did not want
to say, to do things he did not want to do, to deliver and receive
wounds he truly did not want to exchange. That is why none of
us—right, left or center—emerged from that long nightmare without sin."

The last film Reagan made for Warners, *The Winning Team*,
was exactly the kind he had always pleaded Jack Warner to give
him. He portrayed Grover Cleveland Alexander, one of baseball's
immortals. Doris Day, as his wife, received top billing, but the
film, for what it was worth, was Reagan's from start to end, and
gave him a chance to work with some baseball greats. For three
weeks before shooting he had studied daily with Detroit's Jerry
Priddy and Cleveland's Bob Lemon to learn the difference between "throwing from the mound and just throwing."

Grover Alexander had not only been a heavy drinker but had
suffered epileptic seizures. Recalling the dismal failure of *Night
Unto Night*, where Reagan also played an epileptic, Warners
dropped the illness from the script but unfortunately did not alter
it enough for the audience to understand Alexander's problem. As
a result, despite Reagan's and Day's down-home performances,
the story was unbelievable.

When Reagan left the Warner lot on January 28, 1952, for the last time, after fifteen years, there was no gold-watch presentation, no party, not even a word of good-bye from Jack Warner. Reagan's final check was to be sent to him. He left at noon. By two P.M. his name had been removed from his permanent parking place.

21

"HE TELEPHONED ONCE WHEN WE WERE [IN Scottsdale] and asked me for Dr. Loyal Davis and I said who wants to speak to him and he said Ronald Reagan," Edith Luckett Davis recalled of a night in late February 1952. "I thought what the hell's he doing calling Loyal? I didn't know what it was for. I said, 'Just a moment.' I went in and said to Loyal, 'Ronald Reagan wants to speak to you.' And he said, 'Me?' And I said, 'Get to that phone 'cause I want to know what he wants.' Anyway, Loyal went to the phone. He said, 'That's interesting. Are you sure you can? Yes.' And they talked. [After he hung up] Loyal said to me, 'He wants to marry Nancy.' And I said, 'Oh, go on!' He said, 'No, I'm not kidding. He wants to marry Nancy.' And I said, 'That's very exciting, very exciting.'

"Then [Nancy called] and I said, 'Why in hell is that man calling your father for this?' And she said, 'We want to get married, but don't want to marry unless you and Daddy want me to.' And I said, 'Of course. If he's a nice guy and you like him, then I'm sure he's all right.' And she said, 'He is, you'll love him.' And

I said, 'Find out what you want for a wedding present. It can't be extravagant, but I want you to have what you want.' She called back [in a little while] and said, 'I'll tell you what we want. We want a camera that can take moving pictures and a screen that we can show them on, and that's all we want.' And I said, 'Sold.'"

The next day, February 24, an announcement was sent to the press. They were married eight days later, March 4, 1952, by the Reverend John H. Wells at the Little Brown Church in the San Fernando Valley with Bill and Ardis Holden as best man and matron of honor. The ceremony was simple. Nancy wore a plain gray wool suit with a white collar and a small veiled flowered hat that fit close to her head. The press had not been informed and the story had not leaked. After the ceremony, the wedding party drove to the Holdens' home at nearby Toluca Lake where Mrs. Holden had ordered a cake and hired a photographer to take wedding pictures. They spent their first married days at the old Mission Inn at Riverside, California, which Reagan had discovered during the filming of *Storm Warning*. From there they went to Phoenix, Arizona, where Loyal and Edith drove from Scottsdale to meet their new son-in-law. "Meeting . . . the doctor, wasn't the easiest moment I ever had," Reagan later admitted. But the two men got on well. In a very short time, they realized they had more than Nancy in common. Davis was a political man who had always lived a bit vicariously in the theatrical lives of Edith's friends, and no one could help liking Edith immediately because of her easy manner and warm personality. Even so, the saltiness of Edith's tongue took somewhat longer for Reagan to be at ease with.

"I'm always being told [by Nancy and Reagan] to watch my language," Edith laughed. "I guess no one had to remind Nelle Reagan."

With Nancy having been on her own for ten years, asking for parental approval to marry had seemed odd, even to Edith. Her parents had heard she was dating Reagan, but since Nancy had not said anything about him to them during the two years of their courtship, they had not given him much thought. Reagan has said he got the idea during a SAG meeting and slipped a note to Holden. "To hell with this, how would you like to be the best man when I marry Nancy?" Holden had blurted out loud, "It's about time." Eight weeks after the wedding the Reagans announced that they were expecting a baby. A few weeks later it became self-evident.

They moved into Nancy's apartment in Brentwood not far from Zasu Pitts while they looked for a house suitable for a growing family. Reagan did not give up the Londonderry flat until they occupied their first home at 1258 Amalfi Drive in Pacific Palisades (five miles west of Brentwood and only a short drive from Yearling Row Ranch). The seven-room two-story frame house, with rambling roses and bay windows, looked like a builder's rendering of an idealized, clichéd honeymoon cottage. The most distinctive feature of the house was its very ordinariness, hemmed in as it was driveway to driveway with houses on either side of its flat well-manicured frontage. Inside, the rooms were generous (the living room was twenty-five feet by twenty-three feet) and light. Bow windows faced the front, and sliding glass doors led to a rear bricked terrace. There were three bedrooms and a bath upstairs. A bath also adjoined the downstairs den, so that room, in the front of the house, was converted into a nursery.

Missing from the Amalfi Drive house—perhaps with intent— were the glamour, cachet and spectacular views of the places in which Reagan and Wyman had lived. But Pacific Palisades offered untrafficked, wide residential streets, a minimum of smog and was only a short drive to the ocean. With the escalation in prices of Beverly Hills real estate, the Palisades was becoming increasingly popular with upwardly mobile, young film stars (Arlene Dahl and her husband, Fernando Lamas, lived six streets away). The Reagans paid approximately twenty-three thousand dollars, for the house.* A comparable house in Beverly Hills would have been at least double that figure. Nancy was a practical woman; she did not want her husband to have any more financial pressures than necessary. She had at least temporarily retired, and her husband's career was in low gear. Not only had he made his last film on his Warners contract but two weeks earlier had been informed that the third and fourth film commitments on his Universal contract had been canceled. A studio board meeting had been held on January 15, 1952, at which the following memo from the legal department was discussed:

Matters to Review—Ronald Reagan
Expiration of 2nd year of five year contract. This is a multiple picture contract covering five pictures to be made in the five year period, one of which is to be in technicolor, at the

---

* By 1986, a similar house in Pacific Palisades would be worth many, many times that price.

rate of $7,500 per week, ten week guarantee, plus two free weeks [for retakes] in connection with each picture. He rendered services in "Louisa" and "Bedtime for Bonzo." We have exercised our right to terminate the third and fourth employment periods by reason of his refusal to render services in "Fine Day" and "Just Across the Street," respectively.*

When he married Nancy, Reagan had only the commitment to do one more film at Universal. He doubted his wisdom in turning down the ones the studio had sent him earlier, even though he and Nancy had decided he should not accept second-rate material. He talked to Lew Wasserman about the possibility of reactivating his Universal contract, which was easier said than done. He now had two families that would require his support. Jane had been nominated for an Academy Award for her performance in *The Blue Veil*† and had signed a new multimillion-dollar contract, so there was no danger that Michael and Maureen would be in need. But Reagan's background decreed a man must take care of his children. Then there was Nancy, the baby that was due, the house and the high upkeep of Yearling Row Ranch.

The outdoor drama for Pine and Thomas‡ he had so fiercely wanted to make when he lost *Ghost Mountain* had turned up in general release as *The Last Outpost,* an unimaginative epic of the Santa Fe Trail with Reagan in a stereotyped role of a good-fellow Confederate cavalry captain whose brother (Bruce Bennett) is a Union colonel. The script was "rambling, obscure." Reagan rode well and there was lots of action in the last fifteen minutes of the film, too late to save the film from being "an awful lot of talk-talk-talk." Pine and Thomas now offered him a turgid drama titled *Hong Kong.* Despite his and Nancy's decision that he should not make any film he knew was less than good, with Universal still being uncooperative, he agreed to go ahead, but the salary he was paid—forty-five thousand dollars (less MCA's 10 percent commission)—fell a good deal short of the money he had been receiving.

But before filming started, and as a favor to Pine and Thomas,

---

* *Fine Day* was released as *Steel Town.* Both of these scripts were filmed with John Lund in the roles refused by Reagan.

† The award went to Vivien Leigh for *A Streetcar Named Desire.*

‡ William Pine and William Thomas, who produced numerous low-budget films. *The Last Outpost* was released April 8, 1951, for Paramount.

he went into their production of *Tropic Zone*, a Western trans-
planted to a tropical banana-growing country in Central America.
Reagan was a banana expert illegally in fictional Puerto Barran-
cas to avoid political trouble in a neighboring country. Rhonda
Fleming is a banana-farm owner he risks his life to save from ruin
and the skullduggery of villain Grant Withers. The film was "a
pulp fiction affair" and ironically ended up as the second feature
to the William Holden film *The Turning Point* in many theaters.

Hong Kong (*The New York Times* asked in its review, "or was it
Ping-Pong") had Reagan as an ex-GI drifter ("played in his solid
citizen style") who finds himself in charge of a fatherless five-year-
old Chinese boy (Danny Chang). The boy has in his possession a
jeweled idol obviously of great value. Reagan plans to sell the
statue to crooked art dealers and desert the boy, but his better
nature and the child's beguiling personality save the day. The boy
is kidnapped and Reagan battles the law and the crooks to get
him back—which he does—and gets a mission schoolteacher
(Rhonda Fleming) in the bargain.

Prospects were not hopeful. Reagan was forty-four years old,
not an age to suddenly become a John Wayne or a Bill Holden.
He had appeared in forty-five films. Superstardom looked as if it
would always be beyond his grasp. He threw himself into his work
at the SAG while putting the pressure on Art Parks at MCA to
"bring the money" (meaning a paying job).

The juxtapositions in Reagan's life were difficult to place in
perspective. At the same time that he was appearing in films that
were often inane and sometimes worse, having to rattle off dialogue to a chimpanzee, an Indian chief (who spoke no English)
and a five-year-old Chinese boy (with a minuscule vocabulary),
he was debating technical and controversial issues on which the
lives of many thousands of people were balanced. He had also
begun to be invited to give lectures and commencement addresses.
In June 1952, he received a standing ovation from the graduating
class of William Woods College in Fulton, Missouri (a Christian
Church school). His impassioned speech, entitled "America the
Beautiful," was perhaps the only time he would come close to
anything like poetic language. In it he revealed his view of America and his philosophy as an American.* The speech owed much
to Lincoln, much to Will Rogers and much to Louis B. Mayer
("momism," the theme of many Mayer films, was strongly em-

---

*See Excerpts from Speeches, page 539.

phasized). He could not have helped but feel that his potential had never been realized, that the power and charisma he exuded in his SAG dealings and in his speech givings should have been transferred to his image on film.

Jack Dales has said Reagan was an ardent and inspired worker in 1951 and early 1952. The SAG were still in constant negotiation over the television contracts. The blacklisting of members had caused bitter disputes. "He wouldn't get discouraged," Dales insisted. "He would suffer as we all did . . . but, no, he didn't get discouraged. He was always seeking, always seeking, and he didn't necessarily expect to come up with the answers himself. But he would come in, and he would have a dozen different ideas: 'What do you think about this?' 'Have we ever tried this?' Now where he got them from I don't know. Whether he thought them up or whether in the days between times that we would meet he'd talk to other people . . . he was always exploring, and then he would listen most attentively to our reactions to those suggestions . . . he would take criticism very well. I would say, 'That just won't play . . . for these reasons.'

" 'I understand that. Never thought of that.' He wouldn't fight it."

One issue had commanded a great deal of his attention in the early months of 1952. "We [SAG] were fighting for [television] jurisdiction but nothing was going to happen in that jurisdiction," Dales explained. "It was all live, the networks and the advertising agencies controlled television, and we wanted to hold television here, and no studio at that time would touch it [television production] . . . television was their enemy . . . I'm sure they believed that. I'm sure Frank Freeman [Paramount], Eddie Mannix [MGM], Ben Kahane [Columbia] really believed that television had the threat of knocking their studios out of the box, at that time they believed it. And nobody was making product for television.

"So [MCA] came to us [Reagan and the board] and said, 'Do you know what's happening? It's all going to New York. Your membership is going to be a New York membership. Your guys here are not going to get a whiff of it,' which we already knew. [They said] the only reason they brought it [a proposition for MCA to produce television films] to us was that 'We would like to do it [bring television production to Hollywood]. We'd like to go into it, and we'll guarantee to make lots of filmed television *if* you can work it out with us as an agent.' "

That was a shocking proposition for MCA, or any theatrical agency, to make because it was against the SAG bylaws to accept an agent (who took 10 percent of a member's earnings to represent them) as the producer or hiring company.

"Well, we were shocked of course . . . but we thought about it . . . the deal that we made . . . they could not charge their own clients any commission; if they ever put their client in a picture made by them, he had to get the highest salary he'd ever gotten in any picture in his life. It was just loaded with that kind of thing. We were scared that we were going to lose television, and that's the way it started [a waiver that allowed MCA, a talent agency, to become a hiring company]."

Dales called an emergency meeting of the board to consider this flagrantly monopolistic proposition on the night of July 14, 1952. Reagan and six other board members were present. After a lengthy debate, the group signed a blanket waiver stating that MCA could engage in television production and still represent clients.* Occasionally a very limited waiver had been granted by the SAG to talent agencies wishing to produce motion pictures. The MCA "special agreement" for television production was unprecedented.

The minutes of the July 14, 1952, board meeting state: "MCA is hesitant about signing the basic television contract without some sort of assurance that the Guild will not thereafter adopt agency regulations which would prohibit their continuance in both fields. Further meetings were held with Laurence W. Beilenson, representing Revue Productions, and an agreement was reached which permits MCA to enter and remain in the field of

---

*Negotiations had begun on June 6, 1952, between the SAG and MCA. The minutes for that date record: "On Friday 6/6/52 a meeting was held with Laurence Beilenson who represents MCA Artists, Ltd. which is now producing TV presentations under the name Revue Productions, Inc. Mr. Beilenson felt that it might be possible for them to work out a formula with the Guild which would break the deadlock in present negotiations." The week of June 13, 1952, the minutes include the information: ". . . discussions were held with Revue Productions which is in the rather peculiar position of being on both sides of the fence inasmuch as they are agents for actors as well as being producers." On June 30, 1952, there was "further discussion with Mr. Beilenson, representing Revue Productions, who stated that if a deadlock exists, they would still be willing to help break it. In connection with the negotiations with Revue [the proposed waiver] it was pointed out that this is a wholly-owned subsidiary of MCA and that the pattern of agents' interest in production in television, as in the radio field, is well established. Consequently, it appears desirable to recognize the right of agents to engage in TV film production and package show operation, subject to reasonable regulation by the Guild."

The Screen Actors Guild had been one of Beilenson's clients from its inception to his resignation as general counsel in 1949. He had, however, been in the United States Army from early 1942 to 1946. During his absence, his law firm, Beilenson & Berger, represented the SAG.

film television during the life of the present Agency Regulations but prohibits them charging commission to any of their clients who appear in their television films."*

Ten years later, on February 5, 1962, Reagan was called before a Los Angeles federal grand jury to testify in the United States Department of Justice's investigation of MCA's alleged monopolistic practices and the possibility of Reagan and the six other board members having received bribe money or (in the case of the actors) promises of future jobs in television.

"I must tell you," Reagan testified, "that I always told Jack Dales . . . that I felt a little self-conscious about that [the waiver] lest there might ever be a misunderstanding with MCA and sometimes I kind of ran for cover and was very happy to duck a committee duty in these matters."

"Because of the possibility of some conflict of interest that might arise?" the Justice Department attorney, John Fricano, asked.

"That's right," Reagan replied. He added that he had been in favor of the waiver since he felt MCA "filled a great gap in giving employment at a time when unemployment was quite heavy."

> FRICANO: Why then, Mr. Reagan, was Music Corporation of America the only talent company ever issued such a blanket waiver?
>
> REAGAN: Well, that is very easy to recall. . . . We felt we were amply protecting, that if any harm started from this, if anything happened to react against the actors' interest— we could always pull the rug out from under them [MCA]. No great harm would be done before we could ride to the rescue, that our feeling was here was someone that wanted to give actors jobs. . . .
>
> FRICANO: Do you know whether any talent agents applied for blanket waivers subsequent to the time SAG granted one to MCA?
>
> REAGAN: No, I don't.

---

*Reagan was present at these private meetings with Beilenson. William Holden was in Europe filming. Walter Pidgeon met with Reagan, Dales and Beilenson in his absence. Beilenson wrote the author: "At the time of the waiver to MCA, about which you inquire, I had long since ceased to represent the Guild. When MCA asked me to represent it, I accepted on condition that I would not represent MCA in any negotiation with Screen Actors Guild or with any other labor union. Hence, I took no part in the waiver." His name does appear, however, in the minutes of the July 14, 1952, meeting as having met with the SAG's negotiating team on behalf of MCA.

FRICANO: Did Screen Actors Guild attempt to induce agents to enter TV film production subsequent to the time it granted a blanket waiver to MCA?

REAGAN: No, I don't think we ever went out and asked anyone to do that.

FRICANO: That would be consistent with the rationale behind the granting of a blanket waiver, would it not?

REAGAN: No, I don't think the Screen Actors Guild is an employment agency. I think we can well recognize our not putting out blocks in the way of anyone who wanted to produce but I don't think ours was the point of trying to go out to get someone to produce.

FRICANO: In other words, [had] the blanket waiver been asked by talent agents subsequent to 1952 in July when SAG granted the blanket waiver to MCA, such requests would have been considered by the Guild and granted, correct?

REAGAN: If all of the circumstances were the same as, they would be.

Fricano paused dramatically, crossed to the government table, picked up an envelope, and then slowly walked back with it to Reagan.

FRICANO: Did you ever hear it said, Mr. Reagan, that [the] Screen Actors Guild granted a blanket waiver to MCA due to the fact that MCA was willing to grant repayment for reuse of TV films to actors [one of the basic conditions Reagan and the SAG negotiating team were fighting for in their producer-actor contract]?

REAGAN: No sir.

Fricano withdrew a paper from inside the envelope, and read into the record the contents of a letter from Laurence Beilenson to Lew Wasserman which included the statement, "The waiver was executed under a specific set of circumstances where Revue [the name of MCA's production company] was willing to sign a contract giving the Guild members reuse fees when no one else was willing to do so." (Beilenson appears to have been pressing Wasserman to uphold the agreement.)

Fricano stared up at Reagan, waiting.

REAGAN: Well, then I was wrong, but, and I can understand
that, but I certainly, I am afraid when I answered before
that I was under the impression you were trying to make
out that in negotiating a contract we made this as a bargaining point of giving a waver.

FRICANO: Isn't it conceived from this language?

REAGAN: Mr. Beilenson is a lawyer and in charge of negotiations. It's quite conceivable then if he says it in this letter.

FRICANO: Does that refresh your recollection, sir?

REAGAN: I don't recall it, no . . . I don't honestly recall. You
know something? You keep saying 1952 in the summer. I
think maybe one of the reasons I don't recall was because
I feel that in the summer of 1952 I was up in Glacier National Park making a cowboy picture for RKO, Ben
Bogeaus Productions, so it's very possible there were some
things going on that I would not participate in, but I have
no recollection of this particularly* . . . I can only say this.
That in all of my years with the Screen Actors Guild I
have never known of or participated in anything, nor has
the Guild, that ever was based on anything but what we
honestly believed was for the best interest of the actor,
and, however it may look now as to the point of private
negotiations or anything else . . .

In view of what is shown in Mr. Beilenson's letter, it is
very possible at that time, in spite of my not remembering,
it is very possible that we saw an opportunity to break the
solid back of the motion picture industry with regard to
(TV return) residuals and if we saw that kind of thing we
moved in . . .

The 1952 deal with the SAG, undoubtedly won with the help
of Reagan's position within the SAG, made MCA the only company that operated as a talent agency, a producer and a selling
agent. "The deal vaulted MCA to the head of the television industry with advantages that its competitors could never hope to equal
. . . with the granting of the waiver," a Justice Department memo
explained, "the battle [among the Hollywood talent agencies]
took on a one-sided aspect. Since MCA had the rights to as many

---

*Reagan is referring to *Cattle Queen of Montana*, produced by Benedict Bogeaus and starring
Barbara Stanwyck and him. He is faulty in his memory (the statement was made in the
summer of 1962). The film was shot in early summer *1954*, not 1952, and released in
January 1955.

television shows as it wanted, it could also guarantee [its] talent worked in television. Therefore, the talent left the other talent agencies in droves. . . . The central fact of MCA's whole rise to power . . . was undoubtedly the [SAG] blanket waiver."

Insinuations beleaguered Reagan from the time the waiver became public. Did he or did he not receive money or a career boost in exchange for his work in the SAG-MCA dealings? No substantiating proof appears in the six-thousand-page transcript of the Justice Department's investigation into MCA's monopolistic practices, nor in the subsequent Internal Revenue investigation. But certain questions remain unanswered.

Reagan's career and his income took a sharp decline in July 1952. The only chance he had to bounce back and cover his expenses was to get MCA to reactivate his contract with Universal, for nowhere else could he get seventy-five thousand dollars for a film. And, indeed, in January 1953 he was cast by Universal in *Law and Order*, a low-budget Western that co-starred Dorothy Malone and Preston Foster. Reagan played a retired lawman who takes up ranching and then runs into an old enemy-outlaw (Preston Foster) in Cottonwood, Arizona. The citizens and his sweetheart (Dorothy Malone) press Reagan into taking on the task of marshal to clean up the town. His last task as a lawman is to bring in his own brother for murder. Reagan told the press at the time of *Law and Order* (general release, April 1953): "Westerns will never become passé. Trends may come and go, but it's the top Westerns that outdraw 'em all!" *Law and Order* never made it into the galaxy of classic horse operas. It managed to break even at the box office, but *The New York Times* did not review it. "Reagan handles himself easily . . ." *Variety* said. He looked rangy enough and he rode better than most Western actors, but his voice did not have the craggy edge of sage and his eyes did not move fast enough to make anyone believe he was a true Western hero.

His Universal contract for this film paid him the originally agreed salary of seventy-five thousand dollars, a fee considerably out of line in 1953 for a film of the caliber of *Law and Order*. Reagan rode one of his own horses in the movie. He had expanded his operation at Yearling Row Ranch in the short time of its existence. His brood mares included half sisters to such outstanding thoroughbreds as Solidarity and Pedigree. He also raised jumpers and hunters, which he rode and helped train, and announced that the next season would see some of his horses racing at Hollywood Park.

Patricia Ann (Patti) Reagan, weighing in at seven pounds, was born by Cesarean section at Cedars of Lebanon Hospital on the afternoon of October 22, 1952. Nancy had a difficult predelivery that had begun the previous night when she went into hard labor at the International Horse Show at the Pan Pacific Auditorium. For the next six weeks, Reagan stayed home as Nancy slowly regained her strength. He had little to occupy his time because on August 27, slightly more than a month after the MCA waiver negotiations, he had decided to retire as president of the SAG.* He had been the union's president longer than any other person (six of its nineteen years of existence). No reason was given to the press when it was announced he was stepping down.

Dales stated, "He wanted to get out and also he was beginning to be a power within the Guild to the point where he recognized it, that he was having too much influence, that he was able to handle the board. And, I say, *he* recognized it, specifically, in words to me, saying, 'Jack, I'm not comfortable. I'm beginning to wonder, is there anything that I can't get out of the board?'"

He remained on the board and continued to be verbal in his anti-Communist philosophies. "His hatred of the Soviets goes way back," Dales commented. "He's convinced that the world will come to an end, you know, if they get too much power."

As the 1952 presidential election grew near, the Republicans nominated the most popular man in America, General Dwight D. Eisenhower. The general had been born in Denison, Texas (1890); raised in Abilene, Kansas; graduated from West Point; and had ascended meteorically by 1941 to be named chief of army operations in Washington. With the advent of war, he was appointed United States commander of the European theater of operation, commanded the North African landings (November 1942), and in February 1943 became chief of all Allied forces in North Africa. Shortly thereafter, he was made supreme commander of the Allied Expeditionary Force and was largely responsible for the cooperation among British, American and other Allied forces for the integration of land, sea and air operations. At the war's end, Eisenhower was a five-star general and a national hero, but his astounding achievements did not stop there.

After stints as commander of the United States Occupational Forces in Germany and Chief of Staff of the U.S. Army, he had

---

*Walter Pidgeon was nominated to succeed him.

taken a leave of absence from the army to become president of
Columbia University. In December 1950, he returned to the army
as supreme commander of the Allied powers in Europe. The unanswered question was whether or not Eisenhower was a Republican or Democrat. No one knew. The Republican governor of New
Hampshire, Sherman Adams, a member of the Republican committee to draft Eisenhower (who was in Europe and unresponsive
to political requests), wrote the county clerk in Kansas, where the
general maintained his home, to discover whether he had registered his preference. A prompt reply was received.

"Mr. Eisenhower has never voted in this county as far as I
know. . . . Dwight's father was a Republican and always voted
the Republican ticket up until his death, however that has nothing
to do with the son as many differ from their fathers. . . . I don't
think he [Eisenhower] has any politics."

The general's name was written in on several primary ballots
and often only as "Ike." The response was overwhelming. He resigned his command in May 1952, requesting he should also be
allowed to waive his pay, privilege and pension.* The Republicans could not have hoped for a more impressive and attractive
candidate to oppose the Democratic nominee—the intellectual
and energetic liberal governor of Illinois, Adlai Stevenson. The
general was self-assured, "accustomed to command, accustomed
to accommodating rival points of view, accustomed to success and
power, he spoke with unmistakable authority. He carried himself
erect. His blue eyes were penetrating and alert. His gestures conveyed an impression of strength. Eisenhower had presence."

Eisenhower and the Republicans decided on Senator Richard
Nixon for the number-two spot for three reasons: They believed
he could deliver the West Coast; he brought youth to the campaign (Eisenhower was sixty-two, Nixon thirty-nine); and in the
time of the growing anti-Communist hysteria of McCarthyism,
"had there been a medal for hunting Communists in 1952, Nixon
would have received it." Within two months, Nixon threatened to
plunge his party "into a swift descent into oblivion."

When the campaign began, Republicans considered Nixon a
young man destined for great things. One hundred of his supporters (mainly businessmen) contributed two hundred dollars each to
a fund for his personal use. The fund was discovered at the height

---

*Truman acceded to this request with the proviso that all Eisenhower's army rights be
restored on the day following the election should he run and lose.

of the campaign. The Democrats picked up this political football
and ran with it. Nixon tried using claims of "a Communist
smear" to block them, but their footwork was too swift. Placards
reading NO MINK COATS FOR NIXON—JUST COLD CASH greeted
his campaign train. The Republicans were terrified about keeping
him on the ticket, and equally fearful that if they dropped him the
loss of trust in the party would be so overwhelming that they
would lose the election. Eisenhower withdrew to consider the possibilities. Silence followed for several panic-filled days. Then
Nixon decided to take the crisis into his own hands; he bought a
half hour of national television time and made arrangements to
broadcast from the stage of the El Capitan Theater in Hollywood.

Just before the broadcast, New York's Governor Thomas
Dewey telephoned him with an ultimatum: "There has been a
meeting of all Eisenhower's top advisors. They have asked me to
tell you that it is their opinion that at the conclusion of the broadcast tonight you should submit your resignation to Eisenhower."

Nixon replied that it was too late to change his speech. Dewey
suggested he give the prepared speech *and then* "tack on, at the
end, a formal resignation offered to Eisenhower," and added,
"Can I say you have accepted?"

"You will have to watch the show to see—and tell them I
know something about politics too!" Nixon snapped.

Talking in a "tear-choked" voice, Nixon was alternately con-
trite and aggressive. His wife, his finances and his dog, a Spaniel
named Checkers, were put on public view. In a moment of pure
melodrama, he pointed to Checkers (a gift from an admirer to his
children) being held by Pat Nixon and vowed that whatever the
outcome of his crisis he would not give up the dog. He defended
his position and challenged all the men campaigning on the presidential and vice-presidential ballot (a shock to Eisenhower, who
was listening) to reveal their political contributions. He then
leaned in close to the camera, with an earnest, tortured look, his
dark eyes brimming with tears, his hands clenched. "I am submitting to the Republican National Committee tonight, through this
television broadcast, the decision it is theirs to make . . . wire and
write [them] whether you think I should stay or whether I should
get off; and whatever their decision is, I will abide by it." Then,
as an addendum, voice strong again, he signed off with, "And
remember, folks, Eisenhower is a great man. Believe me, he's a
great man. And a vote for Eisenhower is a vote for what's good for
America."

Within the next twenty-four hours, Nixon received "scores of dog collars, handwoven dog blankets, a dog kennel and enough dog food to feed Checkers for a year." He also received more than two million favorable letters and telegrams (sent to the Republican National Committee) and Eisenhower's "blue-eyed smile of benediction."

Reagan, although still registered as a Democrat, voted the winning Eisenhower-Nixon ticket. Reagan himself was installed as honorary mayor of Malibu Lake (the area of his ranch) on May 2, 1953 (with the Republic Studio Orchestra playing a concert of western music in his honor). The next day the announcement was made that he would head the campaign for the reelection of Los Angeles Mayor Fletcher Bowron. He stated that he had taken on the job "because of the threat of good government posed by some of the sinister forces opposing the reelection of Mayor Bowron." He was also approached by Holmes Tuttle, who had a group of California businessmen who wanted him to run for the Senate. "I turned the offer down with thanks. I'm a ham—always was and always will be," he laughed.

As the fifties rocked through the century, stars' staggering salaries and the accelerating fees of the independent producers and directors became a standard by which to measure success. Audrey Hepburn (who had just made *Roman Holiday*) was earning $350,000 a picture and John Wayne had signed a three-picture deal for $2 million. Film budgets soared accordingly. To combat the growing threat of destruction from the little but mighty television screen, the film industry was producing epics, or at least larding budgets so that a chicken could look like a goose (and often more resembled a turkey). In such an atmosphere of high budgets and high rollers, actors of Reagan's modest box-office potential were an endangered species. The performer under contract to one studio swiftly became extinct. Competition was savage for roles in any independent films.

Reagan's expenses were high. The ranch was years from being a money-making proposition, and the horses had to be fed and cared for and the staff paid. He later made statements that he was unemployed for fourteen months (during 1952–53), but he had made *The Last Outpost*, the two Pine and Thomas films and, toward the end of 1953, *Prisoner of War* for Metro-Goldwyn-Mayer. A no-film gap had occurred between May and December of 1953. The MGM film was a grim account of the atrocities practiced on prisoners of war by North Koreans. Reagan appeared as a volunteer for the United States government who parachutes behind enemy lines to check reports of POW brutalities and becomes a prisoner himself. Scenes of "brutal beatings, calculated tortures, senseless killings and other inhumanly conceived treatments, fill the footage," one critic wrote.

Prisoner of War was made in twenty-eight days and released within a few months to cash in on its topicality. Unfortunately, the shocking material was blunted by the hackneyed script and the broad "play acting" of the cast—Reagan included. His salary for the film had been thirty thousand dollars, two thirds of what Pine and Thomas had paid him. Five months after Patti was born, Nancy had tried to return to work (this was the time she claimed the mix-up in names at Columbia). MCA finally got her a low-budget film, *Donovan's Brain,* for United Artists with Lew Ayres and Gene Evans (a remake of the much-filmed Curt Siodmak novel about the scientist who keeps a brain of a dead man alive and then becomes dominated by it). Nancy was paid eighteen thousand dollars for six weeks' work.

By the end of 1953, both the Reagans realized their film opportunities were limited. Television might well have been the answer, but in 1953, the word had the scent of a terminal disease.*

Common sense dictated to Reagan that he stood no chance on Broadway, never having appeared on the legitimate stage. "The MCA trouble shooters," as Reagan referred to them, came up with "another source of loot." Art Parks suggested they help him put an act together and open in Las Vegas. The agency had never lost its power in the nightclub world. Reagan had grave doubts. What would he do? No more than he did at charity benefits, or had done on tour with Parsons, Parks assured him. He added that for a two-week engagement he felt confident he could get him thirty thousand dollars, equal to his salary for *Prisoner of War.* Reagan gave in. Art Parks contacted Beldon Kattleman at the El Rancho Hotel, who agreed to put Reagan on the bill as master of ceremonies with a stripper. Reagan refused. Twenty minutes later, Parks had a more acceptable deal for him at the Last Frontier Hotel.

Reagan would emcee a fifty-minute "revue," as the act was called, and join in with the other performers in songs, dances and

---

*Reagan claimed he refused to consider television in 1953, but he had made appearances with Burns and Allen and on selected anthology series.

jokes. "I'll introduce something new in men's fashions, as well," he told a reporter. "It's a streamlined tuxedo, minus any pockets except for a change slot at the waist. It's in coal black. If the debut doesn't work out, I'll be ready for mourning." The press sensed a good story here, the fading film star fighting to survive. The gossip columns that had ignored him for most of his career now gave him a jab or two in print. He came back with a fifteen-hundred-word article that *Variety* published on January 6, 1954:

> . . . Our business [is] the most ruthlessly competitive there is. . . . A producer can be denied financial backing for one failure, an actor can go from $100,000 price tag, to unemployment on the supposition that a picture's failure was due to his lack of boxoffice appeal. No one questions whether he can act. In fact, everyone will admit he is a superb actor . . . but, because Joe Schmoe, the moviegoer sat up with a sick friend . . . instead of seeing our hero at the Bijou, he faces starvation or a job on television. . . ."

To his old friend Bob Thomas he decried the way studios had cut down their star lists to a minimum, driving "the stars into other mediums." (He added that he was "against the benefit bureaucrats who make their living—and a very good one—by lining up free talent for charity appearances. . . . Whatever happened to the good old American custom of simply giving for a worthy cause? Why does entertainment have to be given in exchange?")

In his new guise as nightclub performer, Reagan was to work with a male quartet called the Continentals, who had appeared on bills at the Waldorf, Cocoanut Grove and Mocambo and been seen on the Ed Sullivan and Milton Berle television shows. "We expected to have to carry Reagan," Ben Cruz of the group confessed. "At first he was rough as a cob. But then he really opened our eyes . . . by the end of the first week [of rehearsals] he was moving like the rest of us. He knew the choreography as well as we did. . . . He was into [self] fitness . . . didn't drink or smoke. He had a daily massage, and on trips from Los Angeles to Las Vegas [stopped for the night] in Barstow rather than complete . . . a too-long drive.

"Nancy would sit through all the rehearsals . . . some up to four hours long, and then all the shows, sipping nothing more than a glass of ice water."

The show was premiered at the Statler in downtown Los Angeles, a businessman's hotel too far from mainstream Hollywood to attract attention. They played two nights there before the Las Vegas engagement, where Reagan, the Continentals, an act called the Blackburn Twins, all supported by a line of gorgeous show girls dressed in South American costumes and two-foot-high plumed headdresses, opened on February 15, 1954. Reagan cracked jokes in an Irish brogue, a straw hat perched on his head, carrying a cane as a prop. He did a barbershop-quintet routine with the Continentals as a silent fifth member. (While the group sang in four-part harmony, they pretended to shave him as he sat on a "chair" formed by the legs of two of their members.) A beer-garden skit followed in which Reagan spoke in a guttural German accent and wore an apron advertising Pabst Blue Ribbon beer, with *"Vos vils du haben?"* incorrectly written across it. From this low he descended into an old-time baggy-pants vaudeville routine where the five men raced around the stage beaning each other on the head with rolled-up newspapers. At the finale, Reagan stood alone, spotlighted center stage in his black tuxedo, and recited a sentimental poem about the glories, sacrifices and contributions made by actors.

The act did not take Vegas by storm. The nightclub critics found him personally ingratiating but the material "third rate" and wondered in print if Las Vegas was now going "to have to suffer a retreating army of fading Hollywood stars."

The desert heat had begun to beat down for the day as the Reagans headed homeward the morning after the last night of the engagement. Reagan had hit rock bottom. "Never again," he told MCA's Taft Schreiber, "will I sell myself so short."

THE
CORPORATE
YEARS

"At one point he was being interviewed on radio at the Stork Club
and the host showed him a picture of
William Holden and some nubile
young thing obviously not his wife.

"'What would you say if I told
you that your best friend, William
Holden, was in here with this girl?'
he asked.

"Ron replied, 'I would say that
that was a composite picture.'"

—EARL B. DUNCKEL

22

REAGAN'S MEMORY WAS WORKING IN PROPER SE-
quence by the time he published his autobiography in 1965. In it,
he places the filming of *Cattle Queen of Montana* correctly between
his nightclub debut, February 1954, and his contract with General
Electric Theater, September 1954. The film featured Barbara
Stanwyck as a crusty cattlewoman who inherits her father's
rangelands and battles Indians and rustlers to protect her livestock. Reagan's character was that of an undercover army officer
sent to track the Indian disturbances. Reagan once claimed the
making of the film was "like playing cowboy and Indian."

Made for RKO, the picture was shot in Glacier National Park,
Montana. Reagan and the cameraman, John Alton, took the train
to the location. Reagan was stunned by the beauty of the "great
northwest" and talked about one day maybe owning a ranch
there. Local ranchers were hired as the film posse and supplied
the horses in the production. Reagan toured the area on horseback and proved to be the top equine expert on the film. He
viewed Stanwyck with reverence, "a great actress and a real pro,"

and returned to Hollywood in high spirits as he entered into negotiations to host a half-hour television anthology series for General
Electric.*

The idea for the show—a continuing star host and a guest star
performer each episode—was sold to G.E. by its advertising company, Batten, Barton, Durstine and Osborne (BBD&O), who
packaged shows through MCA. MCA suggested the format,
which, considering the fierce war then raging between Hollywood
and television, was astounding since the top stars refused to appear on television. "MCA promised us [G.E.] that we would be
able to break that barrier if we could go along with the plan they
had," Earl B. Dunckel later explained. Dunckel had been a news-
paper-man in Schenectady, New York, home of G.E.'s headquarters, when he was asked to join *G.E. Theater* as a "communicator."
Within a short time, he was put in charge of "audience participation." Fred Waring and the Pennsylvanians, who had been with
G.E. for years, had just been canceled. G.E. was looking for a new
format and MCA had found it.

"They were really very smart people," Dunckel continued.
"The plan was essentially to have this half-hour anthology [with a
top star every week]. How they baited the stars in was, one, you
could choose the kind of vehicle you would be in. For example,
Bob Hope could be a Sam Spade–type detective if he wanted to.
(Actually, Jack Benny wanted to do that and did.) The other bait
was that we kept the program for three or five showings, and after
that it's yours."

This meant that the stars would then own the show in which
they had appeared and thus be likely to draw a steady income
from reshowings for many years.†

"MCA was fantastically powerful," one observer commented,
"mainly—oddly enough, because they were great tax people."
And Dunckel added ". . . they would show a star how to save
more of what he earned than anybody else in the world could,
which was the reason, I think that so many flocked to MCA
rather than some of their competitors."

G.E. had been looking for a host for several weeks when MCA
submitted Reagan's name. Reagan claimed the series had been

---

*The first publicity announcement ("New General Electric series starts in September
[1954] with Ronald Reagan as Host") was dispatched on April 21, 1954, but Reagan had
not yet signed his contract.
†The *G.E. Theater* shows are still (1986) being distributed around the world.

created with him in mind, along with a plan for him to go on the road speaking at the various G.E. plants and taking part in their "extensive 'Employee and Community Relations Program.'" But Dunckel has stated:

"We had been very, very definite as to the kind of person we wanted. Good moral character, intelligent. Not the kind with the reputation for the social ramble. A good upright kind of person. We looked at several people. I won't mention who they were.* You don't construct a top-ten program overnight. You don't start right away knowing what the public wants. . . . In a large corporation, if you try something new, your biggest obstacle is your own people. [I then came up with a plan] to have Ron meet and charm these G.E. vice-presidents all over the country so that they would stay off our back long enough for us to get the program moving."

The device of Reagan visiting G.E.'s 135 plants across the country would also be a unique marketing device. G.E. had a staff of more than 700,000 men and women who with their families made up a considerable audience. Dunckel and Reagan met for the first time in New York in August 1954. "There was nothing of the posturing, nothing of the 'I am a star'—he was a regular guy . . . whom I liked instantly . . . Nancy was there with him.

"Ron was going to star in a certain number of vehicles, ones that would be hand-tailored for him or that, reading the scripts, he particularly liked. He was the continuity, the host, the element that tied the whole thing together. We needed that, because [each episode was] so disparate . . . and we needed a focal force in there to hang them all together, to keep them in line."

Reagan's sudden and unexpected good fortune was hard for even him to grasp immediately. The first contract guaranteed him $125,000 a year as host. He was to receive an additional fee for any show in which he took a role, compensation for his company tours and profit participation on episodes in which he appeared after the show was in its fifth replay. Nancy was also to have a part (as supporting performer) in scripts that were suited to her.†

Reagan became host of *General Electric Theater* on Sunday evening, September 26, 1954. The show, emanating from the CBS studios in Los Angeles, was broadcast live from nine to nine-thirty P.M. EST. Not long after, *G.E. Theater* alternated between live and

---

*Edward Arnold and Walter Pidgeon were considered.
†Nancy Reagan played opposite Reagan in three *G.E. Theater* episodes in eight years.

film. Reagan memorized his part as host (about two minutes on the opening show). Regular commercials were interspersed. "We very carefully wouldn't let him do that [the commercials] because it would cheapen his role overall for him to get right down to the nitty-gritty," Dunckel recalled. Nancy appeared opposite Reagan on October 10, when he stepped into his first acting role for *General Electric Theater* as a man on the brink of a nervous breakdown. On December 12, he portrayed a doctor threatened by hoodlums. On January 23, 1955, he turned up (surprisingly) as an officer in the Irish Civil War of 1922 who turns informer to save his life, and on March 13 in a comedy about a motion-picture producer filming a Western version of *War and Peace*. His roles were varied if nothing else.

The initial G.E. tour in August 1954 (before the filming of the first episode) began at the giant turbine plant at Schenectady, New York.* Nothing had prepared him for the vastness of thirty-one acres of factory under one roof. He stood stunned on the balcony above at his first sight of it. The noise of the machines was deafening. Dunckel and another executive led him carefully down the three flights of open iron stairs to the factory floor.

"He couldn't see his hand in front of his face," Dunckel explained. "He couldn't wear [his contact lenses] anyplace where people were smoking or there were any fumes. The irritation was so great that he had to take them out, so he never wore them [on the tours]."

Suddenly a group of workers recognized Reagan. Word spread and the machines ground to a halt. Reagan walked the thirty-one cement acres back and forth for four hours stopping at each machine, talking to almost every one of the plant's factory employees, signing autographs and "generally having a hell of a good time getting acquainted.

"The people were most amusing," according to Dunckel. "The women would come running up—mash notes, autographs and all that kind of thing. The men would all stand . . . looking at him, obviously saying something very derogatory— 'I bet he's a fag,' or something like that. He would carry on a conversation with the girls just so long . . . then he would leave them and walk over to these fellows and start talking to them. When he left them ten minutes later, they were all slappin' him on the back saying, 'That's the way, Ron.'

---

*The company manufactured everything from refrigerators and other appliances to medical and industrial equipment.

"We were going to stay over [in Schenectady] Saturday [for Reagan to rest before going on]. Coincident with this, there was a huge meeting of teachers . . . high school teachers. Meeting at the armory. There were three or four thousand of them. At the last minute their speaker came down ill, and they came to me and said, 'Can Mr. Reagan speak to us Saturday night' . . . I said, in effect, thanks a lot but no thanks. I was thinking, 'My God, this is an area outside of my expertise. I would have to do a lot of research [to write a speech for Reagan].' What did I know about education?

"[Ron] said, 'Dunk, let's give it a try.'

"I said, 'Ron, I haven't got time to [write a speech].'

"He said, 'Don't worry. Don't worry.'

"This was four o'clock on Friday afternoon and he wasn't to speak till Saturday night, but we had all these things going on Saturday morning and through two o'clock Saturday afternoon. He got up there and gave a speech on education that just dropped them in the aisles. He got a good ten-minute standing applause afterward. This is when I finally began to realize the breadth and depth of his knowledgeability . . . everything that went into that mind stayed there. He could quote it out like a computer any time you wanted. He did read widely, and he remembered what he read. He tended to mesh everything in together to get a pattern out of things. It was an amazing *tour de force*. It really was."

Reagan still would not fly unless forced to do so, and so he and Dunckel usually took the train from town to town, a red-eye special that brought them to their destination at dawn, when they would be met at the station and put in one car, their bags in another. They never saw the hotel they were going to until after midnight. All that time, Reagan would be walking plant floors, talking to employees. "In Erie [Pennsylvania], that first trip . . . we got back to the hotel after midnight. The desk clerk said, 'Mr. Reagan, there is a young lady who has been waiting here for you for two and a half hours now.'

"I said, 'Ron, you can't afford it. You're dead now . . .'

"Ron said, 'Dunk, I'd better find out what it's all about.'

"So we went over to her. This was the typical stage-struck small-town girl. She was all set, had it in her mind, tickets and everything, she was going to Hollywood. Ron spent an hour and a half convincing her that, if she was really serious about acting, what she should do is hit the little theater, the local radio and TV stations, the local floor show, whatever. I remember, he kept drumming it into her, 'Always remember, if you can command an audience in Erie, Pennsylvania, you can command an audience anywhere. You don't have to go to Hollywood to prove it.' . . . He saw her to the door. 'Dunk,' he said, 'I'd do almost anything to keep another one of these little girls from going out there and adding to the list of whores out in Hollywood.'"

At another plant, "a bull of the woods showed up. Big woman. She looked Ron up and down and put her face about that far from him and said, 'Buster, I'd love to back you up in a corner sometime.'

"'Well,' he said, 'it would have to be a pretty big corner.'

"The security wasn't a problem in those days. . . . An occasional shop [factory] girl would bare her left breast and want him to sign it."

The tours gave Reagan a new image of himself, as traveling ambassador. By the time of his second tour (the following spring), he was beginning to speak more often in open factory areas or auditoriums or before local groups—the Kiwanis, the Lions, the Rotary, the Elks, the American Legion. He talked about America the beautiful, and the need to retain wholesome values, the family, the country's economic problems, taxes, juvenile delinquency—all the subjects close to the hearts of everyday people. He communicated on their level, never used "highfalutin" language, had a good store of well-told humorous anecdotes. He'd stand for an hour after a speech answering questions and then devote extra time to exchange a few personal words with the people who gathered around him when he was ready to leave.

Whether he wanted to accept the fact or not, he was perceived as a spokesman for management. He never went into details such as employees benefits, and he tried to speak in generalities, translating the employees' questions into his own experience, but he was looked upon as management nonetheless.

"They might ask, 'What do you think of this business of General Electric telling our union to take it or leave it?'

"He would say, 'When I was heading up a union, I recognized that there always came a time when you were at the make/break point and where it had to be one way or the other. All the arguing, all the discussion had taken place. We had passed that stage. Now it was, "Am I going to accept your plan? Are you going to accept my plan? Are we going to go on from here, or is this going to remain a deadlock?" That's essentially what take it or leave it amounts to.'

"[It's] bull, total bull [that he] was reading from three-by-five cards when he was up there giving his talk, 'the talk.'* There wasn't any 'the talk' at all. This is a crock . . . he would occasionally write himself notes. He is a very good writer. . . . He's got this little crabbed handwriting which is hard to read. I can just see him changing a speech to something he is comfortable with. . . . I don't care how many speech writers they have over there at the White House, the end product is his. I'll bet any amount of money on that," Dunckel insisted.

Within a year, Reagan had become "a walking symbol of the company's interest in and responsiveness to its customers and employees." Reagan once asked G.E. head Ralph Cordiner, "Is what I'm saying doing G.E. damage?" Cordiner replied, "I am not ever going to have G.E. censor anything you say. You're not our spokesman. Even though you're going out under our aegis. You're speaking for yourself. You say what you believe."

A few years later he had moved sharply away from talks about Hollywood and America the beautiful and into talks about what was wrong with the country and what could be done (in his opinion) to correct it. At this point, "some people at G.E. said, 'Don't make waves.'"

Dunckel was an archconservative, and as they traveled in trains and cars and stood about waiting for transportation in the nether hours of the day, he would drumbeat conservative politics at him. Reagan still tried to defend New Dealism, and the men had spirited arguments. Finally they agreed that the Democratic party "had turned the corner and gone a different direction. He had not deserted it—it deserted him." The "growing liberal influence in the business world" was also a topic the two men discussed.

Dunckel has said that G.E. had a "left-wing liberal element fairly high up in the organization . . . most of them I don't think were liberals by nature. They were liberals out of fear, particularly those people who read *The New York Times*. It was the first thing they did every morning. All you read in the papers then was the liberal message. The liberals were very, very effective. Reagan was being portrayed in the liberal press as a combination of Attila the Hun and Genghis Khan. . . . Editorially the press commented, 'Here's somebody who hates the little man, who would turn us back to the Dark Ages'—all that nonsense."

---

*Reagan has been accused of giving the same "company" talk on these tours made during his years with General Electric.

Reagan had fallen into a way of life that had marked similarities to his years as president of the SAG. On one hand he was the speaker (less negotiator now) dealing in important issues, and on the other, performing in scripts that did not require great acting on his part. In early 1955, he even managed time to make another Western, *Tennessee's Partner,* for RKO. Reagan was in the saddle again, this time in the thankless role of John Payne's sidekick, Cowpoke, who gets gunned down trying (and succeeding) to save his friend's life when Payne is framed for murder. Payne gave the film whatever few good acting moments it contained. Rhonda Fleming and Coleen Gray looked beautiful, but the "raucous mining town" of Sandy Bar was as phony as Cowpoke's drawl.

Despite her sporadic appearances as an actress, Nancy was often referred to in the press as "the former Nancy Davis of Chicago." This wording implied that she was a society girl whose film career had been a lark, an impression that could well have been circulated by Nancy herself, who never missed an opportunity when being interviewed to mention her father, "the eminent neurosurgeon, Dr. Loyal Davis of Chicago." Edith, however privately revered, was never publicly discussed.

Once Reagan signed with *General Electric Theater,* he and Nancy saw the Davises more often. The doctor and his son-in-law had a growing rapport. Reagan found it easy to stop in Arizona on his way home from a tour. He met and liked Davis's neighbor and good friend Senator Barry Goldwater. And the Davises traveled to the Coast to see the Reagans whenever they could. (Edith recalled that on one trip, the Davises had gone to a church wedding of a friend's daughter in Beverly Hills and Jane Wyman was there. "I went over to her and I said, 'I'm glad to see you, I'm Nancy's mother.' And she said, 'Oh, I'm so glad to meet you. Thank you for being so nice and coming over.' And I said, 'Oh, no, honey. Anybody who wouldn't be nice to you is a fool.'")

Dr. Davis had talked seriously to Reagan about the possibility of a political career. Reagan still feared there was no real future in it for him. He had gone from being honorary mayor of Malibu Lake to honorary mayor of Thousand Oaks (a San Fernando Valley community) and a candidate for mayor of Hollywood. The loss of that election was a personal blow to him. Then, "someone seriously approached me with the suggestion that I run for Congress. That proved to be the last straw! I realized then that I was becoming a Dr. Jekyll and Mr. Hyde, and the two characters were competing to control me."

In the spring of 1956, Reagan continued to remain active on the board of the SAG and was now president of the Motion Picture Industry Council, which was formed as a public-relations group to combat unflattering stories about Hollywood. His tours for General Electric had gained occasional national coverage. He was much more than a salesman or pitch artist. As he was becoming a spokesman for the majority views of big business, so was he growing as a public speaker and media personality. He now made as many as fourteen speaking dates per day on his tours, addressing not only General Electric's seven hundred thousand or more employees but an equal number of representatives of local business and civic groups in the forty-two states in which G.E. had plants and offices.

"From my own viewpoint," commented Reagan, "my kind of an association with a big business firm not only adds half or better to the economic value of my name, but provides a degree of security entirely foreign to the movie business, which is ruled so much by suicidal fluctuations, fads and whims."

In the fall of 1955, Reagan's sense of security had been strong enough for him to begin construction on a new house that would have "everything electric except a chair." General Electric was supplying all the electrical equipment, which included kitchen appliances not yet on the market (a dishwasher with a built-in garbage disposal), a retracting canopy roof for indoor or outdoor dining, and a film projection room. The spectacular site in Pacific Palisades that Reagan and Nancy had chosen was a steep, densely wooded shelf carved into the southern slope of the Santa Monica Mountains, high above the street and affording an unlimited view of Los Angeles and the ocean. The Reagans had asked their architect* to build them a modern ranch house. Interior walls were largely of stone and glass. Every one of the house's main rooms— living room, den, dining room, enclosed patio, master suite and Patti's two-room area—had unobstructed views across the city to the ocean. (In a corner of the patio floor, Reagan had fingered entwined hearts with the initials "NDR" and "RR" while the cement was still wet.) The house (1669 San Onofre Drive) was almost hidden from the street and a massive iron gate ensured further privacy.

Nancy furnished the house with contemporary furniture— large couches, giant tub chairs, low, roomy ebony-and-glass coffee tables—and red splashed everywhere—the upholstery, the drap-

_____
*William R. Stephenson, A.I.A.

ery fabric, the paintings on the wall—set against plush gray car-
peting. Red was their favorite color and Nancy wore it often.
"Nancy and Ronnie are just alike," Edith laughed. "They don't
care—just so it's red . . . it makes her furious and it makes him
upset too, when I say that . . . but [it's] like I tell you—like the
niggers—any color so it's red."

Despite Dunckel's objections to it, "The Speech," as his main
lecture on the horrors of the welfare state became known, was
serving as a bridge for Reagan between show business and the
business of government. The theme that he kept pounding away
at ("Government—staffed by professional politicians and career
bureaucrats—is by nature more wasteful than most human in-
stitutions, and should be reduced to the barest minimum") had
first been hummed by Hal Gross in his early Des Moines days.

Nancy backed everything her husband said. She did not travel
with him on the tours, but they would meet in New York when
they could. The marriage was a good one, better than that of any
of their friends. Reagan never could wait to get home. Nancy
never tired of hearing him speak, but she enjoyed being a wife,
running the house, entertaining, gardening. She took an interest
in whatever he liked most—the horses, baseball, politics. Although well informed, she seldom shared the limelight with him if
he was talking in a group. She had matured well and was more
attractive in her mid-thirties than she had been a decade earlier.
Security and Reagan's tender regard had erased some of the hard-
ness that had formerly narrowed her mouth. The brown wide-
apart eyes that dominated her face were warmer, more vital, the
slim body more rounded. Nancy had a clean, petite beauty, and it
seemed to match up well with Reagan's tall-framed, brawny-
armed, weathered good-guy looks, the crinkly grin and the jaunty
stance. Olivier and Leigh have been referred to as "the golden
couple." From their appearance, Nancy and Reagan might well
have been named "the cowboy and his lady."

"There was a joke about someone listening to Ronnie's spiel
for the G.E. nuclear submarine, and remarking, 'I didn't really
need a submarine, but I've got one now,'" longtime Hollywood
columnist Sheilah Graham remembered. "He believes what he
says and he says what he believes he should say. But he can compromise. He can change from the strongest of his stands. I remember a meeting at the Screen Actors Guild [1952, Graham also
acted from time to time] when he exhorted the members, 'I don't
want to see any of you going over to the enemy,' meaning televi-

sion. The last time I talked with Ann Sheridan [she died in 1967] we discussed this meeting, and she said, 'When I came back to Hollywood after living in New York, I turned on my seven inch set and there was that son-of-a-bitch on television.'"

By 1957, the film industry had tagged him "the Actor in the Gray Flannel Suit." CBS publicity releases referred to him as "a dual personality, devoting at least equal parts of his inexplicable energy to both worlds of acting and business." He spent about sixteen weeks each year on the road, and these tours were the fuel that propelled him forward. G.E. dubbed him "the Ambassador of the Film World." Reagan claimed at one meeting that "the unwashed public" (a phrase he used in an interview) made him aware of what the man in the living room watching television was thinking, "and don't you think that some of their ideas haven't helped in mapping out our programming and television policy . . . and helps make for a sincere performance [by him]."

Reagan had a say in the selection of scripts, and had absolute control over those in which he appeared. The half-hour format, whittled down to twenty-four minutes after Reagan's hosting and the commercials, allowed little in the way of story or character development. Nonetheless, it commanded the viewers' attention and for years enjoyed high ratings. The lack of competition from the other networks during the nine to nine-thirty Sunday night time slot was one factor. Another was the known performers who were guests on the shows: Bob Hope, Jack Benny, Ethel Barry-more, James Dean—the list was impressive. The stories were often entertaining, occasionally gripping and generally well-pro-duced.

By 1958, in the show's fourth season, the program's choice of scripts exhibited Reagan's viewpoints and philosophies almost ex-clusively. The need to lure a major star to television with an extra lump of sugar—a role he or she chose—was unnecessary. Films were in a severe depression and the studios that had not already capitulated would soon begin producing for television themselves. The blacklist had deprived Hollywood of a large segment of its earlier creative and productive force at the same time as it under-mined the former cohesiveness of the studios' production teams. An epidemic of fear had spread throughout the community, and just as Hollywood was terrorized by the words *guilty by association,* so it lived in dread of making a film that might later be banned by groups like the American Legion as being Communist inspired.

The independent producers had stepped in and offered work

and high salaries to stars. But this frequently came at a great cost to the artists, who were assured of only one film at a time and who more often than not had to shoot in foreign countries away from their families and under conditions they would previously, as Hollywood studio employees, never have considered. To cut costs, films were being produced in Spain and Italy, where labor was cheap and union restrictions almost nonexistent. Television, although an undesired alternative, was at least a way to stay home and remain visible.

Reagan's roles on *General Electric Theater* increasingly became either evangelistic or moralistic. One, "No Hiding Place," found him a "wretched Skid Row drunk, who overcomes his craving for alcohol and devotes himself to rehabilitating other human derelicts along the Bowery." Another episode had him and Nancy as an American Indian couple, members of the Turkey Growers' Association, whose son's pet turkey is selected for the Thanksgiving bird at the White House. The boy turns down the honor, but a kindly president arranges for the boy to keep his pet and the family the honor by substituting another bird. In "The House of Truth," Reagan starred as "a member of the United States Information Service in a strife-torn Asian village . . . who is shocked when he learns that Communist agitators have burned the American library . . . but with the help of the oppressed villagers who offer their most-prized possessions to keep the library in operation . . . helps to rebuild the structure."

Earl Dunckel was transferred to another executive job within General Electric in 1956 "because I was so protective of Ron, and very effectively protective . . . against the criticism from the left-wing G.E. executives." George M. Dalen, a former FBI man, took Dunckel's place. Dunckel admitted Dalen "was not as conservative as me, but he was pretty darned conservative."

For two years after *Tennessee's Partner*, Reagan received no film offers. Television performers were "*verboten* on the big screen," he claimed. "It didn't matter that my Sunday night stint was a quick forty-five seconds [the time allotted his introduction and sign-off was closer to two minutes]—I had a weekly show and that was that." This did not reflect the true picture. Reagan also appeared in at least six half-hour G.E. shows a year (plus reruns), clocking up enough film time for two feature films. Columbia Pictures did, however, send him *Hellcats of the Navy*, and he and Nancy decided to accept. For the first time, Reagan had his choice of director, and he chose Nathan Juran, with whom he had worked on *Law and Order*. Juran had been a fine art director before becoming a director in 1952. He had won the Academy Award (Best Art Direction, 1941) for *How Green Was My Valley* and was nominated several times thereafter.* He had not fared that well as a director. His films since *Law and Order* had been low-budget action and horror pictures distinguished only for the professional way they had been photographed and the quality of their sets.

Reagan liked working with Juran. He was low-keyed, respectful, and the two men had much in common. Columbia set a budget on *Hellcats of the Navy* lower than Reagan had anticipated. He had hoped for a big-action patriotic film like *The Wings of Eagles* or *Jet Pilot,* both made that year by John Wayne. Instead, he got a "jingoistic potboiler." The "Hellcats" of the title are the troubleshooters of the submarine service. Reagan played Commander Casey Abbott, sent to Japan during World War II on a daring mission to scout enemy waters for Japanese mines. Nancy was cast as the navy nurse he loves in this, their only film together. Reagan had suffered from a "life long tendency to claustrophobia" (one of the major reasons for his not flying), and the hours spent in the small, cramped (fourteen-man) conning tower of the submarine were hard on him. He has said he could not wait to get out of there at the end of every take. Movie audiences suffered the same feelings. *Hellcats of the Navy* only broke even at the box office. Reagan, thinking his film career had ended, went about his work in television with greater enthusiasm.

The speeches he delivered around the country in 1958 for General Electric had little to do with bringing Hollywood to the people or the people's choice to Hollywood. They dealt mainly with political and business issues. He spoke in Schenectady about "Professional Patriots" (who did not want the Bill of Rights taught in the schools for alleged fear of revolution), in Los Angeles about "Tax Curbs" and in Des Moines on "Business, Ballots and Bureaus" (the evils of burgeoning government). In 1959, however, he cited the Tennessee Valley Authority as a horrible example of governmental excesses. T.V.A. was a $50 million customer for G.E. equipment. The T.V.A. reference was swiftly dropped from any further speeches after G.E. chairman Ralph Cordiner con-

---

*Juran was also art director on *The Razor's Edge* (1946), *Body and Soul* (1947) and *Kiss the Blood Off My Hands* (1948).

ceded—when Reagan asked him—"that the exclusion would make my job easier."*

Ronald Prescott Reagan, the Reagans' second child, weighed in at eight pounds, eight ounces at his birth at 8:04 A.M. on May 21, 1958. Nancy again had the baby by Cesarean section. Reagan had been determined that his son would not be called junior, and therefore the difference in the middle name. The Reagans called their son "Skipper" (and would do so for all the years he lived at home). Reagan was a happy man. His personal life was of the sort he had always wanted, with a wife who thought about him above and before anyone or anything else. His career in television had brought him financial security (more than two hundred thousand dollars a year now), the horse farm was doing well (and had tripled in value), the house on San Onofre was still a dream house (and, with increasing real-estate values and all the additions put in and paid for by G.E., also worth several times what he had paid to build it). He wished he did not have to spend so much time away from Nancy. He thought he should see Maureen (eighteen) and Michael (fifteen) more often; he knew he was a better husband than a father. Nancy was the center of his life, his four children on the perimeter, and he did not see that as bad. He called her "honey," and whenever he phoned her she was *there*. They held hands in public "for real" and were not embarrassed to display their affection for each other before the children or close friends.

What he did not need were complications when he had none and yet another demand on his time that would keep him away

---

*Reagan's reference to the T.V.A. in his speech was as follows: ". . . sacred as motherhood, is T.V.A. This program started as a flood control project; the Tennessee Valley was periodically ravaged by destructive floods. The Army Engineers set out to solve this problem. They said that it was possible that once in 500 years there could be a total capacity flood that would inundate some 600,000 acres. Well the Engineers fixed that. They made a permanent lake which inundated a million acres. This solved the problem of the floods, but the annual interest on the T.V.A. debt is five times as great as the annual flood damage they sought to correct. Of course, you will point out that T.V.A. gets electric power from the impounded waters, and this is true, but today 85 percent of T.V.A.'s electricity is generated in coal-burning steam plants. Now perhaps you'll charge that I'm overlooking the navigable waterway that was created, providing cheap barge traffic, but the bulk of the freight barged on that waterway is coal being shipped to the T.V.A. steam plants, and the cost of maintaining that channel each year would pay for shipping all of the coal by rail, and there would be money left over." Reagan cut this out of the speech he gave on tour. Yet, five years later when he published his autobiography, he included the lengthy paragraph in a reprint of an almost identical speech given in support of Barry Goldwater, which his co-writer, Richard C. Huber, noted, "represents sentiments he has publicly expressed across the nation for the past 15 years [that would place these views as early as 1950]—regardless of political parties or programs that had happened to be in power."

from Nancy even more. But in October 1959, the Screen Actors Guild board, with Reagan and Nancy on it, was determined, as 1960 approached, to press forward in their battle for residuals from old pictures being released to television. Howard Keel was then president, but he had tendered his resignation to accept a role in a Broadway musical, *Saratoga*.

"We knew that [there] was going to be a battle—there was no secret about it," Jack Dales says. "The producers made no secret about it—so we wanted a strong leader, and everybody's mind [the board] turned back to Ronnie Reagan." A meeting of the executive committee (which excluded Reagan) was called—Walter Pidgeon, George Chandler, Leon Ames.

Representing the committee, Jack Dales rang Reagan and asked if he would consider returning for another term as president. "Convinced as I was that my previous service had hurt careerwise, and feeling the upsurge of success in the G.E. Theater after the lean period, I didn't want to answer the question at all—I just wanted to hide someplace. Nancy was even more upset, and felt there was every justification for saying 'No thanks.'" He did not. He said, "Give me a few days to think about it."

He called Lew Wasserman for counsel. To his surprise, Wasserman advised him to take the position. Reagan has never given Wasserman's reasons, but he accepted the SAG nomination as he had almost all the other arrangements MCA had urged upon him.

23

NOBODY OUTSIDE HIS FAMILY COULD REALLY claim to know Ronald Reagan. He could "charm the hell" out of you, but he was an aloof, intensely private man who did not trade stories about his personal life. He now believed that he was a spokesman for the conservative viewpoint and that his voice was important. "An air of dignity" had wafted into his attitude. Helene Von Damm, his secretary during the 1960s, claimed he was "never one of the boys. A Ronald Reagan in a smoke-filled rap session after hours with his staff, or political friends, sitting behind the desk with rolled up shirt sleeves, open collar, feet on his desk, is . . . inconceivable to me. . . . Of course, he inherited an Irish temper and I must admit to having caught him using four-letter words . . . he will blush and utter an embarrassed apology on catching himself."

In speaking to factory workers on his tours, he never dressed down to his audience. He always wore a shirt and tie, the dark hair smoothed immaculately into the modified pompadour (which he retained, although the style was becoming passé). "Funny thing about Reagan," one of his co-workers commented, "he never seemed to sweat." He appeared at the SAG executive and emergency meetings impeccably dressed, although his choice of clothes always looked faintly outdated. This could have been because his frugal nature disallowed casting off anything in good condition or because he felt more comfortable in styles that reflected the Arrow shirt advertisements he had modeled for in the forties.

He returned to the SAG presidency reluctantly. "He felt that, you know, you've done it once, you've done it and it might even be construed as a sign of weakness," Jack Dales says. With Wasserman's nod of approval and the board's coaxing, his name was placed on the ballot without opposition, and he was elected. Almost instantaneously he was catapulted into a series of explosive negotiations with the producers to ward off a strike.

Two main issues were at stake in the SAG's contract demands: one, compensation for films from 1948 onward reissued to television; and two, the establishment of a welfare and pension fund. The issue of past films being sold to television had remained dormant for twelve years (since the last strike) because they were not, at that time, part of the networks' prevalent programming. But in 1959–60, several of the studios were in deep financial trouble; while none of the major studios had put their old films onto television, accusations rose that they were planning to do exactly that.*

Some of the SAG members felt the producers had a point in refusing back pay. "Who the hell ever went back twelve years retroactively? Who the hell ever went back anything retroactively? Maybe back two months. But twelve years. There was a strong feeling that we were out of our minds . . ." The board and a larger group of members did not agree. In addition to the desire for a share of the purchase price, "We [the actors] felt it's going to hurt the actor; his face is on the screen, and the more he's seen, the less he's going to be employable."

A crucial negotiating meeting was held between the Association of Motion Picture Producers and representatives of the Screen Actors Guild on January 18, 1960. For the first time in Hollywood labor history, the presidents of the five major studios participated in the discussions. By the end of the evening there had been no change in the position of either side.

---

*Old Westerns proliferated on television because Monogram and Republic, two of the smaller studios and specialists in the cowboy genre, had released their product.

The meeting was held at the offices of the Association of Motion Picture Producers. Reagan, Dales, the entire board of the SAG, the producers' negotiating committee and the five company presidents—Ben Kahane (Columbia), Barney Balaban (Paramount), Spyros Skouras (Twentieth Century-Fox), Joe Vogel (Metro-Goldwyn-Mayer) and Jack Warner sat around the massive thirty-by-fifteen-foot table. Reagan and Warner were seated facing each other. Skouras acted as general chairman and spokesman for the studios, which he said were not free agents. They had stockholders and boards of directors who claimed the films being discussed were company assets which they owned and no officer of the company was free to give away those rights.

Skouras was standing at the head of the oval table, Reagan was seated just off the curve to his left. It became clear that Skouras was directing his pitch to Reagan. He continued to mount the reasons why they really had nothing *to* discuss. The studios were in a state of emergency. Whatever the revenues might be from old films, the stockholders would demand that they be held against their losses.

Reagan told the Guild membership at the next general meeting that he had replied: "Mr. Skouras, do you mean to tell us now that if we, the whole [acting community], would settle for one percent [of profits from reuse] that you couldn't stay in business with ninety-nine percent? But you could stay in business if you got the other percent?"

"We won't discuss it," Skouras had replied. "It's a nonnegotiable subject."

"Well, we withdrew," Reagan told the thousands of Guild members packed into the vast Hollywood Palladium where Elvis Presley and Frank Sinatra concerts had drawn smaller audiences. "We didn't stop negotiations. We tried it on an off-the-record basis. Everybody knows that a negotiating committee has to make speeches. . . . So every once in a while, when you feel there might be a point to be made, you sort of find yourself out in the hall, and you say, 'What is really your problem?' And he says, 'What's yours?' And you trade notes and go back inside and wind up a deal.

"Somebody once said that in negotiations, you start out asking for the moon, and the other side offers green cheese. When you both get real tired of looking at each other, you settle in the middle of the table for a fair deal for both sides, where you should have settled in the first place.

"Well, we feel that we have proven that we are not asking for the moon any longer." He then told the audience of the board's decision to ask them for authority to call a strike in the hope that would break the deadlock. The strike was called, but not unanimously by any means, and the actors went out. "There was a lot of ferment," Kim Felner of the executive staff admits, "especially among the celebrities. After three or four weeks the regularly working actors, the studio actors, wanted to go back to work. There were a lot of private meetings in stars' homes, and he or she would say, 'Listen, we've got to mediate—maybe if we [the stars] take this position, the rest of the rank and file will come along.'"

"Hedda Hopper led a very conservative force. She wanted to appease the producers," Chet Migden, who was then the SAG's assistant executive secretary, says. "After a month when the actors were out of work and they began to be hit hard in the pocketbook, and they had gotten some points, they felt they should quit while they were still ahead. Reagan came to agree with them."

"Once we were in the strike period," Dales added, "the deal began to sweeten itself. The producers had offered four million dollars to start a pension and welfare plan right [then]. This [plan] started the day that the contract was signed. During six or seven weeks of the strike . . . there were actors who used to come to the office and say, 'This is wrong. We ought to be going back to work. We'll never make up what we're losing. And if you can get television residuals for us in the *future*, that's enough.' There were other actors who said, 'Don't sell us out. To the death, by God!'

"So it was tough . . . [the producers] said, in effect, you are getting retroactive pay. We're putting in four million dollars. *That's* retroactive pay. We're putting in the pension plan."

Fears of an approaching capitulation spread. Bitterness that was to last more than twenty-five years took hold. A paper was circulated with a picture of Reagan "decked out in a Hitler moustache and hairdo over the caption, 'Heil!'"

Then Richard Walsh, head of IATSE (International Alliance of Theatrical Stage Employees) met with Reagan and Dales. Walsh had made statements that he thought SAG was "wrecking the business," and he refused to give them his support. Not only that, but a statement by Walsh appeared in *Variety* and *Hollywood Reporter* that he would get his union triple whatever SAG got in terms of payment for the reuse of theatrical pictures in television.

"Walsh came in with his coterie of [union] leaders and Ronnie just really let him have it," said Dales. "I thought we were going to be in one of those good, old-fashioned fistfights. He said, 'It's the lousiest bit of strike breaking I've ever seen in my life.' That's all it was, was plain strike breaking.

"Walsh was red-faced, and the guys were on their feet. And Walsh—he was no fool—he said, 'Sit down, fellows.' So he said, 'I don't look at it that way. It just was a statement of fact. If it's good enough for you, it's good enough for us. I don't buy your use up of your face. If the pictures are going to be shown there, then they're not making pictures for television; our men are losing work.'" Walsh finally backed down, but Reagan now had problems with his own Guild.

Enter the mystery of the missing minutes. Reagan chaired a general membership meeting on April 18, 1960, to report the progress of the strike negotiations. About three hundred members attended. A transcript of all meetings was required, and one of that meeting was made and eventually "misplaced," and believed lost. Through the years a controversy raged as to what actually happened at that meeting. Some recall it as "a stormy session marked by calls for Reagan's resignation, denunciation of his ties with General Electric and an attack on the agreement [the plan for a pension fund in exchange for any residuals for 1948–59 films re-used for television] as a sweetheart contract selling out to management." SAG member Madelaine Lee recalled Leon Ames as "a heavy," and that members found printed sheets on their chairs with a pressured sales pitch to give in to the producers. Someone else claimed Reagan got so angry he surrendered the chair to Leon Ames, unable to continue. Another SAG member, Frank Maxwell, remembered "vividly" that "the people who had anything to say much against the contract were called out of order . . . and finally the meeting was adjourned at the height of all the debate . . . [it was] a very heated meeting, and I remember being very hot under the collar." Chet Migden, who was also present at the meeting, did not recall any clamor for Reagan to resign or that he turned the chair over to Ames.

The minutes, finally found in October 1980, told a different story. Leon Ames is not listed as having been present and no protest from the membership is recorded. Only a few dissenting votes are noted when a resolution was offered to allow eight feature films [halted in midproduction by the strike] to resume production [pending the final contract ratification]. But these "found" minutes have a traveling history. They were subpoenaed on Reagan's behalf by the Republican party when he announced his intention to campaign for the governorship. Ordinarily, the original typed transcript would have been held in the file and a copy delivered. When the minutes, years later, turned out to be missing, it was assumed that the original transcript had been sent by mistake and never returned. Then, in 1980, a SAG secretary, Joan Hausen, found a concurring typed transcript of the meeting in the 1960 strike-negotiations file. SAG now believed the minutes had been misfiled (all SAG minutes are in large black-leather binders marked by years). The mystery seemed a simple case of careless misfiling. However, on close examination, a further mystery presents itself. The April 18, 1960, minutes appear to have been typed on a different typewriter than that of the other minutes of the same year.

Chet Migden insists, "There are no 'missing minutes.' The minutes were misfiled. They are the official reporter's minutes taken by a court reporter [which might explain the difference in type from the general minutes], probably Noon and Pratt whom we customarily used back then. In any event that's what happened at the meeting.

"People confuse this with another meeting during the strike which was hot. The actors who wanted it over versus those who wanted to stay out. The Guild stayed out . . . Reagan felt it was necessary to establish the actors' right to additional payment for theatrical films on TV. . . . He fought a good fight in negotiations. . . . The issue was emotional and still is. The possibility of getting producers to give up a share of what they already owned was the impossible mountain to climb. . . ."

Reagan claimed that the strike ended in June between "soup and salad" at one of those large Hollywood dinner parties "where some two hundred guests prowl around tables for ten minutes looking for their own names on place cards." Reagan found himself seated next to Anna Rosenberg, employed by the studios as a public-relations adviser in the strike. Whether by coincidence or not, whoever put those two place cards next to each other enabled Reagan to lay out to Rosenberg "exactly what the Guild would settle for" on an easy, social level.

Two days later, MGM's Joe Vogel called Reagan at the Guild asking for a private meeting. Vogel had flown out from New York and Dales and Reagan met him in his room at the Beverly Hills Hotel. "Vogel fancied himself a peace maker," Migden recalled. "He failed." But negotiations were going on at the Producers Association, and four days after the Vogel meeting a deal was struck.

After six months and a loss of many millions of dollars, the actors went back to work. They had sold all TV rights in films they had made from 1948 to 1959 to the producers for two million dollars to establish an improved pension and welfare plan, one half of the producers' original offer.* Somehow, during the long months of negotiation, the SAG had lessened, not strengthened, its bargaining power.

A large faction in the Guild screamed "sellout," feeling the advantage gained by the pension did not balance the loss of wages while they had been on strike and the loss of income they would have received from residuals. Those whose careers were ended by 1959 because of age, changing fashions and the blacklist now had no future income from old films to look forward to, although they were to show up regularly on the late show. Films made *after* 1959 were not generally shown until two decades later, with good economic reason, since film companies did not have to pay out any fees for reuse on pre-1959 films. Despite this, Reagan has always insisted he won a good deal for the SAG.

"It was about June [1960]," Dales remembered, "that he said to me, 'I know I came back for a purpose, and it's been accomplished. I just don't think I should stay. And besides which (and I think this was an excuse) I have a chance to get into producing.'"†

Reagan not only stepped down from the presidency,‡ but he and Nancy went off the board. When he left the Guild offices for the last time as president or board member on July 9, 1960, he said he had "something of the same feeling" he had had the day he walked out of Fort MacArthur, his war service having ended. However, repercussions he had not anticipated were to follow.

Reagan's switch to the Republican party did not happen all at once. But he had crossed the track to the other side in 1950, when he supported Nixon (no matter how surreptitiously) against Helen Gahagan Douglas, and in 1952 he boarded the Republican train during the Eisenhower-Nixon campaign. His vote for Eisenhower had been a comfortable crossover. The last two years of Truman's presidency had been tainted by a scandal of payoffs within the administration, disenchanting many Democrats. And not only

---

*Later, an agreement was made for reuse of films made after that date (1959) with specific percentages.

†Reagan was referring to an offer from G.E. to produce several episodes of the General Electric Theater.

‡George Chandler was elected to replace Reagan.

was the general a great American hero, he had never previously been associated with any political party. Even Jack and Nelle might have understood their son's switch. Now Jack was dead and Nelle was in a nursing home in Santa Monica, no longer interested in her son's politics. Reagan had no one to answer to except his own conscience. In truth, he thought like a Republican, adhered almost wholly to that party's philosophies and principles and no longer believed in many of the things that had once made him a Democrat.

With the passage of the Twenty-second Amendment, limiting the president to two terms of office, Eisenhower could not run for a third term. Had there been no constitutional bar, his closest advisers believed, he would have run again and his popularity would have ensured a victory over any of the likely Democratic candidates. Eisenhower was not overly enthusiastic about Vice-President Nixon as the Republican candidate. He even suggested that Nixon might be better as a secretary of defense. Despite eight years in the White House, the Republicans were still the minority party. Their leaders shared Eisenhower's grave doubts about Nixon's ability to win an election and cited the storm of local protest that had beaten back an attempt to name a street in his hometown of Whittier, California, in his honor. On a visit to Whittier College, his alma mater, only two students would shake his hand.

Nevertheless, enough people believed that he would make an effective president to enable him to win the Republican nomination. Reagan, as a registered Democrat, could not vote in a Republican primary. But as soon as Nixon became the candidate, he joined in his campaign.

The Democratic candidate was John F. Kennedy, and this election was not the first time that he had crossed swords with Richard Nixon. When both sat on the House Labor Committee as freshmen congressmen, they had disagreed so vehemently over the Taft-Hartley Act that they carried their fight outside Congress to a public debate.* Though a Democrat, Kennedy had been considered "a fighting conservative."† He had been running for the presidency since he lost the Democratic vice-presidential vote to Estes Kefauver in 1956. His book *Profiles in Courage* had been a best seller. He had barnstormed the country back and forth, north

---

*Both claimed victory.
† Kennedy campaigned for Congress in Boston, Massachusetts, in 1946 with that slogan.

and south, for three and a half years, speaking at Democratic rallies and dinners, raising money for Democratic candidates in almost every state, and by January 2, 1960, when he declared his intention to run, he was already a national figure.

Kennedy was a well-educated, urbane man, witty, good-looking, brave (a war hero) and so rich no one could ever suspect him of any financial infraction. Young people identified with his youth (forty-three), and his charm, intelligence and energy were indisputable. But in the early stages of the campaign, he was regarded by the liberals with suspicion because of his and his family's close ties to McCarthy (who had died in 1957 in disgrace).* The more conservative Democrats thought him "too young, too rich, too independent, and in too much of a hurry." He was also a Catholic, a "daunting obstacle" to be faced. No wonder Nixon was so confident at the start of their campaign.

Both his own party and Nixon had underestimated Kennedy. He knew just how to run with issues and there was no contest between his personal charisma and his opponent's once they had engaged in their famous television debates. The younger man's vigor, his sophistication, his physical presence were at their best advantage against Nixon's saturnine face and use of standard homilies.

Although he called himself a Democrat for Nixon, Reagan chose this campaign to align himself finally with the Republican party. Reagan's all-involving activities during the first half of 1960—the SAG and his duties for G.E.—kept him from active campaigning, and his public support would have made it appear as though General Electric were endorsing Nixon.

The steadily impassioned Kennedy, with long-legged Texan Lyndon Baines Johnson as his running mate, won the election with the help of the Kennedy organization—hundreds of "effective, intelligent, loyal lieutenants"—but it had not been a landslide. Despite all his shortcomings, Nixon had come closer to winning than the Democrats wanted to believe.†

---

*McCarthy had dated Kennedy's sister Patricia, and Robert Kennedy had been on his staff. John Kennedy had met McCarthy during World War II in the South Pacific and was the only Democratic senator not to vote for the resolution to condemn McCarthy; and in 1952 he contributed three thousand dollars to McCarthy's campaign. Because of his support and friendship to McCarthy, Eleanor Roosevelt had refused to back Kennedy's vice-presidential attempt in 1956, even after he personally appealed to her.

†The Republican party had doubts that Nixon *had* lost. Some of Nixon's supporters wanted him to challenge the results. Nixon refused. "Our country cannot afford the agony of a constitutional crisis—and I damn well will not be party to creating one," he is quoted as having said.

*   *   *

As late as 1961, Reagan was still publicly flailing the issue of Communist infiltration of Hollywood, although McCarthy's downfall and death had happened years before. Under Kennedy, Washington was now a Camelot where nothing ugly ever happened. True, the American Legion published a list of films to be boycotted because some member of the cast or crew had once supported a supposedly Communist front organization. And a reprehensible blacklist did still exist. Few new names had been added since 1957. Hollywood had a new enemy to combat—television—and fighting a "Red invasion" seemed less threatening, at least to the pocketbook.

Yet the speech Reagan was giving across the country under the auspices of General Electric in 1961 was rabidly anti-Communist. He declared that "the Communist party has ordered once again the infiltration of the picture business as well as the theatre and television. They are crawling out from under the rocks, and memories being as short as they are, there are plenty of well-meaning but misguided people willing to give them a hand. . . . Most people agree that the ideological struggle with Russia is the number one problem in the world . . . and yet, many men in high places in government and many who mold opinion in the press and on the air waves, subscribe to a theory that we are at peace . . . the inescapable truth is that we are at war, and we are losing that war simply because we don't or won't realize we are in it.

". . . Only in that phase of the war which causes our greatest fear are we ahead—the use of armed force. Thanks to the dedicated patriotism and realistic thinking of our men in uniform we would win a shooting war. But, this isn't a decisive factor in the Communist Campaign. They never really intended to conquer us by force unless we yielded to a massive peace campaign and disarmed. Then, the Russians would resort to armed conflict if it could shortcut their time table with no great risk to themselves.

". . . The Communists are supremely confident of victory. They believe that you and I, under the constant pressure of the cold war, will give up, one by one, our democratic customs and traditions. We'll adopt emergency 'temporary' totalitarian measures, until one day we'll awaken to find we have grown so much like the enemy that we no longer have any cause for conflict.

"There can only be one end to the war we are in. It won't go away if we simply try to out-wait it. Wars end in victory or defeat. One of the foremost authorities on Communism in the world today [name not given] has said we have ten years. Not ten years to make up our minds, but ten years to win or lose—by 1970 the world will be all slave or all free."

He ended with patriotic fervor:

"In this land, occurred the only true revolution in man's history. All other revolutions simply exchanged one set of rulers for another. Here for the first time the Founding Fathers—that little band of men so advanced beyond their time that the world has never seen their like since—evolved a government based on the idea that you and I have the God given right and ability within ourselves to determine our own destiny. Freedom is never more than one generation away from extinction—we didn't pass it on to our children in the bloodstream. It must be fought for, protected, and handed on for them to do the same, or one day we will spend our sunset years telling our children and our children's children what it once was like in the United States when men were free."

When he gave this speech to the Phoenix Chamber of Commerce on March 30, Loyal Davis was in the audience. After hearing it, Reagan's father-in-law urged him to try his hand at politics. Reagan still resisted. Some said he didn't like the proposed billing—junior senator from California; others felt it was a matter of money—a senator's salary at that time being about one fifth of Reagan's income with General Electric.

That obstacle would soon be removed. In spring 1962, at the end of its eighth season, General Electric decided to discontinue *General Electric Theater* because of the high ratings of *Bonanza* on a competing network in the same time slot. Reagan was now unemployed.

24

THE TOURS INSTILLED IN REAGAN A FEELING OF great wisdom. Tragedy had not often touched his life. The end of his first marriage had been a serious setback. Nelle's recent death on July 25, 1962, had struck him a hard blow, and even with the tender presence of Nancy, it took him several months to recover his usual high spirits. His difficult childhood and youth had prepared him to take tough times in stride. But now they appeared to be over. His years with G.E. had provided a cushion for his future, and through a deal he made shortly after his SAG board resignation he owned a 25 percent interest in the last films he had made for G.E.

One of the first moves that John F. Kennedy made after becoming president of the United States was to name his brother, Robert F. Kennedy, as attorney general. Robert Kennedy turned his immediate attention to the job of routing out antitrust violations, and MCA received the full thrust of his energy. What the attorney general hoped to prove was "that MCA's unique position, achieved through the 'blanket' waiver of being the only organization controlling both a talent agency (MCA Artists, Ltd.) and a television film production company (Revue) is leading inevitably to (a) monopolization of 'Name' talent, and (b) monopolization of television film production. We also hope to prove that the grant of this 'blanket' waiver was effectuated by a conspiracy between MCA and SAG. . . ."

Reagan was subpoenaed to testify in a private session before the grand jury three months into the investigation, on February 5, 1962. The grand jury was looking for a possible payoff by MCA to Reagan for his aid in securing the SAG grant for the lucrative MCA-SAG waiver. Reagan testified for nearly two hours without a break and acquitted himself well. A month later, the Justice Department ordered an audit of both Nancy's (because she had also been on the SAG board) and Reagan's Internal Revenue tax returns for the years 1952–62. (However, the year 1951, a key year if Reagan was repaying a debt to MCA rather than accepting a bribe, was never investigated.) It was shortly thereafter that G.E. canceled *General Electric Theater*.

What with Nelle's death, Reagan spent a stressful summer while the inquiry continued and the IRS audits were being made. Then, on September 18, 1962 (the date that ended MCA's blanket waiver with the SAG), MCA signed a court-ordered consent decree to divest itself of all its interest as a talent agency. (By this time, Revue Productions earned about ten times the yearly volume of the agency.) The attorney general withdrew his bloodhounds and sent them barking at the heels of organized crime.

Earlier in the year, Reagan had at last registered as a Republican. Loyal Davis, Holmes Tuttle and Justin Dart convinced him to run against the more liberal Republican, Senator Thomas Kuchel, in the upcoming primary. Reagan refused. "The whole notion of entering politics was alien to my thinking," he insisted. He wanted to get back to "his kind of work," but he was not being flooded with offers. He no longer had MCA to represent him. He had, in fact, returned to Bill Meiklejohn who, after all these years, was running his own agency again.

Neil had become a top executive with the advertising firm of McCann, Erickson, and had successfully handled many of their television accounts. The firm represented the United States Borax Company, who sponsored a television show called *Death Valley Days*. "The old boy . . . (at that time we called him 'the Old Ranger') who was the host on the show, he got to the place where he was so old that it took more time for us to shoot the forty-five-second opening and forty-five-second close than it did to shoot the half-hour show. Put three words together and he couldn't remember the middle word, or maybe the last," Neil recalled. "U.S. Borax agreed that we were going to have to replace him. Well, the question now becomes—who?

"Dutch had just finished the *G.E. Theater* contract and wasn't doing anything . . . so I suggested to the client, 'What about Reagan?' He said, 'Oh, if you can get him, you're damned right.' Dutch said, 'No way, I don't want to replace [the Old Ranger].' I got the brilliant idea. Why not go to his agent, Bill Meiklejohn, who was not doing so good and between us we set things up."

Neil was in the habit of eating his lunch each day at the Hollywood Brown Derby and had the same booth up front for himself on a more-or-less permanent reservation. "One day in walks Dutch and stops at my table. 'If it wasn't for you, I wouldn't have to be here this noon, dressed up with a tie on,' [he said]. I says, 'What do you mean, because of me?' He says, 'I'm having lunch with Bill Meiklejohn.' I said, 'Well, I hope he's got something for you.'" Reagan then went to join Meiklejohn at his table. "After lunch, Bill Meiklejohn comes over. 'Go ahead and write the contract up and send it over to him. He'll sign it.' He did."

Death Valley, California, is supposedly the hottest place in the world, hotter than the Sahara or the Gobi. That's in the summer, of course. The rest of the year, the temperatures can hit ninety even after the sun goes down, but an occasional wind blows in over the hills swirling the sand into dunes. No one can estimate how many poor souls perished there during the mid-nineteenth century, but the heat hadn't deterred the wagons from passing through in their westward search for gold. In its half-hour segments, *Death Valley Days* retold the legends of this land (adding quite a few new ones in the process). These were the kind of stories Reagan loved to read and see. "It worked out all right," Neil was convinced. "He was happy. There was a little method in my madness that transcended the *Death Valley Days* thing. It kept him in the public eye for what I figured might be helpful."

Neil, along with Tuttle and the others, was in there coaxing him to try his hand at politics, but he continued to resist the idea. Nevertheless, he became more active in the campaigns of other Californians running for office on the Republican ticket. In the summer of 1962, he served as a featured speaker at a fund-raising affair for John Rousselot, an avowed John Birch Society member then running for Congress. Reagan, when questioned about his endorsement of a member of such an extremist group, said he did so "automatically, because he was a Republican." And then he actively campaigned for the extremist candidate Loyd Wright (the same man who had represented Wyman in Reagan's divorce suit) against Thomas Kuchel.

Nancy had been cast in the role of her dreams, wife of a prominent man, but she did not guess the details of the final screenplay yet. Dr. Davis and all of Reagan's old friends kept telling her what a great future her husband would have in politics. She confided to one of her friends, "Ron can't be pushed; he can be coaxed." When Joan Didion interviewed her about this time, she wrote, "Nancy Reagan has an interested smile, the smile of someone who grew up in comfort and went to Smith College and has a father who is a distinguished neuro-surgeon and a husband who is the definition of Nice Guy, the smile of a woman who seems to be playing out some middle-class American woman's daydream, circa 1948. The set for this daydream is perfectly dressed, every detail correct. . . . There on the coffee table in the living room lie precisely the right magazines . . . *Town and Country, Vogue, Time, Life, Newsweek, Sports Illustrated, Fortune* and *Art News.* There are two dogs named Lady and Fuzzy and two children named Patti and Ronnie. . . ."

At forty-three, Nancy's youthfully spare size-six figure and her air of immaculate chic were still intact. Her short red-brown hair with its gold highlights was lacquered to remain in place even in a high wind. She still favored the color red (new red rugs had been added in the house). She liked music you could dance and sing to—Gershwin, Cole Porter—and the singing of Frank Sinatra. She read current novels, and kept up with magazine articles of topical interest. And she truly loved her husband. "I gauge everything by the birth of my children or when I was married," she told her mother's friend Eleanor Harris. "I said, 'Nancy, people just don't *believe* it when you look at Ronnie that way—as though you're saying, "He's my hero." You know what she said to me? She said, 'But he *is* my hero.'"

When asked why Reagan had changed parties, Nancy bridled, "Remember when Churchill left the liberal party to join the Conservatives? He said, 'Some men change their party for the sake of their principles; others their principles for the sake of their party.' Ronnie feels that way about becoming a Republican."

As President Kennedy's term progressed, so did his esteem in the eyes of the nation—and the world. The Kennedys—John,

Jackie, John-John and Caroline, Robert and Ethel and their great tribe, Rose and Joe—were the closest the United States had come to having a royal family. By November 1963, just a few months after the president's forty-sixth birthday, they seemed to be riding an even greater crest of popularity. Nonetheless, Kennedy had made plans to visit first Florida and then Texas to court votes for the upcoming 1964 election. He had lost Florida in 1960, and Texas, though Lyndon Johnson's home state, was in danger of going over to the affluent, extreme Right. His reception had been overwhelming all along the way, and when he arrived in Dallas on Friday, November 22, 1963, he had every reason to believe that Camelot would last longer than "one brief shining moment."

No one understood Kennedy's senseless assassination. The Western world and the new president, Lyndon Baines Johnson, inherited none of his laurel wreaths and all of his unsolved and unfinished problems, not the least of them being the Vietnam War.

In August 1964, American destroyers in the Gulf of Tonkin were attacked by the North Vietnamese and a presidential campaign was in full swing. Johnson stood on a peace platform against Loyal Davis's friend Barry Goldwater, who proposed the use of nuclear weapons, if necessary, to win the war. Ultraconservative Republicans had become united in their support of Goldwater. He was a man "who spoke their language, denouncing Federal matching grants to the states as 'a mixture of blackmail and bribery.'" He accused the U.N. Secretariat of brimming with Red spies ("Get the U.S. out of the U.N. and the U.N. out of the U.S." was one of his campaign chants). He also stated that if elected he would try to remove the Federal government's hand in education, agriculture, urban renewal and social security. He was in favor of an equal income-tax rate for rich and poor.

America's faith in itself was badly shaken with Kennedy's murder. During the three years that he had served, the people had come to believe as he had that the fulfillment of their historic ambitions was within their sight. His murder immobilized the liberals who weren't sure they could trust the new president. People thought of the tough, often vulgar Texan as a power-driven man, and Johnson had less than a year to win the country's confidence.

The Republican party had suffered its own bitter disappointments and setbacks. The conservatives felt betrayed by Eisenhower's administration and still were reeling from Nixon's defeat. They wanted power so badly they could taste it, and in their search for a man who they felt could not only stand up to Lyndon Baines

Johnson but had the charisma to replace him in the White House, they came up with Senator Barry Morris Goldwater.

The senator was charming, energetic and witty. By press standards, "A damned hard man to dislike." A big man (6 feet, 185 pounds), he could stand toe to toe with Johnson and look him straight in the eye. The Arizona sun and his love of the outdoors had given his handsome blond looks a salubrious glow. He laughed easily and liked to kid himself. At one Republican fundraising dinner, he quipped, "Many predict that I might make our finest Civil War President." His father was Jewish, his mother Episcopalian, and he and his brother and sister had been brought up in their mother's faith. On the death of his father in 1929, he left his studies at the University of Arizona to enter the family business, a successful string of Arizona department stores headquartered in Phoenix. He became friendly with Justin Dart, who had been sent to Phoenix by Charles Walgreen, his father-in-law.* Goldwater married a friend of Ruth Walgreen Dart's, Margaret Prescott Johnson, whose father was one of the founders of Borg-Warner Corp., giving him an early connection to big business. A tremendous ambition drove him, and on two occasions (two years apart—1937 and 1939) he suffered nervous collapses that required lengthy "rest" periods. "His nerves broke completely," Mrs. Goldwater admitted.

As a lieutenant colonel during the war, Goldwater ferried planes across the North Atlantic (he had been a pilot most of his adult life) and saw action in the Mediterranean and China-Burma-India theaters. After the war, he became a major general in the air force reserves and was one of the only senators qualified to fly an air force jet. He had started his political career in Phoenix, when he was elected to the city council in 1949. Three years later, aided by an Eisenhower majority, he helped to break the Democratic grip on Arizona by being elected to the Senate.

Reagan had met Goldwater just at the time of this great victory. He could not help but admire and identify with the man. Goldwater was a great outdoorsman, an expert pilot, a confident speaker and a power in his own state. During the next twelve years, Reagan often came to Phoenix and saw Goldwater socially. A lot of the same good-humored political arguments he had once had with Hal Gross and Dick Powell he now had with Goldwater

---

*Barry Goldwater recalls, "The first time I saw Justin Dart he was jerking sodas trying to learn the drugstore business."

and Davis. By 1956, Reagan's friendship with Goldwater was close enough for the Reagans to christen their son with the middle name "Prescott," one of Mrs. Goldwater's family's names.

Goldwater had heard Reagan's 1962 speech to the Phoenix Chamber of Commerce (given elsewhere as well), and he called on Reagan to help his campaign in California. Reagan agreed, but said it would have to wait until his current work was done. He had the *Death Valley Days* season to complete, as well as an NBC-TV picture, *The Killers* (produced by Universal and Revue Productions), based on the Ernest Hemingway short story. The story had already been made into a film in 1946 by Universal and had starred Burt Lancaster (his first movie role) as the man marked for death and resigned to die. Reagan had believed that with *Hellcats of the Navy* his film career was over. But when Bill Meiklejohn suggested he play Browning in *The Killers,* he could not refuse.

This remake was to be a part of Project 120, Revue Productions' series of films for television that would eventually be released to theaters (a new concept in 1964). Reagan was not cast in the Burt Lancaster role (played by John Cassavetes), but as a powerful, violent underworld figure, a type of role—a heavy— that he had never assayed before, and Don Siegel, with whom he had worked on *Night Unto Night,* was to direct. The decision to take the role had taken courage. The character went against the image his public had of him and, although the part was a challenge, he wasn't sure he wanted to be seen as a thug and a murderer. Yet, he accepted the film, which was to star Cassavetes, Lee Marvin, Clu Gulager and Angie Dickinson, and received fifth billing for his supporting part.

The new screenplay lacked the plausibility of the original and had confusing plot shifts. Nonetheless, Don Siegel supplied it with a fast, hard pace and a mood that was reminiscent of some of the early Bogart and Cagney films. In the end it did not work, because Siegel superimposed the realistic violence of a 1964 crime movie upon the background of an earlier period. The use of Technicolor further defeated the somber tone he sought to maintain.

A Ronald Reagan slapping around (*hard*) a beautiful, vulnerable Angie Dickinson, a good-guy Reagan as a crook and murderer, even if he is killed for his crimes in the end of the film, was inconceivable to filmgoers. The film's gratuitous violence barred it from television, the medium for which it had been planned. All in all, *The Killers* was an unfitting finale to Reagan's movie career. And yet he gave one of his better acting performances. Siegel had somehow managed to dent his nice-guy armor. Onscreen he is *not* Ronald Reagan, he *is* Browning, albeit a crime lord with more charm than most.

His work in *The Killers* took only a few weeks. Goldwater had asked for his support, but Reagan was working on another project, his life story (to be titled *Where's the Rest of Me?*), with Richard C. Hubler. It was not to be a typical movie-star auto- biography. It contained very little gossip and revealed almost nothing about his mature private life. What he deemed important was for the world to see him in the light he saw himself—as much more than a movie actor—as a man of serious intellect capable of withstanding tremendous pressure, a former labor negotiator who won major victories for his membership, and a man of good values and a strong belief in Mom, family and God, an unbigoted small- town middle-American boy who had never tried to hide from his roots.

While Hubler was doing the final writing on the book, Reagan decided the time was right for him to make himself more visible in the world of politics. He spoke locally at some Goldwater rallies, and he involved Neil in the senator's campaign.

"I got a call from Ronald one day saying, 'Senator Goldwater is going to call you. He's been getting all kinds of complaints on some TV spots that have been made by the agency that is han- dling him and I told him he should call you,'" Neil recalled. "[The next day] Barry called me . . . I said, 'Well what is your problem?' And he says, 'Well, I'd like to have somebody bring my problem over and show it to you. I'm getting all kinds of crit- icisms on my TV commercials [that he did not communicate well].' I said, 'Well, Senator, first of all, let me say this. You've got an advertising agency, and this really is not Kosher for me to get involved here.' But, I said, 'As long as you're a good friend of my brother's . . . I'll look at the commercial . . . and I'll tell you what I think is wrong with it.'

"Well, he didn't come over. He sent somebody over with the commercial. . . . Here sits Barry in the middle of the davenport between two women. The spot opens with the camera on Barry Goldwater and an announcer's voice-over telling you that Barry Goldwater's going to be interviewed by these two women . . . you don't do a spot with three people on the davenport, because every time that Barry has to now answer this woman over here, he now turns this way, and you've got a great shot of his ear.

"So I told him . . . 'If the other spots are like this, you're throwing money away.'" Despite the fact that Neil felt it would not be ethical to take Goldwater as a client when he had a contract with another company, he suggested he call the New York office of McCann, Erikson and discuss the situation with them. They said, "We'll take the account."

"I traveled with the senator for sixty-five days on his seven-twenty-seven [used for the campaign]," Neil continued, ". . . We had to go into Washington every Sunday and Monday, which was all right because then we could do spots on Monday at the CBS Studio in Washington, D.C. [One Monday] a call came through that Reagan was going to do a speech on CBS but that one of the [Republican] sponsors . . . felt that there were some things in the speech that were counter to points in the Goldwater campaign. . . . Goldwater took the call and then handed me the phone—why he handed me the phone I don't know but I listened to the story again—and then I . . . turned around to Barry and said [this was the day of the night Reagan's speech was to be broadcast coast to coast], 'Well there's one way you can find out whether or not there's anything in this speech that you do not approve of or that's counter to what you have been saying in your campaign . . . we'll get them to feed just the voice portion of the TV show and you can listen to it.' Barry said, 'OK'—I made the arrangements with the network. They fed it through on a spare loop. He listened to it in the control booth and after it was all through, to use an old Barry Goldwater expression, he said, 'What the hell is wrong with that?'"

The speech was released over national television the night of October 27, just one week before the election. Called "A Time for Choosing," it incorporated many of the same themes Reagan had used in his G.E. "Encroaching Control" speech three years earlier and added (or borrowed) some fancy poetic phrases which gave it more grandeur. "You and I have a rendezvous with destiny," he said (without due credit to FDR for the phrase). "We can preserve for our children this last, best hope of man on earth, or we can sentence them to take the first step into a thousand years of darkness." He introduced all his former views on health, housing, farming, industry, commerce, education and government spending.

"If we fail," he ended, "at least let our children's children say of us we justified our brief moment here. We did all that could be done."

One press team called it, "The most successful national politi-

cal debut since William Jennings Bryan electrified the 1896 Democratic Convention with his 'Cross of Gold' speech." Had
Goldwater been given the video to watch and not just the sound
track of this speech, he might have had more reservations about
Reagan presenting it. For Reagan was an actor who had played
this same role in hundreds of previous performances. He knew
how to use each nuance to make a point, to hold the camera, to
make those beyond the camera believe he was speaking directly to
them. Very few political personalities could compete. His old
imitations of FDR had not gone to waste, nor his close study of
Kennedy during the Kennedy-Nixon debates.

Neil says that the speech brought one million dollars of campaign funds. The problem was that Goldwater's followers had lost
heart for their candidate with Reagan's appearance. What they
wanted was a candidate with Goldwater's views and Reagan's
charisma. With Reagan, they would have had both.

Barry Goldwater's attempt for the presidency failed. The nation chose Lyndon Baines Johnson. The day after the November
4, 1964, election, a group of conservatives in Owosso, Michigan,
Thomas Dewey's birthplace, formed "Republicans for Ronald
Reagan."

A movie star had retired from his career, and a political star
had been born.

25

IN THE TARANTELLA OF POLITICS, SOME MEN HAVE the talent to lead, some to follow. Others, knowing they cannot lead and unsatisfied with being followers, become the men who make the music and, upon occasion, pull the strings that make a political star dance. Reagan had many friends who saw in him a man who had the natural ability to attract followers. This quality does not always suggest that such a person is also a leader. That is a gamble political backers take.

Charles E. Cook had been a self-made man. He had been born in Enid, Oklahoma, and brought up in El Paso, Texas, where he had been a bank clerk. At the age of twenty he went to California, and within six years had advanced from bank clerk to bank founder. He had also struck up a friendship with Holmes Tuttle, the used-car dealer. Both men were Republicans active in their party. Both men hankered after power. And both men recognized that they did not have the talent to lead. Of the two, perhaps Holmes Tuttle was the driving force. It had been Tuttle's idea to get Reagan into politics, "not the smoke-filled back room type of thing." Having met him through Justin Dart in the 1940s, Cook has said that Reagan was never interested in state or local politics, or the idea of having to answer to constituents. After Reagan's nationwide television address at the end of the Goldwater campaign, Cook and his brother Howard (his business partner) went into action. Within a matter of six weeks, they and five others got up a pot of thirty-six thousand dollars and asked Reagan to run for governor (of California) in 1966. From that moment, Reagan had his eye on the presidency.

He knew very little about California's problems, especially those indigenous to the northern part of the state. He had never held office on a local or state level. He was, however, willing to learn. Cook has claimed that even as early as 1964, shortly after Goldwater's crushing defeat, Reagan was thinking about announcing himself as a 1968 presidential candidate. Cook and Tuttle worked to convince him his chances would be increased if he had high visibility as governor of California before going for "the big one."

Though still silent on his future, Reagan wasted no time in looking like a candidate. On November 10, less than one week after the 1964 election, he appeared as the major speaker at a meeting of the Los Angeles County Young Republicans:

"We don't intend to turn the Republican Party over to the traitors in the battle just ended [a jab at Kuchel, who had refused to endorse Goldwater]. We will have no more of those candidates who are pledged to the same goals of our opposition and who seek our support . . . turning the Party over to the so-called moderates wouldn't make any sense at all."

By 1964, Reagan's old friend Justin Dart was a powerful figure in California politics. Like Reagan, he thought of himself as a "big-issues guy . . . interested in the national economy and our defense ability, not all these crappy little issues like equal rights or abortion or the Moral Majority or whatever." Dart's language was "habitually littered with profanities ranging from the old fashioned to the coarse," but he had a commanding self-image. When Dart spoke, he expected people to listen—and Reagan did, for he much admired this masculine, shrewd, unsentimental wheeler-dealer, who was at his best "maneuvering behind closed doors."

Through the years, Dart had become one of the party's most aggressive fund-raisers. He both knew the men and women with money and how to get them to make large contributions. His reputation as a king-maker began when he raised so much money for Eisenhower in 1956 that he and the president became personal friends. Reagan was fortunate to have him on his team.

"I don't think he's the most brilliant man I ever met," Dart declared, "but I always knew Ron was a real leader—he's got credibility. He can get on his feet and influence people."

The group around Reagan now included Cook, Cy Rubel, Tuttle, Dart and the men he brought in—oil man Henry Salvatori,* steel magnate Earle Jorgensen, businessman Jack Wrather and Diners Club millionaire Alfred Bloomingdale, whose wife Betsy became Nancy's best friend. Nancy never had a coterie of women friends, but she and Betsy got on well.

Nancy was encouraging Reagan. She knew what it would mean to be a candidate's wife and the idea appealed to her. In 1965 the big question was, Will Reagan run for governor in 1966? Sheilah Graham found Nancy "tense and cautious" during this time, "not the pleasant girl I had known during her brief career in minor pictures at M.G.M. . . . A friend of mine bumped into Nancy at the Saks Fifth Avenue store on Wilshire Boulevard [Beverly Hills] and called to tell me, 'He's running, she was nice to me.' "

Graham was at the Reagans' [in the course of an interview in 1964] when "a telephone call came for him. Ronnie excused himself. He was smiling when he returned. 'A very silly thing just happened. A group of Republicans asked me if I'd be interested in running for Governor.' I thought it was too silly to bother to write about. '. . . It's a wild notion isn't it?' he grinned and was off and running about how the newly elected Democrats were 'leading us to ruin with too much power concentrated in Washington.' "

Neil remembered that ". . . he held out a long time after the suggestion was made to him that he run for governor. The group that got together [including] Cy Rubel, who was at that time chairman of the board of the Union Oil Company, and Holmes Tuttle . . . Ronald trusted Holmes . . . they saw fit to include me in their group during the long sessions up at the house [San Onofre], which used to start at eight o'clock in the evening and wind up at three or four the next morning, talking to him about running for governor. He was very noncommittal. . . . [They asked me to join them] because I was his brother [and thought I might influence Reagan]. . . . I kept a very low profile for the

---

*Henry Salvatori withdrew his support of Reagan when he ran a second time for governor of California.

meetings, but every once in a while he would call me or I'd call him, and then we'd get to talking about that. And then I'd say, 'Well, you really ought to give it serious consideration.'"

If Reagan ran, his opponent would be the incumbent governor (Edmund G.) Pat Brown, a party Democrat with a somewhat lackluster personality. "I have no style and I know it," Brown once confided to a friend. "I'd give anything to have it, but it's just not there." What Brown lacked in personality he made up for in sidewalk politicking—mixing it up with voters, kissing babies, shaking hands. He had also been a good governor, could rely on potent Washington Democrats coming to California to speak on his behalf, and could theoretically count on the registration ratio in the state, where Democrats outnumbered Republicans three to two. The campaign would not be easy. The odds were not in Reagan's favor, and Northern California was not entranced with the idea of an actor for governor. And also before Reagan could get a whack at Pat Brown, he would have to win in the Republican primary against George Christopher, former mayor of San Francisco and a moderate.

By December 1965, Reagan had decided to announce his candidacy, but no public statement was made. He had no previous political experience and "The Friends of Ronald Reagan" (as the group now called themselves) wanted to be sure he would have the best public-relations staff possible. Neil thought the campaign would be handled by his company, McCann, Erickson.

"Ronald called me one day and said, 'I want you to have lunch today. Meet me at the [Cave des Roys] . . . a private club [then on La Cienega and Beverly Boulevard]. . . . So I met him at eleven-thirty, and he comes over and gets in my car and says, 'The people we're going to have lunch with won't be here until twelve. I want to talk to you.' And I said, 'OK.' And he said, 'Now, this is an outfit called Spencer-Roberts.' 'Who is Spencer-Roberts?' 'I don't know,' he said, 'somebody suggested that we might talk to them about handling the campaign. They've handled other campaigns.' I said, 'Well, I thought that I made it plain that this would go through McCann, Erickson.' 'Well, why?' 'So I can keep an eye on it.'"

By the time of this conversation, Stuart Spencer and Bill Roberts were already hired. The final arrangements were that Spencer and Roberts would take care of the purely political areas—speeches, campaigning, press arrangements; and McCann, Erickson would handle all the media advertising.

On the afternoon of January 4, 1966, Ronald Reagan welcomed the press to his hilltop home on San Onofre. He was tanned and smiling as he and Nancy ushered their guests into the living room, "so splurged with color that even [Reagan's] black pants and black loafers seemed exuberant." He also wore a blue-and-green wool tartan jacket, a purple tie and a white shirt. Nancy looked vibrant in a neat red-wool outfit. Spencer and Roberts were determined the Reagans would portray a youthful, confident façade. Reagan announced his candidacy and then settled back on the large comfortable sofa, Nancy by his side, and began talking about his youth in Dixon, Illinois, and how he had come home from Eureka College to no work, and how he had hitchhiked to Chicago and then finally got a job in Davenport, Iowa, as a sports announcer for five bucks a game. He liked telling the story. He told it well and he told it the same way he had told it perhaps a hundred times before. Nancy sat, hands clasped, eyes raised in a loving gaze.

Dutch Reagan had come a long way from the dock at Lowell Park where he had saved seventy-seven lives. Now he believed he might just be able to save a whole state full of people swimming in waters he considered dangerous. A short time later he wrote Mr. Neer, his former Sunday School teacher in Dixon, "Every once in a while I pinch myself . . . thinking this can't be 'Dutch Reagan' here. I should still be out on the dock at Lowell Park."

NOTES

The following abbreviations are used in the note sections:
DET: Dixon Evening Telegraph
DMR: Des Moines Register
LADN: Los Angeles Daily News
LAE: Los Angeles Examiner
LAEHE: Los Angeles Evening Herald and Express
LAT: Los Angeles Times
NYDN: New York Daily News
NYP: New York Post
NYT: New York Times
PI: Personal Interview
SFC: San Francisco Chronicle

CHAPTER 1

Page
11 "Step back": Parsons, *DET*, September 16, 1941.
14 "A torpedo in": PI, Bill Thompson.
15 "Dixon's only outdoor": *DET*, February 4, 1984.
    "On hot summer": Ibid.
    "I always knew": Ibid.
16 "'Louella Parsons Day'": Parsons, p. 160.
    "Louella wants you": Ibid.
    "They've declared a": Ibid.
    "bitter thoughts": Ibid.
    "You remember": Ibid.
    "Thanks, thanks": Ibid. p. 161
    "Ladies and gentlemen": Ibid.
18 "This is an event": *DET*, September 16, 1941.
    "I do not feel": Ibid.
    "This fellow must": Parsons, p. 161.
    "It is with": *DET*, September 16, 1941.
19 "Well—thank you": Ibid.
    "Hi, Dutch": PI, Thompson.

CHAPTER 2

23 "a starved-looking": White, *The Invincible Irish*, p. 77.
24 (fn) "barbarity and atrocity": *National Enquirer*, August 5, 1980.

26 "a clown of a boy": PI.
27 "conducted by mine": *Tipton Advertiser*, April 15, 1887.
    "a ball nine": Ibid.
    (fn) "We think [saloons]": *Bennett Buzzings*, 1898.
28 "Why can't these": Ibid.
    "the ladies of the": Ibid.
    "real joker": PI.
30 "in peaceable possession": "History of Clyde Township," *History of Whiteside County, Illinois*, Bent & Wilson, 1877.
    "at all hazards": Ibid.
    "We were not strong": Daniel Blue entry, Clerk's Office, U.S. District Court for the Northern District of Illinois, 1860.
    "Charles and Alexander [Blue]": "History of Clyde Township."
    "in the teachings": Jane Blue Wilson's obituary, June 7, 1894.
    (fn) "A most wonderful": Note in Reagan Bible.
32 "There was one": Jane Blue Wilson's obituary, June 7, 1894.
    "a couple of nips": *Tampico Tornado*, February 4, 1984.
    "so named after": Ibid.
    "Mr. Reagan": Ibid.
33 "hauling coal to": Ibid.

"pretty much all": Ibid.
"It's time, Nellie": *Bread of Life* (monthly pub. of Ridgewood Pentecostal Church, Gordon P. Gardiner, ed.), May 1981.

34 "the primitive and": *The New Columbia Encyclopedia*, p. 769.
"For such a little": Reagan, *Where's the Rest of Me?*, p. 7.

35 "Jack Reagan has": *Tampico Tornado*, February 7, 1911.
"fat little Dutchman": Reagan, p. 7.
"Now you can": UCLA Oral History Archives.
"horrified from the": *Tampico Tornado*, February 4, 1984.
"[William] really went": UCLA Oral History Archives.

36 "In between all": Ibid.
"I can remember": Ibid.

37 "one of her": Reagan, p. 16.
"engaged in a debate": Ibid.
"sit for hours": Ibid.
"One evening": Ibid. p. 17.

38 "He always protested": Ibid.
"the parades, the torches": Ibid., p. 18.
"I remember six or eight": PI, Gertrude Crockett.

39 "the school closed": *Modern Screen*, 1944.
(fn) "Maureen Reagan": PI, Crockett.

40 "charisma—everyone": Ibid.
"The sun streamed": undated article, Ida Zeitlin.

41. "Evenings Neil and Dutch": *DET*, February 4, 1984.
"racing across the": Ibid.
"What's the": Ibid.
"His dad had": Ibid.
"the thunder of": Reagan, p. 19.

42 "My worst experience" Ibid.
"[On Sundays] we": *DET*, February 4, 1984.
"We was poor": Ibid.

43 "mystic atmosphere": Reagan, p. 20.
"with breathless attention": Ibid., p. 23.

44 "the zest of a": Ibid., p. 20.
"she recited": Ibid.
"Neil seemed always": PI, Jean Kinney.
"scrawny": Reagan, p. 21.
"There was no field": Ibid.
"I got a wild": Ibid.

45 "My mother would": *Bread of Life*, May 1981.
"I can't hope": Perrett, *The '20s*, p. 116.

CHAPTER 3

47 "Dixon was always": *DET*, February 4, 1984.
"the backbone of": Ibid.

48 "the drab hues": Sinclair Lewis, *Main Street*, p. 24.
"We didn't know": *Time*, September 30, 1980.
"gaunt frame shelters": Lewis, p. 31.

50 "As the [three Dixon]": *DET*, undated, circa 1920.

51 "All of us": Reagan, p. 23.
"Everybody thought he": PI, Thompson.
"Dutch was a bit": *DET*, February 4, 1984.
(fn) "The Depression": Reagan, p. 50.

52 "the whole world": Ibid., p. 25.
"the ball appeared": Ibid.
"a glorious, sharply": Ibid.
"with huge": Ibid.
"the miracle of": Ibid.
"who strutted": *Eureka Pegasus*.
(fn) "I hate them": Reagan, p. 25.

53 "Think I'm made": "Dearest Mom," undated article by Cynthia Miller.
"was going to sit": *Modern Screen*, 1944.
"The Klan's the": Ibid.
"Nobody in those": PI, Thompson.

54 "Dixon was no": PI, Violet McReynolds.
"This was a success": *DET*, April 26, 1984.
"Lincoln stood here": Ibid.

55 "[He] would punch": UCLA Oral History Archives.
"a little business": Ibid.
"The pool hall": Ibid.
"When someone": Ibid.

56 "My mother was": PI, Kinney.
"in the cloistered": Perrett, *The '20s*, p. 197.
"Damned on Saturday": Ibid.
"The Lord [will]": Reagan, p. 66.
(fn) "The infallibility of the": PI, Reverend Benjamin H. Moore.
(fn) "The President": Ibid.

57 "Jesus hated prosy": UCLA Oral History Archives.
"Jesus walked barefoot": Ibid.
"People in Dixon": Ibid.
"I was eleven": Reagan, p. 12.

58 "bouts with the": Ibid.
"lusty, vulgar humor": Ibid., p. 14.
"If [Jack] was": Ibid.
"Arise and walk": "Ronald

Reagan's Boyhood Church," March
26, 1984.
"We [Dutch and]": PI, Kinney.
"a personal experience": PI,
Thompson.
59 "My Sunday School": "Ronald
Reagan's Boyhood Church," March
26, 1984.
"phrase might just": *Bread of Life,*
May 1981.
"Everybody loved Nelle": Ibid.
"Well, a kid who": Ibid.
"If Nelle had had": Ibid.
(fn) "the war of the": PI.
60 "She had a way": *Bread of Life,* May
1981.
"She was thin": PI, Isabelle
Newman.
"an old-time pastor": *Bread of Life,*
May 1981.
"Mrs. Catherine Sherer": *DET,*
August 12, 1923.
61 "Electrical entertainer": Ibid.
"This kid of yours": Reagan, p. 27.
62 "No need to put": UCLA Oral
History Archives.
"Jack always wanted": Ibid.
"I took the long": Ibid.
"We [South Dixon]": Ibid.
"extra something": PI.
"As a kid I lived": *Motion Picture,*
November 1937.
63 "There was a dam": Reagan, p. 28.
(fn) "My memory": Reagan to
McReynolds, 1966.
64 "In those days": PI, Thompson.
"I guess you": Letter to Bill
Thompson.
"You're pretty young": *Welcome
Home Mr. President,* Improv Press
and Communications, February 6,
1984.
"Everybody piled": Ibid.
"kitty-corner from": Ibid.
"I kind of had": Ibid.
"He liked it and": Ibid.
65 "He was the perfect": PI,
Thompson.
"How many you": *Reagan's Dixon,*
1984.
"Drowning Youth": *Dixonian,* 1928.
"a sparkling brunette": Reagan, p.
28.
"Dutch had a portable": *The Register
Star,* March 31, 1981.
66 "Oh, that's just": *Welcome Home Mr.
President.*
"hippopotamus": "Meditations of a
Lifeguard," *Dixonian,* 1928.
"She [Margaret] was": Reagan, p.
28.

"I think": Ibid., p. 29.
67 "he had an inside": *Reagan's Dixon.*
"We were poor": UCLA Oral
History Archives.
68 "I was eighteen": Neil Reagan to
Jean Kinney on "Around About."
"Look people straight": *Bread of
Life,* May 1981.
69 "head and shoulders": *Reagan's
Dixon.*
"Clean Speech, Clean": Ibid.
73 "congenial, straightforward":
Perrett, *The '20s,* p. 308.
"You have to start": *Time,* October
7, 1966.
(fn) "made a million": *Washington
Star,* October 3, 1982.
74 "I was stretched out": Reagan
interview, undated.

CHAPTER 4

81 "On that rise": *The History of Eureka
College.*
"I am not ambitious": Ibid.
"We intend to make": Ibid.
82 "The Bible is a": Ibid.
"Religious values": Ibid.
"I fell head": Reagan, p. 30.
84 "annual dancing speech": *The
Pegasus.*
"a tradition": Ibid.
85 "We had a special": Reagan, p. 33.
"perpetually broke": Ibid.
"for the necessities": Ibid.
87 "Just because the": PI, Ralph
McKinzie.
"It's tough to go": Reagan, p. 32.
"Swimming?": PI, McKinzie.
88 "I always let": *Motion Picture,*
November 1939.
"He was indifferent": *Journal Star,*
March 8, 1981.
89 "Affiliated churches": Ibid.
"By questioning": *The Pegasus.*
"as usual": Reagan, p. 34.
"if anybody": Ibid.
"In the second": Ibid.
90 "flew into action": *Journal Star,*
March 8, 1981.
"When the bell rang": Ibid.
"I'd been told": Reagan, p. 36.
91 "We, the students": *Journal Star,*
March 8, 1981.
"police escorts": Ibid.
"The agitation was": Ibid.
"The strike climaxed": Ibid.
92 "Hell, with two": Reagan, p. 37.
"We knew she": *Bread of Life,* May
1981.

"the supposedly original": Reagan, p. 37.

93   "For two and a": Ibid.
"If I had only": Ibid.
"quick end to the": *Journal Star*, March 8, 1981.
(fn) "The situation that has": Ibid.

94   "Bert Wilson was not": Ibid.
"The students were": Ibid.
"presence": *Welcome Home Mr. President*, February 6, 1984.
"of sauntering across": Ibid.
"He stuck with the": Ibid.

95   "Everyone admired Dutch": Ibid.
"drama, sports, and": Reagan, p. 11.
"I was afraid": *Motion Picture*, November 1939.
"serious, well-planned": Reagan, p. 34.

CHAPTER 5

97   "What a football player": *Time*, October 5, 1925.

98   "Outlined against a": Ibid.
"I couldn't believe": PI.

99   "He was always": *Journal Star*, March 8, 1981.
"a last sad date": Reagan, p. 39.

100 "God bless": Ibid.
"mellow, small-town": Ibid., p. 40.
"he'd never paid me": Ibid.
"laid it on": Ibid.
"hashing in the": UCLA Oral History Archives.
"Nelle, I thought": Ibid.

101 "Dutch Reagan's brother": Ibid.
"I sort of had": PI.
"Anytime I heard": UCLA Oral History Archives.

102 "out of a bottle": Reagan, p. 67.
"We tiptoed through": Ibid., p. 41.
"Moon was a natural": PI, McKinzie.
"Bud made the decisions": Reagan, p. 45.

103 "was limited to one": Reagan, p. 44.
"I'm a sucker for": Ibid.
"Eureka opened": *The Prism*, 1929–30.
"nabbed a twenty yard": Ibid.
"and his calm": Reagan, p. 43.

104 "country fashions": *The Pegasus*, November 9, 1929.
"Subdued lights": Ibid., November 23, 1929.
"She always said Dutch": *Bread of Life*, May 1981.

"When our little daughter": Ibid.

105 "Many of us believed": Ibid.
"barely above a": PI.

107 "On what grounds": Leighton, p. 237.

109 "the young attractively": Reagan, p. 48.
"disease": Ibid.
"leading-ladyitus": Ibid.
"in light of the": Ibid.

110 "Sometimes, I would say": *Bread of Life*, May 1981.
"a cheap shoe chain": Reagan, p. 50.
"hole-in-the-wall": Ibid.
"he started telling": PI, McKinzie.
"Moon and I were": Reagan, p. 50.

112 "Rah for Seniors": *The Pegasus*, April 1, 1932.
"Snap of the Late": Ibid., April 9, 1932.
"It seemed there": PI, McKinzie.
"bully them into": Clyde Lyon, Eureka graduation address, 1932.
"hold God and God's": Reverend Ben Cleaver, Eureka graduation blessing, 1932.

CHAPTER 6

115 "the boys could have": *Reagan's Dixon*, 1980.

116 "the Army": Caro, p. 246.
"to combat the ravages": *DET*, March 14, 1932.
"These things": Ibid.
"Paul Rader Pantry": Ibid., July 19, 1932.
"The ridding of old": Ibid., August 20, 1932.

117 "Myrtle, when we get": Walgreen, p. 163.
"just a long": Ibid.
"a game room": Ibid., p. 173.
"the log cabin": Ibid.

118 "I was trying": Reagan, p. 51.
"There it was—": Ibid.
"this was a time": Ibid., p. 53.

119 "Well, you've picked": Ibid.
"a rapid-fire routine": Ibid., p. 54.
"A new deal for": Gies, p. 99.
"somebody to do": Ibid.
"the Vice Presidency": Ibid., p. 94.
". . . because I was": *Time*, October 7, 1966.
"I'm still in favor": Ibid.
"A job, any job": *Time*, January 5, 1981.

120 "If I'm not making": Reagan, p. 54.

(fn) "You don't remember":
Reagan's Dixon.

121 "afraid of the damn": Reagan, p. 55.
"rides were short": Ibid.
"a fellow who told": Ibid.
"where the West begins": Ibid., p. 58.

122 "How does anyone": Ibid.
"thumping and cursing": Ibid., p. 59.
"Not so fast": Ibid.
"Do ye think": Ibid.
"was all alone in an": Ibid.
"We are going into": Ibid., p. 60.

123 "five dollars and": Ibid., p. 61.
"Let the Kid": Ibid.
"It's a wonder there": Gies, p. 98.

124 "set his face like flint": Caro, p. 247.
"that had been afforded": Ibid.
"In Iowa, a mob": Ibid.

125 "[Reagan's] crisp account": *Chicago Tribune,* undated article.
"three meals a day": Reagan, p. 66.
"Would the Lord": Ibid.

126 "king's ransom": Ibid.
"eking by": Ibid.
"just to gild": Ibid.
"to the first": Ibid.
"I've always believed": Ibid., p. 68.

127 "Tea was concluded": Gies, p. 101.
"Mr. Roosevelt": Ibid.
"What are those things": Ibid.
"Let me assert": Franklin D. Roosevelt, inauguration speech, March 4, 1933.
"My friends, I want": Roosevelt, fireside chat, March 12, 1933.
"the quarterback": Lash, Chapter 44, pp. 512–535.

128 "of minor grading": *DET,* November 26, 1933.
"supplies of shovels": Ibid.

CHAPTER 7

131 "Where does that": *Newsweek,* summer 1980.
"as to the *manner* born": PI, Jack Shelley.
"exciting and exuberant": Ibid.
"WHO had only recently": Ibid.

132 "[Dutch] was not": Ibid.
"a cubby hole": Ibid.
"Dr. B. J. Palmer": PI, Herb Plambeck.

133 "It was one of": PI.
"Dutch and Mr. Gross": PI, Plambeck.

"if everyone else": PI, Paul McGinn.

134 "Where are you from?" PI.
"unquestionably Des Moines's": PI, Shelley.
"He was a nice": PI, Chuck Schosselman.
"I'll never forget": Ibid.
"Dutch would clear": PI.

135 "a smart little two-seater": PI.
"a dashing young blade": PI, Shelley.
"Peter [MacArthur] was": PI.
"He was great": *DMR,* February 5, 1982.
"I was so stage-struck": Reagan, p. 71.

136 "insistent hyperthyroid": Leighton, p. 51.
"Her voice . . . was": Ibid.
". . . suddenly I heard": Reagan, p. 71.

137 "It's a called strike": Ibid., p. 78.
"Hartnett returns the ball": Ibid.
"a turntable with": *DMR,* February 5, 1982.
"I knew . . . how": Reagan, p. 77.
"The wire has": Ibid., p. 78.
"red headed kid": Ibid., p. 79.

138 "Leave her alone": PI, Melba Lohmann.
"Are you all": Ibid.
"on a mild, warm": Ibid.
"Dutch called me": UCLA Oral History Archives.

139 "a large living": *DMR,* February 5, 1982.
"The house was": Ibid.
"Club Belvedere was": Ibid.
"with many girls": Ibid.

140 "all [Dutch] ever wanted": Ibid.
"had a yen to be": Reagan, p. 79.
"no particular desire": Ibid.
"had already fought": Ibid., p. 80.
"doing correspondence courses": Ibid.
"vivid descriptions of crowds": *Time,* July 28, 1980.

141 "a huge pool": PI, Richard Ulrich.
"he would have": PI, Ulrich.
"he later waved": PI, Ulrich.
"There was one young": *DMR,* February 5, 1982.
"He [had] bought a Nash": Ibid.

142 "I'd agreed with that": PI, Lois Ulrich.
"the fastest tongue": *DMR,* February 5, 1982.

143 "They used to sit": PI, Ulrich.
"He was handsome": PI, Lois Ulrich.

"Two weeks—": PI, Kinney.
"I took Dutch": Ibid.
145   "I managed to squeeze": Reagan, p. 81.
"soaked to the skin": Ibid.
"If my horse balked": Ibid., p. 82.
"Dutch could stretch": PI, Ulrich.
"flirt with the truth": Ibid.
"I always thought": *Harper's* magazine, March 1936.
146   "When the wind died": Ibid.
"Roads and farm buildings": Ibid.
"from this new Sahara": Ibid.
"They roll westward": Ibid.
"Happy Hollow": *Life,* November 23, 1936.
"as rickety as": Ibid.
"as many as 10,000": Ibid.
"Franklin Roosevelt's Wild West": Ibid.
147   "of grocers' boxes": Ibid.
"kept right on": Ibid.
"their second-hand": Ibid.
"Great Trek to the Pacific": Ibid.
148   "Mr. Roosevelt is the": Gies, p. 138.
"For the first time": Lash, p. 442.
"We have conquered fear": Ibid.
"He arrived at the": Ibid.
149   "no half-and-half": Ibid.
"this generation of": Ibid.
"the greatest political": Ibid.
(fn) "a rendezvous": Ibid.
"men I had been": Gies, p. 137.
150   "He sat across": PI, Joy Hodges Schiess.
151   "come see us": Ibid.
"influential people": Ibid.
"Well, Miss Hodges": Ibid.
"talked [him] into": Reagan, p. 82.
152   "gave sympathetic ear": Ibid., p. 84.
"pick out a scene": Ibid.
153   "How could I tell": Ibid.
"and seeing": Ibid.
154   "some hazing . . . some": Ibid., p. 83.
"I did": PI, Schiess.
"without the glasses": Reagan, p. 85.
"the likeable": PI, Schiess.
"big overgrown kid": Ibid.
155   "Two tests are better": Reagan, p. 86.
"I might not get": Ibid., p. 87.
"I couldn't believe": Schiess
156   "making a bundle": *Holiday* script.
"Mr. Warner [can] see": Reagan, p. 87.
"No, I will be": Ibid.
"WARNER'S OFFER

CONTRACT": Ibid., p. 88.
"HAVE JUST DONE": Ibid.
"then I yelled": Ibid.
"MAY BE SCOOP": PI, Schiess.
157   "The day Dutch got": PI, Shelley.

CHAPTER 8

161   "the burning desert": Reagan, p. 90.
163   "The motion picture": *Fortune,* December 1937.
"a violent hatred": Ibid.
"totalitarian godhead": Robert Rossen, 1963 interview.
"Are you a member": Warner Archives.
164   "Verbal messages cause": Behlmer, p. xi.
"equally short": Lindfors, p. 155.
165   "a shoestring independent": Behlmer, p. 62.
"The studio that had": UCLA Oral History Archives.
166   "What you, the actor": Ibid.
167   "Apparently I was": *The Westmorelands of Hollywood,* p. 117.
168   "fast-talking, high-pitched": Reagan, p. 93.
169   "about chalk marks": Ibid., p. 92.
"plain old everyday": Ibid., p. 94.
"Please be careful": Warner Archives.
170   "To my regret": PI, Schiess.
"knocked off every clay": Regan, p. 94.
"one of the best": *Sunday Mirror,* June 20, 1937.
171   "[Movies are] a specialized": *Westport News,* October 31, 1980.
172   "silly boy": *Fortune,* December 1937.
"Ronnie might . . . [sit]": *Westport News,* October 31, 1980.
173   "We discussed politics": PI, Schiess.
"She's a young": Undated article, circa 1938.
174   ". . . the most exciting": *NYDN,* February 1, 1938.
175   ". . . remember the guy": Reagan, p. 91.
"Miss Parsons plays": *NYT,* January 13, 1938.
"Some place in the": Reagan, p. 95.
176   "Wayne Morris won": Ibid., p. 96.
"I was up at": *Westport News,* October 31, 1980.
177   "It was casually": Ibid.
"fuzzyvisioned": Ibid.
"the second largest": *California,* WPA Works Project, p. 199.

". . . the highest point": Ibid.
178 "a no-nonsense guy": *Life*, June 26, 1964.
"Well, a way has": PI.

CHAPTER 9

179 "the finest, the most": Mayo, p. 258.
"movie cathedral": Ibid.
"This temple of art": Ibid.
180 "the first royal carriage": Ibid., p. 261.
"Do I have to": Reagan, p. 103.
"the sweater girl": *Hollywood Studio Magazine*, March 1981.
181 "monstrous brushes of light": Mayo, p. 260.
"The elite of the movies": Ibid., p. 262.
"so that motion": Kanfer, p. 129.
182 "One of the church": *Bread of Life*, May 1981.
"Christian ways": Ibid.
"Look at your son": undated article, Cynthia Miller.
183 "How is the factory": *Bread of Life*, May 1981.
"the slow careful": Reagan, p. 104.
"with some other actors": PI, Larry Williams.
184 "I soon learned": Reagan, p. 91.
185 "dependable guy, never": PI.
"I became the Errol": Reagan, p. 96.
186 "We realized we had": PI.
"charm and vitality": *Hollywood Spectator*, February 18, 1939.
"impresses and handles": *Variety*, March 8, 1939.
"played his role of": *NYT*, July 4, 1940.
"Scene after scene": Reagan, p. 101.
"Ronald Reagan, as the": *NYT*, August 27, 1938.
"a still worshipping": Reagan, p. 102.
"one of the accolades": Ibid.
187 "from the Bryan Foy": *NYT*, October 26, 1938.
"The cast does not": Ibid.
"friendly name": Ibid.
"who is always": Ibid.
"who can get into": Ibid.
"who plugs along": Ibid.
188 "Ronnie was always": *Photoplay*, circa 1944.
"I don't want to get": PI.

190 "I grew up with": *Photoplay*, circa 1944.
"that was exciting": *Movie Fan*, January 1943.
"with a pencil": PI.
191 "All we had was": *Photoplay*, circa 1944.
"She was a fly-away": *St. Joseph Press*, January 28, 1947.
"I always thought": PI.
192 "My first impulse": *Photoplay*, undated.
193 "When he took me": Ibid.
194 "[Eddie] Albert gives": *Variety*, October 13, 1938.
"Ronald Reagan has a": Ibid.
"All we can say": *NYT*, March 2, 1939.
"in the hope of": *Fortune*, December 1937.
195 "He was a top": Reagan, p. 119.
(fn) "Tracy was born": Warner Archives.
196 "I was playing": Reagan, p. 118.
"He saw my part": Ibid.
"oomph girl": *NYT*, June 23, 1939.
"Staffed by a competent": Ibid.
"Margaret Lindsay and": *Variety*, July 5, 1939.
"Miss Sheridan is": *NYT*, September 4, 1939.
197 "a good scout": undated article, Cynthia Miller.
"loads of fun": Ibid.
"Hope you're feeling": Ibid.
(fn) "Free parking": Warner Archives.
198 "Jane was . . . making": Parsons, p. 161.
"Hot diggity!": Paul Spiegle, *SFC*, November 16, 1939.
"Oh, Louella, won't": *Variety*, November 22, 1939.
"not short enough": Ibid.
199 "breathless tidbits": *SFC*, November 16, 1939.
"and told them how": Ibid.
"Ronald Reagan": *Variety*, November 22, 1939.
"looked exceptionally": *SFC*, November 16, 1939.
"Joy Hodges": *Variety*, November 22, 1939.
"Dutch kept everyone": PI, Schiess.
200 "too-enthusiastic admirers": Ibid.
"Dutch was always": Ibid.
"especially with Washington's": Ibid.
(fn) "a fairly liberal": PI, Reverend Benjamin Moore.

CHAPTER 10

203   "You're anti-Semitic!": *Confessions of a Hollywood Columnist*, Graham, p. 263.
"You're damn right": Ibid.
"and we [didn't]": Warner Archives.
"Too bad I forgot": Ibid.
"So what?": Ibid.
204   "Here, take this": Ibid.
205   "Janie was always intent": PI.
206   "After the easy way": *Motion Picture*, November 1939.
"put in a word": O'Brien, p. 240.
"I've been a great": Ibid.
(fn) "It is a simple matter": Warner Archives.
207   "I was still": Reagan, p. 107.
"sweated out a series": O'Brien, p. 240.
"in ten different": Ibid.
"I really didn't": Reagan, p. 108.
"a great entrance": Ibid.
208   "We walked over": O'Brien, p. 241.
"Hell, I'm a great": Ibid., p. 242.
"I was forty": Ibid., p. 248–9.
209   "a small man with": *Reader*, November 2, 1984.
(fn) "blanket waiver": Ibid.
(fn) "as both agent": Ibid.
210   "shaking down Kosher": *Hollywood Local*, 1983.
"keep labor peace": Ibid.
"There was an attempt": Ibid.
211   "brainstorm": Ibid.
"slipped out of serving": Ibid.
"The Killer": *Reader*, November 2, 1984.
(fn) "the Octopus": Ibid.
(fn) "gobbled up": Ibid.
212   "the black-suited Mafia": Ibid.
"tall, lanky": Ibid.
"Lew was the student": Ibid.
"cold, brusque": Ibid.
"ruthless, hard-nosed": Ibid.
213   "accepted MCA's": Ibid.
"a thrilling experience": Reagan, p. 109.
"I've always suspected": Warner Archives.
214   "lustily tossing harmless": *NYT*, November 9, 1940.
"I MUST REFUSE": Warner Archives.
215   "to something I hope": Reagan, p. 111.
"all the heroes": Warner Archives.
"I figured that under": Reagan, p. 112.
"inability to observe": Massey, p. 259.

216   "He was lining up": Ibid.
"The scene had been": Ibid., p. 260.
(fn) "he broke a leg": Reagan, p. 113.
217   "Vaulting ambition, which": Massey, p. 262.
218   "Here was an Irishman": Reagan, p. 113.
219   "I hope my performance": Notre Dame Archives.
"Don't worry about Jack": Ibid.
"It must have been": Reagan, p. 114.
220   "You will have to eat": Notre Dame Archives.
"I guess we really": Ibid.
"Grand Ball": Ibid.
"a fine letter": O'Brien, p. 249.
"I picked at my food": Reagan, p. 115.
221   "I think that afternoon": UCLA Oral History Archives.
"10 minutes allowed": Notre Dame Archives.
"baggage packed and in": Ibid.
222   "Picture is more than": *Variety*, October 19, 1940.
"If some of it": *NYT*, October 19, 1940.
"It's true, I got": Reagan, 1947 interview.
". . . we will not forget . . .": Leighton, p. 444.
223   "kept him talking": Ibid.
"If I could write": Ibid., p. 445.
224   "Jack, please sit down": *Modern Screen*, circa 1944.
"news tickers": Caro, p. 653.
"The President was": Ibid.
"'Mike, I don't want'": Ibid., p. 654.
"Roosevelt was smiling": Ibid.
"I'm sure he knows": Reagan, p. 115.
"black curse": Ibid., p. 113.

CHAPTER 11

225   "feminine-frivolous": *St. Joseph News-Press*, January 28, 1947.
"I don't know": *Photoplay*, undated.
226   "a viable budget": Ibid.
"Janie always seemed": PI.
"I'd say Janie was": PI.
"Neither Ronnie nor I": *Silver Screen*, August 1941.
227   "One day Scotch": *Modern Screen*, October 1944.
"There was a snobbism": McClelland, p. 224.

"When employed": Powdermaker, p. 279.
"I think Jane started": Morella: p. 42.

228 "Each night as he": Collier, p. 62.
"Even the Republicans": Ibid., p. 63.
"No one was quite": *Westport News,* October 31, 1980.
"The least costly": Collier, p. 63.
"repository of fact": *Westport News,* October 31, 1980.

229 "They had made many": Allyson, p. 95.
"He'll outgrow it": Ibid., p. 96.
"a certain sad": Ibid.

230 "He had a wonderful": McClelland, p. 166.
"I wanted a boy . . .": *DET,* Undated article.

231 "comfortable Reagan": *LAT,* September 24, 1944.
"We don't want": Ibid.
"Jack, I don't think": UCLA Oral History Archives.
"a bright look came": Ibid.
"spoke up": Ibid.
"It was primarily": Ibid.
"Reagan was an": Ibid.

232 "boyish of face": *Time,* April 21, 1961.

233 "I had been warned": Reagan, p. 116.
"Ronald Reagan makes": *NYT,* April 4, 1941.
"to the meat": Reagan, p. 116.
"sort of the Tiffany": Ibid., p. 115.
"some shaky A picutres": Ibid., p. 117.

234 "[The screenplay] seems": *NYT,* June 7, 1941.

235 "the hand movements": Reagan, p. 17.
"Max Rabinovitz": Warner Archives.
"a classly little B": *Variety,* September 3, 1941.
"a frantic newspaper": Ibid.
"Ronald Reagan": Ibid.
"a blazing whodunit": Ibid.

236 "Dear Brynie": Warner Archives.
237 "Dear Hal": Warner Archives.
238 ". . . Before this picture": Ibid.
240 "young, handsome actor . . . he": Ibid.

241 "changing costumes and": Wallis, p. 101.
"I owe Sam Wood": Reagan, p. 119.
(fn) "The woman is": Warner Archives.

242 "Ronnie, have you ever": McClelland, p. 229.
"Bob Cummings plays": *NYT,* February 3, 1942.
"Are you a Catholic?": Morella, p. 50.

243 "because he was afraid": Warner Archives.
"normally . . . amputated": Ibid.
"on the matter of": Ibid.
"from unconsciousness to": Reagan, p. 8.
" 'Lights' . . . I heard": Ibid., p. 9.

244 (fn) "Wood was greatly": Warner Archives.

CHAPTER 12

245 "far more serious": Parsons, p. 161.
246 "aliens, ethnic and": Perrett, *Days of Sadness,* p. 87.
247 "a congressional investigating": Ibid.
"out of real events": Ibid.
"on the edge of": Ibid.
"it's methods . . . were": Ibid., p. 93.

248 "more and more worried": Ibid.
"her Christian duty": *Bread of Life,* May 1981.
"he never felt that": Reagan, *Sincerely, Ronald Reagan,* p. 139.

249 "It's good to be here!" *DET,* November 14, 1941.
"one of the gayest": Walgreen, p. 297.
"cottage": Ibid.
"The fall weather": Ibid.

250 "forthright candor": Ibid.
"movie-goers of this": *DET,* January 26, 1942.
"acknowledged the plaudits": *DET,* November 16, 1941.
"Only once before": Ibid.

251 "While 'International Squadron' ": *DET,* November 17, 1941.
"Ronald Reagan": *NYT,* November 14, 1941.
"Reagan's performance": *NYP,* November 14, 1941.
"excellently spotted": *Variety,* August 13, 1941.
"pulse quickening": *DET,* November 16, 1941.
"an original story": Ibid.
"Each person reacted": Ibid.

253 "He came back": PI.
254 "Ann Sheridan": Warner Archives.
"On Sunday afternoons": UCLA Oral History Archives.

255   "He's really not": Ibid.
      "million dollar contract": Reagan,
      p. 123.
      "Lew Wasserman": Ibid., p. 121.
      "NPM 516": Documents obtained
      through Freedom of Information
      Act.
256   "At noon next": *Time*, February 27,
      1950.
      "limited service—eligible": Reagan,
      p. 132.
      "war mongering": Ibid., p. 338.
      (fn) "who sat with a": Freedom of
      Information Act.
257   "relating to world": Ibid.
      "If Warner Brothers": Ibid.
      "Warner Brothers receives": Ibid.
258   "as one of the": Warner Archives.
      (fn) "The Eptstein boys": Ibid.
259   "high spot in the": Reagan, p. 122.
      "There is quite": Warner Archives.
      "Since we had not": Ibid.
260   "'Kings Row' will give": *New Yorker*,
      February 7, 1942.
      "Warner Brothers": *NYT*, February
      3, 1942.
261   "REGRET TO INFORM":
      Warner Archives.
      "We can't start": Ibid.
      "If we sent you": Reagan, p. 125.
      (fn) "Reagan scores": *Hollywood
      Reporter*, August 14, 1942.
      (fn) "Folks who will": *NYT*,
      September 26, 1942.
      (fn) "The critics take the": Warner
      Archives.

CHAPTER 13

265   "with the wiry": Ibid.
      "Never knew a cavalryman": Ibid.,
      p. 127.
      "Colonel Booker, you": Ibid., p.
      126.
266   "Colonel Booker came": Ibid., p.
      127.
      "The Colonel didn't": Ibid.
      "at a giant rally": Ibid., p.128.
      "to buy something": Warner
      Archives.
267   "My newly acquired": Reagan, p.
      130.
      "I would regret": Ibid., p. 131.
268   "interviewing and": Ibid., p. 132.
      "produced and paid": Warner
      Archives.
269   "July 14, 1941": War Department
      files obtained through Freedom of
      Information Act.

      "October 2, 1942": Ibid.
270   "Release of the": Ibid.
      "an almost reverent": Reagan, p.
      136.
271   "I was in": *NYP*, July 28, 1943.
272   "100 men in one": Wallis, p. 89.
      "We [the company]": Stone, p. 250.
      "each time *he*": Reagan, p. 141.
      "Young fellow, I": Ibid.
273   "What kind of insignia": PI,
      Richard Burdick.
      "we rated as stars": Stone, p. 250.
      "animated debate": PI, Burdick.
274   "a powerful display": *Variety*,
      August 4, 1943.
      "It's socko": Ibid.
      (fn) "Quite frankly": Freedom of
      Information Act.
275   "Broadway strollers flocked": *NYT*,
      July 29, 1943.
      "the unslackening tempo": Ibid.
      (fn) "Irving came West": Wallis, p.
      89.
276   "I RESENT AND WON'T":
      Warner Archives.
      ". . . ARTICLES APPEARED":
      Ibid.
      "MEAN WHAT I SAID": Ibid.
277   "swept up": Reagan, p. 142.
      "another frantic": Ibid.
      "called an emergency": *LAT*, May
      21, 1985.
      "'This is our target'": Ibid.
      "one night when Reagan": Ibid.
      "a minute and a half": Ibid.
      "3 a.m.—Post": Ibid.
      (fn) "a flashing smile": Ibid.
278   "Special instructions": Ibid.
      "DIRECTOR, WAR": Warner
      Archives.
      (fn) "the war would be": *LAT*, May
      21, 1985.
279   "Murky and somber": Morella, p.
      9.
280   "archetypical *film noire*": Halliwell,
      Film Guide, p. 402.
281   "wanted two things": Morella, p.
      78.
282   "Michael [the baby]": Ibid.
      "Heavenly H.Q.": Warner
      Archives.
      "decided to adopt": *LAT*, March
      25, 1945.
283   "only through the": Lash, p. 707.
284   "into . . . the dusty": Ibid.
      "I don't think": Ibid.
      "These Republican leaders": Ibid.,
      p. 710.
      "at 9 p.m. the": Ibid., p. 711.
      "because of the weight": Ibid., p.
      718.

"a certain degree": Ibid.
"I am more sorry": Ibid., p. 721.
285   "Harry, the President": Ibid.
"Hitler's fate—or": Leighton, p. 488.
"All I wanted": Reagan, p. 159.
"'It's all right'" Ibid., p. 161.

CHAPTER 14

289   "hers up, his down": Allyson, p. 96.
290   "We speak of her": Warner Archives.
"DEAR JACK": Ibid.
291   "I felt a great": PI.
(fn) "Notes for talk": Warner Archives.
(fn) "I feel that": Ibid.
292   "Faulkner, as you": PI, Alex Gottlieb.
"During the War": Picturegoer, July 19, 1947.
293   "hemophiliac liberal": Reagan, p. 160.
"wartime contacts": LAT, Undated article.
294   "Politicians have asked": Ibid.
"If Hitler": Douglas, p. 162.
295   "The first order": Ibid.
296   "all of them ready": UCLA Oral History Archives.
"For weeks small": The Story of the SAG, p. 45.
(fn) "little black pay-off bag": Reagan, p. 206.
(fn) "to take down": Ibid.
297   ". . . the Thirties was": Schwartz, p. 103.
"Warner Brothers had": Ibid.
"we find ourselves": Hollywood Reporter, Undated article.
298   "close down the studio": Schwartz, p. 205.
"Ever hear of Benedict": Freedom of Information Act.
"The Alliance's": Schwartz, p. 205.
"one really startling": Ibid., p. 157.
299   "totalitarian-minded": Freedom of Information Act.
"the dissemination of": Ibid.
"The Alliance's": Schwartz, p. 211.
"We don't believe": Ibid.
"right-wing": Perrett, A Dream of Greatness, p. 550.
"Years later": Schwartz, p. 217.
"Like most of the": Reagan, p. 160.
300   "blindly": Ibid., p. 162.
"hell-bent on": Ibid., p. 163.
"observed that more": Ibid.
"became a large wheel": Ibid.

"When I walked": Ibid., p. 154.
(fn) "infiltrated with Communists": Ibid.
301   "as inspiring as mud": Perrett, A Dream of Greatness, p. 56.
"for every shortage": Ibid., p. 57.
"the fighting Quaker": Ibid., p. 58.
"communist-dominated": Ibid., p. 59.
302   "honored": Reagan, p. 192.
"Jimmy Roosevelt was": Schwartz, p. 241.
"Everybody who was": Ibid.
303   "Reagan took a leaf": Ibid.
"It was . . . ridiculous": Ibid.
"when he was": UCLA Oral History Archives.
304   "part of my work": LAE, September 14, 1958.
"As a result of": Freedom of Information Act.
305   "nearly coming to blows": Ibid.
"Due to the nature": Ibid.
"We thought someone": Reagan, p. 195.
"go in for": Ibid.
"opened my eyes": Ibid.
"What are we going": Ibid.
"stated that": Freedom of Information Act.
306   ". . . you referred to": Hollywood Reporter, Undated article.
"two cliques": Freedom of Information Act.
"particularly close": Ibid.
"T-10": Ibid.
"Communist Infiltration": Ibid.
308   "In 'Stallion Road'" Newsweek, April 14, 1947.
(fn) "take care of his": Warner Archives.
309   "no-strike": Reagan, p. 157.
"every movie projectionist": SAG Archives.
"escalating violence": Ibid.
"The inner nucleus": LAEHE, December 9, 1953.
"There was an agenda": Ibid.
(fn) "Three Wise Men": Reagan, p. 168.
310   "was called to the": Ibid., p. 199.
"roughly pulled": Ibid.
"hearing": Ibid.
"Da Silva clutched": Ibid.
"of being raided": Freedom of Information Act.
"I thought he was": Ibid.
"the [Communist] Party": Ibid.
(fn) "fitted with a shoulder": Reagan, p. 200.
311   "It was pretty well": LAE,

September 14, 1958.
"If IATSE puts": SAG minutes,
September 17, 1949.

312 "Reagan had always": Hedda
Hopper, *Chicago Tribune*, undated.
"Reagan was a": *LAEHE*,
December 9, 1953.
"blond, affable": Reagan, p. 206.
"that consideration should": SAG
minutes, October 21, 1946.
"which involved": Ibid.

313 "in the strongest": Ibid.
"to fly stars": Reagan, p. 173.
"burst into tears": Ibid.
"a jolly, Santa": Ibid.
"It doesn't matter": Ibid., p. 175.
"One of us": Ibid., p. 173.
"that jurisdiction over": Ibid., p.
168.

314 "The invitation": SAG minutes,
October 21, 1946.
"round-table": Ibid.
"[I can tell you]": UCLA Oral
History Archives.

315 "whole strike had been": Ibid.
"a put-up job": Ibid.
"I don't think even": Ibid.
"would simply refuse": Ibid.
"The producers, as": Ibid.

316 "mouth piece": Ibid.

317 "[He] took to the": Reagan, p. 208.

CHAPTER 15

318 "Wet your lips": Lindfors, p. 150.
"Warners have a picture": Ibid., p.
151.
"The formula": Ibid.

319 "I heard one studio": Ibid.
"bland and smooth": Ibid., p. 153.

320 "grey, heavy, humid . . .": Ibid., p.
155.

321 "Maybe we'll call": Undated
article.
(fn) " 'You've got two' ": Warner
Archives.

322 "RAN PICTURE LAST": Warner
Archives.

323 "KEEP": Ibid.
"John Van Druten . . .":
McClelland, p. 134.
"stout citizen": *Chicago Tribune*, May
18, 1947.
"Ronald Reagan": Ibid.
"Our highest aim": Ibid.

324 "additional dialogue": *LAT*,
February 23, 1948.

325 "There was a loud": David and
David, p. 17.

326 "I can't stress": Warner Archives.
"Who the hell wants": Ibid.
"Jerry Wald": Ibid.

327 "a certain quality": *Hollywood
Reporter*, October 1948.
"anticipation light": Ibid.
"to eagerly share": Ibid.

328 "We felt so isolated": Morella, p.
117.
"Just sitting there": Ibid.
"Now let us": *LAEHE*, March 31,
1942.

329 "I have a very": Ibid.

330 "conshi camp": Ibid.
"War was more": *Coronet*,
November 1948.
"Lew Ayres [is a]": *LAT*, April 4,
1942.
"some kind of universal": *LAEHE*,
March 31, 1942.

331 "He's one of the": *LAE*, October 27,
1946.
"a spiritually": Irving Wallace,
Coronet, November 1948.

332 "They're up there": Morella, p. 119.
"he haunted the set": Ibid., p. 120.
"The Communist plan": Reagan, p.
186.

333 "Thieves' Paradise will": *LAT*,
December 28, 1947.
"burst into the front": Fagan,
Myron C., "Documentations of the
Reds and Fellow Travellers in
Hollywood and TV," 1951.
"some 300 top": Ibid.
"the Screen Actors": "A Vital
Message for C.E.G. [Cinema
Educational Guild, Inc.] Members
in California—And Your Friend,"
by Myron C. Fagan, 1951.
"There are a number": Freedom of
Information Act.
"a sub-Committee": SAG minutes,
September 12, 1947.

334 "voluntary statement": Ibid.
"In support of our": Ibid.
(fn) "I am not now": SAG Archives.

335 "The thing that I": Ibid.
"some definite": Ibid.

336 "139 So. Camden Drive": Ibid.

337 "We all thought he": Ibid.
"the Hon. J. Parnell": Freedom of
Information Act.

CHAPTER 16

339 "Communists [Jews]": Perrett, *A
Dream of Greatness*, p. 121.

340 "a windy and cheerful": Kahn, p. 11.
"injecting Communist stuff": Freedom of Information Act.
"Ideological termites": Ibid.
"MR. STRIPLING": Ibid.
341 "sauntered jauntily": *Time,* November 3, 1949.
"Anyone attending any": Ibid.
"send them back": Ibid.
"To what extent": Freedom of Information Act.
(fn) "Adrian was a": Schwartz, p. 260.
342 "MR. MURPHY": Freedom of Information Act.
350 "that he is not": SAG Archives.
"whether or not the": Ibid.
"The last Guild": *LAT,* August 17, 1980.
"Anne Revere": Ibid.
351 "to improve the wages": PI, Kim Felner.
"I am sure that": SAG Archives.
"The Guild's position": Ibid.

CHAPTER 17

353 "With Ronnie and": *Modern Screen,* February 1948.
"If this comes": Ibid.
354 "It's a very strange": *Photoplay,* March 1949.
"unostentatiously": Undated article by Ruth Waterbury.
"Lew is the love": Ibid.
"unsurpassingly beautiful": Morella, p. 133.
355 "In recent months": *LAT,* June 29, 1948.
"I suppose there": Reagan, p. 229.
356 "My first meeting": Patricia Neal, *People,* August 10, 1981.
"The day I walked": PI, Virginia Mayo.
357 "paternal": PI, Arlene Dahl.
"Gary Cooper": Ibid.
"I understand": Ibid.
"We did very little": PI, Mayo.
"Reagan was supposed": *Newark Sunday Star Ledger,* June 28, 1981.
"Eddie got so": Reagan, p. 233.
"Reagan was a lonely": *Chicago Tribune,* November 11, 1980.
358 "Supplies of headache": *LADN,* July 3, 1948.
"All actors": Ibid.
(fn) "A playwright who": Ibid.

359 "The conference with": UCLA Oral History Archives.
"The producers": Ibid.
360 "Ronnie acted like": Ibid.
361 "successful conclusion": Ibid.
"They came to": *Citizen News,* December 8, 1949.
"One day you should": McClelland, p. 229.
362 "Dear Jack": Warner Archives.
363 "A single handed": Nicholson, p. 154.
364 "Although I was": Patricia Neal, *People,* August 10, 1981.
"Because Mike was": PI, Mayo.
"You probably will": Warner Archives.
365 "ENGLISH SCHEDULE SET": Ibid.
"He [Reagan] had really hoped": McClelland, p. 158.
"while we have the": Bertrand Russell, *NYT,* November 29, 1948.
"I think it is": Nicolson, p. 255.
366 "Toward the end": William Woods College commencement address, June 1952.
"looking proudly out": Reagan, p. 241.
"It was a thrilling": PI, Mayo.
"To the finder": Warner Archives.
368 ". . . practically everything": Ibid.
369 "Working Pat Neal": Ibid.
"GET PROTECTION SHOTS": Ibid.
"sunshine and warmth": Reagan, p. 240.
"a huge success": Ibid., p. 241.
"On the ride south": Ibid.
370 "I wished that my": Ibid., p. 239.
"WHEN I'VE ALWAYS": Warner Archives.
"pull all the tricks": Reagan, p. 242.
"I accept this very": *LAT,* March 25, 1949.
"most consistent": Ibid.
371 "escorted by her beau": Ibid.

CHAPTER 18

375 "I don't know what": MGM Archives.
376 "Lord knows": Ibid.
377 "the less rebellious": *Variety,* September 8, 1949.
"Nancy Davis": *LAT,* October 1, 1949.
"all the passion": PI.

"a straightforward": PI, Edward
Chodorou.

"Nancy Davis": *Variety*, March 15,
1950.

378   "Only a second": *NYT*, April 23,
1950.

"which are climaxed": *LAT*, May 7,
1950.

"a tough little": Academy of Motion
Picture Arts & Sciences.

379   "A once in a lifetime": *Variety*, June
7, 1950.

"'The Next Voice'": *Cue*, July 1,
1950.

"I never was really": *Look*, October
31, 1967.

"I'm Southern": Edith Luckett to
Jean Kinney on "Around About."

380   "I had no lines": Ibid.

"He asked me": Ibid.

381   "You do the damnedest": Ibid.

383   "In those days": O'Brien, p. 61–62.

384   "Spencer was darling": Edith
Luckett to Jean Kinney on "Around
About."

"Nancy was good": Ibid.

(fn) "the family estate": Leamer, p.
36.

385   "She came to live": Edith Luckett to
Jean Kinney on "Around About."

"I remember one time": Loyal
Davis to Jean Kinney on "Around
About."

(fn) "[Edith] came to": Wallace, p.
2.

(fn) ". . . my driving": Davis, p. 85.

386   "Edith . . . taught me": Davis, p.
228.

"rock-hard": Wallace, p. 6.

"Dad never raised": Ibid., p. 7.

387   "Nancy always handled": Edith
Luckett to Jean Kinney on "Around
About."

388   "pretty is as": Ibid.

"I can remember": Ibid.

"Nancy was never": PI, Gottlieb.

"Whenever I was asked": Edith
Luckett to Jean Kinney on "Around
About."

389   "Always wanted": MGM Archives.

390   "the train pulled out": Jackson, p.
120.

"saw the victim": *The Daily
Princetonian*, December 16, 1941.

"It is odd": Jackson, p. 120.

"a Factory Follies": *SCAN*, May 21,
1943.

391   "the Glamour Gal": Ibid.

"a dreary piece": New York
newspaper *P.M.*, January 6, 1944.

392   "She had been hired": PI, John
Houseman.

"a road jaunt": *Variety*, August 28,
1946.

"nicely sweetened": *Chicago Herald-
American*, October 21, 1947.

"blighting bores": *Variety*, August
28, 1946.

"Sure, I'll see": PI.

393   "The girl knows how": Ibid.

"Nancy was a lady": Edith Luckett
to Jean Kinney on "Around
About."

394   "There was a lot of": PI, Jill
Robinson.

CHAPTER 19

396   "He was an": UCLA Oral History
Archives.

"It was like": SAG Archives, S785.

"You don't seem to": SAG
Archives.

397   "for which I": *LAT*, October 22,
1949.

"Rogers . . . will be": USC
Archives, June 28, 1949.

"This is the kind": Warner
Archives.

"Note outfit Brando": Ibid.

"We have seen": Ibid.

(fn) "I told [Warner]": *LAT*,
October 22, 1949.

(fn) "Ronald Reagan's clothes":
Ibid.

398   "lick the KKK": Ibid.

"There were two": Day, p. 121.

"[It was] the only": Ibid.

(fn) "the entire consular corps":
LAT, December 15, 1949.

(fn) "2,800 people": Warner
Archives.

399   "That's what turned": Warner
Archives.

"idealistic": Ibid.

"There before you": Ibid.

401   "was very much": Reagan, p. 266.

"indicated her": SAG Archives,
3957.

"Lee Bowman": Ibid.

"confusion and distress": SAG
Archives.

402   "It looks": PI.

403   "slovenly and": SAG Archives.

"Hollywood and the": *LAT*,
February 10, 1950.

"One morning I awoke": Reagan
interview.

(fn) ". . . of course": SAG Archives.

404 "America is insisting": Warner
Archives.
(fn) ". . . Day after day": "Inside
Labor," published in *Themis*, official
magazine for Zeta Tau, 1950.
405 "[he] could telephone": *The Mirror*,
January 5, 1950.
"Dear Ronnie": Warner Archives.
406 "Reagan felt he": Ibid.
"I don't know": Ibid.
407 "I talked to Reagan": Ibid.
408 "I've never seen": *Reader*, November
2, 1984.
"package deal": Ibid.
"a staggering compilation": *Saturday
Evening Post*, August 10, 1946.
409 "a good and healthy": Reagan, p.
245.
410 "A good idea": Universal Archives.
"[*Louisa*] must be": Ibid.
411 "He grabbed her": Ibid.

CHAPTER 20

412 "preview showing": *DMR*, August
17, 1950.
"all done up": Ibid.
"They didn't tell": Ibid.
"So many memories": Ibid.
413 "I have another": Ibid.
"Now that was what": Ibid.
"There was quite a": *Welcome Home
Mr. President*, February 6, 1984.
"a firm grip!": Ibid.
414 "Such an experience": Ibid.
"A banquet was": Ibid.
"You must be": *DET*, August 24,
1950.
415 "There's nothing wrong," Bob
Thomas, p. 257.
"It is not the": Ibid., p. 258.
"The secret of": Lambert, p. 257.
"Did you know": *Chicago Tribune*,
September 16, 1950.
416 "decidedly pink": Berkeley Oral
History.
"pink shading into": Ibid.
"If he could win": Douglas, p. 301.
"[Helen] had been": Berkeley Oral
History.
417 "It took the": Ibid.
"particularly vicious": Douglas, p.
323.
"The Pink Lady": Perrett, *Dream*, p.
250.
"A telephone rang": McClelland, p.
229.
419 "a breeding ground": Perrett,
Dream, p. 203.

"He was the master": *Esquire*,
August 1958.
"One night in January": Perrett,
Dream, p. 204.
420 "he suddenly brandished": Ibid.
"McCarthyism": Ibid., p. 205.
"did everything wrong": Reagan, p.
268.
421 "inner workings": UCLA Oral
History Archives.
"made him an interested": Ibid.
"jovial little picture": *NYT*, October
25, 1950.
422 "an animal starrer": *Newsweek*,
March 12, 1957.
"They haven't a": *NYT*, April 6,
1951.
"Reagan gives": *NYT*, January 6,
1951.
"We had a rather": PI, Gene
Nelson.
423 "IT IS OUR": Warner Archives.
"YOUR TELEGRAM": Ibid.
424 "Jack, when I got": Reagan, p. 247.
"Marlon Brando": Graham,
Confessions of a Hollywood Columnist,
p. 257.
"quiet, very quiet": UCLA Oral
History Archives.
"I don't know": Ibid.
425 "rapt attention": Ibid.
"I am addressing": *Variety*, March
16, 1951.
427 "The Board of": SAG board to
Sondergaard, *Hollywood Reporter*,
March 20, 1951.
428 "I think . . . it": Trumbo, p. 570.
"throwing from the": Reagan, p.
272.

CHAPTER 21

430 "He telephoned once": Edith
Luckett to Jean Kinney on "Around
About."
431 "Meeeting . . . the doctor": Reagan,
p. 273.
"I'm always being": Edith Luckett
to Jean Kinney on "Around
About."
"To hell with this": Reagan, p. 269.
"It's about time": Ibid.
432 "Matters to Review": Universal
Archives, January 15, 1952.
433 "rambling, obscure": *Hollywood
Reporter*, April 9, 1951.
"an awful lot": *LAT*, April 13, 1951.
434 "a pulp fiction": *Variety*, December
17, 1952.

"or was it": *NYT*, April 5, 1952.

"bring the money": Reagan, p. 281.

435 "He wouldn't get": UCLA Oral History Archives.

"We [SAG] were": Ibid.

436 "Well, we were": Ibid.

437 "I must tell you": Freedom of Information Act.

(fn) "At the time": Laurence Beilenson, letter to Edwards, October 22, 1986.

438 "The waiver was": SAG Archives.

439 "The deal vaulted MCA": Freedom of Information Act.

440 "Westerns will never": *LADN*, May 28, 1953.

"Reagan handles": *Variety*, April 8, 1953.

441 "He wanted to": Ibid.

"His hatred of": Ibid.

442 "Mr. Eisenhower": Sherman Adams, p. 25.

"accustomed to": Perrett, *Dream*, p. 247.

"had there been": Ibid., p. 250.

"into a swift": Ibid.

443 "a Communist smear": Ibid.

"NO MINK COATS": Ibid.

"There has been a": *Esquire*, August 1969.

"tack on, at the end": Ibid.

"You will have": Ibid.

"tear-choked": Perrett, *Dream*, p. 250.

"I am submitting": Ibid.

444 "scores of dog": Ibid.

"blue-eyed smile": Ibid.

"because of the threat": *LADN*, May 1, 1953.

"I turned the offer": Ibid.

445 "brutal beatings": *Variety*, March 24, 1954.

"The MCA": Reagan, p. 283.

"another source": Ibid.

446 "I'll introduce": *Newslife*, October 11, 1953.

"the stars into": *Hollywood Citizen*, February 15, 1954.

"against the": Ibid.

"We expected to": *LA Magazine*, April 1983.

447 "to have to suffer": PI.

"Never again": PI.

CHAPTER 22

451 "like playing cowboy": Reagan, p. 286.

"great northwest": Ibid.

"a great actress": Ibid.

452 "MCA promised us": Berkeley Oral History.

"communicator": Ibid.

"audience participation": Ibid.

"They were really": Ibid.

(fn) "New General Electric": Ibid.

"MCA was fantastically": Ibid.

453 "extensive 'Employee and'": Reagan, p. 286.

"We had been": Berkeley Oral History.

"There was nothing": Ibid.

454 "We very carefully": Ibid.

"He couldn't see": Ibid.

"generally having a": Reagan, p. 293.

"The people were most": Berkeley Oral History.

455 "In Erie": Ibid.

456 "a bull of the": Ibid.

"highfalutin": Ibid.

"They might ask": Ibid.

457 "a walking symbol": Ibid.

"Is what I'm saying": Ibid.

"some people at": Ibid.

"had turned the": Ibid.

"growing liberal": Ibid.

"left-wing liberal": Ibid.

458 "raucous mining town": Ibid.

"I went over": Edith Luckett to Jean Kinney on "Around About."

"someone seriously": *Hollywood Reporter*, November 1955.

459 "From my own viewpoint": Ibid., April 4, 1956.

"everything electric": *Chicago Tribune*, February 26, 1956.

460 "Nancy and Ronnie": Edith Luckett to Jean Kinney on "Around About."

"The Speech": *Reader*, November 2, 1984.

"Government—staffed": *Life*, May 1967.

"There was a joke": Graham, *Confessions of a Hollywood Columnist*, p. 258–59.

461 "a dual personality": Broadcast Pioneers Library.

"the Ambassador": Berkeley Oral History.

"the unwashed public": Ibid.

"and don't you": Ibid.

462 "wretched Skid Row": Broadcast Pioneers Library.

"a member of the": Ibid.

"because I was so": Berkeley Oral History.

"*verboten* on the": Reagan, p. 329.

463 "jingoistic potboiler": Halliwell,
     Film Guide, p. 630.
     "life long tendency": Reagan, p.
     328.
464 "that the exclusion": Ibid.
     "for real": *Time*, November 24,
     1975.
     (fn) ". . . sacred as motherhood":
     Reagan, p. 345.
465 "We knew that": UCLA Oral
     History Archives.
     "Convinced as I was": Reagan, p.
     313.

CHAPTER 23

466 "charm the hell": Berkeley Oral
     History.
     "An air of dignity": Reagan,
     Sincerely, p. 109.
     "never one of the": Ibid.
     "Funny thing about": PI.
467 "He felt that": UCLA Oral History
     Archives.
     "Who the hell": Ibid.
     "We [the actors]": SAG Archives.
468 "Mr. Skouras": Ibid.
469 "There was a lot of": PI, Kim
     Felner.
     "Once we were": UCLA Oral
     History Archives.
     "decked out in a": Reagan, p. 316.
     "wrecking the business": UCLA
     Oral History Archives.
     "Walsh came in": Ibid.
470 "a stormy session": *Variety*, October
     30, 1980.
     "a heavy": PI, Madelaine Lee.
     "vividly": SAG Archives.
     "The people who": Ibid.
471 "There are no": PI, Chet Migden.
     "soup and salad": Reagan, p. 320.
     "where some two": Ibid., p. 319.
     "exactly what the": Ibid., p. 320.
     "Vogel fancied": PI, Migden.
472 "It was about June": UCLA Oral
     History Archives.
473 "a fighting conservative": Perrett,
     Dream, p. 58.
474 "too young, too rich": Ibid., p. 562.
     "daunting obstacle": Ibid.
     "effective, intelligent": Ibid., p. 563.
     (fn) "Our country cannot": Ibid., p.
     569.
475 "The Communist party": Speech by
     Ronald Reagan, Phoenix, Arizona,
     March 30, 1961.

CHAPTER 24

477 "that MCA's unique": *Reader*,
     November 2, 1984.
478 "The whole notion": Undated
     article.
     "his kind of work": Ibid.
     "The old boy": UCLA Oral History
     Archives.
479 "One day in walks": Ibid.
     "It worked out": Ibid.
480 "automatically, because": *Saturday
     Evening Post*, June 4, 1966.
     "Ron can't be pushed": Ibid., June
     1, 1968.
     "Nancy Reagan": Ibid.
     "I gauge everything": *Look*, October
     31, 1968.
     "Remember when": Ibid.
481 "one brief shining moment":
     Camelot.
     "who spoke their": Perrett, *Dream*,
     p. 595.
     "Get the U.S.": Ibid.
482 "Many predict that": *Washington
     Post*, July 16, 1964.
     "His nerves broke": Ibid.
     (fn) "The first time": Ibid.
484 "I got a call": Neil Reagan to Jean
     Kinney on "Around About."
485 "You and I have": "Encroaching
     Control" speech.

CHAPTER 25

487 "not the smoke": P.I.
488 "We don't intend": *LAT*, November
     11, 1964.
     "big-issues guy": *Washington Post*,
     February 2, 1981.
     "habitually littered": Ibid.
     "maneuvering behind": Ibid.
489 "I don't think he's": Ibid.
     "tense and cautious": Graham,
     Confessions of a Hollywood Columnist,
     p. 258–59.
     "a telephone call": Ibid.
     ". . . he held out": Neil Reagan to
     Jean Kinney on "Around About."
490 "I have no style": *Life*, October 14,
     1966.
     "Ronald called me": Neil Reagan to
     Jean Kinney on "Around About."
491 "so splurged with": Undated article.
     "Every once in a": Ibid.

REPOSITORIES FOR
EARLY REAGAN MATERIAL

Ronald Reagan Home, Dixon, IL
Ronald Reagan Society, Dixon Public Library, Dixon, IL
Private Collection of William C. and Jean Thompson, Dixon, IL
Eureka College, Alumni Files, Eureka, IL
Warner Brothers Film Archives at University of Wisconsin, Madison, WI
Film and Photo Archive, University of Wisconsin, Madison, WI
Warner Brothers Film Archives at University of Southern California
Special Collections, University of California, Los Angeles, CA
Regional Oral History Office, University of California, Berkeley, CA
Screen Actors Guild, Hollywood, CA
Academy of Motion Picture Arts and Sciences, Beverly Hills, CA
Hoover Institution on War, Revolution and Peace, Stanford, CA
International Museum of Photography at George Eastman House, Rochester, NY
The New York Public Library, Newspaper Collection, New York, NY
The Billy Rose Theater Collection, Lincoln Center, New York, NY
Museum of Broadcasting, New York, NY
CBS/Broadcast Group, New York, NY
Television Information Office, New York, NY
Broadcast Pioneers Library, Washington, D.C.
British Film Institute, London, England

BIBLIOGRAPHY

Adams, Harold. *The History of Eureka College, 1855–1982.* Eureka, IL: Trustees of Eureka College, 1982.

Adams, Samuel Hopkins. *Incredible Era.* Boston: Little, Brown, 1939.

Adams, Sherman. *Firsthand Report.* Westport, CT: Greenwood, 1975.

Allyson, June. *June Allyson.* New York: G. P. Putnam's Sons, 1982.

Bacall, Lauren. *By Myself.* New York: Alfred A. Knopf, 1979.

Beaton, Cecil. *Memoirs of the 40's.* New York: McGraw-Hill Book Co., 1972.

Behlmer, Rudy. *Inside Warner Bros.: 1935–1951.* New York: Viking Penguin, Inc., 1985.

Bozarsky, Bill. *The Rise of Ronald Reagan.* New York: Random House, 1968.

Brett, George. *The Fifth Column Is Here.* New York: 1948.

Burns, James MacGregor. *Roosevelt: The Lion and the Fox.* New York: Harcourt, Brace, Jovanovich, 1963.

Cadden, Tom Scott. *What a Bunch of Characters.* Englewood Cliffs, NJ: Prentice-Hall, 1984.

Chambers, Whittaker. *Witness.* New York: Random House, 1952.

Cannon Lou. *Reagan.* New York: G. P. Putnam's Sons, 1982.

Caro, Robert A. *The Years of Lyndon Johnson, the Path to Power.* New York: Alfred A. Knopf, 1982.

Channon, Sir Henry. *Chips.* The Diaries of Sir Henry Channon, edited by Robert Rhodes James, Weidenfeld & Nicolson, London, England, 1967.

Cohan, George M. *Twenty Years on Broadway.* Westport, CT: Greenwood Press, 1924.

Cole, Lester. *Hollywood Red.* Palo Alto, CA: Ramparts Press, 1981.

Collier. *1940—The World in Flames.* London, England: Hamish Hamilton, 1979.

David, Lester, and Irene David. *The Shirley Temple Story.* New York: G. P. Putnam's Sons, 1983.

Davis, Loyal, M.D. *A Surgeon's Odyssey.* Garden City, NY: Doubleday & Co., 1973.

Day, Doris, with A. E. Hochner. *Doris Day: Her Own Story.* New York: William Morrow and Co., 1976.

Douglas, Helen Gahagan. *A Full Life.* Garden City, NY: 1982.

Edwards, Lee. *Reagan, A Political Biography.* San Diego, CA: Viewpoint Books, 1967.

Eells, George, *Hedda and Louella.* New York: G. P. Putnam's Sons, 1972.

Federal Writers' Project of the Works Progress Administration for the State of California, *California: A Guide to the Golden State.* New York: Hastings House, 1960.

Garrison, Winfred Ernest, and Alfred T. DeGroot. *The Disciples of Christ, A History.* St. Louis, MO: Christian Board of Publication, 1948.

Gies, Joseph. *Franklin D. Roosevelt, Portrait of a President.* Garden City, NY: Doubleday & Co., 1971.

Graham, Sheilah. *Confessions of a Hollywood Columnist.* New York: William Morrow and Co., 1969.

————. *Garden of Allah*. New York: Crown, 1970.

Halliwell, Leslie. *Halliwell's Filmgoers Companion*. New York: Charles Scribner's Sons, 1983.

————. *Halliwell's Film Guide*. New York: Charles Scribner's Sons, 1985.

Higham, Charles. *Bette, the Life of Bette Davis*. New York: Macmillan, 1981.

Holmes, T. Rice. *Sir Charles Napier*. Cambridge, MA: Cambridge Press, 1925.

Houseman, John. *Final Dress*. New York: Simon and Schuster, 1983.

————. *Front and Center*. New York: Simon and Schuster, 1981.

————. *Run-Through*. New York: Simon and Schuster, 1972.

Jackson, Katherine Gauss, and Hiram Haydn (ed.). *The Papers of Christian Gauss*. New York: Random House, 1957.

Johnson, Paul. *Modern Times, the World from the Twenties to the Eighties*. New York: Harper & Row, 1983.

Kahn, Gordon. *Hollywood on Trial*. New York: Boni & Gaer, 1948.

Kanfer, Stefan. *A Journal of the Plague Years*. New York: Atheneum, 1973.

Katz, Ephraim. *The Film Encyclopedia*. New York: Putnam Publishing Group, 1982.

Keyes, Evelyn. *Scarlett O'Hara's Younger Sister*. Secaucus, NJ: Lyle Stuart Inc., 1977.

Kitt, H. F. & Co. *History of Carroll County Illinois*. Chicago, IL, 1878.

Lambert, Gavin. *On Cukor*. New York: Capricorn Books, 1972.

Lane, Mark. *Rush to Judgment*. New York: Holt, Rinehart & Winston, 1966.

Lash, Joseph P. *Eleanor and Franklin*. New York: W. W. Norton & Co., 1971.

Leamer, Laurence. *Make-Believe*. New York: Harper & Row, 1983.

Leighton, Isabel, ed. *The Aspirin Age, 1919–1941*. New York: Simon and Schuster, 1963.

Lekwa, Verl L. *Bennett, Iowa, and Inland Township, A History*. In cooperation with the Bennett Community Club, Marceline, MO: Walsworth Pub. Co., 1983.

Lindfors, Viveca. *Night Unto Night*. New York: 1948.

————. *Viveka-Viveca*. New York: Everest House, 1981.

Lyon, Christopher, ed. *The Dictionary of Films and Filmmakers*. New York: The Putnam Publishing Group, 1985.

MacLysaght, Edward. *Irish Families*. Dublin, Ireland, 1957.

MacManus, Seumas. *The Story of the Irish Race*. New York, 1944.

Massey, Raymond. *100 Different Lives*. Boston, MA: Little, Brown, 1979.

Mayo, Morrow. *Los Angeles*. New York: Alfred A. Knopf, 1932.

McClelland, Doug. *Hollywood on Ronald Reagan*. Winchester, MA: Faber and Faber, 1983.

Morella, Joe, and Edward Z. Epstein. *Jane Wyman, a Biography*. New York: Delacorte Press, 1985.

Murphy, George, with Victor Lasky. *Say . . . Didn't You Used to be George Murphy?* London: Bartholomew House, Ltd., 1970.

Napier, Priscilla. *Revolution and the Napier Brothers, 1820–1840*. London: Michael Joseph Ltd., 1973.

Napier, Rosamond Lawrence. *Charles Napier, 1782–1853, Friend and Fighter*. London: John Murray, 1952.

Navasky, Victor. *Naming Names*. New York: Viking Press, Inc., 1980.

Nicholson, Harold. *The Later Years: 1945–1962*. New York: Atheneum, 1968.

O'Brien, Pat. *The Wind at My Back, the Life and Times of Pat O'Brien*. Garden City, NY: Doubleday & Co., 1964.

O'Kelley, M. J., and C. *Illustrated Guide to Lough Gur*. Cork, Ireland, 1978.

Parish, James Robert, and Don Stanke. *The All-Americans*. New Rochelle, NY: Arlington House, 1977.

Parrish, Randall, *Historic Illinois*. Chicago, IL, 1905.

Parsons, Louella O. *Tell It to Louella*. New York: G. P. Putnam's Sons, 1961.

———. *The Gay Illiterate*. Garden City, NY: Doubleday, Doran and Co., Inc., 1944.

Perrett, Geoffrey. *America in the Twenties*. New York: Simon and Schuster, 1982.

———. *Days of Sadness, Years of Triumph: The American People: 1939–1945*. New York: Coward, McCann & Geoghegan, 1973.

———. *A Dream of Greatness: The American People: 1945–1963*. New York: Coward, McCann & Geoghegan, 1979.

Powdermaker, Hortense. *Hollywood: The Dream Factory*. Boston, MA: Little, Brown & Co., 1950.

Reagan, Nancy. *Nancy*, with Bill Libby, New York: William Morrow and Co., 1980.

Reagan, Ronald. *Ronald Reagan Talks to America*. Introduction by Richard M. Scaife, Old Greenwich, CT: The Devin Adair Company, 1983.

———. *Sincerely, Ronald Reagan* (personal correspondence of Ronald Reagan as governor of California, compiled by Helene Von Damm). Ottawa, IL: Green Hill Publishers, 1976.

———. *A Time for Choosing, the Speeches of Ronald Reagan 1961–1982*. Regnery Gateway, Chicago, IL, in cooperation with the Americans for the Reagan Agenda, 1983.

Reagan, Ronald, and Richard Hubler. *Where's the Rest of Me?* New York: Dell Publishing Co., 1965.

Robinson, Edward G., with Leonard Spigelgass. *All My Yesterdays*. New York: Hawthorn Books, Inc., 1973.

Sarris, Andrew. *The American Cinema*. New York: E. P. Dutton & Co., 1968.

Schwartz, Nancy Lynn. *The Hollywood Writers' Wars*. New York: Alfred A. Knopf, 1982.

Stone, Ezra. *Coming Major*. New York: Lippincott, 1944.

Thomas, Bob. *King Cohn*. New York: Bantam Books, 1967.

Thomas, Tony. *The Films of Ronald Reagan*. Secaucus, NJ: Citadel Press, 1980.

Trumbo, Dalton, edited by Helen Manfull. *Additional Dialogue, Letters of Dalton Trumbo, 1942–1962*. New York: M. Evans and Company, Inc., 1970.

Tucker, William E., and Lester G. McAllister. *Journey in Faith: A History of the Christian Church (Disciples of Christ)*. St. Louis, MO: The Bethany Press, 1975.

Walgreen, Myrtle R., as told to Margueritte Harmon Bro. *Never a Dull Day*. Chicago, IL: Henry Regnery Company, 1963.

Wallace, Chris. *First Lady*. New York: St. Martin's Press, 1986.

Wallis, Hal, and Charles Higham. *Star Maker*. New York: Berkley Books, 1980.

Warner, Jack L., with Dean Jennings. *My First Hundred Years in Hollywood*. New York: Random House, 1965.

Warner & Beers, *Maps of Illinois Counties*, 1876.

Webb, Walter Prescott. *The Great Plains*. New York, 1931.

Westmore, Frank. *The Westmores of Hollywood*. New York: J. B. Lippincott, 1976.

White, Patricia Meade. *The Invincible Irish, Ronald Wilson Reagan, Irish Ancestry and Immigration to America.* Santa Barbara, CA: Portola Press, 1981.

Yardley, Jonathan. *Ring, A Biography of Ring Lardner.* New York: Random House, 1977.

Zucker, Irwin, and Mark David. *Ronnie Runs Wild.* Los Angeles, CA: Mark David, 1976.

PERIODICALS

Dixonian (Dixon High School Annual), 1928

The Prism, Eureka College annual, 1929–30

Screen Actor, 1939–85 (published by the Screen Actors Guild)

INDEX